LEVELLING WIND

*Come let us mock at the great
That had such burdens on the mind
And toiled so hard and late
To leave some monument behind,
Nor thought of the levelling wind.*

— W.B. Yeats

LEVELLING WIND
REMEMBERING FIJI

BRIJ V. LAL

PACIFIC SERIES

For our Naati-Pota
Jayan Kenneth, Maya June, Ash Arjun and Ella Saras

To the Future

The living owe it to those who no longer can speak to tell their story for them
Czesław Miłosz

Published by ANU Press
The Australian National University
Acton ACT 2601, Australia
Email: anupress@anu.edu.au

Available to download for free at press.anu.edu.au

ISBN (print): 9781760462666
ISBN (online): 9781760462673

WorldCat (print): 1122806386
WorldCat (online): 1122806645

DOI: 10.22459/LW.2019

This title is published under a Creative Commons Attribution-NonCommercial-NoDerivatives 4.0 International (CC BY-NC-ND 4.0).

The full licence terms are available at creativecommons.org/licenses/by-nc-nd/4.0/legalcode

Cover design and layout by ANU Press

This edition © 2019 ANU Press

Contents

Glossary ix
Acknowledgements xvii
'For the loser now will be later to win' xix
Doug Munro
Ni Sa Bula / Namaskar / G'Day. xxiii

Past Present: Indenture and its Legacy

1. Memories of indenture 3
2. 'Such a long journey': The story of indenture 21
3. The Tamarind Tree 45
4. 'A most callous indifference' 63
5. Transitions and transformations 77
6. Illusion of hope: Aisha and Bhaskar 113
   Padma Narsey Lal
7. 'The burden of remembrance' 135
8. Frequent flyers 149
9. Mr Arjun goes to Australia. 161
10. 'The children of the wind' 181

Future Tense: Witnessing History

11. While the gun is still smoking 201
12. The road to independence 225
13. Where has all the music gone? 251
14. Towards a united future 277
15. George Speight's putsch improbable 299

16.	Laisenia Qarase's missed chance	323
17.	A coup by any other name	349
18.	Entrenching illegality	389
19.	The strange career of a 'clean-up' coup	421
20.	Between a rock and a hard place	453

Retrospection

21.	Exile and a land of memory: Brij V. Lal, Indo-Fijian scholar activist	477
	C.K. Chen	
22.	'Of exits and entrances'	495
	In dialogue with Doug Munro	
23.	ANU made me, but which ANU is mine?	515
Bibliography		537
About the author		563

Glossary

F – Fijian; H – Hindi; L – Latin

aamaa bivah (H)	a special kind of ceremony related to the mango fruit
aapas ke baat (H)	private matters
adda (H)	gathering place
adharmic (H)	morally inappropriate
agua (H)	leader
ahirwa ke naatch (H)	a special kind of Ahir dance, with a man dressed in women's clothes, performed at festive occasions and at weddings; also *lehnga ke naatch*
aja (H)	grandfather
angrezi saheb (H)	white men
arkatis (H)	unscrupulous recruiters
Arya Samaj	Noble Society, Indian Hindu reform movement
awa-gawa (H)	come and gone
aya-gaya (H)	came and went
baanar sena (H)	Lord Hanuman's monkey army
babus (H)	clerk, an educated Indian man
badhiya (H)	good
Badi Beemari (H)	Influenza Epidemic of 1918
badmaash (H)	hooligan
badmashi bund (H)	stop this nonsense
bahini (H)	sister

bahut accha (H)	very good
bahut badhiya (H)	very nice
baigan (H)	eggplants
bajuband (H)	armlet
bakeda (H)	crab (Labasa word)
baksheesh (H)	freebie
bandar (H)	monkey
barbaadi (H)	harm
belo (H)	guest-receiving house; a traditional storage house for farm implements, fertiliser and weedicide
beta (H)	child
bhajan (H)	devotional songs
bhaji (H)	vegetable
bhaloo (H)	bear
bhandara (H)	feast
bhauji (H)	older sister-in-law
bichwa (H)	toe-ring
biraadri (H)	brotherhood
bure (F)	thatched house
chaachi (H)	aunty
chai (H)	tea
chakka panji (H)	hoi poloi
chamar (H)	tanner, low caste
chandali (H)	stupidity
chaplusi (H)	wanton behaviour
chautals (H)	Holi, or Phagwa, festival songs
chini-pani (H)	sugar has turned to water
chori (H)	thievery
chuttar pani (H)	washing your bum with water after visiting the toilet
Court-Kachehri (H)	law courts, judicial proceedings
dabe (H)	flood (Labasa word)

GLOSSARY

dada (H)	older uncle, brother
dai (H)	mid-wife
dakua (F)	Fijian hardwood
dalo (F)	taro
damanu (F)	Fijian hardwood
dandtaal (H)	iron rod musical instrument
desh (H)	nation
devtas (H)	gods
dhandha (H)	occupation
dharamshalas (H)	established centre for spiritual instruction
dhibri (H)	wick lamp
dholak (H)	Indian drum
dhoti (H)	a traditional men's garment; a rectangular piece of unstitched cloth, usually around 4.5 m (15 ft) long, wrapped around the waist and the legs and knotted at the waist
dil roye, beta (H)	the heart cries, son
din maro (H)	to shirk work
Fiji-Baat	a mixture of various Indian languages interspersed with English and Fijian words
Finis coronat opus (L)	the end crowns the work
gaand ke andha (H)	blind as an arse
gaar (H)	arse
ganja (H)	marijuana
ganwaar (H)	country bumpkins
gatka (H)	stick fighting game
gau-mata (H)	mother cow
ghar (H)	house
ghoos (H)	bribe
ghoos-khori (H)	corruption
girmit (H)	indenture, from Agreement
girmitiya (H)	indentured immigrant

gitbit (H)	speaking rapid-fire
gram devtas (H)	village deities
gulgula (H)	Indian sweet
hajam (H)	traditional barber (by caste)
halal (H)	permissible
haram (H)	forbidden
haramil (H)	bastard
hathi (H)	elephant
havans (H)	prayer offerings around fire
hum log (H)	us people
huqqa-pani-bund (H)	social ostracism
iTaukei (H)	Indigenous Fijians
izzat (H)	collective honour
jaanwar (H)	animal
jadu tona (H)	magic, witchcraft
jahajibhai (H)	ship mate, brotherhood of the crossing
jhanjhat (H)	trouble
Jhankar (H)	a weekly film magazine
jhatka (H)	the method of slaughter demanded by many Hindus, Sikhs
jhumka (H)	earring
kab (H)	when
kabarsthaan (H)	graveyard
Kai Idia	Indo-Fijians
Kai Viti (F)	indigenous Fijians
kaitani (F)	foreigners
kaka (H)	uncle, father's younger brothers, cousins
kaki (H)	father's younger brother's wife
kakkus (H)	outhouse
kala pani (H)	dark, dreaded seas
kanganis (H)	middlemen (Ceylon and Malaya)
kasbighar (H)	brothel in the estate lines

kekda (H)	crab, see *bakeda* (Labasa word)
khabardari (H)	alertness
khuda hafiz (H)	goodbye
khula (H)	freed population
koi bat nahin (H)	don't worry
koros (F)	villages
kul (H)	clan
kulambar (H)	CSR overseer
kurmi (H)	cultivating caste
kurta (H)	traditional Indian shirt
kushti (H)	wrestling
kuti (H)	rudimentary hut for religious gathering
lakdi ke mithai (H)	an Indian sweet made of flour and sugar
lathi (H)	walking stick
lathials (H)	guards
lehnga (H)	long skirt worn by women
lehnga ke naatch (H)	see *ahirwa ke naatch*
lovo (F)	a banquet cooked in an earth oven
maan maryada (H)	respect
madarasa (H)	Muslim centre for spiritual instruction
mahajans (H)	money lenders
mai (H)	mother
mai-bap (H)	mother/father, parents, benefactors
maistries (H)	middlemen
mami (H)	mother's brother's wife
mandali (H)	village society
mandir (H)	temple
mardaanagi (H)	Indian manhood
masala (H)	fertiliser, also spice
mataqali (F)	Fijian landowning unit
mausi (H)	mother's sister
mircha (H)	chillies

mohur (H)	single string of gold sovereigns
mulk (H)	homeland
murgi chor (H)	poultry thief, petty person
mutimilelie (H)	may you be mixed with earth
namaste (H)	respectful greeting
narak (H)	hell
nathini (H)	nose-ring
neta log (H)	leaders, community elders
ojha (H)	sorcerer
orhni (H)	shawl worn by Indian women
paal (H)	stitched sacks for mat
pagri (H)	turban
palki-bearers (H)	men who carried people on wheelless vehicles
panchayat (H)	village council
pankah-pullers (H)	fan pullers to keep dignitaries and royalty cool
patoh (H)	daughter-in-law
pawan-bans (H)	children of the wind
Pawan-putra (H)	Son of the wind, Lord Hanuman
payal (H)	anklet
pet khalas (H)	the stomach's gone
pet puja (H)	self-interest
phua (H)	father's sister
poora barbadi (H)	total loss
poora jad pulai (H)	everything
poorbea (H)	eastern
pothis (H)	primary school texts
prashchayat (H)	penance
primus inter pares (L)	first among equals
pujas (H)	devotional prayer offerings
pukka jungali (H)	complete country bumpkin
qassai (H)	butcher
qauwwali (H)	Urdu songs

GLOSSARY

qoliqoli (F)	foreshore
Ram ki marji (H)	God's wish
Ram-Ram (H)	Hindi words of greeting or farewell
rara (F)	manicured open lawn
rasmo riwaz (H)	our own way of doing things
ratoon (H)	second and subsequent cane crop
sab chalta hai (H)	anything goes
sadhu (H)	holy man
saheb (H)	master
sala chutia (H)	you arsehole
salwar kamiz (H)	Indian women's dress
samaj rakshak (H)	guardians of the community
Sanatanis (H)	orthodox Hindus
saris (H)	Indian women's dress
satua (H)	type of homemade sweets
shabaash, beta (H)	well done, son
sharif (H)	honourable
sher (H)	lion
shuddh (H)	'proper'
shukriya ji (H)	thank you, sir
sirdar (H)	Indian male foreman
suar ke baccha (H)	son of a pig
sulu (F)	kilt-like garment worn by Fijian men
suluka (F)	rough, handmade cigarettes wrapped in pandanus leaves
sundar (H)	nice
tabua (F)	whale's tooth
tamasha (H)	sideshow
tanoa (F)	kava bowl
tapus (H)	islands
taukei (F)	indigenous Fijian owners of the land
tehsil (H)	subdistrict

xv

terminat auctor opus (L)	the author finishes his work
terra sacra (L)	sacred earth
tharia (H)	bowl
vanua (F)	land, province
vulagi (F)	foreigner, visitor
yaar (H)	mate
yaqona (F)	kava

Acknowledgements

This book, coming at the end of my professional career, has long been in the making. It began when I went to The Australian National University in 1977 to do my doctorate on the social origins of Fiji's Indian indentured migrants. A decade or so later, military coups and the convulsions they caused drew me to the study of Fijian politics. And in the 1990s, I began, with great pleasure, to live at the interface between history and memory, writing about people and places with no written archives and undocumented lives. All these interests are represented in this book. Just as it takes a village to raise a child, it takes the generosity and assistance of a whole community of colleagues and friends to write a book like this or to pursue a scholarly career more generally. I have been lucky beyond words in this regard.

Given their vast numbers in virtually every corner of the globe, a deeply felt collective expression of gratitude will sadly have to suffice. My colleagues and students in Hawai'i and Canberra, in particular, know how much they have taught and inspired me with their example and friendship. But some names will have to be mentioned. I benefited greatly from Doug Munro's advice and practical help on this project. He has been my first 'reader' for decades. Carolyn Brewer has done a masterly job of editing the manuscript, and Teresa Prowse designed the cover as well as the book with great care and craftsmanship. I am very grateful to Emily Hazlewood, deputy manager of ANU Press, for her careful reading of the penultimate pre-publication draft of the manuscript to remove unnoticed gaucheries of style from it. It has been a pleasure working with all these people. My greatest debt is to Padma, whose love and support over more than 40 years has made this and everything else I have done in my life possible. Without her by my side, I would have had no journey to undertake. Yogi and Niraj, growing up in Canberra where I was learning the alphabets of academia, accepted my obsessions and frequent absentmindedness with good humour (most of the time). And our grandchildren, Jayan, Maya, Ash and Ella, give us balance and perspective about the really important things in life. We hope that someday they will read our words to get some sense of our improbable journeys and their own ancestral beginnings. The words of a Malay proverb come to mind: 'One can pay back the loan of gold, but one will forever be in debt to those who have been kind.'

'For the loser now will be later to win'[1]

Doug Munro, University of Queensland

In a professional lifetime spanning more than 40 years, Brij Lal has written about Fiji and the wider Indian diaspora. He has almost completely confined himself to such specialisations for two reasons. One is that the heart and the head must come together. There has to be immediacy and a sense of involvement before he can warm to a subject. Quite simply, his choice of subject matter stems from relevance to himself and an engagement with his roots. Furthermore, he doesn't want to intrude, as he sees it, on other people's histories. It's an entirely personal decision and he does not object to so-called outsiders studying and writing about Fiji. The result of Lal's 40-plus-year journey into the history and politics of Fiji is a body of writing, notable in equal measure for its quality and quantity. He is bearing witness to his time and place. The impact of his work on his chosen fields will endure.

Selections of this corpus have been presented in three volumes of collected essays. The first—*Chalo Jahaji*—is concerned with the indenture system in Fiji and speaks eloquently of the 61,000 labourers from India.[2] The second—*Intersections*—is testimony to Lal's versatility.[3] Its chapters include autobiography; tributes to others (such as Sir Paul Reeves, the chair of the 1996 Constitution Review Commission, of which Lal was

---

1   Bob Dylan, 'The times they are a-changin'', on *The Times they are A-Changin'* (Columbia Records, 1964), line 17, lyrics available from: www.bobdylan.com/songs/times-they-are-changin/ (accessed 10 April 2019).
2   Brij V. Lal, *Chalo Jahaji: On a Journey of Indenture through Fiji* (Suva: Fiji Museum, 2000; Canberra: ANU E Press, 2012), doi.org/10.22459/CJ.12.2012.
3   Brij V. Lal, *Intersections: History, Memory, Discipline* (Suva: Fiji Institute of Applied Studies, 2011; Canberra: ANU E Press, 2012), doi.org/10.22459/IHMD.11.2012.

a member); discussions of the political situation in Fiji; his thoughts on the deteriorating quality of university life; and broad-brush treatments of the wider Indian diaspora.[4] The book you are now reading is the third, a sequel to *Intersections*, but the emphases are different. Apart from two interviews, the autobiographical content is subsumed in various chapters rather than being chapters in their own right; there is more on the wider Indian diaspora; there are also examples of Lal's creative writing; and, above all, there is more coverage of contemporary Fiji politics.

Here we come to other measures of motivation. What makes Lal keep on writing about the seemingly lost cause of Fiji politics? He explained in *Intersections* that, although he is first and foremost an historian:

> the tumultuous events in Fiji over the last decade have pulled me back to the present, and a considerable part of my time and energy is spent on commentary and analysis of contemporary events in that country. This is time consuming and often repetitive, but it is a responsibility and an obligation that I cannot escape, nor would I want to. Silence in the face of oppression is not an option for me, nor is the defence of democratic values and the rule of law a crime.[5]

It is not that Lal wants, or even tries, to be the conscience of the nation, but there are better ways to go about governing a country.

To read the various political essays in this volume as they emerged over a period of years was sobering enough. To read them sequentially in two or three sittings elicits a more sombre reaction. That is, how could Lal keep on writing about a subject matter so depressing and an unfolding scenario so distressing, recording the unexpected twists and unforeseen turns of Fiji politics as they go from bad to worse—where the rule of law and the independence of the press and judiciary, not to mention the spirit of the constitution, are ridden over roughshod? How does one maintain a sense of equilibrium on a daily fare so cheerless and disheartening? Then there is his (and his wife Padma's) banishment from Fiji since 2010, on the spurious grounds that they are a threat to national security. If the powers that be thought they were going to silence a vocal critic, they completely misjudged the effectiveness of their action.

---

4 ibid.
5 ibid., p. 5.

The negative feelings are moderated by the other subjects that Lal writes about, which you'll find in the first part of this book. Much of it is excursions into the realm of creative writing, which he finds ultimately more satisfying than his academic writing. Here he can let his imagination roam in giving voice to the ordinary people—their hopes and struggles—who are not the usual habitués of history books. Besides, there is life beyond sitting in front of a computer screen or scribbling away. Solace also comes from the joy of reading and his love of good literature, not to mention the happy distraction of watching cricket and enjoying his grandchildren. The inspiration and support from friends has been crucial, for there is no denying the heartache of seeing dreams of a better Fiji disappear, the pain of exile and the ordeal the family has gone through.

Although the political situation in Fiji remains grim, it could be worse. At least there has been nothing like the St Bartholomew's Day massacre, the climax of the French Wars of Religion in 1572. Coming to more recent times, there have been no equivalents of the Reichstag fire, the Night of the Long Knives and Kristallnacht. Speaking of the Nazi onslaught, one is reminded of the lines in Anne Frank's *The Diary of a Young Girl*: 'Where there's hope, there's life. It fills us with fresh courage and makes us strong again.'[6] These words are too hopeful for Fiji's immediate future and it might be thought that Lal is one of the losers in history. As well as being banned from Fiji, his words go unheeded—although not unresented—by the authorities. Then, again, it's worth remembering that nothing is set in stone. It recalls the words of Bob Dylan's 'The times they are a-changin'': 'And don't speak too soon / For the wheel's still in spin.'[7] So, how will 'history' judge the present Fijian Government? When its members lose office, they will suddenly discover that the status and the perks have everything to do with the job and nothing to do with them personally. They will then discover who their 'friends' really are. It's a fair bet that Lal's writings will outlive their deeds and the tables will be turned—or, as Dylan said, 'For the loser now will be later to win'.[8]

---

6   Anne Frank, *Het Achterhuis. Dagboekbrieven 14 Juni 1942 – 1 Augustus 1944* (Amsterdam: Contact Publishing, 1947); *The Diary of a Young Girl*, trans. Barbara Mooyaart-Doubleday (New York: Doubleday & Company; London: Valentine Mitchell, 1952), entry for 6 June 1944.
7   Dylan, 'The times they are a-changin'', lines 14 and 15.
8   ibid., line 17.

Ni Sa Bula / Namaskar / G'Day

> We are but creatures of our origins, and however stalwartly we march forward, paving new roads, seeking new worlds, the ghosts from our pasts stand not far behind and are not easily shaken off.
>
> — M.G. Vassanji[1]

> [F]or the wind passes over it, and it is gone, and its place knows it no more
>
> — Psalm 103:16 (ESV)

Welcome, dear reader, aboard a journey of exploration. First, though, a word or two for the reader new to Fiji. It is an archipelago of some 300 islands in the south-west Pacific, between 15 and 22 degrees south latitude and between 175 degrees east and 177 degrees west longitude, astride the 180th meridian. Most of Fiji's 906,000 people live on the two main islands of Viti Levu and Vanua Levu. Close to 60 per cent of the total population is indigenous Fijian, now called *iTaukei*; about 30 per cent (and declining) is Indo-Fijian and the remainder comprises Pacific Islanders, Europeans, part-Europeans, Chinese, Rotumans and others. Settled about 3,000 years ago by waves of seafarers from the Western Pacific, the islands came into intensive contact with the outside world in the early years of the nineteenth century—which fundamentally altered the course of Fijian history. Christian missionaries of the London Missionary Society arrived from Tahiti via Tonga in 1835, followed by Methodist and Roman Catholic missionaries. Their influence rapidly spread throughout the islands, with the conversion of the native Fijians nearly complete by the latter half of the nineteenth century. Today, Fiji's pre-Christian past is a dim, fading, disparaged memory.

---

1 M.G. Vassanji, *No New Land* (Toronto: McClelland & Stewart, 1991), p. 4.

Other changes followed the arrival of European traders, planters and speculators and random fortune seekers. None was more significant than the British acquisition of the islands in 1874 after previous attempts at cession had been rejected for strategic and financial reasons. Cession put in train a set of policies that shaped Fiji's destiny for over a century. In 1879, the first group of Indian indentured labourers arrived to work on sugarcane plantations to provide the necessary labour force for the economic development of the nascent colony. Sugar remained the major revenue earner for Fiji for almost a century. It is now in decline due, among other things, to bad managerial leadership, lack of foresight and planning, internal political manoeuvrings among various industry stakeholders, and intense competition on the international market. Tourism and remittance are now the principal revenue earners for Fiji. Many former canegrowers whose leases have not been renewed are finding shelter in the mushrooming squatter settlements surrounding urban areas where close to 20 per cent of the population now lives in conditions reeking of desperation and destitution. These squatter settlements are their temporary destination; they most assuredly will not be their destiny, but the first stepping stone on a much longer journey, possibly even beyond Fiji. 'From Immigration to Emigration' may in time become the most apt epitaph for Fiji's Indian community.

Indigenous Fijians, too, were on the move. For nearly a century, colonial policy and traditional customary practices had confined them to the subsistence sector, governed by protective legislation that impeded their mobility and, for the most part, kept them out of mainstream society. But from the mid-twentieth century onwards, forces of change began increasingly to affect their lives. These included the intrusion of a market economy, modern education, urbanisation and, from the 1960s, as the prospect of independence loomed on the horizon, the need for trained workers to staff the bureaucracy of an independent nation. The imperative to catch up with other groups in Fiji, especially Indo-Fijians, also played a part. The fear of being dominated that had clouded their lives since the end of World War II dissipated as their numbers grew to an outright majority of the population. Now, more than 50 per cent of Fijians live in urban or peri-urban areas. They have political power, are dominant in the public service and control the military, and their influence on the affairs of the nation will continue to increase.

Fiji became independent on 10 October 1970, after 96 years of British colonial rule, tethered to its nineteenth-century moorings and hobbled by a political culture divided about the structure of power sharing among the different communities. Fiji had all the paraphernalia of democratic governance: a parliament, political parties, regular elections, but underpinned by the unspoken, though unmistakable, assumption about which ethnic group should hold the reins of national power. When that was overturned in a democratic election in 1987, a military coup overturned the verdict of the ballot box at the behest of the ruling elite, who were unwilling or unable to relinquish power. Three other coups followed, varying in motive and modus operandi—the latest in 2006, which promised to end the country's culture of coups. A new constitution promulgated in 2013 promised to take the country away from its twentieth-century moorings mired in the politics of race and calculations about traditional Fijian power arrangements. Fiji now has a fragile democracy—or rather a semblance of democracy—in which the military, not the parliament, has the ultimate guardian role over the constitution. Whether the promised path to a new future full of opportunity and potential for everyone to live harmoniously in a 'race-blind' society eventuates, remains to be seen. It may be some time yet before Fiji crosses its Rubicon. For the moment, though, in the early years of the twenty-first century, Fiji can only be described as a land of the delayed dawn.

I have spent the better part of my career spanning nearly 40 years trying to understand the history and politics of Fiji, my native country, and the history and culture of the Indian indentured experience from which I have descended. These two together with my recent frequent excursions into the territory of 'faction' writing, at the intersection of history and memory, constitute the cornerstones of my research and writing career. This collection of my essays, which covers all these subjects, is primarily for readers and researchers in Fiji and in the Fijian diaspora more generally. Specialists will have seen them in journals and books, but not lay readers. Many want to know and to understand, and they frequently write to me for advice on where to find material relevant to their interests. Most commonly, it is to see if they can access historical records to trace their roots in India. More often than not, the search is futile because most people have only the vaguest idea about the history of their forebears: the date of their arrival in Fiji, district of origin, the name of the immigrant ship. But the need to know, to understand, to connect, is deep and moving in its own way, especially among children in the diaspora wanting to get some sense of their journeys and destinations. They search websites and databases that whet their appetite for knowledge that provides them with some meaning and context. Many articles reproduced here (after some revision and updating) are available in online publications, but they are often accessible only to those already in the know. And hard copy is hard copy after all, tangible and permanent and real. Old habits die ever so slowly, especially among some of us; unreconstructed remnants of a prehistoric past. I should say that having left the academic treadmill behind, my main purpose here is to make my work accessible to the wider public, and not to improve my chances in the university promotion stakes. That past for me is now truly past.

For readers who might be interested, these essays could provide pointers to my more substantive research publications on the history and culture of the Indian diaspora and on politics and society in Fiji. A list of my major publications that are available online is listed at the end of this volume.

The essays included here are divided into three parts. The first deals with aspects of the indenture experience in Fiji through both factual narrative and creative nonfiction, or 'faction'. The longer narrative essays are followed by creative pieces that seek to explore the inner lived experience not documented in archival sources. Part 2 explores aspects of recent political developments in Fiji and seeks to understand the patterns and processes of change at work. Some of the pieces were written at the time the events described took place or soon afterwards. I have resisted the temptation to substantially alter the tone of the text to preserve its flavour at the time of writing; when the gun was still smoking, so to speak, and the future remained obscure. Part 3 has my reflections on and reaction to events and developments in which I was variously involved personally. It might be likened to an exercise in stocktaking after the end of a professional life.

I should add that the individual chapters in Part 2 of this book were written separately between 2000 and 2016, not only at different times but for different audiences. For these reasons, there is a degree of unavoidable repetition. Mostly it is in the nature of contextualising detail, so that readers will get their bearings and know the background necessary to an understanding of what follows. The other type of repetition is the same episode or discussion occurring in different chapters, although in different words. To simply cut out the repetition, apart from the first mention, could be a strained and artificial exercise. Such a course is not feasible; it would only serve to unbalance the individual chapters and, at worse, to deprive readers of information they need to know in advance of the main discussion. Besides, this is not a book that will be read sequentially, as would a monograph. Readers will be more interested in some chapters than in others, and whatever chapter they choose to read first ought to be complete in and of itself.

I realise now, as I look back over the years, that for a long time, I have been swimming against the tide of passing intellectual fashions. I am a product of my time and place, a member of the mid-twentieth-century generation gradually passing into dotage. The world that formed me has vanished beyond recall. The pursuit of scholarship in the social sciences and the humanities, which was an integral part of my journey and that of my generation, is not the flavour of the month in Fiji (but sadly, not only in Fiji). Reading for pleasure for many is an alien habit. The two-decade-long culture of coups in the country has corroded the creative spirit, and the freedom of speech is severely curtailed in the name of maintaining 'stability'. Authoritarian regimes by their very nature regard the radicalism of free thought as anathematic, dangerous for their survival, to be crushed at the first opportunity. Universities in Fiji, traditionally the site of free thought and critical enquiry, cower in the face of threatened retribution from vengeful political hierarchs controlling the funding purse and demanding compliance. Silence, then, becomes a strategy for survival and, perhaps, even a tool of passive resistance. It might also, as the Chinese philosopher Lao Tzu says, be a source of enduring strength.

The best and the brightest in Fiji, therefore, leave for other shores in search of better opportunities for themselves and their children. Understandably, they pursue those subjects—information technology, accounting, business administration, medicine, nursing and the like—which would improve their chances in the migration stakes. Once overseas, the realities of starting anew in a foreign land take their own toll. All this is perfectly understandable, if also sad. The postindependence Fiji generation has lived through an extraordinary time of triumphs and tragedies, dashed hopes and truncated aspirations, and they are not being chronicled or remembered. We must remember, always, and bear witness to our time and place, for ourselves and for those who will follow us; if we don't, no one else will. That is our obligation and responsibility. Memory must never be allowed to perish. In truth, memory is often all we have with which to contemplate the meaning of our lives and our purpose on Earth. There is no future without a past; the past, as common wisdom has it, is always present. And, as someone has said, remembering imparts possibility to the past, making what happened incomplete and completing what never was. But this may be a forlorn hope. I was distressed, as I was writing this, to learn that nearly half the graduates of the University of the South Pacific are likely to fail a basic English test. Nearly half. The rot starts with the early years of education. Distressing is the right word for this depressing state of affairs.

Still, with all the impediments, the struggle must go on. So, reflect, recreate, write. Winston Churchill was right all those years ago, 'Words are the only things that last forever'[2]—although now, of course, knowledge is also increasingly preserved and disseminated through a variety of other means. Technology is transforming our world and our way of knowing about it rapidly. As a colleague once remarked to me, somewhat too triumphantly for comfort, the hegemony of the written word is finally under siege. That may well be true, though I earnestly hope not. I hasten to emphasise that my words—and I have lived all my life in and around words, that is all I have—belong to yesterday's language. Tomorrow's words, as T.S. Eliot says in the *Four Quartets,* will await another voice, hopefully better and more resonant than mine.

The reader may want to know how 'objective' I have been in selecting and presenting material in this volume. It is a fair question. Throughout my career, I have followed Oskar Spate's advice about being honest with the reader. There is no use pretending impartiality, 'which evades responsibility by saying nothing', and partiality, 'which masks bias by presenting slanted facts with an air of objectivity'. The best thing to do in this circumstance, says Spate, is to declare one's hand so that those who disagree with the writer can see why he or she said this or that.

> The important points are that inference must be based on evidence, as carefully verified as possible, and that the choice shall be made from the evidence, and not from preconceived ideas.[3]

This is eminently fair and sensible, but there are circumstances when neutrality will simply not do. Sides will have to be taken and one's hand declared, as the reader will see from some of the essays in this volume, especially those dealing with the coups in Fiji and the culture of fear,

---

2   Winston Churchill, cited in *PerryMarshall,* n.d., available from: www.perrymarshall.com/12011/winston-churchill-words/ (accessed 31 May 2019).
3   Cited in R.G. Ward and O.H.K. Spate, 'Thirty years ago: A view of the Fijian political scene *confidential report to the British Colonial Office,* September 1959', *The Journal of Pacific History* 25(1) (1990), 103–24, at p. 103, doi.org/10.1080/00223349008572628.

violence and uncertainty they have spawned. My opposition to coups in my native country, whatever their justification or rationale—and they are abundant and relentlessly repeated—is unalterable. There is nothing redeeming or noble about overthrowing the verdict of the ballot box through the power of guns. On this question, I have never been neutral or silent. 'Neutrality helps the oppressor, never the victim,' says Elie Wiesel, the Nobel Laureate and indefatigable chronicler of the horrors of the Holocaust: 'Silence encourages the tormentor, never the tormented.'[4] As I have said before, I live within my history, not outside or above it, and accept all the challenges and opportunities that that brings. I will have it no other way.

A word about the title, which, as the reader will know by now, comes from William Butler Yeats's great poem quoted at the beginning of this volume ('Nineteen hundred and nineteen'). It is an apt description of one of the enduring themes of Fijian history of the twentieth century. It is apt for the experience of the Indo-Fijian community. The institutions, practices and protocols of village India that the Indian indentured labourers had brought with them were transformed—levelled, sometimes beyond recognition—on the plantations and in the lives of the people as they started afresh in dispersed villages across Fiji where they settled. Gradual exposure to the forces of modernity took its own toll, as did technology and travel.

It was no less so in the case of the indigenous Fijians, the *iTaukei*. Traditional institutions based on hierarchy and status came worse off in their protracted contest with the forces of change, including education, urbanisation, a modern cash economy and exposure to the forces of the modern world. The traditional gatekeepers of society lost their relevance and their role. The institutions of public life, the practice of politics and the pursuit of education, based on fraught but expedient assumptions of difference and separation, gave way to the acceptance of the values of a common humanity and a shared destiny. Everyone was slowly becoming a citizen of the Republic of Googlisthan. The world is getting more and more accessible to everyone, which is to be welcomed as the great egalitarian moment of our times, but on the other side of

---

4   Elie Wiesel, 'Nobel Peace Prize acceptance speech', Oslo, 10 Dec. 1986.

the ledger, the forces of change are also levelling the terrain of excellence and merit, the desire to explore the world beyond the horizon, to explore the unexplored wilderness.

Finally, a word about the nomenclature used in this volume. The 2013 Fiji constitution stipulates the use of 'Fijian' as the common name for all citizens of Fiji, and the word *iTaukei* as the name for the indigenous community. This designation—at first resisted by some indigenous leaders—is now being widely accepted. But, until 2013, the usage of the word 'Fijian' was restricted to the indigenous community. Since nearly all the essays included here were written before the promulgation of the latest constitution, I have retained the old usage. I welcome the new terminology of common citizenship, although I am not as sanguine as some that a mere change in name on paper, enforced through a decree rather than through extensive public debate, will necessarily bring about national cohesion or reconciliation. But it is a move in the right direction—a change long overdue, being first mooted in August 1967 by the Indo-Fijian leader A.D. Patel. We will always turn to our past, even our failed, dispiriting past, to understand ourselves why we have become what we are; but our lives will have to be lived in the future, shaped by different forces of change to those to which we have been accustomed. Inclusion, acceptance, understanding and a certain collective unity of purpose, of minds and hearts, will be—will have to be—the way of that future.

In the standard Fijian orthography, 'b' is pronounced as 'mb', as in 'number'; 'c' as 'the', as in 'there'; 'd' as 'nd', as in 'under'; 'g' as 'ng', as in 'anger'; and 'q' as 'ng', as in 'linger'. *Vinaka Vakalevu Sara, Dhanyabad.* Thank you to all those countless good men and women from around the globe whose advice and support have sustained me through all these years of ups and downs chronicled in this book. There is an end to every journey. This is the end of mine. So, dear reader, I take leave, with Graham Greene's words in *The End of the Affair:* 'A story has no beginning or end: arbitrarily one chooses that moment of experience from which to look back or from which to look ahead.'[5]

Brij V. Lal
Brisbane

---

5   Graham Greene, *The End of the Affair* (London: William Heinemann, 1951), p. 1.

PART 1
Past Present: Indenture and its Legacy

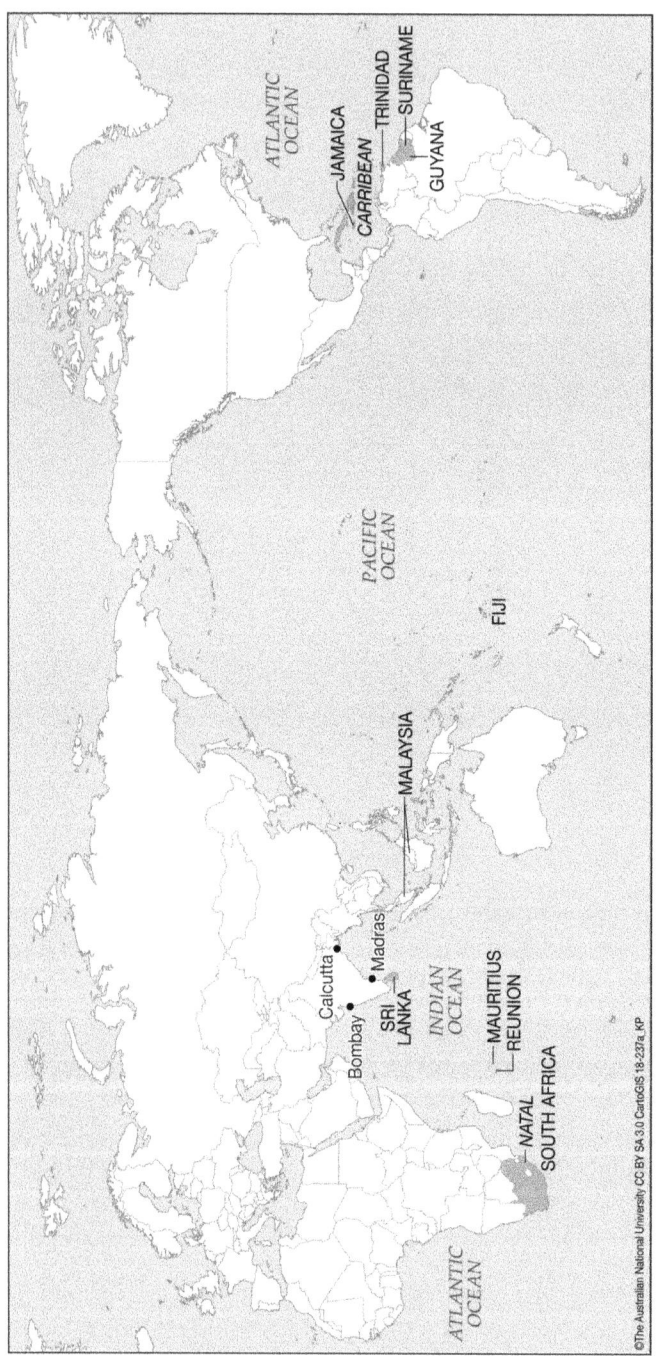

Figure 1. Map of the world showing India and Fiji
Source. © The Australian National University CC BY SA 3.0 CartoGIS 18-237a_KP.

1

Memories of indenture[1]

> How the log came to the mill
> How the tree was defeated and
> Lapped to log
> Really
> Does not matter now.
>
> — Sasenarine Persaud[2]

November 2017 marked the 100th anniversary of the end of Indian indentured immigration to the sugar colonies of the British Empire. The occasion was marked by celebrations and conferences across the Indian indentured diaspora. Much changed in the intervening hundred years, especially in our approach to our past. Once reviled and rejected, indentured immigration is now revered as the foundational cornerstone of our history, the place where it all began. There has similarly been a reevaluation in our attitude to the girmitiyas—*the humble men and women who crossed the* kala pani (*dark, dreaded seas*) *to distant places around the globe. In the following essay, I revisit the ways in which we have understood the* girmit *experience in Fiji and more generally.*

---

1   Originally appeared as 'Avatars of Fiji's girmit narrative', in *Narratives and Identity Construction in the Pacific Islands*, ed. Farzana Goundar (Amsterdam: John Benjamins Publishing Company, 2015), pp. 177–93.
2   Sasenarine Persaud, 'Let the past go pass, my love', in *They Came in Ships: An Anthology of Indo-Guyanese Prose and Poetry*, ed. Ian McDonald, Joel Benjamin, Lakshmi Kallicharan and Lloyd Seawar (Leeds: Peepal Tree Press, 1998), pp. 223–28, at p. 228.

Every so often for the past two decades or so, Indo-Fijians in Fiji and in the steadily growing and vibrant Fijian diaspora across North America and Australasia organise a 'Girmit Divas', on 14 May, to mark the arrival of Indian indentured immigrants in Fiji. Floats and processions are organised, plays performed, specially composed songs sung, poetry recited and school essay competitions held. The occasion has a carnival atmosphere about it, joyous and celebratory, not, as one might expect, solemn and contemplative. The story of *girmit* (indenture) has gone through several 'reincarnations', running the whole gamut from shame in its earliest phase through embarrassment in its middle passage to celebration in the latest, but the underlying narrative is essentially the same, a sad tale stressing suffering and sacrifice on the part of the indentured workers in the most inhospitable of conditions and in the face of impossible odds. Commemoration of *girmit* is for the most part a phenomenon of the postindependence period. It was a dormant issue during the period of colonial rule (1879–1970) for obvious reasons. There was a world of difference between the official rendition of indenture and the collective memory of the indentured labourers.

Colonial officialdom and the Colonial Sugar Refining Company (CSR), the largest employer of Fiji's indentured labour force, saw *girmit* as a positive, ameliorating experience for the labourers. It had brought a people—caught up in the quagmire of misery and destitution in India, imprisoned in a pernicious social system of inequality and oppression— and given them an opportunity for improvement they could not have ever dreamed of in their homeland. The dislocation had come at a cost, to be sure, but it was worth it in the long run. The narrative of (and for) the indentured labourers emphasised the complete opposite: degradation, violence and brutality in a system with no redeeming features at all, reducing everyone to a simple unit of labour to be exploited for the benefit of others. There was in this view no redemption, only rupture. Given the vastly contrasting and deeply contested claims about the nature and meaning of the indenture experience, the subject slipped from public discourse into virtual oblivion, and there it remained for several generations. In this chapter, I discuss the changing nature of both the scholarly treatment and the public imagination of the Fiji indenture experience. But, first, some background.

Indian indentured immigrants were first brought to Fiji in 1879—five years after Fiji became a British Crown colony—as part of first Governor Sir Arthur Gordon's policy to lay the foundations of a reluctantly acquired plantation colony.[3] Indigenous Fijians were prohibited from commercial employment and sources of labour were scarce in other Pacific Islands, embroiled in controversy or tainted with blood. So, Gordon turned to India, which was already a supplier of indentured labour to sugar colonies in various parts of the world (the Caribbean, South Africa and Mauritius). Between 1879 and 1916, over 60,000 Indian indentured men, women and children came to Fiji—the adults on a five-year contract, after which they could return to their homeland at their own expense or on a free passage after 10 years' 'industrial residence' in the colony.

The majority stayed on, encouraged by the government and the planters who were keen to have a large pool of local labour within Fiji. Since indentured emigration was state-sponsored, the Government of India was kept informed about the condition of its subjects in the colony, but in the late nineteenth century, that interest was largely passive and pro forma. From the beginning of the twentieth century, irregularities in the indenture system began to surface to public notice and their exposure brought some amelioration. But when reported sexual abuse of women reached the Indian public and threatened massive civil protest, the Government of India intervened and, ignoring pleas from Fiji, abolished the indenture system. The last indentures were cancelled on 1 January 1920.

Until then, the indentured labourers were confined to their plantation estates in a stringently supervised routine of work in and around the colony's sugar industry. They are for the most part mute and voiceless on the pages of annual reports and other memoranda in the files of the colonial secretary's office in Suva. They appear only as objects of investigation for some breach of the labour regulation or because of violence inflicted and self-inflicted. For these breaches, the indentured labourers themselves were often held responsible. In part, this was inevitable. The labourers were widely believed to be people of bad stock, from the lowest and most wretched sections of Indian society, the flotsam and jetsam of humanity, picked up from the overflowing streets of urban centres and despatched like cattle to the colonies. Nothing much could therefore be expected of people from this kind of socially corrupted and morally compromised background. They got what they deserved.

---

3   K.L. Gillion, *Fiji's Indian Migrants: A History to the End of Indenture in 1920* (Melbourne: Oxford University Press, 1962), Chs 1 and 4.

Bad stock was, of course, part of the ideology that justified the system. The truth was more complex. The immigrants were a representative sample of late nineteenth-century rural Indian society.[4] They emigrated in roughly the same proportion as their size in the total population. Migrants represented all the major castes and classes: higher castes, traders and artisans, agriculturalists and labourers, victims of profound changes taking place in rural India under the impact of the British revenue policy, which induced poverty, dislocation and the fragmentation of land holdings. Famines and droughts added their own share to the increasing rural misery.

The result was a resort to migration to urban centres for employment, making remittances an integral part of the rural economy in the Indo-Gangetic Plain of North India. Men were leaving as well as women. It was from this uprooted mass of humanity on the move that the indentured immigrants came, some undoubtedly victims of fraudulent recruiting practices by the *arkatis* (recruiters), but others in search of better opportunities elsewhere. Many did not envisage a permanent rupture, hoping to return one day. But time passed, memories of India faded and the day of decision never came.

> The passage of time
> has too long been trampled over
> to bear your wistful recollections,
> and you only know the name
> of the ship they brought you on
> because your daadi told it to you.[5]

They were 'coolies' in the eyes of the colonial world, beasts of burden, but some suffered more than others. Women bore the brunt of racism as well as sexism. They were held accountable for the two most obstinate problems of indenture. One was the heart-rending high infant mortality rates, especially in the 1890s, when nearly a quarter of the children could die within the first year of birth. Officials laid the blame for this at the feet of Indian mothers, who allegedly lacked the 'motherly instinct' due in part to their loose morals, rampant promiscuity and poor hygiene.[6]

---

4   Brij V. Lal, *Girmitiyas: The Origins of the Fiji Indians* (Canberra: Journal of Pacific History, 1983).
5   Shanan Yardan, 'Earth is brown', in *They Came in Ships,* ed. McDonald et al., pp. 242–50, at p. 250.
6   Brij V. Lal, 'Kunti's cry', in Brij V. Lal, *Chalo Jahaji: On a Journey of Indenture through Fiji* (Suva: Fiji Museum, 2000; Canberra: ANU E Press, 2012), pp. 195–214, doi.org/10.22459/CJ.12.2012; Ralph Shlomowitz, 'Infant mortality and Fiji's Indian migrants, 1879–1919', *Indian Economic and Social History Review* 23(3) (1986): 289–302, doi.org/10.1177/001946468602300303.

Few attributed the calamity to the nature of plantation work and the routine itself: the absence of child-rearing facilities on the estate lines; the compulsion on women to return to back-breaking field work soon after giving birth; the prevalence of debilitating infectious diseases such as hookworm diarrhoea, dysentery and anaemia to which many, mothers and children included, succumbed in disastrous numbers. These diseases were, by far, the biggest takers of human life on the plantations.[7]

The other major problem afflicting the Indian indentured population was suicide. Suicide was not a major killer but because of its tragic and sensational nature, violent and unnatural, it attracted public attention; and Fiji Indians at the turn of the twentieth century had the highest suicide rate among all Indian labour-importing colonies.[8] For this tragedy, too, women bore the major blame. 'Sexual jealousy' was the catch-all phrase used to explain the cause of death. Proportionately more men than women took their own lives. There was sexual disparity in the recruited population, with a stipulated 40 women migrating to every 100 men. The ratio had been in place since the 1870s and was invariably met in Fiji's case.

But while the recruitment of some women alleviated the disparity somewhat, it did not solve it. Competition for women was an inescapable fact of life on the plantations. Officials alleged that women ruthlessly exploited their 'scarce value'. They reportedly attached themselves to one man, got their rewards in jewellery and other valuable items, moved on to another man and perhaps another, leaving the jilted men to take their lives, most commonly by hanging. No doubt some women trafficked in sex, but suicides had other causes besides sexual jealousy: the cultural prejudice of the dominant towards the minority communities;[9] the collapse of the integrative institutions of society such as family, kinship and community; the violence; the relentless pace of work; and the sense of despair and hopelessness that followed the realisation that the break with India was permanent, and that there would be no return. And most of the suicides occurred within a relatively short time following the immigrants' arrival in the colony.

---

7   See Glenn Fowler, '"A want of care"', in Lal, *Chalo Jahaji,* pp. 237–90; Nicole Duncan, 'Death on Fiji plantations', in Lal, *Chalo Jahaji,* pp. 291–323; Anthony Cole, 'Accidental deaths', in Lal, *Chalo Jahaji,* pp. 324–36; Jane Harvey, 'Naraini's story', in Lal, *Chalo Jahaji,* pp. 337–47.
8   Brij V. Lal, 'Veil of dishonour', in Lal, *Chalo Jahaji,* pp. 215–38.
9   Vijay Naidu, *The Violence of Indenture in Fiji* (Suva: World University Service, 1980).

These were truths revealed in scholarly investigations decades later. In official discourse and imagination, the *girmitiyas* remained beasts of burden from broken backgrounds that had done well for themselves by migrating to Fiji. Instead of holding grudges against the government and the planters, the *girmitiyas* should be grateful for the opportunities that came their way, grateful to be delivered from grinding poverty and social oppression. Indenture had its faults. There were breaches of the penal code, there was violence, but these blemishes were not enough to besmirch the name of the system itself. Officials had come to accept that the 'curtailment of liberty implicit in the system was reasonable and just'.[10] The same narrative persisted after the end of indenture in 1920 when Indians in Fiji began to demand political representation on the basis of equal franchise.[11] The pages of the legislative council debates are replete with words and phrases from European members imputing inferiority to the Indians and demanding observance from them of their proper place in the broader scheme of things in Fiji—at the bottom. Because of their lowly, untutored background, Indians could not possibly be trusted as partners in government, which should, instead, continue to remain in European hands. That was the natural order of things, preordained.

The gaze turned from contempt to pity in the eyes of missionaries and others who began to take an interest in the life of the indentured Indians at the beginning of the twentieth century. For J.W. Burton, the generally well-disposed Methodist missionary, the only salvation for the Indians lay in converting to Christianity, to which cause he expended considerable effort but without success. Burton showed a more sympathetic understanding of the predicament of the Indians and the environment in which they worked, the pressures they endured. He wrote, 'The coolies, however, are not all scum. Among them are to be found, here and there, well-educated men, of good caste and not without refinement.'[12] But these opinions were few and far between; for the missionaries, the best of them were Christian converts and others well versed in Western etiquette.

---

10   Brij V. Lal, *Crossing the Kala Pani: A Documentary History of Indian Indenture in Fiji* (Canberra: Division of Pacific and Asian History, Research School of Pacific and Asian Studies, The Australian National University, and Suva: Fiji Museum, 1998), p. 215.
11   K.L. Gillion, *The Fiji Indians: Challenge to European Dominance, 1920–1946* (Canberra: Australian National University Press, 1977), Ch. 7.
12   J.W. Burton, *The Fiji of Today* (London: Charles H. Kelly, 1910), p. 277; Gillion, *Fiji's Indian Migrants,* pp. 166–67.

Hannah Dudley puts it this way:

> An Indian in becoming a Christian, they [Indians] believe, ceases to be an Indian; he eats meat willingly, drinks water others have been drinking, and breaks other religious laws, the doing of which is considered by them far more heinous than any violation of the moral code. They believe that Christianity is the religion for Europeans and Hinduism is for the Indians.[13]

Mrs Bailey in M.G. Vassanji's masterly novel *The Book of Secrets,* about East Indians in East Africa, expresses a view that would aptly describe the Fiji situation: 'The Indians are half savages,' she says. 'And therefore worse,' her companion agrees. 'You can do nothing with them.' Gone too far the other way for salvation, the Hindus and Muslims are 'incorrigible in their worst suspicions. They will always remain so'.[14] Once again, women incurred the moral censure of the missionaries. Florence Garnham examined the social and moral conditions of the Indians on the plantations and, although sympathetic, wrote of the 'utter abandonment of morals' by young and old alike. 'The life on the plantations alters their [women's] demeanour and even their very faces. Some looked crushed and broken hearted, others sullen, others hard and evil.'[15]

Of all the missionaries and expatriate observers, the most influential was Mahatma Gandhi's confidante and emissary C.F. Andrews.[16] He visited Fiji twice, in 1916 and 1918, and wrote a probing, if also frequently prejudiced, report (in the form of a substantial pamphlet) on his findings. He was, as expected, critical of much of what he saw: the failings of the indenture system; its many irregularities; breaches of the labour regulations; and the need for urgent reform. Perhaps his mind about the evils of the indenture system had already been made up before he left India. The indenture system had to go irrespective of any other consideration. Andrews's account, especially of the abuse of indentured women, who came in for severe treatment in his report, caught the public imagination in India, which led eventually to the abolition of the system.

---

13 Morven Sidal, *Hannah Dudley: Hamari Maa* (Suva: Pacific Theological College, 1997), p. 38.
14 M.G. Vassanji, *The Book of Secrets* (Toronto: McClelland & Stewart, 1994), p. 44.
15 Florence E. Garnham, 'Report on the social and moral conditions of Indians in Fiji', quoted in Brij V. Lal, *Crossing the Kalapani: A Documentary History of Indian Indenture in Fiji* (Suva: Fiji Museum, 1998), p. 162.
16 Hugh Tinker, *The Ordeal of Love: C.F. Andrews and India* (London: Oxford University Press, 1979).

He wrote of the collapse of culture and custom among the immigrants, and the squalid living conditions in the 'lines', which, he said, had the 'morals of the poultry yard'. Andrews wrote:

> The Hindu woman in this country is like a rudderless vessel with its masts broken … being whirled down the rapids of a great river without any controlling hand. She passes from one man to another, and has lost even the sense of shame in doing so.[17]

This portrayal was as harsh as it was unfair, but truth, in the objective sense, was not a part of his purpose or brief. Andrews was engaged in a moral crusade against indenture, and if women had to be demonised to arouse the conscience of India, then that price had to be paid by the victims. That is one of the saddest legacies of the anti-indenture struggle in Fiji and elsewhere.

A similar picture of moral collapse and degradation emerges from Totaram Sanadhya's *Fiji Dwip Men Mere Ikkis Varsh* (My twenty-one years in Fiji).[18] Totaram had come to Fiji as an indentured labourer in 1892 and returned to India in 1913 when Hindi journalist Benarsidas Chaturvedi ghost wrote an account of Sanadhya's time in Fiji. But that account was a polemical text, designed to expose the horrors of the indenture system and to contribute to its abolition. In this endeavour, it was singularly successful.[19] Once again, the treatment of women, especially their sexual exploitation by European overseers, and Indian *sirdars* (foremen), too, played a critical role in awakening the Indian conscience towards the atrocities committed in Fiji and other sugar colonies. Indians as victims is the dominant theme in the narrative. But only that portion of the manuscript that detailed the horrors of the indenture experience, and which could thus aid the anti-indenture crusade, was published. That portion that concerned the social and cultural life of the Indian community in Fiji remained unpublished. Chaturvedi gave that manuscript to Ken Gillion, author of the standard history of Indian indentured migrants to Fiji, who passed it on to his last doctoral student (me). An edited version was published in

---

17 C.F. Andrews and W.W. Pearson, *Indian Indentured Labour in Fiji* (Perth: Privately published, 1918), Appendix, p. 6.
18 Totaram Sanadhya, *My Twenty-One Years in Fiji, and, The Story of the Haunted Line*, ed. and trans. John Dunham Kelly and Uttra Kumari Singh (Suva: Fiji Museum, 1991).
19 Gillion, *Fiji's Indian Migrants*, pp. 147, 158, 174–75.

1994 and revised and reissued in 2012.[20] The manuscript reveals some of the darker aspects of the inner life of the Indian community: the duplicity and deception; the nefarious goings on in the community; and the fraudulence and exploitation by Indian moneylenders and charlatans. But all this remained hidden from the public view for nearly a century.

The abolition of indenture in 1920 marked the end of the first phase of the Indo-Fijian presence in Fiji. The second began soon afterwards with twin projects at the forefront of the community's social and political agenda. The political agenda began with the demand for equal political representation on the basis of noncommunal franchise—that is, a common roll. Indian leaders raised the issue in 1929 when they were first elected to the legislative council.[21] The motion was, unsurprisingly, defeated, whereupon the Indian elected members walked out. They returned later without their demands being met, but the common roll issue would continue as a major political platform for the community over the next half century. Interestingly, the demand for equality was based on the notion of equal citizenship as members of the British Empire irrespective of race or creed. *Girmit* featured little in this discourse or in much else at the time. The eyes of the Indo-Fijian community were firmly focused on the future, not on the past, which had no redeeming features.

On the cultural front, the Indo-Fijians began the massive task of reconstruction to give identity and purpose to a people floundering in the wilderness, unsure of which way to go. A number of voluntary organisations such as the then India Sanmarga Ikya Sangam (TISI) and the Fiji Muslim League were founded in the 1920s to provide moral guidance and leadership to their followers. The older Hindu organisations, the Sanatan Dharam and Arya Samaj, engaged in vigorous (and, in hindsight, futile) debates about the validity and legitimacy of certain rituals and cultural protocols, the proper way to worship, to celebrate life and mourn its passing, as did the Sunnis and the Shias over the correct interpretations of the Qur'an and the proper line of succession following the Prophet Mohammed's death. Temples and mosques appeared in most Indo-Fijian settlements.

---

20 Brij V. Lal and Yogendra Yadav (eds), *Bhut Len Ki Katha: Totaram Sanadyha's Fiji* [in Hindi] (New Delhi: Saraswati Press, 1994); Brij V. Lal, Ashutosh Kumar and Yogendra Yadav (eds), *Bhut Len ki Katha: Girmit ke anubhav. By Totaram Sanadhya* (The story of the haunted line: The experience of *girmit* by Totaram Sanadhya) (New Delhi: Rajkamal Prakashan, 2012).
21 Gillion, *The Fiji Indians*, pp. 137–39.

A new world was beginning to emerge, forged from the remnants of a remembered past but shorn of the arcane rites and rituals of village India. Over time, religion became one of the primary markers of identity in the Indo-Fijian community, drawing boundaries that would become hard to cross or were crossed at considerable personal and social cost. *Panchayats* (village councils) were encouraged in the 1930s, based on the Indian model, to help resolve tension and conflict in the community, but these gave way to more egalitarian councils reflecting the changed realities of Fiji. Indo-Fijian settlements were a haphazard collection of widely scattered households with few settled ideas about the codes for correct conduct so well understood on the subcontinent. Fiji was not India.

Rudimentary schools sprang up, giving children a semblance of education. I have in front of me as I write a rare bound copy of the English–Hindi *Fiji School Journal* from 1929–1934—an official government publication— which contains lessons taught in Indian primary schools throughout Fiji. The content of the curriculum is revealing. Apart from lessons on such basic things as good hygiene and good husbandry, the *Journal* has comprehension lessons about the kings and queens of England, great achievements of English and Western civilisations and technology as well as stories on legendary figures of Indian mythology and more recent history: pride-inducing pieces that pupils were expected to memorise and reproduce on paper. There was near-total amnesia about Fiji's history, and nothing on the historical experience of the Indians in Fiji; this when the majority of the pupils reading the text were Indian. It is as if that past never existed. Instead, Indian children were taught about the remote pasts of England and India. As for *girmit* itself, its 50th anniversary occurred in May 1929. Prominent Indian groups burnt an effigy of 'Mr Girmit' and observed the occasion as a day of shame.[22] Indenture was the site of embarrassing, not inspirational, history.

And so it remained for the next three decades or more. Children growing up in Fiji in the 1950s and 1960s knew little about their foundational past. *Girmitiyas* were on their way out, and those few remaining were often treated as oddities, clad in *dhoti* and *kurta,* with a *pagri* on their close-cropped heads, speaking a variety of dialects incomprehensible to us; they were a people from another place and another time, waiting to die, irrelevant to our needs and times. There was no serious enquiry

---

22 ibid., pp. 120–56.

about them, no effort to listen to their stories. No one talked. By the time attitudes changed and people wanted to know, it was too late. Our cane-farming parents were eking out a meagre livelihood on the outer edges of poverty on a 10-acre (4-hectare) block of leased land.

Neither they nor we had the time, energy or curiosity to enquire about an important but rapidly fading past. It appears important to us now, but it was not then. At school, too, the past pattern of amnesia persisted. There was nothing about *girmit,* or about Fiji for that matter more generally, in the school texts, which were instead full of material on the history and geography of the United Kingdom and later Australia and New Zealand. The children were being prepared for careers as teachers, administrators, managers and civil servants in an independent Fiji that did not need half-baked *babus* (Indian male clerks) conducting enquiries into the country's past and asking troublesome questions.

Two things indirectly provided an added impetus to the rejuvenation of interest in the past. One was the founding of the University of the South Pacific in 1968—an historic event that for the first time placed tertiary education within the reach of most people in Fiji, including children from poor homes. The intellectual ethos and mission of the university were firmly utilitarian: to provide trained workers for a rapidly decolonising Pacific. Nonetheless, its humanities and social science curricula introduced students to aspects of Fijian and Pacific Islands' histories and cultures. It was through these courses that I encountered texts about my own past, in books such as Gillion's *Fiji's Indian Migrants* and Adrian Mayer's *Peasants in the Pacific*.[23] It was an enthralling experience to come across names of people and places and events with which we were intimately familiar but which we had hitherto not seen in written words. My curiosity was further aroused by short stories by authors such as Raymond Pillay, who wrote with insight, sympathy and humour about the inner lives of our people that took us further and further back into the past.[24] *Girmit* was no longer a vague, strange word but one whose resonances could be seen and felt. It was real. We felt connected.

---

23 Gillion, *Fiji's Indian Migrants*; Adrian C. Mayer, *Peasants in the Pacific: A Study of Fiji Indian Rural Society,* 2nd edn (Berkeley, CA: University of California Press, 1973).
24 Raymond Pillay, *The Celebration: Collection of Short Stories* (Suva: South Pacific Creative Arts Society, 1980).

The 100th anniversary of the arrival of Indians in Fiji, in 1979, was celebrated as a national holiday marked by multifaith prayers, music, dance and sports. Surviving *girmitiyas,* well into their twilight years, were sought out and feted on the national stage and their experiences recorded for posterity by radio.[25] They were being honoured, for the first time, for all that they had done for Fiji under the most difficult and inhumane of circumstances. The word *girmit* gained a currency it never had before. Scholars contributed their own share. Ahmed Ali, the then leading Fiji historian at the University of the South Pacific, taped interviews with *girmitiyas* in various parts of Fiji, including in Labasa, my home town.[26] Ali was a Suva-bred boy, Marist-educated, with practically no knowledge of Hindi, so he conducted the interviews with the assistance of others, myself included.

There were no set questions, no systematic interview pattern—the main concern was to obtain the information that could be extracted from very old people with porous memories. The tapes were transcribed, but by whom it is not known; and they have disappeared so that it is not possible to authenticate the accuracy of the transcriptions. For the most part, it contains accounts of pain and hardship, brutality and exploitation. That seemed to be the sum total of the *girmitiyas'* plantation experience. There was no probing about alternative narratives that might suggest diversity and difference in the experience of indenture.

Ahmed Ali's extended introduction made explicit his central thesis that indenture was simply slavery by another name, a 'total institution' whose brutality and violence took unimaginable toll on the *girmitiyas,* psychologically 'infantilising' them. *Girmit* was *narak,* hell, 'as pernicious towards the end as it was in the beginning; violence engulfed life in the *Girmit* lines till abolition'. 'Violence characterized the relations of the ruler and the ruled, between master and servant, and among the labourers.' Murder and mayhem were the order of the day: 'Indentured labourers found strange solace in domestic violence, men against women, and in

---

25   Farzana Gounder, *Indentured Identities: Resistance and Accommodation in Plantation-Era Fiji* (Amsterdam: John Benjamins Publishing, 2011).
26   Ahmed Ali, *Girmit: The Indenture Experience in Fiji* (Suva: Fiji Museum, 1979). See also Doug Munro, 'In the wake of the *Leonidas:* Reflections on Indo-Fijian indenture historiography', *The Journal of Pacific Studies* 28(1) (2005), pp. 93–117, available from: www.usp.ac.fj/fileadmin/files/Institutes/jps/DougMunro.pdf (accessed 5 April 2018).

manslaughter and murder.' All in all, the experience was 'dehumanising', 'brutalising', 'traumatic, destabilising and disorienting in nature', 'an inevitable purgatory towards earthly paradise'.

> The plantation system was a microcosm of the colonial microcosm in which planters prospered. Both were hierarchical and sustained by an ideology of organised racism wherein the person with white skin was master, the dark skin destined to slave for the white master's gain. Violence was endemic in both the colonial universe and the plantation compound.[27]

Ali was hugely influenced by the narrative of indenture authored by Hugh Tinker in his highly influential and emotionally charged 1974 book, *A New System of Slavery*.[28] The title said it all. Indenture was simply slavery by another name. Men and women who came under it were improperly recruited under false promises. On the plantations, violence ruled the day. Elaborate rules on paper governing the system remained largely that, rules on paper, nothing more. The hand of justice remained distant and arbitrary, and this condition persisted throughout the life of the system. Tinker's thesis was widely popular and its appeal persists among both the lay and the scholarly community for it has become an all-encompassing, emotionally appealing explanation of indenture needing no further enquiry or scrutiny. It settles the issue beyond dispute or debate. The slavery thesis, by emphasising suffering and sacrifice with no rewards, also found resonance in the political struggle of Indian communities for full acceptance and equality across the globe, from Guyana and Fiji to Burma, Uganda and South Africa.

Things have moved on. The *girmit* narrative is no longer concerned with the grand moral questions of indenture, with questions of right and wrong and with apportioning blame. Among a newer generation of scholars, the appeal of the Tinker thesis has dimmed. The latest dissension from the slavery thesis comes from Trinidad's Gerard Tikasingh who rejects 'the mythic ideas that indentured immigration was some form of disguised slavery'. Indenture, he argues, was 'a contract for a five-year term of service, for which the worker was paid. It was a contract for a term of

---

27 Ahmed Ali, 'Resisting girmit', in *Girmitiya: Souvenir Magazine of the National Farmers Union* (Suva, 2004), pp. 64–69.
28 Hugh Tinker, *A New System of Slavery: The Export of Indian Labour Abroad, 1830–1920* (London: Oxford University Press, 1974).

service, not involving the ownership of a person'.[29] Violence and brutality in the system are readily conceded, but the diverse experience in different places is also acknowledged. Fiji was not Guyana or South Africa. There was change over time.

Greater agency is accorded to the *girmitiyas* in the making of their own histories. The emphasis in the literature has now shifted to the actual lived experiences of indenture, the ways in which men and women from a variety of social and economic backgrounds coped with the demands made on them, raised families, formed communities and forged new identities from fragments of the new and the old. In Fiji at least, indenture was not a life sentence, as it was in some other places. But it was a limited detention of five or at most 10 years, after which the freed *girmitiyas* set up on their own in settlements of leased or privately acquired lands.

This, then, is the latest avatar of the *girmit* narrative, but it struggles to find full acceptance in popular imagination. Nuance, qualification and subtlety do not travel as well as sharp images and views simply presented in stark, easily grasped words. That, I suppose, is the fate of scholarly discourse in the public arena. But at least *girmit* is no longer an experience languishing in the shadows; a cause for shame and embarrassment. It has become a household word among Indo-Fijians and many indigenous Fijians have also heard of *girmit*. During the 2004 celebrations marking the 125th anniversary of the arrival of Indians in Fiji, it was interesting to observe two rival groups, aligned to two different Indo-Fijian political parties, the Fiji Labour Party and the National Federation Party. Each published separate glossy pamphlets full of pictures and stories about the past and potted biographies of prominent individuals. They organised rallies and ceremonies to mark the occasion. Subtly, each was accentuating the role and contribution of its own selected heroes, each claiming to be the proper inheritor of the legacy of *girmit*. Some used the occasion to differentiate the descendants of the 'pioneer' Indians who came under indenture from the free migrants who came later—to differentiate between *girmitiyas* and non-*girmitiyas*. This has long been a refrain in Indo-Fijian political discourse and the politics of inclusion and exclusion.

---

29   Gerard Tikasingh, *Trinidad During the 19th Century: The Indian Experience* (Trinidad: R.P.L. Limited, 2012), pp. x–xi.

The commemoration of *girmit* has acquired a political edge to it in recent decades as Fijian nationalists have tried to disinherit the Indo-Fijian community of their political rights. Subtly, the *girmit* experience is transformed into a serviceable ideology to demand equal rights for the descendants of the *girmitiyas,* not as a matter of grace from the powers that be, but as a matter of birthright; we have earned our right to belong to this country as full citizens. This is our home, too. We are not here on the sufferance of others. Our existence here is non-negotiable.

> Generations nurtured from my seeds
> will clasp their hands and say
> our ancestors carved those fields
> which have given us meanings
> meanings to stand tall
> This land is ours too.[30]

The quest for acceptance and equality is both legitimate and necessary, but it clashes head-on with another powerful claim: the claim to paramountcy by the indigenous Fijians, premised on the assumption that as the first settlers in the land, their rights, interests and concerns deserve privileged consideration. The paramountcy versus parity paradigm keeps the *girmit* experience as an ideological platform at the forefront of Indo-Fijian political discourse.

Remembering *girmit* is no longer confined to the Indo-Fijian community in Fiji alone. The *girmit* narrative has taken a different turn in recent decades with the increasing size of the Indo-Fijian diaspora in North America and in Australia and New Zealand. There is a palpable sense of the need to know in the new generation growing up in these places. Hardly a week goes by when I do not receive a request from a complete stranger, usually a younger person, often a university student, for information about their roots in India. The need to know is deep and genuine, but the quest often remains unrealised because the information about their ancestors (their district of origin, the name of the ship on which they came, the approximate date of migration) is incomplete. Some younger investigators have made documentaries or short films about their journeys back.

---

30 Rooplall Monar, 'Babu', in *They Came in Ships,* ed. McDonald et al., pp. 203–05, at p. 205.

Others have written poems and short stories and songs about the *girmit* experience, repeating the popular rendition of the past. But, so far, we do not have an extensive literary exploration of the indenture experience, the sole exception being Jogindar Singh Kanwal's Hindi novella *Savera* (The dawn). Fiji has not yet produced an Abhmanyu Anath (of Mauritius), the author of the great novel *Lal Pasina* (Bloody sweat), although Subramani's *Dauka Puran* (Scoundrel's tale), about the postindenture period in Fiji, is a signal achievement.[31] And Fiji compares very poorly with the literary efflorescence of the Indo-Caribbean where novelists, writers of short fiction, poets and playwrights have long been engaged in a massive literary reconstruction of their past. Much of the best Indo-Fijian literary effort, such as it is, is focused on the contemporary period, some of it in a rather incongruous postcolonial mode.

In keeping with the times, the electronic media has entered the scene. Several websites—Fiji Girmit, Girmitunited.org and Fiji Global Girmit Institute—provide access to raw historical data as well as published pieces about various aspects of indentured migration and settlement in Fiji. This is to be welcomed; it is the way of the future. The internet and the visual media will become the new frontiers where the future narrative of *girmit* will be written and debated. The internet, it goes without saying, will reach far larger audiences than the print media can ever hope to match. But there is a negative side to this as well. The internet has sometimes become the vehicle for the propagation of private opinion which passes for scholarship. Emotion overrides thought and reasoned debate. Often it is a case of 'my mind is made up; do not confuse me with facts'. I know of some fairly desperate people being encouraged to apply for an Australian immigration visa and they demand sympathetic consideration on the grounds that their ancestors toiled for the CSR. No chance there.

Some advocate compensation from the British Government for the sufferings Indian people endured under indenture.[32] This is an emotionally appealing cause but legally futile. The labourers came under a contract and jettisoned the right to return when their indentures expired and war-interrupted shipping resumed. Not everyone wanted to return either. 'Most of us regard Fiji as our permanent home,' Indians had told the Secretary of State for the Colonies in December 1927.[33] More than a century later,

---

31 Subramani, *Dauka Puran* (New Delhi: Star Publications, 2001).
32 Gounder, *Indentured Identities*, p. 39.
33 Gillion, *The Fiji Indians*, p. 105.

why would the British Government pay compensation; to whom and how much? But this is a microcosm of a much larger problem of the cyber age: anything goes, at the expense of discrimination and a serious quest for accuracy based on painstaking research. Instant gratification is the order of the day.

In one important respect, things have changed. The *girmitiyas* are no longer viewed as objects of contempt and pity as they had been in the late nineteenth and early twentieth centuries, or as curious, irrelevant oddities, as they were for a generation or two after the end of indenture. They are now figures of reverence in the Indo-Fijian imagination, people from impoverished, improbable backgrounds who achieved great things in the face of very great odds. Their resilience and resourcefulness are celebrated in public discourse. Mythic figures now, they represent nothing less than the triumph of the human spirit over adversity. It has been a long time coming. Former Fiji Indian leader Jai Ram Reddy catches the current consensus of opinion:

> The girmitiyas gave meaning to the ideals of hard work, perseverance, commitment and endurance, and provided the example and inspiration for subsequent generations to emulate. That is the lasting legacy of girmit and the girmitiyas.[34]

And it is well worth commemorating. In the words of Guyana's Sasenarine Persaud:

> Let the wood go to dressing
> And highly polished school
> Of furniture
> Let each kingly grain of sawdust
> Spin jubilantly to the crown of the heap
> Until the jubilant past
> Overtakes everything.[35]

---

34 Jai Ram Reddy, 'Message', in *Girmit's Greatest Gift: Magazine of the Fiji Girmit Council* (Suva, 2004), n.p.
35 Persaud, 'Let the past go pass, my love', p. 228.

2
'Such a long journey': The story of indenture[1]

> But the past must live on,
> For it is the soul of today
> And the strength of the morn;
> A break to silent tears
> That mourn the dream of stillborn.
>
> — Churamanie Bissundayal[2]

Between 1834 and 1920, over 1 million Indian men and women were transported across the seas to serve as indentured labourers to sugar colonies around the world. Most never returned to their homeland. Their descendants today comprise an integral part of the larger mosaic of the Indian diaspora. The history of indenture is no longer an area of darkness as it once was, though there are many aspects of the indenture experience that still await scholarly attention. The following chapter provides the larger historical context of Indian indenture, from recruitment in India to life on the plantations. Fiji in 1879 was the last major sugar colony to import Indian indentured labour. It played a significant role in the struggle to end the indenture system worldwide.

---

1   Originally appeared as 'Indian indenture: Experiment and experience', in *Routledge Handbook of the South Asian Diaspora*, ed. Joya Chatterji and David Washbrook (London: Routledge, 2013), pp. 79–95.
2   Churamanie Bissundayal, 'The arrival: Part 1', in *They Came in Ships: An Anthology of Indo-Guyanese Prose and Poetry*, ed. Ian McDonald, Joel Benjamin, Lakshmi Kallicharan and Lloyd Seawar (Leeds: Peepal Tree Press, 1998), pp. 214–15, at p. 215.

On 9 September 1834, 36 lost-looking Dhangars (tribal people from the Chota Nagpur region) met some recruiters in Calcutta and were asked if they would be willing to go to Mauritius as indentured labourers. The absence would be of short duration and remuneration attractive. Mirich Dwip (Mauritius) was said to be just off the coast of Bengal, and they would be back home before their absence was noticed in the village. The Dhangars agreed, for they had come to Calcutta looking for employment in the first place. Thereupon, they were taken to the chief magistrate at the Calcutta Police Court, who read out and 'explained' the terms and conditions of the contract to be signed. The men affixed their thumbprints on the document, affirming their understanding of what was on offer and that they were emigrating voluntarily. The Vice-President in Council of the Government of Bengal approved the transaction and authorised the departure of the indentured labourers. The tentative venture proved successful after initial teething problems. Between 1 August 1834 and the end of 1835, 14 ships were engaged to transport emigrants from Calcutta to Mauritius. By the end of 1839, over 25,000 Indians had been introduced into the colony. Other colonies elsewhere soon followed suit. Thus began a massive and unprecedented experiment in unskilled labour recruitment and migration. By 1870, Mauritius had 352,401 Indians, British Guiana 79,691, Trinidad 42,519 and Jamaica 15,169.[3] In 1907, Guiana's total population of Indians had swelled to 127,000, Trinidad to 103,000 and Natal to 115,000. By the time indentured emigration ceased in 1917, over 1 million indentured Indian immigrants had been transported across the dark, dreaded seas, the *kala pani,* to the 'King Sugar' colonies in the West Indies, Fiji, Mauritius and South Africa. Their descendants now constitute an important segment of the larger mosaic of the Indian diaspora.

Origins

Indian indentured emigration was started in direct response to the shortage of labour in the tropical colonies caused by the abolition of slavery in the British Empire in 1833 and by the termination of the system of apprenticeship (for six years) under which, until 1838, the planters had been able to obtain slave labour. Once freed, the former slaves understandably refused to return to their old jobs. As one official wrote:

---

3   In this chapter, both Guyana and Guiana are used. Guiana was used prior to independence in 1966. The country is now called Guyana.

> For the greater part ... the Negroes abandoned not only field labour, but service of every kind, almost as soon as they were at a liberty to do so. No present kindness, or memory of past benefits, no persuasion or pecuniary inducements could prevail upon them to remain; and it is to be feared that the time is yet distant when motives of interest, or the press of necessity, will bring them back to serve as agricultural labourers.[4]

The apprenticeship system failed because it was riddled with contradictions and paradoxes, the most important of all being the inherent ambivalence in relations between the labourers and the planters. Once freed, the labourers refused to succumb to the regime imposed on the slaves. The pattern of resistance was the same in the West Indies as it was in Mauritius.

The failure of the apprentice experiment forced the planters to look elsewhere, to Africa and Europe. Between 1834 and 1837, some 3,000 English, 1,000 Scots and the same number of Germans and a sprinkling of Irish were introduced into Jamaica and a smaller number into St Lucia. The emigrants were brought privately on contract for three to five years, although Jamaica also offered a bounty from public funds. But this experiment, too, failed because of the high mortality rate caused by insufficient sanitary precautions, 'the unsuitability of raw, un-acclimatised Europeans for field work in the tropical sun, with the added temptation of unlimited drink'.[5]

Trinidad attempted to procure labour from neighbouring Grenada, St Christopher and Nevis, engaging captains of small trading vessels with a bounty, and the promise of returning labourers to their homes after the completion of their contracts. But the bounty system, with no legal provisions specifying the terms and conditions of service, or making the contract enforceable, 'being ill-contrived and injudiciously managed', also succumbed to failure. The planters then turned to Africa but, given its former history of slavery, this was never a realistic prospect.[6]

---

4   Home Legislative Department (Emigration), A Pros. 14, 8 May 1847, National Archives of India [hereinafter NAI]; also D.W.D. Comins, *Note on Emigration from the East Indies to British Guiana* (Calcutta: Government Printer, 1893).
5   D.W.D. Comins, *Note on Emigration from the East Indies to St Lucia* (Calcutta: Government Printer, 1893), p. 3; House of Commons [hereinafter HC], Parliamentary Paper, 35 (1844), p. 316.
6   See, generally, David Dabydeen and Brinsley Samaroo (eds), *Across the Dark Waters: Ethnicity and Indian Identity in the Caribbean* (London: Macmillan Caribbean, 1996); Bridget Brereton, *A History of Modern Trinidad, 1783–1962* (Portsmouth: Heinemann, 1989), pp. 96–100.

China proved a better prospect. One official described the Chinese labourers in 1844 as:

> well made, robust, and active, inured to field labour, and able to work during the heat of the day, in fact, they are equal to our best Creole field labourers; they are eager for gain, and will do anything for money; they are quiet and very intelligent for their class, and not lazy. They value money, and are shrewd; and I do think no class of men can be better adapted to our wants than they are.[7]

But the very qualities for which the Chinese were praised made them unsuitable as long-term plantation workers. Being 'further developed in civilisation', as one official put it, the Chinese tended to move out of the plantations at the earliest possible opportunity to set themselves as market gardeners and small shopkeepers, becoming in time rivals to the very planters whom they were supposed to serve.

These failures focused attention on India as a reliable and enduring source of labour. In the nineteenth century, India remained the principal source of labour supply to the sugar colonies of the British Empire. An important attribute of the Indian indenture was that it was state regulated, not privately contracted. It was conducted on the basis of a written and supposedly voluntarily accepted contract or 'agreement' (dubbed *girmit* in Fiji), which the emigrants signed (or, more commonly, affixed their thumbprints to) before leaving India. In the early years of indentured emigration, the terms and conditions were not uniform; indeed, they varied widely in content and application. But by the 1870s, a more or less uniform document was in place for all the indentured labour-recruiting colonies. The contract stipulated, among other things, the nature and conditions of employment (dealing principally with work related to the manufacture of sugar cane), remuneration for labour on the plantations, entitlement to medical and housing facilities and, above all, the availability of a return passage to India after a period of 'industrial residence' in the colonies, usually 10 years after the date of arrival. There can be little doubt that the majority of the emigrants intended their excursion out of India to be a brief sojourn, a temporary expedient to cope with their fluctuating economic fortune at home. Many did return: up to 1870, 21 per cent of the emigrants had returned, and in the decade after 1910, one emigrant returned for every two who had embarked for the colonies.

---

7   HC, Parliamentary Paper, 35 (1844), p. 551.

But for the overwhelming majority, an intended sojourn was transformed into permanent displacement in the course of time and in response to the prevailing circumstances.

The early shipments of labourers to Mauritius drew attention to reports of neglect and ill treatment, which led the Government of India, responding to pressure from antislavery quarters, to instruct the Indian law commissioners to provide firmer legislative cover to the operation. These were incorporated in *Act V of 1837*. Among other things, the Act provided that the emigration of contract labourers was to be subject to orders from authorities from India; that the emigrants should be required to appear before an official appointed by the provincial government; that the contract, in English and the mother tongue of the emigrant, must specify wages and the nature of employment in the colonies; that contracts for a period of over five years, which did not include the provision for a return passage, were not to be approved; and that recruiters who obtained labourers through fraudulent means were to be fined or imprisoned.

The imperial dimension

Over the next several years, critics and opponents of Indian indentured emigration pointed to the disparity between the rhetoric on paper and the realities on the ground. Reports continued to reach the public of fraudulence and violence in the recruitment and shipping of labourers and of the terrible conditions of employment on the plantations. For a while, emigration was halted but it soon became clear that the prohibition of emigration could not be maintained for too long. Reports from the colonies acknowledged hardship and problems but claimed that these were exaggerated by the critics. Indeed, they claimed that immigrants in the colonies were better off than their counterparts in India.

The result of the voluminous correspondence between the colonies, the imperial government and the Government of India was the passage of the Government of India's *Act XV of 1842,* the first comprehensive legislation of its kind to provide control and supervision of the trade. The Act provided for the appointment, on fixed salary, of an emigration agent at the ports of embarkation in India. The agent, who might act for several colonies because the recruitment seasons for different places varied, was required personally to examine each emigrant and to ascertain that he or she fully understood the contract they were signing. All the emigrant ships were to be fully licensed by the government and required to conform to certain prescribed standards; dietary and medical supplies for the emigrants were prescribed, as were the accommodation facilities and indeed the length of the voyage itself. The Act was a good start, but it had no provision for the enforcement of the regulations. Nonetheless, this piece of legislation formed the basis for further reforms and amendments in the latter half of the nineteenth century.

Was there room for further government involvement? In 1875, Lord Salisbury, the Secretary of State for the Colonies, wrote to the Government of India enquiring whether, under proper regulation, and with due regard to the interest of the labourers, the Government of India 'might not more directly encourage emigration and superintend the system under which it was conducted'. In Lord Salisbury's view, indentured emigration, properly regulated, would benefit everyone: India, the United Kingdom and the emigrants themselves:

> While, then, from an Indian point of view, emigration, properly regulated, and accompanied by sufficient assurance of profitable employment and fair treatment, seems a thing to be encouraged on grounds of humanity, with a view to promote the well-being of the poorer classes; we may also consider, from an imperial point of view, the great advantage which must result from peopling the warmer British possessions which are rich in natural resources and only want population, by an intelligent and industrious race to whom the climate of these countries is well suited, and to whom the culture of the staples suited to the soil, and the modes of labour and settlement, are adapted. In this view also it seems proper to encourage emigration from India to the colonies well fitted for an Indian population.[8]

Salisbury went on to suggest a number of ways in which the Government of India might intervene directly to encourage and facilitate indentured recruitment and emigration and to reduce its various deficiencies. He urged it to exercise direct control over the type of emigrants recruited by allowing the authorities in India to 'help and counsel' the colonial agents and, in times of difficulty, to even directly recruit labourers themselves. It might also directly involve itself in ensuring that the terms

---

8   Lord Salisbury to Governor-General of India, 24 March 1875, cited in K.L. Gillion, *Fiji's Indian Migrants: A History to the End of Indenture in 1920* (Melbourne: Oxford University Press, 1962), p. 22.

and conditions of the contract the emigrants had signed in India were observed in the colonies by appointing its own agents there. In the last paragraph of his dispatch, Salisbury added:

> Above all things we must confidently expect, as an indispensable condition of the proposed arrangements [that] the Colonial laws and their administration will be such that Indian settlers who have completed their terms of service to which they are agreed as return for the expense of bringing them to the Colonies, will be in all respects free men, with privileges no whit inferior to those of any other class of Her Majesty's subjects resident in the colonies.[9]

Salisbury's dispatch was sent to all the Indian provincial governments for their comment and consideration.[10] With the exception of Bengal, all the other provinces were against the proposals. Bombay feared the loss of labour and therefore loss of revenue. Madras thought that greater involvement on its part could be misconstrued as its support for the colonial planters at the expense of the interests of India. The United Provinces (UP) Government doubted if greater encouragement would necessarily give the colonies the kind of immigrants they wanted. And so the Government of India told the Secretary of State for India that greater involvement was not feasible: 'Our policy may be described as one of seeing fair play between the parties to a commercial transaction, while the Government altogether abstains from mixing itself in the bargain.'[11] Emigration would have an 'infinitesimal effect' on the population of the districts where recruitment was most popular. Moreover, direct involvement might put India in the invidious position of having to reconcile the interests of the colonies with those of the emigrants. Perhaps most importantly, the Government of India feared being held accountable for abuses and irregularities in the recruitment process. It was this reason, more than any other, the fear of being tainted by the evils of the indenture system, that led the Government of India to abolish the indenture system in 1917, despite protest from the colonies.

---

9 ibid.
10 For detailed discussion, see Basdeo Mangru, 'Indian Government policy towards indentured labour migration to the sugar colonies', in *Across the Dark Waters,* ed. Dabydeen and Samaroo, pp. 162–74.
11 Brij V. Lal, 'Leaves of the Banyan tree: Origins and background of Fiji's North Indian migrants, 1879–1916: Vol. 1', PhD thesis (Canberra: The Australian National University, 1981), pp. 73–74.

Origins of indentured labourers

Indian indentured labourers sent to various parts of the world came from different parts of India. Predominantly, they came from the north and embarked for the colonies from the Port of Calcutta. From 1856 to 1861, 66 per cent embarked at Calcutta and 30 per cent at Madras.

South India

South India has probably always been the most migration-prone region of India. Even in prehistoric times, its inhabitants were known to have established contact with other countries. Systematic, large-scale labour migration from this region, however, began in the nineteenth century. The largest importers of South Indian labour were the Colonies of India System—Burma, Ceylon and Malaya. The exact volume emigrating is difficult to ascertain, but according to one source, between 1852 and 1937, 2,595,000 Indian emigrants settled in Burma, 1,529,000 in Ceylon and 1,189,000 in Malaya.[12]

Much of this migration took place under the supervision of the middlemen called *kanganis* in the case of Ceylon and Malaya and *maistries* in the case of Burma.[13] In Ceylon, this system was prominent from the outset while in Malaya it operated alongside indentured emigration. These middlemen, trusted and experienced employees of the plantation or the estate, were sent to their villages to recruit their fellow villagers and kinsmen. They were usually given an advance to cover the costs of recruitment and transportation but the labourers were expected to refund the amount spent on them after a period of employment. The middlemen were not mere recruiters, however; at work they were often the sole intermediaries between the workers and their employers, a position that lent itself to the possibility of corruption and extortion. The absence of comprehensive protective legislation that governed indenture, and the absence of written and legally enforceable contracts served to enhance their grip on the labourers.

---

12   Kingsley Davis, *The Population of India and Pakistan* (Princeton, NJ: Princeton University Press, 1951), p. 99.
13   See, among others, K.S. Sandhu, *Indians in Malaya: Some Aspects of their Immigration and Settlement, 1786–1957* (Cambridge: Cambridge University Press, 1969); N.R. Chakravarti, *The Indian Minority in Burma: The Rise and Decline of an Immigrant Community* (London: Oxford University Press, 1971); R. Jayaraman, 'Indian emigration to Ceylon: Some aspects of the historical and social background of the emigrants', *Indian Economic and Social History Review* 4(4) (1967), pp. 319–59, doi.org/10.1177/001946466700400402.

Malaya was the largest single importer of South Indian indentured labour; some 250,000 between 1844 and 1910. The predominance of South Indians was due partly to the reluctance of the Government of India to sanction recruitment in other parts of the country and the perception that North Indians were 'troublesome elements'. Geography, too, played its part. Indentured immigration to Malaya was different in form, if not in spirit, to that for the sugar colonies. In the case of Malaya, recruitment was carried out by speculators and the private agents of employers, while for the sugar colonies it was carried out by licensed recruiters appointed by the emigration agents and under the supervision, however minimal, of local authorities in the districts. The contract for Malaya was for one to three years; and it was not always a written document. Further, the emigration agents for the colonies assumed responsibility for the cost of recruitment and transportation, while for Malaya, the indentured labourers, like their *kangani* counterparts, had to repay a certain amount from their wages. Finally, because indentured immigration to Malaya was not strictly state regulated, the Government of India was unable, in many cases, to demand the fulfilment of certain conditions stipulated in the *Emigration Act*. In the case of the sugar colonies, for instance, the government was able successfully to insist that 40 women accompany 100 men on each shipment, but was unable to do much in this regard for Malaya.

To the sugar colonies, South India contributed upwards of 290,000 migrants: Mauritius 144,342 (32 per cent of the total); Natal 103,261 (68 per cent); Guiana 15,065 (6 per cent); Fiji 14,536 (24 per cent); West Indies 12,975 (7 per cent); Reunion 2131 (8 per cent); and French West Indies 330 (2 per cent). In the case of Mauritius, about 77 per cent had migrated before 1870. It was a similar story for Guiana and the West Indian islands. Immigration to Natal began in 1860 but increased after the 1880s. The first South Indians went to Fiji in 1903.

In South India, the labourers came from certain regions. Malaya and Ceylon drew their recruits mainly from the Tamil-speaking areas, with a sprinkling of Telugus from Andhra Pradesh and Malayalis from the Malabar Coast. Migrants to Burma came largely from Vizagapatnam and Godavari in Andhra Pradesh and, to a lesser extent, from Tanjore and Ramnad. The sugar colonies drew their immigrants from these areas as well. For Fiji, for instance, most of the South Indian emigrants were recruited in North Arcot, Madras, Kistna, Godavari, Vizagapatnam, Tanjore, Malabar and Coimbatore.[14]

Bombay

Bombay was not a major port of embarkation. The indentured labourers who left Bombay for the colonies, especially before the 1870s, came mostly from Poona, Satora, Ratnagiri, Nagpur and Sawantwadi.[15] After 1870, Bombay and Karachi (mostly Karachi) accounted for 43,221 embarkations. Of these, 36,902 were bound for Mombasa, 538 for Seychelles and 5,781 for other places. The immigrants for Mombasa came mostly from the Punjab region; they were recruited to work on the railways there, and most returned at the expiry of their contracts. In the wake of indentured emigration, small groups of free migrants (traders and artisans), mostly from Gujarat, left from Bombay for other colonies, but theirs is a different history.

French ports

India's French ports accounted for the smallest number of indentured embarkations. Altogether, between 1842 and 1916, 49,890 emigrants boarded the ships there for the colonies.[16] Of these, 20,770 (42 per cent) had left before 1870, of whom 16,000 went to the French West Indies and 4700 to Réunion. After 1870, 29,000 left for the French West Indies, Réunion and French Guiana. Embarkation from French ports was prohibited after the promulgation of the Indian *Emigration Act of 1883*, which restricted departures to the ports of Calcutta, Madras and Bombay.

Calcutta and North India

Calcutta was, of course, the most important port of embarkation for indentured emigrants destined for the sugar colonies. Interestingly, there were few Bengalis among the emigrants; indeed, they were conspicuous by their absence.[17] The overwhelming majority of the Calcutta departees

---

14   See, among others, Surendra Bhana, *Indentured Indian Emigrants to Natal, 1860–1902: A Study Based on Ships' Lists* (New Delhi: Promilla & Co., 1991), pp. 41–49; C.G. Hennings, *The Indentured Indian in Natal, 1860–1917* (New Delhi: Promilla & Co., 1993), p. 21.
15   See G. Geoghegan, *Coolie Emigration from India* (Calcutta: Government Printer, 1874); Panchanan Saha, *Emigration of Indian Labour, 1834–1900* (Delhi: People's Publishing House, 1970); J.S. Mangat, *A History of Asians in East Africa, c.1886–1945* (Oxford: Oxford University Press, 1969).
16   Geoghegan, *Coolie Emigration from India;* HC, Parliamentary Papers, various years; C.L. Tupper, *Note on Colonial Emigration during the Year 1878–1879* (Calcutta: Bengal Secretariat Press, 1879).
17   For discussion of North India, see Brij V. Lal, *Girmitiyas: The Origins of the Fiji Indians* (Canberra: Journal of Pacific History, 1983).

were 'upcountry men'. Before the 1870s, many came from the tribal and plains areas of Bihar. The ship lists for the *Hespres* and the *Whitby*, which left for British Guiana in 1838, show that of the 405 emigrants aboard the two vessels, 72 came from Hazaribagh, 49 from Bankura, 36 from Ramgarh, 27 from Midnapur and 20 from Nagpur. Dhangars furnished 34 per cent of the emigrants, Muslims 8 per cent, Rajputs and Kurmis 5 per cent each, Bauris and Bhuiyas 4 per cent each, and Kshattriyas, Gowalas and Bagdis the rest.

The tribal emigrants proved popular with the colonial planters for their supposed docile disposition and because 'they are willing to turn their hands to any labour whatever, as far as they are capable',[18] for their simple way of life and their adaptability to the hard conditions on the plantations. Further, they were in ample supply in the crowded quarters of Calcutta, where they had drifted in search of employment as their former homeland came under settled occupation. Hindu and Muslim traders, speculators, moneylenders and others in the early decades of the nineteenth century began 'to exploit simple and unsophisticated aboriginals, who were dispossessed of their holdings sometimes by legal process and sometimes by illegal means'.[19] But a high mortality rate of the 'tribals' on crowded and unsanitary voyages and the availability of appropriate employment opportunities closer to home, such as in the Assam tea gardens and the Bihar indigo plantations and coal mines, reduced the attractiveness of employment on the colonial plantations.

The decline in the volume of tribal emigration shifted colonial recruitment northwards into the settled areas of Bihar. Among the largest recruitment districts in Bihar in the 1850s and 1860s were Arrah (Shahabad), Sahebganj (Gaya), Hazaribagh, Patna, Purulia, Ranchi and Chapra (Saran). But these areas also proved a disappointing hunting ground for colonial recruiters in the long run. Like the tribals, these people too were attracted by employment opportunities nearer home. At the same time, encouraged perhaps by the advent of railways, large numbers of Biharis were turning towards Bengal, especially Calcutta, where they were in great demand as *palki*-bearers, *pankah*-pullers, peons, *lathials* (guards) and

---

18   John Mackay, 'Additional memoranda, 22 May 1837, submitted for the consideration of his Excellency the Governor, and to be laid before the Legislative Council, should his Excellency consider it proper', Appendix No. 2, Memorandum on Indian Immigration in *Accounts and Papers: Seventeen Volumes, (5), Colonies: Emigration; Australia; Prisons; West Indies; &c.,* Session 15 November 1837–16 August 1838, Vol. XL, p. 24, no further details available.
19   Lal, *Girmitiyas*, pp. 75–76.

general labourers. The advantage of internal over colonial migration was that it enabled the immigrants to return to their villages in the planting and harvesting seasons.

From the 1870s onwards, the focus of indentured recruitment shifted to the UP of Agra and Oudh, as they were called, and they remained the principal suppliers of labour for the remaining period of indentured emigration.[20] Within the UP, it was the eastern (*poorbea*) districts that furnished the bulk of the emigrants—districts such as Basti, Gonda, Faizabad, Sultanpur, Azamgarh, Gorakhpur, Allahabad and Ghazipur. Many factors explain their popularity: a depressed economy, dwindling property rights, fragmentation of landholdings, subdivision of property, heavy population density, the effects of periodic droughts, floods and famine and, finally, an established pattern of migration. The number of *poorbeas* enumerated in Bengal increased significantly over the last quarter of the nineteenth century: 351,933 in 1880, 365,248 in 1891 and 496,940 in 1901.[21]

Indeed, according to one informed observer, there was hardly a single family in the entire Benares region that did not have at least one member in employment in other places. It was from this uprooted mass of humanity that the indentured emigrants came. In an important sense, colonial emigration was an extension of the process of emigration. Contrary to popular perception, migration was an established fact of life in the eastern districts of UP. In Azamgarh, it was 'known to be considerable', and in Allahabad, 'at all times an appreciable proportion of the population is absent in search of employment far afield'. In Gonda, migration in such adverse 'circumstances was a natural way out of the difficulties with which the population did not know how to cope'.[22]

Migration meant remittance. In Sultanpur, the migrants remitted INR1,627,700 between October 1894 and September 1897. In Azamgarh, the settlement officer noted that in the 1890s, yearly remittances amounted to INR1.3 million, rising to INR2.2 million in years of scarcity.

---

20 For figures for Surinam and Trinidad, see Steven Vertovec, '"Official" and "popular" Hinduism in the Caribbean: Historical and contemporary trends in Surinam, Trinidad and Guyana', in *Across the Dark Waters,* ed. Dabydeen and Samaroo, pp. 108–30, at pp. 112–13.
21 Figures derived from the *Census of India* (1921). For a contextualised study of internal migration, see Ranajit Das Gupta, 'Factory labour in Eastern India: Sources of supply, 1855–1946: Some preliminary findings', *Indian Economic and Social History Review* 18(3) (1973), pp. 277–329.
22 Figures and assessment are derived from *Settlement Reports,* which are, by far, the most comprehensive sources for the study of rural Indian society.

In Ghazipur, an important migration district, emigration since 1901 had assumed 'extraordinary proportions', the proof of which was 'to be found in the immensely increased passenger traffic of the railways, and also in the remarkable amounts remitted to the district through the agency of the post-office'.[23] A result of migration in the district was that labour was becoming dearer each year. Even the cultivating classes no longer relied solely on the produce of their fields, for savings of the emigrants were almost equal to the entire rental demands, the same thing occurring in Ballia and Jaunpur.[24]

It was often asserted by opponents of the indenture system at the time and by popular writers even today that the recruits were either kidnapped or otherwise fraudulently enticed by unscrupulous recruiters into emigrating.[25] This accords with the conventional view that Indians by nature are not migrants but a sedentary people confined to their familiar surroundings by the strictures and protocols of caste and religion. But by the nineteenth century, migration was not a strange phenomenon in rural India. There can be little doubt that a degree of fraudulence and violence was ever present in the recruitment process, as it is even today. Tall tales of easy opportunity awaiting them in the colonies trapped the greedy and the gullible. But deception should be placed in its proper context. The rural population was already uprooted and in search of employment; the recruiters' soothing words made the decision to migrate easier.

Social background

> I have been assured by every native from whom I have enquired, and by most Europeans, that only the lowest castes emigrate, and that nothing will ever induce men of higher class to leave.

Thus wrote G.A. Grierson in 1882.[26] This view has persisted over time and was periodically invoked by the planters and colonial governments to sanction discrimination against their Indian settlers, deny them equal political rights and remind them of their proper place in society—at the bottom. The most comprehensive and exact data on the social background

---

23   Lal, *Girmitiyas*, p. 93.
24   ibid., pp. 93–94.
25   This theme is emphasised in Hugh Tinker, *A New System of Slavery: The Export of Indian Labour Overseas 1830–1920* (Oxford: Oxford University Press, 1993). It is echoed in the published literature on the subject about a generation ago. More recent studies allow greater agency for the recruits.
26   In Emigration Proceedings, A Pros., 12 August 1882, NAI. This view is widely reflected in most official and popular accounts.

of the indentured migrants are from Fiji, and it can safely be assumed that the pattern for Fiji obtained in other sugar colonies as well.[27] Of Fiji's 45,000 North Indian migrants, Brahman and allied castes numbered 1,686; Kshattriya and allied castes 4,565; Bania 1,592; middling agricultural and artisan castes (Kurmi, Ahir, Jat, Lodha) 15,800; menial and low castes (Chamar, Pasi, Dusadh) 11,907; and Muslims 6,787.[28] In other words, the emigrating indentured population represented a fair cross-section of rural Indian society. And this is not surprising, for it was the cultivating castes, without social or institutional protection, that bore the brunt of the deteriorating economic situation in the country in the late nineteenth century: increases in land rent, often demanded in cash rather than kind, increasing fragmentation of ownership rights and subdivision of property, which particularly affected the lower-order cultivators, while the widespread decline in the handicraft industry in UP was ruinous to the artisan class. To many in distress and despair, migration offered a way out. Prolonged absence was not contemplated, but in time an intended sojourn was transformed into permanent separation.

Men migrated as well as women. Migration of men is understandable, but that by rural, illiterate Indian women is less easy to explain. Consequently, stereotype and (male) prejudice become substituted for explanation. It is the common view that the indentured women were people of low moral character, the refuse of society, who fell easy prey to the wily recruiters. C.F. Andrews wrote about Indian-indentured women in Fiji:

> The Hindu woman in this country is like a rudderless vessel with its masts broken ... being whirled down the rapids of a great river without any controlling hand. She passes from one man to another, and has lost even the sense of shame in doing so.[29]

Australian overseer Walter Gill, who saw the last days of indenture in Fiji, wrote that the Hindu woman in Fiji was:

> as joyously amoral as a doe rabbit. She took her lovers as a ship takes to rough seas, surging up to one who would smother her, then tossing him aside, thirsting for the next.[30]

---

27 See, for example, Verene Shepherd (in *Transients to Settlers: The Experience of Indians in Jamaica, 1845–1950*, Leeds: Peepal Tree Press, 1993, p. 47), where she says the Fiji data 'would be replicated in Trinidad, Guyana and Jamaica. What evidence is available supports that assumption'.
28 See Lal, *Girmitiyas*, pp. 68–90.
29 C.F. Andrews and W.W. Pearson, *Indian Indentured Labour in Fiji* (Perth: Privately published, 1918), Appendix, p. 6.
30 Walter Gill, *Turn North-East at the Tombstone* (Adelaide: Rigby, 1970), p. 73.

2. 'SUCH A LONG JOURNEY'

Indeed, so pervasive was the negative stereotype of Indian women in Fiji that they were held primarily responsible for the high male suicide rate, allegedly because they sold themselves to the highest bidder and then moved to the next, leaving the man to take his own life in despair and shame. The records, when read against the grain, tell a different story.

Why women emigrated is lost to us, but scattered data provides some clues. We have already mentioned the pervasiveness of migration in the Indo-Gangetic Plain. Most of the internal migration within India was male dominated, and if the amount remitted to the village was not enough or if the man did not return, the life of the wife could become very difficult. Tolerated for a while, she could be tossed out of the household and forced to fend for herself in times of hardship and difficulty. The following folksong captures some of the anguish of the wife:

> The sun is cruel and bright
> A lot of work is still to be done.
> People have returned to their homes
> Yet no call for meals has come for me.
> Here, in these lonely fields
> I, the unfortunate, work alone.
> My lord being in a distant land
> Who will tell me thy lord has come
> The day of their happiness has dawned.

Constant domestic disputes could be another reason to contemplate escape:

> Alas, I will have to run away with another man
> For my beloved has turned his mind away from me
> How eagerly as I cook rice and dal do I pour the ghee
> But as soon as we sit for dinner, you start quarrelling
> My heart is weary of you
> I put hot fire in the basket
> Carefully I make the bed
> But as soon as we lie down to rest, you start quarrelling
> My heart is weary of you.[31]

To women in desperate, distraught, circumstances the recruiters' soothing words must have been godsend. They left. The tragic story of Sukhdei recounted in Chapter 4 is instructive.

---

31   These two folksongs, which I collected in the UP, appear in Lal, *Girmityas*, pp. 113–14.

Indentured emigration was, by necessity as well as choice, an individualised phenomenon. Nonetheless, there were families migrating on virtually every shipment to the various colonies. In the case of Fiji, 70 per cent of women migrated as individuals, but the remaining 30 per cent migrated as members of families. The majority, 70 per cent of the women, were accompanied by their husbands only, 15 per cent by their husbands and children and 12 per cent by their children only. Some families were formed in the depots at the ports of embarkation and others on the long voyage out and still more on the plantations. The fact that women were prepared to leave a life of drudgery lived on the sufferance of others for distant unknown places across the ocean would suggest that these were women of pride and determination and enterprise and self-respect. These were certainly the values they inculcated in the children and grandchildren.

Once recruited, the potential emigrants would be taken to the district depot, where they would be examined by the district magistrate or his deputy. Around 18–19 per cent would be rejected for various reasons, mostly because they were found to be unfit. At the port of embarkation, a similar percentage would fall off the list because they were found unfit or because they deserted or simply refused to embark. All told, more than a third of those recruited had been dropped or dropped out before the ship left.

The journey from districts of recruitment to the ports of embarkation involved more than just physical relocation. For men and women from the landlocked villages, a journey of several hundred miles was a novel, traumatic experience. Many were seeing the sea for the first time. In the crowded country depots and in the living quarters in Madras and Calcutta, people rubbed shoulders with those of unknown castes, something that would never have happened in the villages regulated by age-old norms and protocols of social intercourse that respected hierarchy and separation. Old adhesives of society were slowly loosening, such as the caste system. Occasionally men and women were finding partners from different social backgrounds. A sense of togetherness, of being passengers in the same boat, was slowly taking shape. As Ken Gillion has written, 'Most of their caste scruples gone, without their traditional leaders and elders and generally without kin, they were resigned to the future and very vulnerable.'[32] New bonds of friendship formed on the long voyages, which could take up to three months on the sailing ships. None was more important than the

---

32   Gillion, *Fiji's Indian Migrants,* p. 67.

relationship of *jahajibhai* (brotherhood of the crossing), which provided a degree of much-needed emotional attachment and security in an alien and alienating environment against the alienations and asperities of the outside world, and which persisted long after indenture itself was over. The process of fragmentation and reconstitution would continue apace on the voyage out and on the plantations in the colonies.

Life and work on colonial plantations

Just as recruitment and shipment of labourers was regulated by legislation, so too were the conditions of employment on the plantations. By the late nineteenth century, a uniform set of rules and procedures had been finalised. The provisions of the Guiana Ordinance of 1891 were closely followed in most other colonies, including the Dutch colony of Surinam.[33] It amplified the precise terms and conditions of employment, the provision of accommodation and medical facilities, sanctions for the breaches of the labour laws, the administration of justice, the terms and conditions of reindenture, and so on. On paper, the ordinance was as comprehensive a piece of legislation as it was possible to imagine, but it was the glaring disparity between the words on paper and the reality on the ground that became the main source of the problem. It was stated, for instance, that indentured men would get 1 shilling per day's work and women 9 pennies, but it took a long time for the workers to achieve this sum. The days absent at hospital were added to the indenture contract. Once contracted to a particular estate or plantation, the labourer could not change his or her employer no matter how genuine the demand for the change. The penal sanctions for breaches of the labour ordinances were more effectively invoked by the planters than by the workers. Indenture was a system of structured inequality between the workers and their employers.

Upon arrival in the colonies, the indentured labourers would be allocated to the various plantations on the basis of orders placed before the colonial government by the planters the year before. Care was taken not to separate families, although on the same plantation, husband and wife could, and

---

33 A copy of the ordinance is reproduced in Brij V. Lal, *Crossing the Kala Pani: A Documentary History of Indian Indenture in Fiji* (Canberra: Division of Pacific and Asian History, Research School of Pacific and Asian Studies, The Australian National University, and Suva: Fiji Museum, 1998), pp. 49–94.

often did, work in different sections. But an effort was made to break up groups of people (who might come from the same district in India, for instance), to prevent strikes. The working day began early. The workers were mustered between 5 am and 6 am, had a hurried breakfast and worked till 4 pm.[34] During harvesting time, the hours could be longer. Most of the work related to the cultivation and manufacture of sugar cane: ploughing, hoeing, weeding, harvesting and planting cane.

The labourers were promised that they would do either 'time work' or 'task work'. The new arrivals were usually allotted time work but as they became accustomed to the working conditions on the plantations, they were assigned task work—a task being defined as six hours of continuous work that an able-bodied man could be expected to accomplish. In Trinidad, by 1913, almost 90 per cent of the work was by task.[35] In most cases, it was the overseer who decided what task was appropriate. Sometimes, tasks were defined on the basis of what a few chosen men could accomplish. And the task could be varied. If a worker accomplished his work in good time, he could return the next day to find his task extended. Sometimes, the standard from one plantation could be applied to another without considering the topography of the fields. And sometimes the workers would be paid nothing at all for a partially completed task.

The labour ordinance provided a very large number of offences for which the employers could prosecute their labourers. In Trinidad between 1910 and 1912, the most important prosecutions included desertion (1,668); absence from work without a lawful excuse (1,466); refusing to begin or finish work (1,125); and vagrancy (983).[36] Other breaches included malingering, using threatening words and breach of hospital regulations. In Fiji, the employers were able to obtain 82 per cent of all the cases that

---

34   See, generally, Gillion, *Fiji's Indian Migrants*; Marianne Soares Ramessar, *Survivors of Another Crossing: A History of East Indians in Trinidad, 1880–1946* (St Augustine: School of Continuing Studies, University of the West Indies, 1994); Shepherd, *Transients to Settlers*; Clem Seecharan, *Tiger in the Stars: The Anatomy of Indian Achievement in British Guyana, 1919–1929* (London: Macmillan Education, 1997); Ashwin Desai and Goolam Vahed, *Inside Indenture: A South African Story, 1860–1914* (Durban: Human Sciences Research Council, 2007); and Marina Carter's many works on Mauritius, including *Voices from Indenture: Experiences of Indian Migrants in the British Empire* (Leicester: Leicester University Press, 1996).
35   Shepherd (*Transients to Settlers*, p. 59) has claimed that '[t]asks were generally preferred in all colonies'.
36   See Ramessar, *Survivors of Another Crossing*, pp. 44–45; K.O. Laurence, *A Question of Labour: Indentured Immigration into Trinidad and British Guiana, 1875–1916* (Kingston: Ian Randle Publishers, 1994), pp. 131–66; and studies in Kay Saunders (ed.), *Indentured Labour in the British Empire, 1834–1920* (London: Croon Helm, 1984).

they brought before the courts. Indentured labourers were punished for not registering their marriages, when the idea of registration probably did not occur to them, especially if their marriages were carried out according to Hindu and Muslim rites. And the labourers knew that they could have a week's pay docked or face a month in prison if they 'committed nuisance' within 60 yards of a stream running through a plantation. Indentured labourers convicted of breaching the labour ordinance could either be fined or imprisoned. Neither, however, was the end of punishment for the indentured labourer, for the planters were legally entitled to recover lost work by extending the contract by the number of days they were absent from the plantation.

Labourers were entitled under the ordinance to lay charges against their employers for assault and battery, nonpayment of wages, not supplying tools or proper rations, using 'insulting language', requiring illegal work, overtasking, falsifying pay lists and so on. But laying charges involved considerable risk. The labourers had difficulty getting permission to leave their plantations. Those who bore the odds became marked men. And there was no guarantee that, after all the risks had been taken, the courts would give them a sympathetic hearing. In Surinam between 1873 and 1916, only 10 per cent of employers who were charged under the labour laws were successful, while the employers were able to secure 75 per cent of the charges they brought against their labourers. When provoked beyond the limits of endurance, the workers either retaliated violently against those in authority—such as by murdering overseers, or striking. But striking was risky at all times, and not easy to organise. The planters had all the power in their hands. The colonial government had a prudent appreciation of the economic contribution of the big companies. The labourers themselves were often disorganised and diffident. When strikes did occur, as Maureen Swan has written of Natal, they were 'short-lived, rarely transcended the accommodation units or work gangs into which plantation work gangs were divided, and were generally concerned with specific abuses of contract'.[37] The strikers were quickly apprehended and dispersed to different locations with the result, as S.J. Reddy has written of Mauritius, 'experience acquired by one group in wresting some concessions was lost as they dispersed to take employment elsewhere'.[38]

---

37 Maureen Swann, 'Indian Indians: Resistance and accommodation, 1890–1913', in *Essays on Indentured Indians in Natal,* ed. Surendra Bhana (Leeds: Peepal Tree Press, 1988), pp. 117–35, at p. 128.
38 S.J. Reddi, 'Labour protest among Indian immigrants', in *Indian Labour Immigration,* ed. U. Bissoondoyal and S.B.C. Servansing (Moka Mahatma Gandhi Institute, 1986), pp. 116–35, at p. 132.

The indentured workers had a prudent appreciation of the reality that confronted them. They often engaged in quiet everyday acts of resistance or adopted strategic accommodation with authority as a way out of their difficulties.

Indenture, clearly was a grim time for those who experienced it: the relentless pace of work on the plantations; the violence; the disease; the frequent indifference of those in authority; the denial of the humanity of the workers. Many were broken by it but many also survived. In some places, such as the Caribbean, indenture lasted for generations, with attendant consequences for social and cultural identity. Links with India were broken for long periods of time. People lived in isolation from their ancestral culture for long periods, losing their mother tongue in the process. Indenture, in short, was a life sentence. But elsewhere, such as in Fiji, it was a limited detention for five or, at most, 10 years, after which the migrants were free to settle on their own or return to India. And contact with India was never really lost.

It was simultaneously an enslaving as well as a liberating experience for many. There were many in the indentured population whose birth had confined them to the lower stratum of Indian society, a fate ordained by divine injunction, it was said, from which there was no escape in this life or the next. To them, migration and indenture offered the possibility of realising their individual humanity. Everywhere they grabbed the opportunity with relish. Indenture was a crucible in which was forged a new society. Old notions of purity and impurity, taboos regarding food, diet, social space, the rituals of prayer and worship collapsed over time to be replaced by new norms and conventions. Caste, as a social institution, became anachronistic; its protocols of approved behaviour unenforceable.[39] Remuneration during indenture was based on the amount of work accomplished, not on social status. The paucity of women necessitated marriages across caste and sometimes religious lines. Everywhere, people continued to 'play' at caste long after indenture had ceased, but its relevance and legitimacy were gone.

Fragmentation was accompanied by the process of reconstitution. Women everywhere played an important part in that process. Women emerged from indenture as productive workers in their own right, enjoying or

---

39 See Chandra Jayawardena, 'The disintegration of caste in Fiji Indian rural society', in *Anthropology in Oceania: Essays Presented to Ian Hogbin*, ed. L.R. Hiatt and Chandra Jayawardena (Sydney: Angus and Robertson, 1971), pp. 89–119.

negotiating a measure of independence that would have been unimaginable in India. They survived the burdens of both racism and sexism. They raised families in often inhospitable circumstances and played a critical role in facilitating 'the transmission and practice of folk religion and of tradition-based sanctions'.[40] In Guiana, writes Jeremy Poynting, women 'were the main preservers of Indian domestic culture,' which, he argues, was 'initially the principal means whereby Indians maintained their identity'.[41] The presence of Indian women in the colonies was important in another way: it discouraged relationships between Indian men and non-Indian women, to varying degrees, in the sugar colonies.

Religion played an equally important role in the protection of Indian culture and identity in the different colonies. It is commonly assumed that the religious practices and protocols of Hinduism and Islam collapsed suddenly on the colonial plantations. This is not true. The various groups of people who went to the colonies brought with them their own family (*kul*) or village (*gram*) deities and the associated rituals and ceremonies. Some involved animal sacrifice while others invoked the dark forces of the underworld. Over time, everywhere, these were replaced by a more universal form of Brahminised Hinduism.[42] And the colonial planters were not always opposed to the perpetuation of the migrants' religious practices. 'As the planters became increasingly dependent on Indian labour,' writes Basdeo Mangru about Guiana:

> they correspondingly endeavoured to make estate life as attractive as possible so as to induce the indentured workforce to prolong their residence through reindenture. One certain way of substituting a temporary sojourn for permanent residence was to permit the Indian labourer to practise his religion, which was an inseparable part of his [*sic*] life.
>
> [Further, to] create a sense of belonging and facilitate reindenture for another five years, some prudent estate managers not only attended the festivals, but generously granted holidays and made regular and substantial contribution towards the festivals.[43]

---

40 Marina Carter, *Lakshmi's Legacy: The Testimonies of Indian Women in 19th Century Mauritius* (Rose Hill, Mauritius: Edition l'Ocean Indien, 1994), p. 142.
41 Jeremy Poynting, 'East Indian women in the Caribbean: Experience and voice', in South Asian Women Writers: The Immigrant Experience, *Journal of South Asian Literature* 21(1) (Winter–Spring 1986): 133–80, at p. 133.
42 See Vertovec, '"Official" and "popular" Hinduism in the Caribbean', p. 114.
43 Basdeo Mangru, 'Tadjah in British Guiana', in *Indo-Caribbean Resistance,* ed. Frank Birbalsingh (Toronto: Tsar, 1993), pp. 13–26, at p. 18.

One festival that was celebrated across all the colonial plantations around the world was Tazia (Fiji), known as Tadjah (Guiana) and Hosein, Hose or Hosay (Trinidad and Jamaica). The festival commemorated the martyrdom of Hassan and Hussein, grandsons of the Prophet Mohammed. Holi, or Phagua, was also regularly celebrated.

In some places, such as the Caribbean, Christianity was able to make significant inroads into the Indian community, promising liberation and the prospect of upward mobility in an environment characterised by closed and low glass ceilings, but in other places, such as Fiji, it was insignificant. In an important sense, religion became a tool of resistance. As Roy Glasgow writes of Guyana:

> The Indian's emphasis upon the value and worthwhileness of his [sic] culture was really a mode of expression of his desire to be treated on terms of equality within the Guyanese universe.[44]

This was successful to varying degrees in different places. In Fiji, within a decade of the beginning of indentured migration, the basic texts of popular Hinduism were circulating among the indentured Indians.[45] These included *Satyanarayan ki katha* (a collection of five stories from the 'Reva' chapter of the *Skanda Purana*), *Sukh Sagar* (a discourse on the different incarnations of Lord Vishnu), popular versions of the Bhagvada Gita, *Danlila* (a devotional verse in praise of Lord Krishna) and, above all, the Ramayana, the story of Lord Rama in some 10,000 lines of verse in the Avadhi dialect of Hindi familiar to most of the North Indian migrants. Rama's story, enacted in the *Ramlilas* and sung communally to the accompaniment of rudimentary music, struck a particular chord with the indentured labourers. Rama was exiled for 14 years for no fault of his own, but he did return; good ultimately triumphed over evil. His story gave the labourers hope and consolation; one day, their ordeal, too, would come to an end.

And it did. All indentured emigration ceased in 1916 and the system was abolished soon afterwards, although in some places, by the beginning of the twentieth century, the peak of emigration was long over. Reports by C.F. Andrews, among others, drew the attention of the Indian public, slowly awakening to nationalist sentiments, to the social problems

---

44   Roy Arthur Glasgow, *Guyana: Race and Politics among Africans and East Indians* (The Hague: Martin Nijhoff, 1970), p. 79, doi.org/10.1007/978-94-010-3213-1.
45   See Brij V. Lal, 'Hinduism under indenture', in Lal, *Chalo Jahaji*, pp. 239–60.

of indenture, especially the abuse of women on the plantations that outraged Indian public opinion and finally forced the Government of India to end indenture despite protests and pleas from the colonies. As Lord Hardinge said:

> No matter how great might be the economic advantages, the political aspect of the question is such that no one who has at heart the interests of British rule in India can afford to neglect it. It is one of the most important subjects in Indian political life today, and its discussion arouses more bitterness, perhaps, than that of any other outstanding question. Indian politicians, moderate and extremist alike, do not consider that the existence of this system which they do not hesitate to call by the name of slavery, brands their whole race in the eyes of the British Empire with the stigma of harlotry.[46]

Upon the expiry of their indenture, the Indian settlers had no alternative but to be independent. Some experimented with other occupations, but limited opportunities, family obligations, kinship ties and lack of education and marketable skills forced most to depend on agriculture; cultivating rice and sugar, principally, but also such crops such as maize, tobacco, sweet potato and yam, in time monopolising market gardening.[47] Expediency, contingency and tolerance born of need or circumstance, rather than social status and prestige, determined relations among the settlers. They built temples and roads and schools, and tried to create a semblance of life on bits and pieces of a remembered past. The old pattern of village India could not be reproduced in the new environment. The emergence of new settlements of freed Indians, with their temples and mosques, rudimentary schools and established homesteads, was also symbolically important for those still under indenture. They served as beacons of inspiration, nurturing the hope that they too would be free one day. It lightened the burden of the relentless plantation routine.

---

46   Cited in Gillion, *Fiji's Indian Migrants*, p. 180. See also Mangru, 'Indian Government policy towards indentured labour migration to the sugar colonies', pp. 171–72. Andrews's role is considered in K.L. Gillion, 'C.F. Andrews and Indians overseas', *Visva-Bharti News* (February–March 1971), pp. 206–17.
47   See, for example, Surendra Bhana and Joy Brain, *Setting Down Roots: Indian Immigrants in South Africa* (Johannesburg: Witwatersrand University Press, 1989), pp. 43–52; Gillion, *Fiji's Indian Migrants*, pp. 136–63; Shepherd, *Transients to Settlers*, pp. 118–49; Seecharan, *Tiger in the Stars*, pp. 147–215; Ramessar, *Survivors of Another Crossing*, pp. 77–118.

Wherever the Indian indentured labourers went, they encountered people who were either indigenous to those places (such as in Fiji) or imported earlier as labourers themselves (as in the West Indies). Relations between the two groups were characterised by prejudice and the suspicion that one was the nemesis of the other. In Trinidad, the blacks could not but notice the degrading conditions in which the Indian indentured labourers lived and worked and their low occupational and social status. The Indians' culture and religion appeared strange and incomprehensible. The Creole and the 'coolie' found little to admire in each other's way of life. 'The coolie despises the negro, because he considers him a being not so highly civilized as himself,' wrote an observer of Trinidad:

> while the negro, in turn, despises the coolie, because he is so immensely inferior to him in physical strength. There never will be much danger of seditious disturbances among East Indian immigrants on estates as long as large numbers of negroes continue to be employed with them.[48]

In other places, the perception of Indians working for lower wages than the blacks poisoned relations. In Fiji, the colonial state prohibited social intercourse between Fijians and Indians and transgressions were punished at law. Everywhere, the seeds of prejudice, suspicion and hostility, planted during the early years of indenture, continued to bear fruit long after the system itself was abolished. Colonial policies exacerbated the gulf between the communities created by culture and history and circumstances beyond their control. The descendants of the Indian indentured immigrants found themselves suffering and living on the sufferance of others, excluded from the corridors of power, disempowered. It was a difficult journey; there was a lot of despair and disappointment along the way. But there was also defiance. In the words of Guyanese poet Rooplall Monar:

> Generations nurtured from my seeds
> will clasp their hands and say
> our ancestors carved those fields
> which have given us meanings
> meanings to stand tall
> This land is ours too.[49]

---

48 Malcolm Cross, 'East Indian-Creole relations in Trinidad and Guyana in the late nineteenth century', in *Across the Dark Waters*, ed. Dabydeen and Samaroo, pp. 14–38, at pp. 28–29. See also Brereton, *A History of Modern Trinidad*, p. 110.
49 Rooplall Monar, 'Babu', in *They Came in Ships*, ed. McDonald et al., pp. 203–205, p. 205.

3

The Tamarind Tree[1]

Jalā hai jism jahāñ dil bhī jal gayā hogā
kuredte ho jo ab raakh justujū kyā hai.

If the body is burnt, so must have been the heart
Why rake the ashes now, what is the search for?

— Mirza Asadullah Khan Ghalib[2]

How indentured men and women lived on the sugar estates, the myriad ways in which they devised strategies to deal with the demands made on them, the plots and intrigues, are lost to us except in the fraying memories of the older generation now rapidly passing from view. How, then, do we write about that past? We do so through the imaginative reconstruction of events and episodes based on stories that have passed down the generations. The following piece of creative nonfiction, or faction as I have called it, is an attempt in that direction.

May 1962. The Tamarind Tree was struck by lightning and razed. Father cried inconsolably. His indentured father had died a few weeks earlier, and now the Tree was gone. We children had no idea about the cause or the depth of his grief. It was not until many decades later that I discovered,

---

1 Originally appeared in *Fijian Studies: A Journal of Contemporary Fiji* 14(1) (2016): 35–49.
2 Mirza Asadullah Khan Ghalib (1797–1869) was a prominent Urdu and Persian poet during the last years of the Mughal Empire. These lines appear in films, poetry and in cultural conversation. I learnt the lines in my Hindi class in primary school, and am quoting from memory. The best source I can find is: *'ilm majaalisii*, p. 106. There are no further details.

through a circuitous route of conjectures, assumptions and reflections, that the Tamarind Tree ground was *terra sacra* for Father, a place of special memories linking him to another past and time. Father was not much of a talker, parsimonious with his emotions like most men of his generation, except when angry. Our conversations, if any, were perfunctory, more in the nature of brisk instructions from him about household chores to be completed before and after school. But that sight of a grown-up man crying like a child remained with me through all the many long years of research and writing about our past. I can still recall father's tattered wet khaki clothes clinging to his body as he stood in the drenching rain in the middle of the compound muttering words of loss and regret that I have now forgotten. He was having his head shaved and a well-tended luxuriant moustache reduced permanently to stubble in bereavement; village old-timers gathering at our place for a week-long period of Ramayan recital and devotional singing followed at the end by a communal vegetarian feast. The details welled up whenever the subject of indenture arose.

The Tamarind Tree was on the banks of the Wailevu River, about a mile down the hill from the headquarters of Labasa's Tua Tua Sector Office of the Colonial Sugar Refining Company (CSR), the main employer of Indian indentured labour in Fiji. My very vague memory is of a tall, gnarled tree, vine-wrapped, standing forlornly in overgrown grass, abandoned. But I saw it when its glory days as the *adda* (the gathering place) of the *girmitiyas* had long been over. For Father, it was different. The Tree had been there for as long as he could remember. It took him back to his own childhood in the immediate postindenture days of the 1920s. How the Tree came to Tua Tua no one really knew. People said it was brought by the early *girmitiyas* sometime in the mid-1890s when cane came to Labasa. Others thought it arrived with the South Indians much later. Tamarind is an essential ingredient in many South Indian dishes. But the question of origin was moot now. Who brought the tree, when, or how did not really matter much to people of father's generation. What mattered was that it was a *mulki* tree, a plant from the original homeland and, therefore, special.

Tua Tua was one of the CSR's earliest sectors in Labasa, and one of the largest and the most prosperous, so people said, full of sturdy thatched homes, solid all-weather roads and rich red soil. Aja, my grandfather, completed his indenture there as a stable hand for the company's draught horses. When it ended in 1913, he moved to Tabia some 5 miles away. But since there was nothing in Tabia then, he continued to walk to Tua

Tua to harvest cane and work as a general labourer on the CSR estates, keeping the connection alive to the place where it had all started for him, the first leg of his Fijian journey. The Tamarind Tree was his touchstone, his indispensable site of communion with his fellow *girmitiyas*—living and dead alike.

I realise now, decades later, why the Tamarind Tree was so fondly remembered by the old timers, and what it meant to them. The Tree connected people to the past and served as a visible reminder of ancestral roots and routes. It was the initial point of entry for the new *girmitiyas* to the Tua Tua Sector. Five or 10 years later, it would be the final point of departure for those whose *girmit* had ended and who were now moving out to newer settlements opening up all around Labasa—miles away from the sugar mill at the Qawa River. The Tree was the site of rest and respite from the relentless pace of plantation work. If the estate lines were decrepit and devoid of any sense of dignity and personal and social space, and full of the company's spies, the Tamarind Tree was a beacon of hope offering fleeting glimpses of freedom and opportunity on the other side of *girmit*. It was symbolically a source of renewal, rejuvenation and reassurance amidst all the confusions of dislocation and rupture. I have no doubt there were hundreds of tamarind, or mango or banyan trees wherever *girmitiyas* were found, in Fiji and other sugar colonies around the world, witnesses to their special moments of triumphs and tragedies.

The departures provoked mixed emotion. Five years of working together in mills, in the cane fields, as domestic servants or as stable hands, and sharing the confined space in the lines, had bred a sense of companionship and camaraderie, a bond of friendship forged in circumstances of great adversity. That communal living, the security borne of collective servitude, was coming to an end. No one knew where they might find land to settle or when they might meet again. They would now be on their own, starting all over again, often without a helping hand. Virgin land would have to be broken and brought into cultivation. Dangers lurked around every corner: flood, fire, wild pigs, theft of property, coercion by fellow men, violence. New relationships would have to be established, often with complete strangers and in unanticipated circumstances. New rules of social engagement would have to be developed, innovative ways found to minimise the inevitable frictions and conflicts in the newly emerging communities as people struggled to establish themselves and find a place they could call their own.

There were good reasons for apprehension, but many also felt a palpable sense of relief that *girmit* was only a temporary detention, not a life sentence as they had feared. For them, the end could not have come sooner. The newly freed were encouraged by stories of men who had farms of their own, grew their own crops and built solid homes. Some were reported to have become big leaders, even moneylenders, in some settlements. Families would come, children married off, schools started and ways found to give the nascent community a semblance of coherence and structure. In time, a new world would emerge, built with fragments from a remembered past but always, in the early days, haunted by the fear of the unknown, and the unthinkable prospect of failure. As people said, with Tolstoyan wisdom, everyone shared in your prosperity, but if you failed, you failed alone. The comfort of a settled, supportive community was some way into the future.

It was under the Tamarind Tree that the newcomers were inducted into the culture and mores of the local estate that was to be their home for the next five years or more. They would be told about the people to avoid, the overseers to be on the lookout for, the way to handle difficult tasks in the fields, tactics to employ to frustrate unfair demands made on them (tools could be damaged, sickness could be feigned, a long time taken to complete a task). They would learn where private pleasures in food and flesh could be safely indulged. For a little something on the side, anything was possible, anything could be arranged, cigarettes, alcohol, even women. Everyone knew who the best pimps and procurers in Tua Tua were. No wonder some *girmitiyas* called the estate lines brothels, *kasbighars*. If some plot had to be hatched about giving a hiding to a *sirdar* or an overseer, if some particularly troublesome *girmitiya* had to be put in his place or brought into line, if some company farm had to be torched in retaliation for violence against the labourers, the Tamarind Tree was the place to meet and plan. The plots hatched there and the secrets shared were safe.

Departures and arrivals, transactions and transitions: the Tamarind Tree was a silent witness to all these, and much more. If only it could talk. From my scarce notes and fading memory, I now recall stories these men heard under the Tamarind Tree about the labyrinthine world of *girmit*. They are partial, private recollections of old men, but they are all I have (perhaps all they had too). Like life itself, there is no single pattern to them, no single theme or narrative. Together, though, they provide an insight into a complex and conflicted world that is now well beyond recall. Ayesha

Jalal, the noted Pakistan-born historian of the Indian subcontinent, has written in the Preface to her book on Saadat Hasan Manto, the writer of the incomparable short story 'Toba Tek Singh', that 'it is possible to chalk out a new interdisciplinary way of reconnecting the histories of individuals, families, communities, and states in the throes of cataclysmic change'.[3] She goes on to suggest that 'Microhistorical detail can illuminate the texture of macrohistorical change'.[4] The cause of historical scholarship would be enriched, Jalal argues, if investigations of historical causation were put on a collision course with the reality of individual lived experience. This essay could be viewed as such a collision course.

As Father talked, memories came flooding back to him in a way that completely surprised him, releasing a floodgate of long-forgotten emotions. They were as vivid and clear to him as broad daylight. He remembered accompanying Aja to the Wailevu market at the Tamarind Tree on Saturdays to sell peanuts, maize, bean and baigan he grew on his 10-acre farm. People from all around Wailevu came, men dressed in the traditional Indian garb of *dhoti* and *pagri* and long flowing *kurta*. Buying and selling was really an excuse for weekly or monthly reunions. After five years of living together in the labour lines during the age of indenture, people had dispersed to wherever they could find a piece of land to rent. There was no rhyme or reason to the way Indian settlements evolved. Contingency and circumstance determined outcomes. Meeting at the market under the Tamarind Tree kept the memories of old companionship alive. What Father remembered from those distant conversations was the clear consensus among the *girmitiyas* that fruits back home in India were always sweeter. They were the best. Indeed, everything about *mulk* (homeland) was golden, perfect: the nostalgia of a displaced people dealt a rough hand by fate. What strikes me now about the *girmitiyas* is how they were a people caught in-between, stranded in the cul-de-sac of a past vanishing before their eyes. They were living in a place they could not escape, making home in a land they could not fully embrace. Theirs was, I suppose, the quintessential dilemma of belonging and attachment, of home and homeland that all migrant peoples face.

---

3   Ayesha Jalal, *The Pity of Partition: Manto's Life, Times, and Work across the India-Pakistan Divide* (Princeton: Princeton University Press, 2013), p. xii, doi.org/10.1515/9781400846689.
4   ibid.

It was at gatherings under the Tamarind Tree that people played at the rituals and ceremonies they remembered from their childhood back in India. Higher-caste men came to the market to have their weekly shave and regular haircut by their favourite *hajam* (traditional barber). The *hajam* would in return get some lentils and rice as compensation. The ritual had to be observed even though everyone knew it to be just that, a ritual. Father said. It was their way of keeping a world alive even though they knew in their hearts that it was for all practical purposes dead. Aja was no exception. Priests dispensed advice about the most propitious days for this *puja* (devotional prayer offering) or that. Sometime in the 1920s, people built a small *kuti* (a rudimentary hut for religious gathering), near the Tamarind Tree, and priests took turns reading the scriptures and officiating at thanksgiving celebrations hosted by families for some piece of good fortune or in anticipation of a blessing—for the birth of a son, for example, for the cure of some mysterious ailment, or for the lifting of a curse. Dates for festivals would be announced and taken to the settlements. Astrological charts would be drawn up for those who wanted them, names for babies suggested. People would make discreet enquiries about the availability of marriageable boys and girls. Marriages were still arranged by parents and community elders, preferably within a prescribed range of castes.

Caste rules were loosening and becoming unenforceable, but it was only a foolhardy person who would publicly breach community consensus about social mores and cultural practices. Father recalled the case of Hirwa who had unwittingly committed the heinous 'crime' of selling a cow to a Muslim. It was automatically assumed that the cow would be slaughtered for meat. The cow was mother incarnate for Hindus. When the news became public, Hirwa was hauled before the elders, asked to do *prashchayat* (penance) and give a *bhandara* (feast) for all his fellow village Hindus as well as a calf to each of the three Brahmin families in the immediate neighbourhood. Breaching important social values could lead to *huqqa-pani-bund* (social ostracism). People would be reluctant to marry into the family. They would avoid attending their funeral and mourning ceremonies. No *mandali* (society) would recite the Ramayana at their place. Cane fields might be torched, people beaten up, womenfolk interfered with. So a feast had to be given, whatever the cost. This could financially cripple the feast giver, as happened with Hirwa. Broke and depressed, he left the village for some unknown place far away, leaving his past behind him. No one ever saw him again. The practice of punishing people using customary ways went with the old timers as the rule of tradition gradually gave way to the rule of law.

For Father, as a young boy, accompanying Aja to the annual festivals held at the Wailevu grounds was the most exciting time of the year. It was the same for children of my generation growing up without radio, television and other inventions now so commonplace. Ram Lila and Holi, or Phagwa, were the main festivals for the largely Hindu community around Wailevu. Ram Lila enacted the story of the Ramayana. For seven days the text would be read by groups of men, from different settlements taking turns, to the accompaniment of rudimentary music (*dholak* (Indian drum), harmonium, *dandtaal* (iron rod instrument)). These could sometimes morph into intervillage competitions to see who best 'sang' the Ramayana. The story of Rama, his childhood, exile and eventually triumphal return, would be acted out by men and boys with the right head gear and multicoloured clothes. People would sit rapt on the sack-covered ground witnessing the gripping drama being acted out before them by their own children or siblings. As a child, I relished playing the role of a monkey in Lord Hanuman's army (*baanar sena*) on its way to conquer Lanka, with my bouncy iron 'tail' wrapped in coloured crepe paper. Our performance would be the subject of much mirthful commentary at home and in school.

Phagwa was a more riotous affair, a festival of colours, celebrated at the end of the agricultural season on the last day of the lunar month. People played with coloured water and sprinkled powder on each other as they went from home to home singing especially composed songs, *chautals*. The climax came with the burning of the effigy of the evil king Hiranakashyap. A huge bonfire would light up the sky for all the neighbouring villages to see. One year, sparks from the bonfire set a nearby cane field alight, damaging several acres of the crop. The cause was disputed by some old timers who thought people from another sector, jealous of the popularity of the Tamarind Tree celebrations, had torched the fields. Another theory had Muslims responsible because they resented the loud musical processions by the mosque, especially during the Friday prayers. Some blamed a family of thieves who were publicly shamed for stealing poultry (*murgi chor*). In typical village fashion, the speculations could be unending. Whatever the cause, the CSR banned the celebrations at the Tamarind Tree for good. Thereafter, Phagwa became a local village-based celebration, and so it remains till today.

Father's recollection of Phagwa reminded me of the Muslim festival of Mohurram (or Tazia) marking the martyrdom of the Prophet Mohammed's grandsons Hasan and Hussain. It was a public holiday in all the colonies that had Indian indentured labour. In the Caribbean, it was invariably associated with drunkenness. On that one day, people were allowed to let their hair down, or, to change the metaphor, let off steam. Some latter-day social theorists see the drunken behaviour 'as an act of resistance' against the planters, but it was probably little more than another excuse to have fun. Was there similar licence in Labasa, I asked Father. Alcohol was restricted to a few well-known and well-connected Indians, and the restrictions were not removed until the 1960s. But other drugs were around, principally *ganja* (marijuana), which old timers of the comparable caste group, *biraadri,* smoked from a hookah in the *belo* (guest-receiving house). We children were not allowed near the building when the *girmitiyas* were talking about private matters (*aapas ke baat*). I still vividly remember plants with serrated leaves at our well that we were told not to touch because they were 'holy'. *Ganja* gradually disappeared with the *girmitiyas*, though now it is making a comeback in some of the more remote parts of the country. *Yaqona*, or kava, became the principal social drink of the community, and alcohol—once drinking restrictions were removed.

Kava (*Piper methysticum*) was the first Fijian item the Indians truly appropriated. It is a mildly narcotic drink, muddy in colour, made from pounded root and stems of the plant. It was surreptitiously bartered with the Fijians who lived at the edge of the sugar estate. In exchange for salt, sugar, rice and spices, the Indians got fish, crab and prawns. These transactions were strictly illegal, for the government forbade contact between the two communities. The exchanges took place at the Tamarind Tree during late weekend afternoons or early evenings when chances of detection were slim. The old timers remembered one Fijian man, Sekope, who was a regular at the Tamarind Tree: roly-poly, frequently shirtless, hairy chested and a very savvy negotiator. '*Hum hiyan ke raja baitho,* I am the king of this place,' he used to say. He might have been; it is difficult to say. People remembered him as an open, friendly man, but what they admired most was his fluency in the local variant of Hindustani, spiced with Fijian words and phrases and Hindi swear words (*sala chutia*, you arsehole; *maadharchod*, mother fucker; *suar ke baccha*, son of a pig; *gaand ke andha*, blind as an arse). The Tamarind Tree transactions crossed barriers and boundaries, but that was all the interaction between the two

3. THE TAMARIND TREE

communities there was. For the most part, the Fijians and the Indians continued to view each other through the prism of prejudice and fear. The gulf suited the purposes of the colonial state.

The demanding plantation routine left the *girmitiyas* little time for idleness or indulgence. But weekends were free and during the drier months people gathered at the Wailevu grounds for fun and frivolity. *Gatka* (stick fighting) was popular but *kushti* (wrestling) was the main sport on the estates. It was familiar and cheap and entertaining and, more importantly, encouraged by the CSR as a way to keep men fit. Sometimes, it was staged as an intersector wrestling competition and sometimes as a contest between the free and those still under indenture. The prize did not matter, Father said, what counted was pride, in oneself and in one's sector. Rahiman, a recently freed labourer from Waiqele, was the champion wrestler widely known throughout Labasa. Big in body and heart, he was the man to beat. Once, a man named Jhagru challenged him to a contest. Everyone thought it would be a quick one-way contest, over in minutes if not seconds. But Jhagru had other ideas. He confided his plan to some close friends who decided to put up a large sum of prize money behind him. Confident as ever, Rahiman's followers backed him with a similarly large sum, feeling almost sorry for his opponent. A large crowd gathered at the Tamarind Tree on the advertised day. As the two men were about to enter the 'ring', word spread that Jhagru had rubbed his body with pig fat. Rahiman, being a devout Muslim, refused even to shake hands with a pig fat–smeared man, let alone wrestle with him and so he forfeited the match, and the prize money. There was consternation in the crowd. Nothing like this had ever happened before, this act of pure provocation. Some applauded Jhagru's cunning audacity ('how did he ever think of *that!*'), while others condemned the cowardly, potentially peace-disrupting act of a cunning *chamar* (low caste).

The hornet's nest had been disturbed. Rahiman's Muslim supporters, especially those who had backed him, were outraged at Jhagru's treachery and the insulting jeers and taunts of his supporters. Resentment had been building up among some Muslims who felt that Hindus were using their numbers to push them around. They were not being consulted on important decisions affecting everyone. They felt taken for granted. It was time to make a stand before they were reduced to nothing. The very next day, they slaughtered a calf in full view of some Hindu women washing clothes at the edge of the Wailevu River and skinned the carcass strung from the branch of a mango tree. News of the slaughter spread like the proverbial wildfire in Wailevu and beyond. For Hindus, slaughtering cattle was bad enough, but doing it in such a brazen manner was provocative in the extreme. Frenzied meetings were held by both sides, and solemn oaths taken to teach a lesson that would not be forgotten for generations. Knives were sharpened and stones and sticks gathered for the inevitable bloody showdown. Someone even had a bucketful of pig's blood to throw down the wells of Muslims for whom the pig is the filthiest of all animals and contact in any form is forbidden. *Haram.* The whole community was on tenterhooks. Nothing less than one's collective honour (*izzat*) was at stake and it had to be defended with blood, if it came to that. Lines in the sand could be so easily drawn and the gauntlet thrown down without a second thought.

Someone had the presence of mind to report the matter to the Tua Tua Sector Office. Mr Sebastian immediately drove to the Tamarind Tree and gathered together leaders of both communities for an urgent meeting. Mr Sebastian was trusted as few other overseers were. Unable to pronounce his name, people had dubbed him Mr Subhas Chand. He had been at Tua Tua for several years. 'This is CSR land', he told the leaders, and no disturbance would be tolerated on it. 'What will the other sectors think? Have you thought of the reputation of this place, your reputations? Do you want to go to gaol for something stupid such as this?' '*Badmashi bund,* stop this nonsense,' he declared. 'No more *kushti* from now on. Kushti *khatam,*' he said with an air of finality as he got up to leave. '*Tum sab ghare jao aur chuppe baitho,* now you all go home and do not disturb the peace.' '*Ji Saheb,* Yes Sir,' people said, feeling suitably chastised. Everyone breathed a sigh of relief that a certain bloody confrontation had been avoided. The leaders regretted the foolishness of their reckless hot-headedness and agreed not to allow things to develop to this stage in future.

A resolution of sorts was reached a week or so later when, at a gathering of both communities under the Tamarind Tree, Jhagru apologised to Rahiman and shared with him half the prize money. Soon afterwards, for reasons unknown at that time, he left Wailevu for Wainikoro in northern Vanua Levu. People later said that this was Mr Sebastian's handiwork. As an experienced overseer and observer of the Indians, he realised that the truce was temporary, like a patch over the puncture of an overheating tyre. Sooner or later, it would erupt. Grief and grievance ran deep among the people, Mr Sebastian had long supervised. It was one trait both the company as well as colonial officials knew and feared: the unpredictable reaction of a people who on the surface appeared so docile. If Jhagru left Tua Tua voluntarily, Mr Sebastian reportedly said, 'there would be no black mark against his name. Nor against his own' for letting matters get out of hand in a place that he knew like the back of his hand. Jhagru agreed; he really had little choice. A few months later, Mr Sebastian was transferred on promotion to another estate.

Father was not alone in his almost mystical reverence for the Tamarind Tree. His recollections led me to other older men in the village, Nikka, Bihari, Mallu, Genda, Digambar, who had their own stories to tell about the Tree. They, too, recalled the festivals, the food and the fun they had as children, making their weekly pilgrimages to the Wailevu market with their fathers. Nikka remembered Madho, an Ahir, a cowherd, who was very particular about caste scruples and practices.[5] The Ahirs had a reputation as tough and independent-minded peasants, never shirking a fight in defence of personal or family honour or when avenging a real or imagined insult. *Girmit* had turned Madho's world upside down. The basic tenets of the old order of village India were gone or had become irrelevant, but he was determined to preserve what he could of the old ways. He would work with men of all castes; in this he had no choice, but he cooked his own meals whenever he could. He would take food and drink only from men of his own caste or those above him. And he managed to create a small fraternity of Ahirs in Tua Tua, a *biraadri* (brotherhood). Its main purpose was to maintain a semblance of Ahir cultural identity. They performed remembered rituals for their *kul* or clan gods and goddesses (*devtas*), celebrated their ancient village festivals, helped each other whenever they could, and performed the *Ahirwa ke naatch,* a special kind of Ahir dance where a man dressed in women's clothes, performed at festive occasions and at weddings. We in Tabia knew it as *Lehnga ke naatch.* Now it is gone, replaced by mindless Bollywood extravaganza and Michael Jackson–style jiggered dancing.

The most important role of the *biraadri* was to arrange marriage for the children. Madho invariably took the lead in the negotiations. Marrying 'down' was out and so was marrying up into castes much higher than your own. It was *adharmic* (morally inappropriate), potentially inviting divine retribution. These caste arrangements were the work of the gods, not of

---

5   'The Ahir are a caste of cowherders, milkers and cattle breeders widely dispersed across the Gangetic Plain.' See 'Ahir', *Countries and their Cultures,* available from: www.everyculture.com/South-Asia/Ahir.html (accessed 16 April 2019).

men, Madho used to say. Old timers, Nikka said, kept a careful mental record of where eligible boys and girls were. Some even arranged marriages as soon as children were born. This was the practice among some castes in village India. Once given, one's word was cast in stone. Sometimes, things could go too far. Once Madho had a man caned under the Tamarind Tree in front of his fellow Ahirs for eloping with a woman of lower caste (*chamar*).[6] Caste pollution he had said, set a bad example. When the senior sector manager, Mr Harriman (Hari Ram to the *girmitiyas*), came to know of the incident, he told Madho, whom he otherwise respected for his leadership abilities, not to take matters into his own hands. '*Hiyan hum sarkar baitho,* here we are the government,' he said. Madho remained Madho to the end, incorrigible and unreformed, but with progressively diminishing authority and influence, a relic of a forgotten past, as people dispersed and new influences came. In time, wealth and education, not caste, became the marker of identity and status.

Labasa sugar plantations had the reputation for excessive violence on *girmitiyas*. Files record men and women travelling long distances, from Nagigi and Wainikoro and Laga, under the cover of darkness to report cases of abuse to the stipendiary magistrate in Nasea town, with no guarantee of redress after all the risks of discovery had been taken. Indian *sirdars* (foremen), oral tradition had it, were the lynchpin of the system. They played pimps and procurers for their masters. In return, they got small favours to make extra money on the side, such as running the estate store or minor moneylending. It was not all one-way traffic though, as I learned. *Sirdars* and everyone else well knew the dangers, as well the limits beyond which it was not prudent to venture. The sharpened cane knife in the hands of an enraged man was the most feared weapon on the plantation, with the killers freely confessing their crimes before facing the gallows. This kind of violence was not uncommon in village India: '*izzat ke sawal hai,* it is the question of one's honour,' people said. Honour, their sense of self-respect, was all they had. It was the way of the peasant world.

Bhukkan was the go-to man to teach someone a lesson. He was the people's enforcer in the sector, as he liked to see himself. His caste had been in this *dhandha* (occupation) even in India, it was said. Perhaps he was from

---

6 'Chamar, widespread caste in northern India whose hereditary occupation is tanning leather.' Members of the caste are included in the officially designated Scheduled Castes under modern India's system of positive discrimination. See 'Chamar: Hindu Caste', *Encyclopaedia Britannica*, available from: www.britannica.com/topic/Chamar (accessed 16 April 2019).

one of those 'criminal tribes' about whom Europeans had written a lot. Bhukkan looked the part too, people said: dark, tall, broad-chested, with a face full of week-long growth and stylishly twirled moustache. He would take care of the offender for a little something. The attack had to be carefully planned over weeks to avoid detection, especially as the lines were full of the eyes and ears of the CSR. And it had to be proportionate to the offence given or crime committed. There was an unwritten code of conduct observed even on remote Fijian plantations, perhaps a remnant of village India. Bhukkan had four or five henchmen who were like blood brothers to him. They would meet under the Tamarind Tree at night in complete secrecy. The nature of the offence would be ascertained and the appropriate punishment determined. Then, over the next few weeks, the movement of the offending man would be closely but unobtrusively monitored, the route he took to work, the time he returned to the barracks, who his close friends were. *Khabardari* (alertness) was the name of the game.

The man giving offence this time was Sukkha, the *sirdar* who liked to make 'cheek-pass' at the women who worked under him. He had an eye for Janakia, Jaggan's wife, making sexually suggestive remarks within her hearing, casually letting his hand roam over his crotch while giving her orders for the fieldwork for the day. Jaggan himself was helpless to do anything. If he remonstrated, he would be isolated from the rest of his coworkers, given a heavier task and perhaps even whipped. He had seen that happen too many times to too many men to take the risk. He knew that no one would come to his assistance as they all feared Sukkha's whip hand and, even more, the overseer's boots. Overseer–*sirdar* collusion was common enough on the plantations, and it was the deadliest of all the possible permutations and combinations of men. Jaggan pleaded with Bhukkan to save his *izzat*. 'I have no one here. You are my *mai-bap, Dada,*' he said, 'my benefactor, sir.' He would do anything for him in return, even sacrifice his life for him. Bhukkan agreed, for a bottle of rum and two fat roosters, to the relatively easy assignment, and a plan of attack began to be hatched at the Tamarind Tree over several nights.

On the designated day, Bhukkan and his men agreed to go to the remotest part of the estate to clean the overgrown drains in preparation for the rainy season. Sukkha came to inspect the work at the end of the day as the sun was about to do down. It was then the men set upon him, dragging him deep into the cane field where no one could see or hear them. They pinned him to the rough ground and took turns urinating in his mouth and all over his body, using the choicest swear words they could think of. '*Sala maadharchod,* mother fucker, you are doing this to your own mothers and sisters? *Haramil,* bastard, what kind of *Jaanwar,* animal are you? *Bhonsriwala,* son of a whore. *Mutimilelie,* may you be mixed with earth.' 'Next time, we will shove this *lathi* up your arse,' they said menacingly. 'And then we will take good care of your wife while you watch.' For good measure, they stripped him of his pants and ordered him back to the barracks pants-less. The humiliation was as complete as it was brutal. The next day, Sukkha asked to be transferred to another estate. No one ever saw him in Tua Tua again.

From *sirdars* the talk moved seamlessly to *sahebs,* the overseers whom the *girmitiyas* called *kulambars,* reportedly coined from the order they barked, 'Call your number'. The names were often recalled formally: Mr Jones, Mr Taylor, Mr Davidson, the Burra Sahebs and the Chota Sahebs, the head and the junior overseers. Some were known only by their nicknames such as 'Tamaatar', for one overseer whose face was perennially red in the bright sun, while another was called 'Ullu' because he seemed clueless most of the time, and another 'Luccha' because of his crude habits (farting loudly in public) and penchant for using mispronounced Hindi swear words, especially about female genitalia. The overseers came in all shapes and sizes, people said, never fitting a single stereotype. If you did your work, completed your task, they left you alone, people said, but if you tried to be a smart-arse, they would quickly find out and give you the hiding of your life, and you became a marked man. Then you were fair game; your fate was sealed.

Some overseers got very attached to the place where they worked and the people they supervised. Some would come to the Tamarind Tree, usually on a Sunday, to tell the people that they were being transferred to another sector and asked them to be as good with their successors as they had been with them. Sometimes those who had served in the sector for a long time would bring along a few loaves of bread and cans of jam or donate a goat as a parting gift, and people would give them homemade sweets, such as *satua* or *lakdi ke mithai,* a particular favourite. Nothing was said, no promises made or extracted but much was understood by both sides. Such strategic exchanges, some anthropologists might say, had powerful symbolic meanings and an internal logic of their own, and were deployed at critical points to achieve desired outcomes. Probably. The *girmitiyas* might have been simple people but they were certainly not simpletons.

Mr Underwood was not one of those *sharif* (honourable) overseers. He was a strange type, Digambar recalled: a man of few words but free and furious with whips and fist, punching and kicking people whenever the mood seized him, screaming at the top of his screechy voice so that others heard him clearly. But that was not the worst thing about him as there were many others around Labasa whose reputation for violence was just as bad. Underwood's real problem was that he had a taste for men. He would paw his prey in some isolated corner of the plantation and buggerise them, certain that his victims would never publicly confess the assault for fear of shame. With time, Underwood got bolder and more brazen, and word of his bizarre behaviour spread beyond Tua Tua.

Something had to be done. Even people from other sectors were beginning to make inquiries; never a good sign. No one had much respect for a buggerised man, a *gandu,* who could not defend his own honour. There was nothing more shaming than being called a sector of effeminate *gandus.* Bhukkan was approached. He convened a meeting under the Tamarind Tree at which several people admitted sexual assault, including Mangal, whom Bhukkan regarded as his own younger brother. They were *jahajibhais* (shipmates) from the *Sangola.* The assaults ascertained, the question was what the punishment should be? Bhukkan had no doubt that it had to be death, and a violent death at that. A lesson had to be taught that Indian manhood, *mardaanagi*, was not to be trifled with.

On the designated day, Bhukkan and his men lay in wait as Underwood made his way on horseback to his favourite spot on the estate behind the mango tree. He fell to the ground as a huge stone hit him on the back of his head. The men dragged him to the middle of the cane field and, filled with murderous rage, hacked him to pieces. They then stuffed dismembered parts of his body into a jute sack, tied it up and buried it in a grave in the overgrown grass at the far end of the field, covering it with shrubs to avoid detection. The gruesome murder shook the CSR. Underwood's depravity was known to his fellow overseers and he would have been transferred to another sector sooner or later, or assigned a nonsupervisory position in the company's local office. That was a common enough practice to deal with the 'rotten potatoes', as the phrase went, before the whole sack was lost.

But a lesson had to be taught to the labourers lest things get out of hand and the company's authority was undermined in the public eye. Strong resolve was called for, and the company left no stone unturned to get to the bottom of the matter, with the support of the local Inspector of Police. The local stipendiary magistrate, Mr Foster, a former CSR overseer, agreed and urged swift action. People had to be put firmly in their place. For weeks, people were beaten or bribed for leads. Payment of wages was withheld and permission refused to the labourers to leave the estate even for brief social visits. Neither were visitors allowed to enter the estate premises. The estate dispensary was allowed to run out of medicine. All recreational activities were cancelled. The Tua Tua estate was in complete lockdown. Many suspected who the deed doer was but no one said anything. Treachery and betrayal at a time like this would bring swift retribution, usually in the form of beheading. And Underwood was a bad man. Then, someone—Chotu, people found out much later, with whose wife Bhukkan was having a torrid affair—fingered him as the most likely culprit. Bhukkan admitted leading the assault as an act of self-defence against egregious provocation. 'First our women, then our men; who is next, our children?' he reportedly said at the trial, but to no avail. He was found guilty of first-degree murder and hanged and his co-conspirators sentenced for life.

The plantation clearly was a place of rough, rudimentary justice. The *girmitiyas* often did not get a fair day in the courts. The mysterious protocols of *Court-Kachehri* (the law courts and judicial proceedings) were beyond them, and cases were decided on the basis of hard evidence adduced, not on hearsay or uncorroborated assertion. Inevitably, the overseers came out on top. But the stories I heard suggested greater complexity. Excesses certainly occurred but they came at a price, everyone realised, and usually at the expense of life. Things could go only so far and no further. Tact was backed by force. It was people like the men who gathered under the Tamarind Tree who maintained a semblance of order at a time of great chaos and confusion that kept the community intact. It was no mean achievement to transform a rag-tag group of people from hundreds of castes, speaking a host of tongues, from different parts of the subcontinent, subjected to servitude on the plantations, into a relatively smoothly functioning community bound by some essential values. It was not until much later that I realised why the names of men like Bhukkan were talked about with such awe and admiration by the old timers. They were their unsung heroes, *samaj rakshak* (guardians of the community).

3. THE TAMARIND TREE

On a fleeting visit to Labasa some years ago, I went to the site of the Tamarind Tree late one afternoon. There was nothing there except the rotten stump of the old Tree among tall, unruly grass. School children walked past the site every day, unaware of what was there once. Not even the teachers at Wailevu Primary knew. It was the same with men cutting cane in adjacent fields and others on horseback or bicycle going about their daily business. The silence was surreal, almost haunting. The past had become past, just like that. It reminded me of so many other things I had seen or experienced, but which were now gone. I remembered the graves of men and women who had died during the wreck of the *Syria* I had seen some years earlier, now lying unmarked and covered by shrub at the edge of the Nasilai Village. I remembered the tall mango tree behind our thatched house in Tabia, which had given us the fruit for our pickles but which had been destroyed after a fire, lit to smoke the bees out from its hollowed base, had been left to smoulder away for months. The land where we had grown up, where so many of our childhood memories were formed, has been reclaimed by its native owners and reverted to bush, obliterating all signs of life and laughter that had once filled the place. Signs of dereliction and neglect abound. That is typical of so many Indian settlements throughout Vanua Levu. There is little consciousness of the past and even less desire to know about it among our people. Everyone is trying to leave, hoping eventually to migrate overseas. My own links to Labasa have become tenuous over the years as members of our extended family left the island to settle in other parts of Fiji. Tabia, the village where I grew up, is now a place of evanescent memories. All the old markers of special moments have disappeared.

Father died nearly 20 years ago. We did not really know him when he was alive; we hardly ever talked about private matters. That was the way things were then. I understand the reason for his grief better now than I did before; the death of the world that formed him. I think I understand the man better, too, his fears and hopes and his sense of his place and purpose on earth. I understand all that, but I also understand why the Tamarind Tree went, why it had to go. It had come to Tua Tua with the *girmitiyas,* and now, ever so faithfully, it was going out with them, taking with it their secrets and stories of their hopes and aspirations. The Tree had given succour and security to men and women from the old world, but it had little meaning or relevance to those who followed them. Its long journey had finally come to an end in May 1962 when it was hit by lightning and razed. *Finis coronat opus.* A reminder of another time and place, its demise lay to rest the ghosts of the past, of people like Bhukkan and Underwood and countless others like them. Befittingly, like so many *girmitiyas,* with its dignity intact, it died a sudden, uncomplicated death, not a long, lingering one. The Tamarind Tree was gone but not forgotten; its ashes would continue to nourish the soil—soul—of father's generation, and mine.

4

'A most callous indifference'

Sukhdei's story

> Death lies on her face like untimely frost.
>
> — William Shakespeare[1]

How do we write about a past where records don't exist, or exist only partially, and memory is not properly archived? Yet, unwritten pasts must be remembered for they, too, are part of our lives. This conundrum confronts all of us who write about the experience of indenture in the late nineteenth and early twentieth centuries. Written records are partial and fragmentary, but often that is all we have to go by. This is where imaginative reconstruction comes in, as in the case of the story that follows. We begin with the documented facts but then put flesh on their bare bones, read against the grain, draw upon similar cases to provide a fuller picture of what happened and why. Factual accuracy is important, but a higher purpose is to capture the truth of the experience through 'true imagination'. Sometimes, the truth of an experience or a fact is best understood in its imaginative version. This is Sukhdei's story, but I have drawn on my lifetime's knowledge of the indenture experience to create a composite picture that, I hope, does justice to the tragic experience of one woman. This is Sukhdei's story, but not hers alone.

---

1   William Shakespeare, *Romeo and Juliet*, in *William Shakespeare: The Complete Works*, ed. Peter Alexander, 902–39 (London and Glasgow: Collins, 1951; reprint 1980), 4.5.28.

There is a spot on the banks of the Sigatoka River a few chains from Ram Sami's village shop that men avoid and try not to walk past at night. Many say they have seen the figure of a frail woman with fraying white hair and dressed in funeral-white clothes wondering aimlessly at various times of the night, lost. Some swear they have heard soft wailing noises at odd hours, and others recall the fragrance of scents sprinkled on dead bodies during funeral ceremonies to keep the stench of death at bay. A mango tree stands forlornly in overgrown para grass. Some old timers remember this as the place where a deranged woman drowned herself. That is all they remember about her and about the remote past of their forebears. The woman's name was Sukhdei. Her death, in the early years of the twentieth century, and the tragic events that led to it were widely talked about in the Indian indentured community right across Viti Levu at the time. The story of complicity and attempted cover-up, the violence and treachery that surrounded Sukhdei's case finally ended in Fiji's Supreme Court, a very rare event almost unprecedented. Who, then, was Sukhdei and what was the true story of her ordeal? This imaginative reconstruction based on fragments of written and oral evidence seeks to answer this question.

Sukhdei, five foot something and a loner, was a *girmitiya* from the district of Mathura, in western Uttar Pradesh. She was seven months pregnant when she came to Fiji in July 1910. She was 18 or thereabouts when she was assigned to the CSR's Tuva Sector. A month after arriving in Fiji, she gave birth to a child (on 16 August) who died four days later. A pregnant unmarried woman would have been a source of great shame to her family and the broader community; the situation was made even worse in this case by the fact that Sukhdei was a Brahmin, of priestly class, from a holy region that was the playground of Lord Krishna. She would most certainly have been tossed out from the village to fend for herself, or killed to avoid giving her family a bad name. At the Emigration Depot at Matiabruj, Calcutta, she was introduced to Ballu, a Fiji-bound immigrant from the district of Benares, and they came together as husband and wife. There must have been many Sukhdeis among the indentured women who easily fell into the recruiters' net and emigrated to the colonies, victims of violence and sexual molestation by their own men, broken and discarded.

Sukhdei was one of 13,596 Indian women who came to Fiji, all adults, as indentured labourers. She was one of 262 from the district of Mathura, and one of 510 who were Brahmin. The majority came as single migrants, though there were about 4,000 who came as members of families.

But whether they came alone or in families, they were all assumed to have fallen into the depths of degradation and vice, as one emigration agent of Trinidad suggested; unsteady, rudderless vessels, as an otherwise sympathetic observer C.F. Andres put it; or immoral doe rabbits, as an overseer in Fiji described them. And they accordingly bore the brunt of the blame for the social ills of indenture. Their faces were hidden behind a veil of dishonour.

Sukhdei's misfortune was not uncommon on the plantations as infants fell to high mortality rates, especially in the wet cane areas of south-eastern Viti Levu. Nearly a quarter of infants in the 1890s died within a year of birth from a variety of ailments including anaemia, respiratory illnesses, diarrhoea and dysentery and the general unsanitary conditions of the lines. Things improved over time, but the danger of death was ever present and tore at the heart of many a family. The *girmitiyas* bore their tragedies stoically, but not so the overseers and government officials who routinely held the mothers responsible, believing they lacked the motherly instinct. Weren't they, after all, the flotsam and jetsam of Indian society, the lowest of the lowest? This deeply entrenched view among the planters, despite much evidence to the contrary, blunted sensitivity to the indentured labourers. Some parents pooled money together to hire a *dai* (maid) to look after their children in the lines while they went out to work, but many mothers also took their children with them to the fields to suckle them during breaks. Exposure to the elements held its own peril.

Two days after the death of her child, Sukhdei was ordered to work crushing stones with a hammer for the railway track being built to cart cane to the recently opened Lautoka sugar mill. Sending mothers to work so soon after childbirth was against the regulations, but on the plantations, especially the remote ones, where official inspections were infrequent and the opportunity to lay complaints limited, it was not the courts but overseers who had the final say. And Sukhdei was desperately unlucky to have Herbert Brackman as her overseer, or *kulambar*.

Brackman was a particularly violent man—volatile, quick to anger at the slightest hint of disobedience, or what he perceived to be disobedience. The possibility of miscommunication or misunderstanding never crossed his mind. In his 30s, he had worked with Kanaka labour in the cane-growing district of Mackay, Queensland, before coming to Fiji to work for the Colonial Sugar Refining Company (CSR). It was rumoured that he had been 'advised' to leave Mackay before things got out of hand because of his rough treatment of the workers under him. At least two overseers had been hacked to death for systematically mistreating their labourers. Brackman had become a marked man. His first posting in Fiji was to the Naqiqi Sector in northern Vanua Levu where, with a free hand, he unleashed what officials called 'a reign of terror' on the sugar estate. He had once poured a pot of hot water on his servant because he was unhappy with the way his breakfast had been prepared. The stipendiary magistrate at Labasa exonerated him of all blame because he had found 'no criminal intent' in his behaviour. Fearing reprisal against him for his violence and brutality, the CSR quietly transferred him to Viti Levu, to the newly opened and remote Tuva Sector where, it was hoped, he would escape official notice. But Brackman was Brackman, a creature of habit who continued with his old ways.

Totaram, Brackman's *sirdar* (foreman) was not much better. *Sirdars* were the lynchpin of the system, the overseers' ears and eyes on the ground, chosen for the role for their ability as enforcers and task masters. On some plantations, they made a little extra by operating a store on the side, with the concurrence of the plantation manager as a reward for loyalty, even though this was strictly against the spirit of the labour ordinance. They could also be relied upon to procure women for the overseers who were invariably young and unmarried. Some were not averse to 'sampling' women under their charge themselves, though the constant fear of a sharpened cane knife in the hands of an enraged man kept matters in check. Totaram, an Ahir cowherder from Gorakhpur, had arrived in Fiji in 1905. He was a big man with a fierce handlebar moustache and a no-nonsense demeanour. A man with a very short fuse, he was feared in the lines. He often talked with his fist, people said. And he had big ambitions for himself too. He knew which side his bread was buttered on, as the expression goes. If he played his cards right, he might be transferred to a bigger sector with greater opportunities for himself. The combination of Brackman and Totaram proved deadly for Sukhdei.

At around 11 o'clock, Totaram came on his routine round of inspection. Seeing Sukhdei resting under a mango tree, he barked, 'What is this? Why aren't you crushing stones? *E tumhar baap ke kam hai,* you are not working for your father.' Sukhdei, weak and bleeding, replied, '*Hamar haal theek nahi hai. Hum nahi sakta e kaam kare,* I am not well. I can't do this work. *Kutch aur kaam deo,* give me some other work.' Totaram interpreted this as insolence, this woman talking back to him like that? Who the hell did she think she was? He advanced towards her, slapped her a few times

4. 'A MOST CALLOUS INDIFFERENCE'

and ordered her back to work. '*Agar hum phir tummhe sustaate dekha to hum tumhar khaal utaar dega,* if I find you shirking work again, I will strip the skin off your back.' Someone uttered a muffled obscenity, but no one did anything, continuing with their work as if nothing had happened. The alleged abuse would be offered as mitigating evidence in Totaram's favour. On his way back, Totaram reported Sukhdei to Brackman when he inquired about work on the new railway track.

When Brackman came on his daily round of inspection around midday and saw Sukhdei resting, he remembered what Totaram had told him and flew into a rage even after Sukhdei had told him about the loss of her child and her weak state. She pointed to her bloodied dress. Could the *saheb* (master) please give her some other work, she pleaded, sobbing? Brackman refused, 'No, I cannot give you other work. Come on, get up. *Jaldi, jaldi.* Quick, fast.' When Sukhdei remained seated on the ground, he walked towards her, grabbed her hair and slapped her face hard. 'You talking back to me like that? I will teach you a lesson you will never forget.' Suddenly, Brackman lost his senses. He was like a man possessed. He lifted Sukhdei and threw her down hard on the stones she was crushing and kicked her several times, as Sukhdei recalled in her testimony to the stipendiary magistrate at Sigatoka. Then the whip came raining down on Sukhdei's sweating bare back. Blood began to ooze from her mouth and back. The beating, fast and furious, went on for several minutes. Once his rage was exhausted, Brackman called out to Kali Das a chain or two away to take Sukhdei to the creek nearby to clean her up of blood and dust. Again, there was complete silence from fellow workers who had all witnessed the attack on Sukhdei.

Brackman's junior sector overseer, A.G. Allen, was aghast at what he had just seen but he was too timid to do anything. Reporting the assault to the estate manager would have spelled trouble for himself and, possibly end his career. 'Snitching' was a punishable crime among the overseers. Allen knew Brackman well, too well, and so did everyone else on the estate, but a 'good' man was hard to find and, as far as the estate management was concerned, Brackman was a good man who maintained discipline among his workers and got the job done. Still, something moved Allen when he saw Sukhdei's terrible blood-stained clothes and heard her sustained sobbing. He pleaded with Brackman to send her to the estate hospital accompanied by Kali Das. Brackman reluctantly agreed but demanded that Sukhdei walk to the hospital some 5 miles away in Nailaga rather than be carried by Kali Das. As soon as he was out of sight of the overseers, Kali Das carried Sukhdei, bleeding and barely conscious, on his back to the hospital. Brackman sent a note with Kali Das to the hospital superintendent that asked T.G. Witton to examine and classify the woman Sukhdei ex-*Santhia II*. He added that she was apparently incapable or else damn lazy and Brackman wanted to know if she was physically capable of work and if so how much.

Witton was new to the Tuva plantation, having arrived there in May 1910, just a few months before the attack on Sukhdei occurred. As a newcomer, he was unacquainted with the way things were done in a remote area like Tuva, unaware of the rituals and protocols of the culture of silence and conspiracy that governed life of the *sahebs* on the plantations. Protecting the good name of the community and closing ranks against any outside intrusion was understood by everyone, if not explicitly stated. But not Witton. He made the 'cardinal mistake' of saying openly that he believed Kali Das's version of events. Brackman had claimed that he had merely 'tapped' her with a fly whisk to get her attention. Witton rejected this outright. He suggested that the wounds he saw could not have been inflicted how Brackman had claimed. He added that he was positive the wounds on Sukhdei's buttocks had been caused by her being lifted up and thrown down on stones. Witton told the District Medical Officer Dr Mullen, when he came around on his weekly tour of inspection, that Sukhdei was black and blue with weals on her back and buttocks. Mullen agreed, suggesting that she had been flayed.

Mullen added that the eight wounds he found on Sukhdei's body were the result of contusion caused by some weapon, probably a stick. Like Witton, he, too, was horrified. He wrote that the facts pointed to a degree of brutality that could hardly be conceived by any man in his right senses, and added that the victim had not been shown to him in the ordinary way but with manifest reluctance. He suggested that Witton had been influenced to cloak the matter. It later emerged that either Totaram, or one of his men, had bribed the hospital orderly to hide Sukhdei from visiting inspectors.

Witton knew that labourers were regularly abused for not completing their task, for malingering, or for damaging field equipment, but this attack was outrageous, beyond anything he had ever seen. And he had seen a lot. He immediately wrote a note to Brackman that he asked Kali Das to deliver. In the note he asked when had Brackman received instructions to put women to work five days after confinement. Witton also castigated Brackman by asking what he thought of himself for ill-treating a woman in such a condition and he added that he thought it would be lucky for Brackman if the woman didn't die. At the same time, Witton wrote that he accepted no responsibility whatever and if anything happened to Sukhdei it was Brackman's fault.

His humane concern was genuine, but it would be used against him in court; his willingness to believe the words of a mere 'coolie' against that of a fellow white man.

The note unsettled Brackman enough for him to write immediately to Witton saying that he didn't understand about the woman's child being dead and adding that he believed she was legally liable for work. He insinuated that Sukhdei had asked for work herself and, when he asked if she was sick or ill, she had said no. In answer to Witton's accusations, he said that he had found Sukhdei lying down at midday, and sent her to hospital against her will. He denied ill-treating her and added that Witton should know that he did not work the women. In an effort to shift the blame, he said that he believed the *sirdar* had handled her roughly when she refused to work but, since he was not there, he felt unable to say. He added that he was sure her husband flogged her in the lines on the Friday morning since he had seen the marks and that the *die* (midwife) who attended Sukhdei had told him that her child had been born quite normally and that the woman was all right. He continued his note to Witton by querying about Sukhdei's sickness, adding that he felt anxious about the woman's health since he had received Witton's note, but denied any responsibility for it in view of the facts. He instructed Witton that he should not be so ready to believe a white man a scoundrel unless he was quite sure of his ground. Finally, Brackman added that if he was not right in sending the woman to work that to please inform him of what he should have done according to the ordinance.

Brackman stuck to his improbable version that Sukhdei had asked for work. Later he added to his story. He said that he had complained to Sukhdei that her person and clothes smelt. According to Brackman, she asked him what she should do about it, since she had no money and no other clothes. When Brackman asked her if she had any soap she told him she didn't. Brackman said he told her to get some soap from her husband, but she replied that her husband was presently in hospital and that he wouldn't give her soap anyway. Brackman reiterated that Sukhdei had asked him to give her work and indicated that she was capable of it.

LEVELLING WIND

Brackman thought he was doing the woman a favour.

The stipendiary magistrate summed it up well. Brackman's assertion that he gave work to the woman at her request is hardly credible, and was denied by her, but if she had asked for it, her request should have been complied with as she was receiving rations. All new migrants were entitled to rations for the first six months. As for the provisions of the law governing the employment of pregnant women, the stipendiary magistrate simply noted that what Brackman had done was not in conformance with the intention of the ordinance. Pregnant women were not to be given onerous tasks and, after childbirth, women were not to be sent to work for up to two months and then only upon medical clearance. That was the letter and spirit of the law, but on remote plantations other realities prevailed.

Brackman could not get Witton's note out of his mind. He had to cover his tracks and quickly. Later that day, he asked Totaram to bring to his bungalow other workers who might have witnessed what took place at midday or had heard about it from others. Hansi, Balchand, Pudar, Hasmat and Ramphal went with Totaram and squatted on the veranda waiting for the big *saheb* to arrive. They were all influential men in the sector and their word would carry weight backed by brute force. It was a very brave or foolish man indeed who went against their wishes or directives. Brackman opened the screen door and came out. Allen was with him. After a round of rough rum, Brackman looked at Totaram and said that if he (Brackman) got caught that will be the end of his life. But if you (Totaram) took the blame, he would pay the fine. He handed two pounds sterling to Totaram to be shared among the witnesses. No one demurred. They all knew only too well the price of disobedience and defiance. They would become marked men and vulnerable to beatings, hard labour and extension of indenture contracts. Better to get along and get out. Resistance came with a heavy price. If bribery did not buy compliance, the threat of violence did. The next day Brackman told Kali Das that if he said anything he would be shot. Kali Das did not say anything. The threat was repeated several times over the week. Brackman thought this was where the matter would rest. He was wrong.

Witton was sufficiently outraged to report the assault to the local police. For his part, Dr Mullen reported it to the Agent-General of Immigration in Suva, the colony's top official responsible for Indian immigrants. He sought the advice of Colonial Secretary Eyre Hutson, the colony's chief administrator a few rungs below the governor, who advised getting more independently verified information from the Resident Inspector of Immigration based at Lautoka. Unable to contact the resident inspector who was on leave, and in any case was leaving government service, the Agent-General of Immigration asked the Inspector-General of Constabulary (IGC) for assistance. The IGC went to Tuva immediately to acquaint himself with the case. He visited Sukhdei in hospital and talked with the stipendiary magistrate. He told Hutson that things on this occasion had gone too far, that Brackman was an uncommonly violent man unfit to work with the labourers under his charge, and that the assault was too serious a matter to be ignored. It should be treated as an aggravated assault and Brackman indicted.

If word of the assault reached India, the consequences for the company and the government could be dire. India, the IGC said, was beginning to take greater interest in the affairs of indentured labourers. Word had reached Fiji that an official delegation was on its way to Fiji to investigate the conditions on the plantations. These were all compelling reasons to take immediate action.

Hutson agreed, and so did the governor. The case eventually came before the Supreme Court in April 1911. The CSR was bent on clearing its name at any cost. And the Supreme Court was the place to do it. Much was at stake including the future allotment of indentured labourers to its plantations. If Brackman was indicted, who would be next? Wouldn't this incite the labourers to lay more complaints against the company? Order and discipline had to be maintained. But Brackman was charged with wounding with intent to do grievous bodily harm and unlawful wounding. What, one wonders, was lawful wounding? Attorney-General Albert Eckhardt KC prosecuted while H.M. Scott, the colony's leading criminal lawyer, appeared for the defence, with Leslie Davidson of Ba, a large sugarcane growing district, who was well versed in cross-examining Indian immigrants. He knew their language and understood their culture. Sukhdei, the first witness, was brought into the courtroom in a wheelchair.

Sukhdei was clearly mentally unwell, deranged, her evidence barely coherent, her recollections vague, contradictory. Indentured labourers were invariably at a disadvantage in a court of law, being unfamiliar with the processes and protocols of the law of evidence and being cross-examined by *sahebs* in an alien language. But this was worse. No, Brackman did not beat her, she told the court. Neither had Totaram. Her husband, Ballu, was the culprit; a point used to significant effect by defence lawyer

Scott. Sukhdei also told the court, improbably, that it was Ballu who had killed the child because he was not the child's biological father. Some of the witnesses who had gone to Brackman's bungalow on the day of the attack had changed their minds and testified that they had indeed seen Brackman assault Sukhdei, but they compromised their evidence by admitting to accepting the bribe. The court rejected their testimony out of hand. Kali Das, who had witnessed the whole episode, told the court that Totaram did not beat Sukhdei, and that he had not seen Brackman assault her either. Witton was upbraided by Leslie Davidson for writing the note to Brackman accusing him of the assault based on what Kali Das had told him. Wasn't a man to be presumed innocent until proven guilty?

Chief Justice Sir Charles Major dismissed the case. He was Fiji's chief justice from 1904–14. Born in the tiny West Indian island of St Kitts, he was a quintessential establishment man, the son of the chief manager of the Colonial Bank of the West Indies and Chancellor of the Diocese of Antigua. He religiously followed the letter rather than the spirit of the law. He had to decide on evidence adduced in court and tested through cross-examination and not on hearsay, he said summing up the case. But many questions remained. Was the chief justice aware, as evidently everyone else was, of Sukhdei's state of mind and body? After all, she had been brought into the court room in a wheelchair several months after she had been attacked. Why was Ballu, Sukhdei's husband, not questioned about allegedly having savagely beaten his wife and killing the infant? Shouldn't he have been sentenced to imprisonment for inflicting such bodily harm on her? How could the discrepancy between what Sukhdei had told the stipendiary magistrate at Sigatoka and what she told the Supreme Court be explained? Why was the stipendiary magistrate himself was not cross-examined? Why had Kali Das changed his testimony? Why did Brackman bribe the workers if he was innocent? Did he not have a history of violence and brutality?

Some years after the Sukhdei incident, bits and pieces of information about it dribbled out. As soon as the severity of the assault had become clear, the ring of silence around Brackman had closed. Totaram was promised promotion to the Lovu Sector in Lautoka. All his needs would be taken care of (women, alcohol, cigarettes, extra bonus). Brackman would personally see to that. Totaram told Ballu to forget about the assault and move on. '*Jo hoi gaye so hoi gaye, bhai,* what has happened, has happened. Now look after yourself. Once Totaram is gone, you will be made the junior *sirdar* with a store to run on the side. If you decide not to go along, don't ever say I did not warn you. Accidents can happen, as you know.' Ballu did. 'Rotten potatoes have no place among us.'

Totaram told Sukhdei not to say anything about Brackman because that would make matters worse for everyone. Totaram added that if it is Brackman today, it could be someone worse tomorrow. He would speak to the *saheb* to assign Sukhdei to domestic duties. And when matters settled down, he would try and get her *girmit* reduced. Some fellow women workers who had witnessed the attack consoled Sukhdei. They told her the story of an overseer on a neighbouring estate who had been set upon by women, pinned to the ground as they took turns urinating on him. Humiliated, the fellow left the estate. They told her that his day would come, *bahini* (sister), adding that *bhgwan ke ghar me der haye, andher nahin* (justice will eventually prevail).

Justice of sorts did prevail. Things did not turn out the way Brackman and his accomplices had hoped. The Immigration Department was convinced that Brackman had indeed committed the grievous assault on Sukhdei. His own previous record of violence and callousness toward the labourers under his charge spoke eloquently about the man's character. The Agent-General of Immigration had said that the callous indifference to the suffering of Sukhdei evident in Brackman's notes was unmistakeable. Sadly, it was not evident to the chief justice. And officials were deeply troubled by Brackman's manner after the incident: no remorse, no sympathy. On the contrary, Brackman bragged to others about how he controlled his workers—with a firm hand and, if force was required, he would happily teach the recalcitrant a lesson they would never forget. As evidence of his successful modus operandi, he often pointed to the absence of strikes on his estate and the paucity of complaints to the Immigration Department. Fellow overseers viewed Brackman with a mixture of horror and muted respect.

The Immigration Department advised Colonial Secretary Hutson, a future Governor of Fiji, to ask Governor Sir Henry May to direct the CSR not to employ Brackman any longer on any of its estates anywhere in Fiji. Hutson explained the situation about Brackman's extremely callous conduct in putting a woman to labour or allowing her to go to labour, even if it was admitted that she asked to be put to labour only six days after childbirth; his cruelty in not having the woman carried to hospital, although she was in such a serious condition that the hospital administrator said that she was very seriously wounded and that he thought her life was in danger upon admission. Brackman failed to inform the hospital administrator that the woman had been assaulted. Instead, he wrote to the hospital administrator that she was either incapable or damn lazy. He neglected to make a report to the police on receipt of the note from the hospital administrator drawing attention to the ill-treatment the woman had received; and Brackman neglected to report the occurrence to the manager of the estate.

Hutson was adamant that if the CSR disregarded the government's advice and continued to employ Brackman it should be told that there would be no further allotment of Indian indentured labourers to any of its estates in any part of Fiji and would result in the cancellation of all indentured allotments to any plantation where he was employed. The governor and the chief justice concurred and so, too, did the CSR.

Brackman's employment with the company was terminated, but that did not end his employment in Fiji. The Vancouver-Fiji Sugar Company in Navua hired him as an office clerk and to do other duties as the need or opportunity arose. Sooner rather than later he would have been restored to his old position. Agent-General of Immigration Coates was outraged. He wrote to Hutson to tell the manager of the Vancouver-Fiji Sugar Company that the government had no intention of rescinding the decision already given as to any further employment of Mr Brackman. Why should the Navua company be allowed to employ Brackman when the CSR had cancelled his contract? Governor May was so advised but he disagreed stating in a letter to Hutson that Brackman had only been barred from being put in charge of indentured labour. That meant that if he was employed as a clerk there was no way to object. Coates told the colonial secretary to inform the Vancouver-Fiji Sugar Company that all allotments of Indian indentured labourers to it would cease if Brackman had any supervisory role over indentured workers.

At the Supreme Court trial, the jury had taken only 20 minutes to arrive at the verdict of not guilty, but they added that Brackman's conduct in putting a woman to work in her condition at such a heavy task was callous in the extreme. It was a mild reprobation of an inhumane conduct. But, the chief justice disagreed. His Honour decided that in the circumstances he would exonerate the accused from the stigma of callousness. What the circumstances were, he did not elaborate, and no one asked, although there was ample written evidence and testimony to the contrary. Brackman realised that his days in Fiji were effectively over. The assault on Sukhdei would haunt him wherever he went, hanging around his neck like an albatross. His notoriety had spread far and wide and he would be a prime target for a murderous revenge attack. The gruesome hacking attack on Overseer Steadman in the Moto district of Ba was fresh in everyone's mind. Bits and pieces of his body were strewn around the cane fields. It was time to move on. Brackman left Fiji on 5 July 1911 and was never heard from again. Sirdar Totaram was reluctantly demoted when the Resident Inspector of Immigrants at Lautoka protested his continued employment as *sirdar* by the CSR. He was sent to work looking after the estates' cows and horses—a stable hand. But not for long. A few years later, he was diagnosed with leprosy and sent to the remote Makogai Island in the Lomaiviti Group where he died and was buried. Kali Das and Ballu both left Tuva some years after their *girmit* ended and nothing was heard from or about them.

And Sukhdei? What a lovely name: giver of happiness. But happiness was not her lot. Hers was a truncated life lived in suffering and on sufferance in a faraway land to which she had come in such hope and anticipation, all dashed so soon. She spent the rest of days as a physically disabled, mentally deranged vagrant around Sigatoka. One day, her body was found floating in the Sigatoka River. Her death was noticed and talked about for years by people who believed she continued to haunt the Tuva district long after she was gone. Her grave is unmarked. Was her death an accident (unknown for a people new to water)? A suicide, a conscious act to end a damaged life drained of dignity and meaning? Or was she deliberately despatched to salve the conscience of fellow Indians who had witnessed the violent attack on her but chose to remain silent or, worse still, accept a bribe to cover the tracks of the perpetrators, a constant reminder of their callousness and cowardice? No one really knew. Sukhdei remained a mystery in death as she had been in life.

5
Transitions and transformations[1]

> Perhaps home is not a place but simply an irrevocable condition.
>
> — James Baldwin[2]

Indo-Fijian culture has evolved and changed over the course of the last century in response to internal developments and external changes. The process has involved adaptation and reconstitution. I trace the broad contours of change through the prism of personal experience and observation. As I say in the chapter, the professional and the personal mingle in the narrative.

Florida, Utah, Montana, Louisiana, Gladstone, Victoria, Eve, Plato, Jacob. Names of esoteric places and famous people, you might say. That they are. But they are also the names of the first Indian children born in Fiji. They were born not in Rewa, Raralevu or Rakiraki, later to become important centres of Indo-Fijian settlement on Fiji's main island of Viti Levu, but on the tiny remote island of Rabi, on planter John Hill's estate—the largest employer of the first batch of Indian indentured labourers in Fiji. The new migrants were sent there because other European planters who had expected to employ them were angry with the government for prohibiting the employment of Fiji labour and so sullenly refused to have anything to do with them. Sir Arthur Gordon, Fiji's first governor and the chief architect of the indenture scheme—he had seen its operation in Mauritius

---

1   Originally appeared as 'Indo-Fijians: Roots and routes', in *South Asian Diaspora: Transnational Connects and Changing Identities*, ed. Rajesh Rai and Peter Reeves (London/New York: Routledge, 2009), pp. 69–107.
2   James Baldwin, *Giovanni's Room* (New York: Dial Press, 1956), p. 92.

and Trinidad where he had been governor before coming to Fiji—was disappointed but not despairing. By the early 1880s, the prospects brightened considerably with the expansion of the sugar industry under the recently arrived Colonial Sugar Refining Company (CSR) of Australia. The company would go on to dominate the sugar industry, and also Fiji's economy, for nearly a century until its departure in 1973.

Between the *Leonidas*'s inaugural voyage in May 1879 and the *Sutlej*'s last in 1916, 87 ships, specially designed to carry human cargo over long distances across treacherous seas, ferried 60,965 men, women and children from Calcutta and Madras to Fiji. They had such magical names, named after great rivers and classical figures: *Danube, Elbe Ganges, Jamuna, Rhone, Avon, Syrius, Pericles, Leonidas.* Remarkably, only one of the ships, *Syria* in May 1884, perished through negligent navigation at a cost of 59 lives, although the long journey itself—three months by sailing ship in the nineteenth century and one month after the advent of steamships in 1904—broke many land-locked lives and disrupted irreparably the settled habits, practices and thoughts of ancient village India. The voyage across the *kala pani* (the dark, dreaded seas), was a great leveller of hierarchy and protocol. But the destruction also contained within it seeds of rejuvenation, for from the fragments of a common past and a cultural predicament a shared destiny and a common destination emerged and forged new bonds. None was emotionally more important or reassuring than the bond of *jahajibhai*, the brotherhood of the crossing, as intimate and comforting as real blood kinship, which men cherished well into their twilight years as a symbol of solidarity against the asperities and alienations of the outside world.

In the end, some 24,000 of the indentured migrants and their families (some born in Fiji) returned to India. The majority stayed on, attracted by the promise of possibilities in their new homeland and the fear of the reception they might receive in India having broken taboos—marrying across caste lines, eating food cooked by unknown hands, doing work considered polluting—taboos still considered sacrosanct at home. Many talked and continued to talk well into old age about returning one day, but the day of decision never came as memories of the past faded and the realities of life in a new place took hold. That new life was fraught. Ancestral wisdom had to be adapted. New pragmatic, cross-caste relationships had to be established. A new geography had to be understood, a new vocabulary mastered.

5. TRANSITIONS AND TRANSFORMATIONS

This the *girmitiyas* and their descendants did, with a mixture of resilience and resignation, often on their own, without a helping hand. In time, their labour laid the foundation of the Fijian economy: illiterate thumbprints most visible in the undulating areas of green cane fields across vast, often inhospitable stretches of previously unturned terrain; in the damp paddy fields of the Rewa and Navua deltas; in the slowly emerging market towns in the cane belts, precursors to modern urban centres; in rudimentary structures on the way to becoming ground-breaking primary and secondary schools; in the steady stream of school children leaving the village environment to enter the world of the professions beyond the imagined horizons of the previous generation.

For a century or so, the self-contained and self-sufficient village community sustained the life of the Indo-Fijians, but that world began to fragment towards the end of the twentieth century. The sugarcane industry for which Indians were brought to Fiji in the first place began to decline through the vicissitudes of the international market, poor planning and lack of foresight among the industry leaders and the nonrenewal of the leased land upon which sugar cane was grown. People in the cane belt left for the mushrooming squatter settlements of urban centres. Internal displacement was accompanied by increasing emigration. The coups took their toll. Following the first military coup of 1987, close to 150,000 left for North America and Australasia, reducing the Indo-Fijian population from around 50 per cent of the national population in the 1980s to around 30 per cent in the early years of the twenty-first century. The outflow was to continue.

The last 40 or so years have been a time of profound change in the life of the Indo-Fijian community. Travel and technology have altered social habits and patterns of thought. The urban drift has transformed the role and place of the village in people's lives. My purpose in this chapter is to look at aspects of the 'first crossing'—the initial rupture—and tease out from this complex and contested history larger patterns of social and cultural change that might help us understand the broad constellation of forces that have shaped Indo-Fijian history and identity and the social development of the Indian indentured diaspora generally. There are many ways of telling this story—for example, through a conventional historical narrative of the type we routinely do. But I want to do something different, something more experimental. I want to be autobiographical, to use the experience and example of my own family history to construct the larger picture, certain that that experience is broadly typical of the community's. In this kind of exercise, the personal and the professional mingle. The narrator is under oath to tell the truth as he sees it.

My direct link with Fiji begins in 1908. That was the year my grandfather came to Fiji as an indentured labourer,[3] one of 60,000 who made the crossing between 1879 and 1916. Aja (grandfather) was lucky in one respect; he arrived in Fiji when the worst abuses of *girmit* were over: the heart-rending infant mortality rates of the 1890s; the excessive over-tasking; the physical violence on the plantations; an uncertain life on the raw edges of extreme vulnerability. In 1907, there were 30,920 Indians living in Fiji, of whom only 11,689 were under indenture. The freed population—*khula*—were cultivating 17,204 acres of land on their own, 5,586 devoted to cane and 9,347 planted with rice. In time, sugarcane cultivation would become the principal occupation of the Indian population.[4] By 1911, of the 40,286 Indians, 27 per cent had been born in the colony, the Fiji-born proportion of the population increasing rapidly with time, until, by 1946, they had become the outright majority of the population, spawning the threat of 'Indian domination' that would bedevil the country's complex political negotiations as it lurched towards independence in the 1960s.

As young children, we heard stories about indenture from Aja and other *girmitiyas*—the hard work at the first break of light; about overseers, both good and bad; the cloistered, unstable family life in the estate lines; the ways in which they attempted to make sense of their predicament. I heard these stories long before I read scholarly accounts of the indenture experience at university. These accounts, most famously Hugh Tinker's *A New System of Slavery,* captured our imagination.[5] I read it in the final year of my university undergraduate studies. That book set the tone of the new historiography.[6] *Girmit* was slavery by another name, nothing more, nothing less, the book informed us. The indentured labourers themselves were gullible simpletons from impoverished rural backgrounds,

---

3   I speak only of my grandfather and not my grandmother because little is known about her background. No one bothered to find out the details of her life. An element of secrecy and shame surrounded the experience of the *girmitiya* women. My own family was no exception in this regard.
4   John Wesley Coulter, *The Drama of Fiji: A Contemporary History* (Rutland, VT: Charles Tuttle and Company, 1967), pp. 90–91.
5   Hugh Tinker, *A New System of Slavery: The Export of Indian Labour Abroad, 1834–1920* (London: Hansib, 1974).
6   For an application of the slavery thesis to Fiji, see Ahmed Ali, *Girmit: The Indenture Experience in Fiji* (Suva: Fiji Museum, 1979).

hoodwinked into migrating by unscrupulous recruiters (*arkatis*), and brutalised by the unrelenting pace of work on the plantations, their sufferings ignored, their women molested by the overseers and *sirdars* (Indian foremen), their families separated, their dignity in tatters.

This rendition of *girmit* was reinforced by the celebrations of 1979, whose overall tone was understandably grim. Until then, the word *girmit* had not been part of the general vocabulary of the Indo-Fijian community. For most people, the word was synonymous with shame and slavery. The word acquired a new vitality during the celebrations as people used it to pry open a past about which much was assumed but little known. But that past was viewed through the lens of the present in which Indo-Fijians were increasingly being marginalised from mainstream public discourse through the vagaries of racial politics. Consequently, a complex and contested history was pressed into the service of an ideology designed to portray Indians as victims of history, without a voice, without agency. The 'whips-and-chains' story is being resuscitated as the 125th anniversary celebration approaches even though the new indenture historiography casts serious doubts about its explanatory value.[7] There is of course undeniable truth in the indenture-as-slavery thesis. Many *girmitiyas* were broken by work, claimed by disease or wrecked by human violence and greed. Suffering and pain were an integral part of indenture. All this is abundantly clear from the historical record, as I have sought to show in previous publications.[8] But it is not the whole story. It is possible to acknowledge hardship while granting *girmitiyas* agency as a people who had a hand in shaping their history.

A central plank of the slavery thesis is that deception and fraudulence played a key role in the recruitment process. Migration was not an integral part of Indian society or psyche, the argument went, and no one in their right mind would therefore ever leave their home for places unknown or unheard of. The Indian peasant was a landlubber, bound to

---

[7] Among others, the works of Clem Seecharan, *Tiger in the Stars: The Anatomy of Indian Achievement in British Guiana, 1919–1929* (London: Macmillan Education, 1997); David Dabydeen and Brinsley Samaroo (eds), *India in the Caribbean* (London: Hansib and University of Warwick, Centre for Caribbean Studies Publication, 1987); Marina Carter, *Lakshmi's Legacy: The Testimonies of Indian Women in 19th Century Mauritius* (Stanley-Rose Hill: Edition l'Ocean Indien, 1994); Surendra Bhana and Joy Brain (eds), *Setting Down Roots: Indian Migrants in South Africa, 1860–1911* (Johannesburg: Witwatersrand University Press, 1990).

[8] Brij V. Lal, 'Murmurs of dissent', in Brij V. Lal, *Chalo Jahaji: On a Journey through Indenture in Fiji* (Suva: Fiji Museum, 2000; Canberra: ANU E Press, 2012), pp. 167–94, doi.org/10.22459/CJ.12.2012.

home and hearth by strict codes of ritually authorised behaviour, not an intrepid explorer of unknown, pollution-threatening worlds. That view is archaic, even for in medieval times, as Irfan Habib and others have shown, peasants moved about in search of better opportunities and to escape the depredations of predatory landlords.⁹ In the nineteenth century, rural India was in the throes of profound change caused by, among other things, the introduction of new notions of private ownership of property, increasing fragmentation of land holdings, deepening indebtedness among the peasantry and the effects of natural calamities. Places in eastern Uttar Pradesh, which furnished 45,000 of Fiji's 60,000 migrants—the remainder came from South India after 1903 when sources in the North had begun to dry up—were particularly adversely affected. As employment opportunities there diminished, people moved about in search of a better life elsewhere.

And so, large numbers left—for the Assam tea gardens, the Calcutta jute mills and factories, the Bihar coal mines and the Bombay textile mills. Between 1891 and 1911, many districts in the Indo-Gangetic plains—Faizabad, Gonda, Allahabad, Azamgargh, Benares—experienced population decline, which officials attributed partly to emigration.¹⁰ In Gonda, migration had become 'a natural way out of the difficulties with which the population did not know how to grapple'; in Sultanpur it was being used to restore 'fallen fortunes or ease off a redundant population which have long been familiar to the inhabitants of the district'; and in Ghazipur:

> immense numbers of people leave their homes every year to find employment in or near Calcutta and in the various centres of industry in Bengal and Assam, while many weavers and others report to the mills of Bombay. The extent of this migration is astonishing, and its economic influence is of the highest importance since these labourers earn high wages and remit or bring back with them large sums of money to their homes.¹¹

The indentured labourers to Fiji and to other places came from this uprooted mass of peasantry. Most of them were registered in their own provinces rather than in large distant cities as critics alleged. But not all

---

9   See Lal, 'A time to move', in Lal, *Chalo Jahaji*, pp. 121–36.
10 This is derived from my reading of the *Imperial Gazetteers*.
11 See F.W. Brownrigg, *Sultanpur Settlement Report* (Allahabad: Government Printer, 1898), p. 6; C.E. Crawford, *Azamgarh Settlement Report* (Allahabad: Government Printer, 1898), p. 7; H.R. Neville, *Ghazipur District Gazetteer* (Nanital: Government Printer, 1908), p. 79.

those who registered migrated. In Gonda and Basti, two large indentured emigration districts, nearly 50 per cent did not migrate, while elsewhere nearly a third remained behind either because they were rejected or because they refused to enlist. The high failure rate gives some agency to the recruited. This is not to say by any means that the unscrupulous recruiters did not snare the gullible and the greedy and the unwary into their nets. They did, but perhaps not to the extent that the slavery thesis holds. Migration to the colonies was, I would argue, an extension of the massive internal movement of people. I vividly remember Aja telling us how he happened to come to Fiji. He was up and about, a young man in his early 20s, when a friend told him about golden opportunities awaiting him in the *tapus* (islands). He eventually ended up in Calcutta, in the batch bound for Guiana (Demerara). That ship was full, so he took the next one to Fiji. I have no doubt that he had no idea what or where Fiji was, but that somehow did not seem to matter to him. He knew that he would be back one day soon, after he had earned enough to get started on his own. But that day of decision never came.

Cultural deracination accompanied slavery in the Caribbean and elsewhere. The experience of indenture, at least in Fiji, was different. Fiji was, after Surinam, the last major importer of Indian indentured labour. By the late 1870s, the darkest period of indentured emigration was over; the period of almost complete break from India became a thing of the past. Fiji was lucky to escape the horrors of its sister colonies in the Caribbean. The *girmitiyas* never completely lost touch with their cultural roots. As early as the 1890s, only a decade after the beginning of indentured emigration, the basic texts of popular Hinduism and folk culture were circulating in the main areas of Indian settlement in the sugar belts of Fiji.[12] These included *Ramchritramanas, Satya Narayan ki Katha, Surya Purana, Devi Bhagat, Danlila, Durga Saptshati, Indra Sabha*, as well as stories from *Baital Pachisi, Salinga Sadabrij* and *Alaha Khand*. The texts were recited communally at social functions and other occasions when people got together. From very early on, Holi (Phagua) and Tazia (Mohurram) were observed as public holidays on most plantations. Religious leaders, both Hindu and Muslim, established centres for spiritual instruction (*kutis* and *dharamshalas* and *madarasas*). Informal gatherings of like-minded men later materialised as cultural and social associations that were to make enduring contributions to the growth and development of the Indo-Fijian community.

12   Lal, 'Hinduism under indenture', in Lal, *Chalo Jahaji*, pp. 239–60.

Religion became both an instrument of survival as well as a tool of resistance. Despite their best efforts, Christian missionaries—associated, in the *girmitiya* minds, with the excesses of the CSR overseers and the racially discriminatory practices of the colonial government—never made much headway in the Indo-Fijian community.[13] They refused to convert because they saw their own religious system as superior. This was in marked contrast to the Indian experience in the Caribbean where Christian missions, especially Presbyterians, enjoyed far greater success among the Indians, providing them, through education, a powerful vehicle for self-improvement and upward mobility.[14] In the Caribbean, a culture weakened by long separation from its ancestral roots and almost total dependence on the plantation system fell easy prey to external temptations; in Fiji the roots, though frayed and planted in a shallower soil, were allowed—through indifference as much as anything else—to nurture themselves unhindered.

There was another important contrast with the Caribbean. Whereas there the indentured labourers and their descendants lived on the plantations for generations—and reminders of the dominant influence of the plantation system are still visible in Guyana—in Fiji, the period of dependence was limited to five, or at most 10, years.[15] The point to underline is that, in Fiji, *girmit* was a limited detention for five or 10 years, not a life sentence for several generations, as it was in the Caribbean and in the case of slavery. Those freed from indenture from the mid-1880s onwards began to establish free settlements, mostly around the sugar mills on the two main islands of Viti Levu and Vanua Levu.[16] These places remain the principal

---

13   J.W. Burton, *Fiji of Today* (London: Charles H. Kelly, 1910) and *The Call of the Pacific* (London: Charles H. Kelly, 1912), recalls his experience of trying to convert Indians to Christianity. See also Andrew Thornley, 'The Methodist Mission and Fiji's Indians, 1879–1920', *New Zealand Journal of History* 8(2) (1974): 137–53.
14   See Dale Bisnauth, 'The East Indian immigrant society in British Guiana, 1890–1930', PhD thesis (Mona, Jamaica: University of the West Indies, 1977), p. 490. See also Arthur Niehoff and Juanita Niehoff, *East Indians in the West Indies* (Milwaukee: Milwaukee Public Museum, 1960), p. 136ff. They argue that Hindus had little difficulty accepting Christ as an avatar of God, like Ram and Krishna. Fewer Muslims converted because the Prophet Mohammed was the last messenger of God.
15   For the Caribbean, see, among other studies, Chandra Jayawardena, *Conflict and Solidarity in a Guianese Plantation* (London: University of London, Athlone Press, 1963); Dabydeen and Samaroo (eds), *India in the Caribbean;* John La Guerre (ed.), *Calcutta to Caroni*, rev. edn (St Augustine: University of West Indies, 1985).
16   See K.L. Gillion, *Fiji's Indian Migrants: A History to the End of Indenture in 1920* (Melbourne: Oxford University Press, 1962), pp. 136–64; Ahmed Ali, *A Society in Transition: Aspects of Fiji Indian History, 1879–1937* (Suva: School of Social and Economic Development, University of the South Pacific, 1976).

centres of Indian settlement in Fiji even today, still dependent in one way or another on the sugar industry. Besides providing the former *girmitiyas* with individual opportunities, the free settlements were symbolically important as beacons of hope for those still under indenture. The rapid growth of free settlements meant that the period of complete isolation for those under indenture was limited, and with time the boundaries, both physical as well as emotional between the indentured and the free, became porous.[17]

It is important to recognise, too, that for many immigrants, indenture, for all its hardships, still represented an improvement on their conditions in India. This was particularly the case with the lower castes who were permanently consigned to the fringes of rural Indian society as untouchables, tenants-at-will and landless labourers with little hope of betterment in this life. The hard work on the plantations was nothing new to them as strenuous physical labour was their lot in India. In Fiji, at least, their individual identity was recognised and their effort rewarded on the basis of achievement rather than a preordained status. For them, the levelling tendencies of the plantation system heralded a welcome change from an oppressive past and promised a future in which they and their children had a chance. Others, perhaps those who were victims of natural calamities, such as famines, floods and droughts, or of exploitative landlords, welcomed the peace and security that the new environment offered them. Reflecting on his indenture days, one labourer told the anthropologist Adrian Mayer in the 1950s:

> The time of indenture was better than now. You did your task, and knew that this was all. You knew you will get food every day. I had shipmates with me, and we weren't badly off when there was a good sirdar and overseer. Of course, if they were bad men, then you had to be careful. But now what do I do? I have cane land, bullocks and a home. Yet every night I am awake, listening to see if someone is not trying to burn my cane, or steal my animals. In indenture lines, we slept well, we did not worry.[18]

---

17 Judith Weller, *The East Indian Indenture in Trinidad* (Rio Piedras, Puerto Rico: Institute of Caribbean Studies, University of Puerto Rico, 1968), p. 65, writes that in Trinidad, by the turn of the twentieth century, immigrants had no difficulty getting passes to leave the estates.
18 A.C. Mayer, *Peasants in the Pacific: A Study of Fiji Indian Rural Society*, 2nd edn (Berkeley: University of Californian Press, 1973), p. 5.

Both oral evidence and archival records indicate some lower-caste labourers, especially *sirdars,* took revenge against their high-caste compatriots for the social oppression they had experienced in India. So, at one level, the *girmitiyas* were all peas in the same pod, but they were also a socially differentiated group from diverse backgrounds and with divergent experiences and expectations of what life was all about, what it had to offer.

Aja became a free man in 1913, after serving his indenture as a stable hand for the CSR in Labasa. Like most of his compatriots, he continued as a mill hand for the CSR for a few years more before leaving with his best friend's wife, leasing a 10-acre piece of land and starting on his own in the newly opened settlement at Tabia. He planted rice, lentils, maize, beans, eggplants, watermelon, pumpkin and peanuts until sugar cane arrived in the late 1930s. It was on that sugarcane farm that we were all born and raised. Now the farm is gone, taken back by the Fijian landowners. Aja went to Tabia not because he had friends or family or fellow caste members or *jahajibhais* there, but because land was available for lease. Geography, the availability of productive agricultural land and its proximity to markets and roads and other facilities, determined the pattern of territorially and spaciously scattered Indian settlements in Fiji, rather than caste brotherhood or religious affiliation.[19] This meant that the pattern of village India, with socially ranked clusters of houses with clear caste-based rules defining access to common facilities, formulating and enforcing rules of appropriate behaviour, could not be reproduced in Fiji.[20] The fragmentation of the Indian village world, begun in the depots of Calcutta and Madras, and accelerated on the plantations, was completed in the postindenture period.

I knew Aja as an old man of perhaps around 80, although he reckoned he was well over 100 in the way most old men do. Some things I can say about his life with absolute certainty, from personal experience, others I deduce from my own reading and research. Aja spoke his own language (a mixture of Bhojpuri and Awadhi) with other surviving *girmitiyas.* He spoke Fiji Hindi with a distinct Indian accent. My Fiji Hindi would be incomprehensible to him. He always wore Indian clothes—*dhoti* and *kurta* and *pagri.* The Indian garment would disappear with him and his

---

19   Although, within a settlement, sub-cultural groups—South Indians, for example—could be found clustered in one part.
20   See Adrian C. Mayer, 'The organisation of Indian settlement in Fiji', *Man* 54(284) (1953): 1–3; also his *Indians in Fiji* (Oxford: Oxford University Press, 1963), p. 28.

generation, replaced by western clothes of shorts and shirt that became the standard for my father's generation. Women's jewellery and finery—*bichwa* (toe-ring), *payal* (anklet), *jhumka* (earring), *nathini* (nose-ring), *bajuband* (armlet)—would also disappear with the *girmitiya* women, replaced by a single string of gold sovereigns (*mohur*), which women displayed as a sign of status and prosperity. In rural areas of Fiji, they still do.

Aja's world, full of ghosts and demons and evil forces that had to be pacified through a variety of precise ritual performances, would disappear with him.[21] He continued to invoke the names of village and clan or caste deities—*gram devtas* and *kul devtas*—for some blessing or to ward off evil or impending misfortune. He still remembered *bhajans* (devotional songs), which he and other *girmitiyas* sang with great fervour on special occasions. Caste as a basis or determinant of social relationship had been jolted in the crowded depots of Calcutta and in the confined cabins of the immigrant ships, finally crashing in the plantations.[22] There, work rewarded productivity, not caste status. Sanctions could not be imposed.[23] Despite all these, Aja continued to practice some minor customs from his childhood perhaps to retain a vanishing connection to a remembered past. So, he never shaved himself but waited every Sunday for a *hajam,* a professional barber by caste, a fellow *girmitiya,* to shave him and collect his fees in kind, usually some rice and lentils.[24] That practice died gradually as the *girmitiyas* moved on and as new forces of change (education, improved communication) entered the community. So, too, did the practice of seeking marriage partners for children from roughly comparable castes.[25]

---

21   See also Steven Vertovec, '"Official" and "popular" Hinduism in the Caribbean: Historical and contemporary trends in Surinam, Trinidad and Guyana', in *Across the Dark Waters: Ethnicity and Indian Identity in the Caribbean,* ed. David Dabydeen and Brinsley Samaroo (London: Macmillan Caribbean, 1996), pp. 108–30.

22   See Chandra Jayawardena, 'The disintegration of caste in Fiji Indian rural society', in *Anthropology in Oceania: Essays Presented to Ian Hogbin,* ed. L.R. Hiatt and Chandra Jayawardena (Sydney: Angus and Robertson, 1971), pp. 88–119; as well as studies in Barton M. Schwartz (ed.), *Caste in Overseas Indian Communities* (Berkeley, CA: Chandler Publishing Company, 1967).

23   Chandra Jayawardena, 'Religious belief and social change: Aspects of the development of Hinduism in British Guiana', *Comparative Studies in Society and History* 8(2) (1965): 211–40, at p. 224, doi.org/10.1017/S0010417500004011. See also Hilda Kuper, *Indian People in Natal* (Cape Town: Natal University Press, 1960), p. 20.

24   Gerad Tikasingh, 'Social change in the emerging East Indian community in late 19th century Trinidad', *Journal of Caribbean Studies* 1(2–3) (1980): 120–39.

25   See Morton Klass, *East Indians in Trinidad: A Study in Cultural Persistence* (New York: Columbia University Press, 1961); R.T. Smith and Chandra Jayawardena, 'Caste and social status among the Indians in Guyana', in *Caste in Overseas Indian Communities,* ed. Schwartz, pp. 43–92, at p. 50.

Life in Fiji must have been very different for Aja and others like him, in some ways a complete contrast to what they had left behind. The physical landscape of an island surrounded by sea, crisscrossed by rivers and streams, full of forbidding forests and numerous hills, must have been alien to a land-locked people from the flat Indo-Gangetic plains. Perhaps the pace of work on the plantations may not have been new to those who came from labouring and farming backgrounds, though its relentlessness, in the absence of a vibrant, organic community, must have been difficult. Within the domestic sphere, traditional notions of proper relations between men and women were renegotiated as women worked alongside men in the fields and assumed other responsibilities that would not have been countenanced in India. Caste, minus its minor ritualistic aspects, had gone, and boundaries of social and cultural inclusion and exclusion were drawn more flexibly. New, pragmatic, cross-caste and cross-religious relationships had to be established in a new environment. In that new environment, the *girmitiyas* were more on their own, more alone, making their way by adapting the metaphors and strategies of a remembered, evanescent past. My enduring memory of Aja is of an old man who looked vacantly into the distance, his near-blind eyes focused on some imaginary point, talking incessantly about the world of his childhood, sometimes crying, wondering about what his friends and family were doing, hankering hopelessly for a past that was truly past, but unable— perhaps not knowing how—to embrace the new world that was his home. He died in 1962.

My father was born around 1918. No one knew the precise date; that did not seem to matter. Whenever asked about it, he would say he was born during the *Badi Beemari* (the Influenza Epidemic) of 1918. His generation grew up in the shadow of indenture. They were formed and deformed by the experience of poverty and uncertainty on the unformed edges of a slowly evolving community, still uncertain of its identity and character but making strenuous efforts to establish and enforce standards recalled from a remembered past. They grew up in a largely enclosed and culturally self-sufficient world. Once indentures had expired, Indians had ceased to be of much concern to the colonial administration. Left to their own devices, the Indian community developed its own voluntary associations and self-help projects—forming voluntary settlement committees to harvest cane, establish temples and mosques, build schools, construct cemeteries, start annual festivals, organise Ramayan recital through village *mandalis*. *Panchayats*—a five-man council of village elders—were started in the 1930s with official encouragement to maintain a semblance of order in village life. They resolved petty issues—resolving boundary disputes, adjudicating fines for damage caused by stray cattle, intervening in family disputes, punishing extramarital relationships—and enforced community standards. Suspicion of alien legal institutions and practices, the cost of court cases, fear of social disapproval and ostracism—a mixture of all of these—forced people to resort to tested ways that had worked in the past. The *panchayats* worked effectively for a while when the village world was still isolated, but lost their authority and rationale in the postwar years as joint families cracked, education and income increased, and improved communication connected the village to the outside world. Now they are a distant memory. Litigation became a prominent, fractious feature of Indo-Fijian life. As it still is.

The self-absorption of the Indo-Fijian community came from the particular circumstances it encountered in the postindenture period—the scattered settlements, the hard struggle on the cane farm, the absence of outside helping hands, the indifference of the colonial state—but it also resulted from a colonial policy that restricted contact with others, most notably and damagingly with the indigenous community. Sir Arthur Gordon's 'Native Policy', as it came to be known, created a separate system of administration—in effect a state within a state—which curtailed Fijian mobility and limited opportunities for employment outside the authorised chief-dominated order, in order, ostensibly, to shield the indigenous community from the corrosive effects of contact with the outside world.[26] When Indians transgressed boundaries and established de facto relationships, Fijians were reprimanded and often fined, and Indians expelled from the vicinity of the *koros* (villages). Deliberate colonial policy designed to keep the two communities in separate compartments compounded the problem of cultural disrespect and suspicion that resulted from racial prejudice and cultural difference. There were some exceptions in some parts of Fiji, but separate development and compartmentalised existence for the two communities was the norm. There was a Fijian *koro* on the outer fringes of our settlement: a row of brooding *bures* surrounding a neatly manicured *rara* (open lawn), but we never entered it for fear—of what, I cannot say. There was a Fijian woman who had somehow adopted my father as her younger brother and was

---

26   For more discussion see J.K. Chapman, *The Career of Arthur Hamilton Gordon: First Lord Stanmore, 1829–1912* (Toronto: University of Toronto Press, 1964), doi.org/10.3138/9781442652699; J.D. Legge, *Britain in Fiji, 1858–1880* (London: Macmillan, 1958).

openly playful with my mother, her *bhauji* (older sister-in-law). We called her *phua* (father's sister), and treated her like a member of the extended family. But that was about it. We children had no Fijian friends.

My father's world, like that of most of his contemporaries, centred upon a 10-acre plot of land leased from the Native Land Trust Board.[27] It was only a lease, so obvious in hindsight, but we never thought that the land wasn't our own, that it wouldn't always be our own. The notion that it might revert to the owners—as it has now done—never once entered our minds. The 10-acre plot was the CSR's idea when, facing labour shortage after the end of indenture, it decided to get out of cane growing and concentrate on milling.[28] The CSR was clever. It wanted to relinquish cane farming, but not control over the industry. It reasoned that with careful husbandry, the limited acreage could be made big enough to be economically viable, but certainly not being enough to make us too big for our boots. On that 10-acre farm, we grew sugar cane and rice, had a cow or two, some goats and chickens for meat and vegetables for domestic use or for selling to neighbours to raise money. That was about it. Like other people in the village, we did not get anywhere very far, but we got by. J.W. Coulter, the American geographer who carried out field research in Laqere, the village across the river from our own, who captured the daily routine of farm life in the late 1930s and early 1940s accurately:

> The regular work of Indian farmers in Fiji is in contrast to the irregular, easy going life of the Fijians. The Oriental rises at half-past five, harnesses his oxen, and plows from six to eight. He breakfasts at home or in the field on *roti* and milk and tea (*roti* is bread made from flour and fried in *ghee*). He resumes plowing until ten; at that time his oxen are unhitched to lie in the shade during the heat of the day. Shortly after ten he milks his cow, and from ten-thirty to twelve hoes weeds or cuts fodder along the ditches or road-side. At noon he lunches on rice, dal or rice curry, and milk. In the early afternoon he hoes again, cuts more grass, or does odd jobs about the house. From three to five he plows. Supper at six consists of rice curry and chutney and milk. There is smoking and

---

27 This is a statutory organisation that leases land to Indo-Fijians and others on behalf of the indigenous landowners.
28 See Michael Moynagh, *Brown or White? A History of the Fiji Sugar Industry, 1873–1973* (Canberra: Australian National University Press, 1981).

conversation by a kerosene lamp until bedtime at eight. In the evenings groups of Indians who have been working in the fields all day trudge home in the dusk, carrying lunch pails.[29]

The details might vary from place to place and from time to time, but the overall picture will be familiar to anyone who grew up on an Indo-Fijian farm. Stanner, who closely observed the Indian community in the mid-1940s, also captures the problems and aspirations of the community accurately. Thousands of families suffered 'under a crushing burden of private debt', he wrote:

> Peasants and labourers lived frugally, worked long hours for extremely low wages or incomes, and saved with desperate application to keep alive, to repay loans and mortgages, to buy freehold land, to remit funds to India, to discharge customary social obligations requiring expensive outlays, and to acquire a competence for old age or return to India.[30]

This last aspect was on its last legs. On the social side, Stanner noted, caste barriers had almost disappeared.

> High and low castes might sit together at school or in other assemblies or live together in unsegregated neighbourhoods. Restriction on vocation and occupation had greatly modified. European dress was widespread among men except in rural areas. Women no longer veiled and their costume, too, had altered. The purdah was unknown. Religious ceremonial had simplified and shortened, especially the ritual purifications, Hindu-Muslim separatism had so far weakened that members of the two religious communities sat together in amity on public committees, often took the same line of policy, co-operated politically (especially on educational matters) and mingled fairly freely socially.[31]

Some old customs, observed by our grandparent's generation, were on the way out. Bill Stanner noted the diminishing relevance of caste in everyday life. There were others. Polyandrous relationships were not uncommon during indenture because women were few and competition for them was intense. But as the sex ratio improved and the community stabilised,

---

29   John Wesley Coulter, *Fiji: Little India of the Pacific* (Chicago: University of Chicago Press, 1943), p. 93. For another account of Indo-Fijian village life, see R.T. Sanders, 'Interlude', in Sir Alan Burns, *Fiji* (London: Her Majesty's Stationery Office, 1963), pp. 149–76.
30   W.E.H. Stanner, *South Seas in Transition: A Study of Post-War Rehabilitation and Reconstruction in Three British Pacific Dependencies* (Sydney: Australasian Publishing Company, 1953), p. 179.
31   ibid., pp. 179–80.

culturally monogamous marriage became the strict rule, the breach of which often led to violence, occasionally murder. During indenture, again because of the shortage of women, Hindu–Muslim marriages were not uncommon—and tolerated—but this practice, too, ended in the postindenture period as the two groups began to establish 'morally correct' behaviour for their followers. Interreligious marriages are rare today. The practice of child marriage, common in my grandfather's generation, and continued from village India, also ceased. The legal age of marriage for boys was increased in 1961 from 16 to 18, and for girls from 13 to 14, though in practice most marriages took place later than the stipulated legal age. Girls' education was still frowned upon. In 1940, only 11 per cent of girls (1,430), compared to 20 per cent of boys (3,607), attended primary school.[32] This situation changed within a decade. In 1959, for example, of the 77,000 pupils in primary schools, 20,000 were Indian boys and 15,000 Indian girls. The remaining gender barriers would crumble soon as the value of education, even if it was not for a career, became entrenched in the community and as the expectations of women's role in the home and in the community at large expanded.

The farm was the only property our parents had, but it was clear that there was no future on it for all the children. We were encouraged to seek alternatives. Education was the key to that quest.[33] Our parents started community schools—nothing fancy, just rudimentary structures of thatched *bures* of bamboo walls and cow dung–plastered floors on a piece of land donated by some generous villager. By 1956, there were 154 Indian schools in Fiji, of which 129 were run by nondenominational settlement committees.[34] Some partially literate village elders assumed the role of instructors in Hindi and elementary arithmetic. Things improved with time and government assistance. I have for some years been interested in the colonial texts that instructed our fathers' generation. I wanted to understand the kinds of ideals and ethos the colonial officialdom tried to instil in them; its conception of the ideal colonial subject.

---

32   Coulter, *The Drama of Fiji*, p. 107.
33   See K.L. Gillion, *The Fiji Indians: Challenge to European Dominance, 1920–1946* (Canberra: Australian National University Press, 1977), pp. 118–29.
34   Mayer, *Indians in Fiji*, p. 9.

I recently came across a copy of texts that were used in Fiji Indian primary schools in the 1930s. They are instructive. Here is just one example from the *School Journal, 1930.*[35] There are stories and anecdotes in it from Indian history about Siddhartha, Rama, Harish Chandra, Tulsi Das, Guru Nanak and so on. The emphasis on things Indian is important; it was a marker of our collective cultural reference point. The government was keen for the Indian population to retain its links with its cultural heritage (and then complain that the Indians did not assimilate into the mainstream colonial society!). The *Journal* also carried stories about Fiji, excerpts from the governor's addresses, announcements about coming events, but these were brief, dry and uninteresting. Much more interesting were the stories about the Empire, *Our Empire,* marked by all the red areas on the *Clarion Atlas.* The geography of Samoa and Hawai'i featured in some of the texts, as did items on Casablanca and the Ford Motor Factory at Detroit. And then there were tips on how to be good citizens, law abiding, respectful of authority, appreciative of the great things that the 'Mother Country' was doing for its children in the colonies. Items on the best way to cultivate maize, banana and tobacco, the precautions to take during hurricanes and floods, the importance of keeping wells clean, were designed to teach people about clean, healthy, hygienic living.

If you were training to be an Indian primary school teacher in 1930, you would be expected to know, among other things: two virtues for which the Chinese are famous; why ANZAC was celebrated; what things the people of Nigeria and Fiji had in common; how the Union Jack came into existence; the names of some of the finest buildings in Auckland; where the missionary John Williams was born; what religious festivals Rumanians enjoyed most and how they celebrated them; how David Livingston got his education; what Florence Nightingale's favourite game as a child was; what pupils knew about the children of Labrador; the importance of the Chrysler Building in New York; the number of talons or claws a cat had. If you were sitting your Primary School Leaving Certificate Examination in 1936, you would be expected to know, among other things: the name of one of the best-known governors of Roman Britain who encouraged the building of houses, towns and markets; the name of the British General who captured Jerusalem in 1917; the name of the brave French Commander who was killed in the same battle as

---

35   The text was produced by A.W. McMillan, an LMS missionary and an inspector of Indian schools in Fiji, who had served in India for many years.

General Wolfe; the name of the Roman Empire revived by Charles the Great; the name of the highest mountain in Australia; the chief export of New Zealand; the capital of Fiji before Suva; two ways in which disease could be spread. Highly relevant, dry and topical things like that! This sort of education was for the chosen elite of the community, the primary school teachers. The idea was not to 'educate' the populace but to train cogs for the colonial bureaucratic wheel. Apart from the court clerks and assistants and interpreters in the district administration, primary school teachers were people of respect and status in the community. Most people of my father's generation aspired to know just enough to read and write letters or sign their names to official documents.

Besides education, the earlier generations devised other ingenious means to erase barriers to social mobility and obliterate marks of social differentiation based on caste or some other such criteria. One way of doing this was the names people gave to their children. *Girmitiyas* had names that a careful observer could use to decipher a person's social status. The lower and middle castes were named after objects, days and months, a particular emotion or event or state of affairs in the household or the village at the time the child was born.[36] Thus, therefore such names as Dukhia and Bipati (sadness/hardship), Gendia and Phulbasia (after flowers), Hansa (a mythical bird), Bhola, Bhullar and Jokhu (simple ones), Mangal, Budhai, Sanicharee, Mangru, Somai, Sukkhu (after the days of the week), Gulab and Gulabi (after a colour), Bahadur, Shera (brave one), Sundar (pretty one). Other names with no particular connotation that I can decipher included Kalpi, Bisun, Tahull, Jaitoo, Jhinul, Chagun, Aleemoolah, Ulfat, Chaitu, Umrai. The *girmitiyas* named their children after gods and goddesses and great mythical figures, which threw the old patterns into confusion, making it difficult to establish one's caste from the names. These names were common in my father's generation: Ram Prasad, Ram Saran, Ram Autar, Arjun, Hari Prasad, Ram Piyari, Bhola Nath, Bihari Prasad, Ganga Din, Jamuna Prasad, Sukh Raji, Suruj Pati, Shiv Lal, Mata Prasad, Tota Ram. No one could tell whether Ram Prasad was a *chamar* (a tanner) or a *kurmi* (cultivator). The higher castes maintained their caste surnames—Sharma, Singh, Mishra—although oral evidence suggests that these names were sometimes appropriated by those below them. Sanskritisation was clearly at work here. Our parents named their children after film stars and famous personalities—Rajendra

---

36   I use only Hindu names here as I am not familiar with the etymology of Muslim names.

Prasad, Raj Kumar, Jawahar Lal, Vijay Singh, Rajesh Chandra, Mahendra Kumar, Satish Chand, Surendra Prasad, Sunil Kumar, Biman Prasad—thus obliterating the last vestiges of distinction.

In some areas, though, distinctions and differences were being institutionalised. This was particularly evident in the fields of cultural and religious identity. With the end of indenture in 1920, a number of religious and cultural associations emerged to provide a semblance of order and regularity to a rapidly stabilising Indo-Fijian community. Arya Samaj and Sanatan Dharam had been established at the beginning of the twentieth century, but the Muslim League and Sangam, the umbrella organisation of the South Indian community, came in 1926. As the community began to set down roots, the different groups engaged in an intense effort to 'define' the proper code of religious conduct, the proper observance of rituals and ceremonies. Conflict erupted. Samajis, followers of Swami Dayanand Saraswati's reformist branch of Hinduism, clashed with the more orthodox, ritual-observing, idol-worshipping Sanatanis.[37] Shia and Sunni Muslims clashed over whether the appropriate successor to the Prophet Mohammed were members of his own family (his son-in-law Ali and his sons Hussein and Hassan) or the Caliphs.[38] Hindu–Muslim tensions, reflecting the political developments on the subcontinent in the interwar period, were visible but restrained. As the divisions hardened and pressure mounted to conform to strictly prescribed codes in food and dress and prayer and worship—not least because of the arrival of religious teachers from India—the more relaxed interaction and easy friendships of earlier years 'when we were all brothers' suffered. Faith became an important marker of identity in time, erasing other markers such as regional origin. And so it has remained.

Indian settlements made a rudimentary beginning in village temples and community halls, but it was the leadership of Indian cultural organisations that made the real difference: the Arya Samaj, the Sanatan Dharam, the Fiji Muslim League and the Sangam. By the 1970s, 80 per cent of all secondary and primary schools in Fiji were 'committee' run, with grant-in-aid from the government. In 1949, the first nongovernment, non-Christian secondary school—the Shri Vivekananda High School—was started by

---

37 Arya Samajis can be likened to the Protestants and the Sanatanis to the Catholics. For more discussion, see John D. Kelly, *A Politics of Virtue: Hinduism, Sexuality, and Countercolonial Discourse in Fiji* (Chicago: University of Chicago Press, 1991); Gillion, *The Fiji Indians,* pp. 102–29.

38 A short history of the Muslim community is in Ahmed Ali, 'Remembering', in *Bittersweet: The Indo-Fijian Experience,* ed. Brij V. Lal (Canberra: Pandanus Books, 2004), pp. 71–87.

the Ramakrishna Mission over the government's initial objection. This proved to be an initiative of singular importance. The graduates of this school went on to be become the leaders of their communities as well as national leaders (Jai Ram Reddy and Mahendra Chaudhry, for instance). Education at the school was imparted in an 'Indian' or, rather, a spiritual milieu, so that students received higher education without losing their cultural moorings.

The language of instruction in Indian primary schools was both Hindi and English (in higher grades). After the abolition of indenture, Hindi was adopted as the official language of communication with the Indian community. Hindi, strictly speaking, was not the 'mother tongue' of the Indians, even North Indians, for whom Bhojpuri, Avadhi and a number of other minor languages were the mother tongue; it certainly was not the mother tongue of the South Indians. Muslims regarded Urdu as their mother tongue while for the Southerners, the three main languages were Tamil, Telugu and Malayalam. These were taught in schools run by Muslims and South Indians; but they were not examinable subjects and were taught more for cultural or religious rather than scholastic reasons. Hindi became the formal language of communication while 'Fiji-Baat', a mixture of various Indian languages interspersed with English and Fijian words, was the spoken language of the community. The tension continues: the language used in newspapers and spoken over the air was not the language most people spoke among themselves. But now there is a growing acceptance of 'Fiji-Baat' as the language of the Indo-Fijian community. Fiji's first major novel (Subramani's *Dauka Puran*) was published in it.[39]

The texts used in the Indian schools were written in Hindi and English. The *School Journal*, which was used in the 1920s and 1930s, had inspirational stories and anecdotes from Indian history, myths and fables.[40] There was nothing in them about Fiji. This was not surprising. Fijian past was contested terrain. There was no common ground that colonialism was beneficial for Fiji, nor any agreed understanding about the legacy of the indenture system. The Indians condemned it while the

---

39   Brij V. Lal, 'Bahut Julum: Reflections on the use of Fiji Hindi', *Fijian Studies* 3(1) (2005): 153–58; Subramani, *Dauka Puran* (New Delhi: Star Publications, 2001); Jeff Siegel, *Language Contact in a Plantation Environment: A Sociolinguistic History of Fiji* (Cambridge: Cambridge University Press, 1987).
40   A.W. McMillan, *Hindustani Handbook: Specially Prepared for Colonial Use: Lessons in Grammar, Key to Exercises, Vocabulary, and Useful Information on Indian Religions, Customs, and Languages (Devanāgari and Roman Scripts)* (Suva: Government Printer, 1931).

colonial officialdom praised it. And Indian parents themselves wanted to know about India and the world. India was the cultural reference point for most Indians. And it remained so for decades. It connected people to a past from which they or their parents had come. In the postwar period, Hindi received a big boost with the publication of Pandit Ami Chandra's *Pothis*—primary school texts that were used in schools throughout Fiji. Again, there was little in them about Fiji or the local environment (though more than what was contained in the *School Journal*). Instead, the books fed a generation of pupils with a steady diet of Indian history and mythology, the heroic deeds of Indian kings and queens (Akbar, Jhansi ki Rani, Latchmi Bai), about great men (Mahatma Gandhi, Harishchandra, Vivekananda), about architectural monuments (Taj Mahal), mixed with snippets from world history (the discoveries of James Cook, Ferdinand Magellan, Christopher Columbus).

These stories entertained and enlightened us, and we read them aloud to our illiterate parents in the evenings, to great appreciation. The English texts were even more remote from the concerns of the local environment. The history syllabus dealt with, among other topics, the history of the Stuarts and the Tudors and of European expansion, the Great Depression, the Corn Laws, the Origins of the World War I, the Unification of Italy and Germany, the rise of Fascism in Italy and the Russian Revolution. The English curriculum introduced students to the classis of European and American literature: novels by Anthony Trollope, Sir Walter Scott, the Brontë sisters, Thomas Hardy, Joseph Conrad, John Steinbeck, the poetry of Samuel Taylor Coleridge, T.S. Eliot, Edgar Alan Poe, and the plays of William Shakespeare (*Hamlet, Macbeth, The Merchant of Venice*). This education broadened our horizons and connected us to new places and new pasts, but we learned nothing about our own place and especially about our own neighbours, the indigenous Fijians. And that gap widened with time.

Our knowledge of English was passive, formal, rudimentary—just enough to read the most basic texts and documents to enable our unlettered parents to grasp the contents of official edicts or commercial dockets. It never became a living functional language, a vehicle of effective communication. We were innocent of its rules of grammar and syntax. Hindi was more manageable. We read Hindi newspapers, and there were many in the 1950s and 1960s. The oldest of them all was the *Fiji Samachar*, first published in 1924 and in continuous circulation until 1974 as a Hindi–English monthly, and after 1955 as a Hindi weekly.

The *Shanti Dut* (Messenger of peace) began in the mid-1930s and a very tame version is still in publication. The 1950s saw an explosion of Indian newspapers in Fiji, reflecting and reinforcing a cultural renaissance in the Indian community: *Jagriti* (New dawn), *Jai Fiji* (Hail Fiji), *Fiji Sandesh* (Fiji news), *Kisan, Sangam*.[41]

These papers were widely circulated in the Indian settlements and were a major source of news and commentary about local and international events. The progovernment *Fiji Times* met its match (at least in the 1950s) with the *Pacific Review*. These weekly outlets were important for several reasons. They provided an alternative reading of official discourse, they interrogated the official agenda and they corrected misinformation, intentional or otherwise, of the official sources. They became especially critical during periods of crisis, such as the 1960 sugar industry strike, in combatting the war of words waged by the CSR and the colonial government. Throughout the 1960s, these newspapers supported the movement for independence broadly opposed by both the Fijians and the Europeans.

Coverage of the Indian subcontinent, its grinding poverty, its 'teeming millions', the failings of its caste system and so on in the *Fiji Times* makes for depressing reading. This angle of coverage was not surprising; it formed the ideological underpinning of the colonial order. The message was: if Indians did not like Fiji, they should go back to India, to the India of destitution and depression. The Indian newspapers, especially the *Pacific Review,* carried more positive stories of development in India and in the developing world, and published articles by leading world writers praising India's history and progress. They also commented favourably on the decolonisation movement then underway in the distant corners of the British Empire, which the *Fiji Times* thought was an unmitigated disaster.[42] Through their coverage of events and people, the Indian newspapers indirectly tried to instil in Indo-Fijians pride in themselves and their culture. The Hindi newspapers also provided an outlet for the widely dispersed creative talent in the Indian community. People regularly contributed poems, short stories and recollections that provided unique insight into the hidden world of the Indian settlements.

---

41   Guru Dayal Sharma, *Memories of Fiji, 1887–1987* (Suva: Fiji Times, 1987).
42   Brij V. Lal (ed.), *A Vision for Change: Speeches and Writings of A.D. Patel, 1929–1969* (Canberra: ANU E Press, 2011), pp. 283–371, doi.org/10.22459/VCSW.11.2011.

5. TRANSITIONS AND TRANSFORMATIONS

Some of them were broadcast over the air as well. The setting up of the Fiji Broadcasting Commission in 1954, modelled on the British Broadcasting Corporation, as a statutory body was a milestone event, not only for the Indians but for Fiji as a whole. Its impact was dramatic. One official wrote:

> In remote areas, Fijians walked for miles to villages where there was a radio receiver. The coverage was very far from complete, but for the first time in History it was possible for message and news and information to reach Fijians in many scattered parts of Fiji at the same time. It was an indication of the influence and value of a broadcasting service.[43]

Radio came to our home in the late 1950s, as it did to most rural homes, and it soon became an indispensable source of entertainment as well as information. Indeed, our routine came to be organised around certain programs the whole family liked to hear: music, current affairs, international news and the national quiz. Different faiths took turns offering prayers and readings from the scriptures at the start of the daily program, followed at specified hours by news and announcements such as death notices, to which close attention was paid. Radio was the only way of knowing about major events in the community. It connected us to people and places beyond the village, lessened our collective sense of isolation and broke barriers and boundaries.

With time came special programs catering for a variety of tastes and interests. Among them were *Giton Bhari Kahani* (Melody-filled stories), *Aaj ke Vishay* (Topic of the day), *Desh ke Log* (People of different lands), *Hamare Maha Purush* (Our great souls), *Filmi Samiksha* (film reviews), *Aap Kitna Jante Hain* (general knowledge). In the evenings came such popular programs as *Bhule Bisre Nagmen* (sentimental songs), *Farmaish* (request for favourite songs), and *Ardh Shashtriye Sangeet* (semiclassical songs). Local talent was recognised and promoted. *Bhajan* (devotional songs) and *Qauwwali* (Urdu songs), poetry and drama and quiz contests were organised. Through these activities, radio promoted a sense of community and common identity among a people widely scattered around the country. Until the 1970s, the Fiji Broadcasting Commission (FBC) was the only radio station in Fiji, and it wielded enormous cultural power. It adjudicated matters of taste, the standard of speech and the topics for broadcast. The Advisory Board comprised the cultural elite of

---

43   Personal communication, Jai Kumar, June 2013.

the community. The language of broadcast was *shuddh* or 'proper' Hindi, and remained so for several decades. The survival of Hindi was due in no small measure to its use on the radio. The discrepancy between the language heard on the radio and what was spoken in everyday conversation was stark. It was not until the arrival of rival radio stations in the late 1970s and 1980s and the advent of phone-in talk shows that 'Fiji-Baat' made a limited appearance on the air. The gatekeepers were gone, but they exercised a profound influence on the evolution of Fiji Indian culture in the postwar years.

Besides radio, the other major impetus for the retention of Hindi in Fiji was the Hindi cinema, which began arriving in Fiji in the early 1930s.[44] By 1933, there were seven cinema houses in the islands, three in the capital, Suva. Among the earliest movies was *Anarkali* (Pomegranate blossom, 1928), a silent film. The steady stream of Hindi movies that followed can be divided into two categories: religious dramas and romantic ones. The religious dramas depicted the epics of Hindu mythology: the stories of Rama and Krishna, the tales of the Mahabharata, *Ajodhya ka Raja* (The King of Ayodhya), *Ram Baan* (The arrow of Ram), *Lanka Dahan* (The destruction of Lanka), *Pandavas*.[45] Romantic movies dominated from the 1950s onwards: *Aah* (Desire), *Barsat* (Monsoon), *Awara* (Vagabond), *Mother India, Ganga Jamuna* (crime drama film), *Pyasa* (Thirst), *Do Bigah Zameen* (A few acres of land), *Waqt* (Race against time). The themes of poverty, exploitation, injustice, of thwarted love and of yearnings for things beyond reach, held great emotional appeal for us, made us realise that our own impoverished condition was not exceptional but was a part of the wider experience of humankind. The great actors and actresses of Hindu cinema became household names: Raj Kapoor, Rajendra Kumar, Dev Anand, Dilip Kumar, Pran, Nargis, Meena Kumari, Vyajantimala, Mala Sinha—parents named their children after them. The plots and dialogues of the films were dissected at length in the villages for weeks. The film songs, of love and loss, of struggle against improbable odds, by Mohammed Rafi, Lata Mangeshkar, Hemant Kumar, Talat Mehmood, Suraiya, Manna Dey and others, were hummed and imitated for years, as they still are. By the 1960s, cinema had become an integral part of the cultural life of the Indian community. People went to see movies, and be seen by others for the fashionable clothes and jewellery they wore.

---

44 Vijay Mishra, *Bollywood Cinema: Temples of Desire* (London: Routledge, 2002).
45 The Pandavas—Yudhistira, Bhima, Arjuna, Nakula, and Sahadeva—are the central characters in the most applauded epic in Hinduism, the Mahabharata.

By the late 1950s and the 1960s, a reading culture was developing in the Indian community. In Suva, the better-known Desai Bookshop sold English-language books and magazines, while the Suva Bookshop marketed books in Hindi, English, Tamil, Telugu, Gujarati and Gurumukhi. In western Fiji, R.C. Bali, the owner of the Ba Book Centre advertised his mission this way:

> For human beings, reading is just as important as education. Education enlightens people, books give them knowledge. People of Ba do not have to wonder. Our Book Centre is full of useful books on religious, social and political subjects as well as wedding decorations. We are waiting for you to come and visit us at least once.[46]

The Hindi novels sold in these bookshops had a profound influence on some of Fiji's future writers. Subramani recalls:

> The first extended prose that I ever wrote was in Hindi at High School. It probably had something of Kushwaha Kant in it, I do not know. Hindi was my original choice made in childhood, and going back to write in it, decades later, was like returning to childhood for important inspiration. It was there, in childhood, I realised the power of books in transporting you to another world, and also the belief that writing was a noble vocation that in some way served humanity.[47]

Subramani was returning to Hindi after decades of writing in English; he had risen to become a Professor of English at the University of the South Pacific. But there were people writing in Hindi from the 1930s and 1940s onwards, publishing small books of poems and devotional songs and contributing bits and pieces to the local weeklies. Among the more prominent early writers were Tavua-based L.B. Master (Hari Bhai Patel), Thakur Dwarka Singh (Korogaga, Nausori), Kashi Ram Kumud (Tavua) and B. Mahabir Mitra (Dam, Ba).[48] In Nasinu, Gyani Das established the Tara Press, from which came a series of books and pamphlets about the life of the Indian community in Fiji. His popular weekly *Jhankar* printed songs from Hindi movies that had a wide circulation and had short stories about social issues in the Indian community. 'Tyagi' is about

---

46 *Fiji Samachar* (Varoka: RC Bali & Sons, 10 November 1966).
47 Subramani, 'Ramcharitraman's country', in *India-Fiji: Experiences to Remember*, ed. Kamal Kishore Mishra and Satendra Nandan (New Delhi: Indian Council for Cultural Relations, 2012), pp. 70–83, at p. 79.
48 Kashi Ram Kumud (ed.), *Hindu Sanskrit Fiji Dwip Men* (Tavua: Privately published, 1965).

an Indian woman who gets pregnant, is disowned by her paramour, is saved from shame and threatened self-inflicted death by a symbolic marriage to a man who calls her sister, and who is eventually accepted by her lover when he realises the error of his ways. This is the constant refrain in the published pieces: truth triumphs in the end, as good does over evil. A full-scale novel-length treatment of the Fiji Indian experience had to wait till much later, and came with the publication of Jogindar Singh Kanwal's *Savera* (Dawn) and Subramani's *Dauka Puran* (Scoundrel's tale). Bharat V. Morris's *Gali Gali Sita Roye* and Kanti Lal Champaneri's *Asha* are shorter prose works now virtually forgotten.

Poets were the early leaders of the Indian cultural renaissance in Fiji. Some, such as Mohammed Shameem, prominent in the 1950s, did not leave a corpus behind while others did. The most distinguished of all was Pandit Kamla Prasad Mishra (1913–1996), revered as the Poet Laureate of Fiji, but who was also a distinguished journalist whose humorous pieces such as 'Mulki ki Rachnayen' appeared in the newspapers.[49] Pandit Pratap Chandra Sharma published his *Pravas Bhajananjali* in 1947, which was reissued in Fiji in 2012. His poems capture small vignettes of everyday life while emphasising the virtues of thrift, industry, perseverance, devotion to faith and family, and pride in one's culture; themes that are common in all Hindi publications about Fiji Indians. Refreshingly, the poet also looks at the faults and failings of his own people, the duplicity of the leaders and the gullibility of the masses, with an ironic sense of detachment. In a telling poem on *girmit*, Pratap Chandra asks his people, brought up on the ideology of grief and grievance, to look within to see what role they themselves might have played in the making of their history; it was, after all the Indian recruiters who fraudulently recruited the *girmitiyas*, it was the *sirdars* or Indian foremen on the plantations who dobbed their own in for punishment by the European overseers. Such revisionism was rare.

The enclosed and socially isolated world of my father's generation began to fracture by the time my generation arrived in the postwar period. The values and practices that had enthralled my father's generation, embroiled them in acrimonious debates with other sections of the community, defined their sense of identity and place, gave them meaning and purpose, had less relevance for my generation. Arranged marriages were, for us, a thing of the past, as were large families (a baker's dozen was not uncommon

---

49   Vivekananda Sharma (ed.), *Fiji's Poet Laureate: Poems of Kamla Prasad Mishra* (New Delhi: Gaurav Prakashan, 1999).

in many families). Daylight marriages of short duration became the norm for us, but were unheard of in the past. Our conceptions of women's role in public and private life would have been alien to the conception of the earlier generations. Compulsory shaving of head and facial hair as a public sign of bereavement was observed, but not enforced. Strict rules about diet—little beer but definitely no beef—were beginning to be observed in the breach. Village moneylenders—*mahajans*—who had exercised such a baleful influence in the past became a distant memory for us as banks spread their tentacles around the country. The great debates of the late 1940s about whether prohibition should continue to be imposed on the Indo-Fijian community—an issue that deeply polarised people and wrecked political careers—meant nothing to us. Whether the meat you ate was *halal* or *jhatka*—an issue that had strained Hindu–Muslim relations in the past—had no relevance for us. Similarly, whether *Sanatanis* (orthodox Hindus) greeting *Arya Samajis* (members of the Indian Hindu Reform Movement) with a *Namaste* rather than the customary *Ram-Ram* would be seen as a sign of defeat or subservience seemed rather silly to my generation. Christmas Day (*Bada Din,* Big day) became for my generation an excuse for exuberant, drunken celebration, eating fresh goat meat and drinking rum—only the poorest of the poor ate chicken or duck on that day—a much anticipated feature of our annual calendar. The older generation mourned the passing of a culturally ordered world that had been built from the memory of a remembered past, but there was little they could do about it.

Improving communication—better roads, bridges and regular public transport—joined us to an expanding world beyond the village horizon. Expectation of what life was—or what it could be—had risen for our generation. By the early 1960s, for instance, primary education was within the reach of most children who wanted it, and secondary education, too, for those who passed their entrance examination. We now could, if we were any good—and our 'goodness' was judged solely on the basis of our performance in external examinations—contemplate a lowly career in the public service, in the banking sector, in the sugar industry as trainee overseers and in the teaching profession; possibilities that were beyond even the imagined horizon of our parents. In the early 1960s, university education was restricted to a select few—perhaps 10 a year—who were sent on government scholarships to New Zealand (rarely to Australia) to train as high school teachers, administrators and economists. They were the cream of the crop, who returned from overseas after a few years, proclaiming themselves culturally disoriented, misfits, ill at ease among their own people. For all their idiosyncrasies, though, they made a huge impression on youthful minds, representing possibilities that could be ours if only we tried hard enough. Many became our role models.

But all this changed with the founding of the University of the South Pacific in 1968. That event must be counted as one of the turning points in the modern history of the Pacific Islands.[50] It opened up opportunities for higher education to thousands of children from poor homes who would almost certainly have otherwise missed out. It brought us into contact with people from other parts of Fiji and from other parts of the Pacific, which had, until then, remained forbidding names on paper, nothing more. A new generation had come of age at a critical time in the region's history as islands were on the eve of independence. We were trained—and destined—to play an important part in our future.

Our world was more diverse than that of our parents. Those who went to Christian or urban schools lost the Hindi language, were more exposed to modern influences and were more at home in cross-cultural friendships. Those of us who went to rural schools or schools run by various Indo-Fijian cultural organisations retained firmer links with our culture and language. This, I now realise, had its obvious advantages, but it also imposed limitations that dawned upon me much later. Just as we went to predominantly Indian schools, Fijian children went to predominantly Fijian schools—Queen Victoria and Ratu Kadavulevu. In 1960, when I was in grade two, there were only 88 non-Fijians in the colony's 325 Fijian primary schools, and only 53 non-Indians in Indian primary schools.[51] We thus grew up engrossed in the ethos of our own society, untouched by cross-cultural influences, completely ignorant of the values, interests and concerns of the Fijians, and blind to the complex, inner impulses of their society. And yet, we were a part of the generation that was called upon to play an important role in national life in the postcolonial era—as teachers, administrators, politicians. No wonder Fiji has faltered so often in its recent journeys.

---

50   More discussion is in Brij V. Lal, 'Laucala Bay', in *Pacific Places, Pacific Histories: Essays in Honor of Robert C. Kiste,* ed. Brij V. Lal, (Honolulu: University of Hawai'i Press, 2004), pp. 237–58.
51   Burns, *Fiji,* p. 230.

We were the last generation of Fiji school children to complete high school before independence. We were the last to study the colonial curriculum. Senior Cambridge was the exam high school children sat until New Zealand Entrance came in the late 1960s.[52] Once again, the emphasis was on learning other people's pasts and experiences. So in geography we had lessons on Burma, Central China, Malaya, Singapore, Manchuria, East Anglia, the Midland Valley of Scotland, about Brittany, Denmark and the Mediterranean coastlines of France, about California, the Canadian maritime provinces, the corn belt of the United States, Florida and the St Lawrence Valley, about the Snowy Mountain Scheme, irrigation farming in Renmark, South Australia, the transport problems of the Cook Islands—they had transport problems there?—the relief maps and the sheep industry in New Zealand and Australia. I did not do well in geography because, among other things, I did not know the name of the highest mountain in Australia. I knew that it began with a 'K', but wasn't sure whether it was Kosciusko or Kilimanjaro. Coolgardie and Kalgoorlie confused me. And, try as we might, we could not spell Murrumbidgee. What kind of a name was that?

In history in the lower grades, we studied the rise of the Liberal Party in New Zealand, the importance of the refrigeration industry to New Zealand agriculture, the Wakefield scheme, the Maori Wars (as they were then called), about John Macarthur, the merino sheep and squatters, the effects of the Victorian gold rushes and the rapidly expanding wool industry—topics like that. In higher grades, we left the Antipodes to focus on the grand themes of modern history. So, we studied the unification of Italy and Germany, the Crimean crisis and World War I, the Bolshevik Revolution, the rise of Adolph Hitler and Mussolini, the emergence of the trade union movement in Great Britain and, briefly, the rise of new nations in Asia. Pupils ahead of us by a few years studied the causes of the 1929 Depression, the Partition of Africa, the social reform policies of Gladstone and Disraeli, the significance of the *Import Duties Act 1931*, the Gold Standard, the Abdication Crisis, the Irish Free State.

In our English classes at secondary school, we studied both literature as well as language. Language was dry, antiquarian, but literature was something else, good, solid, untrendy stuff that would be dismissed today as hugely Eurocentric: novels, short stories, poems and plays by John

---

52 I have written more about this in *Mr Tulsi's Store: A Fijian Journey* (Canberra: Pandanus Books, 2001), pp. 59–80.

Steinbeck (*The Pearl*), William Golding (*Lord of the Flies*), Emily Brontë (*Wuthering Heights*), Joseph Conrad (*Lord Jim*), William Wordsworth (*Daffodils*), Samuel Taylor Coleridge (*Ancient Mariner*), Edgar Alan Poe (*Raven*), D.H. Lawrence (*The Snake*), William Shakespeare (*Hamlet, Macbeth, Merchant of Venice, Romeo and Juliet*), T.S. Eliot (*Love Song of J. Alfred Prufrock*). The list does not end there. Reading, broadening our imaginative horizon was fun, but writing short composition pieces could be tricky. For instance, a long meaningful paragraph on modern art, the astronauts, western films, the bottle drive of collecting for Corso, about the main stand at a flower show, the case for or against television (when we had no idea what this creature was), a climbing adventure, baby sitting or, of all things, a winter morning. In hot, humid Tabia of all places! A few years back, I met a man in Brisbane who had sat the Senior Cambridge Examination in the mid-1960s. There was an essay question on the 'Phenomena of the Beatles', the music group. Not paying heed to the spelling, he proceeded to write a long and (he thought) a meaningful paragraph on the 'Phenomena of the Rhinoceros Beetles!' With misunderstandings like this, it was a miracle that he or anyone passed external exams, and with good marks too.

We were introduced to the global sweep of the human experience in history and literature, to the creative genius of the great minds of the world, but I am not at all sure we understood what we were reading. The subject matter was alien. We read to set standards; cramming was what was required of us to pass exams, not free-ranging exploration of the new worlds that the books were opening before us. We were taught to learn, not question. This was the value of colonial education. Still, for all their cultural biases, the western texts opened up new worlds for us. They awakened our imagination, emphasised our common humanity across boundaries of culture and race, and sowed the seeds of future possibilities. The idea of the fundamental oneness of humanity has remained with me. So, I don't cringe at the colonial texts we learnt parrot fashion; I am grateful for the windows they opened.

The metaphors of our own culture and allusion to our own past had no place in higher colonial learning, although in primary school we learnt Hindi and learnt about our ancestral culture and history, about various gods and goddesses and the heroes and heroines of Indian history. We had enough of the language to read the Ramayana and Hindi newspapers to our unlettered parents. The language connected us to our cultural roots. Indian school children played an important part in keeping the culture alive. There was no Hindi in high school in the late 1960s. I regret that now, but it did not seem to matter then. And I have, through private effort, continued to read, write and speak Hindi. But the sense of loss is palpable among those who have no Hindi at all. Some, now in middle age, are trying to learn the language.

More regrettable, for me, is the complete absence of Fijian culture and history in the curriculum. We heard occasional hair-raising anecdotes about the notorious cannibal Udre Udre who reportedly ate 100 humans, marking each feast with a stone heaped in a pile, or about Ma'afu, the mercurial Tongan, who nearly colonised Fiji, and Cakobau who so gracefully ceded the islands to Great Britain. But that was about it. Fijians remained for most of us objects of fear and suspicion—their names invoked by mothers to send unruly children to bed. 'If you don't go to bed, Timoci will take you away.' We all had a Timoci in our families. To us, all Fijians were peas in the same pod. We did not, until quite late in life, know about the inner configuration of Fijian society, its rituals and ranking systems and precise protocols, its political divisions and rivalries. I am sure it was the same with the Fijians who saw Indo-Fijians as *Kai Idia,* an undifferentiated group descended from an enslaved past. For many of them, Gujaratis and *girmitiyas,* the Kurbis and the Madrasis were one and the same thing. That said, the postcolonial generation is becoming more aware of things Fijian, thanks to an increasing number of multiethnic primary and secondary schools, the multiethnic university campus in Suva, and broader social interaction in the workplace and in the community at large. In their attitudes and relationships, their habits and moods, the Indo-Fijians, while retaining their 'Indian-ness', are becoming more conscious of the 'Fijian-ness' in their hyphenated identity.

There was nothing in primary or secondary education about Fiji history, so that generations of children grew up knowing virtually nothing about their past. History—and the humanities generally—was for no-hopers; bright students did the hard sciences. But there is, I think, another reason for the absence of Fiji from the curriculum. There was no shared understanding of the country's past, no consensus on its commonalities. Thanks to colonialism's stratagem, there was not one Fiji, but three— each with its own distinct place in the colonial compartment. While one group lauded colonial rule, the other castigated it. One demanded primordiality as the basis of political culture, the other espoused secular, egalitarian ideology as the principle of political relationships. One asserted paramountcy as the principle of political representation, the other wanted parity. One owned the land, the other was effectively landless. And so the divisions went. No wonder the educators edited history out of the textbooks. Learning someone else's history was safer. Fiji has paid a heavy price for the ignorance of its history.

For Indo-Fijian children, education became a profound agent of social change, just as indenture had been for the *girmitiyas*. The classroom was a great leveller of hierarchy. Before World War II, education, especially higher education, was largely the prerogative of the wealthy and the well-connected in the Indo-Fijian community. Wealth, status and power came from owning property or proximity to officialdom. The early generation of leaders came from this privileged background: lawyers, landowners, businessmen such as Badri Maharaj, the Grant family, the Deokis, the Ramrakhas, the Mishras, the Singhs of Ba, the Sahu Khans, the Tikarams. But the expansion of educational opportunities opened up the field to children from poor, nondescript backgrounds. Talent and merit became the markers of success and ladders to power, and that has remained the case. The old, well-established families, whose names were once synonymous with status and sophistication and fame and fortune, have gone and are now largely forgotten.

By the 1970s, Fiji had become a different place to what it had been during our childhood. Once the 10-acre leased land had been the sole source of livelihood for most Indian families in the cane belt. By the 1970s and 1980s, it had become increasingly inadequate and nonremunerative, forcing people to seek cash employment in urban areas. Soon, most families had at least one person working outside the farm. The situation worsened from the mid-1990s onwards with the nonrenewal, under the 30-year *Agricultural, Landlord and Tenant Act,* of agricultural leases.[53] Nonrenewal often meant the end of sugarcane farming on the expired leases, leading to a large-scale relocation of former canefarmers. Most of them moved to mushrooming squatter settlements fringing the major urban centres of Fiji where now between 15 and 20 per cent of Fiji's population resides. New occupations had to be learned. Many former canefarmers turned to market gardening. The comfort and solidity of village life with its practised routine was gone. In some squatter settlements, the Fijian landlords demanded cash payment from Indo-Fijians for holding religious ceremonies. As a result, in some cases, the screening of religious videos became a substitute for the actual performance of a *puja*.

---

53 Padma Narsey Lal, *Ganna: Profile of the Fiji Sugar Industry* (Lautoka: Fiji Sugar Commission, 2008), pp. 125–26.

Videos began to arrive in Fiji in the mid-1980s. They accelerated the 'privatisation of pleasure' and the further narrowing of the circle of engagement in the community. The dwindling of community elders and the slippage of knowledge of rituals associated with certain ceremonies (birth, death, marriage) increased reliance on the video for guidance. The advent of Bollywood cinema in the 1990s and the ready availability of Indian television sit-coms deepened the dependence. People learned about fashion and 'proper' dress codes from television. Wedding ceremonies in rural settlements reflected the influence of Indian television as people took their cue from the subcontinent. In a curious kind of way, India once again became a cultural reference point for some of the younger generation.

Urban drift by both Fijians and Indians fractured boundaries and fostered cross-cultural contact. Sports were more ethnically integrated. Soccer, once a predominantly Indian game, boasted many Fijian players. Rugby Sevens, with exclusively Fijian players, attracted a national following, with most Indo-Fijians basking in the reflected glory of the national team's international success. Western popular culture (dance, music, films) forged relationships across the ethnic divide. A visible change occurred in the student composition of Fiji's primary and secondary schools. A generation ago, these were predominantly one ethnic group or another. Now they are, as a general rule, ethnically mixed. Some schools in Suva that were once predominantly Indian are now predominantly Fijian. There is little or no Hindi in Fiji primary and secondary schools, certainly not as an externally examinable subject, in contrast to the situation a generation ago. There is greater attraction to and affinity with western values. English, for many Indian children in urban areas, is now the principal language of communication and creativity; it is effectively their mother tongue. Knowledge of Hindi, where it is found, is passive, and reserved for occasions of formal cultural performance. A fluent mastery of the Devanāgari script is a rarity, as is the knowledge of literature in Hindi, something intimately familiar to the children of the immediate postwar generation.

The relegation of Hindi can also be explained by the new reality confronting the Indian community in Fiji; the corrosive culture of military coups in the country since 1987. The Indian community was the principal target of the coups, carried out in the name of protecting the interests of the indigenous community.[54] Emotionally uprooted and feeling unwanted, the immediate reaction of the Indians was to leave the country for other shores: Australia, New Zealand, North America.[55] The Indo-Fijians numbered around 50 per cent of the population in 1987. Their proportion of the total population has now been reduced to around a third, and it continues to decline further due to continuing migration and a low birth rate. Absolute Fijian dominance of the population is now an established fact of life in Fiji, which will have consequences for the future of minority communities there, including the pressure for a greater knowledge and awareness of things indigenous Fijian.

The centre of gravity of the Indo-Fijian community has shifted—to Sydney, Melbourne, Brisbane, Auckland, Wellington and Vancouver. Virtually every Indo-Fijian family has someone living in one or more of these places. A new community of the 'twice banished' is forming in the diaspora. The older members, direct migrants, still have connections with Fiji, visit it as often as they can, contribute funds for various causes—it is the home of their childhood memories. But this is no longer so for the younger generation, growing up in a western country, acquiring the skills and language of western culture. Fiji is their parents' land, not theirs, just as India was our indentured grandparents' home, not ours. Fiji for them is a place of curiosity, a fractured memory of a place of turbulence, perhaps a tourist destination, but little more. Growing up in western countries, they are navigating questions of identity and belonging in a complex, conflicted world, balancing an equation in which Fiji is a diminishing emotional presence. For them, lines of bipolarities are blurred and notions of here–there, local–global, traditional–modern, centre–periphery are conflated. They are at home exploring and maintaining multiple relations—familial, economic, social, organisational, religious and political—that span several borders, connecting them to one or more societies simultaneously. A new community is emerging whose precise character is difficult to describe and whose future is unclear, but which is becoming increasingly more visible.

---

54   Brij V. Lal, *Power and Prejudice: The Making of the Fiji Crisis* (Wellington: New Zealand Institute for International Affairs, 1988); Surendra Prasad (ed.), *Coup and Crisis: Fiji a Year Later* (Melbourne: Arena Publications, 1988).
55   Kishore Chetty and Satendra Prasad, *Fiji's Emigration: An Examination of Contemporary Trends and Issues* (Suva: School of Social and Economic Development, University of the South Pacific, 1993).

> It is not now as it hath been of yore;—
> …
> The things which I have seen I now can see no more.[56]

As we grew up, the world of our parents began to recede into a vanishing past; joint families, proper and periodic observance of rituals and ceremonies, the comforting bonds of a cohesive community, family solidarity, respect for age and authority, politeness in the presence of pandits, extreme carefulness in the management of money, healthy fear of the unknown. The gap widened with time in much the same way as it had done when our parents moved away from their parents' world. The change was inevitable—and liberating. And it continues unabated. As mobility increases and modernity touches nearly every aspect of life, the Indo-Fijians are becoming more aware of their complex and confusing identity. Living in a society corroded by the ravages of racial politics, they continue to nurture the roots of their Indian cultural heritage as a matter of pride and choice, though perhaps not with the reverence and understanding of their parents and grandparents. Indian music, dress, food and art are being interpreted and reinterpreted through a different and distinct sense of lenses, touched by modernity and the inevitable forces of globalisation that would have been feared and forbidding to the earlier generation. Western cultural values, alien and alienating to our forebears, also continue to be embraced and incorporated, not the least because they open up doors to other opportunities.

Perhaps what will surprise the earlier generations most, as they peer down the corridors of time—surprising in view of the prejudices and stereotypes and entrenched attitudes that had to be overcome—is the way in which their descendants have accommodated themselves to the ethos and mores of a society deeply informed by its indigenous past in ways they could not, or were perhaps unable and unwilling to embrace. They will be surprised at the extent to which their children and grandchildren have taken to drinking *kava,* enjoying Sevens Rugby, eating *lovo* food, wearing the *sulu,* conversing in the Fijian language and being familiar with Fijian cultural protocols. They will be disbelieving of the depth of interracial friendships in the community. They will, I am sure, marvel at the long, troubled, unpredictable, confusing, depressing and exhilarating journey from being an Indian to being an Indo-Fijian.

---

56 William Wordsworth, *Ode. Intimations of Immortality: From Recollections of Early Childhood* (Boston: Lothrop and Company, 1884), lines 6 and 9.

6

Illusion of hope: Aisha and Bhaskar[1]

Padma Narsey Lal

> Real courage … is when you know you're licked before you begin, but you begin anyway and you see it through no matter what.
>
> — Harper Lee[2]

The sugar industry was the reason why Indian indentured labourers were brought to Fiji in the late nineteenth and early twentieth centuries. For nearly a century, it formed the backbone of the country's economy, but in recent decades its fortunes have dwindled, and it faces an uncertain future due, among other things, to the nonrenewal of agricultural leases, the end of the preferential access to the European market, poor milling infrastructure, and politicised decision-making at all levels of the industry. In this chapter, Padma Lal looks at the human cost of the suffering and uncertainty that cane growers face. The experiences of Aisha and Bhaskar are replicated throughout Fiji where people continue to live with an illusion of hope. Padma Lal gathered material for this chapter as part of a research project on the Fiji sugar industry in 2002–03, but it captures the reality of the sugar industry for the preceding decade as well.

---

1   Originally appeared as 'Aisha', in *Bittersweet: The Indo-Fijian Experience*, ed. Brij V Lal (Canberra: Pandanus Books, 2004), pp. 287–303; and 'Bhaskar' appeared as 'Bhaskar's dilemma', in *Ganna: Portrait of the Fiji Sugar Industry*, Padma Narsey Lal (Lautoka: Sugar Commission of Fiji, 2008), pp. 171–78.
2   Harper Lee, *To Kill a Mockingbird* (Philadelphia, PA: J.B. Lippincott Company, 1960; New York, NY: Warner Books, 1982), p. 115.

Aisha

Aisha had just returned from the field to meet with me. Her deeply creased forehead, calloused hands and well-worn old blue ankle-length *lehnga* (long skirt), a white blouse and tattered *orhni* (shawl worn by Indian women) signalled that she was a struggling daughter of the soil. Aisha is a rarity in Fiji: she is an Indo-Fijian woman cutting cane. Until recently, cane cutting was an all-male, all-Indo-Fijian, occupation. But things have been changing in recent years. Now, many indigenous Fijians are working as 'substitute' cutters, often to raise money for community projects back home in the islands or on the mainland. For Indo-Fijian men, cutting cane now is an occupation of last resort. But an Indo-Fijian woman cutting cane? And a woman close to 70, at a time when people retire to savour their hard-earned sunset years enjoying grandchildren, dispensing advice to younger members of the family.

Aisha tells me she took up cane cutting after her husband died soon after the 1987 coups. The cane-cutting gang of which the family had been a member for several decades began to play up, exploiting her vulnerability. Sometimes, for no obvious reason, her crop would be the last cut. Sometimes, her cane would not be cut at all. So, both out of sheer desperation and to ensure that her voice was represented in the cane-cutting gang that made important decisions, she joined the gang and took up cane cutting herself. Village life has its undoubted virtues, I realised as I listened to Aisha, but it can also be brutally cruel for people who are poor and vulnerable, particularly today in Fiji when people seem to have lost all sense of compassion and appear to have become more selfish, focused exclusively on their own narrow, self-serving interests.

I had gone to Aisha's house to attempt to capture a typical cane-farming scene and an atypical cane-cutter's story; scenes that belong to another era, not likely to survive for much longer, despite all the talk of reforms in the sugar industry. Aisha sat down on the bench under the mango tree outside the *belo*—a traditional storage house for farm implements, fertiliser and weedicide used in the cane fields. She slowly undid her *orhni* wrapped around her head to provide some protection from the hot sun, and put it back over her shoulders and the blouse. Rural Indo-Fijian women even today cover their heads as a gesture of respect in the presence of strangers or elders. She wipes her perspiring face with the *orhni* and then we begin to talk.

'*Beta* what can I tell you,' she says with a tinge of sadness and regret. 'I am happy working and living here. This is where I've lived since I married Somu's father.' Somu was her eldest son who was still on the farm with his own family—a common scene in many cane families, usually following the son's marriage and the tension that develops with the daughter-in-law. Somu's father, as happened in many Indo-Fijian cane-farming families, had allowed his son to build a separate house on the farm. 'This is the only place I know. This has been our home for as long as I can remember. My late husband and all his 13 brothers and sisters themselves were born on the cane farm.' Aisha and her 10 brothers and sisters grew up on a cane farm not far away. 'That was the only world we knew. But now,' she says, 'it is a *kabarsthaan* (graveyard) of memories. Some part of me dies every day.' After a short pause she says:

> Past is all I have. There is no future for me here. My lease will expire next year. I don't know what will happen then. Where will we go if the lease is not renewed? There has been no word from the Native Land people.

She turned her head away from me and looked into the distance with tears in her eyes. My eyes, too, were moist.

Aisha is not alone in this predicament. Agricultural leases have begun to expire in large numbers since 1997 when the first of the leases automatically renewed some 20 years ago under the *Agricultural and Landlord and Tenant Act* (ALTA) expired. Since then, over 5,500 native ALTA agricultural leases have expired. Of the expired ALTA leases some 4,160 were cane leases and just over 20 per cent of these cane leases have been renewed to sitting tenants or their children as either cane land (743) or residential leases (105). The overwhelming majority—over 50 per cent—of the tenants, many of whom can trace their link to the expired lease for several generations, had to uproot their families, in some cases even their houses, to start all over again somewhere else, repeating the experience of their *girmitiya* ancestors a century ago—unskilled, unwanted, uprooted, on the move again.

'My children want me to go and live with them overseas,' Aisha says. Her two sons are abroad, one in Sydney and one in Auckland. They are among some 80,000 Indo-Fijians who have left Fiji since the 1987 coups for greener pastures in Australia, New Zealand and North America. Her sons want to sponsor her, though at her age a successful emigration visa cannot be guaranteed. Like so many people of her age, Aisha is apprehensive about making the move. 'What will I do there?' she asks. 'I have lived on this farm since I got married 50 years ago. Even though Somu's father is no longer on this earth, his soul is still here. I cannot leave him.' These simple, heartfelt words captured the essence of village family relationships that seem now to belong to another era.

'*Maan maryada,* respect, *rasmo riwaz,* our own way of doing things, are important to people of my age, *beta,* child,' Aisha continues unprompted. She has met children born and raised overseas and doesn't seem to like what she sees. She cannot relate to them. 'They do not seem to have the same respect for the elders as we used to have in our time.' I know exactly what she means, having lived in Canberra for the last decade and seeing how the younger generation interacts with their parents and relatives. The clash of values between two competing traditions, Indian and western, inevitably produces friction that can rupture relationships. No subject is taboo and young people express opinions in words and gestures that are at odds with values of deference and respect that we grew up with. From sex and sensuality, from individual rights to relationships—all get talked about in public, without embarrassment. It can be a very disconcerting experience for people from a more traditional background.

> Here I have my independence. I can go where I want to and when I want. I have people to talk to in my own language. What will I do overseas? English *baat jaanit nah hai,* I will become totally dependent on my children.

Seeing what a feisty and proud woman she is, I knew an overseas lifestyle was not for her. She would be a totally lost soul in the soulless suburbia of Auckland or Sydney. Listening to Aisha reminded me of my own father-in-law's experience. We had sponsored him to come to Australia to spend some time with us. We had hoped for an extended visit of several months, but soon after arriving in Australia, he began to miss his routine, his friends and relatives, even his animals. Being unlettered, he could not understand the new world around him, could not communicate with his grandchildren in his own language. He missed his beloved Tabia desperately, and returned after just a few weeks.

'This cane farm is my soul,' Aisha says when we return to the subject of cane farming:

> just as it was for my father and grandfather. I am a daughter of a *girmitiya*, grew up on a cane farm, married a canefarmer and had all my children on the cane farm. My husband too was born on a cane farm, a grandson of a *girmitiya*.

Aisha has vague memories of stories that old people told about the past. Like many in Fiji, she has no knowledge of where in India her ancestors came from, when, on what ship. That kind of knowledge was not valued then, and much of it is regrettably lost to history now. But she remembers that her family were always farmers, unlike some who had moved to the towns and ventured into other professions.

> *Khoon pasina se hum log e jamin ke sawara banaya hai, beta,* we have cared for this land with our blood and sweat. I never thought that after living a lifetime on this piece of land, I would ever have to contemplate finding another abode.

In that struggle, too, Aisha is not alone.

Aisha's farm has seen better days, I realise as I look around. It is not very lush nor properly weeded. It has an unkempt look about it. No new cane plants can be seen. I assume that the uncertainty of lease renewal has led to a lack of investment of time and energy in the farm, and the use of little fertiliser. It is a common enough response throughout the country. As leases expire, families wait during the grace period pondering their future. The grace period is nothing more than an extension of their agony. Not knowing whether they will be there the following year, growers just rely on the *ratoon* (second and subsequent) cane crop. In 2003, less than 10 per cent of the farmers had planted any new cane in contrast to the almost 80 per cent before the coups of 1987. The evidence of decline and decay is visible everywhere.

'Who in their right mind would plant cane today?' Aisha says reading my mind. 'Plant cane is too expensive. With *ratoon* all you need is to put in some *masala* (fertiliser) and weedicide and you can still get some returns.' During the 2002–03 farm survey, I was aware that in times of uncertainty farmers, particularly those whose leases were close to expiry, used small amounts of fertiliser, the bare minimum, far less than the recommended rate for *ratoon* crops. It was an understandable, if unfortunate, response for in the end productivity suffered.

'I should face reality,' Aisha says with sad resignation.

> After all, leased land is leased land. Leases will expire someday. It is just that I did not ever think that this day will come for me. We had no problems with renewals in the past. We did not even have to pay any goodwill nor did we have to run around to get our leases renewed. Before, our leaders had negotiated renewals on our behalf. Why is it that our *neta log* (elected leaders) today are unable to negotiate lease renewals on our behalf?

Before I could say anything, she continued unprompted.

> Everyone has to now pay goodwill. This time the *mataqali* [Fijian land-owning unit] has asked for $5,000 goodwill. We were lucky because we had to pay only $5,000 for a 10-acre block. Our neighbour had to pay $10,000 for his six acres. Hanif across the road paid $15,000 for his 10 acres.

I know that Aisha is forgetting that most of them did pay goodwill or premium, as they called it, to the chief. What is different now is that goodwill is also demanded by the Native Lands Trust Board (NLTB), which it euphemistically calls payment for New Lease Consideration. According to the NLTB, the new lease consideration is supposed to 'reflect the value of improvements on the land at the date of expiry' and 'landowners' goodwill to again give up their exclusive possession' of land. The tragic irony in this escapes the decision-makers. The very same people who made the improvements are now being asked to pay for the improvements they had made or else risk nonrenewal.

'I can afford to pay the extra goodwill because my farm is one of the more productive ones,' Aisha continues. Her land is Class I, which means cane yield is over 85 tonnes per hectare. From the Fiji Sugar Corporation records, I know that the annual cane output from her 10-acre (4-hectare) land has always been well over 500 tonnes. She is among fewer than 30 per cent of the growers in Fiji producing such large volumes of cane. Most growers in her sector and elsewhere produce fewer than 100 tonnes a year. 'I will be able to get a loan from the Sugar Fund and they know that I can pay off the goodwill from my cane income,' says Aisha. 'Many of my neighbours are in worse situations: *bahut kharaab haalat hai un ke.*' She mentions the names of two families who had to relocate when their leases were not renewed, and they could not pay the goodwill demanded by the *mataqali* and the NLTB.

6. ILLUSION OF HOPE

Aisha considers herself lucky despite all the gloom and doom around her. She accepts her fate, her kismet with equanimity. 'My children live abroad. They are very successful. And all that because of the income from the cane.' She does not deny that the cane farm has been good for her and the family. Income from cane had sustained the family all these years, and continues to do so even today. Money from sugar cane made it possible for all the children to get educated, all but one having gone to university. Her house is made of concrete and her vegetable garden provides her daily requirements of beans, *baigan* (eggplant), *bhaji* (vegetables) and *mircha* (chillies). She makes her own coconut oil for cooking.

One grandson lives with Aisha. She worries about his future constantly. His parents had died in a car accident, and she has looked after him ever since he was a baby. He unfortunately did poorly at school and failed the Fiji Junior. He cannot get a job in town. The job market is glutted with graduates. 'Now-a-days, everyone wants a diploma or a certificate to hire someone for even a clerk's, or a salesman's job.' The grandson has three little children of his own. His prospects for migrating are low because one of his children is mentally handicapped. Besides, he has no marketable skills. The hope is that his children will be able to migrate. It is the hope of most Indo-Fijian families.

'I know I do not have long to live, but where will Ramu go?' Aisha asks forlornly. 'What will he do if the lease is not renewed?' But she is optimistic, as most desperate people can be, hoping against hope that her lease will be renewed, just as it was the last time. Her bigger worry is how will her grandson survive on the land. 'There are too many changes in the air,' she says.

> This restructure, that restructure. I hear the company (FSC) wants to get rid of rail transport. The daily radio talk is so confusing to people like us. And they speak in a language that poor illiterate people like me find hard to understand.

This year Aisha, like many others, had to convert from rail to lorry because FSC could not supply enough rail trucks on time, or, if supplied, the growers could not be sure if their cane would reach the mill within 48 hours as required. In recent years much of the cane reached the mill 48 hours after being harvested. With every day's delay, recoverable sugar decreases as the cane deteriorates. 'For generations our cane was transported via rail. This is the first time in a hundred years that this did not happen,' says Aisha. 'But we are happy that the Council had arranged FSC to pay some compensation for the extra cost of transporting cane by lorry.'

It may not be the last time if FSC has its way. FSC has deliberately neglected the rail system, and uses this as an argument to encourage farmers to use lorry transport, even though they clog up the road traffic. This is ironic. Elsewhere in the world, rail systems have been strengthened since they are found to be a highly cost-effective mode of transportation when high-volume goods have to be moved. It seems that the government, which has a 68 per cent share in the corporation, has provided a perverse incentive to the FSC to deliberately not invest in the rail system. Currently, the FSC pays a small lorry conversion rate; a rate that increases with 'air distance' and not the actual distance travelled by road. The rebate or conversion rate is nowhere near the actual cost of lorry transport. Perhaps the FSC has been able to get the government to surreptitiously reduce the sharing formula between the miller and the growers, just as the increase in the export tax from 3 per cent to 10 per cent did. Everyone knows that the FSC had been arguing for a reduction in the sharing formulae stipulated under the Denning Arbitration and the Kermode Award.

Aisha's thoughts wander back to one of her real concerns and she says playfully with a chuckle:

> What will happen when I am no longer on this earth? How will my grandson manage with cane farming, particularly harvesting? We are lucky because I cut my own cane with the help of Ramu. I can beat any young men of today in cutting cane, *Jawaan admin ke garda khawaye sakit hai.*

I know she is fortunate because she and her grandson both cut cane. They do not use hired cutters. This is not very common today. Before the 1987 coups, most families used to cut their own cane, today less than one in two Indo-Fijian families do so. Others rely on substitute cutters. Because of the shortage of cutters—another indirect effect of mass migrations since the coups—it is a substitute cutters' market. Substitute cutters are demanding a lot higher rate for the cutting of cane than has been agreed to by the gang and lodged as part of the Memorandum of Gang Agreement (MOGA).

Under MOGA, members agree amongst themselves before the start of the harvesting season about the schedule of farms to be cut in the first, second, third and, if necessary, fourth rounds, and the rates that growers would pay for the harvest of their cane. Despite the agreement, substitute cutters can demand almost double the MOGA rate for cane cutting as well as additional funds for buying things like shoes, knives, billycans and food. One gang in the Labasa district demanded $5 a day for green cane on top of the MOGA rate of $7 per tonne for green cane and $6 a day for burnt cane in addition to the $6 per tonne provided for in the agreement. Such a pricing system encourages the burning of cane before harvest.[3] Substitutes, who are assured $12 per tonne, often force growers to burn their cane to lighten their own work. This demand, together with regular mill breakdowns and a late start to the cane-crushing season, puts added pressure on growers to burn their cane. It is not surprising that today more than half the cane delivered to the mills is burnt, compared to 15 per cent before 1987. Burning cane is not without risk; farmers may end up paying a penalty if the cane is not delivered within 48 hours. Delays occur with the frequently troubled lorry or rail delivery system. During the crushing season, cane trucks are found sitting in the sun for hours beyond the Passover points,[4] with every hour of delay meaning lower sugar extraction.

'I know the industry is not doing too well,' Aisha tells me. 'Nothing like this used to happen during CSR days. We used to complain about the price of cane we got then, but at least our cane was cut and delivered on time.' Memory is playing tricks on her, for it was not just during CSR days but before the coups under the FSC that cane was delivered within a reasonable time, when they could get cash advances as well as advice about best farming practice from the FSC. Nothing of this sort happens today. As a cost-cutting measure, the FSC stopped all extension work couple of years ago, and discontinued giving cash advances. Now even the banks are reluctant to lend to canefarmers because of possibility of the nonrenewal of leases and other uncertainties caused by the FSC arbitrarily declaring that it would accept only a portion—2.8 million tonnes of cane of an estimated 3.4 million tonnes. Shortage of funds perhaps could be another reason why few farmers are not planting new cane, and applying the bare minimum of fertiliser. Planting cane requires money, as does good husbandry. Very few farmers have ready cash.

---

3 By burning cane farmers could jump the scheduled harvest and delivery queue, as mills give priority for burnt cane delivery.
4 'Passover Point' is in the mill yard where cane is technically 'handed over' from the farmer to the miller.

There is regular news of the mills breaking down, worsening the situation with the approaching rainy season. This causes deep concern to Aisha and many farmers like her. It is perhaps out of desperation that some farmers burn their cane to 'jump the queue' and get their cane quickly to the mills. But this does not help the farmers or the industry. While burning per se is not the problem, delayed burnt cane means mills cannot produce grade one sugar. And regular customers of Fiji sugar are getting wary of buying poor-quality sugar. Recently, even a trusted customer from the United Kingdom had rejected Fiji's sugar.

'We all have known about these problems for years. No one seems to be doing anything,' Aisha says with subdued anger.

> Everyone is blaming everyone else. The company (FSC) says the problem lies with us the growers because we burn the cane. But we feel we are the victims. The company does not give us the quotas on time, the rail system is unreliable, the mills keep stopping and the cane is not moved quickly enough in the yard. Go to the mills and see it for yourself. There is always a backlog of rail and lorry in the mill yard. You can see the trucks and lorries queued up for hours, sometimes days. You may even find lorry drivers sleeping under their lorries and wherever they can find some protection from heat and dust and rain.

She is speaking the truth. I am aware that at times the queue is so long that lorry drivers have to stay in the mill yard for two to three nights, with their wives or sons bringing in food; lorry drivers relieving themselves in the nearby bushes or in between the rakes of rail trucks. There is only one toilet—at the mill gate—which too does not function most times.

'On top of all this,' Aisha continues, 'we hear of outside threats of lower price for our sugar. What have we done to deserve this? Why is the world against us?' These, I know, are not merely threats but a likely eventuality after 2006, when the current Cotonou agreement expires. Under this agreement, previously known as the Lome Convention, Fiji's export amount was guaranteed in perpetuity, but not the price. The European Union—our main trading partner under the World Trade Organization (WTO)—is under considerable pressure to remove price support. Recently, major sugar suppliers—countries such as Australia, Brazil and Thailand—have taken the EU to the WTO Tribunal to make them remove the price subsidies that Fiji and other African, Caribbean and Pacific (ACP) countries have enjoyed for some of their commodities. 'Tell me, what should we do?' There is very little that can be done, as Fiji is a price taker and the push for globalisation is like a tornado. There is very little that a small country like Fiji can do. But surely, domestic issues such as mill breakdowns, delays in quotas and land lease renewals can be tackled.

'Have you talked to political leaders about this?' I ask tentatively. This touches a raw nerve. Aisha *chaachi* (aunty) is fed up with politicians. And she has a lot to say about them as well. 'They are feathering their own nests,' she says bitterly.

> *Pet puja,* self-interest. They are all playing games, scoring points off each other. They want us to believe they are genuinely interested in the farmers' welfare when they do not give a damn what happens to us. If they did, wouldn't you expect the Unions, the Council (Sugar Cane Growers Council) and the politicians to work together to help farmers. No, they would not. *Ek bole aam to dusara bole imli.* They cannot agree amongst themselves. If anything, you can always count on someone to stand up and contradict whatever is being said by someone else in the interest of the growers and the industry. Look what happened when the leases began expiring in 1997. Instead of working with the landowners to negotiate renewal of leases, some politicians encouraged farmers to leave their farms. In some cases even before their leases had actually expired. They were given all sorts of promises, promises of tickets to migrate, new aid money. After listening to them, some of the farmers from places like Wainikoro and Daku left their homes and their farms in 2000. Went to makeshift Valelawa camp, with faith in their leaders. Some whose leases had expired refused to be resettled at new sites in Naduri because our leaders had promised them bigger things. They stayed in makeshift houses, without jobs or land, with nothing to support their families. Children could not go to school. After waiting for months some of the families had to put their tail between their legs and go back to their own villages to start all over again. We all know that politicians' promises are like a sieve. Nothing stays.

'But do our people ever learn?' I interrupted Aisha.

> No they do not. Even though people realise that for us Hindustanis to live peacefully in this country we have to work together with the *Kai Vitis,* indigenous Fijians. Many people vote for the party that preaches racial policies rather than the party that represents cooperation and multiracialism. Look at what happened in recent by-elections.

I wonder if Fiji has lost its chance of 'being the way the world should be'.

Aisha's thoughts again return to her own immediate family, to her grandson's future. I realise, as she speaks, that this is something that really haunts her, the future of her grandson. 'How will my grandson make a living?' His future on the farm is not bright. He will have to learn new things, focus on producing cane with high amounts of sugar. Otherwise, his income will decline, because under the new cane payment system, the price he will get will depend on the amount of sugar contained in his cane. He will have to be extra careful with his farm management practices so that he produces the best output of sugar. He will have to choose appropriate sweeter varieties. He may have to think about getting contract harvesting because not many people in his sector might want to cut cane. Substitute cutters do not cut cane properly, often leaving large amounts of stump, the sweetest part of the cane on the ground. He will have to learn new skills in bookkeeping. In short, he will have to reinvent himself.

But I know that even if he were to reinvent himself, the future of the sugar industry would remain uncertain unless the government swallows some bittersweet pills and substantially reforms the industry as a whole. For one, the FSC has to be totally revamped. To do this, more than organisational restructuring is needed. Reorganising the FSC is like rearranging the deck chairs on the *Titanic*. Reform is needed all along the production, harvest, transport and milling chain. In the milling sector, changes are needed all the way from the top management (the board and the senior management) to the field—the field officers, the locomotive drivers and the mill workers.

Management at all levels has been allowed to deteriorate. From my analysis of FSC's milling performance and reports from the ground, it seems as if there the rot has set in to every part of the industry. The FSC has been running at a loss since 1999, even though the gross revenue has increased steadily. In 2002 the FSC made a record loss of $24 million, largely because of poor management decisions, allowing the recovery of sugar already contained in the cane produced by growers to decrease from the 90 to 94 per cent before 1989 to less than 85 per cent, and in one mill area to even as low as 78 per cent. There were also reports of corruption in the way quotas were allocated in the field. I received many reports throughout the mill areas that locomotive drivers deliver more trucks to certain areas than were released from the depots, with the locomotive drivers 'selling' the 'extra' trucks for $2 to $3 each.

If this is true then it is no wonder that some growers have to wait for hours and days for their harvest quotas, when their neighbouring gangs are able to finish their harvests well before the season is over. Every day's delay in quota and trucks means an increase in the cost of the cane harvest, because they have to provide extra *yaqona* (kava), tea, *gulgulas* (Indian sweets) and in some cases even meals while the gang waits around for the quotas to be delivered by the field officers. Such delays could add additional costs of anywhere from $100 to $200 to farmers such as Aisha. While this may not be that critical for Aisha, for small farmers producing less than 100 tonnes a year, the delays could mean an additional $2 to $3 a tonne in harvest costs. This, together with farmers not paying particular attention to farm husbandry, could mean that many farms may become financially unviable—even with the current price regime that Fiji enjoys of two to three times the world price. What will happen when the preferential EU prices end in 2006? But I keep these thoughts to myself.

'As long as my grandson continues to work on the farm and rely on himself,' Aisha says with vague, fatalistic hope, 'and continues the good practices he learned from me and my husband, I think he will be alright.' The quiet dignity and inexhaustible patience of women like Aisha— whom I began calling *chaachi* halfway through our talk as a heartfelt gesture of affection and respect—is touching in ways that words cannot express. Innocent people caught in a tragedy not of their making, living in a world over which they have no control, living in vanishing hope and on the sufferance of others.

'*Khuda Hafiz, beta,*' Aisha *chaachi* says to me as I take leave in the gathering darkness. 'I am glad I do not have long to live. *Bhaut din nahin bacha hai. Insha Allah.*'

Bhaskar's dilemma

'What more do we have to cope with,' thinks Bhaskar, a fourth-generation canefarmer in Fiji. Little does he realise that problems such as these in the milling and processing sector are nothing compared to what is really in stock for him and other canefarmers. Sadly, the worst is yet to come.

For months, Bhaskar has been worried, and at times even depressed, about what has been happening in the Fiji sugar industry and how he is going to support his family. He is one of the 15,510 active growers in Fiji who produced about 3.2 million tonnes of sugar cane in 2003. He is about 52 years old with a wife and three children to support—one of whom is mentally handicapped. The family lives in a small house made of corrugated iron on their 10-acre cane farm of rolling-to-hilly land. The house has no running water or electricity. Land is leased from the Native Land Trust Board. Bhaskar's lease, which was last renewed for 30 years under the Agricultural and Landlord and Tenant Act (ALTA), is due to expire in 2012. He does not know if his lease, which is one of about 70 per cent of all cane farms leased from indigenous Fijians, will be renewed. Judging by the recent trends in the industry, ever since 2003 when over 50 per cent of leases were not renewed, he does not have very high hopes.

Bhaskar's concerns about the future of his family grow more acute by the day, as he hears about the ongoing woes in the industry—mill breakdowns, cutters sitting around idle waiting for their daily quota, sugarcane lorries queued up at all mills, rampant cane burning. He knows that such incidents are not that uncommon in the sugar industry. Similar news of mill breakdown or burnt cane was reported by FSC even before the first coup in May 1987. The difference today is that such news is almost a daily occurrence. That, too, within just a few weeks of the start of the crushing season, when farmers and others know that the mills should be operating efficiently following necessary maintenance that would have occurred after the close of the previous milling season last December. The Fiji Sugar Corporation, the sole miller, has had some five months to do the yearly maintenance and service the different machines. But this year the 'maintenance period' does not seem to have had much effect on the mill operating hours.

Before the May 1987 coup, Bhaskar does not remember mills shutting down for more than a day a week, if that. Every mill had regular stoppages for cleaning and unexpected repairs, but on average mill operating hours were usually around 144 hours a week. Today, FSC would be lucky if the Lautoka Mill, where Bhaskar sends his cane for crushing and processing, runs for less than half that amount of time; Lautoka is the newest mill and with the most advanced machinery and technologies. Yet, it is the worst performing mill.

Such problems with the mills have flow-on effects, which further affect Bhaskar's bottom line. With mills stopping, there are long queues of 7-tonne lorries for almost a kilometre. Lorry drivers sometimes find themselves waiting for a full day to unload their cane, not to mention having to put up with personal discomfort, particularly when there are no amenities readily available. Delays in unloading also mean that lorry drivers end up making only a single trip a day instead of at least two trips, adding further to the cost of harvesting and transport. Further, regular mill breakdown results in the extension of the crushing season beyond the 22–24-week season, and into the beginning of the rainy season around the November–December period. Rain also means delays in cane harvesting as well as difficulty in delivering cane via lorries on unsealed roads through sloppy or reclaimed swampy land—all adding to the increasing costs of harvesting and transport borne by the farmers.

Bhaskar's and other farmers' woes do not stop there. Regular mill stoppages also mean there is delay in getting harvest quotas out to the cane cutters. Post the 1987 coups, cane cutters could be sitting around idle as late as 9 am. Before 1987, cane cutters would have had by then at least three hours of cane cutting under their belt, and getting ready to have a break for tea or grog and some *gulgula* or biscuits. Since 1987, growers still had to supply drinks and snacks irrespective of whether a full quota of cane cutting had been completed or not. Cane-cutter efficiency had decreased by almost 50 per cent. This, too, was also not unknown to the industry—but nothing was being done.

However, it is a cutters' market. Bhaskar knows this too well from first-hand experience. After his brothers migrated to Australia in 1989, he could not find regular cane cutters. He had to resort to hiring substitute cutters, usually people from the outer islands who were often lured into coming to the mainland during cane-harvesting seasons to raise money for their church, school or some other project for the village. It being the cutters' market also means that Bhaskar is at the mercy of the demands of casual cutters. He has to provide not only a place for them to stay but also three meals a day, not to mention other in-kind supplies such as a billycan, and a cane knife. In addition, he has to provide a bonus of several dollars per tonne of cane over and above what the 'harvesting gang' of growers would have decided during the annual gang meetings prior to the cane-harvesting season. Under the MOGA a gang sets the harvesting rate as well as harvesting schedule for the growers who belong to that gang.

These agreed and officially recorded rates with the Sugar Commission of Fiji (SCOF) do not bear much resemblance to the real cost of cane harvesting that growers have to meet. Many a time cane cutters also demand the burning of cane to ease their own effort. After 1987, almost 50 per cent of cane supplied to the mills was burnt, as compared with less than 20 per cent burnt cane before the first coup. In 2002, over half of the cane was burnt; in the 2006 season, 52 per cent of total cane supplied was burnt.

Before the 1987 coups, Bhaskar's harvesting gang usually comprised farmers or their relatives, and gangs relied on each other's family members for their cane harvesting. The gang used to work as a team, as a 'family', helping each other out on farm and off farm. Today, his gang, like almost all others in the country, comprises 'substitute cutters', who are not necessarily related to the cane growers, or have much experience in cane cutting let alone cane farming. No wonder the cutter efficiency declined from 350 tonnes per cutter pre-1987 to less than 200 tonnes per cutter in 2002. After all, outsiders do not know much about cane cutting, often leaving some 10–15 per cent of cane from the ground uncut, usually the sweetest part of the cane.

The industry, it was estimated in 2003, lost about $11 million due to poor harvesting practices. Such losses no doubt all add to the increasing cost of cane production and the farmers' bottom line.

Today harvesting and transport costs account for more than 50 per cent of the total cost of about $44 per tonne of cane delivered to the mill gate, which is almost a third more than $35 a tonne a couple of decades ago. Before the 1987 coups, the harvesting and transport cost was around a third of the average total cost. This meant that an average farmer in the Lautoka mill area who supplied about 150 tonnes lost over $1,500 a year compared to what he used to make 20 years ago for the same volume of cane. Bhaskar, producing about 250 tonnes a year, would have lost approximately $2,500 due to such inefficiencies.

Farm productivity has also decreased considerably, mainly due to the practice of using hired labourers to work on the farm. Instead of cane farming being a family affair, today the majority of farms rely on the use of hired labour, largely because of the migration of family members who normally would have worked on the farm. The use of hired labourers, often with little supervision from farm owners, has also meant the common occurrence of *din maro,* where labourers shirk work, putting in less than expected effort for a day's pay, or cutting corners when applying fertiliser or weedicide. Bhaskar knows that when he uses *masala,* fertiliser, he can easily apply about 12 bags a day, whereas, with hired labour, he can expect no more than six to seven bags a day. This, together with farmers' reliance on crops of over five to six years instead of newly planted cane on at least a quarter of the field, has resulted in a decrease in farm productivity, costing the industry almost $30 million a year in foregone production.

Further, all canefarmers get hit by a double whammy because of poor milling efficiency. Regular mill breakdowns also mean poor mill efficiency and thus a reduced level of recovery of the sugar contained in sugar cane delivered by farmers such as Bhaskar. The sugar recovery rate has been reduced from about 86 per cent in 1972 to about 80 per cent in 2004; in 2002, the average sugar recovery rate was as low as 76 per cent.

Each percentage decrease in sugar recovery means, at the 2003 sugar prices and the current volume of cane processed by FSC, a total loss of about $1.5 million. During the period 1986–2000, on average $6 million worth of sugar already produced in sugar cane was annually lost through milling 'wastes', bagasse,[5] mud, molasses and waste water; 70 per cent of this loss was borne by the farmers.

Bhaskar recalls the days before the 1987 coups when every part of the industry—cane cutters, lorry operators, locomotive drivers, mill workers (crushing/processing)—all worked in harmony. He proudly remembers the Fiji sugar industry being regarded as better performing than the Australian and even the Mauritian sugar industries. In the face of the EU's sugar trade liberalisation, Australia and Mauritius reformed their industries to the point of being among the best performing in the world. Fiji, on the other hand, has regressed to the lowest 15 per cent of the world's producers.

The new loan of $85 million that Fiji Government obtained from the Exim Bank of India in 2002 may bring about much-needed improvements, even if one questions the logic in obtaining such a loan at this time when Fiji is about to lose its preferential market access into the EU. Bhaskar wonders if the problems can be turned around with new machines replacing old ones. An analysis of FSC's own mill-operating performance shows that the recent poor performance of the mills was due largely to poor management and little or no accountability at all levels of decision-

---

5   Bagasse is the dry pulpy fibrous residue that remains after sugar cane has been crushed to extract the juice.

making—from factory floor, to mill management, to the FSC Board. In addition, nepotism and the discriminatory practices of the management in appointing mill workers based on ethnicity rather than merit have contributed to the problems. Thus, there is doubt if one can expect much improvement in milling operations with the installation of new machinery without also accompanying improvements in management.

But poor management does not seem to have stopped. In 2004, the local radio carried news that certain mill managers were reprimanded for not performing, or for poor accountability of activities, which resulted in the mill having serious breakdowns. What was most disturbing was that one of the mills that reported regular breakdowns and poor performance was the oldest mill, but which used to be one of the best performing ones in the country, despite being the oldest mill, until a new manager came on board in the 1980s.

The FSC reported a profit in 2006 following several years of losses. Bhaskar finds this hard to believe, particularly when the FSC has got a new loan to repay and most of the mills have more than usual breakdowns and shut downs. Further, the volume of cane produced in 2006–07 has been low compared to previous years because of the decrease in the number of active growers due largely to expiry of leases and the eviction of farmers from the cane belt. Bhaskar wonders if this is just paper profits generated by some creative accounting to show that the industry is being turned around under the Bainimarama Interim Government.

Bhaskar finds this reported profit even harder to believe when the price received from the EU has decreased by at least 5 per cent, the first of a few further decreases as a result of the expiry of the Cotonou Agreement, which replaced the original Lomé Convention. Fiji, like other ACP countries, is now scheduled to lose its favourable conditions of two to three times the world market prices, although the preferential access may remain. This must surely affect the bottom line of the FSC, not to mention the growers, the landowners and the economy as a whole.

With the projected decline in EU prices, canefarmers in Fiji can expect to see a decline in their gross income of at least 20 per cent. With such a decline in gross income, Bhaskar thinks he may still be able to survive and cover his costs plus still have about $1,500 net income, but not many farms will remain afloat. He will be one of about 2,000 farmers in the Lautoka mill area who expect to remain financially viable. It is reported that almost a quarter of the farmers are not expected to even meet their cash costs of farming, let alone cover other 'in-kind' costs, when the price reduces by almost 25 per cent. On the other extreme, after the projected reforms in the EU's own agricultural setup, which may result in Fiji's price decreasing by about 39 per cent, almost two-thirds of the farms would become financially unviable at farm-cost structures by 2004. Bhaskar knows that his family is heading for hard times as a net income of $1,500 would put him well below the basic national poverty line.

With such changes in the farming sector, major structural changes are expected in Fiji, affecting many rural towns. Bhaskar knows from his sister living in Tavua that towns such as hers and adjacent Ba and Rakiraki are already suffering. Many retail shops in these towns are no longer operating, and there is even talk of some of these areas becoming 'ghost towns'. Not only would the farmers' own income decrease, there is also very little hope of finding alternative employment in rural areas as the whole rural economy will decline. Unless farmers are able to reduce their farming, harvesting and transport costs, there is no future prospect for sugar in Fiji.

But there is very little chance of achieving lower costs unless farmers revolutionise their farming practices—major replanting must be carried out, improvement in hired labour productivity must occur, and efficiency in harvesting and transport must take place. There have been increased efforts to encourage farmers to plant new cane, make greater use of mechanical harvesters as well as lorry transport instead of rail. Much of this, it was hoped, would have occurred with the use of the $350 million Adjustment Cost project funding that the EU was to provide. This funding has been put on hold as a result of the 2006 coup and events following it. It seems there is little hope in the industry of seeing major improvements in farm productivity or in the morale of farmers in the country generally. As Bhaskar said, '*Jab dil toot gaya tab kaise dil lage ganna ke kisani mein,* once you have lost all faith then how can you put your heart into cane farming.'

Bhaskar knows that with expected decline in his income, his family is heading for real hardship. Living on the farm, at least the family could grow some of its own basic food and even make its own coconut oil for cooking and family use. But he does not know how he will pay for things such as his kids' schooling with changes to his cane income in the future. Even though in Fiji there are no fees in primary schools, there are always the building fees, clothes and books to pay for. And then there are the occasional medical expenses or transport costs of coming into town to got to banks, or to go to the local hospital.

Bhaskar wonders if the time has come for him and the family to leave farming and move to Suva, as so many other farmers from his village have done since 1997. As their farm leases expired, many families dismantled their houses, or at least whatever they could take, and migrated to Suva. Some families had gone to live in squatter areas in Suva on land that belongs to the state. Only the fortunate families, those that had some savings, or were supported by relatives, were able to get 5-acre (2-hectare) agricultural plots in places like Navua or Nausori. Reports suggest that these displaced families are doing well. Many of the resettled farmers, who were able to obtain blocks of land to farm in Navua or even near the Nausori Airport, took up planting *dalo* (taro) and vegetables for the local markets. Today, when given the choice of going back to cane farming even with extended land lease, these resettled canefarmers all refuse point blank. And with good reason too—they are reported to be earning a lot more than what they did on their cane farms.

This is a real dilemma for Bhaskar. He, too, feels he must leave cane farming. He does not have the heart to uproot his family. But, most importantly, he does not know where to go. He regrets not completing high school, like his two brothers who did and became school teachers. Their skills, as science mathematics teachers, were very much in demand overseas and they had no difficulty getting permanent resident visas. His eldest brother, Ram Bahadur, left Fiji to reside in New Zealand, following the then prime minister David Lange's decision to open the doors of his country to people of Indo-Fijian origin. He migrated two years after the first coup in May 1987. His second brother, Sanjeev, 10 years younger, left after the 2000 coup, frustrated and anxious for the future of his young family of three. His brothers had sponsored Bhaskar's family for migration. But because of his handicapped child, Australia had rejected the application. Fate always seems to work against those who already have very few choices in life.

Bhaskar realises he does not have enough savings to move to Suva or even to the Lautoka–Nadi corridor and make a fresh start. He will have to find a place to live. But renting in urban or peri-urban areas is very expensive. In any case, he will have to find a job first before he can support his family in any urban area. He thinks that at his age, with little education, no one will give him a job. He thought of trying to get a piece of agricultural land. But that, too, seems to be out of reach today. Two years ago, lease on a 5-acre block of state land at Waituri, near Nausori airport, was available for $4,000. Today, for same piece of land the lease sale price is almost $20,000–$30,000. He knows he cannot raise such amounts from the Fiji Development Bank or any of the commercial banks. Bhaskar does not have any savings that would be required as a down payment or assets to use as collateral. Perhaps, he thinks, he may ask one of his brothers now living abroad to lend him some money. But, being a proud man, he is reluctant.

In the meantime, Bhaskar hopes that ongoing talks about diversification of the sugar industry become a reality and cane farming remains a profitable venture as the FSC generates more electricity to sell to the Fiji Electricity Authority, or the FSC begins to produce ethanol as biofuel. Perhaps with the increase in global crude oil prices to almost US$100, ethanol production for cars and cogeneration might become financially viable and the demand for sugar cane would continue, if not for sugar than at least for ethanol or the electricity made from it.

Diversification into these other commodities could become a reality if the industry stakeholders—the FSC, farmers, the landowners and the government—can also agree on a partnership formula and then seriously take steps towards diversification, just like Mauritius had done once it became clear that the EU sugar trade liberalisation was going ahead. The last time they talked about forming a stakeholder-based company in 2002, to encourage landowners to have equity in the sugar industry to encourage renewal of land leases, the initiative fizzled out because politics, and perhaps greed, got in the way and the stakeholders could not agree amongst themselves on an equitable sharing formula. Bhaskar wonders if it is going to be any different in the future. In the charged atmosphere following the December 2006 coup, he wonders if the interim government and other stakeholders are capable of making rational decisions. He thinks not. Judging by the proposal to establish another sugar mill in Seaqaqa by the interim government at a time when the sugar prices are declining, farmers are leaving in large numbers, and the production, harvesting and transport costs are skyrocketing, there seems to be little hope of seeing any objective and rational decision any time soon.

What the future holds for families like Bhaskar's is anyone's guess. Perhaps it is *Ram ki marji,* God's wish. Bhaskar, a staunch Hindu, leaves his fate in God's hands. But also being a realist, he knows he has to do something, as nobody else will. But what?

7

'The burden of remembrance'[1]
Nandu's shadow

> I feel you die a little
> each time the phone rings unexpectedly
> tearing the flying sunlight
> and shadows of spring afternoons.
>
> — Tessa Morris-Suzuki[2]

'*Ram Ram kaka*,' Kamal, my nephew, said in an early telephone conversation from Labasa. Early morning calls in Canberra usually bring unwelcome news. 'What's up, *beta*,' I ask, with some trepidation. 'Nand Lal *dada* died this morning.' 'From?' 'Heart attack.' 'Where?' 'At home.' 'Funeral *kab?* When?' 'Thursday.'

That is two days from now. My first instinct is to pick up the phone and book a flight to Fiji immediately. But then I quickly realise I can't go because I am banned from entering the country. It hurts deeply at moments like this, not being able to fulfil the instinctual urge to say the final farewell to family and loved ones in person. And Nandu, our older cousin, was an integral part of our lives growing up in Tabia. He was our

---

1 Originally appeared as 'Nandu's shadow', in *Fijian Studies* 12(1) (2014): 73–83.
2 Tessa Morris-Suzuki, 'A matter of time', in *Peeling Apples* (Canberra: Pandanus Books, 2005), p. 1.

last surviving link to our early beginnings as a community in Labasa. His passing marked the end of an era for us, and I want to be there in person to bear witness to the moment.

I want to call, but there is no telephone at home. Kamal had called from the Labasa Post Office. He had gone to town to place a Death Notice on Radio Fiji. The routine was familiar to me. Three close family members would be notified through the broadcast, and listeners urged to pass the sad news on to friends and extended family members. *Sun ne wale kripeya is khabar ko* so-and-so *tak pahuncha den*. I can clearly visualise the scene unfolding in the village. People would start gathering at Nandu's house as soon as they received the news. A corrugated iron shed would be quickly constructed, people would bring food as a fire would not be lit in the house until after the cremation, and someone would be dispatched to arrange firewood for the ceremony the following day. Transport would be organised to take the body to the hospital mortuary. The police would be notified and the death certificate obtained before the cremation. For 13 days, the traditional period of mourning, people would come every night to sing *bhajan* (devotional songs), and provide company and comfort to the bereaved family. Then, gradually, life would return to normal.

'A thousand fantasies / Begin to throng into my memory'[3] of people and places, remembrance of things past, long gone and forgotten but now jolted by this sad news. Nandu lived across the road from us. He was not an original Tabia resident, unlike us. The family had moved to Wavu Wavu, 15 or so miles (24 kilometres) away sometime in the late 1940s, but had retained its share of the family land in Tabia where they planted rice, made oil from coconuts on the farm, grew peanuts, bean and maize. Sugar cane came later. In the late 1950s, the family began to break up as the boys married and had families of their own. As the extended family disintegrated, the family land was parcelled out to the boys. Nandu got the Tabia portion as his share, and he moved there soon afterwards. Until then, he had been for us a remote relative from a distant place; an infrequent visitor. After the move, he became part of our extended family. With time, we lost touch with the Waiqele mob.

---

3   John Milton, *Comus* (1637), in *The John Milton Reading Room: A Mask Presented at Ludlow Castle 1634*, pp. 105–06, available from: www.dartmouth.edu/~milton/reading_room/comus/text.shtml (accessed 18 April 2019).

Nandu was a constant presence at every family function; when distant relatives were visiting or when there was a *puja* (devotional prayer offering) or a Ramayan recital at home. He would be the go-to person for us at major events such as weddings and funerals, our *agua* (leader), the orchestra conductor, our conduit to the outside world. Father was, of course, the head of the family, but he was a shy, reserved person, clueless about the machinations going on in the village. It was no wonder that people called him *Sadhu* (Holy man). Nandu, on the other hand, was a man-about-town, so to speak, with a finger in every village pie. He knew which way the village wind would blow almost before everyone else. And we trusted him; we had no choice.

'Let us not burden our remembrance with / A heaviness that's gone.'[4] Every Christmas, Nandu would come home very early in the morning to slaughter the goat for the occasion. He was our family *qassai* (butcher), as none of us was either old enough or brave enough to kill the animal ourselves. We could manage chickens and ducks, messy though it all was; the frightened, uncomprehending eyes, the squirting blood and feathers flying about, the headless, lifeless body on the ground; but goats were another matter. Things had to be done in a certain way. Several pairs of hands were required to pin the animal tightly to the ground to prevent it from thrashing about as the knife sliced its throat, the muzzle had to be tied shut with a piece of rope or cloth to prevent the animal spewing undigested grass, the streaming blood (for curried black pudding) had to be collected properly in a *tharia* (bowl), sprinkled with salt to hasten coagulation. The limp body of the dead animal then had to be strung to a branch strong enough to bear the weight, the skinning had to be done in a particular way to avoid damaging the skin, which could later be used for making *dholak* (Indian drum), and the cutting up done carefully to avoid penetrating the stomach causing the messy spillover of its contents. Nandu was a slaughterer of considerable experience. As compensation, he would invariably take the head and the stomach. Mother once remarked that instead of slicing the throat close to the head, Nandu was cutting it closer to the shoulder of the animal and so taking a larger portion. But there was nothing anyone could do about it.

---

4   William Shakespeare, *The Tempest*, in *William Shakespeare: The Complete Works*, ed. Peter Alexander, (London and Glasgow: Collins, 1951; reprint 1980), pp. 1–26, 5.1.205–06.

Nandu was the most avid movie fan in the village. He would see every movie that came to the two Labasa theatres, the Majestic and the Elite—what improbable names in this most rustic of Fiji towns. Of all the people I have ever known, he had the most phenomenal memory for the plot, the dialogue and the songs. He would give us a blow-by-blow account for hours, make comparisons with other films he had seen. He knew the names of all the actors and actresses (Nimmi, Nalini Jayant, Suraiya, Ashok Kumar, Dilip Kumar, Raj Kapoor, Pran), what they wore, what they looked like, who spoke the best lines. He would imitate the dialogue to our unbounded delight. We hardly ever went to town, some 9 miles (14.5 kilometres) away; cinema was simply beyond our reach. Nandu was our only link to that world of magic and fantasy. He was not only a movie buff, he was also a 'bush' movie historian. He would regale us with side-splitting tales of the old timers going to the movies for the first time when they began arriving in Labasa in the late 1930s. Once, some of them quickly opened their umbrellas in the theatre when they saw rain on the screen! On another occasion, they all got up with their palms folded in prayer when they saw the image of Lord Rama on the screen. It might have been the film *Ram Baan* (Ram's arrow). Some of them began ducking and weaving in their seats, swaying from one side to the other, to avoid the arrows flying on the screen. They took sides with the main characters, getting visibly agitated with the villains, shouting them down, interrupting the dialogue. These and similar stories would be later recounted by some unkind Viti Levu people to remind us, the people of Labasa, of our rustic beginnings and innocent social habits, to put us in our proper place—at the bottom of the social ladder.

Jhankar (weekly film magazine). Every Saturday, Nandu would cycle to town and buy a copy of the weekly magazine published by Tara Press, *Nasinu*. Loose-leafed, these would contain the lyrics of our favourite film songs (*Nain mile nain hue bawre, chain kahan mere sajan sawren*), which we would immediately commit to memory and hum for the rest of week, news about forthcoming releases and who was acting in them, publicity material on stars (*Kalakaar ki parichay*), information about how films were made (*Filme kaise banti hain*). We read about the role of camera men, sound engineers, mike men, make-up men, but with no precise idea of what or who they were. The weekly also had a question and answer session with the editor, Gyani Das, with such delicious enquiries as 'Which is a greater intoxicant, alcohol or love?' We, of course, had no idea; we had experience of neither. 'Can a sightless man fall in love like the rest of us?'

'Love was a matter of the heart, not sight,' the readers were told. 'What do women cherish the most?' Answer: 'Once their unblemished character, now jewellery.' Nandu kept most issues of the magazine. They are with me now, a priceless archive of vanished memories.

Besides *Jhankar,* he also bought Hindi newspapers. There were several with, as I now recognise, different ideological bents. *Shanti Dut* (Messenger of peace) was timid. *Fiji Samachar* was progressive but politically neutral. Nandu always bought *Jagriti* (The new dawn), with its distinctly and unapologetically pro-Indian bias, instilling in us pride in our culture and history, stiffening our spine, asking us to stand up for our rights against the CSR, for example, and against petty acts of racial discrimination practised by the colonial government. Being a colonial subject was nothing to be proud of. I now recognise in the journal the faint origins and character of my own political thinking. *Jagriti* was an integral part of the project of cultural rejuvenation in the Indian community. We would read the news aloud to our illiterate parents, and occasionally at village gatherings. Sometimes, discussions would go long into the night, especially if it touched the sugar industry, our lifeline.

Radio came late to the village, sometime in the 1950s. By then, the shadow of indenture was receding and we were beginning to find our feet on the ground. Schools were being founded in most Indian settlements: Tabia Sanatan Dharam School was established in 1945, and Nandu was among its first pupils, present at creation, so to speak, and full of stories, real and imagined, about life in the pioneering days. I first went to Tabia Sanatan in 1959.

'A hunter of shadows, himself a shade.'[5] Along with all his good deeds, Nandu was also an inventor of tall tales. Everyone in the village, especially children, was afraid of the dark. The night world, we believed, was full of unseen evil forces: *bhoot-pret* (ghosts and evil spirits), *shaitan* or *satan* (ghost), *churail* (female ghost). We all believed in *jadu tona* (magic and witchcraft), and feared the worst if we incurred someone's wrath. Unnatural deaths were a particular cause of concern. If someone committed suicide or drowned, the soul would continue to linger on in the world until its appropriate, predestined time of departure, 'Doom'd for a certain term to

---

5   Homer, *Odyssey* 11. 572, trans. Samuel Butler, *The Internet Classics Archive,* 800 B.C.E., available at classics.mit.edu/Homer/odyssey.html (accessed 18 April 2019).

walk the night.'[6] Nandu would tell us about someone always jumping off the Vunibacea Bridge at midnight, and we assumed it was Ram Lal's wife who had drowned in the river. He would talk about soft, wailing noises at a particular road junction, leaving no doubt in our minds that it was Pati Fua's son, Shiu, who had hanged himself from the branch of a mango tree in a gully over his wife's affair with a neighbour. He would tell us about seeing lights swaying in the distant hills at certain times of the night. And he would warn us to avoid taking a certain path after dark because it was the favourite gathering place for ghosts. Any noise in the dark, even if it was from a mongoose scurrying across fallen mango leaves, would induce scrotum-shrivelling fear in us. If we had to run some errand at night, we always did it in company, never alone. Nandu enjoyed our discomfort, he told us many years later. When my brothers and I reflect on those distant days, we realise how gullible, how innocent, we were.

Kama Sutra delights

Nandu was a favourite of unmarried boys in the village who got their introduction to the business of bees and birds from him. It is blush-making even now to recall the detailed instructions and advice he gave within our earshot about positions and techniques and the wonderful pleasures possible in the bedroom, although we were too young to fully grasp everything he said. A few copies of well-thumbed Hindi books of sex and romance were known to be secretly circulating in the village. I suppose every village had its Nandu, who could talk about a subject taboo at home. The business of turning boys into men was always left to someone like Nandu. The practice persists to this day. Girls got their instructions and advice in sexual matters from some senior sister-in-law in the village who had similar licence. Nandu also fancied himself as a Lothario. Behind his back, we called him Andoo Bhaiya, Brother Randy Bull. We all heard muffled rumours about his 'fence jumping' with Dhannu's second wife, much younger than him, from somewhere in Nasarawaqa. He always found some excuse to walk past our house to the cane farm where she often worked. People exchanged knowing glances about his movements, about what he was up to, or would soon be. There was much more going on in the cane fields besides hoeing and weeding.

---

6   Shakespeare, *Hamlet*, in *William Shakespeare: The Complete Works*, ed. Alexander, pp. 1028–72, 1.5.10.

7. 'THE BURDEN OF REMEMBRANCE'

Several furrows were being ploughed at the same time. There were, in truth, quite a few Lotharios in the village as I found out later, as there still are: probably more now as kava-crazed men are unable to perform. The whispers of what went on in the village beneath the tranquil veil and under the cover of darkness never ceases to amaze me. That world was invisible to outsiders.

I left the village, first to go to high school in town and then to university in Suva. With each passing year, my distance from village folk increased. I was getting engrossed in a world of books and ideas beyond even the imaginative horizon of most family and friends. I was becoming a stranger among them. Whenever I returned, a party would be organised and Nandu would always be invited home, and sometimes he would invite himself. We would drink late into the night and play cards. Playing cards was the favourite pastime of most village folk when we were growing up (*Tanni, Raja Pakad, Seven Hands*). Even now, when I get together with my brothers, we invariably play the card games of our childhood and laugh about the many cheating tactics we learnt from people like Nandu. Reunions were joyous occasions but there was not much conversation about what I was doing. Instead, during family get-togethers, I would often be regaled with some embarrassing incident from my past, such as wetting my pants on the first day of school, parents approaching our family with marriage proposals for me with several acres of freehold land as 'dowry', the girls, now women with children of their own, still enquiring about me and my whereabouts, or getting into a 'hissy fit' with some old village woman who joked about wanting to marry me. Sitabia, from across the river in Laqere, was particularly mischievous. My older sisters-in-law even now recall her antics and my embarrassment. Nostalgia was all we had in common, but it could take us only so far. Later, my brothers also left for Suva for jobs or education though their connection with the village was less tenuous than mine.

With the departure of the boys, life at home began to change slowly. Pitaji (Father) became increasingly dependent on Nandu. While the boys were still at home, they would read and interpret official documents for him, whether they were notices from the Native Land Trust Board about the renewal of lease or cane payment notices from the Fiji Sugar Corporation about how much money was deducted for what purpose (cost of fertiliser, delivery services, cane inspection). Now, Pitaji had to turn to Nandu for help. He began demanding payment in cash or kind, usually the latter in the form of cigarettes, *yaqona,* a chicken or two if some writing or calculation was involved. 'Nothing free now,' he would say. Pitaji had the distinct impression that Nandu resented intrusions on his time and was increasingly uneasy about it. It was very painful then, but I can now understand Nandu's reaction. He saw us moving on to better jobs and careers, to newer worlds full of promise and opportunity, while he remained stuck in the village. Village life for us was limited detention; for him, it was a life imprisonment. He had his own young family to look after, daughters to marry in due course, and boys to send to secondary school. He resented assisting with the education of someone else's children.

The distancing showed itself in unexpected ways. Nandu was the president of the village of Ramayan Mandali. As president, he decided the order of the Ramayan recital, and we began to be allocated the most inconvenient times, close to school holidays or festive occasions. Nandu himself, an avid reader of the Ramayan, began missing sessions regularly as if he did not care anymore. More troubling was the allocation of the sequence of cane harvesting. Every year, before harvesting began, the village cane committee would meet to decide the order of harvesting. Nandu was on that committee. Everyone tried to avoid the rainy season, which set in around late October. The feeder roads would then become unserviceable, and the rivers and creeks would swell up, which would make truck crossing difficult. Those farms located on slopes furthest from the main road and those that were in low-lying areas and subject to flooding were harvested first. But old principles of allocation were being discarded for no apparent reason. Nandu began demanding 'something on the side' for a 'proper' decision. And he began demanding money for the odd green jackfruit on his farm that our family picked for food. It was the same with coconuts. It was not so much the money as it was the attitude that it expressed; a broad hint of an altered relationship that troubled Father.

Pitaji was too old to do the backbreaking work in the cane field. Arthritis had taken its toll, his back was giving in, and age was beginning to have its effect. We all decided that it would be best to ask Nandu to take over the farm on a sharecropping basis. He would keep half the proceeds after expenses and we would have the other 50 per cent. At first, it worked well, but over time things changed. Nandu began deducting expenses for small amounts of family labour, hoeing and weeding, and began charging exorbitant amounts for fertilisers and weed killers, which he bought from his friends rather than from the sugar company itself. Money was changing hands beneath the counter. Most visits to the town were charged to the cane account. All the expenses were carefully written down in a notebook, but Pitaji was illiterate and there was no way to verify them. It was Nandu's words against others. We all recognised that something was awry, but there was little we could do from overseas. We contemplated selling the farm and buying a small house near the town, but Pitaji was a village man through and through. He had his routine and his favourite animals. It was his place; that is where he belonged. 'In the town, I will just be waiting to die,' he would often say.

'With useless endeavor, / Forever, forever, / Is Sisyphus rolling / His stone up the mountain!'[7] It was not a good time to be a farmer. The price of cane was down. 'Pocket change' is what most canegrowers got after the expenses were deducted. Even worse, many leases were not being renewed. At first we thought the Fijian landowners wanted their land back so that they themselves could enter cane cultivation. That happened in some places, surprising us with how good Fijians could be if they put their mind to farming. But, as usual, the picture was much more complicated. Many interests were at play. Someone was always ready to pounce on someone else's tragedy. We had heard that in Soi Soi and Laqere some farmers had surreptitiously approached individual landowners with a *ghoos* (bribe) to reserve the land adjacent to theirs to cultivate either for rent or on a sharecropping basis. Outsiders had no idea about this side of village life, but old certainties and assumptions about good neighbourly relations were disappearing rapidly. We were, once again, becoming a collection of individual families rather than a cohesive community with common purpose and common identity. The displaced farmer, if he was young and able, would then look for another place, usually in a remote part of the island to start all over again. More commonly, the farmers would leave cane farming altogether, migrate to Viti Levu and settle in the mushrooming squatter settlements near major towns and cities, or acquire a piece of abandoned Crown land on the outskirts of Nausori or some other town and grow vegetables for the local market. This would be the first stop in a long and unpredictable journey of displacement. Seeing people on the move reminded me of an earlier journey of desperation and displacement, the journey of our indentured forebears. History can cruelly repeat itself.

---

7   Henry Wadsworth Longfellow, 'The house of Epimetheus', in *The Masque of Pandora and Other Poems* (Boston, MA: James R. Osgood and Co., 1876), pp. 21–27, V, 86–89.

The idea of playing a similar game of bribery and betrayal also entered Nandu's head. His own piece of land was around 5 acres (2 hectares), and if our family land were added to his, the acreage would substantially increase to 15 (6 hectares). He would get our very productive rice farm in the bargain as well as the hilly part for grazing goats. His chance came when our lease was up for renewal and Father turned to Nandu for advice and assistance with the paperwork. Nandu thought of doing what others had done before him, approaching the landlord Sirsa, a chief in the Tabia koro. We, of course, had no idea who the landlord was. We were leasing our land through the Native Land Trust Board, which acted as the intermediary between the tenants and the landowners. This arrangement had its advantages. It avoided face-to-face confrontation. It reduced the possibility of corruption; once the rent was paid and the papers signed, the tenant would be left alone. But it also meant that both the tenants and the landlords were 'faceless' to each other, just names on a piece of paper. So when the life of leases was threatened, we could not approach the landlord for some consideration because we didn't know who he was.

Nandu approached Sirsa through the local shopkeeper Hari Prasad. Hari was not a local but a recent arrival from Wailevu. I did not know him, but people talked about him as someone agile, a doer and deliverer. For a certain 'cut', he could secure deals that no one else could. And he delivered for Nandu. Precisely how much money was involved is not known, but it would have been at least $5,000, which Hari loaned for a substantial 15 per cent interest. That, people said, was 'the going rate' in the village. Nandu told Pitaji that the landlord had decided not to renew the lease because he had some other, as yet unknown, plans for it. The news devastated Pitaji. This was ancestral property. This was the first and the only thing his indentured father had owned in Fiji. This was the land on which he was born, where his children were born. This was the only world he knew.

'Fire in one hand, water in the other.'[8] Nandu appeared solicitous, muttering soothing words about how this was the way things were going everywhere. Entire villages in Daku, Wainkoro, Lagalaga and Nagigi had been uprooted and returned to bush, the families left to wander about the island or migrate to Viti Levu for good. He then broke the news that he had been asked to take over the land on a sharecropping basis for

---

8   This quote is attributed to Rābi'a al-'Adawiyya (713–801 AD), a Muslim saint and great woman Sufi mystic.

the landlord, which he had 'reluctantly' agreed to do. 'But what would happen to us?' Pitaji asked. 'Where would we go?' Nandu assured him that he would remain where he was for a small residential rent. That was the least he could do. As for income, well, we, his children, could all contribute, which would easily see him through. 'Thank God, you don't have too many more years to go.' He was right about that. Pitaji died a few months later.

Hari Prasad, the shop owner, was watching and learning from the deals and betrayals going on all around him. He began to have bigger dreams himself. Selling goods on credit to the struggling canefarmers was small change, and Hari wanted to catch a bigger fish. There was no bigger fish in Tabia now than its biggest landlord, Sirsa. He was the man to cultivate. Hari opened the doors of his shop to him. 'Anything for you, *Bosso*,' he would say to Sirsa. 'Money is nothing among friends.' He could buy anything he wanted on credit, with no requirement for timely repayment: cartons of tinned mutton and fish, bags of flour and rice, dozens of cartons of sweet drinks. Hari arranged for the delivery of corrugated iron and wood for the construction of a new house for Sirsa. His children received gifts of fancy floral shirts and sandals and bales of cloth for *sulu* (kilt-like garment worn by Fijian men). Sirsa, everyone knew, was a big man; now he lived like one, and he wanted the world to take note. *Hum hiyan ke raja baitho,* I am the king of this place. He even began dreaming about a political career for himself. Hari encouraged him.

After a year or so, Sirsa's credit with Hari mounted to around $20,000. It was time for Hari to make his move. He began to ask for repayment. But Sirsa had no money, and the banks would not lend him any either. This suited Hari perfectly for he did not really want money. He had his eyes on Sirsa's land. He told Sirsa he would look after a man he counted among his closest friends and write off the debt in return for a 60-year lease on all his Tabia land for minimal rent. Sirsa was relieved. 'No problems, Bro. *E sab jamin ab thumar baitho. Koi parwah nahin.* All this land is now yours.' The next day, Hari and Sirsa went to the law offices of Shiri Chand and had the verbal agreement transformed into a formal document, accompanied by ample supplies of whisky and beer at the Grand Eastern Hotel. Hari was now not only the village's sole shopkeeper and its leading moneylender, he also became its largest 'landowner'. And he had big plans about developing cane and rice production as well. He also had plans to grow melon, cucumber, pumpkin, cabbage and other vegetables for the Nasea market. He was preparing for the future. He had heard that 'diversification' was the way to go.

Small tenants with poor production records would have to make way for more enterprising ones, and Hari had plenty to choose from. Nandu, he decided, was among those who would have to go. Where would he go, he asked Hari. 'But did you think about that when you took over Munnu's land?' Hari asked. Munnu was Pitaji's name. *Jaise karni, waise bharni,* you shall reap what you sow. Hari captured the standing crop to reclaim his loan. Nandu was literally left penniless. With nothing in Tabia to look forward to, he began to think about moving to Viti Levu. He knew some other distant relations who had relocated to the Nausori hinterland. Five-acre parcels of Crown land, once earmarked for rice growing, in places like Waituri, were available for leasing. He might be able to persuade someone to lease a piece that he could work as a sharecropper until he could buy one himself. His son, Rudra, returned with the good news and preparation began to dismantle the lean-to house for shipment to Suva. The day before they were due to take the ferry from the Nabouwalu jetty, Nandu died of a sudden heart attack.

'No trophy, sword, nor hatchment, o'er his bones, / No noble rite nor formal ostentation.'[9] The funeral was a paltry affair. About 20 people came, mostly elderly village folk. The younger ones had gone to work in the town, and extended family members from other parts of Labasa returned home the same day. In the past, they would have stayed around a little longer to grieve with the family or to help if it was needed. The body had been brought home in a wooden coffin, not on the traditional homemade stretcher of split bamboo poles and coconut leaves covered with white cloth and carried in an open truck. It was all very much as I had expected, though I was told that the customary 13-day mourning period was not observed. And immediate family members did not have their heads shaved as a sign of bereavement. These customs were on their way out all over Fiji, along with so many other ceremonies and rituals that had once been important to us but had now become irrelevant and burdensome—victims of rapidly modernising times.

---

9   Shakespeare, *Hamlet*, 4.5.210–11.

7. 'THE BURDEN OF REMEMBRANCE'

Nandu's death marked the end of a world of which I was once a part. He had through the years seen the emergence of a new community from a bedraggled collection of men and women who settled in Tabia after their indentures had expired. They had cleared the land, created farms, established families, gave shape to a nascent community and nourished its soul through education, cultural festivals and rituals. He had connected us, a generation later, to that past and revived in us, at least in me, an interest in its myriad dimensions. He had seen the village grow from nothing and then he had witnessed the old ties that bound the community slowly disintegrate from the corrosive effects of modernity beginning to push at the outer edges of the village. I was aware of Nandu's petty acts of duplicity and greed. He was no saint, but I don't have any bitterness towards him now. We all have our Nandus. We are a people like that, limited and pragmatic, adept at making 'a peaceful seepage into every opening left unclosed and a tenacious defence of every position once occupied', as the anthropologist W.E.H. Stanner put it more than half a century ago.[10]

I wonder, as, in a distant and wintry Canberra, I think of that vanished world, whether anyone among those who gathered to mourn Nandu's death really knew who Nandu was, where he had come from, whether in that mourning for a man, they might also be mourning the end of a time that was gone for good, never to return.

So sad, so strange, the days that are no more.[11]

---

10 W.E.H. Stanner, *The South Seas in Transition: A Study of Post-War Rehabilitation and Reconstruction in Three British Pacific Dependencies* (Sydney: Australasian Publishing Company, 1953), p. 179.
11 Alfred, Lord Tennyson, 'Canto IV', in *The Princess: A Medley* (New York, NY: American Book Co., 1896), pp. 68–88, line 35.

8
Frequent flyers

> I have an idea that some men are born out of their due place. Accident has cast them amid certain surroundings, but they have always a nostalgia for a home they know not … They may spend their whole lives aliens among their kindred and remain aloof among the only scenes they have ever known. Perhaps it is this sense of strangeness that sends men far and wide in the search of something permanent, to which they may attach themselves.
>
> — W. Somerset Maugham[1]

After the coup of 1987, more than 150,000 mostly Indo-Fijians left Fiji for other countries, principally North America and Australasia. The best and the brightest have left and many more would if they only could, draining the country of the talents and skilled manpower it can ill-afford to lose. There is by now much information available on the sociology and economics of migration from Fiji, but rather little is known about the extent of rupture and emotional trauma that displacement entails. The following story aims to capture the private experience of a couple of Indo-Fijians who migrated to Australia.

One by one they all went, selling their dream houses on Vale Levu Street in Tamavua's Namadi Heights. Once the pride of the most desired suburb of Suva, the place now looked deserted, unkempt, full of household rubbish on the side of streets and stray dogs wandering aimlessly looking for food. Soon after 1987, Ram and his wife Sashi had migrated to Vancouver,

---

1   W. Somerset Maugham, *The Moon and Sixpence* (New York, NY: George H. Doran Company, 1919; London: Vintage, 1999), p. 177.

Anish and Chitra left for Auckland and Ravi and Vikashni for Canberra. 'This trickle will turn to a torrent, you just wait, Bro,' Ram had said to me one day. And he was right too. It was not too long after the May 1987 coup that long queues formed in front of Australian, New Zealand and American embassies. Anyone who could leave was leaving. 'Immigration to Emigration, that should be the title of your next tome, Doc,' Anish had said. Ram, Anish and Krishna were my school mates from Labasa Secondary, sons of struggling canefarmers, like myself, but who had all done well. They had finished their commerce and law degrees in Auckland and Wellington, and were steadily climbing the local corporate ladder. Getting ahead in the quickest possible time was their main preoccupation. They felt genuinely sorry for me and my choice of a career as an historian.

'Why history when you could have done anything you liked?' Ram had wondered aloud once. 'Do law, Bro,' Ravi advised me. 'It is not too late yet.' 'And what, become a liar?' I had responded half in jest. 'Well, better a rich liar than a pious pauper,' he replied with a chuckle. 'Making a difference is what life should be about,' I had added, somewhat pompously. 'Yes, Mahatamaji. Making a fast buck will do me,' Anish had said, tapping me gently on the shoulder. True to their vocation and ambition, the three bought the best blocks on the street and built their dream homes modelled on architectural designs imported from Sydney and Auckland, double-storey structures with polished *dakua* and *damanu* (Fijian hardwood) floors, impressive barbeque sets, liquor cupboards full of the best imported spirits and wines, framed Monet and Picasso prints on the walls and the best local handicraft strategically displayed in the living room. It was their version of high living with class. What really upset them most about Rabuka's coup was that it so rudely disrupted their dreams of living long and well in this part of town. 'Fuck Fiji,' Ram had said when he was leaving. 'It is losing this house that really pisses me off.' 'And to see some bloody Fijian living in it,' Ravi had spat out bitterly.

For a while, we lost touch with each other as we all went our different ways. A few years after migrating, I heard that Ram had died in a horrible road accident while driving from Vancouver to Edmonton. I did not know Sashi well. Anish is doing well in Auckland and we meet every so often, but he has made a new start and Fiji is falling off his mental map. 'Why hanker for something that will never be yours,' he once wrote to me. I knew many migrants who felt that way about Fiji. Ravi remained close because we lived in the same town for a while when I returned to Canberra after a spell in Hawai'i before he moved to the western Sydney suburb of Newlands. A slightly idealistic streak in him appealed to me when Fiji was full of lawyers with no conscience or public mindedness. Vikashni was distantly related, the eldest daughter of Uncle Shiu Prasad of Waiqele, and that kept the link alive. Shared anxieties about starting afresh in a new place, the lurking fears of failure and losing face, the common demands of raising a young family in an unfamiliar cultural environment, had cemented the bonds.

Ravi and Vikashni and their two young children lived in Canberra's southern suburbs, in one of the outer affordable suburbs of the town where many young, starting families had homes. Nappy Valley they called it. Vicki had no difficulty finding a job as a nurse at the local hospital, and the two children were enrolled in Duffy Primary. Ravi was less lucky. He was without a job. He found it difficult to break into the fairly close-knit Australian legal profession. The leading law firms were full, so he was told, and there was no vacancy at the office of the Director of Public Prosecutions where migrant lawyers tended to get a start. He did odd jobs as a consultant, which in truth meant menial, mind-numbing work most lawyers passed on to their lowly subordinates. But mostly he stayed at home, picking up kids from the school and doing odd jobs around the house. Once a week he stuffed junk mail in the neighbourhood mail boxes. On weekends, he worked at the Jamieson Shopping Centre as a trolley collector, meeting and swapping stories with men from similar backgrounds from different parts of the world: Sudan, Croatia, Turkey, Ethiopia. Meeting these men helped Ravi know that he was not alone in his depression and desperation. Although from different parts of the world, they all shared similar experiences: frustration at not having their qualifications recognised, difficulties with children's expectations of parents, trying simply to survive with dignity.

Ravi was always on the quiet, almost withdrawn, side, but there was no hiding his unhappiness. In Fiji he was an up-and-coming lawyer, someone people looked up to, a figure of respect in the community, a trustee of many community schools, with a career in politics in the offing. In Australia, he had gone from being a little somebody to a big nobody, and prospects for improvement in the immediate future did not look bright. But he had his family to think of. Abhay and Apeksha had no future in Fiji, and he had no right to stand in their way. At least Vicki was employed. And Ravi tried to console himself that he was not alone in his predicament.

Vicki could see that Ravi was unsettled, and that disturbed her deeply. The last thing she wanted was to see him unhappy. She knew the sacrifices his family had made to see him through the law school. He was the first one in the family to finish secondary school. His parents had borrowed money to send him overseas, hoping that a foreign degree might give him a head start. In the typical Indian way, it was expected that after completing his law degree Ravi would help out with the education of his younger brothers, all bright boys with the potential to go places. That was the way things were done in Labasa, people getting out of the unending rural misery by standing on the shoulders of those who had gone before them. But, after 1987, it was thought best for Ravi to migrate so that he could one day sponsor all of them. Everyone was thinking that way.

Soon after Ravi had migrated, his father died of the heart attack he suffered when he had been told one day that his lease would not be renewed and that he would have to vacate his 10-acre (4-hectare) plot (to be leased out, it was later learnt, on a sharecropping basis, to the ever avaricious neighbour Mr Ram Jattan, who had quietly instigated the nonrenewal). Ravi knew then that his plans to settle down permanently in Australia would have to be put on hold for a while. Uppermost in his mind was the welfare of his elderly mother, Auntie Sukhdei. There were no close relations nearby to look after her. Migration papers would take a long time to be processed. Even if she did manage to leave, what would she do in Australia, someone illiterate in English and unfamiliar with western culture, cooped up in a suburban home with no Indo-Fijians in the neighbourhood? Ravi had seen some elderly lost-looking people passing time in shopping malls during winter, lonely, objects of pity, gawking vacantly at the passing human traffic. 'Waiting to die,' one of them had said to him one day.

'Maybe, you should return to Fiji for a while, Rav,' Vicki volunteered to Ravi one day. Ravi just looked at her somewhat startled by the suggestion. 'I mean, for a short while till Mum is settled down. I will manage things here.' 'But what about Abbie and Apes?' Ravi asked. 'Oh, they will be fine. They are like their father strong, or maybe I should say stubborn like a mule,' she said as she planted a kiss on his cheek. 'Oh Vick,' was all Ravi could manage. It was a brave and heartfelt gesture of support, but Ravi knew how hard it would be for Vicki raising two kids all by herself, running a household and working full-time. But he also knew in his heart that Vicki made sense.

A week or so later, Ravi rang Daven, his former law partner in Suva, to see if there was still a place for him there. 'Just for a short while till things settle down. May be a year or two at the most.' 'For as long as you want, Bro,' Daven said encouragingly. 'The business is down, but we could do with a good litigator. And you were just about the best we had.' 'Flattery will get you somewhere big one day,' Ravi replied relieved.

Ravi returned, rented a flat in Augustin Street and started where he had left off. The office staff welcomed him back warmly because they admired his kindly and compassionate ways. There was sympathy for him, perhaps more like pity. Soon life set into a routine. But charm and the excitement that had so animated life on the Vale Levu Street appeared to have deserted the city. Many of his close friends had left, were leaving, or making plans to go. Real estate prices were plummeting. The streets looked forlorn, full of potholes and filth, houses were unpainted and covered with soot and shops full of shoddy goods. His former suburb was a ghost of its earlier self; the promise of the early years disappearing without a trace. The old moral order seemed to be collapsing too. Incest cases had increased dramatically, the newspapers regularly carried horror stories about the sexual abuse of children, prostitution, suicide cases because of failure in exams or because of tangled love affairs, increasing divorce rates and domestic violence. Something in society was snapping—the sense of order and purpose and cohesiveness. Everyone seemed to be for themselves. Perhaps these had always existed, but they were becoming more visible now. Ravi found the sight of young girls and women from broken homes congregating at the Triangle or at the post office early in the evenings distressing.

Days were easy to pass, while he was occupied in the office or appearing in the courts. And there was the ever-present *tanoa* (kava bowl) and regular lunches at the Cottage, the local eatery. Nights were a nightmare for Ravi. It was not as if Augustin Street did not have nocturnal charms of its own. It was full of men, like Ravi, early to middle age, whose families were safely 'parked' outside the country but who had returned to resume their old jobs. There was plenty of duty-free liquor around, and boozy dinner parties were a regular feature of the street. Women were in plentiful supply too, single mothers, girls from desperately poor homes, university students earning much-needed cash on the side. 'Buyer's market,' everyone said. Some men were secretly glad to have their wives out of the way so they could indulge their perverted sexual fantasies. But this was not Ravi's way.

He was a light drinker, and he missed his family. In an old-fashioned way, he believed sex outside marriage was sinful. He resolved that he would try and visit Vicki and the kids once every six to eight weeks.

These reunions were in the beginning joyous occasions. The kids enquired enthusiastically about 'relos' back home: Nana, Nani, about the neighbours and the kids, about Tipu their dog, and Rani the cat. Vicki cooked food that Ravi liked: spicy lamb and crab curry, various varieties of dhal. They frequented the Belconnen and Fyshwick markets for fish and fresh fruits and vegetables. Ravi went to Abhay's soccer matches and to Apeksha's musical performances. They hiked in the Brindabellas, had picnics at the Cotter Dam. Occasionally, they drove to Sydney for the weekend, and the kids enjoyed Darling Harbour. Vicki introduced Ravi to her friends, most of whom were working at the hospital. 'The mystery man,' they would joke. 'Here today, gone tomorrow.' An elderly man had said to him, 'Be careful young man, Vicki is a real head turner.' Vicki blushed, but Ravi never doubted her fidelity. Time flew. Before they knew it, it was time to return home. The goodbyes were heart-wrenching. Then the routine returned.

Both Ravi and Vicki knew that they would have to find ways of occupying themselves apart from work. Ravi joined the Rotary Club, Suva East Branch. Rotarians were progressive people doing good things, helping raise funds for scholarships, buying computers for schools and organising book bins for the community libraries. There was regular fellowship, which kept Ravi informed and connected. Periodic forays into the countryside, whether it was a drive to Rakiraki through Monasavu, or exploring the lush, craggy mountain ranges of the Serua-Namosi hinterland, opened up new areas that had been hidden to him, and to most people in Fiji. Some Rotarians were from Australia on various assignments in Fiji, and they brought along Australian newspapers and magazines to the 'make-up' sessions, which kept Ravi reasonably well informed about events in Australia.

Vicki, too, was keen to escape the ever-threatening loop of loneliness, and in this she was encouraged by her friends at work. She cut her hair short and began wearing skirts and pants rather than the traditional *salwar kamiz* (Indian women's dress), which had been the cornerstone of her sartorial repertoire in Fiji, attracting disapproving looks from some of her Fiji friends. She began to take cooking lessons at a friend's house in Garran, both out of choice as well as necessity. Abhay and Apeksha complained that their friends at school always made funny faces at them at lunch time. They did not like the smell of curry and roti. Some had called them 'curry munchers'. 'Why can't you be like other mums, for a change,' Abhay had once snapped at her, more in frustration than anger. 'Pasta would be good for a start.' Vicki was hurt, but not surprised. After all, they were the ones who had come to this country, and they should adjust and not always insist on hanging on to the old ways. And so she had a go at Italian, Greek and Lebanese cuisine. She also joined the Mums for Duffy Soccer Club, for which Abhay played. The club prepared sandwiches and coffee and tea for the weekend matches and little munchies for the boys. Sometimes she would accompany the team on their weekend retreats to Cooper's Creek. She became a member of the Duffy Parents' Association and helped out at the weekend fetes. Then there was the Duffy Mothers' Book Club, which met on the first Tuesday of every month. All the weekend activities were exhausting, but Vicki didn't complain. As things fell into a pattern, she actually looked forward to her various activities.

A new world was beginning to open up to her, expanding her horizon in unanticipated ways. She had a new and widening circle of friends, mostly Australians. That she found refreshing because most Fiji women had few interests outside home and most were caught in the 'keeping up with the Jones's' world. Vicki found her Australian friends curious about Fiji. Several of them had visited the country and wanted to know more. Mrs Swinstead, the wife of the former Westpac manager at Lautoka, asked Vicki to give talks about Fiji to her friends in the University of the Third Age. At first, self-conscious, she quickly read up on whatever she could find in the Woden Library, and shared her thoughts and experiences, gaining confidence each time she gave public addresses. She talked about the Indo-Fijians, how they got there, the Colonial Sugar Refining Company (CSR), the coup. She helped her friends' kids with their school assignments about Indian religion and culture, about which she briefed herself surreptitiously. Vicki was what you might call your model migrant: sensitive to the local environment, eager to learn new ways, to contribute whatever and wherever she could, ever ready to 'have a go'.

Abhay and Apeksha too were adapting in their own ways. At first they were shy. Their English was not fluent, and they had a lot to learn about Australian culture and ways of doing things. But in no time, they had mastered the lingo and the local dress code, including pierced ears, trendily torn jeans and spiky hairstyles. Abhay was a natural at sports; good in soccer, as most Fiji boys are, but getting better at cricket too.

Apeksha took to popular culture like duck to water. She caught up on shows like *Home and Away* and *Shortland Street*. She went over to her friends' places for sleepovers, and boys came to Abhay's place, drinking coke and eating ordered pizzas, lying about on the floor watching videos and playing Nintendo. Vicki bought a second-hand billiard table, which kept the boys at home within her earshot.

Ravi's visits were still looked forward to, but not with the same anticipation as the first visits. Fiji was weighing Ravi down, sometimes against his own will. The daily news of harassment somewhere, the religious bigotry, the glass ceiling in the public service, the increase in incidents of violent burglaries, the regularly interrupted water supply and electricity, the palpable sense of despair among his people. In the courts, he did cases involving incest, rape, attempted suicide and domestic violence—all on the rise. It was all coming apart at the seams right in front of his eyes. So much promise, he thought to himself, so much of it gone to waste so quickly. When visiting Canberra, he continued worrying about events back home. But the children, and latterly Vicki too, had been showing less and less interest in what was happening in Fiji.

When Ravi mentioned this to Vicki one day, she replied, 'Well, Rav, sometimes to move forward, we have to switch the lights off, shut the door and move on.' It was not that she did not care about Fiji, but now there were so many other things to think about. The children, for example. 'Do they care about anything?' Ravi asked. They seemed to him to be obsessed with mundane trivia. 'They do, Rav, but it is not easy being a teenager in this society.' Vicki knew about the drug problems and teenage pregnancies plaguing the local schools, and was thankful her children were safe in the company of good, clean friends. She was watchful and observant. Nothing escaped her. When Ravi mentioned seeing Abhay with a stubby in his room, Vicki said, 'Count your blessings if the worst they are doing is beer.'

There were many things that upset Ravi, but he realised there was no point raising them. Kids were staying up regularly till long past midnight watching television. Their rooms were a health hazard, with clothes, empty coke cans, junk food wrappers and magazines lying around. There was never any offer of help with housework or in the kitchen. Ravi dreaded talking to his children, fearing their sharp, snappy responses. Once he asked Abhay about his school work, and he had replied, 'Not that shit again, Dad.' 'But that's why we came here, Abbie, for you guys.' 'Don't put the guilt trip on me, man. Look, school is not the end of the world. If I stuff up, so what? There's heaps of other things I can do.' Apeksha lived in a world of her own and, knowing her temper tantrums, Ravi thought it best to leave her alone. This was no way to live family life, but he seemed helpless.

When Ravi mentioned his conversation with Abhay to Vicki, she felt genuinely sorry for her husband. This was no way to talk to their father, she agreed. 'I will talk to him,' she promised. But there was a deeper point lurking in Ravi's head. What hurt him most was that he could not talk to his own son in a language that he could understand about things that really mattered to him. He simply could not enter his son's world, try as he might. All he had was his own experience to go by. 'That's all I know, Vick,' he said one day. 'All we can do is to be here for them when they need us,' Vicki replied. 'That's all, and hope that things will come good.' 'Thank God, we at least have each other,' Ravi said. When Ravi came over in the early days, Vicki would adjust whatever she had on in her calendar to suit Ravi's schedule. His happiness and satisfaction were her priority. But now she had her own routine, which she was loathe to break. Thursday evenings would be her yoga classes. On Fridays she went to the gym. Then there were regular outings with her friends. On these occasions, Ravi would have to make do with whatever was left over in the fridge or order a pizza for himself. Cooking was never his forte. In Suva, his house girl took care of all his domestic chores. All he had to do was to issue the order for the day. His grocery shopping was done for him. His clothes were washed and ironed, shoes polished. But in Australia, all these chores he had to do by himself.

Small things magnified the growing difference. Vicki, very health conscious, would have a light dinner of salad and soup, perhaps, or even Asian noodles, whereas Ravi had gotten used to home-cooked roti and spicy curry. He was indifferent about breakfast and lunch, but dinner had to be taken in the traditional Indian style, eaten with fingers. He really couldn't ask Vicki to cook every evening for him, and yet he missed his routine. Vicki had her own favourite television programs, soaps and serials, which she watched religiously, asking friends to tape the ones she missed for whatever reason. She would try to get Ravi involved by telling him about the various plots and how they were connected, but they had little meaning for him. Once or twice he thought to himself: 'The world is going to the dogs, half of humanity is mired in desperate poverty and here everyone is glued to meaningless, juvenile love entanglements.' Whenever he tried to switch on to the news channels, he felt that his family was merely tolerating him. 'I have had a hard day,' Vicki would say, a cue to watch something light before retiring to bed. Local stories that stirred public opinion and filled the airwaves meant little to Ravi. Kangaroo culling was big news, which had been picked by animal liberation people in many places, including Japan, as did passionate stories about the closure of primary schools in emptying suburbs, the construction of jails and roads close to inhabited areas, stories about the wayward ways of local and national politicians, about refugees and boat people and asylum seekers. What mattered most to him, Fiji, was hardly ever mentioned in the news and yet Ravi knew that Fiji was churning.

In the early days, Ravi could talk to Vicki about Fiji, but now her interests were captured by things closer to home. She cared deeply about what happened in the neighbourhood about which Ravi could not care less. For Vicki, Fiji was beginning to fade from her mental radar, just as it was beginning to imprison Ravi. Family connections too were becoming tenuous. Many of both Ravi's and Vicki's families and friends had already migrated, or were planning to. Vicki saw little point in hanging on to the memories of a place that had caused such rupture and anguish in their lives. Vicki became gradually aware of Ravi's unsettled behaviour and tried to introduce him to her friends from work. Once or twice she organised barbeques at home. She invited him to drinks after work, to the occasional Sunday picnics at Cotter. Her friends were decent, well-meaning people but with limited experience. They asked simple questions about Fiji and told him about people from there they had met. The outings were nice, but they only temporarily alleviated Ravi's growing sense of isolation. 'Pity about Fiji, mate. It didn't have to be a four letter word,' a man once said to him. It was a cue to change the subject.

Reestablishing links with the Fiji people might help, Vicki thought, and on several occasions they drove to Sydney to participate in festivals, musical evenings and fundraisers for various causes. Ravi knew some of the people, but they had all moved on. Some of them talked about house prices, playing the share market, golf and overseas holidays. Full of pretension, living well for them was the best form of revenge. Fiji was furthest from their minds. Others remembered the trauma surrounding their departure from Fiji and said, and hoped, that things would never improve there. Revenge and retribution was what they wanted. For Ravi, there were few points of contact and exploration.

One day, about two years ago, Ravi distinctly sensed that his visits were not as warmly welcomed as they once had been. The children now barely acknowledged his presence. Fiji was fast becoming another country to them. They were losing the language and whatever they had learned of traditional Indian culture. They now only vaguely recalled the names of their younger cousins and extended family members. They lived in a virtual world of their own. And Vicki had created a network of friends and associates who were a vital source of support and encouragement for her. They were almost like a family, perhaps even closer than the family she had back in Fiji.

Now sometimes the kids asked, 'When are you returning to Fiji, Dad?' The question spoke not of concern but of relief at the return of routine unhindered by the presence of a vanishing figure in their lives. Ravi realised, sadly, that he was a guest in his own home. 'We can't go on like this, Vicki,' he said one day. 'This is no way to live a family life. I seem to have become a stranger to my own children.' The growing distance between Ravi and Abhay and Apeksha had not escaped Vicki. And she understood, although it was unspoken, that Ravi would prefer Vicki to live with him in Fiji. 'This is home now, Ravi,' she said to him. 'We have nothing back in Fiji.' 'But what will I do here,' Ravi asked, not really expecting an answer, wondering aloud. He had a job in Fiji, a lifestyle he liked, some friends with whom he had shared much over the years. Despite everything that had happened, he still had a presence in the community. People looked up to him, and he liked helping out whenever he could: filling forms, witnessing documents, giving free legal advice to community and charitable organisations. Life had a purpose and a meaning beyond simply the act of living.

'It's always about you, isn't it?' Vicki said.

> Always. 'What will I do?' Have you thought about us, me and the children? What will we do there? Abbie and Apes are still in high school. I can't simply abandon them just like that. They are too young to be left alone.

And they had other obligations to meet as well. They had just renovated their house, with a big loan from the bank. The new car had to be paid off. Apeksha was preparing to spend an exchange year in Japan, and money would be needed for that as well. And Vicki had a secure, satisfying job, which she was grateful to have. Ravi knew that Vicki was sensible and rational. Why would anyone give up a secure job to return to uncertainty?

They talk about bloodless coups, Ravi thought to himself, but some things are worse than death. He was exaggerating, but only just. The thought of rupturing his relationship with Vicki never once entered his mind, despite all the turbulence and uncertainty of recent years, nor did the thought of keeping two kitchens, as the expression goes, ever enter his mind. 'You play the hand you are dealt' was almost his motto. He thought he would remain a commuter, a frequent flyer for the foreseeable future.

Postscript

But then, two years later, fate intervened in the form of George Speight. The fraudulent Fijian nationalist overthrew another democratically elected government, derailing the process of reconciliation that had promised to restore hope and opportunity to an ill-fated Fiji. 'Indians are different,' he told the world with a smirk. 'They act different, they eat different and they smell different. They are heathens.' 'They will reduce this place to rubble,' Daven, Ravi's law partner, said of the coup makers, 'and finally claim this country as their own. Fiji for the Fijians, finally.' 'Democracy is indeed a foreign flower here. We have no place in it,' he said ruefully on another occasion. 'We will never belong, Bro, never be invited to belong.' He was selling his law practice to relocate to Auckland. 'Life is too short for this shit.'

Labasa was emptying, reverting to bush, as people were moving to the mushrooming squatter settlements around Suva. Joining the exodus were Ravi's own brothers and nieces and nephews, embarking on the first step of a journey that would eventually take them to foreign shores. Auntie Sukhdei's death finally settled the issue for Ravi. Fiji, with its unending saga of violence and treachery and racial hatreds, lost its hold on his soul. It no longer felt like home anymore. There was nothing left for him in Fiji. I'd rather be a little nobody in Australia than a big somebody over here, Ravi finally resolved. Life would not be a bed of roses there, he would have to learn and listen hard again, reconnect with his family, reenter their world on their terms, not his own. 'I will always have my memories,' Ravi thought to himself, as he packed up, thinking about his childhood, chasing his cousin around the cane fields, meeting Vicki, the birth of his children. He knew of the long and lonely road ahead, full of unpredictable twists and turns, but he was glad to give up the life of a frequent flyer. He was finally going home.

9

Mr Arjun goes to Australia[1]

> What we have once enjoyed we can never lose …
> All that we have loved deeply becomes a part of us.
>
> — Helen Keller[2]

Emigration is now a permanent theme in the life of the Indo-Fijian community. Anyone who can, wants to leave. This piece once again touches on the theme of the trauma and tragedy of migration explored in the previous chapter. Soon after the coup of 1987 and the convulsions that followed, many Indo-Fijians sought desperately to emigrate, leaving behind elderly parents and relatives who did not meet the criteria for emigration. Some visited their children and grandchildren later, only to realise a gulf now separated them from their children. Mr Arjun's experience will find resonance in the lives of many others.

I seldom visit Tabia now, the village of my birth and childhood. The place is a labyrinth of haunting memories of happier, more innocent times better left untouched. But on the rare occasion I do, I always make an effort to see Arjun Kaka. Now in his late 70s, he is the only one in the whole village who has a direct connection to my father's generation—the last link to a fading past. He knows my interest in history and we talk endlessly about past events and people at every opportunity. Kaka is unlettered and a vegetarian and teetotaller. Everyone in the village knows him as a man

---

1 Originally appeared in Bruce Connew, *Stopover: A Journey of Migration* (Honolulu: University of Hawai'i Press, (2007), pages unnumbered.
2 Helen Keller, *The Open Door* (New York, NY: Doubleday, 1957), p. 131.

of integrity, a man with a completely unblemished reputation. His wife died about a decade ago and he now lives on the farm with the family of his deceased son. The other three boys, bright and educated, migrated to Australia after 1987. He misses them desperately, for this is not the way he had wanted to spend his twilight years. He now wished one of them had remained behind. There is no telephone in the house and the letters from his children are rare. He wonders about his grandchildren, how old they are, what they look like, if they remember him, ruminating like old men usually do.

A few years ago, covering a general election, I went to Labasa and visited Kaka. 'Why don't you visit Krishna and the other two boys, Kaka,' I said after he had mentioned how badly he missed his children. 'At my age, *beta,* son, it is difficult,' he said sadly. 'You know I cannot read and write. Besides, my health is not good.' 'Kaka, so many people like you travel all the time,' I reminded him. 'Look at Balram, Dulare and Ram Rattan.' Formerly of Tabia, they had moved to town when their leases were not renewed. Kaka nodded but did not say anything. Then an inspired thought occurred to me. I was returning to Australia from my sabbatical a few weeks later and could take Kaka with me. When I made the offer, his face lit up, all the excuses forgotten. They were excuses, really, nothing more, a deep desire to travel but not knowing how. '*Beta, e to bahut julum baat hai,*' he said, 'this is very good news indeed, son.' He embraced me. 'You are like my own son. Bhaiya [my father] would be very proud of you.' If truth be known, since dad's death, I had regarded Arjun Kaka as a father figure.

'Have many people left Labasa in recent years?' I asked Kaka. There was a time when going to Suva was considered 'going overseas', an experience recounted in glorious and often embroidered detail for years. Australia and New Zealand were out of the question. 'The place is emptying day by day, especially since all the *jhanjhat* (trouble) started.' He meant the coup. 'There is no growth, no hope. Young people, finishing school, leave for Suva. No one returns. There is nothing to return to.' '*Dil uth gaye*', Kaka said, 'the heart is no longer here.' Kaka's observation reinforced what I had been told in Suva. There was hardly a single Indo-Fijian family in Fiji that did not have at least one member abroad. 'The best and the brightest are leaving,' a friend had remarked in Suva. 'Only the *chakka panji,* hoi poloi, remain.' The wealthy and the well-connected had their families safely 'parked' in Australia and New Zealand, he had said. An interesting way of putting it, I thought, suggesting temporariness, a readiness to move again if the need arose. I had heard a new phrase to describe this new phenomenon: frequent-flyer families. Those safely abroad talked of loyalty and commitment to Fiji, of returning one day, but it was just that, talk, nothing more. I felt deeply for people who were trapped and terrorised in Fiji, victims of fate, living in suffering and sufferance.

As the news of Kaka's planned trip to Australia spread, people were genuinely happy for him. At Tali's shop the following evening, Karna bantered. '*Ek memia lete aana, yaar,* bring a white woman along with you.' '*Kab tak bichari patoh tumhar sewa kari,* how long will your poor daughter-in-law continue to look after you?' 'Learn some English words,' Mohan advised. 'Thank you, goodbye, hello, how are you, mate.' He was the village bush lawyer. 'Make sure you are all *suit-boot*, well-dressed, not like this', referring to Kaka's khaki shorts and fading floral shirt. 'We don't want others thinking that we are *ganwaar,* country bumpkins.' 'Which we are,' Haria interjected to mild tittering. Bhima wondered whether some of the *kulambars* (Colonial Sugar Refining Company (CSR) overseers) were still alive and whether Arjun Kaka might be able to meet some of them in Australia. Mr Tom, Mr Oxley, Mr Johnson.

Mr Tom: now there was a name from ancient history. He was the first white man I ever saw. Tall, thin, white hard hat, his face like a red tomato in the midday sun, short-sleeve shirt and trousers, socks pulled up to the knees, the shirt pocket bulging with pens and a well-thumbed notebook. The overseers had a bad reputation as heartless men driven to extract the maximum from those under their charge. Was that true, I wondered. 'Well the company was our *mai-bap,* our parents,' Kaka said. 'You did what you were told,' Bhima chimed in. 'The *kulambars* were strict but fair.' So it wasn't all that bad? I wanted to know more. Bhima continued. 'As far as they were concerned, we were all the same, children of coolies. They didn't play favourites among the farmers. Look at what is happening now.' I had no idea. 'Look at all the *ghoos-khori,* corruption.' He went on to explain how palms had to be greased at every turn—to get enough trucks, to get your proper turn to harvest. 'In the old days, if you did your work, you were left alone.' Nostalgia for a simpler, less complicated time perhaps, I wondered, but said nothing.

People in the village had very sharp memories of the overseers. Mr Tom drank kava 'like fish', Mohan remembered. 'And chillies', Karna added. 'A dozen of those "*rocketes*", no problem. *Chini-pani, chuttar pani.*'[3] We all exploded with laughter. Overseers, I learnt, were expected to have some rudimentary Hindi because the farmers had no English. But sometimes their pronunciation of Hindi words left people rolling with laughter. Bhima recalled Mr Oxley once asking someone's address. '*Uske ghar kahan hai,* where is his house?' But the way he pronounced *ghar—gaar—*made it sound like the Hindi word for arse: 'Where is his arse!' Kaka recalled Mr Tom visiting Nanka's house one day wanting to talk to him. But Nanka had gone to town. Mr Tom asked Nanka's son whether he could speak to his mother. Instead of saying '*Tumar mai kahan baitho,* where is your mother, *mai*', he accidentally added the common swear word, *chod* (to fuck): '*Tumar mai-chod kahan baitho,* where is your mother fucker?' Which left Mrs Nanka tittering, covering her mouth with her *orhni,* shawl, and scuttling towards the kitchen. Mr Tom froze, his face blood red, when he realised his faux pas, practically sprinting to his landrover. '*Sala chutia,* you arsehole', he muttered to himself in a mixture of fear and frustration at his loose tongue. It could have cost him a lot of trouble.

This warm reminiscence of ageing men from another era brought back memories that until now had vanished. I recalled the excitement, every three months or so, of the CSR Mobile Unit coming to the village. On the designated evening, the entire village would gather in the school compound, sit on sheets of *paal* (stitched sacks), cover themselves with blankets in the colder months and watch a tiny screen with grainy pictures perched at the end of a landrover. At the outer edges of the compound would be placed a put-put-put droning generator to provide power to the machine. Sometimes, the documentary would be about a model Indian family, sometimes about some aspect of the sugar industry or good husbandry. 'This is Ram Prasad's family', the voice-over would announce in beautifully cadenced English, which we all secretly admired. Then we would see an overseer, in a hard white hat, his hands on his hips, talking to Ram Prasad, in short sleeves and khaki pants; his amply oiled hair neatly combed back, not saying much, avoiding eye contact with the overseer. Ram Prasad's wife would be at a discreet distance by the kitchen, wearing

---

3   *Chini-pani* in the cane belt meant 'sugar has turned to water', meaning the sugar content is down, which is what allegedly the overseers at the mill weighbridge told the farmers, cheating them of a fair income. *Chuttar pani* refers to washing your bum with water after visiting the toilet—a reference in this case to Mr Tom's probably agonising toilet sessions after eating so many hot chillies.

lehnga (a long skirt worn by women) and blouse, her slightly bowed head covered with an *orhni* (a shawl worn by Indian women), while school children, in neat uniforms with their bags slung around their shoulders, walked past purposefully. The moral was not lost on us. We too could be like Ram Prasad's family—happy and prosperous—if only we were as dutiful, diligent, hardworking and respectful of authority as them.

Occasionally we would see documentaries about Australia. We did not understand the language, partly because of the rapid speed at which it was spoken, but the pictures remain with me: of vast golden-brown wheat fields harvested by monster machines, hat-wearing men on horseback rustling up cattle in rough, hilly country, wharves lined up with huge container carriers, buildings, tall beyond our imagination, and streets choked with cars crawling like ants. Pictures of parched, desolate land puzzled me. It seemed so harsh to us surrounded by nothing but lush tropical green. I sometimes wondered how white people, who seemed so delicate to us, could live in a harsh place like that. But the overwhelming impression remained of a vast and rich country. It was from there that all the good things we liked came: white purified sugar we used in our *pujas* (devotional prayer offerings), the bottled IXL jam, the Holden cars. The thought that we would one day actually live there was too outrageous to contemplate. And we did not.

I also remembered the annual school essay competition. The CSR would send the topics to the school early on in the year. Usually, they were topics such as 'Write an Essay on the Contribution the CSR Makes to Fiji', or 'How the Sugar Industry Works'. The brighter pupils in the school were expected to participate and turn in neatly written and suitably syrupy pieces. I was a regular contributor. One day during the morning assembly, our head teacher, Mr Subramani Gounden, announced that I had done the school proud by winning the *third* prize in the whole of Vanua Levu! The first one ever from our school, and the only one for several years, I was later told. I vividly recall trooping up to the front to receive my certificate scrawled with a signature at the bottom. Such success, such thrill. It was at university that I realised how unrelenting and tough-minded the CSR was in the management of the sugar industry, but at primary school, we were immensely grateful for the tender mercies that came our way. We were so proud that on the prize-giving day we had an overseer, no less, as our guest of honour. Mr Tom was a regular and much honoured presence.

One day I asked Arjun Kaka what he thought Australia might be like. '*Nahin Jaanit, beta,* I don't know. There must be a lot of people like us there,' he said. 'Why do you say that?' I asked somewhat perplexed. 'You know white people. They can't plant and harvest sugar cane, build roads or do any other hard physical work like that. All that is our job. They rule, we toil.' Kaka spoke from experience, but I assured him that white people did indeed do all the hard work in Australia. They planted and harvested cane and wheat, worked as janitors and menial labourers, drove trucks, buses and cars. Kaka remained unconvinced. 'It must be cold there?' he enquired. I tried my best to explain the seasons in Australia. Knowing the Canberra weather in summer, I said, 'Sometimes it gets hotter than Fiji'. 'But how come then white people there don't have black skin? Look at us: half a day in the sun and we become black like *baigan,* eggplants.' 'You will see it all for yourself, Kaka,' I said and left it at that. This old man is in for the shock of his life, I thought to myself. His innocence and simplicity, his complete lack of understanding of the outside world was endearing in a strange kind of a way. I made a mental note of things I would have to do in the next few weeks: get Kaka's passport and visa papers ready, ask Krishna in Sydney to purchase the ticket. Then I left for Suva, promising to inform Kaka of the date of travel well in time. I would see him in Nadi.

Kaka was relieved to see me again in Nadi. This was his first visit to Viti Levu, the first out of Labasa actually. In the late 1990s, the Nadi International Airport resembled a curious mixture of a marriage celebration and a funeral procession as people arrived in the busloads to welcome or farewell friends and family. Men are dressed in multicoloured floral shirts and women in gaudy *lehngas* (long skirts) and *salwar kamiz* (women's dress) and *saris.* I notice a family huddled in one corner of the airport lounge. One of them is leaving. I can quite imagine the scene at their home the previous night. A goat would have been slaughtered and close family and friends invited to party long into the night. The puffed red eyes tell the story of a sleepless night. A middle-aged woman, presumably the mother, prematurely aged, with streaks of grey in her dishevelled hair, is crying, a white handkerchief covering her mouth. And the father, looking anxious, sad and tearful, is chatting quietly with fellow villagers, passing time.

This is a regular occurrence these days: ordinary people, sons and daughters of the soil, with uncertain futures, leaving for foreign lands. A trickle is turning into a torrent right before our eyes. To an historian, the irony is inescapable. A hundred years ago, our forebears had arrived in Fiji, ordinary folk from rural India, shouldering their little bundles and leaving for some place they had not heard of before but keen to make a new start. A hundred years later, their children and grandchildren are on the move again: the same insecurity, the same anxiety about their fate. No one seems to care that so many of Fiji's best and brightest were leaving. Some Fijian nationalists actually want the country emptied of Indians. Kaka noticed my contemplative silence. He had read my thoughts. He asked, '*Beta, e desh ke ka hoi?* What will happen to this country?' It was an interesting and revealing formulation of the problem. He hadn't said '*hum log*', a communal reference to the Indo-Fijians. He had placed the nation—*desh*—before the community. I wished Fijians who were applauding the departure of Indians could see the transparent love an unlettered man like Kaka had for the country.

Arjun Kaka seemed nervous as we entered the plane: this was only the second time he had ever flown in a plane. The first time was when he flew from Labasa to Nadi to catch the flight to Sydney. Kaka was watchful, nervous. 'So many seats, *beta*,' he said. '*Jaise chota saakis ghar*, like a mini theatre.' Not a bad description, I thought to myself. 'And so many people! Will the plane be able to take off?' I watched him say a silent prayer as the plane began to taxi. 'Everything will be fine, Kaka,' I reassured him. 'Yes, *beta*, I just wanted to offer a prayer,' he said smiling. Sensing my curiosity, he said, 'Oh, I was just saying to God that I have come up this high, please don't take me any higher just yet.' We both smiled at the thought.

Half an hour after take-off, the drinks trolley came. I asked for a glass of white. Knowing that he was teetotaller, I asked Kaka if he would like anything soft. 'No, *beta*, I am okay. *Sab theek hai.*' 'Nothing? What about soft drinks, tomato or orange juice, water?' 'At my age, you have to be careful,' Kaka said to me some minutes after the trolley had gone. 'I have to go to toilet after I have a drink. Can't contain it for too long.' '*Bahut jor pisaap lage.* But there is a toilet on the plane, Kaka,' I reassured him, gently touching his forearm. 'Actually there are several, both at the front and back of the plane.' That caught Kaka by complete surprise. A toilet on the plane? 'You can do the other business there, too, if you want,' I continued. But Kaka was unwilling to take the risk. Later I realised a possible reason for his hesitation: if he did the other business, he couldn't wash himself with water—toilet paper he had never used.

When lunch was served, Kaka refused once again. He was a strict vegetarian, a *sadhu* (holy man) to boot. 'You can have some bread and fruit, Kaka,' I said. He still refused. 'You don't know what the Chinese put in the bread,' he said. In Labasa, all the bread was made by Chinese and a rumour was started, probably by an Indo-Fijian rival, that they used lard in the dough. I did not know but it did not matter to me. In the end, Kaka settled for an *apul* (apple) and a small bunch of grapes. 'I am sorry, Kaka, but I have ordered chicken,' I said apologetically. '*Koi bat nahin*, don't worry,' he said. Everyone in his family ate meat, including his wife. He was its only vegetarian member.

My curiosity was aroused. How did Kaka become a vegetarian and a teetotaller? Most people in the village were not. I noticed that the palm of his right hand was deformed, his skin burnt and his fingers crooked. 'Kaka,' I said, 'if you don't mind my asking, how did that happen?' 'It is a long story, *beta*,' he said. 'But we have three hours to kill,' I replied. This is what Kaka told me. Soon after he got married, he had a large itchy sore on the back of his right palm. Someone had obviously 'done' something. Magic and witchcraft (*jadu tona*) were an integral part of village life, I remembered. One possibility, he said, was his neighbour, Ram Sundar, who might have spread the rumour that Kaka had leprosy, the most dreaded social disease one could imagine; a disease with a bad omen. If Kaka went to Makogai Hospital (for lepers, in the remote Lomaiviti group), the whole family would be ostracised, no one would think of marrying into it. There would be no invitations to marriages and festive occasions. Social pressure would force the family to move to some other place to start afresh, as far away from established settlement as possible. If Kaka had leprosy, he would have to move from the village and Ram Sundar would then finally realise his dream of grabbing Kaka's adjacent 10-acre (4-hectare) farm. Such cunning, such heartlessness, and here was the outside world thinking that warm neighbourly relations characterised village life.

The extended family—because their reputation would be singed too by this tragedy—decided that something had to be done soon about Kaka's condition. Rumour was spreading fast. Instead of going to a doctor—no one in the village did or really believed in the efficacy of western medicine—his *girmitiya* father sent him to an *ojha* (a sorcerer) in Wainikoro some 30 or so miles away to the north. The *ojha*, Ramka, was famous—or dreaded—throughout Vanua Levu. He had once saved the life of a man, Ram Bharos, who had gone wild, squealing like a mouse sometimes and roaring like a lion at others, clenching his teeth and hissing through closed lips, because he had faltered trying to master magic rituals that would enable him to destroy people and cattle and property, even control the elements. To acquire that power, Ram Bharos was told—by whom it was not known—that he would have to eat a human heart sharp at midnight. Nothing was going to deter Ram Bharos from realising his ambition. He killed his own aged father. At night, he went to the graveyard, opened his father's chest with a knife and put the heart on a banana leaf. After burying the body, he walked to a nearby river, with the heart in his hands, and waded chest-deep into the river. Then something frightening happened. He saw a man shrouded in white walking towards him. Suddenly there was a blinding flash of light. Ram Bharos stumbled, forgot the names of deities he was supposed to invoke. He went mad. Ramka cured him partly, restoring a semblance of normalcy to Ram Bharos's damaged personality. This sounds like an improbable story, but I believed Kaka. Labasa, dubbed the Friendly North, has its dark side as its residents know only too well.

It was to this famous *ojha* that they had taken Arjun Kaka. In a dimly lit room, Ramka did his magic. He rubbed Kaka's damaged palm with fat and turned it over the over the fire for a very long time, chanting words in a language that was incomprehensible to him. By the time he had finished, the skin had been charred. A few days later, the bones had twisted. But Kaka was 'cured', he did not have leprosy, the family's honour was saved, and the farm remained intact. Ramka asked Kaka never to touch meat and not have pork cooked at his home. That was how Kaka had become a vegetarian.

Magic, witchcraft, sorcery, belief in the supernatural, the fear of ghosts and devils, blind faith in healers and magic men; it all recalled for me a world that the *girmitiyas* had brought with them and of which we all were a part, but which now belonged to an era long forgotten, for the present generation nothing more than a figment of a twisted imagination. And this man, from that world, was going to Australia! 'I have forgotten the details, *beta*,' Arjun Kaka apologised. 'You are the first person to ask me.' I am glad I did. After Kaka had spoken, I recalled the pin-drop silence of unlit nights in the thatched bure (*belo*) where we slept, the fear-inducing scurrying of nocturnal animals on dry leaves around the house, stories of swaying lights in the neighbouring hills, soft knocks on doors at odd hours, the mysterious aroma at night of perfumes usually sprinkled on corpses, streaking stars prophesising death somewhere, wailing noises across the paddy fields and shimmering figures in the mangrove swamps. We dreaded nights.

At Sydney airport, Krishna met us. I gave him my phone number and promised to keep in touch. Kaka had a three-month visa and I told him that I would visit him in Sydney. After we embraced, I headed for Canberra, determined that I would do everything I could to give Kaka a memorable journey to Mr Tom's country. About a month later, Krishna phoned me. Kaka wanted to talk to me. '*Beta,* I am going back soon. I would like to see you before I return.' 'But you have a full three-month visa.' 'Something inside tells me that I must return as soon as possible.' A premonition of some sort? His world of magic and sorcery came to mind, and I realised there was no point arguing or trying to persuade him to change his mind. I left for Sydney the following day.

Krishna and his wife had gone to work and the children were at school when I reached the house. It was immediately clear to me that Kaka was a lost man, uncomfortable and anxious. I reminded him of his promise to tell me the full story about his Australian experience. '*Poora jad pulai.* Everything.' What he missed most, Kaka said, was his daily routine. In Tabia, he would be up at crack of dawn, feed the cattle and have an early breakfast before heading off to the fields. Even at his age. In the evening, after an early shower at the well, he would light the wick lamp (*dhibri*) and do his *puja.* He missed his devotional songs on the radio, the death notices in the evening. He would not be able forgive himself if someone dear to him died while he was away. Kaka often wondered how Lali, his beloved cow, was. He treated her tenderly, almost like a human, a member of the family. For him not looking after animals, especially cow (*gau-mata,* mother) was a crime.

In Fiji, Kaka was connected, was part of a living community. He had a place in the wider scheme of things. But not here. 'I sit here in the lounge most of the day like a deaf and blind man. There is television and radio, but they are of no use to me.' 'What about walk in the park, a stroll in the nearby supermarket?' I asked. Kaka recalled (for him) a particularly hair-raising experience. One day Krishna had left him in the mall of a large supermarket and had gone to get his car repaired. At first Kaka was calm, but as time passed, surrounded by so many white people, he panicked. What if something happened to Krishna? He did not have the home address or the telephone number with him. How would he find his way home? He tried to talk to a young Indian man—who was probably from Fiji—but the man kept walking, muttering to himself. 'He probably thought I was a beggar or something.' From that day on, Kaka preferred to remain at home. For a man fond of the outdoors, active in the field, this must have been painful. 'It is torture, *beta*. Sitting, eating, pissing, farting. That's all I do all day, every day.' I felt his distress.

Did Krishna and his wife treat him well, I wanted to know. It was an intrusive question, I know, but I wanted to be helpful. 'Oh, they both are very nice. *Patoh* makes vegetarian dishes and leaves them in the fridge for me. I have a room to myself. My clothes are washed. On the weekends, they take me out for drives.' But there was something missing, I felt. '*Beta*, it is not their fault but I don't see much of them. Babu [Krishna] goes to work in the morning and *Patoh* does the evening shift. By the time she returns, it is time for bed.' The 'ant-like life', as Kaka aptly put it, was not his cup of tea. 'Getting established in this society is not easy Kaka,' I said. 'But things improve with time.' 'That's true, but by then, half your life is over. These people would have been millionaires in Fiji if they worked as hard as they do here.' 'They do it for the future of their children, Kaka.' He nodded. 'I know, I know.'

Kaka felt acutely conscious of himself whenever he did anything, constantly on the guard. Back home, he would clear his throat loudly and cough out the phlegm on the lawn. Everyone did it. Here his grandchildren giggled and covered their mouths with their hands in embarrassment. In Tabia, Kaka always wore shorts at home. Here, on several occasions, he felt undressed, half naked, when Krishna's friends came around. 'I could see that both Babu and Patoh were sometimes uncomfortable.' Sometimes, the people he met at *pujas* and other ceremonies, especially people from Viti Levu, laughed in jest at his rustic Labasa Hindi.

> They find us and our language backward. '*Tum log ke julum bhasa, Kaka*,' they would say to me mockingly, uncle, you folk [from Labasa] have a wonderful language: '*awa-gawa*, [come and gone, when they say *aya-gaya*], *dabe* [flood, *baadh*], *bakeda* [crab, *kekda*]'. They find it funny, but after a while I find the mocking hurtful. So I don't say much, not that I have much to say these people anyway.

In Tabia, Kaka had his own *kakkus* (outhouse) where he could wash himself properly with water after toilet, but here he would sometimes spill water on the toilet floor or accidentally leak on it, causing mustiness and a foul smell. He would then feel guilty and embarrassed. Kaka found the accumulation of small things like this making himself conscious, ill at ease in the house. No one ever said anything, but he felt that he was a bit of a nuisance for everybody, especially when Krishna's friends came around.

Kaka was desperate for news from home, any news. There was nothing about Fiji, let alone Labasa, on television and only brief snippets on one or two radio stations, which he invariably missed because he did not know how to use the dial. 'At home, I knew what was happening in Fiji and the world, but here I sit like a frog in a well. It is as if we do not exist.' I understood his puzzlement. Fiji—Labasa—was all he knew. His centre of the universe was of no interest and of no consequence to the rest of the world. 'That is the way of the world, Kaka,' I tried to assure him. 'We are noticed only when we make a mess of things, or when there is a natural disaster or when some Australian tourist gets raped or robbed.' Some of the people he had met, especially the older ones, hankered for news from home, but the younger ones were too preoccupied with life and work to bother.

Television both entertained and embarrassed Kaka. He couldn't watch the soaps with the entire family in the room. The scantily clad women, the open display of skin, the kissing, the suggestive bedroom scenes, the crude advertising (for lingerie, skin lotions) had him averting his eyes or uttering muffled coughs. Sometimes, unable to bear the embarrassment, he would just retire to his room on the pretence that he was tired, and then spend much of the night sleepless, wondering about everything. He liked two shows, though, and enjoyed them like a child. One was David Attenborough's natural life programs. He did not understand the language but the antics of the animals and creatures of the sea he did not need words to understand. These programs brought a whole world alive for him. He remembered the animals his *girmitiya* father used to talk about: *sher* (lion), *bhaloo* (bear), *hathi* (elephant), *bandar* (monkey). He had seen pictures of them in books, but to see live animals on the screen was magical. And he liked cartoons, especially the Bugs Bunny shows. They made no sense to him at all—or to me—but that was their charm, characters skitting across the screen speaking rapid-fire (*gitbit*). He would laugh out aloud when no one was watching.

These were the only programs Kaka could watch with his small grandchildren. Otherwise there was no communication between them. The children were nice; '*sundar*' is how Kaka described them. They made tea for him and offered him biscuits and cookies, but they had no Hindi at all and Kaka knew no English. He would caress their heads gently and hug them and they would occasionally take him for walks in the park nearby, but no words were exchanged. '*Dil roye, beta,*' Kaka said to me, 'the heart cries, that I cannot talk to my own flesh and blood in the only language I know. I hope they will remember me and remember our history.' Krishna was making an effort to introduce his children to Indian religion and culture through the weekend classes held at the local *mandir,* but it was probably a lost cause. History was not taught in many public schools, certainly not Pacific or Fijian history, and I wondered how the new generation growing up in Australia, exposed to all the challenges posed by global travel and technology, would learn about their past. I did not have the heart to tell Kaka, but I know that his world would go with him, just as mine will, too. Our past will be a foreign country to children growing up in Australia.

Once or twice, I took Kaka out for a ride through the heart of Sydney, pointing out the monuments, Hyde Park, Circular Quay, the museum and the Mitchell Library, but Kaka had no understanding and no use for the icons of Australian culture. For him, the city was nothing more than a concrete jungle, one damn tall building after another. I took him for a ride in the country, playing devotional Hindi music in the car (which he enjoyed immensely). Kaka had imagined Australia to be clogged with buildings and people, but the long, unending distances between towns both fascinated and terrified him. In Labasa, an hour's journey was considered long; the idea of driving for a couple of days to get from one place to another was alien to him. And the geography too fascinated Kaka: the dry barren countryside wheat-brown in December, the bleached bones of dead animals by the roadside, the rusting hulks of discarded machinery and farms stretching for thousands of hectares. 'How can one family manage all this by themselves,' he wondered. 'How can you grow anything in this type of soil?' And he wondered how, living so far apart on their farms, the people kept the community intact. I said little: he was wondering aloud, talking to himself. On our return journey, Kaka said sadly that he wished his wife could have seen all this with him. I wished that too. I could sense that he was missing her. Kaka remained silent for a long time.

I was still unsatisfied that Kaka was happy with all that Krishna and I between us had been able to show him. Then it came to me that Kaka might like to visit the Taronga Zoo. It was an inspired thought. Kaka was like a child in a lolly shop. The animals he had seen on the television screen he now saw live with his own eyes: giraffe, rhino, tiger, leopard, lion, cobra and elephant. I was so glad that he was enjoying himself, pointing out animals to me, saying: 'Look, look', with all the excitement of an innocent child. As we approached the monkey section of the zoo, Kaka stopped, joined his palms in prayer and said '*Jai Hanuman Ji Ki*, Hail to Lord Hanuman', the monkey god, Lord Rama's brave and loyal general, who had single-handedly rescued Sita from Ravana's clutches. He was excited to see a cobra. '*Nag Baba*,' he said reverentially, the snake god. When I looked at him, Kaka smiled but I couldn't tell whether his display of quiet reverence for the monkeys and cobras was for real or was it for my entertainment! I knew that the old man certainly had an impish sense of humour.

As we were having a cup of tea at the end of the zoo visit, sweetening it with white sugar, Kaka wondered where that was manufactured. The next day, I took Kaka to the CSR refinery. He was thrilled. As already mentioned, we considered white sugar 'pure', enough to offer to the gods in our *pujas* and *havans* (prayer offerings around fire). A supervisor gave us a good informative tour when he found out that Kaka was from Fiji. Kaka was impressed with how clean the place was and how new the machinery was, nothing remotely like the filthy, stench-producing sugar mills in Fiji. We also visited an IXL jam factory on the way. Jam and bread were a luxury for many poor families in rural areas of Labasa, to be enjoyed on special occasions, such as birthdays. The standard food in most homes was curry, rice and roti, with all the vegetables coming from the farm itself.

The visit to the sugar-refining factory rekindled Kaka's interest in the CSR. He wondered whether any of the *kulambars* were still alive. 'We could find out,' I offered. It would mean a lot of research work, but I wanted to do it for this man who meant so much to me. I rang the CSR head office in Sydney. There was nothing on the overseers. Evidently, once they finished with the company, they disappeared off the record books, a bit like the *girmitiyas* about whom everything was documented when they were under indenture, and nothing, or very little, when they became free. Was there ever an association or club of former Fiji overseers, I wondered. The lady did not know but promised to find out. She rang an hour or two later to say that I could try Mr Syd Snowsill. He was the leader of the Fiji pack in Sydney. The name seemed vaguely familiar; he was, from memory, the spearhead of the Seaqaqa Cane Expansion project in the early 1970s. A gruff voice greeted me when I rang. When I explained the purpose of my enquiry, he became relaxed. '*Bahut accha,* very good. Who are you after? Anyone in particular?' I volunteered three names: Mr Tom, Mr Oxley and Mr Johnson. 'I see,' Mr Snowsill said chuckling and with some affection, 'all the Labasa *badmaash* gang, eh, the Labasa hooligans.' He did not know the whereabouts of Mr Oxley and Mr Johnson, but Mr Tom—Leslie Duncan Thompson—was living in retirement in Ballina. 'His name will be in the local telephone book,' Mr Snowsill said as he wished me good luck. '*Shukriya ji,* thank you Sir. *Namaste,* or should I say *Khuda Hafiz,* goodbye!' 'Both are fine.'

If you do not know it, Ballina (Bullenah in the local Aboriginal language) is one of the loveliest places in Australia. A rural sugarcane-growing community of fewer than 20,000 acres in subtropical northern New South Wales, by the enchanting bottle-green Richmond River and surrounded by a sea of rippling cane fields for as far as the eye can see; tidal lagoons and surf beaches nearby. It was the kind of place I knew that Kaka would like; rural cane country since the 1860s, and the people, friendly and genuine, in the way country folk generally are. And he did, as we drove on the Princess Highway through small, picturesque seaside towns, beaches, thickly wooded rolling hills along the roadside, across a gently gathering greenness in the distance.

Mr Tom was certainly in the book when I checked the next morning. His address was a retirement home on the outskirts of the town, on a small hill overlooking the river. I didn't ring but drove to the place to give Mr Tom a surprise. My mental picture of him remained of a tall, thin man, barking orders. Kaka was smiling in anticipation, perspiring slightly. We waited in the wicker chairs in the veranda as the lady at the front desk went to get him from the dining table across the room. As he walked towards us, I knew it was Mr Tom—tall, erect, with a bigger waist now, face creased, and the hair gone, but not the sense of purposefulness. 'Yeash,' he drawled. When I explained why we had come and told him Kaka's name, he beamed and hugged him, two old codgers meeting after decades, slapping each other gently on the back. '*Salaam, saheb,*' Kaka muttered. '*Salaam, salaam,*' Mr Tom replied excitedly. '*Chai lao. Jaldi. jaldi,* bring some tea, quick-fast,' he said to no one in particular. Perhaps he wanted us to know that he still had Hindustani after all these years.

'*Tum kaise baitho?* How are you?' Mr Tom asked Kaka. Before Kaka could reply, Mr Tom said, '*Hum to buddha hai ab,* I am an old man now'. I translated for Kaka. After a while, the names came to Mr Tom: Lalta, Nanka, Sundar (he pronounced it Soonda). He especially asked after Udho, the de facto headman of the village, who was one of the few from Labasa to volunteer for the Labour Corps during World War II. He had died some years back. 'Too bad,' Mr Tom said. 'He was a good man.' He asked after Kaka's family, about the school.

> I haven't been to Labasa since leaving, but hear it is a modern place now, not bush place like it used to be. They tell me the roads have been tarsealed and people have piped water. No longer a *pukka jungali*, complete country bumpkin, place, eh. You people deserve every bit of it.

'*Seaqaqa kaise baitho, Arjun?* How is Seaqaqa?' Mr Tom asked Kaka. That was the project on which he had worked with Mr Snowsill. It had been launched with great hope of getting Fijians into the sugar industry. Half the leases were reserved for them. When Kaka told him that many Fijians had left their farms or subleased them to Indo-Fijian tenants, Mr Tom seemed genuinely sad to learn that all the effort that he and other overseers had put in had gone to pot.

> It was done all too suddenly. They wanted to make political mileage out of it. Win elections. All that *tamasha,* sideshow. That's no way to run this business. We needed to have proper training for them, proper husbandry practices in place. You can't just pluck them out the bush and make them successful farmers overnight. Ridiculous.

'Farming is a profession, son,' Mr Tom said to me, 'just like any other. It is not everyone's cup of tea.' Mr Tom said that the CSR should have remained in Fiji for another five to 10 years to effect a good transition, train staff properly, and mostly to get politicians to see the problems of the industry from a business angle. 'But no, everything had to be done in a rush. You got your independence and you didn't want white men around telling you what to do anymore. Fair enough, I suppose.'

Then Mr Tom asked about the current situation. He had read that the industry was in dire straits. 'I am afraid it is true, Mr Tom,' I said. Most leases in Daku, Naleba, Wainikoro, Laga Laga—places Mr Tom knew so well—had not been renewed, and the former farms were slowly reverting to bush. Mr Tom shook his head. 'Sad. So much promise, shot through so early.' He asked about the farmers. Those evicted were moving out, many to Viti Levu, starting afresh as market gardeners, vegetable growers, general labourers and domestic hands. '*Girmit* again, eh? Unnecessary tragedy. Why? What for? We have all gone mad.'

I asked Mr Tom about something that had been on my mind for many years. 'Why didn't the CSR sell its freehold land to the growers when it decided to leave Fiji? It would have been the right thing to do, the humane thing to do.' Mr Tom acknowledged my question with that characteristic drawl of his, 'Yeash'. And then bluntly:

> We couldn't give a rat's arse about who bought the land. All we wanted was *nagad paisa,* cash. Fijian leaders understood very well that land was power and didn't want the CSR to sell its freehold land to Indians. Over 200,000 bloody acres or so. Indian leaders in the Alliance went along, trying to please their masters, hoping for some concessions elsewhere. The Fijians and the Europeans—Mara, Penaia, Falvey, Kermode: that crowd—had them by the balls. We in the company watched all this in utter incomprehension and disbelief, but it wasn't our show. We were so pissed off with the Dening Award.[4] And then there was the Gujarati factor, did you know?

I didn't.

> Some of your leaders feared that if Indian tenants got freehold land, Gujarati merchants would get their hands on them by hook or crook. To some, the Gujaratis were a bigger menace than Fijians and Europeans. Such bloody short-sightedness. Son, some of your suffering is self-inflicted. Harsh thing to say, but it is true.

After a spell of silence, Kaka wanted to know about Mr Tom's life after Tua Tua. From Tua Tua he had gone to Lomowai and did the rounds of several Sigatoka sectors (Kavanagasau, Olosara, Cuvu) before moving to Lautoka Mill as a supervisor. Taking early retirement, he returned to Australia and after some years of working in Ballina's sugar industry, he 'went fishing', as he put it, travelling, taking up golf and lawn bowling. I vividly recalled lawn bowling as the game white people, in white uniforms and white shoes, played at Batanikama. Wife and children? Kaka wanted to know. The wife had died a few years back, which is when he moved to this place.

---

4   Reference to the award by Lord Dening, Britain's Master of the Roll, which favoured the growers against the millers and which led eventually to CSR's departure from Fiji in 1973.

The children were living in Queensland. 'There is nothing for them here.' Kaka wondered if Mr Tom still had that fearsome taste for hot chillies. '*Nahin sako,* Arjun, can't do it anymore. *Pet khalas,* the stomach's gone. And what do you do, young man?' Mr Tom asked me. When I told him that I was an academic in Canberra, he smiled. '*Shabaash, beta,* well done, son. Boy from Labasa, eh! Who would have thought! From the cane fields of Fiji to the capital of Australia, and a professor to boot! Good onya, son.'

We had been talking like this for an hour or so when the topic of the coups in Fiji came up. Mr Tom had been outraged by what had taken place. There was broad sympathy in conservative Australia for the coups. They were seen essentially as the desperate struggle of the indigenous community against the attempted dominance of an immigrant one. But Mr Tom was different.

> I wrote letters to the local papers, gave a few talks and interviews on the radio. No bloody use. Look, I said, you don't know the Indian people. I do. I have worked with them. I understand them. They made Fiji what it is today. They have been the backbone of the sugar industry. You take them out and the whole place will fall apart. Just like that. What wrong have they done? How have they wronged the Fijian people? Their only vices are thrift and industry.

He went on like this for some time. I was not used to hearing this kind of assessment from people in Australia. Mr Tom was refreshingly adamant, defiant.

'Yours must have been a voice in the wilderness, Mr Tom,' I said.

> Bloody oath, yes. You talk about immigrant people ripping natives off. Bloody well look at Australia! Look what we have done to the Aborigines. Snatched their land, made them destitute, pushed them into the bush, robbed them of their rights. Bloody genocide, if you ask me. What have the Indians done to Fiji? They worked hard on the plantations so that the Fijians could survive. What's bad about that? If I had my way, I would bring the whole bang lot here. We need hardworking people like you in this country.

Mr Tom had spoken from the heart. 'Let me not go on, because all this hypocrisy lights me up.' 'Mr Howard would not approve,' I said. 'What would these city slickers know,' Mr Tom said dismissively. 'They don't know their arse from a hole in the ground, if you ask me.' I had heard many a colourful Australian slang—blunt as a pig's arse, knockers, spitting the dummy—but this one was new. I smiled, and appreciated Mr Tom's unvarnished directness.

9. MR ARJUN GOES TO AUSTRALIA

It was time to go. Once again, Kaka and Mr Tom hugged. 'Well Arjun, *nahi jaano phir milo ki nahin milo,* don't know if we will ever meet again. Look after yourself and say salaam to the old timers.' With that we headed back to Sydney. I told Kaka all that Mr Tom had said. 'Remember *beta* what I told you: many *kulambars* were tough but fair. We were not completely innocent either: *Chori, Chandali, Chaplusi,* thievery, stupid, wanton behaviour.' I was impressed, even touched, by Mr Tom's directness and his principled uncompromising stand on the Fiji coups. I had not expected this sort of humanity in a former *kulambar,* whose general reputation in Fiji is still rotten.

I dropped Kaka at Krishna's place and returned to Canberra. I was going to Suva for a conference in a couple of months' time and promised to see him then. Tears were rolling down his stubbled cheek as he hugged me. '*Pata nahin beta ab kab miliho,* don't know son when we will meet again.' I didn't know it then, but it was the final goodbye. A month after Kaka had returned Krishna rang to say that he had died—of what precisely no one knew. I was devastated, speechless for days. The last link to my past was now gone, the last one in the village who had grown up in the shadows of indenture, gone through the Depression, the strikes in the sugar industry, World War II. I felt cheated. I still feel his loss.

When I returned to Fiji, I knew that I had to go to Labasa. Perhaps it is the ancient urge to say the final goodbye in person. I wanted to know the exact circumstances of Kaka's death. Only then, I knew, could I bring closure to my grief. He was very happy to return home, back in his own house, back to his daily routine, people told me. Then one day, all of a sudden, Lali, the cow, died. Kaka was distraught; she was like family to him. He used to talk to her, caress her forehead, dutifully feed her para grass every morning and afternoon, wash her once a week. He had bought Lali many years ago with his wife, Dhanraji. Perhaps he was really talking to Kaki through Lali. Now a loved link to that past was gone. He was heartbroken. In fact, he had died from a massive heart attack. The last words Kaka spoke before he collapsed, one of his grandchildren remembered, was '*Dhanraji sabur karo, hum aait haye,* Dhanraji wait, I am coming.' With Kaka gone, one more familiar Tabia signpost had disappeared from my life. After a brief moment of promise, the place once again became a labyrinth of haunting memories.

10

'The children of the wind'[1]

A journey to Chattisgarh

> We made no inquiries about India or about the families people had left behind. When our ways of thinking changed, and we wished to know, it was too late.
>
> — V.S. Naipaul[2]

18 May 1901. Chiriya. Father's Name Kuru. Age 17. A Bhumihar from the village of Bandarchua in Lohardaga district of Bihar, boarded the SS *Fazilka II* for Fiji. He was an indentured labourer, one of 60,000 who went to Fiji between 1879 and 1916. He was recruited upcountry; precisely where and in what circumstances is not known. But the rest of the details are clinical, precise and authoritative, brushed clean of the dusty, murky details of history. From his village, Chiriya was taken to Purulia Depot in late March and from there transported to Calcutta. A few days later, he appeared before Fiji's Emigration Agent, A.C. Stewart, who certified that:

---

1 Originally appeared in *South Asia: Journal of South Asian Studies* 16(2) (2013): 297–307.
2 V.S. Naipaul, 'Two worlds', Nobel Lecture, 7 December 2001.

the Man above described has appeared before me and has been engaged by me on behalf of the Government of Fiji and is willing to proceed to that country to work for hire; and that I have explained to him all matters concerning his engagement and duties.[3]

This, Stewart said confidently, was also 'done at the time of registration by the Registering Officer appointed by the Indian Government'. All matters properly explained to an unlettered 17-year-old by an important *angrezi saheb* (white man) with a myriad other matters to attend to! On 4 May, the Depot Surgeon at Calcutta certified that 'we have examined and passed the above-named Man as fit to emigrate; that he is free from all bodily and mental disease; and that he has been vaccinated since engaging to emigrate'. His superior officer, the Surgeon Superintendent, agreed. All the protocols and procedures of inspection and registration completed, the Protector of Emigrants on 18 May authorised his emigration: 'Permitted to proceed as in a fit state of health to undertake the voyage to Fiji.' A month later, Chiriya arrived in Fiji. And, then, promptly disappears from the record books forever, his name erased from the pages of history.

I began my journey in search of Fiji *girmitiyas* well over 30 years ago, in 1977, as part of my doctoral dissertation on the origins of Fiji's north Indian migrants. During the course of my research, I read and coded each and every one of the 45,000 Emigration Passes and computer-analysed them. It was an unimaginably tedious, eyesight-destroying task, sitting by myself and reading reels upon reels of microfilm in the darkened basement of the Australian National Library in Canberra—month after month. Each important piece of information in the pass—caste of the migrant, his or her district of origin and district of registration, sex, next-of-kin—had to be coded and entered individually on a specially designed sheet of paper and analysed using the computer. It had to be done. Each pass considered individually. Perhaps in some subconscious sense I was paying homage to those who had crossed the *kala pani*, the dark, dreaded seas, to come to Fiji, to give us all a new beginning, and who were the foundational spring of our own lives.

It was during that exercise, with bits and pieces of information supplied by my father about his indentured father's background in India, that I had discovered my paternal grandfather's Emigration Pass. Using information

---

3   This, and subsequent references in this paragraph, are from Chiriya's 'Emigration Pass', National Archives of Fiji, Suva.

in it, I had visited his village in Bahraich district during my year-long fieldwork in India in 1978, and reconnected with my ancestral family; much to my father's unbounded delight but to my very mixed emotions. Ganga water, which I had brought back in a Teachers whisky bottle, remained one of his most prized possessions till his last days. It was kept in a green tin box underneath his bed amidst important family documents; holy water from the holiest of rivers from his father's land, drops of which were ritually poured on the lips of dead relatives to wish the departed soul well on its next journey.

Now, 30 years later, I am embarking on another journey of discovery. Chiriya was my Nana, my mother's father. I never knew him in the way I knew Aja, my paternal grandfather, who died a grand old man when I was 10; a picture of him remains vivid in my mind. But Chiriya Nana died very young, when my mother was just a little child. She had only the dimmest memory of him, unable even to recall what he looked like. My mother and her youngest siblings, two sisters and a brother, were brought up in various parts of Labasa by some distant relations now gone and forgotten, in circumstances about which not a word was ever said but about which much was understood. Chiriya remained just a name to us, nothing more. There are no photographs, no mementoes. My mental archive of Nana was blank.

Until about two decades ago.

It all came about in an unexpected way. My reputation as the genealogist of the *girmitiyas* spread far and wide with the publication of my first book, which presented the fruits of my doctoral research, *Girmitiyas: The Origins of the Fiji Indians* (1983).[4] Soon afterwards, I began receiving enquiries from people, at first few but then increasing rapidly in volume, about their ancestral connections to India and whether I could help them locate the Emigration Passes of their great-grandparents. Often the enquiry was futile because the information was vague and scanty. The name of the person was remembered and of the ship too, but there could be dozens of Gajadhars or Bisuns or Autars on the same ship. The name of the district of origin could make all the difference but the response often was, 'he came from somewhere around there', meaning the eastern districts of Uttar Pradesh (Basti, Faizabad, Gonda and the like). The need

---

4 Brij V. Lal, *Girmitiyas: The Origins of the Fiji Indians* (Canberra: Journal of Pacific History, 1983).

to know, to reconnect, is genuine and in its own way deeply moving. There is a certain poignancy to the desperate search for roots, but what is lost is now lost forever.

These enquiries bring me back to Chiriya Nana and the need for me to 'do something' to fill the gap in that side of our family's history, if for nothing else than for my late mother. A child growing up without ever knowing her parents is a haunting thought. If I don't do it, no one else will. I had nothing to go on except conversations with old folk in the village and older members of our extended family, now all gone. Slowly, over the years, fragments of a picture emerge. Nana served his indenture as a train driver's helping hand in the Tua Tua Sector. He most certainly was not a 'train driver', as some people vaguely claimed. That was a white man's job. Aja had also served his indenture as a stable hand in the same sector, which leads me to wonder if the two men knew each other—probably not. After his indenture ended, Aja settled in Tabia on leased land as a small-time cultivator of rice, lentils, peanuts, maize and other such crops until sugar cane arrived in the 1930s.

Nana settled across the Laqere River in a place called Nuk Nuk. The place is now covered in thick bush with no sign of previous human habitation at all. As children, we knew of Nuk Nuk as Nana's place, but also as a place of bad memories, haunted, a place to be avoided by children. Nuk Nuk is completely cut off from the village of Laqere. Why Nana settled in this remotest of places, away from all his fellow Indians, remains a mystery. Nana's heart was not in farming, it was said. He spent all his time fishing in the sea nearby, a loner at peace only with himself, a recluse. That was a puzzle because interdependence and cooperation were the only way an Indian village functioned. People had to work together to plant, to harvest, to celebrate life and mourn its passing, but Nana seemed to relish living on the outer edges of society. He had some close family members living in the neighbouring settlements and that for him was enough.

After Nana's death sometime in the late 1920s or early 1930s, the extended family fractured. Some went to Dreketi in southern Vanua Levu to work as copra cutters on Don Bull's coconut plantation. Others followed. From Dreketi they went to Savusavu to copra cutting jobs on the Vulagei Estate, and there they remained for the rest of their lives. Distant relatives are still scattered around the place. We had no contact with them at all. Savusavu might as well have been on a distant island somewhere far away in the Pacific. There were no roads linking Savusavu to Labasa, the local town,

10. 'THE CHILDREN OF THE WIND'

and a boat journey was hazardous and taken only in the rarest or most desperate of circumstances. Rumour had it that some younger members of the family had gone 'astray'. One of them was said to have married a Fijian or a part-European, which was then simply unheard of in Tabia. But all that was distant news. Caught up in our own world, we forgot about our extended maternal family in other parts of the island.

***

In 2009, while researching at the National Archives in Fiji, I decided to look for Nana's Emigration Pass, but there was little to go by. All I had heard was that Nana had arrived 'a few years before' Aja did in 1908. Which ship, which district, which year: nothing was known. All I had was Nana's name. I began working back from the 1908 Emigration Passes of the *Sangola II* to the Emigration Passes of the *Ganges*, which had come to Fiji in 1900, some 22 ships earlier. Since the passes are organised alphabetically, the search was not so arduous. I looked at all Men's Emigration Passes beginning with the letter 'C'. If there was more than one Chiriya among the thousands who arrived in Fiji between 1900 and 1908, my quest would be dashed, for I would then have no means of knowing which one was Nana. Lady Luck smiled upon me. For all those years, there was only one Chiriya: my Nana, all of five feet and four inches tall, a labourer, with the distinguishing feature on his body being a scar on the left forearm. And he was only a lad of 17 when he enlisted for Fiji.

Armed with all this information about Nana, I knew I would one day attempt to visit his village, just as three decades earlier I had gone to Bahraich to visit Aja's place. It was a journey I would have to make in memory of my mother. But precisely when, I was not sure. Once again providence intervened. Siddharth Kak, the founder of the Surabhi Foundation in Mumbai, wanted to 'bring to life' *The Encyclopedia of the Indian Diaspora,* published in 2006, of which I was the general editor. That volume provides, so far, the most comprehensive treatment of the growth of the Indian diaspora from precolonial to modern times. Siddharth rang to enlist my (readily given) support to make 10 or so documentaries on Indian communities scattered around the globe, with the support of the Indian Ministry of External Affairs. I was a little concerned about the Indian Government's involvement; concerned that the series might be used as syrupy propaganda for the glorious achievements of the Indian diaspora, but Siddharth's reputation for integrity and probity is solid and reassuring. I would act as an historical consultant to the project, help make contacts, suggest themes and lines of enquiry but would otherwise remain uninvolved.

After a series of long telephone conversations over several weeks, Siddharth suggested that the last documentary should be about the diaspora's search for its roots in India, and that I should be one of the subjects of the story. The prospect was intriguing but in view of my heavy commitments in Canberra, I doubted if I would be visiting India anytime soon. Fortuitously, an invitation came from the University of Hyderabad to give the keynote address to a conference on the Indian diaspora there. I could accomplish two things at once. Siddharth set filming arrangements in motion when I told him. Aditi Dave, the producer for this documentary, sent me a series of questions and suggestions she wanted me to consider, and asked for Nana's Emigration Pass so that she could make the travel arrangements, liaise with local officials and decide on shooting locations.

Aditi contacted the Resident Commissioner of Lohardaga to enquire about the location of Bandarchua. At first, there was great confusion. There is a place by that name in Lohardaga's Samdega district, she was told, but there is also one in Jaspur district in Chattisgarh. Which one was it? Lohardaga and Jaspur are neighbouring districts now in two different provinces. A series of hectic emails ensue. Luckily, a piece of information in the Emigration Pass saved the day. Bandarchua on the Emigration Pass was in the *tehsil* (subdistrict) of Khunkuri. There was only one *tehsil* by that name, and it was in Chattisgarh! We were all relieved.

The physical boundaries of this region had changed several times in recent decades. In preindependent India, Bihar was a large sprawling province covering several linguistic and geographic areas. After independence, as state boundaries were drawn up, certain places had been shifted from one province to another. Parts of Sirgooja, for instance, which was also known as Lohardaga, had been moved into Madhya Pradesh. In 2000, new language-based states were created. Among them was Jharkhand, the heartland of tribal India, with Ranchi as its capital and Lohardaga as one of its districts, and the other was Chattisgarh, with Raipur as its administrative centre. Bandarchua, I discovered, was one of 99 nondescript villages in the *tehsil* of Khunkuri.

From Hyderabad, I flew to Ranchi via Delhi, and met up with the Surabhi documentary team: Aditi, Sudiksha Dhooria, Kaushik, the camera man from Calcutta, camera attendant Shyamal, production person, Rupesh, and the driver Binod. All of them looked so young, none over their mid-30s. Their purposefulness and professionalism impressed me. Their minds were fully on the work at hand and there was no time to waste. We drove around central Ranchi looking for batteries and other items, had lunch in a surprisingly pleasant air-conditioned restaurant, and then went to the Deputy Commissioner's office for consultation and direction. Kamal Kishore Soan, an Indian Administrative Service (IAS) officer, was giving an audience to local leaders, both men and women, who had come to complain about matters of local importance, such as delays in the disbursement of allocated funds for rural projects. He despatched them with great speed and tactfulness while we waited and watched. The camera crew told me to look attentively at the proceedings. Seriousness was writ large on my face as they went about their business. It was close to six o'clock and the day's proceedings had still not finished. Soan postponed our meeting till 8.30 pm at his official residence. Long days and very late dinners were common fare in those parts, and in India generally, I quickly discovered. At the residence, there was more shooting, more staged conversation, more helpful advice about who to see in Jaspur Nagar—where we would be heading the following day. His obligation to us was completed around nine o'clock, and Soan rushed off to another engagement, a wedding reception.

We left for Jaspur Nagar soon after dawn on a five-hour drive. Some mirthful scenes from earlier Indian journeys returned. The roads were clogged with dangerously overloaded, gaudily painted trucks with 'Horn Please', and 'Awaz Do' written prominently at their backs. One which split my sides said, 'I am Horning, R U'. A constant feature of travelling on Indian roads was the incessant hooting and tooting when overtaking a vehicle or when alerting pedestrians or animals to the oncoming traffic. I was amazed at the nonchalance with which chickens and goats and cows crossed the road—as if they owned the damned thing. Live and let live was the principle there. What would happen if you hit a chicken, I ask. '*Poora barbaadi,* total loss,' someone says. Not only would the driver have to pay for the dead chicken but its owner would demand the income foregone. If the chicken had lived on for another five years, she would have produced so many scores of eggs and so many dozens of chooks and compensation would be demanded for these as well. Some owners would insist that even their roosters laid eggs, someone said to much mirth. 'This is India, *yaar. Sab chalta hai,* anything goes.' 'What if you hit a goat?' 'God help you,' Kaushik says, '*Double barbaadi.*' 'And what if you hit a person?' 'Don't stop, for God's sake, drive fastest to the nearest police station, otherwise they will kill you and burn your vehicle.' It sounds a bit overly dramatic but I got the picture. I had been similarly advised about driving in the highlands of New Guinea some years back.

I had always imagined this part of India, its geographical heartland, to be tropical green full of forested hills and large rivers and animals about which we had read in our primary school texts: *bhaloo* (bear), *sher* (lion), *hathi* (elephant), *bandar* (monkey). Forested hills were in the far distance on both sides of the road though not verdant, but the plains areas had been cleared for agriculture. The rivers were low and virtually stagnant. It was the dry season and there were only brown stalks of harvested rice in the hazy heat and swirling dust in the distance. Along the road in the shade of large mango trees people were idly standing around. I learned that there was no local employment in the hot season. Someone told me that about 60 per cent of the population was engaged in seasonal migration. It is history repeating itself. In the late nineteenth century, large numbers from this region were heading off to the Calcutta jute mills, Assam tea gardens, even to the Bombay textile mills, for employment. The districts that featured prominently in early colonial migration to Mauritius and the West Indies, in particular, were the Bihar districts of Arrah, Sahebgunj, Ranchi, Hazaribagh, Patna, Chapra and Ghazipur (in eastern Uttar Pradesh). As supplies in these areas dried up, recruitment moved up north-eastern Uttar Pradesh districts of Basti, Azamgarh, Gorakhpur, Faizabad, Gonda, Bahraich and others. It is difficult to imagine now but a region that seemed so desolate and diminished was the site of massive migration 100 years previously. People shook their heads in disbelief when I told them this.

We stopped at a *chai* shop on our way. The camera crew wanted to shoot me talking to local people as if asking for directions to Bandarchua. I approached the owner, a dark man in old, tattered clothes. He shook my hand and was eager to talk but baulked when he saw the camera crew. Aditi told him the purpose of our conversation. The man looked at me quizzically and invited me inside for a private conversation. '*Aapas ke baat*,' he said. 'Are you from the government?' he asks. 'No,' I say. 'From the police?' 'No.' 'Will I get into trouble if I talk to you?' I was perplexed by the man's anxiety, his furtive glances to see who might be watching. By now, crowd of onlookers had gathered. I went out and talked to them in my surprisingly fluent Hindi and explained the purpose of my visit to their part of the world. They listened attentively and nodded their heads in appreciation but with absolutely no idea where Fiji was or if people from this region had gone overseas (or anywhere else for that matter). That was an unthinkable thought. The *chai* shop owner was clearly pleased at the crowd's reaction and told me the direction in which I had to travel and the time it would take to reach there. All this was really for the camera. We took several shoots because instead of looking at me, the man kept smiling and giving side glances at the camera!

After the shoot, we had tea. The man brought my cup himself, a mark of respect for a visitor. I dreaded this. Indian tea is not tea but milky syrup, and I am diabetic. I was acutely conscious of my erratic observance of dietary restrictions on this trip, which would infuriate my family. The man looked at me with appreciation and anticipation. I closed my eyes and took a tiny sip—nothing more than making contact with the cup with my lips. When the man turned towards the kitchen, I quickly dumped the tea in a stagnant drain nearby. '*Theek tha?* Was it okay?' the man asks. '*Bahut badhiya!* Very good!' I say. By this time, I was practised at telling small lies to keep my sanity and my health intact. And by this time, too, I also knew the routine of road travel in India. Toilet paper is an essential item to be carried in your personal luggage at all times. I couldn't squat in the privy and I hadn't used water for toilet since I left my village in Labasa over 40 years ago! We carried several bottles of water with us, although I know that what is good for health is not necessarily good for road travel. A full bladder on a bumpy road is, well, not pleasant, to put it politely. I have difficulty 'taking a leak' in public, even in a secluded area. Where and how will I wash my hands? And 'doing the other business' in the open is simply impossible to imagine, with flies buzzing around and people looking in your direction. Indian public toilets are a dreadful mess and to be avoided at all times. Better to have an empty stomach and an empty bladder, I decided.

I was perplexed by the *chai* man's initial reluctance to speak with me and wondered why as we resumed our journey. Kaushik filled me in on the details of something I had heard in Ranchi. The country through which we were travelling was Naxalite country. The Naxalite or Naksalvadi movement began in West Bengal in the late 1960s inspired by the doctrines of Mao Zedong. A loose coalition of complementary interests, its initial aim was the redistribution of land to the landless through armed struggle. Prominent among its early leaders and supporters were people from the tribal heartlands of Bihar and Madhya Pradesh, places such as Jharkhand and Chattisgarh. The movement attracted notoriety through the beheadings of landlords and other acts of terror and violence. A few days before we arrived in Ranchi, newspapers had carried reports of three beheadings of police informers; people taken from their homes in the middle of the night, interrogated, found guilty, killed and their bodies returned to their families. Just like that: retribution and revenge were swift and brutal, which explained the *chai* man's hesitation to talk to me. 'Is this is a terrorist group?' I asked. 'No,' I was told, 'here everyone is either a Naxal or a Naxal sympathiser, even government ministers.' As I saw all the destitution and poverty around me, I could understand why. 'If I was living here, I would be a Naxal too,' someone piped up from the back of the car.

Kaushik, the camera man, was hawk-eyed for shoot sites. We stopped several times as he walked out briskly to survey the scene, the light, the shade. Then he would set up his camera and give the thumbs-up for me to perform. I walked purposefully looking into the distance with a solemn expression on my face, and said my piece in clear, authoritative tones. There is little room for ambiguity and nuance in television talk. 'Keep it simple, Sir,' Aditi advised me. But one take was never enough. Something invariably went wrong. There was someone in the background. I had used my hand to waive off an insect hovering about my face as I spoke. There was noise from a truck on the road. I looked too tense for the part. Could I please redo my bit one more time? One more time became several more times on virtually every shoot.

The routine was draining. Gradually, I became aware of the cultural difference between me as a scholar and the crew as film makers. They had their scripts and their questions. They did not seem overly interested in what I said but rather in how I said it, how it would all look on film, the scenes people would remember. 'How will this all fit into the overall picture,' I asked Aditi. 'Don't worry, Sir,' she said, 'leave it to me.' I did; she was the expert. They were so solicitous, so respectful, so innocent-looking. They listened to me politely, shook their heads respectfully in the quintessential Indian way, but I knew they would do exactly as they had decided.

Apart from some breezy banter, we didn't talk much on the drive. There was not much to share. The documentary team was about half my age. Their taste in contemporary culture and music was alien to me. They sometimes talked about the antics of this hero or that heroine, about a particular scene from a famous recent movie, but I was lost. I had resumed seeing Hindi movies after a lapse of two or three decades, but by then everything had changed, the characters, the concerns, the whole scene. At the Hyderabad conference, I had chaired a session on Bollywood and the Indian diaspora. Farhad Khoyratti, from the University of Mauritius, gave a deeply learned paper titled 'Choosing Bollywood: A phenomenological reading of the contemporary Indian diasporic adoption of the Bollywood text with focus on Mauritius', and a highly animated but very knowledgeable Jorge Diego Sanchez from the University of Salamanca in Spain spoke on 'What's after *Bend it Like Beckham?* Representations and challenges of the women of the Indian diaspora in British cinema'. They spoke enthusiastically about such films as *Hum Aap ke Hain Kaun?* (Who am I to you?), *Dilwale Dulhania Le Jayenge* (The big-hearted will take away the bride), *Kabhi Khushi Kabhie Gham* (Sometimes there's happiness, sometimes there's sorrow) and many more with similarly jaunty titles.

Sitting in the moderator's chair, I felt like a cultural Neanderthal. I knew nothing about contemporary Indian cinema, which was the subject of such learned discourse at the conference and in scholarly gatherings generally. There was a whole new world out there about which I was completely innocent. How had this come to pass, I wondered. What about movies that moved my generation: *Pakeeza* (Pure), *Waqt* (Time), *Guide, Sangam* (Confluence), *Madhumati, Ganga Jamuna, Mother India* and the greatest of them all, *Pyasaa* (Wistful)? Shah Rukh Khan, I learnt, was a major Bollywood star, but what about Dilip Kumar or even Rajesh Khanna? Kajol and Kareena Kapoor were the latest female heart throbs of the screen, but what about Waheeda Rehman and Zeenat *Dum Maro Dum* Aman, of my youthful years, the stuff of our romantic dreams and fantasies? I felt stranded in a rapidly vanishing past, a remnant in my own lifetime. I kept my thoughts to myself. The sense of being lost and being irrelevant to the world around me had been with me for some time, and the distance between the past the present increased daily.

'What do you like about India, Sir?' Aditi asked me, trying to start a conversation after a long silence. 'Your cricket team,' I said with a chuckle. It was a cruel joke, I know, because the much vaunted Indian cricket team had been a total wipe out in Australia, a cause for much national anguish. We laughed and compared notes about who should be in and who should be out of the Indian national team. But Aditi's question touched something deep in me, though I could not quite put my finger on it. I still cannot answer that question. Many Indians of the colonial Indian diaspora carry in their heads a rather fossilised, idealised image of India as a land of great myths and legends, of heroic figures and the great epics with which they grew up, especially the Ramayana. They would be in for a rude shock as they passed through modern airports as good as any in the world, as they travelled along modern highways in Hyderabad and Bangalore, for instance, or shopped in swanky outlets in most metropolitan centres. You did not have to go to London to shop at Marks and Spencer—these prestigious names were now common in India. Craze for things *phoren* (foreign), once so common and so irritatingly insistent, is now firmly a thing of the past.

I detected in most people with whom I spoke a quiet sense of pride in being an Indian. They might want to visit other countries but India is where they would live. It is their home; they want no other. Aditi went to the United Kingdom to do a course in journalism and could easily have stayed on there, but she returned 'to her own place', where her friends and family were. This experience is not uncommon. There is even a major Bollywood movie about it, *Swades: We the People*, if I recall correctly, about a man returning to his native land to apply his foreign-learned skills to improve the life of his people. I don't see the country through rose-tinted glasses; the newspapers are full of reports about corruption and violence, communal tensions are real, and poverty still stalks large parts of the country. But there is a genuine, unyielding commitment to resolving the nation's myriad problems through the values and practices of democracy. And that, when you think about it, is no mean achievement in the developing world. That would be one answer to Aditi's difficult question.

For the first time in my life, I was travelling fully equipped with an iPhone and an iPad, much to the puzzled bewilderment of my family who know me at home as a complete technological innocent. 'From nineteenth century straight to the twenty-second, eh,' my brother Kamla quipped. But these gadgets were a godsend on this journey. They enabled me to switch off and retreat into my inner world. This I did by listening to the music of those long gone days of my childhood. There was Mukesh's *Ye Mera Diwanapan Hai,* sung on the screen by the inimitable Dilip Kumar in the film *Yahudi* (Jew). I realised quickly as I fiddled with my iPhone that other artists have also sung that song, and I spent hours comparing the various renditions. I similarly spent time with other favourites, such as *Aaj Jaane Ki Zid Na Karo* (Please don't insist on leaving today), famously put to music by the immortal Farida Khanum and with Talat Mehmood's songs of love and loss, *Aye dil mujhe aisi jagah le chal.* Hindi music of a certain vintage has the capacity to touch the deepest places in my heart, to reduce me to tears with its haunting melodies. I didn't think Aditi or

10. 'THE CHILDREN OF THE WIND'

any of the other youngsters would understand this, but this is also an integral part of my Indian heritage that has formed me and without which I would be incomplete and all the poorer.

As dry paddy fields flash by, old memories of childhood return: the dry rice fields on which we played fierce games of soccer with balls made from rolled up paper, of the backbreaking work during the planting and harvesting seasons, of the grizzled old *girmitiyas* congregating at our home once in a while, smoking *suluka*, rough, handmade cigarettes wrapped in pandanus leaves, or chewing tobacco, singing *bhajans,* devotional songs, and reminiscing about their past in a language none of us understood. What a journey they had undertaken; from this place in the middle of nowhere to sugar colonies thousands of miles away. What moved them? Why did they leave? I simply don't know. As an exile myself now, I can quite imagine their anguish at not being able to return to the place of their birth even for a visit, dying in a land they never fully embraced. I think of my mother, betrothed at 13, married at 16, bearing eight children, all except one at home, the trauma and taunts she endured because she did not conceive during the first three years of her marriage, but ending her life as a respected member, *kaki* (father's younger brother's wife), *mami* (mother's brother's wife), *mausi* (mother's sister), *phua* (father's sister), of the entire extended family scattered all around Vanua Levu, a renowned singer of wedding songs and a fount of knowledge about the proper rituals to follow for the different *pujas.* Above all, I think about Nana, 17 years old, no more, who took his fate in his hands, shouldered his small bundle of worldly possessions, and left for an unknown place called Fiji.

We arrived in Bandarchua mid-morning. We had decided to do two days of shooting here, but word had been received the previous evening that the Maoist Coordinating Committee had declared a strike the following day. That would mean that all public roads would be blocked by the Naxalites. Everyone knew that vehicles which breached the roadblocks would be fair game, blown up by improvised roadside devices. But I had to be in Ranchi to catch the plane back to Australia the day after so shooting would have to be sped up. As Kaushik set up his camera, a crowd gathered around us. We were an item of great curiosity; film crews are rare in this part of the world. Word quickly gets around about the purpose of my visit and people were curious about who my family might be. I met Mr Narayan Prasad Gupta, the Deputy Sarpanch (Chair) of the village council and Mr Ram Kishore Saipaikra. When I explained why I was there, Mr Gupta asked for my *titol.* He means my caste name. Lal does not help; it is not a caste name. I mention Nana's caste, Bhumihar. That, too, is of no use. I am not disappointed. I had not come to Bandarchua with any expectation of finding Nana's relatives here. After all, there had been no contact for well over a century. Merely to find the place he came from would be enough for me, more than enough.

I walked around. The land was flat and dry as far as the eye could see, dusty and shimmering in the heat. The village centre where we had stopped had several tattered shops selling soft drinks and cheap goods for the locals. Shop signs were painted in bright colours, in both English and Hindi. People were generally well dressed in shirts and long pants; the old familiar garb of *dhoti* (traditional men's garment) and *kurta* (traditional Indian shirt) were not much in evidence—a sign of modest prosperity perhaps? There was a television in one of the shops, and a teenager, knowing that I am from Australia, told me that Australia has just won the toss and could bat first in what would be the final Test. He knew many of the Australian players by name, and was full of praise for David Warner, Ricky Ponting and Michael Clarke. '*Phir se barbadi*, bad luck again,' I say light-heartedly. The boys laughed, knowing the barbed truth of my comment. Many people carried mobile phones, and music from the radio was everywhere. Bandarchua may be remote, but like the rest of India, it is not isolated. It is a part of V.S. Naipaul's *India: A Million Mutinies Now,* the title of one of his books about contemporary India.[5]

'What kind of ridiculous name is Bandarchua? Monkey-Rat,' I ask Mr Gupta, slightly puzzled. 'It is not Bandarchua, it is Bandarchuan.' 'And that means?' 'In olden days,' Mr Gupta continued, '*kuan* (well) was called *chuan*. There was a *chuan* in the village where monkeys from the forest would come for a drink every day. That is how the village got its name.' 'Does that *chuan* still exist?' I am curious. 'Oh, yes,' Mr Gupta said. 'It is very near my house.' We take the tar-sealed road for a few kilometres from the town and veer off on to the dry paddy fields. A kilometre or so later, we come to the *chuan*. It is still there after hundreds, perhaps thousands of years—a small round hole, a metre in diameter, no more, full of greenish water with a few, stray rice stems floating in it. I commented on its neglected state. It might just as well be another watery hole in the ground anywhere in India. Both Mr Gupta and Mr Saipaikra nodded their heads in sadness. 'There is no consciousness of history among our

---

5   V.S. Naipaul, *India: A Million Mutinies Now* (London: Heinemann, 1990).

people anymore,' Mr Gupta said. '*Itihas se kutch parichay nahin,* it is all money, money, money.' 'It is the same everywhere,' I replied. *Sabhi jaghe aisa hi hai.*

I wanted to commemorate my visit to this historic place by planting a mango plant we had brought along with us, at Siddharth's suggestion. A colleague (anthropologist Chris Gregory) familiar with the region later told me that the mango tree was the right choice. It is associated with fecundity, fertility and auspiciousness. Tales abound of barren women falling pregnant after eating a mango. Having planted the tree, Chris informed me, I would have to go back and arrange an *aamaa bivah*, a special kind of ceremony related to the mango fruit, when the first fruits appear. I doubt if it will be anytime soon. Perhaps my children will complete the return journey for me, though I know in my heart of hearts that it is an idle thought; their interests and aspirations are different to mine. History, the search for ancestral roots so profoundly important to me emotionally, holds little interest for them. A spade materialised from a nearby home, we dug a hole by the roadside adjacent to the *chuan* and planted the tree in Nana's memory.

Then we left. Tears welled up as I walked back to our waiting vehicle, my journey complete. I came in search of my Nana's place, and I had found it in this desolate landscape. I felt my (late-middle) age, and the passage of time. Suddenly I became conscious that I am a Nana myself now, of 13-month-old Jayan. He is our pride and joy, taking his first tentative steps into the world as we move inexorably towards our twilight years. We likely won't be around when he comes of age. I wonder about the world in which he will grow up, the influences that will shape his life, whether he will remember *his* Nana, show curiosity about the old man's history and heritage, his journeys and transformations. I would not be surprised if he thinks his Nana's odyssey is beyond comprehension, a figment of someone's imagination; born on a farm to unlettered parents, growing up without electricity, piped water or paved roads, being taught in primary school in open thatched huts, reading at home by flickering kerosene wick lamp, passing strange external exams and managing mysteriously to escape the world of poverty and destitution to a life of learning in the West. My journey will appear as improbable to Jayan as my Nana's appears to me, and probably just as intrinsically fascinating.

Who precisely was Nana was still unresolved in my mind as we headed back to Ranchi in the gathering darkness. Was he a Bhumihar, as his Emigration Pass says, member of a powerful landowning caste that ruled the roost in these parts, people of high rank and powerful connections associated with violent attacks on Dalits and other lower-caste communities for demanding better wages and other rights, people who are regularly targeted by the Naxalites? And why would the son of a Bhumihar migrate? Had Nana escaped from the village for some crime he had committed? Had a girl from another caste been impregnated, inviting swift and severe retribution? Was there a drought in the region which forced young men to seek new prospects beyond the village? Was he at odds with the law? I can only ask these questions; I have no answers. And in the absence of hard evidence, the possibility that Nana was a Bhumihar must remain open.

But another possibility was inadvertently suggested by Mr Gupta. He did not know any Bhumihars in the district; perhaps he was reluctant to identify them for fear of an attack, but there used to be a group known as Bhuinhars in the area, all now gone or absorbed into the settled agricultural community. And who were these people? These were the aboriginal settlers of the land, subsequently displaced by Aryan migrants, and now scattered in small numbers throughout Uttar Pradesh, Bihar and Madhya Pradesh—but once concentrated in the Chota Nagpur plateau, the tribal heartland of India. There were different types of Bhuinhars, differentiated from each other by rank, rituals and tradition. Some were patronised by the rulers while others were shunted to the periphery. Some assimilated with the new migrants from the north in the eighteenth and nineteenth centuries while others lived at the edge of forests as hunters and gatherers or as shifting agriculturalists who regarded working for wages beneath them. Agriculture was not in their blood; they disdained the routine of settled life. Some went into gold panning in rivers and streams nearby, and moved on when prospects there dried up. There was something else about the Bhuinhars I read somewhere later that stuck in my mind; that they liked to live in isolation from the rest of the world, preferring the company of their own close kith and kin. Nothing mattered more to them than their independence and freedom of movement. *Pawan-bans* (the children of the wind) they sometimes called themselves, establishing indirect connections to Lord Hanuman, *Pawan-putra* (the son of the wind).

10. 'THE CHILDREN OF THE WIND'

All this would explain Nana's otherwise peculiar behaviour perfectly: why he preferred to fish rather than work on the land, why he settled in remote Nuk Nuk, far from the civilised world of Tabia and Laqere. Perhaps as a young lad he was out and about, looking for work, met a recruiter who promised him milk and honey in the *tapus* (islands), perhaps not far away, fell into the recruiter's trap and left. Ethnographic literature on the castes and tribes of central India in the late nineteenth century suggest that the Bhuinhar are a dark-brown, well-proportioned race, with plentiful black, straight hair on the head, but with little hair on the face. Of middle height, they have compact, light-framed figures and are capable of very hard work. This will do me as a mental picture of the Nana I never knew.

The past is now truly past. Whether Nana was a Bhumihar of the settled dominant agricultural community of Bihar, or a restless Bhuinhar wanderer of the forested hills of central India matters little. His secrets, the fears and ambitions that drove him from this place to faraway Fiji, went with him. But I am glad I made the return journey for him, and especially for my mother. I desperately wish mother were alive to hear the news of my visit to her father's distant homeland. I would like to think that Nana would be pleased that his wanderlust and free spirit continue to flow in the veins of his grandchildren now scattered around the globe: like him, children of the wind. I leave Bandarchuan with '… memories vague of half-forgotten things / Not true nor false, but sweet to think upon'.[6]

---

6 William Morris, 'March', *The Earthly Paradise* (New York and London: Routledge, 2002), lines 42 and 43.

PART 2
Future Tense: Witnessing History

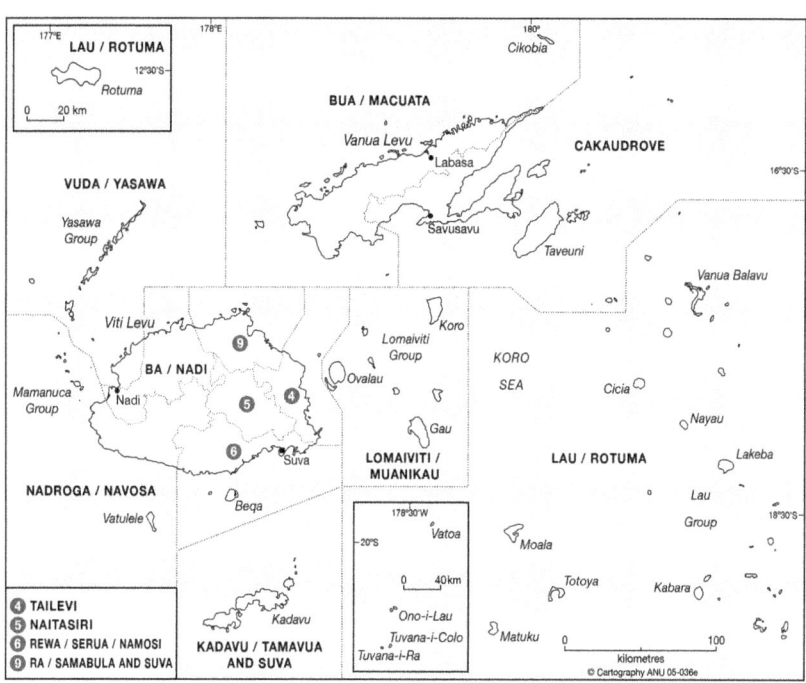

Figure 2. Map of the Fiji Islands
Source. © The Australian National University. Cartography ANU 05-036e.

11
While the gun is still smoking[1]

> History is the long struggle of man, by the exercise of his reason,
> to understand his environment and to act upon it.
>
> — Edward Hallett Carr[2]

Throughout my research and writing career, I ranged freely between matters more historical and topics in contemporary history, from writing on the experience of indenture to the analysis of general elections in recent times. Often I was a close observer from the sidelines, but on some occasions I was actively involved in political issues, such as my role as a commissioner on the Reeves Constitution Commission in the mid-1990s. In the 1999 general elections in Fiji, I actively campaigned for the National Federation Party in support of its commitment to making the 1997 Constitution work. All this raises the question about whether I can write 'objectively' on events in which I was intimately involved. There is also a school of thought that holds 'contemporary history' to be a contradiction in terms, advocating the view that 'proper' history can be written only after the dust has long settled and the guns are silent. I address these questions here.

---

1   Originally appeared as 'While the gun is still smoking', in *Pacific Lives, Pacific Places: Bursting Boundaries in Pacific History*, ed. Brij V. Lal and Peter Hempenstall (Canberra: The Journal of Pacific History, Inc., 2001), pp. 70–87.
2   Edward Hallett Carr, *What is History?* (New York, NY: Random House, 1961), p. 178.

'A lot of history is concealed autobiography,' the distinguished Australian historian Ken Inglis once wrote.[3] That observation rings true to me. So, too, does E.H. Carr's contention that every historian is in some sense 'a social phenomenon, both the product and the conscious and unconscious spokesman [sic] of the society to which he belongs'.[4] And Jim Davidson seems right as well when he says that the 'initial impetus towards the study of modern history not infrequently derives from the students' own sense of involvement in his [sic] own society'.[5] The nature and quality of that engagement, I would argue, shape our understandings and assumptions about the world we live in, and frame the identity, orientation and style of our work. I do not wish to suggest a simple mechanistic correlation between class, ideology and intellectual work. History is a liberal, broad-minded discipline of multiple, overlapping identities, which admits a variety of approaches, techniques and sources. Its boundaries are porous and flexible. What I do suggest is a dynamic dialectical relationship between social and historical experience and intellectual endeavour, underlining the fundamental truth that we live in our own histories.

The subject of this chapter is contemporary history, eyewitness history and participant history. It is necessarily autobiographical, as these projects usually are,[6] but I use my experience to raise issues about the limitations, attractions and opportunities that present themselves to historians who live at the interface of history and practical action. What forces and impulses pull them in the direction of practical engagement? Does participation or engagement hinder or help one's understanding of the society's history? How does it affect the analysis and interpretation of the event in which one is a participant? Does engagement provide new

---

3   Ken S. Inglis, assisted by Jan Brazier, *This is the ABC: The Australian Broadcasting Commission, 1932–1983* (Melbourne: Melbourne University Press, 1983), p. 1.
4   Carr, *What is History?*, p. 35.
5   J.W. Davidson, 'Understanding Pacific history: The participant as historian', in *The Feel of Truth: Essays in New Zealand and Pacific History*, ed. Peter Munz (Wellington: AW & AH Reed, 1969), pp. 27–42, at p. 34.
6   For typical examples, see Arthur Schlesinger, Jr, 'The historian and history', *Foreign Affairs* 41(3) (1963): 491–97, doi.org/10.2307/20029635; 'The historian as participant', *Daedalus* 100(2) (1971): 339–58; David Butler, 'Instant history', *The New Zealand Journal of History* 2(2) (1968): 107–14; Davidson, 'Understanding Pacific history', pp. 25–40.

insights into the dynamics of the practical affairs of state, or does it simply reinforce existing prejudices? There is, in my case, the added complication of being a historian participating in the affairs of my own country.[7]

Participant and eyewitness history of the types I discuss here, without drawing a sharp distinction between them, are decidedly out of fashion even, or especially, among historians. The conventional, not to say unconvincing, objections are well known. Participant and eyewitness accounts are partial and biased; they distort; they lack perspective; they are unable to separate matters of residual moment from matters of cardinal importance; they are, at best, the first primitive draft, a small building block, nothing more, in the larger edifice of later historiography produced in the course of time by detachment and objectivity. Attachment, it is argued, constricts accuracy; and advocacy, of whatever kind, is the stuff of propaganda. History should be objective, not reductionist or directly utilitarian in intent, and the historian should try to tell 'how it actually happened'. Disapproval also comes from cultural relativists and the new social historians who decry the narratives of 'total' history and the search for complete explanation, wary of creating structures and imposing interpretations that suffocate variety and deny diversity. Scepticism, doubt, ambiguity, tentativeness and partiality of knowledge, a firm belief in the impotence of human reason and the injustice of universal moral judgements, are markers of this discourse. These words and concepts would seem incongruous to most participant historians. And *their* organising concepts—political power, the nation state, democracy, human rights, for example—and *their* efforts to search for patterns and meanings, to create structures that unite and enlarge the common space, are dismissed as hopelessly obsolete, relics of a past long gone and mercifully forgotten. I exaggerate slightly, but the suspicions and the tensions are real.

In the Pacific Islands many scholars, including historians, have been active participants in the affairs of their societies. Nowhere in the region has this been more marked than in my own country of Fiji, where the list is impressively long. The drift began with Rusiate Nayacakalou, trained in anthropology at the London School of Economics by Raymond Firth and tenured at Sydney, who gave up a promising academic career to return to

---

7   As opposed to, say, Jim Davidson, O.H.K. Spate, Harry Maude, Ron Crocombe and David Stone were all expatriate advisors and experts. Alan Ward, who engaged as a consultant to the Waitangi Tribunal in his native New Zealand, also worked as an advisor and consultant on land issues in Vanuatu and Papua New Guinea. See Peter Hempenstall, 'Tasman epiphanies: The "participant history" of Alan Ward', *The Journal of New Zealand Studies* 4–5 (2005–06): 65–80, doi.org/10.26686/jnzs.v0i4/5.107.

Fiji to head the Native Land Trust Board.[8] Isireli Lasaqa, with a doctorate in geography, left an academic position at the University of the South Pacific for a senior position in the Fiji public service.[9] Ahmed Ali gave up academia for national politics, followed by Satendra Nandan, Tupeni Baba, Jo Nacola, Meli Waqa, Ganesh Chand, Isimeli Cokanisiga, Biman Prasad and, for a while, Wadan Narsey. I mention only the names of those who took the direct plunge from university teaching into parliamentary politics, but many Fiji staff, both Fijian and Indo-Fijian, have long been politically active in a variety of capacities. One hopes that in due course some of them will reflect on their transition and transformations and tell us how their training and experience as academics has tempered their practical work.

Participation came naturally to the generation of students attending the University of the South Pacific in its salad days of the 1970s. The regional university, which opened in 1968, was required by its founding mission to train people to meet the anticipated development needs of a rapidly decolonising region. A Programme Planning Seminar at the Laucala Bay Campus in May 1968 took its cue from the Charter of the University, which provided that the objects of the University shall be:

> the maintenance, advancement and dissemination of knowledge by teaching, consultancy and research and otherwise and for the provision at appropriate levels of education and training responsive to the well-being and needs of the communities of the South Pacific.[10]

At the seminar, 'the decision was taken to adopt the general organisation of groups of discipline located within Schools of broad developmental rather than the more common departmental and faculty structure'.[11] The initial schools, which have been renamed since, were Education, Natural Resources, and Social and Economic Development.

---

8 Rusiate Nayacakalou, *Leadership in Fiji* (Melbourne: Oxford University Press, 1975), p. v.
9 Lasaqa wrote a book, *The Fijian People: Before and After Independence, 1959–1977* (Canberra: Australian National University Press, 1984). Ratu Sir Kamisese Mara, in the Preface, writes:

> Dr Lasaqa is an academic who has the sobering experience of finding himself being translated into the field of administration and he has distinguished himself in both. But this means that he has been able to bring to his writing of his book both intellectual and practical disciplines, and his academic studies have been tried and tempered in the field (p. v).

Lasaqa himself does not reflect on this beyond saying that he is attempting to represent the Fijian point of view.
10 University of the South Pacific, *Calendar 1983*, p. 315.
11 ibid.

The developmental intellectual climate set the framework of learning in practical ways. Specialisation was discouraged; a broadbased education was deemed the best preparation for training future administrators and teachers. The actual political environment of decolonisation provided an affirming context for the intellectual course charted by the new university. My own evolution as an historian engaged in practical issues derives largely from that experience.

Like other Pacific Island historians—Sione Latukefu, Malama Meleisea, John Waiko—I focused on the history of my own people for my first piece of sustained graduate research, writing my dissertation on the social and cultural background of the Indian indentured migrants to Fiji. At the same time, I expanded my research to include the workings of contemporary politics, which began through a series of election studies and commentaries. Living in Fiji, and called upon to comment on the political campaigns, I could not, nor did I want to, escape the challenge and opportunity to participate, albeit as an interested bystander, in contemporary debates in my own country; and what could be more interesting than covering a heated political campaign? With time, an incidental interest evolved into a major professional preoccupation, resulting in a series of detailed political studies, and culminating in my appointment to the Fiji Constitution Review Commission in 1995. That appointment itself was preceded by several years of active opposition to the coups of 1987 and the divisive public culture of governance they spawned. From the very beginning, I was opposed to the overthrow of the Labour Coalition Government. I felt then, as I feel now, that there was something profoundly wrong about overturning the verdict of the ballot box by the bayonet.

The coups presented, for me, a deep political as well as moral crisis. One either supported the coups or opposed them. There could be no middle ground. I lost patience with those who treated the coups as an 'on the one hand and on the other' kind of discourse. Perhaps I spoke too firmly, but at least there was no doubt in anyone's mind about where I stood. Taking a stand! Those words have a familiar ring to those caught in the middle of a fray—both participants and historians. My opposition intensified with time. I intervened through radio and television interviews, mostly unsuccessfully, to correct what I construed to be misrepresentations and misconceptions. I learnt the rude lesson that in the public domain facts, when they get in the way of a dramatic story, are not welcome. Complex facts do not engage the public imagination, which wants simple, vivid, preferably provocative answers to quotable 'newsworthy' questions, delivered in attractive sound bites. By intervening the way I did, I may have compromised my objectivity, but I remained staunch in my support for liberal, representative democracy while emphasising the need to acknowledge and celebrate constitutionally recognised sacred and important institutions of Fijian society. In this respect, I share Oskar Spate's wise advice to declare one's hand to the readers:

> The impartiality which evades responsibility by saying nothing, the partiality which masks its bias by presenting slanted facts with an air of cold objectivity—these are a thousand times more dangerous than an open declaration of where one stands; then at least those who disagree can take one's measure with confidence: 'that is why he said thus' … The important points are that inference must be based on evidence, as carefully verified as possible; and that the choice shall be made from the evidence, and not from pre-conceived ideas.[12]

This is the approach I used in my *Power and Prejudice: The Making of the Fiji Crisis* (1988).[13] I was a target of the coup perpetrators because of my ethnicity and political stance; the book was written while the gun was still smoking. Nonetheless, I brought to my analysis the training and approach of the historian. I gathered all the available evidence as assiduously as I could against which I tested a number of prevailing hypotheses, many of which failed to measure up. One such, which had reached melodramatic proportions soon after the coups, saw the American Central Intelligence Agency (CIA) as the principal instigator of the overthrow of a left-leaning government supposedly hostile to American strategic interests in the Pacific. The presence in Fiji around the time of the coups of some senior American officials, alleged to be veterans of coups in other parts of the world, added fuel to the fire.[14] Nothing that I saw convinced me that the hypothesis was tenable. Americans may have known, perhaps given a knowing wink or looked the other way when they knew that something was afoot, but they did not mastermind the coups. The search for the extent of foreign involvement, I argued, should not be allowed to distort

---

12 R.G. Ward and O.H.K. Spate, 'Thirty years ago: A view of the Fiji political scene: *Confidential Report to the British Colonial Office*', *The Journal of Pacific History* 25(1) (1990): 103–24, at p. 103, doi.org/10.1080/00223349008572628.
13 Brij V. Lal, *Power and Prejudice: The Making of the Fiji Crisis* (Wellington: New Zealand Institute for International Affairs, 1988).
14 James Anthony, a Fiji expatriate living in Honolulu, was the principal proponent of this theory.

the larger picture. Often those who pursue the theory of external causation pay insufficient attention to the role of local forces and local leaders in the making of their own history.[15]

Three decades later, I have no reason to change my view, but at the time I was accused of being a puppet of the State Department for not holding the United States responsible for the Fiji crisis. Another hypothesis portrayed the coup as a simple racial conflict, between indigenous Fijians and Indo-Fijians, an assertion of indigenous power against an economically powerful and demographically preponderant immigrant-derived community. On the surface, the hypothesis sounded convincing, but was superficial upon closer analysis. Ethnicity was both a cause as well as a scapegoat of the crisis. I saw the coups as flowing from a complex interplay of a range of factors, none of which themselves could be sufficient. I argued:

> The Fiji coups were more about frustrated politicians bent upon recapturing power lost at the polls than they were about ethnic prejudice, the importance of the latter cannot be—and here it is not—lightly dismissed. I argue further that the basic reasons for the coups will be found not so much in the machinations of outside agencies—which no doubt played a role in aiding and abetting forces opposed to the Coalition Government—as within the dynamics of local history and politics, and in the actions and machinations of specific individuals within Fiji without whose active participation nothing could have been accomplished. It is possible to discern the premonitions of the present crisis in the silent footsteps of modern Fijian history; but to argue that the coups were historically predetermined is to falsify a very complicated story and misjudge its essence. There was nothing really inevitable about the Fiji coups. In the ultimate analysis, the Fiji crisis was caused by a complex combination of incipient class conflicts, provincial tensions among the indigenous Fijians and deep-seated racial antagonisms long embedded in the very structure of Fiji's society and politics.[16]

Almost 30 years since this analysis was first drafted, many books, some by participants, have been published and some new information has come to light, but my fundamental thesis stands. At least, I stand by it. Indeed, I am tempted to say that it grows stronger as new information comes

---

15   Lal, *Power and Prejudice,* p. 36.
16   ibid., p. 7.

to light. An important reason is that I wrote the account as a trained historian. We do not deal with certainties but with probabilities. We try to draw conclusions from the facts, as carefully and objectively assembled and verified as possible, rather than fit them into preconceived conclusions. No one explanation by itself 'will satisfactorily account for the complex character of the Fijian crisis', I wrote in 1988, nor was 'it desirable to put the Fijian story into the straitjacket of political and social theories derived from other contexts and experiences'.[17] This is no unique insight; it is simply sound historical practice of the type we employ in the course of our regular work.

While historians are good at predicting the past, they by and large make bad prophets, especially historians of the contemporary scene. Engrossed in the details and drama of events unfolding before their eyes, they miss the wood for the trees. I was no exception. When I wrote, I was deeply pessimistic about Fiji returning to normalcy in my own lifetime. In 1988, the architects of the coup were in power, implementing policies designed to entrench Fijian paramountcy. The economy was on the brink of collapse. Fiji was out of the Commonwealth. Capital drained out of the country and people queued outside foreign embassies seeking visas for permanent migration. The army was on the streets. The opposition was demoralised. The world did not seem to care. But Fiji, within a decade, returned to embrace a new constitution, without violence and bloodshed, to launch the country tentatively in a new direction of inclusive multiracial democracy, only to have it shattered by George Speight's intervention—another case of historians not seeing what was coming. With hindsight, I should have glimpsed the shape of future developments. I had argued that provincial tensions, class interests and individual ambitions for power had led to the coup, along with ethnic fears. It should have been apparent that once the fears that had sparked the crisis had gone, these interests and concerns would have, in the course of time, gone on their own divergent paths. I should have seen that the politically expedient unity of Fijian interests was a chimera; that politics among Fijians, like any other community, were driven by vested social interests and personal ambitions. And my knowledge of history should have taught me that authoritarian structures imposed on a populace through force do not enjoy a long and happy life.

---

17 ibid., p. 6.

11. WHILE THE GUN IS STILL SMOKING

As I read the accounts of the coups, including my own, long after the dust had settled and the army returned to the barracks, I am impressed by the depth and detail of the narratives produced while the gun was still smoking. They convey passion, urgency and immediacy that are difficult for me to conjure up now. The authors argue different theses. There were few points of agreement between them then, and they remain as far apart even now. Time has not erased the difference, and it never will. The idea that one day when all the facts are available, when the first primitive drafts of contemporary, or eyewitness, history have been transformed by a master historian into a standard, universally uncontested account, about the full significance of what happened in the past, is mere fantasy.[18] Three of the earliest accounts of the coup were written by professional historians.[19] The imprint of their training and approach is clear. The texts are well documented, but they also rely on types of evidence that go beyond the narrow range of sources typically deployed in conventional political histories.

My own analysis draws upon newspaper accounts and other published sources in the public domain. But it also draws upon other material, much of which is now probably lost to posterity: handbills, draft copies of speeches, transcripts of radio broadcasts, television footage and interviews. In the future, those wanting to know the initial reaction of the people might turn to the handbills distributed on the streets of the major towns and centres. I reproduced two in my book to give the reader a sense of what was being said and heard as the crisis was unfolding. They capture some of the anxiety, frustration, suppressed anger and trauma at the time in a way that a latter-day historian working from conventional sources might be unable to construct. I also used personal observation: the shops clogged with frenzied people buying emergency food supplies; shop windows barricaded behind hurricane shutters; the commandeered vehicles speeding along deserted streets; anxious, armed, balaclava-clad

---

18 Among the influential historians of the past who hold the hope of ultimate history is Herbert Butterfield. See his *History and Human Relations* (London: Collins, 1951):

> If we consider the history of the historical writing that has been issued, generation after generation, on a given body of events, we shall generally find that in the early stages of this process of reconstruction the narrative which is produced has a primitive and simple shape. As one generation of students succeeds another, however, each developing the historiography of this particular subject, the narrative passes through certain typical stages until it is brought to a high and subtle form of organisation (p. 10).

19 Besides me, see Deryck Scarr, *The Politics of Illusion: Military Coup in Fiji* (Sydney: NSWU Press, 1988); Robbie Robertson and Akosita Tamanisau, *Fiji – Shattered Coups* (Sydney: Pluto Press, 1988).

soldiers atop strategic buildings; long queues seeking to emigrate; hushed conversations in cars. These are the kind of details a future novelist writing about this event might find to be of primary importance. A contemporary historian, especially one working in societies where the culture of preserving the historical record is undeveloped and unappreciated, carries the dual burden of being an archivist and an observer as well as an interpreter of events.

Eyewitness history also provides the historian with the opportunity to corroborate evidence through interviews—a technique that is unavailable to those working on more remote periods. A case in point is the role of the judiciary in resolving the early stages of the first (May 1987) coup. The matter was understandably shrouded in secrecy, encouraging rumours and false impressions about what was happening at Government House. What advice had the judges given the governor-general? Had their advice been sought? What was the legal status of the suspended constitution and other authority flowing from it? Wanting to find out, I rang the chief justice at his residence, and, much to my surprise, he readily agreed to see me that very morning. When I met him, the chief justice not only gave me a detailed account of the difficulties he had encountered in contacting the governor-general—he gave me the names of individuals impeding that effort—he also gave me a copy of the high court judges' submission to the governor-general, which is reproduced in my book, *Power and Prejudice*.[20] The judges' advice that the 'purported suspension of the Constitution of Fiji by the military regime which has assumed de facto power is illegal and invalid', and that the independence constitution 'remains in force and unchanged', when it finally reached the governor-general, changed his mind. He proclaimed himself deeply disturbed by the 'unlawful seizure of members of my government … which must not be allowed to continue'. The role of the judiciary was a crucial one, and one which I would not have understood properly without the assistance of the chief justice. I would be surprised if the chief justice would still be able to recall all the details and the emotion as vividly as he did a few hours after the event.[21]

---

20 Lal, *Power and Prejudice*, p. 81.
21 In pre-electronic days, when people often kept daily diaries and wrote letters with greater frequency, such details might be there for the taking by later historians among private papers, assuming, of course, that these were preserved for posterity.

I would not today be able to write the book I wrote in 1988. Is that an indictment of contemporary history? I do not think so. My own response is well put by David Butler:

> If one is trying to summarise an event as it seemed at the time, trying to get the facts together, the less one is contaminated by posterior wisdom, by looking back at the events with a knowledge of the consequences, the greater the force and immediacy of one's narrative.[22]

Events and emotions that loomed large at a critical moment in time have a reality and identity of their own, irrespective of their place in the later assessment of history. Their meaning and importance, ethnographic historians will argue, should not be contingent upon the meaning placed upon them by posterity. To 're-present what actually happened in its specificity'[23] is important in its own right. But, having said that, I am also mindful of Doug Munro's contention that 'contemporary or participant history should not necessarily be regarded as intrinsically deficient or as de facto primary source material for future historians'. And neither, he argues, is there a perfect time to take stock: one always writes from the perspective of the time of writing.[24] 'Historians,' as Greg Dening has reminded us, 'live with the certainty that they will one day become someone else's historiography.'[25]

Writing about your own society as a participant historian requires great sensitivity and tact and a certain degree of self-censorship. The quest for truth and objective understanding has to be balanced against the demands of other, sometimes equally, demanding factors. In a small island state, everyone is known to virtually everyone else, and news travels fast on the coconut wireless. Criticism and adverse comment, no matter how justified, are often taken personally. And they can easily be misconstrued in a country like Fiji, which has two contrasting traditions of discourse.

---

22   Butler, 'Instant history', p. 109.
23   Greg Dening, *The Bounty: An Ethnographic History* (Melbourne: University of Melbourne, 1989), p. 109. Dening argues:

> History is a way of knowing, an act of consciousness, constantly repeated, never the same, always relative to the language in which it is expressed, always relative to the audience to whom it is given, itself a cultural artefact of an age other than the one whose story it tells. History is reductionist insofar as it transforms the totality of the past into words.

24   Personal correspondence, 5 July 2000.
25   See Greg Dening, 'Reflection: On the cultural history of Marshall Sahlins and Valerio Valeri', *Pacific History Bibliography and Comments* (Canberra: Journal of Pacific History, 1986), pp. 43–48, at p. 45.

One, practised by the Indo-Fijian community, is at home in open, robust, democratic debate. The other, rooted in traditional communal culture, is presented in subtle, indirect ways, conscious of the rank and status of both the speaker and the person spoken about. Commenting on electoral politics in Fiji in the early 1980s, I was acutely conscious of the need to be cautious in my comments and analysis for fear of being misunderstood or, worse still, labelled. I practised a degree of self-censorship in my public comments though not in my writing, performed in the safety of a foreign university. In a divided society such as Fiji, everything is seen and assessed through the prism of ethnicity. Public memory is racially archived. Birth and death certificates register ethnicity; one is asked to indicate one's ethnic identity when opening a bank account or when taking out a driving licence. Upon leaving and entering Fiji, the citizens are required to declare their ethnic identity. In South Africa, the immigration forms distinguish five categories of ethnicity. In Fiji, the number is seven.

Markers of ethnicity are everywhere. In the mid-1990s, the National Bank of Fiji was on the verge of bankruptcy, brought about by breathtakingly bad management. The matter was raised in parliament by the Indo-Fijian Leader of the Opposition, Jai Ram Reddy. The indigenous Fijian Foreign Minister (Filipe Bole) attributed the criticism to racism because the employees were Fijians and Rotumans.[26] When some opposition Indo-Fijian Members of Parliament criticised French nuclear testing in French Polynesia, Rabuka denounced the critics as anti-Fijian, because his (Fijian) government had tried to cultivate relations with the French. I dared to suggest that Ratu Sukuna's policies had, at least in part, disadvantaged many ordinary Fijians because he saw no value in academic education for his people—as distinct from chiefly Fijians, who, thus equipped, could then go on to perpetuate chiefly dominance—while other ethnic groups were marching ahead in the professions. I was labelled anti-Fijian for my audacity to criticise the work and legacy of a high chief.[27] Physical distance now diminishes the impact of these criticisms, but they can be oppressive and dangerous to those living with them on a daily basis.

---

26 See Brij V. Lal, *Another Way: The Politics of Constitutional Reform in Post-Coup Fiji* (Canberra: Asia Pacific Press, 1998), p. 54; Roman Grynberg, Doug Munro and Michael White, *Crisis: The Collapse of the National Bank of Fiji* (Suva: USP Book Centre, 2002), pp. 42, 148.

27 For an example of distorted criticism, see Ropate R. Qalo, *Small Business: A Study of a Fijian Family* (Suva: Privately published, 1997), p. 5; 'The stamp of the man: Initial impressions', *Journal of Pacific Studies* 22 (1998): 207–12.

Academics resolve the dilemma in several ways. Some present their views openly, without being overly concerned about the consequences. Isireli Lasaqa, analysing the development dilemmas facing the Fijian people, writes forthrightly about 'Fijian life and thought, Fijian needs and aspirations, how they see their neighbours, and the Fijian scene and beyond'.[28] If one is labelled a racist for representing a racial point of view, so be it. Some attempt a 'middle course between partiality on the one hand and impartiality on the other', satisfying no one, while others take the grandiose view that 'there is a lot to be said on both sides'.[29] Some resort to anonymous but editorially sanctioned essays in the newspapers, getting their ideas into the public arena without revealing their identity. This approach, to me, seems cowardly. Others have used the path of fiction to circumvent the dilemma. The best exponent of this approach in the Pacific Islands is Epeli Hau'ofa. His justifiably well-known satire, *Tales of the Tikongs*,[30] deals with the problems of aid, development, corruption and mismanagement, and conflict between traditional customs and modern attitudes, in the tiny island of Tiko. The issues are identified, and the message gets across without the messenger being persecuted. Sudesh Mishra's searing poems on the coups and subsequent developments also achieve the same goal, but whether his work is read by those who are its target is another matter.[31]

Participation enables one to see history in the making. It is a sobering experience to see how 'truth' emerges from a vast, chaotic mass of experience and activity, how small things get magnified, torn out of context and used in unexpected ways that change the course of history. One example will suffice. In 1982, Jai Ram Reddy, the leader of the National Federation Party (NFP), was fighting a tough election against the ruling Alliance Party, which, for its part, wanted to wean away sufficient Indian voters from Reddy's party to destroy, once and for all, the NFP's claim to be the voice of the Indian community.[32] The campaign was closely contested, tense. In the course of one speech in Labasa, Reddy

---

28   Lasaqa, *The Fijian People,* p. xii.
29   The quotes are from David Thomson, *The Aims of History: Values of the Historical Attitude* (London: Thames and Hudson, 1969), p. 27. Without meaning to be unfair to him, I have the sense that Ahmed Ali held back from pursuing a searching enquiry into Fiji politics in the 1970s because he had been closely allied to the Alliance Party under whose banner he would enter national politics later.
30   Epeli Hau'ofa, *Tales of the Tikongs* (Auckland: Longman Paul, 1983).
31   See Sudesh Mishra, *Tandava* (Melbourne: Meanjin, 1992); and his poems in *With Heart and Nerve and Sinew: Post-Coup Writing from Fiji,* ed. Arlene Griffin (Suva: Christmas Club, 1997).
32   See Brij V. Lal, 'The Fiji General Elections of 1982: The tidal wave that never came', *The Journal of Pacific History* 18(2) (1983): 134–57, at p. 150, doi.org/10.1080/00223348308572463.

said that Mara was so desperate for Indian votes that he would even open a toilet block in order to capture Indian votes! A harmless enough remark given the context, but printed in the papers next day, it aroused more emotion and acrimony than I had ever seen before. Reddy, many Fijians said, had committed a serious breach of protocol, which in ancient times would have seen him clubbed. He had insulted not only a great man, but also insulted the *vanua* (province) of Lau, of which Mara was the paramount chief and the Fijian people generally. How dare an Indian suggest that a high chief like Mara would ever stoop so low to get Indian votes. Seizing the moment, Mara said in a deeply injured tone that those who had attacked him will not be forgiven or forgotten. Protest marches were held throughout Fiji, demanding Reddy's resignation. Racial rhetoric reached dangerous levels. Up went the call for Fijian unity. Reddy lost the election, winning 24 seats to Alliance's 26, but his words remained firmly in people's minds for a long time. Indeed, a few months after the election, at a meeting of the Great Council of Chiefs (GCC), opened for the first time by a reigning monarch, the chiefs vented their anger at the remarks made by *kaitani* (foreigners), and passed resolutions demanding Fijian dominance in parliament.[33] A stray comment, uttered in the middle of a heated campaign, inflamed racial passions and brought Fiji to the brink of potentially explosive political conflict. Such is the nature of politics in an ethnically divided society.

The participant historian also learns from personal experience that sometimes the public record does not reflect reality, and may in fact be contrary to it. When that happens, should the participant expose the facts and face the consequences, knowing that left uncorrected the historical record would forever remain distorted? One example will suffice. During the course of public hearings organised by the Fiji Constitution Review Commission, I was attacked several times by a number of nationalist Fijians, who questioned my credentials and credibility and integrity to be on the Commission. The attacks were vicious and hurtful, accusing me of being an incompetent, anti-Fijian bigot. They were broadcast on television and published in newspapers, and people still remember the incident several years later. The Commission expressed full confidence in me, but I was discomfited by such brutal and unfounded attacks, especially when I could not respond without damaging the standing of the Commission. Much later, when I met one accuser in an airport lounge, and another at a

---

33   See Brij V. Lal, 'The 1982 Fiji National Election and its aftermath', *USP Sociological Society Newsletter* 5 (1983): 3–17.

social gathering, I gently asked why they had been so hard on me. The first, wrapping his arms around my shoulders said that he was trying to 'soften me up', a routine tactic politicians use against all new opponents, trying to get their measure. That came as a surprise to me. The other, equally frank, regretted attacking me, but revealed a personal agenda. He was contesting a by-election in Tailevu, one of several caused by the disqualification of Adi Samanunu, as a member of the Fijian nationalist organisation Vanua Tako Lavo Party, a nationalist Fijian political organisation. Attacking me, he said, would assure him automatic publicity and national news coverage as a champion of the Fijian people, standing up against this 'smart Indian'. Not that it did him any good, because he lost the by-election by a huge margin.

Serving on the Commission also made me realise how limited, and limiting, media coverage is or can be. Things are done on the run, deadlines have to be met, there is limited space in the news column, the story, important in its own right, does not have 'sale' value. Often, only the sensational bits and pieces get reported, and even then they are torn out of context. For instance, the future historian of the Fiji's constitutional evolution will read, from the newspapers, that the reason why the Commission was unable to submit its report on time was that Tomasi Vakatora and I were bitterly opposed to each other and were unable to agree on the most important points.[34] I will not deny that we had our difficult days, but the reason for the delays had nothing to do with us: the delays were caused by the sheer amount of work we were asked to accomplish. For the record, the main details about the structure of the executive and legislative branches of the government were resolved by January 1996, several months before we submitted our report! This fact will be known only to those who care to comb the record of the Commission rather than relying on newspapers. Sometimes, what is said never comes to light, again distorting the public record. Let me illustrate this with an example. One prominent advocate of separate representation for Muslims, then a civil servant, asked for a private audience with the Commission to plead his case. The request was granted. He repeated the usual arguments: Muslims were a separate group, apart from the larger Indian community into which they were

---

34   Doug Munro, in a review of my book *Another Way*, likened my working relationship with Tomasi Vakatora to that between the German Stresemann and the Frenchman Briand, as a meeting of minds between two seeming irreconcilables who put aside national differences in the quest for the greater cause of a lasting peace in Europe. Munro's review appeared in the *Pacific Economic Bulletin* 14(1) (1999): 115–17.

lumped for the sake of administrative convenience. He also favoured making Fiji a Christian state, largely to win the support of the Fijians for his cause. How could he, a Muslim, agree to Fiji becoming a Christian state? Was there not a contradiction here? His response, his exact words were, 'No, because Islam is a heresy of Christianity anyway! Christians we don't mind, it's the Hindu gatekeepers we cannot abide.'

There were many others like him, saying one thing in public and another in private for reasons of pure political expediency that perplexed me. Take the Sunday Ban, for instance, a strict observance of the Sabbath, which came into force in 1988, proscribing all unauthorised commercial and recreational activity on Sunday. Many people, including, especially, indigenous Fijians, suffered from the ban on public transport, making it difficult for them to attend church or go to hospitals or access other essential services, and the closure of shops denied them the normal foodstuffs such as bread, tea, sugar—all staples in the countryside. They wanted the ban removed, they said in private, but in public they remained steadfast in support of it. It was a similar situation on provincial representation. Many Fijians in private deplored its deleterious effects, sowing the seeds of provincial division and rivalry, impeding the development of an effective national political party not tethered to local provincial interests. They wanted us to recommend reversion to the constituency-based electoral system of the precoup era. Yet, these same individuals remained disconcertingly silent in public or actively joined the chorus to retain the status quo. In a meeting of the Joint Parliamentary Committee, one participant arguing for change pointed out the absurdity of Filipe Bole not being able to stand from Suva, where he lived, but standing from Lau, where he was born but where he had not lived for decades. Many members agreed with the absurdity of the situation but voted against the proposal. The public heard that the Fijian Members of Parliament were unanimously in favour of retaining the provincial system of election. Some of the most eloquent defenders of the status quo were among the most passionate pleaders for change in private.

For an historian, it is interesting as well as instructive to see how history is understood and used at the popular level. I was both impressed and dismayed by what I saw and heard during the Commission's hearings. Historical facts and events were often invoked in support of various demands. Often, the seemingly incontrovertible truth being presented was either wrong or misleading, acquired through hearsay, prejudice masquerading as principle, but the submitters did not know or care. The most troubling example of this was the Soqosoqo ni Vakavulewa ni Taukei (SVT) submission, which used, unacknowledged, some 30 quotations from my book *Broken Waves*.[35] Wrenched out of context, the words were used to support themes that directly contradicted my own position. So, Governor Sir Murchison Fletcher is quoted saying that Indians who had gone to Fiji had come from 'the most ignorant and backward part of India', and he saw danger in 'placing power in the hands of untutored people'. But Fletcher wrote this to argue the more limited position that Indians were not worthy of equal franchise. Sir Maynard Hedstrom, an implacable foe of Indo-Fijian demands for political equality, is quoted approvingly. The 'British race', Hedstrom was quoted as saying, must continue to govern Fiji to safeguard the paramountcy of Fijian interests, because 'the Indian race has not yet in modern times completely proved its capacity for self-government'. And yet the same person wanted more native land to be converted to freehold title! The GCC resolution of 1933 is quoted: 'The immigrant Indian population should neither directly nor indirectly have any part in the control or direction of matters affecting the Fijian race.'[36] The chiefs were asserting the right to complete unfettered internal self-administration, but now those words were stretched to mean denying the Indo-Fijians equal political rights. Ratu Epeli Ganilau is quoted as objecting 'to being ruled by Indians, as we always have regarded British to be sole foundation of honour, justice and fairness'.[37] But Indians were not demanding the right to rule Fijians; they wanted equality with other British subjects. The context of these quotations is missing, the political and ideological logic behind them ignored.

Elementary errors of composition and argument are accompanied by more serious and deliberate misreading and manipulation of history. I will cite two examples mentioned most frequently to the Commission to illustrate the point. One concerns Lord Salisbury's Despatch of 1875, in which the Secretary of State for India asked the Government of India whether it would, after consultation with the various provincial governments, intervene to facilitate the recruitment and emigration of Indian indentured labourers to the British colonies.[38] In return, the India

---

35 The SVT's remarkable submission is among the Commission's papers at the National Archives in Suva.
36 Great Council of Chiefs, Proceedings, 1933, Resolution 19, C.P. 8/34.
37 In SVT's submission to the Fiji Constitution Review Commission. I was a member of that three-member commission chaired by Sir Paul Reeves of New Zealand.
38 See Brij V. Lal, *A Vision for Change: A.D. Patel and the Politics of Fiji* (Canberra: ANU E Press, 2011), pp. 5–6, doi.org/10.22459/VC.11.2011.

Office promised to ask the colonies to grant the Indian settlers 'rights and privileges no whit inferior to those of any other class of Her Majesty's subjects resident in the colonies'.[39] The provinces declined the request, the Government of India advised London accordingly, and the matter was dropped. The SVT argued that the promise made in the Despatch also lapsed, forfeiting any claim to legal authority. But this reading ignores the crucial fact that the intention of equality was never abandoned by India. In fact, it underpinned India's policy on indentured emigration throughout. Indeed, in 1910 the value of the Indians as permanent settlers was recognised. It was agreed in correspondence between India and Fiji that equal civil rights had been granted to the indentured immigration in Fiji and that any measures that lead towards lowering the political status of the immigrants or reducing their economic freedom would have involved a breach of faith with those affected.

The vagueness of the promises in Salisbury's Despatch is contrasted with the firm assurances given in the Deed of Cession by which the leading chiefs of Fiji ceded the islands in 1874.[40] That important document has been invested with a range of meanings, beyond the weight the document itself can reasonably be made to carry. It has come to be seen as a document of trust between the Fijian people, a compact, a solemn pledge, a charter that not only promised to protect Fijian rights, but also guaranteed the paramountcy of Fijian rights over all. What many Fijians wanted, they told the Commission, was an unequivocal restatement of that right, fulfilling a solemn pledge made by Queen Victoria. To those unfamiliar with the document, the supposed promise of paramountcy and the British failure to fulfil it would seem a grave breach of trust. But, in fact, the words 'paramountcy of Fijian interests' are nowhere mentioned—not even once—in the Deed of Cession. The Deed acknowledges the unconditional surrender of the islands to the United Kingdom, promises to promote 'civilisation and trade' in the islands, while Fijian rights 'shall be recognised so far as is and shall be consistent with British Sovereignty and Colonial form of government'.[41] All claims to financial liabilities made by the chiefs would be carefully scrutinised according to principles of justice and sound public policy.

---

39   ibid., p. 6.
40   See Brij V. Lal, *Broken Waves: A History of the Fiji Islands in the Twentieth Century* (Honolulu: University of Hawaii Press, 1992), pp. 11–12.
41   The full text is in the Appendix to R.A. Derrick, *A History of Fiji* (Suva: no publisher, 1950).

11. WHILE THE GUN IS STILL SMOKING

Throughout the twentieth century, the colonial government and especially the local members of the 'British race' continually invoked the concept to forestall Indo-Fijian claims for elected political representation on the basis of universal franchise and a common roll. To acquiesce in that project would be to relinquish a solemn pledge to the Fijians and safeguard their own vested interests, allowing political change to proceed at a pace acceptable to the colonial establishment. Nonetheless, the concept of paramountcy was used in a broadly protective sense. That is, in matters pertaining to the internal structure and administration of Fijian society— determination of land and chiefly titles, the drawing of traditional land boundaries, the allocation of the roles and responsibilities within society, sanctions for breaches of traditional, customary practices—the Fijian people themselves, through their customary elders and the GCC, would exercise the paramount power. In this protective sense, it was intended to shield the Fijian people from the demands and corrosive pressures of the modern world. As independence approached, paramountcy was transformed from a protective sense to an assertive one. The Fijian leaders began to argue that the paramountcy of Fijian interests could only be guaranteed if Fijians had political paramountcy. Legislative and constitutional safeguards were deemed to be insufficient. A concept, not found in the document to which its origin was attributed, was transformed from a protective instrument into an assertive tool for political dominance, and invested with historically unsustainable meanings and symbolism.

My second example is the now famous Wakaya Letter, which was also invoked before the Commission on numerous occasions.[42] This was a letter, signed by the members of the Fijian Affairs Board, the administrative and policy advisory arm of the GCC, and which had as its members all the highest ranking chiefs of Fiji, including Ratu Mara. It was presented to Nigel Fisher, the Parliamentary Undersecretary of State for the Colonies in 1963. The signatories demanded certain preconditions before Fijians would discuss even the possibility of independence. Fiji, they said, had a special relationship with the British Crown, which had to be clarified and codified. Fijian ownership of native land should be guaranteed, in consultation with the GCC. The Fijian Affairs Board should have veto power over all legislation affecting Fijian rights and interests. Fijian wishes for Fiji to be declared a Christian state should be recognised, and the Public Service should ensure racial parity in the public sector. 'Subject to a satisfactory resolution of the issues we have raised in the foregoing

---

42   A copy is reproduced in Lal, *Broken Waves*, p. 189.

memorial,' the signatories concluded, 'we would be prepared to initiate, in co-operation with the other principal races, further moves towards internal self-government.' The fact that Fijian leaders cooperated actively in the movement towards greater self-government from the mid-1960s onwards suggests that their preconditions had been met, if not in full. The Wakaya Letter was only a negotiating document. But many people kept reminding the Commission of the document in support of their claim for political paramountcy, and especially in support of making Fiji a Christian state. It was difficult to convince the people that the Wakaya Letter was designed for a specific purpose for a particular moment, and that its import was now purely historical, superseded by another compact—the constitution that gave Fiji its independence. Assertions get transformed into unassailable facts before your eyes, one learns quickly; historical truth is a matter of perception.

A participant is privy to information given in a variety of ways: a heavy hint, a slanted joke, a throwaway remark masking a serious point or indicating a point of view to be noted, malicious gossip of no permanent value but clearly intended to harm an opponent (though it is of permanent value to the perpetrator!). It is often assumed, although seldom explicitly articulated, that things are being said in confidence. Much of this kind of evidence can be discarded or forgotten. But some information, from recounted conversations, and eyewitness accounts about important players or critical events and episodes, raise troublesome questions. Uttered in confidence, or the expectation of confidence, how does one use it, especially if it relates to something of great public importance? An example. During the 1999 election campaign, Sitiveni Rabuka claimed that he had not acted alone in carrying out the coups, that in fact he was the 'fall guy' who had refused to fall. He named some of the co-conspirators and left others unnamed.

A year later, through his authorised biography, he implicated Ratu Sir Kamisese Mara in the precoup machinations, recounting a conversation he had had with Mara on a golf course where Mara had tried to sooth the nerves of a clearly worried colonel about the possible intervention of foreign countries, especially the United States and the United Kingdom in the event of a military coup in Fiji, by saying, 'Leave these to me'.[43] For the record, Mara has denied the conversation. The accusation caused an uproar in Fiji, but Rabuka's account was a public secret in Fiji long

---

43   See John Sharpham, *Rabuka of Fiji: The Authorised Biography of Major-General Sitiveni Rabuka* (Rockhampton: Central Queensland University Press, 2000), p. 105.

before it appeared in print. Some years ago, he had told me—and several other people as well—what his recent biographer has since revealed: that his biography, if ever one was written, should be titled 'The Fall Guy' or 'The Kleenex Man', the allusion to being used and then discarded like paper tissue. As an historian, I noted his remark, because in my own account of the Fijian coups, I had written generally that Rabuka could not have acted alone, and that circumstantial evidence pointed to the involvement or, at the very least, the acquiescence of others. But important as Rabuka's information was, I could not use it. First, I could not document or verify it. Second, since the information was given privately, and thus off the record, Rabuka could, if he so chose, deny it, leaving me to face the very likely prospect of a libel action. So both personal interest as well as ethical concerns about broadcasting the contents of a private conversation led me to commit the information to my files.

I was chastened from an earlier experience, when a speaker flatly denied saying what he had, in fact, said. In the early 1980s, a former Fijian colleague from the University of the South Pacific visited the East-West Center in Honolulu. During the course of an informal presentation, he was asked about the increasing rate of Indo-Fijian emigration, and its effects on the Fijian economy. The sooner more of them leave the better, he said, to uneasy laughter from the audience. I thought the remark inappropriate. I cannot now recall when or how I recounted this conversation to an acquaintance. The next day, to my horror, an Indian candidate at the Civic Auditorium in Suva recounted the substance of my conversation, alleging that the Fijian candidate was anti-Indian. The accused candidate, of course, denied the allegation the next day, and threatened a libel action. Fortunately, the allegation was never repeated, and soon swamped by other issues and forgotten, but the pragmatic need for discretion has remained with me ever since.

The possession of privately acquired, potentially explosive information creates its own problems. The obligations of scholarship, the disinterested pursuit of knowledge and truth should require full disclosure. This obligation, however, has to be assessed in the context of other competing obligations. Will the release of the information do more harm than good? Might it, for example, lead to civil strife, loss of life, poison race relations, affect the welfare of innocent people caught in the cross fire, or bring down a government? The question is: who is to act as arbiter? What right does the possessor of important information have to withhold information from the public? The answer can never be clear cut. In my own case as a Constitutional Commissioner, there are certain things that my oath of secrecy requires me never to make public, however important they are. Some discussions treating sensitive issues were never recorded. Such was the case with the proceedings of the Joint Parliamentary Committee, which deliberated on the Reeves Commission Report and produced the draft constitution. Recording the proceedings, it was felt, would impede free flow of discussion, and make people wary of the fact that their words were recorded, which might harden positions. In the Commission's own deliberations, discussion was recorded without attribution for the very same reason. But having said that, I should state that the substance of what I saw or was told and believed, I have reproduced in an indirect, allusive way, without specifying details. This is unsatisfactory, to be sure, but there does not seem to be any way around it.

There is an unmatchable excitement about doing contemporary history. One sees events in the raw, unprocessed, unfolding haphazardly, with little sense of where they might lead. One thrills to the particularities of events, to their uniqueness and integrity. Human beings can never be reduced to abstract categories no matter how subtle or intricate they appear. One sees how history is created, and how messy and unpredictable the process is. Often what one reads in the media or in the official reports is not how one saw it at the time. One becomes acutely aware of how only a tiny fragment of what happens finds its way into the historical record. One learns painfully how complex seemingly simple things can be. One becomes aware of the role of contingency, fortuity, ignorance, chance and stupidity in human affairs. Participation humanises history, and reinforces belief in human agency. It is humbling to realise the limits and limitations within which instantaneous choices are made.

One begins to develop a more sympathetic understanding of human frailties and human ambitions. Fijians who want political power to control their destiny are not necessarily racist chauvinists, but people who feel besieged, threatened, caught in the grips of forces beyond their control. They are saddened by the sight of their cherished world of childhood vanishing before their eyes, hurt to see things they believed to be beyond comment—the institution of chieftainship, for example—dragged into the cauldron of ordinary debate, thus debasing their culture. They want political power, enabling them to adjust to the world at their own pace. That is the romance of the idea. The Indo-Fijians do not necessarily want power to dominate others. They want equal rights, as human beings, to live with dignity and freedom. They invoke universal principles and their enormous contribution to the country in support of their claims, while Fijians support theirs by invoking the arguments of cultural uniqueness.

Can I be objective about what I write as a participant historian? Partial or biased scholarship is not the peculiarity of any one period or of a particular type of scholarship. As Walter Laqueur puts it, 'Violent prejudices are nursed and maintained more easily in sheltered academic surroundings than on the political stage, which provided on many occasions welcome corrections and may even teach patience and tolerance.'[44] 'The only completely unbiased historian,' says David Thomson, quoting Mark Twain, 'is the Recording Angel, whose works are unpublished: and even he, said Mark Twain, doubtless has convictions which, to Satan, might look like prejudices.' Thomson goes on:

> If prejudice is inevitable, and it comes from the 'spirit of the age' as well as from more individual inclinations, it should perhaps be welcomed and made use of. It may be argued that it is, indeed, as indispensable to the historian as is resistance to the autocrat who knows that, without resistance to his rule, he has no leverage to rely on. The battle against his own prejudices can be invigorating for the historian and an aid to him in his battle to find the truth. But only a few bold spirits among professionals accept the subjective element in historiography as not regrettable and not merely unavoidable, but as positively vitalizing and perhaps indispensable to it as an intellectual endeavour.[45]

Meaningful participation requires attachment and commitment and an informed and long-term engagement with the subject of one's research. And it can never be undertaken from intellectual inertia.[46] But these qualities are coming under threat from the changing culture within the academy. Financial cutbacks to universities have demanded increasing rationalisation of resources. Classes become bigger and teaching loads

---

44 Walter Laqueur, 'Introduction: Historians in politics', in *Historians in Politics*, ed. Walter Laqueur and George L. Mosse, (London: Sage Publications, 1974), p. 1.
45 Thomson, *The Aims of History*, p. 28. See also W.H. Walsh, *Philosophy of History: An Introduction* (New York: Harper Torchbooks, 1958): 'There is no such thing as history free from subjective prejudice' (p. 112). He went on:

> Inside any given set of presuppositions, historical work can be more or less well done. The history served by party propagandists to encourage the faithful and convert the wavering is bad history not because it is biased (all history is that), but because it is biased in the wrong way. It establishes its conclusions at the cost of neglecting those certain fundamental rules which all reputable historians recognise: scrutinise your evidence, accept conclusions only when there is good evidence for them, maintain intellectual integrity in your arguments, and so on. Historians who neglect these rules produce work which is subjective in a bad sense; those who adhere to them are in a position to attain truth and objectivity so far as these things are attainable in history (p. 114).

46 See Isaac Deutscher, 'From the Introduction (1961)', in his *Stalin: A Political Biography*, 2nd edn (New York: Oxford University Press, 1966), pp. x–xi.

increase, reducing the already limited time for research. In an age of outsourcing, research funding is increasingly becoming outcome oriented. Relevant research, related in some way to Australia's (or the United Kingdom's or the United States's) national and strategic interests, gets priority. And when the currently fashionable research agenda—governance, poverty reduction, capacity building, structural reform—passes, emphasis moves on to some equally fashionable and equally transient topics.

Some of this policy-related work is important, but counterproductive when it is allowed at the expense of more fundamental, long-term, culturally informed research. The culture that nurtures participant history is also challenged by the current intellectual fashion in fields such as cultural studies which:

> unsettles, destabilizes, and complicates the discourses of the humanities', where the 'line between words and things, subject and object, inside and outside, humanity and nature, idea and matter becomes blurred and indistinct, and new configuration of the relation of action and language is set in place.'[47]

This kind of exercise may be stimulating in a graduate seminar, but unhelpful when dealing with the practicalities of the real world.[48] Generally, people, I have come to believe, want to entertain the possibility of hope, of change and progress, rather than dwell in the quagmire of self-pity and despair, disabled by doubt. They want clarity, not complication; stability, not uncertainty; rules, not anarchy. But they also want the simplicity that evades truth—that denies the complexities, contradictions and dynamics. That is what makes our task demanding—to get clarity and subtlety; clarity that includes discomforting exceptions and gaps in the evidence. We want to be able to write so that those who were there say, yes, that is the way it was—and learn something. Participant historians learn to live with the inescapable truth that we all live in our histories. V.S. Naipaul has written, 'The world is what it is; men who are nothing, who allow themselves to become nothing, have no place in it.'[49] These words provide participant historians with both their challenge as well as their opportunity.

---

47 Mark Poster, *Critical Theory and Poststructuralism: In Search of a Context* (Ithaca: Cornell University Press, 1989), pp. 9–10.
48 See also Alan Ward, 'Comfortable voyagers? Some reflections on the Pacific and its historians', *The Journal of Pacific History* 31(2) (1996): 236–42, at p. 238, doi.org/10.1080/00223349608572821.
49 V.S. Naipaul, *A Bend in the River* (New York, NY: Knopf, 1979), opening line.

12

The road to independence[1]

> Footfalls echo in the memory
> Down the passage we did not take
> Towards the door we never opened
> Into the rose-garden.
>
> — T.S. Eliot[2]

The Union Jack came down for the last time in Fiji on 10 October 1970; exactly 96 years after Fiji had become a British Crown Colony. Prince Charles, representing the Queen, was on hand to deliver Fiji's constitutional documents to the new Prime Minister, Ratu Sir Kamisese Mara. Foreign dignitaries from some 30 countries watched and applauded the new nation on its way, among them astronaut Michael Collins representing President Nixon, New Zealand's Prime Minister Sir Keith Holyoke, and the leaders of Samoa, Tonga and the Cook Islands. In Suva Harbour, warships from four navies watched the unfolding proceedings. Throughout the country, school children flew the new miniature independence flag—navy blue with the Union Jack on the left top hand corner and Fiji's coat of arms on the right.

---

1   A version of this paper was presented to a conference on nation building at the University Kabangsan Malaysia, Bangi, Malaysia. I have referenced it lightly, but for those needing further guide to the literature, the main works cited here should be sufficient. Originally given as a lecture in a symposium on Nation Building at Univrersiti Kabang Malaysia, Bangi, 2010 (revised).
2   T.S. Eliot, 'Burnt Norton', *Four Quartets* (London: Faber and Faber, 1958 [1943]), 1.11–14.

Independence did not mark an abrupt or angry rupture of relations between the United Kingdom and the new nation, but rather the continuation of the journey Fiji began at the time of Cession in 1874, Prime Minister Mara assured his guests and the nation. 'We became dependent in a warm spirit of friendliness and trust and we become independent in the same warm spirit.'[3] 'Nothing that is happening today,' he continued, 'can change the warm feelings of our people for the Crown, the United Kingdom and its people.' In this respect, Fiji's experience of decolonisation resonated with the wider Pacific experience. Independence there came late, was orderly, peaceful and amicably negotiated, leaving largely intact the colonial structures and the ideological underpinnings that sustained them.[4] The contrast with the experience of Southeast Asia and most parts of Africa could not have been greater.

The peaceful transfer of power was welcome, not least because it had seemed a distant dream just a year before, but it left the major problems facing Fiji unresolved, shelved. The consultations about independence were held in secrecy in Fiji, and the constitutional agreement reached in London was never subjected to public debate. Deeply held views about the structure of the electoral system, for instance, which had bedevilled Fiji politics throughout the 1960s, were put on hold for fear of disrupting the feel-good atmosphere accompanying independence. The fears and anxieties of the different communities, their contested understanding of what the new independent state should be about, were camouflaged under a thin veneer of contrived national unity. Fiji at independence was not so much a cohesive multiracial nation as it was a wary coalition of ethnic groups each with their own distinctive, often divergent and sometimes diametrically opposed understandings of their role and place in the national polity. Controversial issues were avoided, elided or silenced by self-censorship or threats of retribution. They would return to haunt the nation. The tragedy of Fiji at independence was that it was trapped by a failed past and unable to articulate an encompassing vision for all of its people that enlarged the common space of citizenship.

---

3   Ratu Sir Kamisese Mara, 'Message from the Prime Minister', in *Fiji Independence Souvenir Magazine,* 1970. On Mara generally, see Deryck Scarr, *Tuimacilai: A Life of Ratu Sir Kamisese Mara* (Adelaide: Crawford House Publishing, 2008).
4   J.W. Davidson, 'Constitutional change in Fiji', *The Journal of Pacific History* 1 (1966): 165–68, doi.org/10.1080/00223346608572086; Peter Larmour, 'The decolonization of the Pacific Islands', in *Foreign Forces in Pacific Politics,* ed. Ron Crocombe and Ahmed Ali (Suva: Institute of Pacific Studies, 1983), pp. 1–23. A detailed documentary study of Fiji's decolonisation is in Brij V. Lal (ed.), *Fiji: British Documents on the End of the Empire* (London: The Stationery Office, 2006).

12. THE ROAD TO INDEPENDENCE

Fiji's colonial self-image, and its self-image at the time of independence, was of a stable three-legged stool.[5] The three legs were the indigenous Fijian, the Indo-Fijian and the European communities. Each of them was seen as distinct and separate in their culture, history and economic position, largely homogenous in their own internal social and cultural configurations, but interlinked to the overarching national structure, making their unique contribution through their own separate channels. The indigenous Fijians provided the land for economic development; the Indo-Fijians provided the labour and Europeans the capital. Since the contribution of the three groups was deemed to be equally valid, no one group alone (except the indigenous Fijians, but more about that later) was to enjoy privileges and rights greater than others. Equality of group representation, irrespective of size, was to be the basis of political representation. And the colonial state positioned itself as the neutral, benevolent, disinterested arbiter of conflict.

This was a comforting, self-serving, metaphor for a complex, conflicted reality. None of the three ethnic groups was homogenous. Religious and cultural divisions racked the Indo-Fijian community. Europeans feared being swamped by part-Europeans (as they were called) with whom they were lumped together for voting purposes. Class and regional differences divided the Fijians, as they do today. There was no equivalence—or balance, to use the colonial vocabulary—between Indo-Fijian labour on the one hand and European capital on the other. Nor was colonial rule as benevolent as its advocates argued. The metaphor served the interests of the colonial officialdom, but did great disservice to Fiji's complex history. It is to the evolution of that complex history that I now turn.

Let us begin at the beginning to understand the origins of the problems that confronted Fiji throughout the twentieth century. The foundations of modern Fiji were laid when it became a British colony in 1874. Reluctantly acquired, Britain expected Fiji to become economically self-sustaining in the quickest possible time. But the conditions for rapid economic development were absent. European planters, numbering around 2,000 in the mid-1870s, were insolvent and despondent. Indigenous Fijians were dispirited and restless, having lost a third of the population to an

---

5 J.L.V. Sukuna, *Fiji: The Tree-Legged Stool: Writings of Ratu Sir Lala Sukuna*, ed. Deryck Scarr (London: Macmillan Education, 1983). For Sukuna's life, see Deryck Scarr, *Ratu Sukuna: Soldier, Statesman, Man of Two Worlds* (Basingstoke: Macmillan Education, 1980).

epidemic of measles accidentally introduced from Australia. Large parts of fertile Fijian lands were being claimed by European settlers, often for a pittance. And there were demands on Fijian labour, too.

Fiji's first substantive governor, Sir Arthur Gordon, promulgated a set of policies that settled Fiji's future for more than a century. He began a system of 'indirect rule' designed, he said:

> to seize the spirit in which native institutions had been framed, and develop to the utmost extent the capacities of the people for the management of their own affairs, without exciting their suspicions or destroying their self-respect.[6]

To that end, he formalised a Council of Chiefs to advise him on Fijian matters. The Council, constitutionally entrenched in the 1997 Constitution, but disestablished in 2009 by Fiji's coup leader Commodore Frank Bainimarama, was the supreme advisory body to government on matters affecting the Fijian community. Under various constitutional arrangements following the military coup of 1987, it nominated the president and vice-president of the Republic, and its nominees in the Senate enjoyed the power of veto over all legislation affecting Fijian land, customs and customary rights.

Second, Gordon's policies ensured that 83 per cent of all land remained in Fijian hands in inalienable right. Without a secure ownership of land, Fijian society would eventually disintegrate, Gordon believed. Today, as Crown land has come under the jurisdiction of the Native Land Trust Board (created in 1940), more than 90 per cent of all land in Fiji is owned by the indigenous community. Gordon decreed that the Fijian people should be freed from the pressures of commercial employment and allowed to progress at their own pace in their own traditional surroundings, paying tax in kind rather than cash, and tending to their lifestyle in their age-old fashion. For nearly a century, the Fijians had their own separate court system, their own provincial administration, native regulations and strictly observed schedule of work in the villages. Their isolation from the mainstream of colonial society was almost complete.

---

6   Arthur Hamilton Gordon, *Paper on the System of Taxation in Force in Fiji. Read before the Colonial Institute* (London: Harrison, 1879), p. 178; see also J.K. Chapman, *The Career of Sir Arthur Hamilton Gordon: First Lord Stanmore, 1829–1912* (Toronto: University of Toronto Press, 1964), doi.org/10.3138/9781442652699; J.D. Legge, *Britain in Fiji, 1858–1880* (London: Macmillan, 1958). See also David Routledge, *Matanitu: Struggle for Power in Early Fiji* (Suva: Institute of Pacific Studies, 1985).

12. THE ROAD TO INDEPENDENCE

Gordon's policies were well-intentioned, but over time they became encrusted in orthodoxy.[7] A once fluid situation, represented by dynastic wars and warring chiefdoms, was frozen by fiat, uniform codes and practices imposed on a diverse and complex society where none had existed before, and certain collaborating regions privileged in leadership and social status over others. Chiefly hierarchy and privileges were entrenched and enforced at law. Gordon had intended his policies to be reviewed after 25 years; enough time, he felt, for a distressed community to achieve some stability. But when the moment came, officials baulked and the opportunity for review and reform was missed. Sadly, Fijians watched, cocooned in their subsistence sector, as the world around them changed and moved on.

From the very beginning, Fijians were led to believe that in the colony their interests would be 'paramount', and the phrase 'paramountcy of Fijian interests', mistakenly attributed to the Deed of Cession, was often invoked both by the Fijians themselves and by European settlers to block change not determined by themselves. But the phrase was intended to be used in a protective sense. That is, in the management of Fijian affairs, the government would give 'paramount' importance to the views of the Fijian people and their leaders. Over the course of the twentieth century, though, the phrase came to acquire another, more assertive, meaning—that in the broader scheme of things, Fijians would enjoy rights and privileges over and above those of their fellow citizens.

To solve the problem of capital, Gordon turned overseas. Having seen the success of plantation economies in the Caribbean and Mauritius—he had been Governor of Trinidad and Mauritius before coming to Fiji—he chose the plantation economy as his preferred mode of economic development, and sugar cane as the plantation crop. He invited the Australian Colonial Sugar Refining Company (CSR) to extend its operations in Fiji, which it did in 1882, and remained there until 1973.[8] In time, the CSR became the monopoly producer of sugar in Fiji, with considerable political influence in the affairs of the colony. To work the plantations, Gordon imported Indian indentured labour. Between 1879, when emigration began, and 1916, when it ended, more than 60,000 men and women and

---

7   Peter France, *Charter of the Land: Custom and Colonization in Fiji* (Melbourne: Oxford University Press, 1969).
8   Michael Moynagh, *Brown or White? A History of the Fiji Sugar Industry, 1873–1973* (Canberra: Australian National University Press, 1981).

children arrived in the colony.[9] When their five-year contracts expired, the government encouraged them to stay on. Most did. From the experience of indenture emerged a new society, more egalitarian, enterprising and driven by desperation, and seeking, as anthropologist W.E.H. Stanner put it, 'peaceful seepage into every opening left unclosed and a tenacious defence of every position once occupied'.[10] Isolated, struggling, self-absorbed and vulnerable, the Indo-Fijian community was just as caught up in its own internal affairs, changing and adjusting to the requirements of their new adopted homeland, and just as myopic about its long-term interests as the Fijian community.

Indentured emigration was sanctioned by the Government of India on the broad understanding that the indentured labourers who decided to settle in the colonies would enjoy rights equal to the other British subjects there. This assurance was periodically reinstated, as in 1910:

> The whole tenor of the correspondence between India and the colony shows that it was on this condition that indentured immigration in Fiji has been allowed in the past, and any measures leading towards lowering the political status of the immigrants or reducing their economic freedom would, in our opinion, involve a breach of faith with those affected.[11]

Throughout their political struggle in the twentieth century, Indo-Fijian leaders would continue to cite the principle of parity in support of their cause.

After the end of their indentures, the freed Indians settled on leased land, and continued to work mainly in the sugar industry as growers and mill workers, as their descendants did for several generations. The community diversified and grew; outnumbering the indigenous Fijians in the total population in the mid-1940s and spawning publicly aired and politically charged fears about 'Indian domination'.[12] But while remaining on the land, the Indo-Fijians established schools, often without state assistance,

---

9   K.L. Gillion, *Fiji's Indian Migrants: A History to the End of Indenture in 1920* (Melbourne: Oxford University Press, 1962); Brij V. Lal, *Chalo Jahaji: On a Journey of Indenture in Fiji* (Suva: Fiji Museum, 2000; Canberra: ANU E Press, 2012), doi.org/10.22459/CJ.12.2012.
10   W.E.H. Stanner, *South Seas in Transition: A Study of Post-War Rehabilitation and Reconstruction in Three British Pacific Dependencies* (Sydney: Australasian Publishing Company, 1953), p. 179.
11   Brij V. Lal, *A Vision for Change: A.D. Patel and the Politics of Fiji* (Canberra: ANU E Press, 2011), p. 6, doi.org/10.22459/VC.11.2011.
12   K.L. Gillion, *The Fiji Indians: Challenge to European Dominance, 1920–1946* (Canberra: Australian National University Press, 1977).

seeing education as the way out of the vagaries of life on leased land. In time, most settlements had a primary and even a secondary school whose students filled the junior ranks of the civil service, and from the 1950s onwards, the professions as lawyers, doctors, nurses and accountants. Fijians, too, had their own schools but their educational success was limited. Cultural factors, emphasising group solidarity and the virtue of subordinating individual interests to communal interests, rural isolation and poor educational facilities played a part. Moreover, Fijian leaders actively discouraged 'academic' education for ordinary Fijians. The few opportunities for higher education were reserved for people of chiefly rank. As the starkest example of this, the Great Council of Chiefs (GCC) declined to offer a university scholarship to Rusiate Nayacakalou, a commoner who later emerged as the most brilliant Fiji-born social scientist of the twentieth century.[13]

If the disparity in educational opportunities for the two communities was one problem that would haunt Fiji in future, another was the monoracial character of its schools. The Queen Victoria School was exclusively Fijian while most schools in the sugarcane belt were predominantly Indo-Fijian. Multiracial schools were mostly Christian and in urban areas. The children of the two communities, then, attending their own racially oriented schools, and firmly tethered to their own cultural ethos and values, had no opportunity to acquire a knowledge of each other's culture and language, and of any understanding of the deeper impulses that drove them. And yet, students from these schools would be called upon later to play a vital role on the national stage; a task for which, by virtue of their cross-culturally limited education, they were spectacularly ill-suited. It is no wonder that Fiji has faltered in its postindependence journey. The tragedy is that little is being done even now to rectify the situation

The tiny European population occupied the apex of the colonial, social and economic pinnacle. They dominated the retail and wholesale commerce of the colony, owned copra plantations and shipping companies and occupied pride of place in the colonial administration. They had their own racially segregated clubs and exclusive voluntary associations and schools. In the twentieth century, they began to move to urban towns

---

13   Stewart Firth and Daryl Tarte (eds), *20th Century Fiji: People who Shaped the Nation* (Suva: USP Solutions, 2001), pp. 131–32. The GCC is an entirely indigenous Fijian body, traditionally of hereditary chiefs, whose role has been to advise governments on matters pertaining to the Fijians. It appoints the president, the vice-president as well as 14 of the 32 members of the Senate (Upper House).

and centres. The community was not homogenous, though, with fine lines of demarcation differentiating the various nationalities that comprised it. Europeans of all hues saw themselves as superior to part-Europeans who, for political purposes, were grouped with them. In the late nineteenth and early twentieth centuries, some prominent Europeans, dissatisfied with the policies of the local government, tried to have Fiji annexed to New Zealand, but when that alternative vanished, they agitated for a privileged place in colonial politics. Paramountcy for Fijians, Parity for Indo-Fijians and Privilege for Europeans: these three conflicting ideas informed the political discourse in colonial Fiji.

Political representation

From the very beginning, the electoral system in Fiji was race based.[14] The colonial government saw this as natural and desirable. In part, it reflected its own interests; with the three communities locked in their own separate compartments, the colonial government could play the role of an impartial referee. Certainly, the government did little to encourage the communities to forge common, multiracial links among themselves. Europeans were given the right of elected representation in 1904, Indo-Fijians in 1929 and indigenous Fijians in 1963. Before then, Fijian representatives in the Legislative Council were nominated by the GCC. Each group had equal representation irrespective of population size. Under the Letters Patent of 1937, which remained in force until 1963, the three communities had five representatives each. Three of the five Indo-Fijians and Europeans were elected by their group and two nominated by the governor, while all five Fijians were nominated by the chiefs.

This arrangement was frequently questioned after World War II to make the political structure reflect more accurately the demographic, social and economic changes sweeping Fiji, as well as Whitehall's commitment to gradual self-government for the colonies. Specifically, advocates of constitutional change wanted elected representatives to be more directly involved in policy formulation. This agitation for constitutional change was led, not by Indo-Fijians, but by a group of Europeans. Their goal was not to remove racial representation; they wanted that maintained.

---

14   Brij V. Lal, *Broken Waves: A History of the Fiji Islands in the Twentieth Century* (Honolulu: University of Hawaii Press, 1992); Ahmed Ali, *Fiji: From Colony to Independence, 1874–1970* (Suva: School of Social and Economic Development, University of the South Pacific, 1977).

The Europeans wanted the system of nomination abolished for everyone, including the Fijians. Fijians were opposed to the extension of election. Why change the system of government when that system was working satisfactorily, they asked? A democratic system of government did not suit the Fijian people.[15] A universal franchise would be open to abuse and corruption and manipulation by selfish individuals. Chiefs were the natural leaders of their people and it was un-Fijian to trust critical decisions to commoners. Fijian fears about the security of their rights were exacerbated by the rapid increase in the Indo-Fijian population, which exceeded the indigenous population for the first time, with the Fijian Affairs Board asking Whitehall to take a firmer line with Indo-Fijian politicians and others agitating for constitutional reform. Colonial rule had been good for the indigenous community. It had preserved their social and cultural institutions, their way of life. They therefore saw no need for change.

Indo-Fijian leaders disagreed. They accepted that the rights and privileges of the indigenous community should not be questioned. Minority rights should be protected, but, as A.D. Patel, the leading Indo-Fijian member of the Legislative Council, put it in 1946, minority communities had 'also to appreciate and realise the fact that you cannot expect or hope for privileges and rights in excess of those enjoyed by the majority'. He continued to argue for a nonracial common roll form of voting. He had pursued this idea since the late 1920s, and would continue to do so throughout his political life. A common roll, he believed, was the only way forward for a racially divided society, the only way 'a common denominator of a political outlook will be developed'.[16] But he agreed that a common roll could not be introduced unless everyone accepted the idea. His plea fell on deaf, indeed hostile, ears. Forty years after his death, a common roll became a reality in Fiji, though he would have never approved of the manner of its introduction—through a military coup and a decreed constitution. Its introduction was facilitated by the fundamental demographic change in Fiji in the late twentieth century, which saw the indigenous community become the outright majority of the population, putting paid to fears of Indian dominance for good.

---

15   Brij V. Lal, 'The decolonisation of Fiji: Debate on constitutional change, 1943–1963', in *Emerging from Empire? Decolonisation in the Pacific,* ed. Donald Denoon (Canberra: Division of Pacific and Asian History, The Australian National University, 1997), pp. 26–39.
16   See Lal, 'The decolonisation of Fiji', p. 29.

Murmurings of change

Lack of a consensus about the pace and direction of constitutional change suited the colonial government, placing it in the happy position of not having to take a stand or propose initiatives on a controversial issue. Privately, though, its views were deeply divided. Among many there was instinctive sympathy for the Fijian position and a marked lack of it for Indo-Fijians. There was an understanding of the Fijian predicament leavened with a good deal of romanticism about the Fijian way of life.[17] The fact that Fijian leaders looked to Britain for guidance, after having reposed complete trust in her institutions and policies, increased the sense of obligation and responsibility correspondingly. The government had little understanding of the impulses that drove the Indo-Fijians, for whom colonial rule was not the solution but the cause of Fiji's problems. Remembering the hardship of indenture and acts of petty discrimination, they saw little of value but much to criticise in colonial rule. And they were not averse to airing their grievances outside the colony, much to the irritation of colonial officials.

There was an Indian problem, many agreed, but it could just as easily have been labelled a 'Fijian problem'. As Governor Grantham told London in 1946:

> Apart from the relative growth in population, it might be better termed the Fijian problem, since it is rather a question of raising the Fijian so that he [*sic*] is able to hold his own with the Indian in the modern world, than holding back the Indian so that he does not outstrip the more easy-going Fijian.[18]

Fijian interests should be protected, the Commissioner of Labour told the Legislative Council in 1946, but the Fijians had 'reciprocal obligations to the other races in this colony to recognise their economic and political aspirations and facilitate their attainment'. The Europeans and Indo-Fijians had made their contribution to the colony 'and they are entitled to be admitted into full membership of the Colonial family'. To be sure, there were divisions and distinctions, but the:

---

17   G.K. Roth, *Fijian Way of Life* (Melbourne: Oxford University Press, 1953).
18   Governor Grantham to Colonial Office (CO), 28 August 1946, Despatch 104, CO series 83/252.

interests of the three races are not as so many independent threads, but strands which are interwoven into one economic fabric which are interwoven into one economic fabric; and each strand is essential to the strength of the whole.[19]

To those who invoked real or imagined promises to the Fijian people, he replied:

> The obligation of the Government to the Fijians can be stated comprehensively in a few sentences; we must preserve all that is good of their culture, but not outworn customs and ways of life; we must give them the opportunities and the means to expand that culture; we must protect them from exploitation and disease; and otherwise so govern and lead these people as ultimately to achieve their full integration into the political and economic life of a composite society comprising all the races of the Colony.[20]

In the 1950s, official sluggishness began to yield with the appointment of Sir Ronald Garvey (1903–1991) as governor. Garvey, an old Pacific hand, was independent-minded, self-confident and acutely aware of the local realities. Garvey wanted to move the constitutional train along because he was convinced:

> fairly steady, progress is being made [towards common citizenship]. Both colour and social barriers are being broken down and the desirability and, indeed, inevitability of unity is taking shape. It is a policy which I constantly preach myself and it is having its imperceptible effect throughout the whole community.[21]

In 1954, Garvey asked the GCC to consider directly electing three of their five representatives to the Legislative Council to give the Fijians an experience of electoral politics. He told the chiefs that the 'chiefly system on which so much depends should march with the times and should not ignore—for too long—the modern trend of democracy'.[22] To those who invoked the Deed of Cession in support of gradualism and permanent paramountcy of Fijian interests, Garvey responded with characteristic but unprecedented bluntness. He said in 1957:

---

19   Commissioner of Labour, in *Fiji Legislative Council Debates*, 1946.
20   ibid.
21   Ronald Garvey to CO, 4 October 1956, CO series 83 1036/9.
22   Ronald Garvey to GCC, 10 October 1954.

Surely the intention of this Deed, acknowledged and accepted by chiefs who were parties to it, was that Fiji should be developed so as to take a significant place in the affairs of the world but that, in the process, the rights and interests of the Fijian people should be respected. To read into the Deed more than that, to suggest, for instance, that the rights and interests of the Fijians should predominate over everything else, does no service either to the Fijian people or to their country. The view, for the Fijians, would mean complete protection and no self-respecting individual race wants that because, ultimately, it means that those subject to it will end up as museum pieces. The Indians are equally eligible to have their interests respected. By their work and enterprise, the Indians in Fiji have made a great contribution to the development and prosperity of their country, and to the welfare of its people. They are an essential part of the community and it is unrealistic to suppose that they are not or to imagine that the position of Fijians in the world today would benefit by their absence.[23]

Lull before the storm

Governor Garvey approached the Colonial Office in 1956 with fresh constitutional proposals. His ultimate goal was common Fijian citizenship, he said. Perhaps his most radical proposal was a 'Multi-Racial Bench' of four members, one each from the three main racial groups and one to represent 'other races' such as Chinese and other Pacific Islanders, all of them elected from a colony-wide constituency. This was the first time that such a proposal had been made. But Garvey was not supported by his more cautious, conservative officers. The opponents argued that the concept of a multiracial bench would be opposed by the Europeans and Fijians who would see the proposal as 'the thin edge of the wedge' driving towards a common roll, paving the way for reforms far too radical for the colony to bear. And would not members not elected by their own group be seen as puppets of the group whose votes elected them? Garvey was undaunted, saying that 'if we are aiming at a growth of a consciousness of Fijian citizenship overbidding differences of race and religion, I think it has considerable merit'.[24] Maintaining the status quo was no solution to Fiji's political problems.

---

23 Ronald Garvey, quoted in the *Fiji Times,* 15 October 1957.
24 Garvey to CO, 4 October 1956.

Garvey's proposal was discussed by the old colonial hands in London—the 'back room boys', Garvey called them derisively—who raised all the tired old arguments about the need for Whitehall to keep a firm grip of the initiative and act just in advance of pressure, but only just. The racial factor had to be considered. 'It is true that constitutional advance does not wait upon a country's demand, but the circumstances of Fiji are rather special and to go too fast would … play into the hands of the Indians.'[25] 'If there is no pressure for a change, we should be the last to stimulate it', was the advice of one Colonial Office hand. Garvey's motive was questioned. Was he actuated by the desire to end his term of office by 'some significant advance'? The Secretary of State replied to Garvey's proposals on 20 March 1956:

> It seems very unwise to do anything to encourage it [constitutional reform] to grow more quickly unless we have some fairly clear idea where we are going. In some respects Fiji is a very difficult proposition from the point of view of constitutional advance. We are all, very naturally, inclined to think of such advance in terms of British institutions, leading in the direction of an elected assembly, universal adult suffrage, the party system, the vesting of executive power in unofficial Ministers and so forth. Yet we are learning by experience elsewhere that the traditional British pattern, however suitable for places of a certain size, is difficult to work out in small territories, even where there is a homogenous and relatively well advanced population; it is still more difficult to apply in such a place as Fiji, where race means more than party, and where a dilemma is created by the numerical preponderance of the Indians on the one hand and our obligations to the Fijians on the other. It may well be that what we ought to aim at in Fiji is some form of constitution which differs from the traditional pattern. In this connection you may like to look at the enclosed document about another of our problem areas—Mauritius—not because the ideas which are being tried out there are necessarily all applicable … but as an illustration of the fact that new ways are being sought to establish forms of democracy and of representative institutions in places where the conditions favourable to the 'Westminster model' do not exist.[26]

---

25   ibid.
26   Secretary of State to Sir Ronald Garvey, 20 March 1956, CO series 83 1036/10.

Garvey was disappointed, but not surprised. The fears of the floodgates were, in truth, groundless, he said. In taking the initiative, he reminded the Colonial Office, he was 'not playing with a scorpion's tale'. His modest proposals would have resulted in 'some quickening of interest in a direction where we are failing to make progress even though we are far better equipped than many who have raced ahead of us'.[27] If Fiji were to wait for integration to take place at the local government level, before proceeding to any constitutional change, 'we shall have to wait a long time for progress in that direction'. When recommending the appointment of a commissioner to advise on constitutional matters, Garvey said, he was not thinking of anyone entirely unfamiliar with Fiji. He had in mind Sir Arthur Richards, now Lord Milverton, a widely respected former governor, who had engineered the creation of the Native Land Trust Board.

By the late 1950s, Fiji was a very different place to what it had been at the beginning of the decade. The working class had begun to organise. A series of lightning strikes in the 1950s, culminated in the December 1959 riots that shook Fiji. A crippling strike in the sugar industry was in prospect, after a peaceful interlude of nearly two decades. The population was increasing rapidly and becoming better informed about events in Fiji and overseas, thanks to a thriving print media and the advent of the radio. Fijian soldiers were returning to Fiji after four years of service in the Malayan jungles. Two major commissions of enquiry were under way, one by geographer O.H.K. Spate into the economic and social problems facing the Fijian people[28] and another, by Sir Alan Burns, into the natural resources and population trends in the colony, both recommending a fundamental change of direction.[29]

The government could no longer afford to stall or stonewall. In his budget address to the Legislative Council in 1960, the new governor, Sir Kenneth Maddocks (1907–2001), tested the waters by suggesting the need for constitutional reform, hoping that the next election (in 1963) might be held under a new Letters Patent. The aim was to give more responsibility to unofficial members and pave the way for a ministerial system of government—called the Member System—under which unofficial members of the Legislative Council would be invited to

---
27 Garvey to CO, 4 October 1956.
28 O.H.K. Spate, *The Fijian People: Economic Problems and Prospects* (Suva: Government of Fiji Legislative Council Paper 13, 1959).
29 Sir Alan Burns et al., *Report of the Commission of Enquiry into the Natural Resources and Population Trends of the Colony of Fiji* (Suva: Government of Fiji Legislative Council Paper 8 of 1961).

undertake a supervisory role for a collection of government departments, contribute to policy formulation and oversee its implementation, all under the principle of collective, cabinet-type responsibility.

The government's constitutional proposals were debated in the April 1961 sitting of the Legislative Council, with the motion being introduced by the acting colonial secretary. His tone is almost pleading, begging European and Fijian members to have an open mind on reform. For the first time, the government was taking the lead, somewhat along the lines that Garvey had envisaged in the 1950s. He asked the members to 'try and establish for ourselves a long-term objective'. The winds of decolonisation were moving closer to the Pacific. Samoa was on the verge of independence and Fiji could not afford to be indifferent. 'I know it would be nice to consider Fiji in a vacuum and isolated and do as we wish, but unfortunately we cannot.' He continued:

> We are part of the world and there are forces moving which, whether we like it or not—and I know many of us do not like it—are going to have a profound influence on us and on our future. We need to consider these forces; what they are and what steps are necessary to meet and mould them to our ends. We want to do it in our own unhurried time. We do not want to wait till the forces are built up against us and we have to do things as a matter of urgency. Let us think ahead, see what is coming, be ready for it and do all that we have to do in our own time, and by our own choosing … do not let us forget the forces outside. It is no good forgetting them; they are there and they are real.[30]

By 'forces out there', the government meant the pressure from the United Nations' Committee on Decolonisation, which watched developments in Fiji closely, to the irritation of the colonial government as well as Fijians and Europeans.

Then the colonial secretary turned to those who always tried to clinch the no-change argument by saying that the advocates of change were a minority, and that the majority of the people were satisfied with the status quo. He is worth quoting at length:

> [A]lmost everything starts with a minority. Minorities have a way of growing, and when minorities have a popular idea, any Government which ignores such a minority does so at its peril. A minority can be likened to a small stream. It is there, something

---

30 *Fiji Legislative Council Debate,* April 1961.

quite small and water is soft. It can be used for many purposes. If you dam the stream the waters build up behind the dam so you build a bigger dam, but one day you cannot go on and the burst comes. We do not want a burst here. What we want is to look together into the future and be sure that this stream of ideas, this minority perhaps, this thing called democracy is not dammed up or held back but is guided to our purpose. We want no burst dam.[31]

Unsurprisingly, the Indo-Fijian members supported the motion while Europeans opposed it. But what mattered more now than ever before was the reaction of the Fijian leaders. Fijian opinion was not as solidly against change as in the past. Although the majority opposed the motion, they did so for quite different reasons. Among those who remained unconvinced of the government's policy was Ratu Kamisese Mara, the ascendant Fijian political leader and Fiji's first prime minister. The government's policy was ill-conceived and ill-timed, he said, because it ignored the spirit and implications of the Deed of Cession and the special place of the Fijian people in their own country. The chiefs had ceded Fiji 'to be part and partial of the United Kingdom', in the same way that the Channel Islands and the Isle of Man were integral parts of the UK. That special relationship was recognised in the title Fijians used to refer to the Queen: *Radi ni Viti kei Peretania*, the Queen of Fiji and of Great Britain. Ratu Mara urged caution and gradualism. Constitutional development should follow, not precede, social and economic integration. Ratu Penaia (1918–1993), another high chief and future Governor-General and President of Fiji, agreed: no constitution, no matter how good, would work unless there was a common background of accepted principles.

The government listened politely, knowing that it had no alternative but to take the lead, though without embarrassing the Fijian members. It sought to allay their fears without compromising the principle of constitutional reform. Ratu Mara's contention about the Isle of Man was rejected. The two island groups had completely different histories and unique relationships with the United Kingdom. The government denied that its proposals detracted from the promises of the Deed of Cession, and assured the Fijian leaders that it would entrench provisions regarding the native ownership of land as well as others that touched upon customary matters. To the argument that social and economic integration should

---

31 ibid.

precede political reform, the government argued that 'unity does not have to grow from the bottom. In fact, when there are present communities speaking different languages, having different religions, living mostly in a different economy and having different customs', unity 'can spread downwards'. Suva was not doing anything that London itself had not adopted as official policy. The colonial secretary reminded the Legislative Council that as early as 1943 the United Kingdom had pledged itself to 'guide Colonial people along the road to self-government within the British Empire,' adding that 'it is no part of our policy to confer political advances which are unjustified by circumstances or to grant self-government to those who are not yet trained in its use'.[32] For Whitehall, though, the latter qualification had reached the end of its life.

In 1963, Fiji got new Letters Patent that provided for an enlarged Legislative Council, consisting of 19 official and 18 unofficial members,[33] the three main communities had six members each—the principle of parity was preserved—four elected from racial rolls and two nominated by the governor. Property qualification for voters was abolished and, for the first time, a universal franchise was extended to the Fijians. The issue after 1963 was not if self-government and independence would come to Fiji, but rather the terms and conditions upon which they would be acceptable to its various ethnic communities.

The road to independence

By the mid-1960s, the political landscape of Fiji had altered dramatically. Fijian fears, alluded to above, intensified. The industrial disputes of 1959 in Suva and in the sugar industry in 1960, aroused or, rather, reinforced the threat of Indo-Fijian domination. The calls for reform in the Fijian system of administration—for traditional structures to be loosened to enable greater personal enterprise among those Fijians who wanted it, for the natural resources of the country to be used in an economic way for the benefit of the country as a whole, for the system of Fijian administration, which had kept the indigenous community isolated from the mainstream, to be overhauled—startled a people used to gentle counselling, flattery and effusive praise for their traditional way of life. Their leaders expressed their

---

32 *Fiji Legislative Council Debates,* July 1961.
33 Norman Mellor and James Anthony, *Fiji Goes to the Polls, The Crucial Legislative Council Elections of 1963* (Honolulu: East-West Center Press, 1968).

anger, and London listened. 'I see no future in the Burns recommendation that the Fijian administration should be wound up as soon as possible,' wrote Julian Amery, Undersecretary of State for the Colonies in 1960.

> The Fijians are determined to resist any move in this direction. They realise that whatever its defects the tribal system does provide a leadership capable of defending the Fijian communal interest against what they regard as the Indian threat. Without their chiefs they would be leaderless.[34]

Still, Fijian leaders realised that they could not go on resisting whatever constitutional proposals the government presented. And so the Fijian Affairs Board, the executive arm of the GCC, presented their views in a document that subsequently came to be known as the Wakaya Letter.[35] In it, they stated their preconditions for constitutional reform. Addressed to Nigel Fisher, the Parliamentary Undersecretary of State for the Colonies, the letter reminded the Crown of the special significance of the Deed of Cession for the Fijians. It was the Fijian view that 'the possibility of severance of this link with the Crown—a link forged in a spirit of mutual trust and goodwill—should never be contemplated'.[36] Before any further constitutional changes were considered, the letter stated, the terms of the relationship, which they mistakenly likened to the relationship between Britain and the Channel Islands, should be clarified and codified. The letter went on:

> There would have to be a precise restatement of the guarantee on Fijian land ownership. We visualise that the Native Land Trust Legislation should not be changed or added to without the prior consent of the Sovereign and the agreement of the Council of Chiefs. We also stand by the expressed desire of the High Chiefs in the preamble to the Deed of Cession that Fiji should be a Christian state and that therefore no constitutional or administrative changes should take place that would deviate from that intention. The provision of the Fijian Affairs Ordinance that all legislation affecting Fijian rights and interests should be referred to the Fijian Affairs Board or, on the recommendation of the Board, to the Council of Chiefs, should be retained and likewise the Governor's direction to the Public Service Commission to work towards a balance of the races in the Civil Service.[37]

---

34 Julian Amery, Undersecretary of State for the Colonies in 1960, CO series 83 1036/612.
35 A copy of the Wakaya Letter is reproduced in Lal, *Broken Waves*, p. 189.
36 ibid.
37 ibid.

12. THE ROAD TO INDEPENDENCE

If these concerns were addressed, the letter concluded, the Fijian chiefs would consider contemplating further constitutional changes.

The letter was a negotiating document, designed to extract the maximum concession from the governments in Suva and in London. The Colonial Office was sympathetic to Fijian concerns but firm about the need not to ignore the interests and concerns of the nonindigenous communities. The government in Suva privately assured the Fijian leaders that the special position of the indigenous community would be safeguarded, and not placed under 'the heels of an immigrant community', to use the words of Governor Derek Jakeway (1915–93) who was himself active behind the scenes helping the Fijians to organise politically.

Europeans used to a privileged position in the colony's affairs felt insecure about their place in any future constitutional arrangement. The 1959 Suva riots, multiracial in character and overtly anti-European in intent, had shaken them as never before. Alone, they knew they stood little chance of maintaining their disproportionate representation in the Legislative Council; and they had few friends in places where it really mattered, such as Whitehall. Hence, they sought closer alignment with the Fijian leadership. Understandably, it was an alliance of mutual convenience. The Europeans needed the political protection the Fijians could provide, and the Fijians, appreciating the Europeans' vulnerability, knew they could always count on European support against the Indo-Fijians. This alliance of interest against the threat of a perceived common enemy would last the rest of the decade and, indeed, well into independent Fiji. It was formally institutionalised by the Alliance Party, which emerged in 1965, and was backed by the Fijian Association.

The Indo-Fijian scene was energised by the return to the Legislative Council, after the absence of more than a decade, of A.D. Patel. Patel, Indian-born but a Fiji resident since 1928, was a leader of unequalled intellectual brilliance; a Gandhian at heart, a fierce and fearless critic of colonial rule and an untiring advocate of a common roll.[38] He united the usually fractious Indo-Fijian community and formed Fiji's first political party, the Federation, in 1963. Two ideas lay at the heart of Patel's political vision. One was independence, or at least a large measure of internal self-government eventually leading to independence. If Samoa and the Cook

---

38 ibid.

Islands, small, vulnerable and resource-poor, could become independent, why not Fiji, he argued? Independence was a matter of time, Patel believed, not if but when it came, and he wanted Fiji to be prepared for it.

The other idea was a common roll. He had been its advocate from the beginning. A communal roll, which Fijians and Europeans wanted, would be ruinous for the country.

> Of all the people, Indians are bitterly opposed to communal representation because they have seen its painful result in the course of time. It may not be very serious now, but as time goes on, once people get used to the idea of racial separation, racial attitudes harden and people start thinking in racial terms and racial interests which leads not to one nation but, in the course of political developments, it leads to claims of several nations.[39]

A 'communal roll', he continued:

> symbolises divided loyalties, and inhibits the formation of secular parties, with success in politics depending on reflecting communal interests and prejudices. Compromise will be rendered difficult and relative party strength may be frozen for long periods because a party can grow only with an increase in the size of the community upon which it is based.[40]

On the other hand, a common roll would 'encourage the citizens to organise political parties along national lines and in the long run compel everyone else to think in terms of his country rather than a particular race, community or religion'. It was 'only through making one nation out of Fiji that we can achieve the sort of future we want for everybody'.[41]

The passion with which Patel pursued the idea was reciprocated by the passion with which its opponents—which included all Fijian and European leaders—rejected it. The system of communal representation was well established in Fiji; it had worked well, they argued; a system of guaranteed racial representation produced no fears of any one group dominating others; it realistically accepted the differences of culture, language, custom and religion. These two positions illustrate the two contrasting, even diametrically opposed, visions of Fiji; and they have continued to haunt Fiji's subsequent political history.

---

39   Lal, *A Vision for Change,* p. 189ff.
40   ibid.
41   ibid.

12. THE ROAD TO INDEPENDENCE

The final phase

In July 1965, the Colonial Office convened a constitutional conference, and invited the elected representatives of the three communities to London.[42] All the established positions were expressed, with Europeans and Fijians agreeing only to limited internal self-government and the Indo-Fijian delegation hoping for a final blow to colonial rule in Fiji. Important advances were made. The Legislative Council was expanded to include 36 members: 14 Fijians (nine elected on communal roll, three on multiracial cross-voting and two nominated by the GCC); 12 Indo-Fijians (nine communal and three cross-voting); and 10 Europeans (seven communal and three cross-voting). The system of cross-voting was seen as a limited concession to a common roll in which multiracial electorates voted for seats reserved for candidates of different races. The Fijian and the European delegations were delighted with the outcome, and for good reason: the Europeans' privileged position was maintained, and the Fijians had, for the first time, got two additional seats. Fijian–European solidarity was consolidated.

The Indo-Fijians were disappointed with the outcome of the conference. They had lost parity with the indigenous Fijians.[43] The communal roll had been maintained, their plea for at least partial introduction of common roll had fallen on deaf ears. And the Indo-Fijian community was now more isolated than ever, electorally segregated from the other communities. The Fijian roll, for instance, was expanded to include all the other Pacific Islanders and the European roll enlarged to accommodate the Chinese. Why should the Chinese be on the European roll when they had culturally less in common with Europeans than the Indo-Fijians? Patel asked. But to no avail.

He accused the Colonial Office of not playing a fair mediating role at the conference (preoccupied as it was at the time with the crisis in Aden), by not persuading the Fijians and Europeans sufficiently to accept at least a partial common roll and by effectively capitulating to combined European and Fijian pressure. I am presently investigating the thinking of the Colonial Office, so can only provide a tentative assessment of the subject. But my overwhelming impression is that London had a deep

---

42   Davidson, 'Constitutional change in Fiji', pp. 165–68.
43   Lal, *Broken Waves*, pp. 195–200.

sympathy for the Fijian people and was concerned not to let them end up in a secondary position in any future political arrangement. Their rhetorical advocacy of Westminster democracy was secondary to their concern for Fijian feelings. London also had a prudent appreciation of its dependence on Fijian security forces to maintain law and order.[44]

Nor did London share the vision of Fiji as a cohesive multiracial nation. Julian Amery reported confidentially to the Colonial Office in 1960 that 'the Fijians and Indians are more distinct as communities than Jews and Arabs in Palestine, Greeks and Turks in Cyprus or even Europeans and Bantu in South and Central Africa'.[45] Understandably he did not add that London itself was partly responsible for this unfortunate state of affairs. It was 'impracticable to think in terms of a single Fijian nation or of a common roll at any rate for the foreseeable future', he advised. The concept of a 'single multiracial community as the goal towards which Fijians and Indians alike should strive' was illusory, he added. 'The Fijians will no longer accept this; and the more we lay the emphasis on multi-racialism, the more suspicious they will become that we plan to sell them out to the Indians.' Indeed, Amery recommended setting up a separate system of administration for Indo-Fijians, as a counterpart to the separate administration for the Fijians. In view of this, Patel's vision for Fiji was doomed from the start.

In September 1966, 15 months after the constitutional conference, Fiji went through another election, for the first time on party lines: the Indo-Fijian–based Federation Party and the Fijian Association–backed, nominally multiracial Alliance Party. Both parties won handily in their constituencies, the Alliance winning two-thirds of the Fijian communal votes and the Federation a similar percentage among the Indo-Fijians. Ratu Mara became the chief minister. The 1965 constitution had produced the result both Suva and London wanted, and neither saw any reason to review the constitution that the Federation Party had accepted under protest. The new government jettisoned the bipartisan approach of the past. Patel feared that unless the constitution was reviewed, the entire Indo-Fijian community would be consigned to 'the wilderness

---

44   Robert Norton, 'Accommodating indigenous privilege: Britain's dilemma in decolonizing Fiji', *The Journal of Pacific History* 37(2) (2002): 133–56, at pp. 153–54, doi.org/10.1080/002233402200 0006574.
45   Julian Amery to CO, 8 November 1960, CO series 83 1036/612, in Lal (ed.), *Fiji: British Documents on the End of Empire,* pp. 37–39.

of frustrated and possibly endless opposition'. And so, on 1 September 1967, the Federation Party walked out of the Legislative Council when its motion for constitutional change was defeated.

The ensuing by-election was fought in an intense atmosphere of great bitterness and tension.[46] When the Federation Party won all the Indo-Fijian communal seats (and with increased majorities, too) many hard-line Fijians threatened violence, bringing the country to the edge of a potentially dangerous crisis. But cooler heads prevailed and emotions subsided, but the message was clear: the 1965 racially unbalanced constitution would have to be reexamined, and the wishes of the Federation Party could not be ignored. Nor, on the other hand, could Fijian views be discounted. Apprehending the gravity of the situation, Governor Jakeway urged Mara and Patel to resume dialogue. In August 1969, representatives of the two parties met in Suva for a series of confidential discussions. There, each party stated its views about the constitution and possible ways out of the current impasse. But Patel died in October, to the relief of both the government and many in the Alliance party.[47] His successor, Siddiq Koya, had neither the intellectual depth nor the commitment to the vision of Fiji as a genuinely nonracial society.

In the confidential discussions, common ground was reached on many issues. To allay Fijian fears about their rights, the Federation Party proposed an upper house, the Senate, where the nominees of the GCC would have the power to veto any legislation that could, even remotely, affect Fijian interests. The Federation Party also proposed to go into independence without an election to avoid acrimony that an election campaign would inevitably entail, because it felt that Ratu Mara, then widely popular, was the best leader to be at the helm to effect a smooth transition to independence, and because the Federation Party itself was diffident about the broad acceptability of its own leadership.[48] In truth, they acknowledged that all the power was on the other side, and that they would have to accept the role of opposition for a long time into the future.

---

46 James Anthony, 'The 1968 Fiji By-Elections', *The Journal of Pacific History* 4(1) (1969): 135–38, doi.org/10.1080/00223346908572151.
47 Ratu Kamisese Mara, *The Pacific Way: A Memoir* (Honolulu: University of Hawaii Press, 1997), p. 97.
48 See Lal, *Broken Waves*, pp. 200–06; and Confidential British Documents in Lal (ed.), *Fiji: British Documents on the End of Empire,* Ch. 6, Documents 141–66.

On one issue, though—the composition of the legislature and the method of election—the two parties disagreed. The Federation Party presented its case for a common roll, though without the conviction or authority of the past. Predictably, the Alliance opposed the idea, while promising an open mind on a common roll as a long-term objective. Both parties decided to defer the issue until the impending constitutional conference in London, with the Federation agreeing that, in the event of an impasse, it would accept a formula 'approved and settled by the British Government'. Lord Shepherd, Minister of State for Foreign and Commonwealth Affairs, who was in Fiji to witness firsthand the progress of the local negotiations, was clearly delighted by the Federation's concessions—as, of course, was the Alliance Party. He insisted that the consensus be formally recorded. The consensus was that:

> if no agreement was reached and circumstances remained as at present, it would be necessary that the constitutional instruments for independence should reflect, subject to any formal changes arising from independence, the provisions of the existing Constitution.[49]

That is, the same constitution that the Federation Party had rejected in 1965 as 'undemocratic, unjust and iniquitous'! In their quest for an orderly transition to independence, the party leaders had sacrificed their long-held principles for political expediency.

The penultimate conference paving the way for Fiji's independence was held in London in April 1970. The result was a compromise—if not compromised—constitution. Fiji was to have a bicameral legislature with an appointed Upper House (Senate) and a fully elected Lower House (House of Representatives) of 52 seats, with 22 each reserved for Fijians and Indo-Fijians and eight for the general electors (Europeans, part-Europeans, Chinese and Others). Of the 22 seats reserved for the Fijians and Indo-Fijians, 12 were to be contested on communal (racial) rolls and the remaining 10 on national (cross-voting) seats (which meant that candidates themselves were required to be Fijians, Indo-Fijians and general electors, but they were elected by all registered voters). In the House of Representatives, then, Fijians and Indo-Fijians had parity. The Europeans' privileged position was also preserved: with only 4 per cent of the population, they had 15.4 per cent of the seats, whereas Fijians

---

49 Lord Shepherd, 'Fiji Constitutional Conference', 22 April 1970, Foreign and Commonwealth Office (FCO) 32/572, no. 112, in Lal (ed.), *Fiji: British Documents on the End of Empire*, pp. 486–89.

and Indo-Fijians had 42.3 per cent of the seats each. European overrepresentation was accepted, indeed advocated, by the Fijian leaders who knew from experience that Europeans would always support them, as they had invariably done in the past. In the 22-member Senate, the principle of Fijian paramountcy was explicitly recognised by giving the eight nominees of the GCC the power of veto over all legislation affecting Fijian interests and privileges.

The independence constitution, then, represented a continuity with Fiji's racially divided past. It assumed that 'race' or ethnicity, was, and would long remain, the most important determinant of political behaviour of the people and that Fijians would control political power if they remained united and voted solidly as a racial group. And there was a tacit assumption among many leaders that, for their own physical safety, Indo-Fijians would not aspire to political leadership.

The tragedy of independent Fiji was that the assumptions upon which the constitution was based proved untenable. New forces of change came with urbanisation, a modern cash economy, internal and external migration, multiracial education and a media that questioned the primacy of race in the political system.[50] The idea of ethnic solidarity that Fijian leaders had taken for granted at the time of independence began to fray as internal debates about the structure of power within the indigenous community spilled over into the public arena. A new generation was emerging for whom race had little to do with the vagaries of daily life. Old, exhausted orthodoxies privileged in the new constitution had long outlived their usefulness. Hobbled by a fractured history, Fiji failed to come to terms with the rapidly changing realities of the postcolonial era. An ill-fated past had come home to roost. It was not until 30 years later when the umbilical cord with the structures and assumptions of the twentieth-century political culture of Fiji would finally be severed—through a military coup.

---

50   Michael Taylor (ed.), *Fiji: Future Imperfect* (Sydney: Allen & Unwin, 1987).

13

Where has all the music gone?[1]

On the whole it is better to explore history rather than
to repress or deny it.

— Edward Said[2]

It is not enough to stand at a tangent of other
peoples' conventions;
we should be the most unforgiving critics of our own.

— Tony Judt[3]

[There is a] difference between the silence after the music,
and the silence when there is no more music.

— Vincent O'Sullivan[4]

Fiji's postcolonial journey has been a fraught one. The euphoria of a smooth transition to independence in face of the fear of violence and upheaval belied the truth of the actual state of affairs in the country, about the fears and hopes of the different ethnic groups, about the structure of power sharing and

---

1 Originally appeared in *The Contemporary Pacific* 23(2) (2011): 412–36.
2 Edward Said, *Culture and Imperialism* (New York, NY: Knopf, 1993; New York, NY: Vintage Books, 1994), p. xxiv.
3 Tony Judt, *The Memory Chalet* (London: William Heinemann, 2010; London; Vintage, 2011), p. 216.
4 Vincent O'Sullivan, untitled chapter, in *Notes Towards a Biography: John Mansfield Thompson*, ed. Margaret Clarke with Jim Collinge and Martin Lodge (Wellington: Steele Roberts, 2003), p. 164.

the like. Unresolved questions came to the fore in 1987 when the country had its first military coup to overthrow a duly elected democratic government ostensibly in the name of protecting the interests of the indigenous Fijians. This chapter provides a personal exploration of the broad contours of Fiji's fluctuating political fortunes in the postindependence years.

On 10 October 2010, Fiji marked the 40th anniversary of its independence from the United Kingdom after 96 years of colonial rule. It was a predictably subdued affair. The guest of honour, Sir Michael Somare of Papua New Guinea, failed to turn up for the celebrations. There was, in truth, little to celebrate. The Public Emergency Regulations in place since April 2009, when the constitution of the country was abrogated, severely curtailed mobility and free speech, threatening retribution to anyone who questioned the conventional wisdom of the day; all this in marked contrast to the joy and optimism that attended the severance of the colonial umbilical cord in 1970. What a tumultuous 40-odd years it had been in the ill-fated history of this otherwise richly endowed country: coups and constitutional crises, state-sponsored constitutional engineering, more coups and endless cul-de-sacs. The prospect of stability, peace and prosperity at the time of independence, the sense that Fiji, as a multiethnic society, might have a lesson to teach similarly situated countries in the developing world at the end of colonial rule seems like a bad dream now. What was once thought to be the fate of newly independent countries in Africa and Latin America whose fledgling democratic values were regularly subverted by the military in the name of good governance has now become an integral part of Fiji's postcolonial narrative. And there is no end in sight to its unpredictable future.

I was in my final year of high school when Fiji became independent. I remember the occasion vividly. Lollies were distributed at the morning assembly along with miniature plastic navy blue Fiji flags, the Union Jack came down for the last time as we dutifully recited 'God Save the Queen' for the last time, speeches were made by Mr Sukru Rehman, Chairman of the school's Board of Governors, and by the District Commissioner, Mr Dodds, and words were spoken about achieving independence with tolerance, harmony and justice and about the legacy the British were leaving us: a sense of fair play, the rule of law and the fundamentals of parliamentary democracy. It was a quietly proud moment in our youthful lives and we were told never to forget the wonderful legacy our colonial masters were bequeathing us. I did not know it then that I would spend my entire life variously engaged with Fiji's history and politics. I am

13. WHERE HAS ALL THE MUSIC GONE?

a part of the history I now seek to understand. I cannot and do not claim detachment and objectivity. But I will say that what I express is not entirely idiosyncratic, that in ample measure it reflects the opinion and experience of a section of the community from which I come, and those of the generation of which I am a part. In the sounds of my footsteps many would, I am sure, recognise the echoes of their own.

The late 1960s, as the previous chapter has shown, were one of the most dynamic decades in Fijian history, comparable in some senses to the 1990s; full of animated debate and discussion about what kind of political culture was appropriate for a multiethnic society such as Fiji. Opinion was genuinely divided. The National Federation Party (NFP), with its base in the Indo-Fijian community, advocated a nonracial common roll of voting with one person, one vote, one value. The Alliance, nominally multiracial but solidly backed by the Fijian and European communities, wanted nothing less than the retention of full communal (that is, race-based) rolls. The NFP wanted Fiji to become independent with an elected Fijian head of state, while the Alliance was lukewarm about independence and wanted ties to the British monarchy maintained. Questions were asked about such sensitive subjects as the role and place of traditional social and cultural institutions in the fabric of the wider society, and about the social, cultural and institutional impediments to change and growth in Fijian society.[5]

These were questions that I came upon much later at university. Living in rural Labasa on the island of Vanua Levu, in a village without running water, paved roads or electricity, where the radio was still a novelty in many households and newspapers an expensive luxury only a few could afford, we lived largely in blissful ignorance. We had few means of finding out what was going on in the world. We had no contact with Fijians who lived on the outer edges of our settlement, no comprehension of their concerns, aspirations and needs just as they were innocent about ours. We were preoccupied with making do with whatever little we had, which was very little indeed. More than national politics, the affairs of the sugar industry, then under the mighty Colonial Sugar Refining Company (CSR), were of much greater concern to us. The sugar industry sustained us. It was

---

5   O.H.K. Spate, *The Fijian People: Economic Problems and Prospects* (Suva: Legislative Council Paper 13/1959); C.S. Belshaw, *Under the Ivi Tree: Society and Economic Growth in Rural Fiji* (London: Routledge and Kegan Paul, 1964); Raymond Frederick Watters, *Koro: Economic Development and Social Change in Fiji* (London: Clarendon Press, 1969).

our lifeblood. It was the reason why we were in Fiji. The news of national politics came to us via the occasional Hindi newspapers such as *Jagriti, Shanti Dut* and the *Fiji Samachar*. More immediately, it came through occasional visiting politicians, important men, impressively dressed, who talked about independence, about pride and sacrifice, about a new future; things that few of us actually understood or contemplated. That luxury was denied to us by our desperate economic situation. Our cane-growing village was solid Federation country. It was 'our party'. It had fought the CSR on our behalf. It carried our hopes and aspirations. There were a few Alliance supporters in the village, such as my eldest brother, for which I was sometimes taunted at school as a traitor to our community; but since such people were few and far between, they were generally tolerated as misguided men with misplaced loyalties. Harmless.

At high school, politics were taboo, even in the higher grades. The colonial protocol of separating politics from education was strictly observed. It was as if nothing was happening in the country that truly mattered to us. In our school debates, we chose (or rather our teachers chosen for us) topics such as 'Alcoholics should have no place in society' and 'Why students should be allowed to wear thongs to school', but nothing more serious.[6] Politics were a dangerous, destabilising territory, best left unexplored. The colonial educational bureaucracy kept a close, watchful eye on what went on in the classroom, and we were all focused on preparing for the final exam, which would determine our fate and our school's ranking in the colonial prestige system. In our history classes, we learned about the unification of Germany and Italy, about the causes and consequences of World War I and the Russian Revolution, but nothing about Fiji itself, or the broader Pacific region for that matter. Colonial rule was no longer fashionable and its defence problematic. The irony is glaringly obvious now. Here we were, people who would inherit the challenges and opportunities of independence, its next generation of leaders, completely unaware of important developments taking place all around us. And as products of largely mono-racial schools, we would be called upon to play national leadership roles on a multiracial stage for which we were spectacularly ill prepared. No wonder, Fiji foundered on its postcolonial journey.

---

6   Brij V. Lal, *Mr Tulsi's Store: A Fijian Journey* (Canberra: Pandanus Books, 2001), p. 70.

Fiji embarked on this postcolonial journey as we entered university. The opening of the University of the South Pacific in Suva must count as one of the turning points in modern South Pacific history, availing higher education to masses of students from poor homes who would have, before then, been deprived of the opportunities of tertiary education altogether. Higher education in colonial Fiji was the privilege of a selected elite— usually a dozen or so scholars sent to Australia and New Zealand to study 'useful' subjects in preparation for careers in the teaching profession and in low-level administration. The university was for us an enlarging and enriching experience, but there was no more informative about what was going on in political circles in Fiji. Once again, we had our sports, hiking, social and cultural clubs, we staged plays, read poetry, went bushwalking; but serious discussion of politics was absent, or confined to a few individuals. The Indo-Fijians generally assumed that their Fijian counterparts were supporters of the Alliance Party while they, in turn, suspected us of being Federation sympathisers. Given that the political parties were essentially race based, we were conscious of the ever-present danger that any criticism of a political party could easily be interpreted as a provocative attack on an ethnic group; and so, the boundaries remained intact, and we kept our thoughts largely to ourselves.

Other Pacific Island students, from Samoa, Tonga, the Cook Islands and the Solomons, talked proudly of their 'history' as a beneficial and nourishing influence in their lives. They had a history to celebrate, which had a coherence borne of ancient heritage or forged in response to colonial rule (the Mau movement in Samoa, Maasina Rule in the Solomon Islands, the monarchy in Tonga). Their obvious pride in their 'national identity' was a source of envy for us. We had no overarching sense a common identity; we were 'Indians' and 'Fijians', separate in our conceptions of the past and divergent in our understanding of the present. We hardly spoke each other's language. Our memory was racially compartmentalised. While one group lauded the policies of colonial rule, the other rejected it. In our vision of what Fiji as a multiethnic society should be like, we were poles apart, symbolised most immediately in the different attachments to communal and common roll systems of voting. Our traditions of political discourse were different: one was open and robust, the other hedged in by a careful observance of rituals and protocols of hierarchy. The space of common concerns was small although in the lived experience of daily life, social boundaries were freely breached. For us, history could not serve a serviceable ideology of nation building as it could and did for many of our Pacific neighbours. There was little we could agree on.

This was the unspoken reality on the ground, but our national myth evoked a different image. The early years of independence were warm and fuzzy. We had become independent without strife. Our links with the British monarchy remained intact. The old colonial pattern of political representation, with paramountcy for Fijians and privilege for Europeans was maintained, with Indo-Fijians having to content themselves with the illusion of parity in the overall scheme of things. We were paraded before the world as a model of multiracial democracy. 'The Way the World Should Be', Pope John Paul II had intoned on a fleeting visit to the country in 1985. That became our national mantra, shamelessly self-promotional. But deep inside us, I am not sure if we really believed this myth. Independence had arrived peacefully, but none of the deep underlying problems about power sharing, land leases, the underpinnings of affirmative action, had been resolved. We were reluctant to look into the abyss that faced us in the eye.

In truth, we had merely papered over the cracks and fractures that lay just beneath the surface. There were certain assumptions and understandings that underpinned the independence order that lay unexplored lest we discovered the hollowness that lay beneath the centre of our public life. Race, we were repeatedly told, was a fact of life; in truth, it was on its way to becoming a way of life. Every issue of public policy came to be viewed through the prism of race. You were asked for your race when you opened a bank account, took out a driving licence, left or entered the country. In the awarding of scholarships, in promotions in the public service, race became a consequential factor in the national equation of affirmative action. 'Blood will flow,' Ratu Mara said menacingly, if Fijian sensitivities about land and leadership were ever breached.[7] Race serviced a convenient political ideology, but it was also deeply flawed. Neither the Fijians nor the Indo-Fijians were homogenous communities. That much was obvious to us. There were interests and concerns that transgressed communal boundaries in many parts of Fiji. Nonetheless, the overall architecture of national life was race based.

---

7   These sentiments were commonly expressed by Ratu Mara and other Fijian leaders throughout the late 1970s and 1980s, especially at tense election rallies such as in 1982.

Expatriate academic analysts scratched the surface and developed the theory of 'three Fijis'.[8] There was some truth in this characterisation although fundamental structural changes in the economy were surreptitiously unsettling established orthodoxies. The Fijians were behind in some sectors but considerably ahead in others (ownership of land, timber and marine resources, for example). The Fijian Government of the day adopted an affirmative action policy in favour of indigenous Fijians in the field of education, which affected us most directly. An education commission in 1969 had recommended that 50 per cent of all government scholarship should be reserved for indigenous Fijians and unexpended funds designated specifically for Fijian educational projects.[9] Fijian disadvantage in education, and in the professions generally, was a direct result of the policies and visions of an earlier generation of Fijian leaders, principally Ratu Sir Lala Sukuna, who thought the place for his people was in the subsistence sector in the villages under the guidance of chiefly leadership, and that higher education was to remain the preserve of the chiefly elite.[10] In the abstract, the policy of racial balance made sense, but it was quite another matter at the personal level to see Fijian students getting scholarships on far lower marks than Indo-Fijian students. That policy of discrimination inevitably bred resentment. We felt as if we were the stepchildren of the state. In the civil service, senior Indo-Fijians stared blankly at the glass ceiling.[11] The feeling of disappointment was muted, but it was real. A few years after independence, the warm mantra of multiracialism espoused by the leaders seemed strangely cold.

Things went from bad to worse after the mid-1970s. In 1974, former Alliance Junior Minister Sakeasi Butadroka founded the Fijian Nationalist Part with its motto, 'Fiji for Fijians'. The following year, he moved a provocative motion in parliament on the fifth anniversary of Fiji's independence to have the Indians deported from Fiji, with the expense of relocation to be paid by the British Government.[12] In hindsight, the motion seems ludicrous, a rhetorical flourish of the Fijian nationalist

---

8   E.K. Fisk, *The Political Economy of Independent Fiji* (Canberra: Australian National University Press, 1970).
9   Sir Philip Sherlock et al., *Education for Modern Fiji: Report of the 1969 Fiji Education Commission* (Suva: Government Printer, 1969).
10 See Lala Sukuna, *Fiji: The Three-legged Stool: Selected Writings of Ratu Sir Lala Sukuna*, ed. Deryck Scarr (London: Macmillan Education, 1984).
11 Brij V. Lal, *In the Eye of the Storm: Jai Ram Reddy and the Politics of Postcolonial Fiji* (Canberra: ANU E Press, 2010), pp. 145, 197, doi.org/10.22459/ES.11.2010.
12 Brij V. Lal, *Broken Waves: A History of the Fiji Islands in the Twentieth Century* (Honolulu: University of Hawaii Press, 1992), pp. 235–38.

fringe, nothing more. But at the time, it had a powerful, unsettling effect on us. In 1974, Idi Amin had expelled long-settled Indians from Uganda for no other reason than their industry and hard-earned prosperity. If it could happen in Uganda (and expulsion of Indians had taken place in Burma earlier), there was no obvious reason why it could not happen in Fiji. The Alliance Government's political point-scoring response to the motion, condemning Butadroka but affirming support of the rights of all citizens, not only Indians, who were its specific targets, deepened our sense of alienation. This was especially felt when it became clear that the motion's sentiment, in varying degrees, was shared fairly widely in the Fijian community according to Ratu David Toganivalu, himself a man of widespread cross-cultural friendships. For the first time, many Indo-Fijians began to feel that Fiji might not, after all, be their permanent home. The Canadian Prime Minister Pierre Trudeau's more liberal, skills-based migration policy opened doors that began to attract many. A gradual drift began.

Two years later, the tremors of the earthquake started by Butadroka were felt when the Alliance lost the general election in April 1977 with 25 per cent of the Fijian votes going to the Nationalists. Five months later, the Alliance recaptured its natural constituency by effectively jettisoning its multiracial philosophy and embracing an openly ethnic one. The Alliance learnt anew the truth of a central assumption that underpinned the independence settlement; that Fijians would remain in power provided they remained united. Henceforth, the main preoccupation of the Alliance would be the preservation of Fijian ethnic solidarity. A similar consolidation was taking place on the Indo-Fijian side. Having won the April elections by the narrowest of margins (two seats), the NFP tried for four days to have a coalition government with the Alliance, an offer the party flatly refused. The dithering allowed Governor-General Ratu Sir George Cakobau to appoint a minority government headed by Ratu Sir Kamisese Mara. The NFP's delay in forming government and its internal but well-publicised leadership skirmishes were blamed for the appointment of the minority government but everyone knew privately that an 'Indian' prime minister would not be acceptable to Fijians, proclamations of democratic principles and multiracial values notwithstanding.[13] One by one, all the founding Indo-Fijian members of the Alliance Party left, or were forced to leave on one pretext or another, finding a welcoming home in the NFP

---

13   Lal, *In the Eye of the Storm,* pp. 142–71.

headed by its new leader Jai Ram Reddy. Reddy had not been part of the bitter ideological fights of the preindependence era. He wanted all Indians united under one umbrella, precisely the goal that Ratu Mara had in mind for the Fijians. Racial polarisation was almost complete. We could feel it in our bones.

In 1982, things nearly boiled over. Indo-Fijians had joined hands with some western Fijian leaders disgruntled with the Alliance Government's development policies, especially about the lucrative pine industry, and nearly succeeded in toppling the Fijian Government. Racism raised its ugly head again. Calls were made to deport Indo-Fijian leaders, refuse renewal of leases to Indo-Fijian tenants unless they agreed to Fijian political control, and amend the constitution to enshrine Fijian paramountcy. Crises were manufactured, and events staged to arouse people's emotions. Old timers will remember the *Four Corners* program and the Carroll Report.[14] Once again, the reluctance of the Fijian establishment to concede power or to share it, except on its own terms, was on full display. The tensions generated by the political debates percolated down to the grassroots, subtly influencing (and infecting) cross-cultural attitudes and perceptions. There was cordiality in public but a great deal of circumspection in private. Not everything, however, was as the Alliance narrative portrayed it to be. Villages and settlements were changing in significant ways as the tentacles of the modern cash economy reached the hitherto isolated sections of the community.[15] Travel and technology were transforming urban attitudes and relationships. More and more children were attending multiracial schools, and people of all ethnicities were feeling the effects of a stalled economy and lengthened unemployment lines caused, in part, by World Bank–inspired policies. A multiracial working class was haphazardly in the making. The old polarities and binary oppositions were making less and less sense.

One result of the dissatisfaction with the existing orthodoxies and power arrangements in the country was the formation of a (nominally) multiracial Fiji Labour Party in 1985. Rhetorically left leaning, it was, in fact, cautiously pragmatic or pragmatically cautious, but its emergence posed a potential threat to the established order of things Fijian where

---

14 See Brij V. Lal, 'The Fiji General Elections of 1982: The tidal wave that never came', *The Journal of Pacific History* 18(2) (1983): 134–57, at p. 150, doi.org/10.1080/00223348308572463.
15 R. Gerard Ward, 'Native Fijian villages: A questionable future?' in *Fiji: Future Imperfect*, ed. Michael Taylor (Sydney: Allen & Unwin, 1987), pp. 33–45.

the conventional wisdom held that the business of leadership was the prerogative of chiefs. Its criticism of the eastern chiefs who had dominated Fijian political discourse for much of the twentieth century caused further alarm in minds used to deference and acquiescence to duly constituted authority. It came as little surprise that the Fiji Labour Party–National Federation Party coalition, which won the 1987 general election, was swiftly deposed by the Fijian military in the name of the 'Fijian race'. I argued at the time that the coup was more than the simple racial contest that it was made out to be by the supporters of the coup and by the international media; that it was more about defeated politicians taking back power by any means possible.[16] This narrative lacked traction in those emotionally charged days when 'race' was the privileged explanatory factor of the coup.

The story of the two 1987 coups is too well known to be retold here. The wounds they inflicted on the body politic, social fabric and interethnic relations were profound and enduring. The daily harassment of people, mostly Indo-Fijian supporters of the coalition, including members of my own extended family, broadened the religious bigotry and fanaticism that found its culmination in the infamous Sunday Ban. Along with the threatened nonrenewal of leases and the rampant discrimination in the public service, a deep wound was left on the Indo-Fijian psyche. The sense of rejection and humiliation was deep; just how deep would become clear a few years later. I think I misjudged the depth of the hurt. The 1999 general elections were the first time that Rabuka had to seek Indo-Fijian support to govern. Under the 1990 Constitution, which was completely race based, he only had to court the Fijian electorate, but there were 25 'Open' (that is, nonracial), seats under the 1997 Constitution.

The Indo-Fijians rejected his overtures for partnership in opening a new chapter in Fiji's political evolution. All his achievements in helping give Fiji the most liberal constitution it ever had counted for little. I campaigned vigorously throughout the country for the Rabuka–Reddy coalition parties, explaining the contents of the new constitution and why it needed to be given time to prove its worth, how it was paving the way for a new future for Fiji away from its preoccupation with the politics of race. To be sure, there were good reasons why the Rabuka Government was unpopular—his administration was riddled with corruption and

---

16   Brij V. Lal, *Power and Prejudice: The Making of the Fiji Crisis* (Wellington: New Zealand Institute for International Affairs, 1988, reprinted 1990).

mismanagement and scandals that nearly drove the country to the brink of bankruptcy. Politics of patronage were the order of the day. A new era was beckoning, I argued, but all this fell on deaf ears. The electorate wanted revenge and retribution. Rabuka had done something terribly wrong and he could not go unpunished. Mahendra Chaudhry, the Labour leader, understood the Indian psychology well and exploited it adeptly for his own purposes, even though it was his support that had enabled Sitiveni Rabuka to become prime minister in 1992 in the first place. But sadly, it turned out to be a pyrrhic victory for him.

The 1987 coups sent important messages to the Indo-Fijian community. As Rabuka said at the time, they could live in Fiji and make as much money as they wanted, but they should never aspire to political power, which should always remain in Fijian hands.[17] The Indo-Fijian community was caught in a cul-de-sac. With very little to fall back on—the land leases were expiring at a rapid rate, there was rampant discrimination in the public sector—many Indo-Fijians began to contemplate migration, which had started in earnest soon after the May military takeover. A trickle turned into a torrent. Precise figures are understandably uncertain, but a conservative estimate would put the numbers of those who left after the first coup at over 120,000. The size of the Indo-Fijian population as a result has declined from around 49 per cent in 1987 to around 30 per cent now. And the decline will continue well into the future through a continuously falling birth rate and unceasing migration.[18]

This huge demographic transformation is full of important implications. To start with, the fear of 'Indian domination' that had so plagued the dynamics of Fiji politics since the end of World War II, when the Indo-Fijians for the first time exceeded the indigenous Fijians, has gone forever. You can feel this in the texture and tenor of ordinary conversation with Fijians who know in their hearts that Fiji is once again 'their country'. This transformation has demonstrated the potential for the reconfiguration of Fiji politics. It has, for instance, opened up more space for democratic debate among Fijians about such sensitive topics as chiefly titles and inheritance—for example, in ways that would have been unimaginable during the reign of the paramount chiefs in the early

---

17 Eddie Dean and Stan Ritova, *Rabuka: No Other Way* (Sydney: Doubleday, 1988), pp. 11, 35–37.
18 In the Fijian census of 2017, racial categories of enumeration were dropped so it is impossible to be precise about the ethnic composition of Fiji's population. The figure of 30 per cent is widely suggested by experts.

years of independence. In the 1990s, there was a proliferation of Fijian political parties, each with their own specific agendas that opened up and re-energised the discussion of intra-Fijian issues.[19] The carefully nurtured artefact of 'Fijian unity' was visibly fractured, aided by the departure from the political stage of the paramount chiefs who had once wielded an overarching, unifying influence over their people. The disappearance of the traditional gatekeepers of knowledge and information and the advent of modern technology: radio, television, the internet, and the visual and print media added to the fracturing of 'Fijian unity'.

The bulk of those who left were people of talent and education whose skills were in great demand overseas, especially in Australia and New Zealand: doctors, nurses, accountants, science teachers, mechanics, businessmen. The best and the brightest have left, are leaving and will continue to leave. On that there is general consensus. Among the migrants are members of my own family: three brothers in Brisbane, a sister in Darwin and nieces and nephews and cousins scattered around the globe. Those who remain in Fiji do so for reasons of business, lifestyle or enduring commitment, but have their families and their investments safely 'parked' elsewhere: the word is theirs, not mine. Some who are overseas talk of retiring 'back home', but few so far have taken the opportunity of becoming permanent residents or citizens. They are keeping their options open: once bitten, twice shy. Among those leaving are people who in the normal course of events might have been expected to take a more moderate, longer-term view of the future. Their departure affected the power base of the NFP, playing an important part in its downfall in the 1999 elections. Those who remained and who could not leave—unskilled workers, farmers, the elderly—who had nothing to lose by demanding the sky, fell prey to the demagoguery and vaguely emancipating, empowering rhetoric of the Fiji Labour Party. Among those left in Fiji are the desperately poor with few hopes and little opportunity. They will continue to be vulnerable to the entreaties of opportunistic politicians preying on the needs and aspirations of the truly desperate. And the young will continue to migrate through family sponsorships, arranged marriages or other means. Many are taking courses at tertiary institutions in the hope of improving their chances in the migration stakes.

---

19 Alumita Durutalo, 'Elections and the dilemmas of indigenous Fijian politics', in *Fiji Before the Storm: Elections and the Politics of Development*, ed. Brij V. Lal (Canberra: Asia Pacific Press, 2000), pp. 73–92.

The creation of the Fijian diaspora in Australia and New Zealand, in particular, is an important recent social phenomenon. We are not talking about 'migrant communities' in the old sense of a rupture of a more or less permanent kind. They might more accurately be described as 'transmigrant' communities whose links with their former homelands are never severed but nurtured in a variety of novel ways. People maintain contact with friends and family back home through the internet (emails, Facebook), through regular telephone conversations (via Skype) and through periodic visits. Air travel is not as prohibitively expensive as it once was, and physical proximity helps: Australia and New Zealand are just a few hours away by plane. People help with scholarships, refurbishment of temples and schools, medical supplies and relief efforts during the natural calamities that visit Fiji with mundane regularity every year. Clusters form around places of origin in Fiji (Ba, Labasa) or around religious or cultural affiliation (Sangam, the Muslim League, Sanatan Dharam and Arya Samaj) to provide more targeted assistance in times of need. This sort of contribution is difficult to measure but it is real, and it is increasing. The principle of gift-giving is no longer the preserve of 'traditional' societies much studied by anthropologists.

Many migrants left Fiji in emotionally difficult circumstances, giving up secure jobs that once held the prospect of promotion and permanency, selling homes and other property for a fraction of their normal price, rupturing relations built over generations, taking a journey into the unknown from which, they know, there will be no return. The pain of dislocation is real if never fully expressed. Understandably, their attitude towards those whose policies led to their displacement in the first place is suffused with a mixture of bitterness and deep anger. Many became strong supporters of the Fiji Labour Party and vocal critics of the more moderate and consensus-building strategies of its opponent, the National Federation Party. Jai Ram Reddy's plea to make a fresh start, to let bygones be bygones, fell on deaf ears. Labour's red-hot, punitive rhetoric was more to their liking. It came as little surprise that many Indo-Fijian residents in Australia and New Zealand also became vocal supporters of Frank Bainimarama's latest coups for a variety of motives, not the least of which was revenge. Fijians had caused a lot of misery to Indo-Fijians in the past, enthusiastically endorsing the nationalist rhetoric of previous coups. Now it was time for them to 'taste their own medicine', as the phrase goes in Fiji. There is a reluctance amongst many to believe anything but a positive narrative of the ongoing Fijian saga. That is, whatever the present state of affairs, Bainimarama will come good in the end. He, therefore, needs support, not opposition. Angered by my opposition to the latest coup, some Indo-Fijians in Sydney petitioned Vice-Chancellor Ian Chubb to fire me from the University for my publicly aired and widely disseminated views.

While migration was proceeding apace, there were other developments in the 1980s and 1990s that were aiding the alienation of the Indo-Fijian community in Fiji. Among them were the Rabuka Government's avowedly pro-Fijian policies, especially during its first term, when he seemed overtly indifferent to the concerns of the Indo-Fijians. Rabuka allocated government funds to enable Fijian landowning units to purchase freehold land on the market but appeared to do little to address the anxieties of Indo-Fijian tenants who were evicted from expiring leases. Scandals rocked the government. The economic rationalist policies of Finance Minister Jim Ah Koy affected all workers, Fijian and Indo-Fijian alike, especially at the lower levels. Jobs were lost, and unemployment lines lengthened. The man who had committed the coup was now embarking on a course that was compounding Indo-Fijian misery.

The expiry of the 30-year agricultural leases under the *Agricultural Landlord and Tenant Act* in the 1990s caused havoc in the Indo-Fijian farming community.[20] Leases were not renewed partly because Fijian landowners themselves wanted to enter the industry in which until then they were bystanders. But land was power, too, Fijian power; around 83 per cent of the land was owned in inalienable right by Fijians. People like Marika Qarikau, the Fijian nationalist manager of the Native Land Trust Board, realised this early and used land as a blunt instrument to extract maximum political concessions from the Indo-Fijians. Tenancies would be renewed, the message went out, if Indo-Fijians accepted the principle of Fijian political control. The threat of nonrenewal of leases came at a particularly inopportune time for struggling farmers: the ancient milling structures were collapsing, husbandry practices had deteriorated, tonnage per acre produced was low, and the preferential access to the European Union under the Lome Agreement was about to expire. It was always in the nature of the leases that they would end one day, and the theoretical possibility was held constantly at the back of the mind of the growers. But the reality, when it finally eventuated, was different. The experience of uprooting after generations of living in a place and

---

20 Padma Narsey Lal, *Ganna: Portrait of the Fiji Sugar Industry* (Lautoka: Fiji Sugar Commission, 2009), Chs 6 and 7.

then seeing your formerly productive farm revert to bush, of having to start afresh in a new occupation in a new place, often amongst complete strangers, was wrenching. It left many deeply traumatised and unforgiving of those whose policies had brought about their demise as cane growers, including members of my own extended family.

Ironically, many positive things were happening in the country concurrently, the most important of them being the review of the racially lopsided 1990 Constitution, which Rabuka, along with Jai Ram Reddy, played a genuinely important role in establishing. It was a courageous move, going against the grain of nationalist Fijian opinion completely averse to any concession in the direction of political partnership with the Indo-Fijian community. The 1997 Constitution was a genuine improvement over its previous counterparts. There was limited but important movement in the direction of nonracialism. Race had been removed as a factor in the allocation of affirmative action programs. The constitution had significant human rights provisions. Most importantly, the power-sharing arrangements of the constitution ensured that Indo-Fijians, if they won a sufficient number of seats in the House of Representatives, would, as a matter of right, not charity, be entitled to an invitation into Cabinet. This is what the community had been struggling towards for nearly a century, and the opportunity was now within its grasp. But in the countryside, emptying from the nonrenewal of leases, and in the mushrooming squatter settlements fringing the main urban centres of Fiji, where memories of deprivation and displacement were fresh and deep and the struggle for sustainable living was getting more difficult by the day, constitutional reform counted for little. The constitution won't put food on the table, opportunistic politicians told the people, who believed them. Among them was a former university academic, now a senior academic administrator.

Chaudhry's Fiji Labour Party was the clear beneficiary of the gradually growing reservoir of Indo-Fijian hurt and grievance.[21] He won the 1999 general elections by annihilating his old enemy, the NFP, which failed to win a single seat. Apart from anything else, the Indo-Fijian electorate was unforgiving of NFP's embracing of Sitiveni Rabuka. Grudges run deep in the Indo-Fijian psyche. But the Chaudhry Government lasted only a year in office when it was toppled from office in a quasi-military

---

21 Jon Fraenkel and Stewart Firth (eds), *From Election to Coup in Fiji: The 2006 Campaign and its Aftermath* (Canberra: ANU E Press, 2007).

coup by insurgents led by the improbably self-styled Fijian nationalist George Speight. It was a dark moment for Fiji, but darker still for the Indo-Fijian community, which saw, yet again, a government elected by them overturned by force. It did not matter that the causes of the Speight insurrection were complex and had more to do with intra-Fijian rivalries and struggles for power. The overthrow simply reinforced the feeling of rejection and marginalisation already well entrenched in the broader narrative of the Indo-Fijian experience in the postcolonial period. This ignored the fact of Chaudhry's rather abrasive style, developed in the cauldron of Fiji's combative trade union movement, his ill-advised confrontation with the media, his untimely and reportedly unilateral pursuit of policies of land reform which could have been postponed to more propitious times. The fact that a prime minister of Indo-Fijian descent had been overthrown was enough for many. Chaudhry, it should be emphasised, was not the cause of George Speight's insurrection, though he might have contributed to it unwittingly.

What followed made matters even worse, deepening Indo-Fijian disenchantment with the unfolding events. An interim administration set up by the military and led by the merchant banker and former head of the Fiji Development Bank Laisenia Qarase, which morphed into a new political party, the Soqosoqo Duavata ni Lewenivanua (SDL), won the general elections in 2001 and remained in power until 2006. The tragedy was that Qarase, in his first term, had not learned the lessons of Fiji's recent history. Everything he did repudiated the spirit of consensus building of the 1990s. He openly courted the Fijian nationalist fringe to remain in power.[22] He gave the Fiji Labour Party miniscule portfolios of no significance, which Labour rightly refused, seeking a Supreme Court ruling on the numerical composition of the multiparty Cabinet. The fundamental thrust of his government's policy was to address the concerns and needs of the indigenous Fijian community to the exclusion of virtually everything else. His reading of the Fijian scene was as dated as it was blinkered, premised upon the notion that the Fijians were the disadvantaged community needing special assistance while Indo-Fijians were the well-to-do ones. This, when every piece of objective, verifiable evidence showed that poverty and disadvantage paid no respect to ethnic boundaries but freely transgressed them, This, at a time when rural Indo-Fijians comprised some of the most disadvantaged groups in Fiji society

---

22 Jon Fraenkel, Stewart Firth and Brij V. Lal (eds), *The 2006 Military Takeover in Fiji: A Coup to End all Coups?* (Canberra: ANU E Press, 2009), doi.org/10.22459/MTF.04.2009.

(as shown in various studies by Wadan Narsey). His 'Fijian Blueprint' promised massive assistance for specifically Fijian projects.[23] His education policies directed special assistance to Fijian-run schools when many urban Indian-run schools had more Fijian students than Indian but which missed out because they were not Fijian institutions. The overall narrative of the first Qarase Government was Fijian empowerment and Indo-Fijian disempowerment.

After the 2006 elections, and looking ahead to his last term in parliament with an eye on his place in history, Qarase tried to make amends for his errant, explicitly race-based politics of the past. He now honoured the spirit of the power-sharing provisions of the 1997 Constitution by giving Labour nine senior ministries in his Cabinet. Labour ministers in Cabinet felt there was a genuine effort to make power-sharing work. Qarase himself was, as he told me, full of praise for his Labour colleagues in Cabinet. The mood among Indo-Fijians, and in the country at large, was buoyant, filled with optimism that at long last Fiji might be turning the corner of racially divisive confrontational politics. But by then, Chaudhry, the Labour leader, was completely disaffected. He thought, unlike most other people in Fiji, that the elections had been rigged. There may have been inconsistencies here and there, I thought at the time as I covered the campaign and the week-long voting, but nothing that would have changed the outcome of the election. As party leader, he wanted to allocate portfolios to his ministers, and he wanted them to be accountable to him rather than to the prime minister as the Westminster convention requires. This was crude politics designed to destabilise the multiparty government. When his ministers balked, punishing them in the name of party solidarity became Chaudhry's relentlessly pursued prime concern. At that point, the multiparty government was doomed.

Qarase did not help his cause by attempting to fulfil some of his controversial campaign promises, which could, and should, have been left for consideration later in the life of his government, if implemented at all. These included returning the ownership of the foreshore to the indigenous owners (the *Qoliqoli Bill*), which deeply angered developers, hoteliers and non-Fijians generally; investigating the basis of land purchases in the nineteenth century with a view to returning illegally or fraudulently acquired lands to the traditional owners; and, most

---

23   'Blueprint for the Protection of Fijian and Rotuman Rights and Interests, and the Advancement of their Development', presented to the GCC by Qarase, 3 July 2000.

controversially, bypassing established judicial procedures to release from jail people convicted of coup-related crimes. The story is more complex than it is possible to discuss here, suffused as it is with a variety of motives. None of the bills actually came before parliament, but the damage to the government's reputation for probity and fairness was significant, providing powerful ammunition to its critics. Among these critics was Commodore Frank Bainimarama, head of the Fiji military. His wrath focused particularly on the use of the Compulsory Supervision Order to effect early release of prisoners, convicted for their role in the mutiny in November 2000 in which several loyal soldiers lost their lives, and which nearly claimed the life of Bainimarama himself. He was angry, too, at the prospect of facing a reduction in the size of the top-heavy military force recommended in a White Paper commissioned by the government. There were issues also surrounding the length and duration of Bainimarama's contract. Deep personal animosity between military commander and prime minister did not help. For these and other reasons, Bainimarama unleashed his coup on 5 December 2006.

Fijian anger at the overthrow of a Fijian Government, elected with overwhelming indigenous Fijian support, was understandable. No one had ever contemplated the possibility of a Fijian military confronting a Fijian government, or the uncultural humbling and humiliation of the central institutions of Fijian society, the Great Council of Chiefs (GCC) and the Methodist Church. The reaction of the Indo-Fijian community was revealing. In 1987 and in 2000, there was immediate outrage: strikes were threatened or mounted, trade unions mobilised, international sanctions sought. But there was none of that in 2006. There were many reasons. To begin with, there was the nature of the coup itself. The 2006 Fiji Coup would have to be one of the most advertised coups in the history of the world, announced several years before it actually materialised: a coup by haemorrhage. When the dénouement finally came, it was received not so much with surprise as with relief that the deed was finally done. It was not a coup, Bainimarama said; it was a 'clean-up' campaign. The catchphrase caught on; it resonated in the experience of many who had witnessed or been victims of the bourgeoning bribery and corruption in Fiji. *Baksheesh* was fast becoming a way of life in the country. Reports of government largesse being channelled to constituents for political, vote-buying purposes were well known. Many genuinely believed that Bainimarama meant business when he promised to halt the looting of the public purse for political purposes.

A new dimension to Indo-Fijian thinking was added in January 2007 when Labour leader Chaudhry joined the military administration as its finance minister. There are many in Fiji who believe that Chaudhry was in on the game from the very beginning—a charge he denies vehemently, and for which he must be taken at his word. Nonetheless, throughout the steadily building crisis, Chaudhry was quietly seeking audience with Bainimarama after hours, keeping his powder dry, keeping abreast of the latest developments and taking every opportunity to criticise the Qarase Government and his own ministers in it. Perhaps, like Bainimarama, Chaudhry was haunted by a past that had denied him his just dues and he was determined not to forgive his enemies. Chaudhry was the leader of the Indo-Fijian community and many, for that reason alone, followed his lead. There were other Indo-Fijian leaders, of the NFP, for instance, who opposed the coup, but theirs was a minority voice. Perhaps Chaudhry thought he might be able to use his vast political experience to steer the novices in the military regime into a desirable direction—the tail that might wag the dog—but in this view, he was seriously mistaken. A year later, he was unceremoniously dumped from the military Cabinet, but by then the damage brought about by his involvement had been done. Chaudhry's participation had given the military regime a certain cloak of much-needed legitimacy at a time when it mattered most. Bainimarama had been able to buy off valuable time to consolidate himself in power and fend off criticism at home and from abroad. Chaudhry now finds himself hobbled on the margins, taking occasional pot shots at various government policies from his website. His once strongly organised community is similarly disabled.

The Indo-Fijian business community switched sides in quick time, which comes as no surprise. When the coup took place, many were heard to say that the country would bounce back to normalcy within six months. It did not, which forced them to take a longer-term view of things, including courting elements of the military. There were some who supported the new regime because of their experience with corruption in the previous administrations, but for many, money making was their main priority, the end that any means could justify. The authoritarian environment suited their purpose. Some are known to have direct access to the members of the shadowy Military Council. The commitment of the business community to Fiji is suspect. It has been so for a while. Many have moved their nest eggs safely elsewhere, to Australia and New Zealand, where many also have permanent residence. Businessmen with conscience and commitment have been rare in Fiji.

More surprising has been the reaction of the Indo-Fijian moral community. After the obligatory disapproving tones, many Indo-Fijian religious leaders quickly fell in line. The head of the largest Hindu organisation in Fiji, the Sanatan Dharam Pirtenidine Sabha of Fiji, declared quiet support for the stated goals of the coup. The Acting President of the Arya Samaj, the wife of a high court judge, joined the military administration's National Council for Building a Better Fiji and urged an understanding of the military regime's plans for Fiji. From Western Viti Levu, the perennially changeable politician Swani Maharaj, a member of several political parties in the past, gave similar assurances of support. The South Indian cultural organisation Sangam expressed opposition while the Fiji Muslim League, whose leaders were close to the Qarase administration, maintained strategic silence. But the overall narrative was of compliance.

A part of the reason for the support was pragmatic. There were personal business interests to consider. The regime in power had to be courted to receive special grants and other favours for schools and community projects because it looked likely that the regime would remain in power for longer than originally thought. But an important part of the reason for supporting the regime was grievance and grudge. People remembered the excesses of the Sunday Ban of the late 1980s, the mindless acts of religious vandalism, the burning of mosques and temples and other places of worship, with the support of the leaders of the Methodist Church— the Reverends Tomasi Raikivi, Manasa Lasaro and Viliame Gonelevu, to mention just three. For this reason, many welcomed Bainimarama's punitive approach to the Methodist Church leaders. It was the same with the humbling and humiliation of the GCC, which had supported coups in the past and which many thought was anachronistic in the modern era. Why should this body alone decide who should be the President and Vice-President of Fiji?

In the past, academics and tertiary students played prominent roles in rallying public opinion against the coups. But now, with one or two notable exceptions, they took a back seat. In the early days, many of them were seduced by the 'clean-up' campaign message; their strategic silence quietly encouraged by the leadership of these institutions of higher learning fearing reprisals, if nothing else. Many actually believed in the possibility of the Bainimarama Coup being a good coup, a means to an end, the end being the creation of a better governed, race-neutral society. They were prepared to give the new regime the benefit of the doubt over Qarase and Chaudhry, two old practitioners of race-based politics.

A focus on personalities detracted from the fundamental principles at stake; a military coup had deposed a democratically elected government. Qarase and Chaudhry may fall under the proverbial bus tomorrow, but the sanctity of the ballot box must be guarded at all times. Others offered old, tired extraconstitutional justifications such as the need to sometimes go outside the law to protect it. Students took their cue from their teachers. Their seeming indifference and apathy was dismaying, their involvement in the great issues of governance almost nonexistent. Perhaps, many were simply focused on acquiring the right qualifications to emigrate. Others saw opportunities for themselves and thought it undesirable to 'rock the boat'. Edward Said's words are apposite:

> You do not want to appear too political; you are afraid of seeming controversial; you need the approval of a boss or an authority figure; you want to have a reputation for being balanced, objective, moderate; your hope is to be asked back, to consult, to be on a board or prestigious committee, and so remain within the responsible mainstream; someday you hope to get an honorary degree, a big prize, perhaps even an ambassadorship.

Said goes on to say that 'if anything can denature, neutralize, and finally kill a passionate intellectual life it is the internalization of such habits'.[24]

From Fiji's émigré community there came unexpected support for the coup, particularly from retired Indo-Fijian expatriates. Many had left Fiji, or been forced to leave it, in singularly unfortunate circumstances in the late 1980s; some summarily dismissed from the public service for suspected harbouring of procoalition sympathies. Now in their retirement, they wanted to return to help set things right, to make Fiji a true, nonracial democracy, albeit on exorbitant consultants' salaries, almost obscene by local standards. Some were clearly opportunistic, yearning for a brief moment in the sun before the inevitable twilight. But there were also among them technocratic ideologues who had little confidence in the institutions and practices of electoral politics to deliver desired outcomes. They had no time for wicked politicians who played the race card to win elections. Voters could not be trusted to know what was in their own best interests. Elections were problematic: low voter turnout endemic in developing countries, corruption and scandals rampant, alienation of people from the processes of governance growing. Democracy may

---

24 Edward Said, *Representations of the Intellectual* (New York: Chatto and Windus, 1996), pp. 100–11.

not be the most appropriate form of government for all societies. They, therefore, threw their weight behind the so-called 'Peoples Charter', a document full of motherhood statements that might as well have been lifted straight from any Good Governance 101 course, to put the country onto autopilot, leaving elected politicians only to dot the i's and cross the t's. The Charter has now become the military regime's roadmap, its foundational document, but it is observed more in the breach as the regime tramples upon principles of natural justice and basic human rights in order to entrench itself. The Charter supporters are caught in a bind: they can neither condone the excesses of the regime their participation helped to legitimise, nor can they condemn it outright. Like most Indo-Fijians, they too are marooned in a cul-de-sac.

Some responses are easily categorised, but others are not. There are many Indo-Fijians, perhaps the majority, who have no view either way, whose standard of life has not changed much at all since 2006, quite the contrary, who live precariously on the charity and sufferance of others. People who have endured enough upheaval in their lives for the last two decades hope that this too will pass soon so that they can get on with their lives. It is resignation borne not of indifference or fatalism, but of experience, an endless cycle of promises made and broken. I should at this point declare my own hand. I have been a strong opponent of military coups in Fiji. I was as opposed to them in 1987 as I was in 2006. For me, there is something deeply immoral (quite apart from being illegal) about overturning the verdict of the ballot box by the bayonet. The history of the world shows that coups don't solve problems, they merely compound them. Violence as an instrument of policy is always counterproductive. And I believe deeply that the intellectual classes (but not they alone) have the sacred responsibility to speak truth to power. If we don't, who will? I did that in my own small way, speaking and writing against coups and their consequences for Fiji and for which I paid the price. I was interrogated by the military in November 2009 and expelled from the country, the land of my birth. There is no rancour or bitterness; if that is the price that had to be paid for standing up for the values of democracy and the rule of law, then I am glad I paid it.

Four years after the 2006 coup, the Indo-Fijian community, diminished and demoralised, is caught between a rock and a hard place. The rhetoric providing the initial justification for the coup rings hollow now. The 'clean-up' campaign has yielded few results except more embarrassment for the military regime and its bungling Fiji Independent Commission

Against Corruption (headed by a serving military officer). Like the Qarase administration, the military regime too has used the Compulsory Supervision Order to affect early release from prison of people convicted for various coup-related crimes, including the manslaughter of civilians, thus denting its moral claims over the regime it deposed. It is now clear that the military will only countenance a new political order in which it will have a visible and permanent presence. A militarised democracy is in the offing. Burma, as a comparison, comes to mind. There are many Indo-Fijians who, having supported the coup thus far, feel that there can be no turning back. They have burned their bridges with the Fijian community. They know that they are seen by others, fairly or unfairly, as aiding and abetting the coup through various acts of omission or commission. If the coup fails, they know they are done for, and so out of desperate necessity they back Bainimarama because they know that he is the only one who stands between them and anarchy. Indeed, some are beginning to embrace him as their real leader, not Chaudhry or anyone else.

The impulses underlying this kind of thinking are understandable but wrong-headed and in truth counterproductive. Rhetoric of nonracialism aside, the Bainimarama Coup is morphing into a 'Fijian' coup as many Fijians take up opportunities left by the departing Indo-Fijians and as province after province lines up to 'apologise' to Bainimarama for opposing his regime. The presence in the interim administration of such notable former coup supporters and members of the hard-line Taukei Movement as Inoke Kubuabola and Filipe Bole is reassuring to them. Bainimarama has vowed not to allow 1987-era politicians to stand for elections in the future and yet has rewarded two of them with senior positions in his administration. There is talk of nonracial equality but not a word has been said about opening up the almost racially exclusive military to non-Fijians. The ethnic imbalance in the public sector is glaring. Military personnel increasingly take up senior civilian positions. Commodore Bainimarama promises to address the perennial land-lease problem by making available unused Fijian land on 99-year leases for agricultural purposes. It sounds an attractive proposition on paper, but it is like locking the stable door after the horse has already bolted. The sugar industry is dying, and no amount of artificial resuscitation will revive it. Places in northern Vanua Levu—Wainikoro, Lagalaga, Naqiqi, Coqeloa—are emptying at a depressingly rapid rate as people move into the congested squatter settlements principally in the Suva–Nausori corridor where an estimated one-third of the total population now lives, often in wretched conditions.

Yet, those displaced from the farming country say they will never return to the perpetual uncertainties of the past. The umbilical cord is severed for good. Many are contemplating an overseas future for their children.

For the Indo-Fijians, as indeed for Fiji as a whole, the last 40 years have been a time of frustration and bewilderment, the promise of independence gone awry. A large part of the problem lay with the architecture of the independence political order itself. It was constructed on the pillars of ethnic compartmentalisation while, with time and with the advent of new forces of change, 'race' largely lost its relevance in daily life to all but the leaders who continued to embrace it a 'as a fact of life'. When power was finally wrested from the ruling elite at the ballot box, the military was unleashed to win it back. In a strange twist of irony, the military, which was nurtured as the ultimate bastion of power for the Fijian establishment, returned in 2006 to destroy its very foundations. It now looks unlikely that it will never completely disappear from the political scene. Power concedes nothing without a struggle and, once out, soldiers do not voluntarily return to the barracks. The intense and deeply felt debates over the last 40 years about strengthening the institutions of parliamentary democracy—electoral systems, political parties, constitutional protection of rights, institutional mechanisms for strengthening the participation of citizens in the governance of the country—seem, in the end, to have been a wasted effort. There is poignant irony in the fact that a community committed broadly to a nonviolent Gandhian approach to politics, and which itself had been a victim of coups in the past, now endorses, however indirectly or tangentially, violence as an instrument of public policy in the desperate hope of a better outcome for itself. But one of the lessons learnt from history is that coups do not solve problems, they compound them.

The Indo-Fijian community itself has changed almost beyond recognition in the last 40 years. The self-contained, self-sustaining rural community built around the sugar industry is uprooted and adrift. The settlements in the cane areas that once hummed with life—local sports competitions, festivals and festivities—now look empty and forlorn. The land has ceased to be the sole source of livelihood for most families, including my own. Villages are now essentially residential sites. There is a deep yearning among most young people, still stranded in rural areas, to leave for someplace else. The rapid transformation of the rural scene is eroding a culture and a way of life that once formed the bedrock of Indo-Fijian society and provided a direct link to its foundational past. Cut from its cultural moorings, with declining support and sustenance from its roots, the community is vulnerable, much more at the mercy of forces of change beyond its control. It is, in truth, living on the sufferance of others. In the early 1970s, migration would have appeared a very distant prospect for most Indo-Fijians. It was something that only the wealthy and the well-connected might contemplate. It is a daily occurrence now, uppermost in the minds of most people, if not for themselves then certainly for their children. The community is emotionally uprooted. It is often said with some truth that there is hardly a single Indo-Fijian family in Fiji that does not have at least one member abroad. The emotional centre of gravity has shifted. Perhaps in time, 'from Immigration to Emigration' may become the dominant narrative in the overall experience of the Indo-Fijian community, its Fiji sojourn a momentary stopover in the life of a people condemned by fate to scatter around the world. By then, people of my generation would have moved on. In the words of John Dryden, 'Not Heav'n itself upon the past has pow'r; / But what has been, has been, and I have had my hour.'[25]

---

25   John Dryden, *Imitation of Horace,* Book iii, Ode 29, lines 71–72.

14

Towards a united future[1]

Report of the Fiji Constitution
Review Commission

> All the great things can be expressed in single words: freedom,
> justice, honour, duty, mercy, hope.
>
> — Winston Churchill[2]

In 1996, the Fiji Constitution Review Commission handed down its report on its review of the postcoup 1990 Constitution with recommendations for the basis of a new Constitution that met the needs of Fiji as a multiethnic society. The Commission recommended a gradual but decisive shift towards a nonracial political culture. Many of the Commission's recommendations were incorporated into the 1997 Constitution, except those relating to the election to and composition of parliament. The 1997 Constitution was overthrown by the Fijian military in 2009. What Fiji's future might have been like if that constitution had a different fate will never be known. 'What might have been' must remain some of the saddest words in the English language. This chapter provides a summary of the work of the Commission and its thinking behind its recommendations. I was one of the commissioners on the three-person Fiji Constitution Review Commission. In the larger perspective of history, the

---

1   Originally appeared in *The Journal of Pacific History* 32 (1997): 71–84.
2   Winston Churchill, cited in Robert Rogers, 'Second thoughts', *Who Goes Home: A Parliamentary Miscellany* (London: Robson Press, 2012), n.p.

work of the Commission will be seen as a signal achievement of compromise and consensus in the most difficult of circumstances, and whose vision for Fiji was fundamentally progressive and far-sighted.

On 6 September 1996, the Fiji Constitution Review Commission submitted its report on the review of Fiji's 1990 Constitution to the country's president, Ratu Sir Kamisese Mara. Four days later, the report, nearly 800 pages long and containing some 694 recommendations, was laid on the table of Fiji's Parliament.[3] This chapter, which is in the nature of an executive summary of the Constitutional Review Report, attempts to present the thinking as well as the reasoning behind the Commission's recommendations, which sought to point Fiji in a new direction. As a coauthor of the report, I have borrowed freely and extensively from the text to preserve its flavour and to protect its integrity.

Origins of the Fiji Constitution Review Commission

The 1990 Constitution, decreed into existence by President Ratu Sir Penaia Ganilau five years after the military coups of 1987,[4] with no popular participation in its formulation or its implementation, was assumed by its authors to be an interim document. Section 161 of the Constitution provided for its review at the end of seven years after the date of its promulgation, that is, before 25 July 1997. After the 1992 elections,[5] which brought the Soqosoqo ni Vakavulewa ni Taukei (SVT) to power and Major-General Sitiveni Rabuka to the prime minister's chair, the government and the opposition started discussions on the review of the constitution.

A Joint Parliamentary Committee was set up to make recommendations on how the review process should be undertaken. After protracted discussions, the joint committee recommended, and both Houses of

---

3   Report of the Fiji Constitution Review Commission (Sir Paul Reeves, Tomasi Rayalu Vakatora and Brij V. Lal), *The Fiji Islands: Towards a United Future,* Parliamentary Paper, 34 (1996).
4   There were two coups in 1987. The first one was on 14 May 1987. This was the main coup. There was another one in September, which severed Fiji's links to the UK Monarchy. So, when I talk about the 1987 coups, I lump them together to make the larger point about turbulence, etc. When I discuss the May coup, I mean the first coup.
5   See Brij V. Lal, 'Chiefs and Indians: Elections and politics in contemporary Fiji', *The Contemporary Pacific* 5(2) (1993): 275–301.

Parliament unanimously agreed in September 1993, that a commission of inquiry should be set up to review the constitution. Parliament also unanimously approved the terms of reference for the Commission, but further progress was disrupted when the SVT Government fell in November 1993.[6]

Early in 1994 the SVT returned to power with an increased majority, and resumed discussion on the constitutional review with the opposition parties. The most important unresolved issue was the membership of the Commission. Eventually, it was agreed that the Commission would consist of three persons, one appointed by the government, one by the opposition, and a chairperson to be an independent person from outside. The government nominated Tomasi Rayalu Vakatora, a former senior public servant, a Senator, a government minister and the Speaker of the House. The opposition nominated me, an academic specialist on Fiji history and politics. Both sides agreed on Sir Paul Reeves, former Anglican Archbishop and ex–Governor-General of New Zealand, as chair. The three commissioners received their commissions on 15 March 1995 and the two legal counsel assisting them (Alison Quentin-Baxter and Jon Apted) on 19 May. The Commission commenced its work in early June.

The terms of reference, themselves an historic achievement of consensus and compromise, considering the bitterness and hostility generated by the coups, required the Commission to recommend constitutional arrangements that would meet the present and future needs of the people of Fiji, and promote racial harmony, national unity and economic and social advancement of all communities. Those arrangements had to guarantee full protection and promotion of the rights, interests and concerns of the indigenous Fijian and Rotuman people, have full regard for the rights, interests and concerns of all ethnic groups in Fiji, and take into account internationally recognised principles and standards of individual and group rights. In accomplishing this task, the Commission was expected to have scrutinised the constitution, facilitated the widest possible debate on its terms and, after ascertaining the views of the people, suggest how the provisions of the 1990 Constitution could be improved upon to meet the needs of Fiji as a multiethnic and multicultural society. The terms of reference were wide-ranging, prompting some critics to wonder what they actually meant and whether they could be reconciled

---

6   See Brij V. Lal, 'Rabuka's Republic: The Fiji Snap Elections of 1994', *Pacific Studies* 18(1) (1995): 47–77.

into a workable formula. These thoughts also crossed the Commission's mind, which devoted a great deal of time early on to analysing the text as well as the implications of the terms of reference.

Unlike previous commissions of enquiry, such as the Street Commission of 1975 and others set up in the immediate aftermath of the coups,[7] the Reeves Commission was required to review the whole constitution, not only the provisions relating to the electoral system and the composition of parliament. The review, then, was to be a fundamental, wide-ranging exercise, covering, besides the two critical areas just mentioned, the functioning of parliament, the relationship between the executive and the legislative branches, institutions of government and the mechanism for improving accountability and transparency in them, the administration of justice, citizenship, ethnic and social justice issues, rights of communities and groups, the operation of local government bodies, public revenue and expenditure, emergency powers, and a Bill of Rights, among others.[8]

To accomplish the task, the Commission took an early decision regarding the modus operandi of its work: as far as possible, the process of consultation would be open, transparent and inclusive. To ascertain the view of the people, and thus fulfil one of the requirements of the terms of reference, the Commission decided to hold public hearings throughout the country to receive submissions. That exercise, exhausting and exhaustive, lasted from July to November 1995. More than 800 written and oral submissions were received from individual citizens, community, religious, cultural and various interest groups, and all political parties. The overwhelming majority of the submissions were made in public, and are available to the public;[9] but some individuals, for various reasons, chose to speak to the Commission in confidence, and these naturally form part of the closed record. The Commission also invited specific individuals, heads of statutory organisations and other prominent individuals in public life to share their experiences and views privately. At the same time, the Commission commissioned papers from local and overseas researchers on a range of topics, to deepen its knowledge of the local social and economic environment and to better understand international

---

7   The first of these, set up in July 1987, was chaired by former Alliance Government Attorney-General Sir John Falvey, which produced a divided report.
8   Bills of Rights in Fiji have been included in various versions of the constitution. They are not stand-alone Bills.
9   These have been microfilmed by the Pacific Manuscripts Bureau at The Australian National University and are accessible to all researchers.

conventions and constitutional arrangements for power sharing in other jurisdictions. The Commission visited three of them, Malaysia, Mauritius and South Africa, to find out firsthand how they had resolved the problem of political representation in their multiethnic societies. While all these various sources of information were enormously helpful in facilitating an understanding of the task at hand, no one source was privileged over any other.

Fiji's constitutional arrangements

It is neither possible nor desirable to cover all the major areas contained in the Commission's report. For the purposes of this exercise, two sets of issues will be discussed. The first, and perhaps the most critical, concerns the election to and the composition of parliament. That question lay at the centre of the 'web', and was at the forefront of all the submissions. It was the one area of central disagreement between the major political parties and the two major communities. The second relates to the functioning of the institutions of government and issues of social justice and human rights.

From the outset, the Commission believed that unless the systemic nature of Fiji's constitutional problems was clearly understood, there was little hope of devising constitutional arrangements that would not give rise to the same problems in the future. From the evidence before it, the Commission concluded that it was Fiji's constitutional arrangements that had hampered the process of nation building and impeded effective cooperation among the various communities, which otherwise had shown a remarkable capacity for tolerance and respect for each other's cultural and religious traditions while sharing the values and interests they had in common.

Fiji's problems, the Commission concluded, arose from four features of the country's constitutional arrangements. Two were understandable responses to Fiji's multiethnic society—the principle that Fijian interests should be paramount, and the communal system of representation in parliament—and these two reflected the Westminster system of government that Fiji inherited at the time of independence: the role of political parties and the principle that a government must command the support of a majority in parliament. All these underpinned both the 1970 and the 1990 constitutions.

The principle that Fijian interests should always remain paramount had been expressly enunciated by the colonial government since the early years of this century, partly reflecting genuine concern for the position of the indigenous Fijians, partly serving to deflect the Indo-Fijian demand for equal political representation, and partly serving as a tool to guide political change at a pace acceptable to the colonial state. Nonetheless, the principle was widely accepted and became part of the political culture of Fiji. As Fiji moved towards self-government in the 1960s, the principle of political paramountcy became the focus of negotiations among the main political actors in the colony. The Fijian view was that the principle that Fijians' interests should be paramount could only be secured if they had political paramountcy as well. As other communities already dominated the economy, Fijian leaders pointed out, it was only fair that Fijians should dominate in government. For their part, Indo-Fijian leaders agreed to the entrenched legislative protection of Fijian land ownership, culture and separate system of administration, but did not see the paramountcy of Fijian interests as involving an ongoing commitment to secure the reelection of a predominantly Fijian government. If the democratic process provided for in the constitution gave the opportunity, Indo-Fijian leaders saw no reason why they should not join other groups, including some Fijians, in voting in a government in which they could participate. Differing interpretations of the meaning of Fijian paramountcy, then, was one contentious issue.

Another was the system of representation in parliament. From the very beginning, the electoral system in Fiji has been communal, the seats always allocated among the various ethnic communities. This arrangement grew out of the colonial government's view that, in an ethnically divided society, separate representation of different communities was natural and desirable. And the system enabled the government to keep the differences apart as much as possible, thus accentuating its own role as an impartial and indispensable mediator of disputes among the communities. Until 1966, Fiji had only a communal roll, with voters in each community electing members belonging to that community. Later, the communal rolls were complemented with cross-voting rolls, allowing members belonging to each community to be elected by all voters. This system also represented a compromise between the Fijian and European desire for communal representation from the communal roll and the Indo-Fijian commitment to the principle of a nonracial common roll. The compromise spawned more problems than it resolved.

14. TOWARDS A UNITED FUTURE

The third feature of Fiji's political arrangement was that all its parties were essentially ethnic. The National Federation Party (NFP), formed in the aftermath of the 1960 strike in the sugar industry, was based in the Indo-Fijian community, able to attract only a motley number of Fijian supporters over the years. The Alliance Party, formed in 1965 at the behest of Governor Sir Derek Jakeway, was a Fijian-dominated party supported by the Fijian Association, the General Electors Association and the Indian Alliance. The Alliance was more multiracial, but at each successive election, the ethnic basis of the two main parties became increasingly clear.

The final feature of Fiji's political arrangements was the Westminster system, where the prime minister is the leader of the party or combination of parties that can command majority support in the Lower House. The Cabinet is drawn exclusively from that coalition or party. Through its direction of the departments and other government agencies, the government of the day has effective control of policy. Because of its majority in parliament, it can secure the passage of its budget and other legislation. If the party in power is defeated in a general election, the control of government passes to the winning party.

1970 and 1990 constitutions

These arrangements were reflected in both the 1970 and the 1990 constitutions. The 1970 Constitution, negotiated by the leaders of the two main political parties, the Alliance and the National Federation, was an 'interim solution'. The method of election had proved a major stumbling block in the negotiations leading to independence. Unable to break the impasse, the leaders agreed to defer the question of the electoral system to an independent commission. Meanwhile, the 1970 Constitution provided for a 52-seat House, of which 22 were to be Fijian, 22 Indian and eight General Voters (that is, those classified neither as Fijians nor Indians). Of the 22 Fijian and Indian members, 12 were to be elected on the communal roll and 10 by cross-voting; three of the General Voters were to be elected from the communal roll and five from the national roll.

At the beginning, hopes were for the development of multiracial politics. In the 1972 elections, both the Alliance and the National Federation Party made genuine attempts, although with limited success, to attract voters from all communities, but as time went on, communal politics gained ascendancy. This was not surprising, but a logical consequence of the constitutional arrangement in place in Fiji, combining the Westminster system with communal representation. The communal system provided little incentive or opportunity for either voters or candidates to concern themselves with the problems of other communities. Communal sentiments were reinforced. It followed that those elected from the national (cross-voting) seats, representing national constituencies, were not regarded as really legitimate representatives of their own communities. Political parties, predominantly ethnic in character, focused their energy on the community whose interests they were formed to promote. The stress on communalism meant that those parties that were originally committed to multiracialism were inevitably driven back to promoting mainly or only the interests of the community from which, historically, they derived their support.

From this followed the most serious problem of all: the role of ethnic parties in forming government. Because the political parties, responding to the communal system of representation, drew their support mainly from one community, government by one party was seen essentially as ethnic government. The defeat in a general election of the governing party by another party or coalition supported mainly by another ethnic group was seen as the defeat of one community by another. This is precisely what happened in Fiji. In 1987, when the Alliance was defeated by a coalition of the NFP and the Fiji Labour Party (FLP), many Fijians thought that their community had been defeated, and that they were deprived of the political paramountcy, which they saw as essential in safeguarding their interests. Because so much weight was placed on political paramountcy, the Fijians were unwilling to accept the outcome of the election. Fijians saw the defeat of their party as a breach of the Indo-Fijians' tacit acceptance of the principle of Fijian political paramountcy, but the Indo-Fijians saw no inconsistency with their recognition of this principle, as they understood it, with seeking to become government. The result of this mutual incomprehension was the military overthrow of the Coalition Government on 14 May 1987.

Yet the outcome of the 1987 election was entirely consistent with the nature of the 1970 constitutional arrangements. No constitution based on democratic principles can guarantee that a particular party will always remain in office. Nor can it guarantee that the party that wins a majority will always be the one representing a particular ethnic community. The very essence of a democratic system is the ability of elections to change the government, to maintain their accountability and responsiveness to the people. The process of change, which is both natural and inevitable, has been evident in Fiji.

The 1990 Constitution reflected what Fijians believed to be the remedy for their political predicament. There were significant departures from the 1970 Constitution. The size of the Lower House was increased to 70, and there was no longer parity of representation between Fijians and Indo-Fijians. The 37 seats for the Fijians gave them an overall majority. Indo-Fijians were allocated 27 seats, and Rotumans, previously part of the Fijian electoral roll, were given one seat. The number of General Voter seats was reduced from eight to five, and the roll enlarged to include Pacific Island voters who had been previously on the Fijian roll. The prime minister was required to be a Fijian, and the president an appointee of the Great Council of Chiefs (GCC). All seats were to be filled by voting on communal rolls. There was no provision for cross-voting, so that no single ethnic community could affect the selection of members to represent any community but its own. The Upper House of 34 consisted of 24 nominees of the GCC, one of the Council of Rotuma and nine appointed by the president to represent the other communities. A number of positions were reserved for the indigenous communities, and affirmative action policies required specific attention to their needs.

The 1990 Constitution was a drastic response to what had been seen as a drastic situation. Its underlying assumption was that if Fijians had more than half the seats in the House of Representatives, they would be able to maintain their hold on political power. An indigenous Fijian party winning all the 37 seats would have the necessary majority to form a government. Splinter Fijian parties would submerge their differences and come together in the interests of the larger Fijian cause. And Rotumans and General Voters could be counted upon for their support. That was the hope, but, in reality, there was considerable divergence of interests across occupations and regions in Fijian society, created by the effects of the monetary economy, which no amount of political engineering could hide. Even with the benefit of weighted representation, Fijians could not form government without the support of independent members and members of another party. Nor was the governing coalition able to maintain its own unity in all circumstances, most clearly seen in the defeat of the SVT-led coalition in November 1993.

The lesson was clear. First, the goal of permanent Fijian political unity was unrealistic and efforts to peruse it in the context of a rapidly changing environment had a high cost for Fijians themselves. Second, in the absence of unity, even a constitution as heavily weighted in favour of Fijians as that of 1990 might not prevent a minority of Fijians from joining with an Indo-Fijian party or parties to form a government. And third, trying to keep a predominantly Fijian government in office in perpetuity might not be the best way of securing the paramountcy of Fijian interests. In short, the assumptions and understandings that underpinned the 1990 Constitution proved untenable. Fiji would need to chart a new course to move away from the cul-de-sac of communal politics and ethnic compartmentalisation.

Charting a new course

The Commission was convinced, after listening to submissions, that the people of Fiji wanted all communities to play some part in the Cabinet, and that the voters should be able to cast votes for at least some candidates belonging to communities other than their own. They disagreed on the means of achieving that end and the pace in the direction of multiethnicity, but the broad goal was widely shared. The Commission agreed that progress towards the sharing of power among all communities was the only way to resolve some of Fiji's constitutional problems, the only way to attain racial harmony, national unity and the social and economic advancement of all communities. Constitutional arrangements that promoted the emergence of multiethnic governments should be the primary goal. Such arrangements should protect the rights and interests of all citizens, particularly of the indigenous communities. They should provide incentives to political parties to strive for the goal of multiethnic cooperation, and for the political process to move gradually but decisively away from the communal system of representation. The principle of Fijian paramountcy should be recognised, as in the past, in its protective role, in securing effective Fijian participation in a multiethnic government, along with members of other communities, and in securing the fruits of affirmative programs of social and ethnic justice based on a distribution of resources broadly acceptable to all. Fijian interests should not be subordinate to the interests of other communities. Ultimately, however, the best guarantee of the interests of all ethnic communities was a constitution that gave all political parties a strong inducement not to espouse policies that favoured the interests of one community over others. Instead, it should encourage them to see the important interests of each community as national interests that have to be met through the concerted efforts of all.

This goal of achieving an inclusive, democratic, open and free multiethnic society is reflected in a number of the Commission's early recommendations. Fiji should be named The Republic of the Fiji Islands, which would give all Fiji citizens, if they wished, the opportunity of calling themselves by the common name of 'Fiji Islanders'. The constitution should accord the Fijian, Hindi and English languages equal status and, wherever possible, provide services to the public in all three languages. The preamble should be broadly acceptable to all its citizens, touching upon the history of Fiji's multiethnic society and its shared beliefs and values. Perhaps most important, the values and principles that should be taken into account when forming governments should be stated in a Compact, an artefact of moral as distinct from legal force. These include respect for the rights of all individuals, communities and groups, including those protecting the traditional ownership of Fijian land and the observation of lease arrangements between landlords and tenants; the right to freely practice religion, language, culture and traditions; the right of the indigenous communities to governance through separate administrative systems; political freedom and full and equal citizenship rights for all; respect for the democratic process; fair and inclusive government and the need to negotiate in good faith to reach agreement, to resolve differences and conflicts of interest; recognition of the principle of the paramountcy of Fijian interests as a protective principle to ensure that the interests of the Fijian community are not subordinated to the interests of other communities; and the need for affirmative action and social justice programs to secure equality of access to opportunities, amenities and services for the Fijian and Rotuman people, as well as other communities and for all disadvantaged groups, to be based on an allocation of resources broadly acceptable to all ethnic communities.

Institutions of government

The values and principles mentioned above were given concrete constitutional form in the Commission's recommendations on the structure of government. They represented significant shifts from both the 1990 and the 1970 constitutions. To begin with, the Commission recommended that the Bose Levu Vakaturaga (BLV) should not only be recognised in the constitution, as was the case in the 1990 Constitution, but that its composition, powers and functions should be further specified. There was widespread support for this view, reflecting the respect that institution is accorded for its preeminent role in Fijian affairs. Some Fijians wanted to return the BLV to its original status, restricting its membership predominantly to chiefs. The Commission regarded that view as impracticable and inconsistent with contemporary reality. It recommended that the BLV should consist of a mix of members nominated by the three confederacies and those elected by the provinces, besides five ex-officio members including the president, the heads of the three confederacies and the Minister of Fijian Affairs. The BLV should continue to be an advisory body, though with the important functions of nominating candidates for the office of president, and exercising veto power over amendments of the entrenched legislation relating to Fijians, Rotumans and the Rabi Island community or any other legislation the attorney-general certifies as affecting Fijian land or customary rights. To exercise its functions impartially, the BLV should be independent not only from government but also from any political party. It should have its own secretariat and relative financial autonomy as well as electing its own chairperson. The Indo-Fijian community also wanted a body similar to the BLV for itself. The Commission recognised the need for such a body but felt that this was a matter for the Indo-Fijian community to take up in the first instance. It could be conferred statutory or constitutional status if it proved its utility as a representative body of Indo-Fijian opinion.

The Commission recommended the retention of the Office of the President, largely with the same powers as the holder of the office of governor-general in the Westminster tradition. This meant that executive power would rest with the Cabinet, and the president would be bound to act on the advice of ministers. The ceremonial role of the presidency would be important, with the holder of the office expected to symbolise the unity of the nation, command the loyalty and respect of all the communities and be seen to be impartial in the discharge of duties. There would be clearly spelt out matters on which the president could act in his or her 'own deliberate judgement', but within the bounds of the conventions of the parliamentary system of government. Most submissions agreed that the president should continue to be an indigenous Fijian, an important symbolic recognition of Fijians as the indigenous people of the land, but they also suggested that this be balanced by the constitutional provision that there should be a vice-president who should be a non-Fijian. The president (and the vice-president, who would be the president's running mate as in the American system) would be elected without debate by the Electoral College comprising both Houses of Parliament from a list of three to five names submitted to it by the BLV. There would be a President's Council of 10–15 distinguished citizens of all ethnic communities and walks of life to give the president their well-informed, nonpartisan views on issues of national importance, without in any way imposing constraints on the actions of the Cabinet.

The Commission recommended the retention of the bicameral Westminster system, which has been in existence in Fiji for nearly 30 years, but suggested significant changes in both the composition of the two Houses as well as the method of election. Both the Houses should be elected. The Upper House, to be renamed Bose e Cake, should be comprised of 35 members, two each from the 14 Fijian provinces, one from Rotuma and six appointed by the president on the advice of the Electoral Commission to represent communities and groups unrepresented in parliament (religious and cultural groups, women, youth). Members of all communities would have a very strong sense of territorial identity through both birth and residence as well as shared or complementary interests. Time and again, the Commission was told by members of all communities belonging to a particular area that 'here, we all get on well together'. In the rural areas, most people were able to speak both Fijian and Hindi; indeed, in several places, some Indo-Fijians indicated to the Commission their desire to make their submissions in the Fijian dialect of the area. For these reasons, the Commission recommended that members representing the provinces in the Bose e Cake be elected by voters from all communities resident in the province, thus helping to strengthen the sense of common identification with the province and their economic and, sometimes, social interdependence. Provincial concerns would be articulated from provincial rather than narrow racial perspectives. In terms of its powers and functions, the Bose e Cake would be similar to a house of review in the Westminster tradition.

The arrangements for electing members of the House of Representatives attracted the greatest amount of attention nationally and internationally— understandably so—as it would not only be the main legislative organ of the country but also because the party alignment of its members would determine which party would form the government and which party leader would become prime minister. The Commission approached the delicate issue of the election and composition of the House with certain objectives in mind: they should encourage the emergence of multiethnic governments; comply with international standards of equal suffrage; be based on a more open system of representation, and provide a gradual but decisive means of moving away from the present constitutional arrangements. Applying these criteria made it clear that the Fijian system of communal representation was anachronistic and generally contrary to international practice. A study of the voting systems of 150 of the world's 186 sovereign states by the International Parliamentary Union in 1993 showed that in only 25 states some members were elected or appointed to the legislature to represent particular groups, but in each case, the number of special seats was very small in comparison to the size of the legislature. In Fiji, all the seats were elected on a communal roll.

Many submissions supported the present arrangements, and many Fijians wanted to see them even more heavily weighted in favour of the indigenous communities. Equally, there were many submissions, from individuals and groups of all communities, which wanted at least some seats to be filled by candidates elected by voters on a nonracial basis. Many advocated returning to the cross-voting seats under the 1970 Constitution, but that arrangement was fraught and only marginally successful in bringing about more conciliatory and less communally based politics. The community found it hard to accept that members elected mainly by the votes of other communities really represented the community to which the seat belonged. Consistent with its view that the people of Fiji should make a gradual but decisive break from the present arrangements, the Commission recommended a 70-seat Lower House, to be called the Bose Lawa, made up of 45 seats elected from open constituencies (with no constitutional restriction of race for voters or candidates) and 25 from reserved seats allocated as follows: 12 Fijians (including Pacific Islanders), 10 Indo-Fijians, two General Voters and one Rotumans. Communal representation is not in itself inconsistent with international standards, especially if it operates within the framework of individual choice and the principle of equal suffrage, but the Commission saw the reserved seats as a transitional measure to be discarded over the next decade or so. Hence any deviation from the principle of equality could be accommodated within the 'margin of appreciation' that international law allows to states in applying international human rights standards. The allocation of reserved seats was broadly based on population figures, while taking account of historical and other factors that had affected the present and past allocations of communal seats. The point was that the allocation should be seen to be fair and acceptable.

The 25 reserved seats represent approximately 36 per cent of the total number of seats in the Bose Lawa and the open seats 64 per cent; the minimum necessary to allow them to act as a spur to the development of multiethnic politics. As a further incentive to the emergence of multiethnic government, the Commission recommended that 45 open seats should be elected from 15 three-member constituencies. Boundaries of these constituencies were to be drawn in such a way as to ensure that, as far as possible, and while taking into account the traditional criteria such as geographical features, existing administrative and recognised traditional areas, means of communication and mobility of population, the constituencies should be heterogeneous. That is, they should be composed of members of different communities, the object being to force political parties to appeal for votes for their candidates from communities other than the one in which they were based. The chances of a candidate or candidates of a community-based party succeeding would depend on the extent of support from other communities. The level of heterogeneity would naturally vary, given the nature of population distribution in Fiji—some places were predominantly Fijian and some predominantly Indo-Fijian—but the principle of multiethnicity should be borne in mind in designing constituency boundaries. The Commission took as the measure of heterogeneity the inclusion within the constituency of a mixed population ranging from a more or less equal balance between Fijians and Indo-Fijians, to a proportion as high as 85–95 per cent of one community and 10–15 per cent of the other. The average distribution was 60 per cent of one community and 40 per cent of the other. The evidence before the Commission suggested that it was entirely possible to draw boundaries in Fiji in a way that achieved reasonable heterogeneity.

Along with open seats and heterogeneous constituencies, the electoral system could also play an important role in promoting multiethnic cooperation. Students of politics have long realised the crucial role electoral systems play in shaping the behaviour of political parties, the strategies they employ to win elections and the incentives they provide in rewarding one outcome and punishing another. Fiji, like most ex-British colonies, inherited the British voting system at independence. That is the plurality system known as first-past-the-post (FPP) under which the winning candidate is the one who gets the greatest number of votes. A logical system when the choice is between only two candidates, the FPP is widely considered unfair and iniquitous where there are more than two candidates. It also denies voters the possible range of preferences they may have among them. Because of the disadvantages of plurality systems, various modifications have been proposed over the years to ensure that a winning candidate gets an absolute majority of the votes cast, that is, more than 50 per cent, and several of these were mentioned to the Commission for its consideration.

Acknowledging the critical role the electoral system plays in determining political outcomes, the Commission identified and ranked a number of criteria against which to evaluate the various available options. These, in their order of importance, included the encouragement of multiethnic government; recognition of the role of political parties; incentives for moderation and cooperation across ethnic lines; effective representation of constituents; effective voter participation; effective representation of minority and special interest groups; fairness between political parties; effective government; effective opposition; proven workability; and legitimacy. All electoral systems meet some of these criteria, and some more than others. The Single Transferable Vote (STV), which was recommended by the Street Commission in 1975, for example, mitigates against the winner-take-all outcome of FPP, and achieves a better proportionality of seats to votes than does FPP. But, by requiring an extremely low threshold to get elected—in a three-member constituency, a successful candidate would need no more than 25 per cent to get elected—and by privileging the representation of community interests, it fails to meet the commission's most important electoral criteria—the promotion of multiethnic governments. The List System Proportional Representation allocates seats to parties in proportion to the number of votes cast for the party, and while it has considerable merit, its one weakness is that by treating the whole country or major regions of a country as a single constituency, it fails to provide the important links between the voter and his or her member. It also provokes fears of small parties exercising disproportionate influence in the governance of the country.

In the Commission's view, the Alternative Vote (AV), also known as the Preferential Vote, best met all the criteria it identified as being relevant. The AV is based on the same principle as second ballots, but avoids the need for a second election at a later date. It is in effect a refinement of the FPP system in that it requires voters to rank candidates in order of preference. To be elected, a candidate must have a majority of the votes cast, that is, 50 per cent plus one. If no candidate reaches the threshold when first preferences are counted, then second and third preferences are counted and allocated. The process of elimination continues until one of the candidates has obtained the required quota. The AV provides an incentive for vote pooling by requiring the winning candidate to obtain more than 50 per cent of the votes. In heterogeneous constituencies, this threshold increases the need for the winning candidate to have multiethnic support. The system allows parties to trade preferences. Again, only moderate parties with conciliatory policies will agree to trade preferences, and be able to persuade their supporters to honour the agreement. The system therefore encourages the emergence of such parties. Constituents are effectively represented, at least in so far as candidates represent territorial constituencies and citizens are given considerable opportunity to affect the outcome of the poll by expressing preferences among individual candidates. As a majoritarian, not a proportional system, AV is likely to encourage the emergence of a strong party or preelection government. The Commission recommended that the AV system be used in multimember constituencies, but there is nothing stopping its use in single-member constituencies. I should add parenthetically that in the 1999 General Elections, the spirit of the AV system, in which like-minded parties would trade preferences and put those whose policies they found repugnant last, was breached by the FLP. With winning at any cost as their main goal, they gave first and second references to parties such as the Christian Democrats with whose policies they completely disagreed, thus putting their former coalition partner NFP, now their rival, last. They won a pyrrhic victory in the elections.

As mentioned, the Commission recommended the retention of the Westminster system for Fiji. The people were familiar with its workings and conventions. Nonetheless, its adversarial nature, pitting an 'Indian' opposition against a 'Fijian' government, elicited comment in the submissions. The Commission noted that in Fiji very often an opposition criticism of a government proposal, no matter how valid or rational, was portrayed as an Indian criticism of Fijian performance. People asked the Commission to suggest ways of minimising the harmful effects of this aspect of the Westminster system and to allow the House to use the talents of all its members to good advantage in a collaborative way. Fortunately, Commonwealth countries, including New Zealand, have devised such ways by setting up sector committees that permit all members of the Lower House, except ministers or assistant ministers, and whether belonging to the government or the opposition, to take part in national decision-making. Sector committees are structured in such a way that all departments and other government agencies come within the supervision of some committee. The Commission recommended that in addition to the existing standing committees (such as the Standing Select Committee on Sugar and the Public Accounts Committee), there should be five standing select committees—each dealing with one of the following sectors: economic services, social services, natural resources, foreign relations and administrative services. These committees would systematically scrutinise all areas of government activity, and consider Bills referred to them by parliament. Their overall membership should reflect the balance of the parties in the House, with the chairperson and the deputy chairperson to come from opposite sides of the House.

All these various ways—from the Compact, through the method of electing parliament from open heterogeneous constituencies using the AV system to the establishment of sector select committees—are designed to achieve an open, representative, inclusive and multiethnic government that protects the interests and addresses the concerns of all communities and groups within the overarching framework of a democratic system. That was the only way all the people of Fiji could aspire to realise for themselves and their children a prosperous and united future.

Issues of governance and accountability

While questions surrounding the election of parliament understandably occupy the centre stage in any constitutional review, there are other areas of considerable importance that impinge on the daily lives of the people that need attention. These include, among others, provisions relating to the acquisition and deprivation of citizenship, fundamental freedoms and rights, the independence and functioning of the judiciary, the enforcement of accountability in the performance of the public sector, and access to state services on a nondiscriminatory basis. Often in these areas, the Commission was required not so much to formulate new proposals as to modernise or revise the existing ones in the light of new international conventions and practices that have been adopted over the last decade or so.

To illustrate, the 1990 Constitution already had a Bill of Rights, called Fundamental Rights and Freedoms, adapted with few changes from the one in the 1970 Constitution. But the independence Bill of Rights was in a form developed by the Foreign and Commonwealth Office and included, with only slight variations, in the constitutions of most former

British colonies. It naturally reflected British caution about including individual rights in a judicially enforceable constitution. Individual rights and freedoms were seen as already enshrined in common law. The emphasis was not on affirming their existence but on protecting them from unjustified interference by the state. The Commission recommended that in keeping with modern trends, the constitution should affirm rights and freedoms in positive terms, that these should be judicially enforceable, binding the legislative, executive and judicial branches of government at all levels, and that they should not conflict with the international human rights standards but rather give effect to them where appropriate. It recommended the creation of a three-member Human Rights Commission to educate the public about the nature and purpose of the Bill of Rights, make recommendations to government about matters affecting compliance with human rights and exercise any other functions conferred to it by Act. The Commission adopted a similar approach to the issue of citizenship. Fiji's existing citizenship laws reflected the thinking of an earlier generation and were in some important respects not only archaic but also in breach of modern conventions. The independence constitution and its 1990 counterpart allowed noncitizen women the automatic right to acquire Fiji citizenship upon marriage to a Fiji male citizen, but did not accord the same privilege to noncitizen husbands. Whatever the reason for that discrimination in the past, it is no longer acceptable. Nor did the earlier constitutions make specific reference to the rights of children. Most women's groups who made submissions were adamant that discrimination against women and children had to go, and the Commission agreed.

In the Westminster system, a vital corollary of the power of politically appointed ministers to direct government policy is the expectation that the administration of that policy will be carried out economically, efficiently and effectively by politically neutral and impartial state services. Although the objectives of economy, efficiency and effectiveness in state services have a long history in Fiji, they have never been expressly required in the constitution. Because these objectives are so fundamental to the functioning of all state services, the Commission felt that they should be reflected in a constitutional provision. A related issue, to be considered alongside the ones mentioned above, was the 'fair treatment' of each community in the number and distribution of entry appointment. The 1970 Constitution directed the Public Service Commission to 'ensure that, so far as possible, each community in Fiji receives fair treatment in the number and distribution of offices to which candidates of that community are appointed on entry'. The 1990 Constitution obliged the government to ensure each level of each department comprised not less than 50 per cent Fijians and Rotumans, and not less than 40 per cent members of other communities. But this quota has not been observed, nor, to be fair, is it possible to achieve at *every level* within *every department.* Indo-Fijians complained of a significant reduction in their numbers in the state services, particularly at senior levels. They expressed concern at falling Indo-Fijian representation in the police force and their almost total absence from the armed forces. Whatever the reason—occupational preferences, emigration—the Indo-Fijian complaint was well founded. The Commission concluded that while efficiency, economy and effectiveness should be the principal objectives in managing state services, some more appropriate account must be taken of the overall representation of different ethnic groups at all levels in all the various state services.

To that end, the Commission proposed a new general provision in the constitution along the following lines. In recruiting and promoting members of all state services belonging to the executive branch of government, including the public service, the Fiji Police Force and the Republic of Fiji Military Forces, and in the management of those services, the factors to be taken into account include the need to ensure that government policies can be carried out effectively; the need to achieve efficiency and economy in all the state's services; the need to make appointments and promotions on the basis of merit; the need to provide men and women and members of all ethnic groups with adequate opportunities for training and advancement; and the need for the composition of each service, at all levels, broadly to reflect the ethnic composition of the population, taking into account, however, occupational preferences.

Closely related to the provision of state services is the issue of ethnic and social justice. Section 21 of the 1990 Constitution explicitly enjoins the government to introduce affirmative action programs for the Fijian and Rotuman communities that were perceived to be lagging behind other communities in terms of their achievement in some sectors, notably education, commerce and participation in higher levels of the public service. These policies have had an effect. In 1985, Fijians made up 46.4 per cent of established civil servants, Indo-Fijians 48 per cent and General Voters and expatriates 5.6 per cent. The corresponding figures in October 1995 were Fijians 57.3 per cent, Indo-Fijians 38.6 per cent, and General Voters and expatriates 4.11 per cent. In 1995, of the 31 permanent secretaries, 22 were Fijians, six were Indo-Fijians and three General Voters. Indo-Fijians accepted the principle of affirmative action to redress imbalances in the public sector but wanted them to include disadvantaged members of all communities, not just the indigenous people. Their submission drew attention to the growing poverty among sections of their people, and their growing numbers in squatter settlements fringing towns and cities. The Commission agreed that the government needed to continue implementing policies and programs to reduce inequalities between different ethnic communities, but since there are areas in which other communities are also disadvantaged, social inequalities should not be neglected. It recommended a social justice and affirmative action program for Rotumans and Fijians and other ethnic communities, and for men as well as women, to provide effective equality of access to education and training, land and housing, participation in commerce and all aspects of service of the state at all levels, and other opportunities, amenities and services essential to an adequate standard of living. Furthermore, the program should be authorised by an Act (following parliamentary debate), which specifies the goals of the program and the identity of the persons or groups it is intended to benefit, the means by which those goals would be achieved, performance measures for achieving the efficacy of the program, and the criteria for the selection of the members of the group entitled to participate in the program. In short, to be effective, affirmative action policies should be transparent, properly debated and carefully monitored.

Generally, for state services and institutions to be effective and impartial, they need to be subject to strict rules of accountability. The Commission received many submissions proposing constitutional provisions to prevent official corruption and to achieve higher ethical standards from those holding important offices of state. They were not accusations against ministers or state servants; they were about public confidence in Fiji's system of government and the integrity of its leaders. Existing statutes, regulations and orders contained ethical standards and rules that applied to state servants, members and officers of statutory bodies, but the Commission was convinced of the need to go further. It therefore proposed an 'integrity code' for the president, the vice-president, ministers and all members of parliament, and all constitutional office holders, which would require them not to place themselves in positions in which they have or could have a conflict of interest; compromise the fair exercise of their public or official functions and duties; use their offices for private gain; allow their integrity to be called into question; endanger or diminish respect for, or confidence in, the integrity of government; demean their office or position. These principles should be enshrined in an Act of Parliament, which would make detailed and specific provisions to deal with the various kinds of conflicts of interest in the context of Fiji's particular circumstances. The Commission also recommended the strengthening of the Office of Ombudsman to investigate allegations of corruption or mismanagement of public office. In an important and innovative recommendation, the Commission recommended the creation of a new Constitutional Offices Commission, which would recommend to the president the appointment of the ombudsman and the auditor-general and directly appoint the solicitor-general, the director of public prosecutions, the secretary-general to parliament, the supervisor of elections and the commissioner of police.

A future constitution, the Commission felt, should be generally acceptable to all citizens; guarantee the rights of individuals and groups and promote the rule of law and the separation of powers; recognise the unique history and character of Fiji; encourage every community to regard the major concerns of other communities as national concerns; recognise the equal rights of all citizens; and protect the vital interests and concerns of the indigenous Fijian and Rotuman communities, and all the other groups, within the inclusive and overarching framework of democracy. The consequences of any other approach are too sad to contemplate.

15
George Speight's putsch improbable[1]

Chiefs and thieves and other people besides.

— George Speight[2]

George Speight's improbable intervention in Fijian politics through an attempted putsch opened fresh wounds in Fiji's body politic. Ostensibly carried out to depose a government headed by an Indo-Fijian prime minister, it had other causes with deep roots in traditional Fijian politics and hidden political agendas. The country was held to ransom for 57 days and the siege finally ended with the intervention of the Fijian military. Speight was not the principal instigator of the crisis but the figurehead for other individuals and interests. Speculation about the actual masterminds of the putsch continues while Speight languishes in jail unlikely ever to taste freedom again. The putsch now seems like a bad dream but, at the time, it unleashed much fear and confusion that threatened to damage the country irreparably.

Around 10 am on 19 May 2000, seven armed gunmen, led by George Speight, stormed the Fiji Parliament taking Prime Minister Mahendra Chaudhry and his ill-fated government hostage. May 19 marked the government's first anniversary in office. The seizure of parliament followed a series of protest

---

1   Originally appeared as 'Chiefs and thieves and other people besides: The making of George Speight's coup', in *The Journal of Pacific History* 36(3) (2000): 281–93.
2   Words spoken by George Speight in a radio interview when asked who was being his attempted putsch.

marches by a variety of Fijian nationalist groups variously opposed to the People's Coalition Government and committed to its overthrow. Still, the hostage crisis seemed improbable. Speight, a part-Fijian failed businessman due to be arraigned in court on a bankruptcy charge, was a little-known player on the local scene. And, unlike 1987, no recognisable group or institution claimed immediate responsibility for the deed, including the recently revived Taukei Movement headed by the perennial dissident Mohammed Apisai Tora. In 1987, the Royal Fiji Military Forces, under then Lt Col Sitiveni Rabuka, took responsibility for the coup and he was, in turn, held accountable for it. The May 1987 Coup, it can be argued, was carried out on behalf of, and blessed by, the Fijian establishment.[3] In 2000, Speight and his men carried out a coup against the Fijian establishment. If 1987 was about shoring up indigenous Fijian power and preserving Fijian political unity, this later coup has had the effect of fostering Fijian political fragmentation on an unprecedented scale. Speight's dramatic intervention has altered the fundamental dynamics of Fiji—and indigenous Fijian—politics.

The hostage crisis left in its wake an impressive list of casualties. The 1997 Constitution, approved unanimously by a parliament dominated by indigenous Fijians, blessed by the Great Council of Chiefs (GCC) and warmly welcomed by the international community, had been abrogated.[4] Ratu Sir Kamisese Mara, President of the Republic of Fiji, a central figure in contemporary Fijian public life and a paramount chief in his own right, was asked by the army to step aside, while the Republic of Fiji Military Forces assumed executive control of the country. Ratu Sir Kamisese Mara was sent to his home province of Lau, after the presentation of a customary forgiveness-seeking *tabua* (whale's tooth), under the cover of darkness, guarded by soldiers, on a patrol boat heading towards the Lau Sea. It was a sad end to a distinguished though not uncontroversial career, marking the final eclipse of the long reign in Fiji politics of powerful paramount chiefs tutored for national leadership by the colonial government in the years following World War II.[5] The democratically elected government headed

---

3   The literature on the 1987 coups is vast, but for two accessible interpretative essays, see Stewart Firth, 'The contemporary history of Fiji: A review article', *The Journal of Pacific History* 24 (1989): 242–46, doi.org/10.1080/00223348908572619; and Barrie Macdonald, 'The literature of the Fiji Coups', *The Contemporary Pacific* 2(1) (1990): 198–207.
4   The making of the 1997 Constitution is covered in Brij V. Lal, *Another Way: The Politics of Constitutional Review in Post-Coup Fiji* (Canberra: Asia Pacific Press, 1998).
5   The four great chiefs of the latter half of the twentieth century groomed for leadership by the British were Ratu George Cakobau, Ratu Edward Cakobau, Ratu Penaia Ganilau and Ratu Kamisese Mara.

by Mahendra Chaudhry was unceremoniously and unconstitutionally dismissed, the prime minister endured the longest period of captivity in modern Pacific Islands history, his freedom—or unfreedom—curiously overshadowed by other struggles for power taking place in Fijian society.

The crisis also tainted the reputation of once sacred institutions of Fijian society in previously unthinkable ways. Among them was the military, with a proud record of service in the jungles of the Solomons in World War II, in Malaya against the Chinese communist insurgents in the 1950s, and as peacekeepers in the Middle East in the 1970s. In the face of the coup, the army stood divided and confused, unable or, worse still, unwilling to uphold the constitution or protect the security of the state. The security forces were shown to be infected by the viruses of provincialism and regionalism.[6] Had martial law not been declared when it was, the army might well have fragmented into factions, each defending their own *vanua* (land, province) and chiefs. The GCC, seeking in recent years to enlarge its role and status as the guardian of national, not only indigenous Fijian, interests, failed the test of *national* leadership. They sympathised with Speight's ambition for the Fijian people, but then backed President Ratu Sir Kamisese Mara to lead the country out of the crisis. They vacillated while the country awaited their wise counsel, which never came. Their deliberations got embroiled in traditional confederacy and provincial politics, their proceedings dominated by younger, more assertive chiefs wanting their own place in the Fijian sun, leading to further division and fragmentation. As army spokesman Col Filipe Tarakinikini put it, the chiefs 'are riddled with personal agendas'[7] and incapable of impartial, decisive action.

However it is looked at, the hostage crisis-cum-coup was a disaster for Fiji. The economy, which was just beginning to recover from the downturn of the 1990s, was once again poised on the precipice.[8] The crisis cost the government millions in lost revenue, and the government's Microfinance Unit, in a paper prepared for the military, predicted a trade deficit of $400 million. With trade bans in force, the gross domestic product (GDP) was predicted to suffer a reversal of 13 per cent, exports decline

---

6   See Army spokesman Col Filipe Tarakinikini's statement on *fijilive*, 14 June 2000: 'The army is just a reflection of society, so what is happening there [fragmentation] is happening in the army as well; you can't deny that.'
7   Interview with Col Filipe Tarakinikini, in the *Australian*, 14 June 2000. See also the *Daily Post*, 9 June 2000 for a similar view from Marika Qarikau, manager of the Native Land Trust Board.
8   For more discussion, see *Pacnews*, 9 June 2000; and the *Sunday Sun*, 4 June 2000.

by 22 per cent and imports by 20 per cent. Already, hundreds of workers, often those at the bottom of the economic ladder and, therefore, the most vulnerable had been laid off, especially in the handicraft, garment and tourism industries—and more would follow. Even if no trade bans were imposed, unemployment was expected to rise by 6 per cent, and some 7,000 workers were likely to be retrenched. Local investors would flee the country in the wake of riots that ravaged the commercial district of Suva, and their foreign counterparts would be equally hesitant investors.

Some costs, though, were less easily measured. Within the indigenous Fijian society, for instance, old assumptions about the traditional structure of power were questioned in novel and potentially significant ways. It is almost a truism now to say that this crisis, as it unfolded, became more about intra-Fijian rivalries than about race. Even Speight himself admitted that 'the race issue between Fijians and Indians is just one piece of the jigsaw puzzle that has many pieces'.[9] In this respect, it is unlike the crisis of 1987, which was seen largely as an ethnic conflict between Fijians and Indo-Fijians. Then, there was much sympathy for the Fijian 'cause' across the Pacific, whereas after the May 2000 Coup there was condemnation.[10] Some argued that Mr Speight represented the interests of the Kubuna Confederacy against the long ascendancy of the traditional hierarchies of the Koro Sea. Fijian political analyst Jone Dakuvula's claim to this effect brought upon the local television station broadcasting his remarks the wrath of the Fijian mob allied to Speight.[11] Then, as the crisis dragged on, the western chiefs, long aggrieved about their absence from the national centre of power, threatened to secede from the state of Fiji, failing which they promised to settle for a much-cherished and long-demanded fourth confederacy, the Yasayasa Vaka Ra.[12] The west, they said, drove the engine of the national economy. Sugar, pine, gold and tourism were produced from its soil, and they wanted representation in national councils proportionate to their contribution to the national economy. The east–west divide existed, but it was not a sharp, clear line.

---

9   Interview with George Speight in the *Fiji Sun,* 10 June 2000.
10   There are some notable exceptions, though, including Cook Islands' Geoffrey Henry (*Cook Island News,* 27 May 2000) and New Zealand Māori lawyer Anthony Sinclair (*fijilive,* 3 June 2000), who declared, without irony: 'We believe that revolution is a legitimate part of the democratic process'.
11   Information such as this is a part of the public record, broadcast by *fijilive,* hence it is not necessary to provide documentation. A copy of the transcript is at the Centre for the Contemporary Pacific, The Australian National University.
12   This is discussed at length in Simione Durutalo, 'Internal colonialism and unequal regional development: The case of Western Viti Levu', MA thesis (Suva: University of the South Pacific, 1985).

Instead, it was extensively crisscrossed by marriage and kinship ties that blurred distinctions of old.[13] The threatened secession of Western Viti Levu was followed by a declaration of partial autonomy by the province of Cakaudrove, which proposed to set up a separate Tovata State, but the declaration lacked conviction or authority.[14] What it did indicate, however, was the willingness of the Fijian people to consider options unthinkable in the twentieth century.

Race relations were severely strained just when things looked to be on the mend following the successful review of the constitution: the scars of the present crisis—reflected in the images of looting and violence on the streets of Suva; the fleeing of terrorised Indo-Fijians from parts of the Rewa Delta to safe havens in Western Viti Levu; the destruction of schools and desecration of places of worship; the unruly Fijian mob roaming neighbourhoods around the parliamentary complex. Those scars would take a generation to heal. There are also deeper questions here than I can deal with; questions about culture and history and identity. The Fijian, the *taukei,* the indigenous owner of the land, who has lived side by side with his/her Indo-Fijian neighbour, still regards him/her as a *vulagi,* a foreigner, welcome to stay and enjoy the hospitality of the host but knowing full well whose house it is.[15] Even the chiefs of Western Fiji, who have—or should have—a better understanding of Indo-Fijian fears and aspirations and who oppose Speight, want Fiji to be declared a Christian state so that Hindus, Muslims and Christians can all solve their problems in the proper Christian way. They blame Australia and Britain for introducing Indians to Fiji, without appreciating the purpose for which they were brought. Indo-Fijians, now fourth or fifth generation, are hurt to be still regarded as outsiders in the land of their birth, threatened with the denial of equal citizenship and equal protection of the law. Sometimes, those who applaud the indigenous Fijians for maintaining their culture and tradition ask the Indo-Fijians to subjugate theirs in the cause of assimilation. Salman Rushdie, writing about the Fiji crisis makes a telling point. 'Migrant people do not remain visitors forever,' he has written. 'In the end, their new land owns them as their old land did, and they have a right to own it in their turn.'[16]

---

13   *Fiji Times,* 10 June 2000.
14   *Sunday Times,* 11 June 2000.
15   For more discussion of this concept, see Asesela Ravuvu, *The Facade of Democracy: Fijian Struggles for Political Control, 1830–1987* (Suva: Reader Publishing House, 1991).
16   Salman Rushdie, in an article in the *New York Times,* 8 June 2000.

The 2000 crisis was far worse than its 1987 counterpart in terms of violence and damage to property. In 1987, the army was held responsible for the maintenance of law and order. To its credit, it did manage to contain the mobs. In 2000 the mobs had a free hand, directed, if they were directed at all, by invisible hands in the parliamentary complex, armed and energised by Speight's racial rhetoric, terrorising the rural Indian countryside for food and fun, as they had done in the hinterland of Nausori. The main targets were Indo-Fijians in outlying rural areas; their cattle slaughtered and root crops stolen. After 1987, some 70,000–80,000 people migrated from Fiji, most of them Indo-Fijians. They now live in Australia, New Zealand, Canada and the United States. It is often said that there is hardly an Indo-Fijian family in Fiji that does not have at least one member outside. Kinship has become a multinational or transnational corporation, sustaining those left behind on money remitted from abroad. After 2000, many more would leave—the doctors, the computer technicians, mechanics, the accountants. In short, virtually anyone who was accepted outside would go, draining the country of skills it could ill-afford to lose. 'I would rather be a dog in America than an Indian in Fiji,' said a man whose house had been demolished and his possessions taken by Fijian mobs. He was not alone in holding that thought.

The public face, though not perhaps the principal instigator, of the crisis was Speight. He was a businessman with a career littered with failures in Australia and Fiji (and possibly elsewhere as well)—I called him a failed businessman and that description stuck. The 45-year-old Speight was wandering on the fringes of the local commercial circles on the eve of the coup.[17] He had been sacked by Agriculture Minister Poseci Bune as Chairman of the Fiji Pine Commission and the Hardwood Corporation. Shortly before he stormed parliament, he had been negotiating on behalf of the American company Trans Resources Management to win a tender for harvesting the country's massive mahogany forests valued at over $300 million.[18] The government chose instead the Commonwealth Development Corporation, with a proven record in the exploitation of natural resources. Speight was declared an undischarged bankrupt and was about to face court proceedings when he launched his assault on parliament. Clearly, Speight had his own private grievances, which he carefully hid behind a fiercely nationalist rhetoric. Like Sitiveni Rabuka in 1987, Speight portrayed himself as a faithful servant of the Fijian cause,

---

17 For a profile of Speight, see the *Fiji Times*, 23 May 2000.
18 See the *Sunday Times*, 11 June 2000.

an anointed saviour of the Fijian 'race'. Speight, however, is no Rabuka, as even his most ardent supporters admit. Indeed, an important reason why the international community—as seen in Australian Foreign Minister Alexander Downer's reaction—had been so severe in its condemnation of Fiji was because of Speight as the face of indigenous Fijian nationalism. A part-European of Fijian descent, Speight, with head shaved, was articulate, engaging, bantering with the international media; still, he was an unconvincing Fijian hero.

But it would be a grave mistake to see Speight as acting all on his own. If he were, the crisis would have had a limited and inconsequential life. Behind him, in the shadows, were individuals and groups, writing his speeches, devising position papers, building up the mass support base and orchestrating the crowds—people who had little to lose but everything to gain from the overthrow of the Chaudhry Government. Among them were politicians defeated at the last elections or otherwise excluded from power, who were seeking redress and probably revenge. Apisai Tora and Berenado Vunibobo come readily to mind. The Fijian Opposition Leader, Ratu Inoke Kubuabola, was there as well, and so, strangely enough, were factional leaders of Fijian political parties in coalition with Chaudhry's Labour Party. The Fijian Association Party's Adi Kuini Vuikaba Speed was deputy prime minister, but Ratu Cokanauto Tua'akitau was with Speight's group. Apisai Tora, the founder of the spectacularly misnamed Party of National Unity, wanted Chaudhry's head, but three members of his party were in the Cabinet.

Speight was also supported by people like himself, young businessmen on the make, who rode the gravy train of the 1990s, benefited from opportunistic access to power, secured large, unsecured loans from the National Bank of Fiji, but then found their prospects for continued prosperity dimming upon the election of a new government. Prominent local businessmen-cum-politicians in the previous Soqosoqo ni Vakavulewa ni Taukei (SVT) government supported the destabilisation campaign.[19] For them, the Chaudhry Government had to go before it managed to entrench itself. In this group of the ambitious and, upwardly mobile, I would also include what one might call the 'Children of 1987'. This group included those who benefited from the post-1987 racially based affirmative action programs—sanctioned by the 1990 Constitution—in

---

19 In the papers, Fiji businessmen Kanti Punja and Jim Ah Koy, among others, have been identified, but both have denied involvement.

the award of scholarships, promotions in the civil service and training opportunities. They were the children of privilege, sons and daughters of the well connected. Many of them had come of age in the mid-1990s, at the height of the SVT Government's reign.[20] This new generation of fast-tracked Fijian middle class had a narrow, limited experience of multiculturalism, and little taste or patience for it. They contrasted starkly with an earlier postindependence generation of the 1970s, which grew up working in a multicultural environment, dedicated to professionalism and the principles of good governance, under governments publicly committed to a unifying vision.[21] The 'Children of 1987' did not understand or approve of the spirit of the 1997 Constitution.

While the indigenous Fijian middle class, or at least sections of it, provided the brains for Speight's agenda, the Fijian social underclass provided the brawn. The bedraggled unemployed, unskilled Fijian youth armed with sticks, knives, bamboo spears, stones and some with guns, who looted, burned and trashed Suva, terrorised the countryside and acted as a human shield for Speight and his men, had little understanding of the larger, hidden personal agendas and complex forces at work. They were in some sense the human casualties of globalisation and economic rationalism and, more immediately, the victims of the structural reform policies pursued by the Rabuka Government in the 1990s. They could not understand why they remained behind, mired in poverty and destitution, while others had moved on. Without hope and without a future, they fell easy prey to Speight's mesmeric rhetoric and easy solutions: get rid of the Indians, revert to tradition, put Fijians in political control, and all would be well. Speight gave them a purpose, an explanation, a mission and a brief spot in the Fijian sun. They in turn responded enthusiastically to his clarion call of racial solidarity.

How did this crisis come to a head? To understand this, it is necessary to look at events over the previous 12 months, beginning with the 1999 General Elections, which took place under the revised 1997 Constitution.[22] Chaudhry's Labour Party won 37 of the 71 seats in

---

20 Good representatives of this cohort would include Speight's legal advisor Ratu Raquita Vakalalabure, Ro Filipe Tuisawau, Saimone Kaitani, and Ratu Timoci Silatolu, among others.
21 Among them would be names such as Josefata Kamikamica, Mosese Qionabaravi, and Savenaca Siwatibau, among others.
22 I have discussed the elections in *A Time to Change: The Fiji General Elections of 1999* (Canberra: Department of Political and Social Change, Research School of Pacific and Asian Studies, Regime Change and Regime Maintenance in Asia and the Pacific, Paper no. 23, The Australian National University, 1999).

its own right. Together with his other Coalition partners, the Party of National Unity (PANU), Fijian Association Party (FAP) and Veitokani ni Levenivanua Vakaristo (VLV), the People's Coalition won altogether 58 seats. The unexpectedly large victory was due to two factors: an effective campaign against the outrages and excesses of the Rabuka Government, of which there were many, and a sharp, carefully calibrated focus on the bread-and-butter issues affecting ordinary working and middle-class people. Labour promised to roll back the unemployment-causing structural reform programs of the Rabuka Government, introduce minimum wages, lower interests on housing rates, provide social security for the elderly, and resolve the long-festering issue of expiring agricultural leases. These uncosted but electorally appealing policies were effective on the hustings, but they came to haunt the party when it came to power. The opposition National Federation Party (NFP), Fiji's oldest political party long the champion of Indo-Fijian interests, which did not win a single seat, opportunistically kept the government's heel close to the fire. To counteract criticism and keep its support base from fragmenting, the Chaudhry Government embarked on a hectic program of legislative reform, setting up commissions (Education and Human Rights), instituting inquiries (into corruption) and staffing statutory organisations with competent staff (Housing Authority).

The appearance of movement and change was impressive, but it also embroiled the government in a hugely counterproductive tussle with the media. Small things were magnified in an atmosphere already rife with suspicion and distrust about the government's motives.[23] Why did Chaudhary appoint his own son, not a civil servant, as his personal assistant on the public pay roll? Here was a man who, as long-term secretary of the Fiji Public Service Association, had been scathing of nepotism and corruption in previous governments, but, once in power, had begun to ignore his own wise counsel about transparent governance and public accountability. There was nothing illegal in the appointment: a prime minister can, of course, appoint anybody he or she wants. But the perception of the government favouring its own was created stuck, despite repeated denial. Fijian civil servants, appointed under the Rabuka Government when ethnicity and loyalty were privileged over merit and seniority, complained about being unconsulted or marginalised in important decision-making. Faced with intensifying opposition, the

---

23 See, for example, Eugene Bingham, 'Fiji tragedy woven from many strands', *New Zealand Herald*, 3–4 June 2000.

governed battened down the hatches. To every question and all opposition, it chanted—to its opponents with constant, arrogant regularity—the mantra of having a mandate to do what it had promised in its election manifesto. The government did have a mandate, but its mandate was one among many mandates in Fiji. The parliament is not the sole source of all power in Fiji: the Native Land Trust Board has its mandate to look after native land; the GCC has its own mandate under the constitution; the army its own. It was the failure, or perhaps the unwillingness, to balance the complex equation of competing mandates that compounded the government's problems. Chaudhry's own forceful personality, forged in the long years spent in the trade union movement, also played its part in galvanising the opposition. Chaudhry is a highly intelligent and resourceful person, tenacious and uncompromising (confrontational to his opponents), a born fighter who was a painful thorn in the side of the Rabuka Government for years. He was feared by Fijians, but not trusted. He was a strong and decisive leader of a generally weak Cabinet, and his opponents, rightly or wrongly, saw his unmistakable imprint on every policy decision of the government.

Another problem facing the government was the fractious nature of the People's Coalition itself. As mentioned, the Coalition was a loose structure made up of four parties: Labour, PANU, FAP and VLV. Some of these parties espoused philosophies directly contradictory to Labour's. The VLV, for example, wanted to make Fiji a Christian state and to have an urgent review of the 1997 Constitution to address the concerns of the Fijian people, both of which Labour repudiated.[24] Indeed, soon after the elections, Bune of the VLV threatened to lead a coalition of Fijian parties against Chaudhry—until he was inducted into cabinet reportedly at Ratu Sir Kamisese Mara's behest. PANU had its own agenda for western Fiji, as did the FAP for south-eastern Viti Levu, its stronghold. But what they all had in common was their adamant opposition to Sitiveni Rabuka, both for who he was and what he had done. He was not forgiven for the coups of 1987 by one side, and punished by another for breaching the traditional protocol regarding the appropriate place for commoners in the traditional Fijian social hierarchy dominated by chiefs. Opposition to a common enemy, then, rather than commitment to a common agenda, brought the disparate groups together. And when that enemy (Rabuka) was defeated, the difficulties of internal cohesion came to the fore, almost

---

24 Lal, *A Time to Change*, pp. 14–15.

immediately after the election. Chaudhry rightly took steps to become prime minister; his party had an outright majority in parliament. The FAP cried foul, accusing Labour of reneging on a deal that a Fijian, one of its own members, would be chosen prime minister by the Coalition. Chaudhry was helped unobtrusively and opportunistically by Ratu Mara who urged the Fijian parties to rally behind Chaudhry, but Chaudhry's ascension also split the Coalition. A faction of the FAP disregarded Adi Kuini's leadership and informally aligned itself with other Fijian opposition parties, eventually going so far as to back Speight. Tora became a fierce rabble-rousing critic of the government, expressing his disgruntlement by leading a revived Taukei Movement. So the Chaudhry Government was buffeted by its opponents and hobbled by internal divisions, speaking on crucial issues with discordant voices.

The issue that united the Fijian opponents of the new government was land. Land has always been a sensitive issue in Fijian politics.[25] The question has always been the use rather than the ownership of land. At the time, 83 per cent of all land in Fiji—3,714,990 acres—was held in inalienable rights by indigenous Fijians, 8.2 per cent was freehold, state freehold was 3.6 per cent and crown or state land around 5 per cent.[26] Much of the country's agricultural activity—in particular sugar cultivation—was carried out on land leased from Fijian landowners. The country's 22,000 cane growers, the overwhelming majority of whom are Indo-Fijians, leased native land under the *Agricultural Landlord and Tenant Act*. This Act, which came into existence in 1969, provided for 30-year leases whose renewal was negotiated between the tenants and landlords upon the expiry of the leases. These leases were beginning to expire and some, but by no means all, landlords wanted their land back either to cultivate the land themselves, rezone it for commercial or residential purposes, or use the threat of nonrenewal to extract more rent. They were led by the head of the Native Land Trust Board, Marika Qarikau. He was, by all accounts, a hardline, abrasive nationalist who used every means available—from addressing the provincial councils to using the network of the Methodist Church—to rally Fijian landowners behind him and against the government. The

---

25 See Brij V. Lal, *Broken Waves: A History of the Fiji Islands in the Twentieth Century* (Honolulu: University of Hawaii Press, 1992), pp. 224–27.
26 For more discussion, see Josefata Kamikamica, 'Fijian native land: Issues and challenges', in *Research Papers of the Fiji Constitution Review Commission,* Vol. 1: *Fiji in Transition,* ed. Brij V. Lal, Paul Reeves and Tomasi Vakatora (Suva: Suva: School of Social and Economic Development, University of the South Pacific, 1997), pp. 259–90.

Native Lands Trust Board (NLTB) was Qarikau's power base and he, too, claimed a mandate to protect native Fijian land. Three weeks after the coup, Qarikau circulated a 20-page 'Deed of Sovereignty', which demanded, among other things, the return of all state and freehold land to native ownership.

Chaudhary did not contest the landowners' desire to reclaim their land. Nor, on other hand, could he—or any government for that matter—ignore the human plight of the tenants; unskilled, uneducated, poor, evicted from land their families had cultivated for four or five generations. The government offered the displaced tenants $28,000 to start afresh in some other occupation, and about $8,000 to landlords who repossessed their former leasees' land to become cultivators themselves. Meanwhile, it also resuscitated the idea of a Land Use Commission (LUC), mentioned in his party's manifesto, but with a history going back nearly 40 years, to work with landowners to identify idle land and to put it to productive use, including, if possible, the resettlement of displaced tenants. With the NLTB on a warpath, the government went directly to the Fijian landlords. Early in 2000, it sent a delegation of Fijian landowning chiefs to Malaysia to familiarise themselves with the work of a similar commission there. The chiefs returned impressed, but by then Qarikau had already orchestrated a move among the provincial councils to reject the concept outright. Poseci Bune, Minister of Agriculture, recalled the malicious misinformation spread among the people. In one province, he was told, the LUC was a ploy by Chaudhry to bring Indians to Fiji. Apparently Air India had expressed an interest in opening an office in Suva. But this was a false front. The main aim behind setting up an Air India office was to bring Indians from India to settle on land identified for development by the LUC. Faced with this malicious propaganda, the government then did what it should have done earlier: it took the proposal to the GCC, which approved it in principle but asked the government and the NLTB to develop it further cooperatively. It was a hard-fought victory for the government.

Just when the government seemed to be gaining an upper hand, as shown in generally approving polls, Tora's Taukei Movement resurfaced in Western Viti Levu, fuelling and galvanising extreme Fijian opinion against the government. The Cakaudrove Provincial Council passed a vote of no confidence in the government, and others followed. Ratu Tevita Bolobolo, Tui Navitilevu, formed a landowners' council, Matabose ni Taukei ni Vanua, attacking the government and threatening nonrenewal of leases. Ratu Tevita had lost to Labour in the 1999 General Election. Taniela Tabu, former Taukei Movement stalwart and a trade unionist with a chequered career, formed the Viti National Union of Taukei Workers and attacked the Chaudhary Government for Indianising the public service. The charge was baseless—the upper echelons of the public service, and nearly 90 per cent of the permanent heads of government departments, were dominated by indigenous Fijians—but effective among many Fijians already distrusting of the government. The Christian Democrats labelled the government—in which it was partner—anti-Fijian over its hesitation to renew the work visa of expatriate Fiji TV head Kenneth Clark, because the Fijian provinces held the majority of shares in the company headed by Clark.

The protest movement, small and disorganised at first, gained momentum and focus as May drew near. The government continued to chant the mantra of mandate and refused to acknowledge that trouble was in the offing, dismissing the marches as the work of a few miscreants and misguided people. Police Commissioner Isekia Savua's public warning to the government to raise its political antenna to catch the grumbling on the ground was ignored, and Savua was chastised for daring, as a public servant, to advise the government on questions of policy. Convinced that its policies were beginning to bear fruit and were popular with the electorate, which had learned the hard lessons of 1987, the government adopted a business-as-usual approach as tension mounted around the countryside. Ignoring all the warning signals, the government sent the Commander of the Military Forces, Commodore Frank Bainimarama, to Norway on an official trip. The police commissioner was on holiday, and the president was in Lau celebrating his 80th birthday. When the parliament met on 19 May 2000, marking the first anniversary in government, no special security precautions were taken, no special police forces were deployed around the parliamentary complex. While the police force focused on the 5,000 protest marchers heading from downtown towards Government House to present a petition to the president, Speight and his men stormed parliament around 10 am. The assault was led by 20-year SAS veteran Major Ilisoni Ligairi and members of the Counter Revolutionary Warfare Unit he had set up at the request of the 1987 coup leader, Sitiveni Rabuka.

At 1:20 pm on 19 May, Speight spoke to a stunned nation:

> I want to make clear that these actions set forth the foundations for change once and for all in the affairs of the country of Fiji as desired by the indigenous people of Fiji in their desire to achieve self-determination and control of their future destiny in all matters pertaining to their livelihood and the affairs of the

Republic of the Fiji Islands. We executed our actions this morning, there were a small number of us but as I speak and as I sit to make these announcements to you I speak on behalf of every individual member of the indigenous Fijian community. Through these actions I am stressing ownership, am asserting control and I am asserting executive power over Fiji. We have revoked the Constitution and have set that aside. We have revoked the powers of the President of the Republic of Fiji. The executive control of this country of ours currently resides in my hands.[27]

Soon afterwards, he announced the make-up of his administration. All, without exception, were known nationalists, including many 'Children of 1987'. Ratu Timoci Silatolu (FAP, Rewa) was appointed Prime Minister, Ratu Naiqama Lalabalavu (SVT, Cakaudrove) was made Minister of Fijian Affairs, and Ratu Rakuita Vakalalabure (SVT, Cakaudrove) Minister of Home Affairs. Three others had no portfolio: Simione Kaitani (SVT, Lomaiviti), Isireli Leweniqila (SVT, Tailevu) and Levani Tonitonivanua (Nationalist, Serua). Speight himself had his eye on the presidency, but that was not officially announced. A fuller list, announced two days later, demoted Silatolu to Deputy Prime Minister, but added the more recognisable names of Berenado Vunibobo, Ratu Tu'uakitau Cokanauto and Ratu Inoke Kubuabola. Whether the individuals had agreed to serve in the Speight administration is not known, but there is no doubt that they sang the same nationalist tune as the architects of the coup.

Speight had hoped for a speedy acceptance of the proposals. A meeting of the GCC would be convened, the proposed list of names presented and endorsed, the hostages released, and the country run by a *taukei* civilian administration. But events took a different, perhaps unexpected turn. Late in the afternoon of 19 May, as a rampaging mob burned and looted Suva, President Ratu Sir Kamisese Mara declared a State of Emergency. 'There are democratically recognised avenues for airing grievances in accordance with the laws and the Constitution,' Mara told an anxious national television audience. 'I urge all those who lay claim to be leaders of this dissenting group to follow lawful means in raising their dissent.' His words fell on deaf ears. The president lacked the resources to enforce his will. The army was still in the barracks, divided in its loyalty, and the police force was confused, under-resourced and effectively leaderless and, in the view of some, silently colluding with Speight's supporters.

---

27   This quote is from an extract on the internet site, *fijilive*.

After being persuaded that Rabuka did not have foreknowledge of the coup, Ratu Mara engaged him as his mediator with Speight. Rabuka was an occasional golfing partner of Speight and the hijackers had reportedly trained on his estate in Vanua Levu. Some of them were from his own province of Cakaudrove. As events unfolded, Rabuka's lack of involvement in the May uprising became clearer; he was almost a bystander in the unfolding drama. Of all the major players on the Fijian side, he was the only one who stood uncompromisingly by the constitution. Mara suggested, through Rabuka, that Chaudhry should voluntarily step down in favour of an indigenous Fijian. Deputy Prime Minister Tupeni Baba was the name Mara had in mind as the Fijian replacement. Speight welcomed the suggestion, but asked Mara to step down as well. When Rabuka conveyed that demand to Mara, the president agreed to oblige, but only if that was the decision of the GCC. Speight also wanted to meet the president but Mara refused unless the hostages were released first. As Mara recalled:

> He was going to tell me that if I don't follow what he says, he will start executing hostages one-by-one and when I said what does he really want I was told that he wants me to step down and allow his group to run the country. I said I will not be able to oblige.[28]

But while refusing dialogue under duress, Mara gave Speight and his supporters in a nationally televised address his 'personal guarantee as executive head of the Republic that the issues you have raised will be dealt with fully and your position as the indigenous community will be protected and enhanced'.[29] This was an important victory for Speight; the president had conceded the need to amend the constitution to 'protect and enhance' Fijian interests. But Mara wanted to achieve that goal through constitutional means. More was still to come. Mara also hinted that Chaudhry might not be reinstated as prime minister.

> I can't say that I will put back the government that caused all these problems … What I intend to do is to talk to them (government members) and say 'you've seen what has happened' so what's your possible solution.[30]

---

28 Radio Fiji transcript, n.d.
29 *fijilive*; a hardcopy of the release is in my possession.
30 See the *Fiji Sun,* 23 May 2000.

Whatever Mara's motives, his public doubts about Chaudhry's return to government served to strengthen the hostage takers' resolve that their goal was now within reach. Wittingly or unwittingly, the president had shown his hand. He was—or was seen to be—essentially on the same side as the broad spectrum of Fijian nationalists; they differed only in their methods.

While Mara sought to assert his executive authority, Speight began to build a human fortress around him by busing in hundreds of supporters from south-eastern Fiji, men, women and youth. They sang and danced and cooked food on the grounds of the parliamentary complex; food (cattle and root crops) stolen from Indo-Fijian farmers in the Rewa Delta were brought to Suva in police vans. The carnival atmosphere kept up the spirit of the gradually increasing crowd, but their presence in large numbers also ruled out a hostage-rescue operation. When the police force sought to control the crowd at the parliamentary complex, they were chased away by armed youths. The crowd gave the impression of a growing groundswell of support for Speight, especially to the international community; Speight himself emerged as an articulate and effective manipulator of the media.

With the deadlock between Mara and Speight, all attention shifted to the meeting of the GCC convened on 23 June. What transpired in that deeply emotional meeting is not known, although it was later reported that the Tailevu chiefs presented a *tabua* to the GCC to seek forgiveness for Speight's insulting remarks about them; Speight wanted the chiefs to justify their decisions, saying they had lost touch with the grassroots whom he now claimed to represent. After two days of talk, Ratu Mara was able to sway them to his side. He assured the chiefs that he would return the country to normalcy but would address the concerns that Speight and his supporters had raised with him, though by what authority he did not say. The chiefs agreed. They expressed full confidence in the president and the vice-president, endorsed Mara as the leader of his proposed interim administration but asked that his proposed council of advisors include some of Speight's group. The chiefs asked for the hostages to be released immediately and stolen arms surrendered to the army. They also recommended a pardon for all those involved in the hostage takeover. And finally, they urged Mara to:

give full and urgent attention to the grievances as raised by the various Taukei groups during the recent protest marches with special attention given to ensuring that the position of President and Prime Minister together with other senior government positions (unspecified) shall always be held by indigenous Fijians and Rotumans.[31]

Speight had got most of what he wanted, but he was still unsatisfied. He wanted not pardon but complete amnesty. And there was always the hint that he expected to hold office in a new government. Mara agreed to consider it, but only after a proper trial. Speight was not satisfied with an amendment to the 1997 Constitution as the chiefs had recommended; he wanted it abrogated. And, knowing Mara's political cunning, he wanted the president to step down as well, fearing that he might appoint people who were personally loyal to him to his council of advisors.

Mara proceeded with his plan to assume executive control. With Chaudhry incarcerated, the Labour Coalition had elected Ratu Tevita Momoedonu as its interim leader and spokesman. Mara swore him in as acting prime minister 'solely to enable me to take three steps'.[32] The first was to advise the president under Section 99 (1) of the constitution to dismiss all Cabinet ministers, paving the way for him to appoint a caretaker prime minister and other advisors. The second was to advise the president to prorogue parliament, buying him time to 'set things in order'. And the third was for the acting prime minister to tender his resignation, handing over the executive authority to the president to run the country in the absence of a prime minister, a Cabinet and a sitting parliament. Ostensibly to save the constitution, the president sacrificed the prime minister and his duly elected government. Chaudhary, Mara said, 'is not only absent from duty but also he's unable to perform the functions of that office'. He invoked Section 106 of the Constitution:

> The President may appoint a minister to act in office of another minister, including the Prime Minister, during any period or during all period when the minister is absent from duty, or is for any other reason unable to perform the functions of the office.

---

31   Press release, George Speight Group (GST), Suva, n.d. A copy in my possession.
32   Mara's Press conference of 27 May is reported on *fijilive*, 29 May 2000.

Mara's action was constitutionally flawed.[33] The constitution, following the normal Westminster convention, severely limits the power of the president to act without ministerial advice. The constitution does prescribe the circumstances in which the president may act in his or her own deliberate judgement, but as far as the dismissal of a prime minister is concerned, Section 109 (1) of the Constitution explicitly states:

> The President may not dismiss a Prime Minister unless the Government fails to get or loses the confidence of the House of Representatives and the Prime Minister does not resign or get a dissolution of Parliament.

Chaudhry was a hostage; he had not vacated his office, and he still enjoyed the confidence of the House. He was still prime minister. But Mara had assumed otherwise 'as a matter of political reality', to use the fateful words of Chief Justice Sir Timoci Tuivaga who advised him.[34] In hindsight, it seems that Chaudhry's fate was sealed the moment Speight and his gunmen entered parliament. Sadly for him, neither the president nor the chief justice was prepared to stand by the constitution or the democratically elected government. The chief justice's behaviour invited the wrath of the Fiji Law Society, which accused him of acting hastily in assuming that the 1997 Constitution was in fact abrogated. His authorship of a decree—Administration of Justice Decree—that abolished the highest court in the land, the Supreme Court, made Timoci Tuivaga a judge of the Court of Appeal of which he was previously not a member and where he would now take precedence when they sat, were severely criticised by the society. 'The eyes of the profession, the nation and the world are upon the judiciary,' Peter Knight, the President of the Law Society, reminded the chief justice.

> It cannot be seen to openly condone criminal activity. It should as a matter of record [note] that it will continue to occupy and function in its judicial role in the same uncompromising manner as it had done prior to 19 May.[35]

The chief justice remained unmoved.

---

[33] For the advice of three eminent Australian constitutional lawyers (George Williams, The Australian National University, Cheryl Saunders, the University of Melbourne and Dennis O'Brien, who drafted the constitution), see *fijilive,* 26 May 2000.
[34] Chief Justice Sir Timoci Tuivaga to Peter Knight, President, Fiji Law Society, 14 June 2000. The letter has not been published.
[35] Fiji Law Society to Chief Justice, 9 June 2000. A copy of the unpublished letter is in my possession.

Ratu Mara's action was equally controversial, having decided on his own, shortly after the takeover of the parliament, that the 1997 Constitution needed to be amended to accommodate the views of the Fijian nationalists. Yet, two years before, the president had praised the constitution as a fair and just charter for the nation. Perhaps Mara sensed that the Fijian opinion generally supported Speight's revolution and, as in the past, he wanted to be where his people were. As Mara had said so often, a chief without his or her people's support is not a chief. In 1982, Mara had behaved in a similar manner, refraining from condemning a motion passed by the GCC demanding Fijian control of parliament.[36] Be that as it may, Mara's action dismayed many, among them the United Nation's Special Envoy Sergio Vieira de Mello and Commonwealth Secretary-General Don McKinnon, who were reportedly 'stunned by Mara's endorsement of Speight's nationalist views'.[37] And Minister of Education Pratap Chand reminded Mara that the effect of his intervention would be to 'legitimise the overthrow of a constitutional and democratically elected Government by terrorists'.[38] But Mara was determined to pursue a course of action from which he would not be deterred while the world speculated on his motives.

On the streets, where Speight's men marauded freely, these constitutional manoeuvres mattered little. On 28 May, they trashed the local TV station, which ran a program drawing attention to the partial, provincial base of Speight's support. In the melee that followed, a police officer was shot dead and shots were fired at the president's residence. It was a night of nightmares. The following day, Speight's supporters planned to march from the parliamentary complex to the president's house demanding his resignation. The march was called off at the last minute on the advice of the army, which feared a violent conflict with rumours of Lauans in Suva gathering in support of their paramount chief. Despite his public pronouncements, the president's authority was weak. The police were outgunned. And the army was divided and unwilling to back the president fully. Part of the reason, according to Commodore Bainimarama, was that emotionally many soldiers were in Speight's camp but did not support the methods he had used. And many were not prepared to risk their lives for

---

36 Discussed at length in Lal, *Broken Waves*, p. 250.
37 This is from a Suva-based Australian Federal Police report, forwarded to me by Sarah Creighton of the *Sydney Morning Herald*, on 25 May 2000. See also Gwynne Dyer, 'Democracy vs ethnicity in Fiji', *Japanese Times*, 1 June 2000.
38 Letter written on 27 May 2000, and published on *fijilive*, 29 May 2000.

a man, Ratu Mara, whom they distrusted for a variety of reasons. They regarded Mara as the man who stood between them and the goal of Fijian paramountcy; an autocratic leader who, in Speight's words, was 'imposing his will and controlling the Great Council of Chiefs through fear as he has done to the Cabinet, the civil service, the *vanua* over the years, despite the will of the people'.[39] Speight, like many others in Fiji, suspected that the president harboured dynastic ambitions, that he supported the Chaudhry Government because his own family members were in it. Mara, for them, was part of the problem, not part of the solution. He had to go. When that decision had been reached, four senior army people, led by Commodore Bainimarama as well as Ratu Mara's son-in-law and former army Commander Ratu Epeli Ganilau, approached Mara late at night on 29 May in the traditional Fijian way, presented him with a *tabua* in forgiveness and asked him to step aside.

Commodore Frank Bainimarama assumed executive leadership and imposed martial law at 6 pm on 29 May. An immediate curfew was imposed. A new military council was appointed to run the country for up to three years, during which a new constitution would be drawn up and elections held under it. The army named Ratu Epeli Nailatikau as its choice for prime minister. But it was a poor choice that added fuel to the fire. Speight and his supporters saw in his nomination the continuation of the Mara dynasty and the Fijian establishment, although Nailatikau himself came from a high-ranking chiefly family of Bau. Speight's group had at first welcomed the military's intervention. 'I suppose for the maintenance of law and order and for the safety of the lives of the public that was the only option for the military to take,' Ratu Timoci Silatolu told Radio Fiji on 30 May. 'And we are keen to negotiate with them, someone who understand the hostage situation—an institution that is totally Fijian.'

The optimism of a breakthrough, however, was short lived. Speight's group wanted the new interim administration to be dominated by their followers. The opposition forced the army to delay naming its military council and withdraw Nailatikau's name. As the third week of the crisis drew to a close, the impasse continued. The military attempted to consolidate its support among the provinces by promising that their demands for political paramountcy would be accommodated in the new constitution. Speight himself might not have found a place in the civilian administration, but

---

39   See *fijilive*, 23 May 2000.

his supporters and most certainly his vision would. Speight had achieved much. The most significant of which was the acceptance, among a broad cross-section of indigenous Fijian opinion, that the spirit that underlay the 1997 Constitution, of the spirit of multiethnic cooperation, of equal rights under the law, of equal citizenship and of enlarging the common space through representative democracy. And this in a country divided along racial lines for so long.

Fiji had travelled that route before under the 1990 Constitution, ending up in a cul-de-sac. Speight and his supporters wanted self-determination for indigenous Fijians,[40] but they had to have autonomy—and veto power in parliament—over matters of internal governance since independence. They had to have intact their traditional chiefly institutions, including the GCC, and other separate administrative systems set up for their governance under the Fijian Affairs Act. Invoking international conventions on the rights of indigenous people was similarly unhelpful.[41] The clear inference from them was that at the national level, the political and other rights of indigenous peoples were on exactly the same footing as those of other members of society. These conventions saw the special rights of indigenous peoples as distinct communities supplementing the fundamental human rights and freedoms they already enjoyed and shared with other citizens. Nothing in these conventions gave an indigenous person superior or paramount rights in taking part in the government of the country. Fijian nationalists wanted Fijian paramountcy recognised as a right, but there was no basis on which the paramountcy of Fijian interests or Fijian political paramountcy could be elevated into a right. Concepts of 'self-determination' and 'sovereignty' gave no support to that proposition. They wanted numerical dominance in a democratically elected parliament. But no constitution could guarantee political paramountcy of a particular ethnic group in a multiethnic state, unless, of course, it abandoned all claim to being democratic. The 1990 Constitution was weighted in favour of Fijians, but even it could not regulate the distribution of political power among Fijian parties. For that reason it could not ensure that Fijians would always be able to form an exclusively or predominantly

---

40   See his interview in the *Fiji Sun,* 10 June 2000.
41   The two conventions most commonly cited are the *ILO Convention No 169 on Indigenous and Tribal Peoples* and the draft *Declaration on the Rights of Indigenous Peoples*. For a discussion of their application to Fiji, see Report of the Fiji Constitution Review Commission (Sir Paul Reeves, Tomasi Rayalu Vakatora and Brij V. Lal), *The Fiji Islands: Towards a United Future* Parliamentary Paper, 34 (1996), pp. 40–48.

Fijian government. The Rabuka Government fell in 1993 because of political fragmentation among indigenous Fijians, and it fell for a similar reason in 1999. As provincial and regional sentiments were reinforced, the fragmentation would continue.

Speight lamented the 'gradual erosion of things that are important to Fijians in their own country'.[42] This erosion had been taking place for many decades. In the early 1980s, Fijian geographer and administrator Isireli Lasaqa had sounded similar warnings about the gradual disintegration of rural Fijian society:

> The weakening of Fijian social organisation and kinship ties as a means of providing some measure of social welfare to its members … the encouragement of an enquiring mind and a willingness to question tradition, rather than a passive acceptance of fate.

The social system, Lasaqa said:

> Has become increasingly coarse so that more and more elderly Fijians pass through … and cannot derive much support and benefit from the system. In other words the kinship links have weakened and the younger generation, with their increased commercial sense, greater individual needs, and commitment to their nuclear family, are either unwilling or unable to look after their aged relatives.[43]

Two decades later, the problems remain. The solution? Army spokesman Tarakinikini said:

> The social problems facing our country cannot be solved by putting in place a constitution that guarantees 100 per cent the rights and paramountcy of indigenous Fijians in this country. It will not safeguard, it will not ensure, that indigenous Fijians will succeed. The only way we indigenous Fijians will succeed is to make sure that we make sacrifices today for the sake of our prosperity tomorrow.[44]

---

42 See the *Fiji Sun,* 10 June 2000.
43 Quoted in Brij V. Lal, 'Rhetoric and reality: The dilemmas of contemporary Fijian politics', in *Culture and Democracy in the South Pacific,* ed. Aiono, Fanaafi Le Tagaloa and Ron Crocombe (Suva: Institute of Pacific Studies of the University of the South Pacific, 1992), pp. 97–116, at p. 111.
44 Talk on *Radio FM 96,* 4 June 2000.

Forces of social and economic change cannot be arrested by the barrel of the gun. The ultimate, inescapable truth is that Fiji is an island, but an island in the physical sense, alone.

CoupNews.com

'Some shots were fired, a man is at the gate
The rebels are led by one George Speight.'

So silently proclaims the internet,
Mother of all opinion and the elusive fact.

We all read the same text, the same lead pieces,
Policy documents and inflammatory speeches

About Christian State and Political Paramountcy,
'Fiji for Fijians': the mantra of Fijian orthodoxy

'These Indians smell different,' says Mr Speight,
Fanning the embers of racial hate.

'As coolies you came, so you must remain,
Political equality? Dream on in vain.'

Mobs dance to the music of racist beats,
Supporters celebrate on shuttered streets.

The army dithers, the police is nowhere in sight,
The looting continues well into the night.

'Family shopping,' a grinning man remarks,
Amidst damaged goods and broken glass.

Trapped, terrorised among the charred remains,
Shop owners contemplate their losses and gains.

Years of toil gone up in smoke,
Just like that, incinerating all hope.

Shops will be rebuilt, shelves restocked,
But what about lives whose dreams are dashed?

This act of madness in the month of May,
Will haunt us yet for many a long day.

Brij V. Lal

16

Laisenia Qarase's missed chance[1]

In George Speight's shadow

George Speight's putsch, even though it failed, cast a long pall on Fiji politics. Laisenia Qarase, a merchant banker and long-term head of the Fiji Development Bank, was appointed leader of the interim administration tasked with paving the way for the next elections. But instead of learning the lessons of the past, he pandered to the whims and demands of the Fijian nationalist fringe, promulgating race-based policies and seeking constitutional entrenchment of Fijian political control. He won the 2001 General Election narrowly over the Fiji Labour Party, but abused the spirit of power sharing embedded in the 1997 Constitution. The Qarase Government fell into the quagmire of ethnic politics, and Qarase lost the chance to forge a new path for Fiji, in the process ruining his political career.

Fiji went to the polls two years after the last election in May 1999, which had elected a Fiji Labour Party–led People's Coalition to government.[2] That government was overthrown in a civilian coup led by George Speight on 19 May 2000.[3] Fifteen months of confusion, anxiety and violence later, the worst in modern Fijian history, Fiji went to the polls again, under the 1997 multiracial constitution, which Speight and the Fiji military forces had declared abrogated, but which had been upheld by the

---

1 Originally appeared in *The Journal of Pacific History* 37(1) (2002): 87–101.
2 For the 1999 general elections, see Brij V. Lal (ed.), *Fiji before the Storm: Elections and the Politics of Development* (Canberra: Asia Pacific Press, 2000).
3 My analysis of the coup is in 'George Speight's putsch improbable', Chapter 15 of this book.

High Court and subsequently by the Fiji Court of Appeal. The holding of the elections was a significant achievement in the circumstances, but instead of resolving the country's political difficulties and healing wounds, it ended up polarising ethnic relations even further, embroiling major political parties in an acrimonious debate about power sharing mandated by the constitution. Fiji's agony continues.

A record 26 mostly indigenous Fijian political parties registered to contest the elections, but only 18 fielded candidates for the 71-seat Lower House. Interim Prime Minister Laisenia Qarase's Soqosoqo ni Duavata Lewenivanua (SDL), launched on the eve of the elections, won 32 seats; deposed Prime Minister Mahendra Chaudhry's Fiji Labour Party 27; the coup-supporting Conservative Alliance Matanitu Vanua (CAMV), among whose successful candidates was Speight himself, 6 seats; the National Federation Party (NFP) one; the breakaway New Labour Unity Party (NLUP) formed by Tupeni Baba, Deputy Prime Minister in the People's Coalition Government, two; and independents two.[4] The smaller splinter parties failed to make an impact. What was surprising was the failure of the more established parties that had fared well in the past, including the Fijian Association Party (FAP), a senior partner in the People's Coalition Government, and the Soqosoqo ni Vakavulewa ni Taukei (SVT), the party in power for much of the 1990s.

Speight, still awaiting trial for treason, cast a long shadow over the campaign. Fijian political parties competed with each other to court his supporters, promising to fulfil his agenda of enshrining Fijian political paramountcy in perpetuity. Otherwise, there was little public enthusiasm for the election. The electorate was genuinely pessimistic and apprehensive.[5] On the Indo-Fijian side, there was a pervasive feeling of fear and anxiety, the memory of 19 May 2000 still fresh. 'Fijians will do whatever they want,' a voter told me. 'What's the point of voting?' The low voter turnout—78.6 per cent—and a surprisingly large number of informal votes, indicated indifference or protest. On the Fijian side, where the voter turnout was equally low, there was dismay and disillusionment

---

4   In terms of votes, Fiji Labour Party won 226,000 first preference votes, or 35 per cent of the valid votes cast, SDL 169,000 votes, NFP 66,000 votes, Conservative Alliance 64,000 votes and, New Labour 29,000 votes.
5   *Pacific Islands Report*, 15 August 2001.

at the large number of parties, with divergent and sometimes diametrically opposed agendas, despite the effort of the Methodist Church to forge a semblance of political unity.

Public confidence in the most important institutions of the state was at its lowest ebb, their reputation for professionalism, independence and integrity tainted or otherwise compromised. Among them was the police force. The *Daily Post* summed up the popular perception.

> The force remains under-paid, badly equipped, lacking in skills, demoralised, lacking in a leader with the moral authority to preach to his men and women, let alone the people of Fiji. The force under Mr [Isikia] Savua, has been linked with complicity in last year's political crisis. Many a police officer has said that the police did not act when they were needed during the riots in Suva city because they had not received the relevant instructions from the top.[6]

Isikia Savua was eventually cleared of illegality and complicity in the coup by a closed tribunal headed by the chief justice, but without abating public scepticism.[7] One observer called the inquiry 'a fraud' facilitated by the chief justice, a 'person who has come under attack from legal sources in Fiji and internationally for facilitating the abrogation of the constitution and for continuing to frustrate legal challenges to the abrogation of the constitution'.[8] Labour Party President Jokapeci Koroi accused Savua of having 'deliberately misled the government by giving assurances that there was nothing to worry about. Mr Savua must go'.[9] Savua continued as police commissioner, although with a tarnished reputation.

The army, too, had diminished in public esteem. It managed to restore law and order after the hostages were released after 56 days of incarceration, but not before it was shown to be infected with indiscipline, insubordination and provincialism. The army's Counter Revolutionary Warfare Unit, established by Sitiveni Rabuka after the 1987 coups, was instrumental in the execution of the coup. Several senior military figures professed public sympathy for Speight's agenda but disapproved of his method, though precisely what method they would have approved was not specified.

---

6   *Daily Post,* 31 August 2001.
7   *Fiji Sun,* 11 August 2001.
8   Private correspondence with a leading Fiji lawyer.
9   *Fiji Sun,* 13 August 2001. Poseci Bune, Agriculture Minister in the People's Coalition Government, said 'Savua was the leader of the coup that failed to turn up': *fijilive,* 24 August 2001.

In November 2000, a section of the army mutinied, killing five soldiers and injuring scores of others. The violence the army unleashed to quell the mutiny remains a source of great bitterness and tension in the Fijian community, uncomprehending of the possibility of a Fijian army spilling Fijian blood. President Josefa Iloilo granted immunity to the regular soldiers, while mutineers awaited trial.

Another institution that lost credibility for independence and integrity was the judiciary, with a local daily pleading with the judges to 'wake up, grow up and, importantly, stop bickering'.[10] The role Chief Justice Sir Timoci Tuivaga played or did not play—the advice he gave the president in resolving the crisis that later proved to be unconstitutional, his early acceptance that the constitution had been abrogated, his authorship of a decree abolishing the Supreme Court—became matters of intense public dispute, leading the Fiji Law Society to call for his immediate resignation. The chief justice rebuked judges who disagreed with his interpretation or otherwise showed independence and rewarded those who sided with him. His unexpectedly harsh attack on Justice Anthony Gates of the Lautoka High Court, who had upheld the constitution, was typical. Tuivaga accused Gates of not 'recognising and respecting the hierarchy of administrative power and authority with the judiciary of this country', and advised him to 'explore other work environment[s] where the rules of administrative propriety do not apply'.[11] Tuivaga defended himself. 'I have been Chief Justice for 20 years, in the driver's seat, and I know what is good for this country and what I did was good for the country.'[12] He had accepted the de facto government as 'a matter of political reality', and intervened to 'ensure that the maintenance of law and order and justice in this country was not to be frustrated by any ineffective administrative court machinery'.[13] The Fiji Court of Appeal, however, thought otherwise.

The social costs of the political crisis were visible. These included poverty, joblessness, prostitution, growth in the number of squatter settlements fringing major urban centres, people evicted from expiring leases living in makeshift camps in Valelawa in Vanua Levu and at the Girmit Centre in Lautoka, women from broken homes, single mothers, and the unemployed (because of the closure of garment factories established under lucrative tax

---

10 Editorial, *Fiji Times*, 29 August 2001.
11 *Fiji Times*, 28 March 2001.
12 *Daily Post*, 1 September 2001.
13 Chief Justice to President of Fiji Law Society, 14 June 2000. High Court file CJ/WF/9.

regimes in the 1980s). There had been a marked increase in the suicide rate, particularly among women since the crisis of 2000.[14] Many workers had suffered from pay cuts and reduced working hours.

The economy, which was beginning to show signs of growth after the 1999 elections, had suffered a severe downturn, with a projected 1 per cent growth rate. Foreign investment had dried up, while many local big businesses had moved their financial assets overseas. A few large ones continued to operate in Fiji as foreign companies. Investor confidence, severely shaken by the crisis and continuing uncertainty about Fiji's political stability, would take a long time to return. The economy would also suffer from the huge cloud over the sugar industry, which provided over 40 per cent of the country's export earnings and 15 per cent of the gross domestic product. The sugar industry employed nearly 150,000 people.[15] The anticipated loss of preferential access to the European Union was a problem.

But the more immediate issue was the fate of farmers whose leases under the *Agricultural Landlord and Tenant Act* (ALTA) had begun to expire. The Act, which came into force in 1976, granted 30-year leases to tenants, and established a semblance of stability in the agricultural—especially the sugar—sector. The government and the Native Land Trust Board wanted the ALTA replaced by the *Native Land Trust Act* (NLTA) because they saw ALTA as favouring tenants by making the termination of expiring leases more difficult and remuneration for landlords less attractive. The essential difference between the two was that NLTA provided for rolling 5–30-year leases, not a minimum 30-year leases, giving landowners the opportunity to reclaim their land earlier if they so wished.[16] Under ALTA, the rent was assessed at a fixed 6 per cent of the unimproved capital value, while under NLTA, it was assessed at the current market value and a percentage of production, to the benefit of landowners. Other provisions of the ALTA generally favoured the landowners. The land problem was inevitably politicised, both by the leaders of the farming community as well as by those representing the landlords, to the detriment of the economy. Many

---

14   *Pacnews,* 31 August 2001.
15   See Padma Lal, 'Land, lomé and the Fiji sugar industry', in *Fiji before the Storm: Elections and the Politics of Development,* ed. Brij V. Lal (Canberra: Asia Pacific Press, 2000; Canberra: ANU E Press, 2012), pp. 111–34, doi.org/10.22459/FBS.12.2012.
16   See Padma Lal, Hazel Lim-Applegate and Mahendra Reddy, 'Land tenure dilemma in Fiji: Can Fijian landowners and Indo-Fijian tenants have their cake and eat it too?', *Pacific Economic Bulletin* 16(2) (2001): 106–19.

leases not renewed were lying idle, slowly turning to bush, while the displaced tenants, dismayed to see their life's work ruined, sought shelter in refugee camps and alternative employment.

The fabric of national society was strained. On the surface things looked calm—people went about their business, intermingled in the workplace, on the sports field, around the *yaqona* bowl, more of it more visible in parts of Fiji not directly traumatised by the events of 19 May. But hidden behind the rhetoric of multiculturalism and reconciliation lay deep suspicions and raw prejudices—more widespread than in Fiji's recent past. People once of genuinely moderate views sought shelter in extremist ethnic camps. Many Indo-Fijians, although politically opposed to Chaudhry, supported him as 'their only hope' against the Fijian nationalists. Many Fijians similarly supported Qarase. Some saw the widening divide between the two ethnic groups as confirming the pattern of race relations in Fiji's history, but that would be a mistake. The two communities had cooperated in the past—for example, in the review of the 1990 Constitution. And there was genuine regret on all sides at the racial turn Fiji politics had taken.

In Fiji, race relations tend to get polarised at election times. The race card has long been a part of the zero-sum game politicians have played. A semblance of normalcy returns as political tempers cool. While relations are tense, it would be a mistake to draw a picture of two solidly united groups, at the edge, at each other's throat, ready to explode. For the truth is that both the communities are internally divided by class, regional origins and culture. Not all Fijians, for instance, want the 1997 multiracial constitution revoked, or Fiji to be turned into a Christian state. Some demand special affirmative action programs for Fijians, while others do not. Some wanted Speight and his co-conspirators pardoned while others insisted on a proper trial. The deeper cracks, the confederacy and dynastic politics that surfaced in the aftermath of the coup, are still there, papered over for the moment. Fijian leaders recognise that the political unity of all Fijians under a single banner is an evanescent dream. Fijians rallied behind Rabuka in the early 1990s only to fragment later. Large numbers supported Qarase in this election but signs of division are already beginning to emerge.

Strong support for Chaudhry among Indo-Fijians should be read in a similar light. They rallied behind him because of the spectre of violence and discrimination that threatens them at the hand of the Fijian nationalists. But deep divisions exist. In this election campaign more than in previous ones, there was open talk of the difference between Gujaratis and the descendants of the *girmitiyas,* and between North and South Indians. The NFP was portrayed as a party of the Gujaratis and the South Indians. Several community leaders spoke with dismay about the damage that reference to regional and cultural origins during the election campaign has done to social relations at the local village level. Whether, or how, the internal frictions and divisions manifest themselves in future political realignments will be watched with interest.

It is not surprising, in view of these developments, that turnout at the polls was low; a mark of fear, apathy, indifference and protest and, possibly, the absence of fear of noncollectable fines for not voting. Many Indo-Fijian voters also stayed away because of intimidation, fearing reprisal from Fijian landlords as well as nationalists if they voted for Labour. The percentage of invalid votes was a staggering 11.69 per cent compared to 8.69 per cent in 1999. The campaign itself lacked the verve and excitement normally associated with election campaigns in Fiji. There were a few large rallies in selected centres, but most of the campaigning was done in small pocket meetings. Television advertisement played a larger role this time than before, featuring party manifestos and policy positions. There was lengthy debate among leaders of all the major parties, generating more heat than light. Interestingly, all the major parties used the internet, several with their own websites, to publicise their manifestos and accomplishments. The internet was largely for overseas supporters and fundraisers as few outside the major urban centres in Fiji had access to computers. The calibre of candidates among Indo-Fijians was markedly inferior to the 1999 line-up, featuring a lacklustre list of retired school teachers and public servants and others looking for a second career. This was in marked contrast to the calibre of Fijian candidates, especially in the SDL, which featured accomplished, if politically inexperienced, professionals, most of whom had served in the interim administration. Fijians see a future in politics; Indo-Fijians do not, at least not with any expectation of taking a leading part in the nation's affairs.

The road to the August elections began with the hijacking of the Fijian Parliament on 19 May,[17] holding members of the People's Coalition Government hostage for 56 days. The takeover of parliament was accompanied by an intense period of confusion and violence, during which

---

17 See Chapter 17.

the major players struggled to impose their will. Speight and his wide circle of supporters, defiant and uncompromising, sought to have themselves installed as the new government, preferably with the endorsement of the Great Council of Chiefs (GCC). A number of appointments to an interim administration were in fact announced but then abruptly withdrawn or revised when negotiations failed. Besieged President Ratu Sir Kamisese Mara, sought, albeit unconstitutionally, to wrest control of the unfolding events, offering an olive branch to the rebels with the promise to review the constitution to take account of their concerns. He failed because the rebels saw him as part of the problem, an ageing, imperious leader unwilling to give up power, out of touch, seeking personal advantage for himself and harbouring dynastic ambition. Unable to stamp his customary authority, Mara vacated office under armed protection on 29 May, allowing the army to impose martial law and a curfew in the urban areas.

Following Mara's resignation, the army installed a military government headed by Commodore Voreqe (Frank) Bainimarama. He became Executive Head of Government, advised by a Military Court of Advisors. Their main aim was to secure the release of the hostages and the return of stolen weapons. After a long and frustrating series of meetings with the rebels, the military managed to negotiate the Muanikau Accord, which freed the hostages. The rebels were promised amnesty if they surrendered arms stolen from the military's armoury. But when the rebels reneged, making further impossible demands from their new holdout at Kalabu, the army, its reputation already bruised and battered by the hostage crisis, its inaction the subject of derisive comment about its much-vaunted professionalism, retaliated with a brutality that shocked the Fijian community. The army eventually subdued the rebels and established a semblance of law and order, but its brutal tactics left a legacy of bitterness among Fijians, planting the seed for a violent mutiny several months later.

On 3 July, the Interim Military Government announced a 19-member Cabinet to run the country till 2002, by when, it hoped, a new constitution would be in place and fresh elections held under it. The military saw the main task of the interim administration as rehabilitating the economy and drawing up the terms of reference for a new Constitution Review Commission. The Commission would 'consider particular constitutional issues of concern to indigenous Fijians',[18] including strengthening the role

---

18 *Pacnews,* 3 July 2001.

of the GCC 'in the national affairs of the State'; a race-based affirmative action for Rotumans and Fijians, and recognition of traditional and customary laws of the indigenous community. The Commission began hearings in mid-August 2000, but met immediate public opposition, both for the manner in which it was appointed, by an unconstitutional interim administration without consultation with the major political parties, and for the composition of its membership. The four Indo-Fijians on it were all Christians—a tiny percentage of the Indo-Fijian community—none enjoying the confidence of the community they purported to represent. The chair of the Commission was Asesela Ravuvu, a long-time advocate of Fijian paramountcy and one of the vocal hardline Fijian nationalists.[19] His presence and utterances compromised the Commission, with the Indo-Fijians boycotting the hearings en masse.

The Commission was suspended in January 2001 following a High Court ruling upholding the 1997 Constitution and declaring its appointing authority, the interim administration, illegal. A small four-member subgroup prepared a summary report that, for the most part, blamed the Indo-Fijians for the problems facing the Fijian people. They were *vulagi* (visitors) who should, but did not, accept their proper culturally sanctioned role to serve, or at least be subservient to, the *taukei* (the owners of the land). Indo-Fijians used 'democracy, equality, and human rights to discourage and outmanoeuvre Fijian political efforts and aspirations to regain that nationalism and the power which had been ceded in 1874', the report argued.[20] The Indo-Fijians, moreover, 'did not consider the Fijian people's demands for the paramountcy of their interests and the return of all government authority into Fijian hands'. The solution to Fiji's political problems? Fijians 'must rule it [Fiji] and feel secure that they shall not be dominated in their own house. This is the only solution to long term political stability, peace and prosperity'. The political leadership of the country should always remain in Fijian hands, the authors argued 'within a time frame to allow others to be eventually assimilated and accepted as Fijians'.[21]

---

19 For his nationalistic views, see Asesela Ravuvu, *The Facade of Democracy: Fijian Struggles for Political Control, 1830–1987* (Suva: Reader Publishing House, 1991).
20 A copy of this report, which has never been released to the public, is in the author's possession.
21 *Fijilive*, 17 September 2001; Constitution Commission/Panel Report, *Seeking Cooperation, Toleration and Understanding of our Diversity: A Model of the People's Constitution.*

Qarase promised to be guided by the spirit of the report, adding provocatively that since Fijians owned 83 per cent of the land, they should have proportionate dominance in parliament.[22] Whether the report would bear the desired fruit remained to be seen. A constitution that breached international human and civil rights conventions, as the Fijian proposal promised to do, would be rejected by the international community. The international response to the racially discriminatory 1990 Constitution was proof enough of that, and global commitment to the protection of human rights had strengthened in recent years. For their part, the Indo-Fijian community would reject any attempt to marginalise them, paving the way, yet again, for a long period of boycotts, sanctions and continued political instability.

On the economic front, the government promised a number of initiatives to revive a stagnant economy. It proposed to lower the corporate tax rate, introduce accelerated depreciation allowances, lower duty rates on construction materials and capital items, permit exporters access to world priced inputs, and introduce a duty suspension scheme for all regular exporters with a record of compliance.[23] Four months later, following the example of the post-1987 initiatives, the Qarase administration embarked on a 'look north' policy, seeking export markets and fresh investment input from East Asia.[24] Fiji backed Japan's effort to become a permanent member the United Nations Security Council, and supported China's membership of the World Trade Organization. China gave the Royal Military Forces US$1.8 million, and Japanese aid similarly increased. But many of the Asian tigers are a humbled group now and unlikely to invest in Fiji to any significant degree, especially in an atmosphere of political uncertainty.

These initiatives were overshadowed by, or subsumed under, the interim administration's 'Blueprint for the Protection of Fijian and Rotuman Rights and Interests, and the Advancement of their Development', presented to the GCC by Qarase on 3 July 2000. The blueprint proposed to transfer all crown or state land to the Native Land Trust Board, set up a Land Claims Tribunal to 'deal with long-standing historical land claims' for 'land acquired for public purposes', establish a Development Trust Fund for Fijian training and education, give Fijian landowners more

---

22   *Fiji Times*, 22 August 2001.
23   Fiji Interim Government, press release, 15 August 2000.
24   Fiji Interim Government, permanent release, 4 December 2000; *Fiji Times*, 5 December 2000.

royalties for resources extracted from their lands, the payment determined by the Cabinet and not parliament, exempt Fijian-owned companies from company tax for a period of time, reserve 50 per cent of the licences (import, permits) for Fijians as well as 50 per cent of government contracts. These initiatives were not new. Many such schemes had been tried in the past and failed, but the administration was less concerned about the internal coherence and viability of its proposal. It was more attuned to the blueprint's certain appeal among Fijian voters.

In July 2000, the administration announced a 'Blueprint for Affirmative Action for Fijian Education'.[25] Long on vision and rhetoric but short on specifics, the blueprint proposed a 10-year affirmative action program for the:

> development of a new generation of indigenous Fijians, proud of their traditions and cultural heritage, and imbued with a hunger for education for individual development and success; and of a national society with indigenous Fijians competing successfully in all fields of endeavour towards national socio-economic development.

The aim was:

> to develop and transform all Fijian schools into centres of cultural and educational excellence to promote, facilitate and provide the quality education and training Fijian students need for their own individual development, and to adequacy equip them for life in a vibrant and developing economy. To inculcate into Fijian parents the understanding that education is the key to success in life and to therefore place the education of their children highest on their list of priorities.

These would be realised through the establishment of an advisory Fijian Education Board, strengthening community participation, providing access to quality education and training at all levels, upgrading the qualification of Fijian teachers, mounting special programs to meet the needs of Fijian school leavers, strengthening education in rural areas, and providing for a system of review to monitor the progress of the aims of the blueprint.

---

25 'Blueprint for Affirmative Action for Fijian Education', presented to the GCC by Qarase, 3 July 2000.

Fijian education has long been a national problem. Failure rates, especially at secondary and tertiary levels have been alarming for years, despite nearly four decades of affirmative action. An estimated 90 per cent of Fijian students dropped out between 1988 and 2000. In 1988, 11,000 Fijian children enrolled in Class 1, but 13 years later only 1,247 were in Form 7. There has been little proper accounting for the failure rate, and the allocation of more money may not necessarily solve the problem. The interim administration's 'racial' approach neglected certain complexities of educational activity in Fiji. Only Fijian schools, so designated, were eligible for funds earmarked for Fijian education. Yet, there are many non-Fijian schools that Fijian children attend; in some instances—for example, Pandit Vishnu Deo Memorial School in Samabula and DAV Girls College and Suva Sangam High—they comprise the largest numbers. Yet, these schools do not qualify for special assistance, discouraging Fijian parents from sending their children to non-Fijian schools, shielding them from a competitive learning environment they would inevitably encounter later in life.

The interim administration had its critics who saw the blueprint as 'Qarase's ploy to pay off militant elements who were behind the May 19 [2000] event'. Dr Isimeli Cokanasiga of the Fijian Association Party argued that the blueprint would 'not benefit Fijians who were hardworking, successful, talented, smart and ambitious', but those who were 'blue-blooded, losers, lazy, dumb and ambitious'.[26] But Qarase was undeterred. His policies, backed by all the advantage of incumbency, proved popular among Fijians and accounted for the party's victory in the elections. Buoyed by popular support and unable to form a united Fijian political front, Qarase, a politically inexperienced merchant banker of mixed record, launched his own political party, the SDL, in May. Qarase targeted the Fijian voter as his first electoral priority, and unashamedly committed the public purse to that end.

There was much movement and activity on the Labour side as well. Released from captivity, the members of the deposed government pleaded their case to the international community already outraged by Speight's coup. Australia, New Zealand and the United States responded with trade and 'smart' sanctions banning coup supporters from entering their countries. In July, Labour filed a case in the Lautoka High Court before Justice

---

26 *Fiji Times*, 13 November 2001.

Anthony Gates challenging the abrogation of the constitution.[27] It argued that the attempted coup of May 2000 was unsuccessful, the declaration of a state of emergency invoking the doctrine of necessity by President Ratu Sir Kamisese Mara unconstitutional, and the purported abrogation of the 1997 Constitution void. The People's Coalition Government remained the legitimate government 'in view of the [inability of the] interim military government and Speight's group to reach an agreement on governing the country'.[28] For its part, the interim administration argued that the applicant, Chandrika Prasad, a farmer fleeing terror in Muaniweni in south-eastern Viti Levu, who had sought temporary shelter at the refugee camp at the Girmit Centre, and in whose name Labour had instituted the legal proceedings, had no *locus standi* to mount the court case. His action was an 'abuse of process', 'scandalous, frivolous and vexatious'.

Justice Gates, however, thought otherwise. He agreed that the coup had failed. 'It never achieved any legitimacy,' he declared, because it had breached established procedures for amending the constitution. He then turned to the contentious 'doctrine of necessity', upon which the state rested its case. The doctrine justifies extralegal intervention in exceptional circumstances, through military takeover, for instance, to preserve peace, order and a semblance of government when the state is paralysed. But it cannot be used to legitimise or consolidate the extralegal usurpation of the power of the state. Gates ruled:

> The doctrine does not permit necessity to be used as a means of subverting the existing constitutional structure either by abrogating the existing legal order or by bypassing the path laid out for lawful amendment … Whatever is done however should be done in order to uphold the rule of law and the existing constitution …

> Necessity cannot be resorted to in order to justify or support the abrogation of the existing legal order. The doctrine is valid only to protect not destroy.[29]

The interim administration, too, was illegal, in Gates's opinion.

---

27 *Republic of Fiji and AG vs Chandrika Prasad 2000,* High Court Action No. HBC 0217.00L, Lautoka.
28 ibid. See also George Williams, 'The case that stopped a coup? The rule of law and constitutionalism in Fiji'. *Oxford University Commonwealth Law Journal* 1(1) (2001): 73–93, doi.org/10.1080/14729342.2001.11421385.
29 Chief Justice Anthony Gates, High Court of Fiji at Lautoka, Civil Jurisdiction no. HBC 0217.00L, 15 November 2000'. A transcript is in my possession.

> [The] rule of law means that the suspended state of affairs and the constitution return to life after the stepping down of a responsible military power and after the conclusion of its work for the restoration of calm for the nation. The nation has much for which to be grateful to the military, and may yet have further need for its assistance to maintain stability. There is no constitutional foundation of legality for the interim administration.[30]

The pre–May 19 2000 parliament was still in existence. Mara still remained president. The 'status quo' was restored. Parliament should be summoned by the president at his discretion but as soon as possible.

Gates's was a courageous decision that caught the interim administration, and most people in Fiji, by surprise. Nonetheless, to its credit, and against the advice of some hardliners, parliament agreed to appeal the decision before the Fiji Court of Appeal, Fiji's highest court after the abrogation of the Supreme Court following the May 2000 Coup. The full bench met in March, chaired by Sir Maurice Casey of New Zealand and consisting of Justices Ken Handley of Australia, Gordon Ward of Tonga, Sir Maori Kapi of Papua New Guinea and Sir Ian Barker of New Zealand. The interim administration was represented by two Queen's Counsel (Nicholas Blake and Anthony Molloy) and the respondents by Australian legal academic George Williams and the high-profile human rights lawyer Geoffrey Robertson, QC. The appearance in the court case of such a distinguished cast ensured high drama and unusual international interest.[31]

The court first considered the state's contention that the abrogation of the constitution was justified because the electoral system—preferential voting—had produced an outcome detrimental to Fijians, that the first-past-the-post (FFP) method of voting would have given a more balanced result, that 1997 Constitution had weakened protection of indigenous Fijian rights guaranteed under previous constitutions, 'so that the new government under an Indo-Fijian prime minister could disregard and erode the rights of indigenous Fijians'.[32] On the system of voting, the court concluded that under the FFP system, one of the Fijian parties, the SVT, would have won more seats (from 8 to 17), and Labour three

---

30 ibid.
31 *The Republic of Fiji and AG vs Chandrika Prasad 2000*, The Court of Appeal, Fiji Islands on Appeal From the High Court of Fiji Islands Civil Appeal No. ABU0078/2000S. High Court Civil Action No. 217/2000, available from: www.fijihosting.com/pcgov/docs_o/chandrikaprasad_ruling_appeal.htm (accessed 4 May 2018).
32 ibid.

fewer (34 instead of 37), but overall the People's Coalition would have won 45 seats (increased to 47 with the addition of two VLV candidates to the Cabinet). 'Whichever system had been used, the voting figures would have made the FLP the largest individual party by a substantial margin.' The court similarly rejected the claim that Fijian rights could be eroded by the government of the day, noting the iron-clad guarantees in the constitution. No significant issue touching indigenous concerns could be passed without the consent of the Fijian people themselves, specifically without the support, in the Senate, of 9 of the 14 senators nominated by the GCC.

> [Any] attempt by the government to change the law in relation to land or to indigenous rights by stealth was impossible under the 1997 Constitution and any suggestions that it needed to be replaced on that ground cannot be substantiated.

Nor did the court uphold the doctrine of necessity as a justification for abrogating the constitution.

Had a new legal order been created by the coup? Had the revolution succeeded? The interim administration argued that it had. It was now firmly in control of the country, the machinery of administration was functioning, the population had acquiesced. Fiji's continued diplomatic relations with the international community also attested to its legitimacy and authority. The court ruled otherwise. Several human rights and community organisations had presented affidavits showing curtailment of basic freedoms. The existence of emergency legislation inhibiting public expression of dissent was proof enough of continuing public disquiet about events in the country. 'The people must be proved to be behaving in conformity with the dictates of the de facto government,' the court concluded, and the interim administration had not furnished convincing evidence to support its claim, thus failing the test of acquiescence. Summing up, the Fiji Court of Appeal ruled that the 1997 Constitution remained the supreme law of the country. It had not been abrogated. And the parliament had not been dissolved but prorogued on 27 May for six months. But on one issue—whether the president had in fact resigned of his own accord—the court ruled that he had, contradicting Gates's judgement. Mara was no longer President of Fiji. Vice-President Ratu Josefa Iloilo had assumed the office of president.

The much-anticipated decision of the Fiji Court of Appeal did not create the havoc in the country that some had predicted (or hoped for). Instead, the GCC, the interim administration and the military, after some public misgivings about its ability to maintain law and order, agreed to respect the decision. What was the way forward? The court's decision divided the Labour Party. One faction, led by Deputy Prime Minister Tupeni Baba, preferred a broadbased government of national unity from among the members of the deposed parliament. Baba, a politician of thwarted ambition with a shaky power base, whose strident criticism of Chaudhry's style was public knowledge, would lead that government with other Fijian parties, including the SVT. What Fiji needed, he said, was more breathing space to heal the wound of the coup, not another acrimonious election in a heightened atmosphere of racial tension. Chaudhry disagreed. He would never agree to be a part of any government which included people who were 'connected even remotely' to the coup.[33] Chaudhry changed his tune after the election, though, when he explored the possibility of having the Christian Alliance, Speight's party, in a multiparty government led by him. The national interest, Chaudhry said, 'Would best be served if we were to go for fresh elections'. Accordingly, Chaudhry advised the president to dissolve parliament after reconvening it to deal with constitutional issues raised by the opposition parties.[34] Astonishingly, in his letter to the president, he even agreed to jettison the Alternative Vote system, of which he had been a staunch advocate. 'The People's Coalition has an open mind on this and is prepared to discuss changes to bring back the FFP system.'[35]

The president disregarded the advice of both the factions. Instead, he listened to the senior officers of the army who met him soon after the appeal court's ruling. The military expected the president to observe the spirit of the constitution but added emphatically that 'as a matter of national interest we cannot afford to have Mr Chaudhry and his group back'.[36] The army, now a central part of the Fijian political equation and the ultimate guarantor of public security, could be ignored only at the country's peril. Even Chaudhry's own colleagues agreed, including his deputy prime minister, Adi Kuini Speed, who urged her former leader to

---

33 *Pacnews,* 5 March 2001.
34 *Fiji Sun,* 30 May 2001.
35 People's Coalition Government, media release, 7 March 2001. Dr Jonathan Fraenkel argues (private correspondence) that Chaudhry's willingness to jettison the Alternative Vote system was a 'shrewd move'. Chaudhry 'knew full well that the preferences gained in 99 would not be forthcoming, but the FLP might get a plurality of the vote'.
36 *Fiji Sun,* 4 March 2001.

'use good sense and realise that it is going to be very unstable if he returns as prime minister. It will be very dangerous because of what has happened'.[37] In an act of astounding constitutional contortion, President Iloilo swore in his nephew, People's Coalition Minister Tevita Momoedonu as acting prime minister, and asked him to advise dissolution of parliament, which Momoedonu did. Iloilo accepted the advice and Momoedonu's prompt resignation and reappointed the Qarase's caretaker administration to prepare the country for general elections. Chaudhry challenged the constitutionality of the president's action, but was unsuccessful.

The announcement of elections in August paved the way for the next phase as political parties geared up for elections. Fragmentation and confusion were the order of the day. The People's Coalition fractured. Tupeni Baba resigned from the Fiji Labour Party in May to form his own New Labour Unity Party, accusing his former leader of trampling on 'dialogue, compromise and consensus', of being insensitive to Fijian concerns and problems, and of an absence of 'fair and equitable distribution of power' within the party. Chaudhry, Baba said bluntly, was a 'dictator'. The disunity among Fijians was worse. In Western Viti Levu, Apisai Tora, ever mercurial, formed yet another political party, the Bai Kei Viti, to challenge the Party of National Unity he himself had launched to contest the 1999 elections. Competing for the same vote, on an almost identical platform, they cancelled each other out, thereby decreasing the western Fijian voice in national affairs that both were keen to secure. The SVT regrouped under the leadership of Filipe Bole, but it was pale shadow of its former self, unsure of its identity, uncertain about its future direction, confused about its electoral tactics and strategy, and contradictory in its political pronouncements.

The Fijian Association, under its ailing leader, Adi Kuini Speed, was divided and drifting, unable to articulate a coherent vision. The Nationalist Vanua Tako Lavo party had its predictable agenda for Fijian nationalism and political control was appropriated by other 'mainstream' political parties. Among them was the newly formed Conservative Alliance Matanitu Vanua party, conceived on the island of Vanua Levu by supporters of Speight and the coup. The party wanted the 1997 Constitution replaced with one that gave Fijians political control. 'We can't have immigrant people run the government; political control must

---

37 *Fiji Times,* 5 March 2001.

be related to the ownership of resources that fuels Fiji,' thundered one of its leaders, Ratu Rakuita Vakalalabure.[38] The party rejected ALTA, demanded greater landowner control over the exploitation of natural resources (forests, fisheries, minerals), and compensation for past government projects on alienated Fijian land. It also wanted Speight and his co-conspirators granted amnesty. Speight, the party claimed, was not a terrorist but a political prisoner, not a traitor but a hero of the 'Fijian cause', a latter-day Sitiveni Rabuka.

Qarase's SDL, launched on the eve of the elections, was the mainstream Fijian 'nationalist' party. Its unabashedly pro-Fijian agenda and deep animosity to Chaudhry, which intensified as the campaign progressed, increased its appeal among Fijian voters. The SDL portrayed itself as the party best positioned to realise the aims of the Speight Coup, trumpeting the wealth of bureaucratic and technocratic talents among the rank of its candidates. It, too, would review the constitution to entrench Fijian paramountcy. It would set up a Land Claims Tribunal to investigate land claims by landowners. The Fijian blueprints were its manifesto for the indigenous community, and the SDL committed itself to its full implementation. And the Qarase administration blatantly used the advantage of incumbency to the maximum, practising pork-barrel politics at its worst (or best), improving roads, building bridges, donating money to schools in marginal Fijian constituencies, providing farming implements, brush cutters, outboard motors and generators.[39] Loyalists were placed in strategic decision-making positions in the public service and statutory organisations. And the powerful Methodist Church lent the party its own considerable support, 'threatening eternal damnation for those not supportive of whomever it support[ed]'.[40] Well-funded, sharply focused, uncompromising and strident in its defence of Fijian interests, the SDL easily outgunned its Fijian rivals.

The advantage of incumbency apart, Qarase was helped by the division and lack of drive in other Fijian parties. A good example was the performance of the SVT. Its new leader, Filipe Bole, a veteran politician, adopted a moderate, multiracial stance. He defended the 1997 Constitution and criticised Qarase's nationalist rhetoric. Bole also saw no problem working

---

38   *Fiji Sun,* 5 September 2001.
39   See *Sunday Times,* 2 September 2001. Also Ro Alipate Mataitini, 'Forked tongues', a paper presented to the Fiji Workshop held in Canberra at The Australian National University, 19 November 2001.
40   Mataitini, 'Forked tongues'.

with Chaudhry. The party's manifesto emphasised social and economic issues—health, education, jobs, infrastructure, reforming the value added tax (VAT) system and helping first time home buyers[41]—making it virtually indistinguishable from its rivals with an identical menu of promises. Ema Druavesi, the formerly ardent Fijian nationalist secretary of the SVT, called Qarase's blueprints 'racist', saying that a 'national leader should project an image of a leader that respects and looks after the nation, irrespective of ethnicity, religion, or political differences'.[42] This, from a party once led by the coup leader Sitiveni Rabuka, left many Fijian's shaking their heads.

But many in his own party did not share Bole's vision. Among them was former SVT leader, a coup-supporting nationalist, Ratu Inoke Kubuabola, for whom there was a 'Fijian consensus that the 1997 Constitution does not adequately safeguard the indigenous rights and aspirations'.[43] On Chaudhry, Kubuabola declared the Labour leader:

> must accept reality; he is not a man of peace, he is for confrontation; he is trying to take what is not his for the taking. The reality should tell Mahendra Chaudhry why he just doesn't qualify to lead this country.[44]

Mere Samisoni, the SVT candidate for Lami, was an ardent supporter of the Speight Coup, supplying food to rebels at the parliamentary complex.[45] Berenado Vunibobo, with nationalist leanings, was likewise linked to the Speight camp. He was, moreover, a member of the Constitution Review Commission, which wanted the constitution changed. The SVT also suffered the indignity of its sponsorship by the GCC being severed on the eve of the elections. The party, which had started with much promise and which had been in power throughout the 1990s, was clearly hobbled by doubt about its purpose and identity, unable to articulate a vision that resonated with its primary constituency, the indigenous Fijians. That role had been usurped by the SDL. And the SVT's newly minted but generally unconvincing politics of moderation were undermined from within its ranks and attacked by other Fijian parties.

---

41   *Daily Post,* 29 July 2001.
42   ibid., 4 May 2001.
43   ibid., 16 August 2001.
44   ibid., 24 August 2001.
45   See Mere Samisoni, 'Thoughts on Fiji's third coup d'etat', in *Coup: Reflections on the Political Crisis in Fiji,* ed. Brij V. Lal and Michael Pretes (Canberra: Pandanus Books, 2001), pp. 39–46.

Labour's success was also due to its own innate strengths as well as the weaknesses of its opponents. Among its opponents was the New Labour Unity Party formed by Tupeni Baba.[46] For a while, Baba's prospects looked bright, but not for long. Baba was unable entice to his new party other senior members of Labour equally displeased with Chaudhry's style and who had been reprimanded for indiscipline and purported insubordination (Krishna Datt and Pratap Chand, for example). Baba, a former academic prone to ponderous intellectualising, had no political base of his own, and Labour supporters accused him of treachery at a time when unity was imperative. The party's new style election campaign, featuring pop singers and football players, was ridiculed by an electorate demanding, and accustomed to, a more serious approach to political campaigning. Baba's handing out of food parcels to squatters and other urban poor, smacked of vote buying, similar to the tactic adopted by the SDL. Perhaps most damaging of all to NLUP's claim to be clean and transparent was the revelation that a convicted fraud, Peter Foster, had bankrolled the party's campaign to the tune of $200,000.[47] The revelation mocked Baba's call for transparency, accountability and good governance, and he paid the price. Baba lost his seat, although two of his colleagues won.

The other major threat to Labour was the NFP. In 1999, the NFP had won a third of the Indo-Fijian votes to Labour's two thirds. The NFP thus had much ground to cover, but it was not up to the task. One problem was leadership. The retirement from politics of its long-term leader, Jai Ram Reddy, had left a huge gap. The resignation of Biman Prasad, an academic economist and newcomer to politics, just two days after being elected leader compounded the problem. His replacement, Attar Singh, a trade unionist, was unable to erase the image of a weakened, drifting party searching for a leader. The NFP's moderate and conciliatory approach, its emphasis on social and economic issues, which looked suspiciously like a copy of Labour's manifesto, lacked appeal in an atmosphere charged with racial tension. Chaudhry could, and did, claim the mantle of Indo-Fijian leadership.

The NFP's electoral tactic of highlighting its role in the political and economic development of the country—its role in the achievement of Fiji's independence, in the Dening Arbitration, which had caused the departure

---

46 *Fiji Sun,* 2 June 2001.
47 *Pacific Island Report,* 13 August 2001. Peter Foster was jailed for 18 months by a British court in 1996 for his role in a fraudulent weight-loss scheme. He fled to Australia while on parole.

of the Colonial Sugar Refining Company (CSR) from Fiji, in the negotiation of the *Agricultural Landlord and Tenant Act,* its role even in the successful review of the 1990 Constitution—carried little weight with voters reeling from unemployment and poverty, and profoundly ignorant of history. The NFP's traditional support base had eroded over the years, captured by Labour—the sugarcane growers were with the Labour Party–affiliated National Farmers Union, as were public servants, teachers and workers. The emigration of thousands of Indo-Fijians since the coups of 1987 had robbed the party of supporters who might have been more sympathetic to NFP's moderate stance and multiracial vision. Labour's claim that the NFP was yesterday's party, supported by rich businessmen some of whom had allegedly supported the Speight coup, did not help. In the end, the NFP was unable to capture the imagination of people looking for a party to lead them into the future, not one harking to its past glories.

The other minor Indo-Fijian parties were similarly ineffectual. Among them was the Justice and Freedom Party, formed after the May 2000 coup.[48] Holding the United Kingdom and Australia responsible for the introduction of Indians to Fiji, and by extension their present troubles, the party demanded compensation from them as well as permanent residence for Indo-Fijians in Australia. The plight of Indo-Fijians in the camps in Lautoka and Vanua Levu served to heighten the appeal of the issue. But the single-issue party failed, its cause emotionally appealing but legally unsustainable. The indentured workers had come under a contract, an agreement, which entitled them to return to India at the end of five years, at their own expense, or at government expense after 10. Most had chosen, voluntarily, to stay on in Fiji, acquired Fiji citizenship and participated in the affairs of the country as full citizens. To be sure, indenture was a harsh, brutalising experience, but it was not slavery, at least in the technical sense. Voters sympathised with the party's cause but rightly thought its realisation impractical.

Labour triumphed not only because of the weakness of its opponents. Chaudhry is an astute, skilful politician, perhaps the most adroit in the country, and now the only Indo-Fijian political leader of national stature. Many rallied to him for that reason, just as many Fijians supported Qarase. To some, Chaudhry appeared arrogant and confrontational, but his supporters saw him as strong, fearless and principled. There was

---

48   *Fiji Times,* 7 August 2001.

an enormous amount of emotional sympathy for what Chaudhry and his colleagues had endured at the hands of the parliament hijackers: the humiliation and brutality and the imminent threat to their lives. And yet, despite it all, they had remained undaunted. As Chaudhry told his rallies, 'They put a gun to my head and I didn't flinch. Why should you be afraid to vote for me?'[49]

Leadership aside, Labour's other trump card was its record of government. They had removed the VAT on essential food items, generated employment (6,400 jobs) and investment (FJ$300 million worth of hotel projects approved), improved infrastructure, cracked down on tax evaders, achieved a remarkable 6.6 per cent of economic growth, and had a FJ$47 million budget surplus in just the first three months of 2000. They were overthrown not because they had failed but because some vested interests (and others who felt otherwise marginalised) felt threatened. They wanted to complete the task they had begun. They had done nothing wrong; they were the wronged party. The Indo-Fijian electorate listened sympathetically, understood the message and responded overwhelmingly in support, especially those who were desperately poor and without hope. The Fijian nationalists' shrill attack on Chaudhry stiffened their resolve.

The election produced a stalemate, with neither SDL nor Labour winning an outright majority of seats. Both parties then began negotiations with the Conservative Alliance, the moderates and the independents to form a multiparty government required by the constitution. Chaudhry's action in seeking a coalition with the party whose members had masterminded the coup against his government a year earlier was full of irony, but then, in 1992, Chaudhry had supported Sitiveni Rabuka, the author of the 1987 coups.[50] Initially, the Conservative Alliance grossly overplayed its hand by demanding amnesty for Speight and his co-conspirators, a voice in Senate nominations and, most improbably, deputy prime ministership. To their credit, both Qarase and Chaudhry flatly refused the amnesty demands. Realising their strategic error, the Conservative Alliance dropped their demands and agreed to join Qarase's SDL Government—political opportunism winning over political principles. Qarase also

---

49   I attended the rally at which Chaudhry uttered these words.
50   See Brij V. Lal, *Another Way: The Politics of Constitutional Reform in Post-Coup Fiji* (Canberra: Asia Pacific Press, 1998).

successfully enlisted two independents (Savenaca Draunidalo and Marieta Ringamoto) and New Labour Unity Party's Kenneth Zinck to his side.[51] He had formed a multiparty government.

That, however, was not enough. The Constitution (Section 99) provides that the prime minister:

> must establish a multi-party cabinet. In establishing the cabinet, the prime minister must invite all parties whose membership in the House of Representatives comprises at least 10 per cent of the total membership of the House to be represented in proportion to their members in the House.[52]

If the party declined the invitation, the prime minister could then nominate members of his own party or a coalition of parties to fill the places in the Cabinet.

As the leader of the largest party in parliament, Qarase was thus constitutionally obliged to invite the Labour Party to join his Cabinet. This he did, reluctantly, hoping that Chaudhry would decline the invitation. According to the formula provided for allocating the number of seats in the Cabinet in the Korolevu Declaration,[53] Labour was entitled to eight of the 20 Cabinet seats and SDL 12. Qarase, who had already rejected the idea of working with Chaudhry as an anathema, argued that Labour's and SDL's policies were diametrically opposed, as they indeed were, and that Labour's inclusion in Cabinet would be a prescription for political paralysis.

> The policies of my Cabinet will be based fundamentally on the policy manifesto of the Soqosoqo Duavata ni Lewenivanua, as the leader of this multi-party coalition. Our policies and your policies on a number of key issues of vital concern to the long-term stability of our country are diametrically opposed. Given this, I genuinely do not think there is sufficient basis for a workable partnership with your party in my Cabinet.[54]

---

51   Zinck has since been sacked by his party, but, at the time of writing, still continues to be a member of the Qarase Cabinet.
52   Republic of Fiji, *Constitution 1997*, S99 (5).
53   The document is published as Parliamentary Paper, 15 (1999).
54   Letter is reproduced in the *Daily Post*, 20 September 2001.

Chaudhry, however, thought otherwise. He accepted the invitation. 'What fool in politics would like to be in opposition when he can be in government,' he observed.⁵⁵ Personal differences between the two leaders were of secondary importance, Chaudhry wrote to Qarase:

> We believe that common conviction on rebuilding the nation in a spirit of reconciliation must supersede all else. The issue of policy difference can be resolved in a frank and fair discussion designed to reach consensus and understanding.⁵⁶

Qarase was unmoved, employing additional arguments to keep Chaudhry out. He argued now that Chaudhry had laid down conditions that he found unacceptable. Chaudhry, he said, wanted to have a hand in the allocation of Cabinet portfolios. He wanted to act as 'opposition' within Cabinet, thus undermining the principle of consensus and collegiality. Chaudhry denied conditionality, and pressed for urgent negotiation, pointing out that as prime minister he had invited into his Cabinet parties whose policies, too, were different from Labour's but who had managed to form a coherent government. When Qarase refused, Chaudhry sought the president's intervention.⁵⁷ But the frail president, increasingly dependent on advisors openly sympathetic to the cause of Fijian nationalism, refused, swearing in Qarase and his Cabinet. Chaudhry took the matter to the Fiji Court of Appeal.

Qarase's intransigence was the predictable result of many factors. Among them was his personal antipathy to Chaudhry. Qarase would have been able to work with another Indo-Fijian leader, his supporters say, less abrasive, less confrontational, someone like Jai Ram Reddy. But personality is only a part of the equation. Political survival is at stake too. Qarase knows that if he does not deliver on his electorally appealing but poorly costed promises to the Fijians and appease the nationalist fringe—small but powerful, capable of immediate mobilisation, and ready to take to the streets to be heard—he will suffer the same fate as his predecessors. He raided the public purse to bolster his campaign, and he succeeded, but that is an unsustainable approach. Qarase's main aim was to keep Fijians united and on his side. To that end, he worked hard to coopt all potential Fijian adversaries and dissidents into his circle. Apisai Tora, the opportunistic western Fijian rebel, had been appointed to the Senate. Ratu Tevita

---

55 *Fiji Times,* 11 September 2001.
56 Chaudhry's letter is reproduced in the *Daily Post,* 17 September 2001.
57 See the *Daily Post,* 21 September 2001 for Chaudhry's letters.

Momoedonu, another westerner, had been appointed Fiji's Ambassador to Beijing. Ratu Epeli Nailatikau, the amiable but ineffectual high Bau chief and loyal deputy prime minister in the interim administration, had been appointed Speaker of the House of Representatives. The President of the Methodist Church, Reverend Tomasi Kanailagi, a powerful figure in the Fijian community and privately a staunch supporter of the coups, had also been rewarded with a seat in the Senate. The nationalist chair of the Constitution Review Commission, Asesela Ravuvu, was there as well. Ratu Finau Mara, the drifting, jobless son of the former president, had been made the roving Ambassador to the Pacific Islands. Sooner rather than later the cooption strategy would run its course, the well would run dry. What then?

Keeping his Fijian fragile constituency united and on side may not prove practicable in the long run. There was grumbling in government ranks. The Conservative Alliance had given Qarase 6–12 months to deliver on his promises. They demanded that the government facilitate the transfer of sovereignty over Fiji to the country's second-tier chiefs (who had supported the coup), declare Fiji a Christian state, return all Crown Schedule A and B land to their original owners, and entrench Fijian political leadership in perpetuity. The deep-seated social and economic tensions within the community would surface, as they had often done. There were deep fractures along provincial, rural–urban and class lines that had defeated previous efforts at unity. Racially based affirmative action policies, deeply contested by other communities, would face scrutiny when results did not match expectations. Rewriting the constitution to accommodate the nationalist sections of Fijians would be fraught. Investor confidence and economic growth would be stifled in an atmosphere rife with racial discrimination. Qarase's assurance to other communities, especially the Indo-Fijians, that they had nothing to fear from his government, that their legitimate political rights would be protected, rang hollow in the face of his nationalist pronouncements. The politics of ethnic chauvinism and confrontation would continue to keep Fiji in a state of perpetual turmoil. Qarase, a weak leader beholden to groups with divergent agendas and aspirations, cooped up in an opportunistic coalition of convenience, discovered, sooner rather than later, that winning the elections was easier than governing a deeply polarised country. He was riding a tiger he could not afford to dismount. His fate was sealed.

17
A coup by any other name[1]
The road to a military coup, 2006

> [I]f civilization is to survive, one is driven to radical views. I do not mean driven to violence. Violence always compromises or ruins the cause it means to serve: it produces as much wrong as it tries to remedy. The State, for example, is always with us. Overthrow it and it will come back in another form, quite possibly worse. It's a necessary evil – a monster that continually has to be tamed, so that it serves us rather than devours us. We can't do without it, neither can we ever trust it.
>
> — Ian Milner[2]

Following his victory in the 2006 General Election, Laisenia Qarase sought to make amends for his past mistakes by appointing a genuine multiparty, multiethnic Cabinet, giving Labour substantial portfolios. But the Labour leader Mahendra Chaudhry remained outside Cabinet seeking to influence or rather direct his Cabinet colleagues from the outside. He became a painful thorn in the Qarase Government's side. The other was the military leader Frank Bainimarama who sought the removal of the government for his own

---

1   Originally appeared as 'Anxiety, fear and uncertainty in our land', in *The Round Table: The Commonwealth Journal of International Affairs* 96(389) (2007): 135–53.
2   Ian Milner, 'Conversation with Charles Brasch', *Landfall* 25(4) (1971): 344–72, at p. 349. I am very grateful to Doug Munro, Hank Nelson, Vicki Luker and Stewart Firth for their stringent and astute comments on a draft of this paper. But they are not responsible for its contents, I am.

personal reasons but who justified his intervention as a 'clean-up' coup. Far from the truth, but it gained traction in the public opinion. Incessant warfare between two civilian leaders made Bainimarama's task all the easier.

Fiji experienced the whole gamut of emotions over the course of a fateful 2006. The year ended on the unsettled note on which it had begun. Fiji was yet again caught in a political quagmire of its own making, hobbled by manufactured tensions, refusing to heed the lessons of its recent tumultuous past, and reeling from the effects of the military coup of 5 December, Fiji's fourth since its first on 14 May 1987. Ironies abound. A Fijian army confronted a Fijian government, fuelling the indigenous community's worst fears about a Fijian army spilling Fijian blood on Fijian soil. The military overthrow took place exactly 19 years to the day after frustrated coup maker of 1987, Sitiveni Rabuka, had handed power back to Fiji's civilian leaders, Ratu Sir Penaia Ganilau and Ratu Sir Kamisese Mara, paving the way for the eventual return of parliamentary democracy.

This coup, like the previous ones, deposed a democratically elected government. Perhaps more importantly, it peremptorily sidelined the once powerful cultural and social institutions of the indigenous community, notably the Methodist Church and the Great Council of Chiefs (GCC), severing with a startling abruptness the overarching influence they had exercised in national life. Politicians who had supported past military coups in Fiji transformed themselves overnight into fearless defenders of democracy because, this time, they found themselves on the other side of the barrel of a gun.

However, some victims of previous coups, such as Labour leader Mahendra Chaudhry, accepted ministerial portfolios in a military-appointed interim administration on the grounds of serving the national interest; victim of coup one day, beneficiary the next. The GCC initially opposed the coup but then, in early January, it backed Commodore Frank Bainimarama and pledged 'to work together [with the military] for the betterment of the nation'.[3] In a similar fashion, the powerful Methodist Church, to which the overwhelming majority of indigenous Fijians belong, reversed its initial opposition and endorsed the coup as a part of God's plan for Fiji.[4] To complete the chaotic saga of limited transition to quasi-civilian rule, Bainimarama, initially disavowing a political role, accepted appointment

---

3   *Fiji Times*, 14 January 2007.
4   God's name, it has to be said, was invoked by virtually every major player on all sides in the crisis.

as interim prime minister while remaining military commander, with the full support of a visibly ailing and curiously ineffectual President Ratu Josefa Iloilo.

In between the talks of coup and confrontation, Fiji had its share of high drama caused by an intense election campaign in May and the installation soon thereafter of a multiparty power-sharing Cabinet that promised, despite the initial teething problems, to take the country towards a new era of genuine multiethnic cooperation that its people so desperately wanted but which had remained elusive. The military coup put paid to all that. This chapter traces the political roots and routes of Fiji's latest constitutional crisis.

The flashpoint between the military and the government in January 2006 came at the end of a long and troubled relationship. A 'cold war' between the two had begun as early as 2003 when it became clear that Bainimarama was a 'no-nonsense personality' who would not toe the government line.[5] An early indication came in 2004 when he single-handedly took on both the president and the prime minister and reversed a government order to reduce the sentence for soldiers involved in a mutiny in November 2000. In May of that year, five senior military officers alleged that Bainimarama was plotting to overthrow the government.[6]

In retaliation, the government quietly initiated moves to have the commodore replaced. These were unsuccessful and relations between the two deteriorated rapidly. People close to the government, some even part of it, who were variously implicated in the attempted coup of 2000[7] were released from jail after a brief period (some for as little as under a fortnight) under the Compulsory Supervision Order, and others on dubious medical grounds. Among them were former Vice-President Ratu Joape Seniloli and Ratu Naiqama Lalabalavu, the paramount chief of Cakaudrove (Tui Cakau), leader of Laisenia Qarase's Soqosoqo Duavata Lewenivanua (SDL) coalition partner, the Christian Alliance

---

5   See *The Review Magazine*, 15 July 2003, which described Bainimarama thus:

   Although he shuns the limelight, Bainimarama can come out firing if he believes he is being underestimated or unappreciated. He is said to be a "silent thinker" who thinks long-term. To his credit Bainimarama always seeks the advice of his officers—and also taps on the experience of those who have held office before him. He is definitely not a Yes-Man.

6   *The Review Magazine*, 1 June 2004. The allegation proved, in the end, to be true.

7   Brij V. Lal, *Islands of Turmoil: Elections and Politics in Fiji* (Canberra: Asia Pacific Press, 2006), pp. 185–231, doi.org/10.26530/OAPEN_459301; 'Fiji's Constitutional conundrum', *The Round Table: The Commonwealth Journal of International Affairs* 372 (2003): 671–85, doi.org/10.1080/0035853032000150663.

Matanivanua Party, and Minister for Fijian Affairs. The military insisted that the 'real' players in the 2000 crisis were walking free while the 'small fry' were being caught in the net. Others implicated were safely out of the country on plum diplomatic postings, such as Ratu Inoke Kubuabola, posted to Malaysia as Fiji's High Commissioner (now in Tokyo),[8] and Isikia Savua, the controversial police commissioner in 2000,[9] who was cleared of misconduct and dereliction of duty in a closed trial headed by former Chief Justice Sir Timoci Tuivaga,[10] and who later served in New York as Fiji's Permanent Representative to the United Nations.

Having installed Qarase as the interim prime minister after the George Speight crisis of 2000, hoping that he would form a lean and corruption-free government, Bainimarama expressed disappointment that 'politics as usual' had prevailed. Qarase, a commerce graduate, had been the head of Fiji's Development Bank (FDB) for 15 years (1983–98) before heading the Fiji Merchant Bank. His headship of the FDB had been controversial, as he was accused of authorising doubtful loans for racially skewed projects. 'He betrayed our trust when he went back to team up with the very people who caused the political instability of 2000,' said Bainimarama. 'Though George Speight is in prison, the policies that he made are now being adopted by the Government and also the very people behind him are in parliament making decisions for the nation.'[11]

Revelations of a massive scam in the Ministry of Agriculture involving millions of dollars to purchase votes in the 2001 General Election under the guise of pro-Fijian affirmative action policies hardened his opposition against the government. Bainimarama fingered Attorney-General Qoriniasi Bale for particular criticism. 'He was not voted in by the people but [came in] through the Senate.' He raised questions about Bale's competence and integrity. 'We know Qoriniasi Bale's record and involvement in some trust funds a few years back that saw him being disbarred for some time.' His appointment as attorney-general was 'frightening'. 'Corruptive practices' had to end, Bainimarama said in his quiet, determined way, and the sooner the better.[12]

---

8 He was a self-acknowledged key player in the 1987 coups and a silent supporter of the one in 2000.
9 Savua watched while Suva was looted and burned by Speight-supporting mobs.
10 Tuivaga had also drafted a decree abrogating the constitution soon after Speight's coup in 2000.
11 Interview, *Fiji Sun*, 1 November 2006. It's not strictly true that Speight actually 'made' any policies, although he did advocate hard-line pro-Fijian sentiments, many of which were appropriated by the government.
12 *Fiji Sun*, 1 November 2006.

Qarase defended his government. 'The Commander makes many untruthful allegations against the Government,' he said.

> He regularly expresses unsubstantiated accusations about widespread corruption. My position is very clear. The Government has taken a very strong position against corruption. Draft legislation to combat this is being prepared. In the meantime, law enforcement authorities must be allowed to do their duty when allegations are made. Those making the allegations against the Government must provide evidence to the Police.[13]

In this war of words, public sympathy seemed to lie with the commodore, for 'evidence' of corruption (or mere incompetence and sheer carelessness) was everywhere, though prosecutions were difficult to initiate. Entrenched positions publicly aired in acrimonious tones made compromise and genuine dialogue difficult.

The military's condemnation of the government crystallised around two controversial Bills the government sought to bring before parliament.[14] One was the Promotion of Reconciliation, Tolerance and Unity Bill 2005.[15] The government argued that the Bill was intended to heal the wounds of the past resulting from the events of 2000. The principle underlying the Bill was restorative, not retributive, justice. Its aim was to promote 'tolerance and genuine unity' among the people to prevent 'the perpetration of politically-motivated [sic] violations of human rights in Fiji'.[16] Those who had suffered 'gross violations of human rights and civil dignity' would receive reparations. But the provision that inflamed not only the military's but civil society's vehement opposition to the Bill concerned the 'granting [of] amnesty to persons who make full disclosures of all facts relevant to acts associated with a political, as opposed to purely criminal, objective during the crisis'.[17]

---

13   Laisenia Qarase, 'Address to the Nation', 1 November 2006.
14   All Bills presented to the Fiji Parliament are available on the internet and on the website of the Fiji dailies. The third Bill, the *Indigenous Land Tribunal Bill*, was also on the military's list but did not get much airing.
15   *Promotion of Reconciliation, Tolerance and Unity Bill 2005*, available from: www.fijibure.com/recon.htm (accessed 21 May 2019).
16   ibid., 3(1)e.
17   ibid., 3(1)d.

Rightly or wrongly, the amnesty provision came to be viewed as a device to pardon the coup perpetrators. The hasty release from jail of those convicted of various coup-related crimes increased the public's suspicion about the government's real, unstated intentions. It was also argued that the Bill's amnesty provision was in fact intended to circumvent the country's generally robust judiciary whose proper role it was to adjudicate matters of such importance. How could there be reconciliation without justice, many asked?

Faced with sustained vocal pressure from a wide cross-section of the community, the government withdrew the Bill, promising to take account of the concerns that had been raised. Ultimately, yielding to pressure, the government decided 'categorically', to use Qarase's word, to drop the amnesty provision. By dropping the provision after months of insisting that it would not be removed or amended under any circumstances, Qarase caught the nation by surprise and briefly reclaimed some of the ground he had lost to Bainimarama. The concession was an act of political expediency, not an act of genuine compromise. Expedient or genuine, the concession came too late. By then, the military had already decided to overthrow the government.

But the question was asked: if the much-criticised amnesty provision was dropped, what remained of Bainimarama's objection? Self-preservation was said to be the answer. If the Reconciliation Commission, which the Bill proposed to set up, was established, the commodore's violent suppression of an Army mutiny in November 2000, which nearly claimed his life and which resulted in the brutal death of rebel soldiers, would be scrutinised. Many in Fiji believe that Bainimarama is 'haunted' by the mutiny— indiscipline and insubordination in the ranks of the military, its violent quelling, the attempt on the commodore's life—and read his subsequent behaviour in the light of that fact. Questions would also be asked about the commodore's role, as then head of the military government, in the dismissal of President Ratu Sir Kamisese Mara in 2000. To his detractors, the commodore's public pronouncements on the Bill were suspect, carefully camouflaging personal interests behind the publicly appealing rhetoric of guarding the national interest.

The other piece of legislation that the military opposed (as did the opposition parties and commercial organisations such as the Fiji Hoteliers Association) was the Qoliqoli Bill (2006) designed to transfer 'all proprietary rights to and interests in *qoliqoli* [foreshore] areas within

Fiji fisheries waters [and] vest them in the *qoliqoli* owners'.[18] By this process, the marine area from the foreshore to the high-water mark would be declared 'native reserves', for the unfettered use and enjoyment of the resource owners. The tourism industry reacted predictably with outrage, prophesising its collapse because of the uncertainty that the Bill would introduce into the negotiations between the hotel owners and the numerous *qoliqoli* owners. Others argued that the state was hastily divesting itself of a major resource, which it should develop for the benefit of the entire nation, including the resource owners. 'Thousands upon thousands of vacant and re-possessed land are not being used, making Fiji the world's largest producer of weeds and grass,' remarked Deputy Opposition Leader Bernadette Rounds.[19]

Many *qoliqoli* boundaries are uncharted or unregistered and the critics, including the military, felt that the Bill would accentuate conflict among Fijians when registration started. But the government, which went to the elections promising to introduce the Bill in parliament if it was returned to power, claimed that it had majority Fijian support for the Bill. After all, over 80 per cent of indigenous Fijians had voted for the SDL. The real implications of the Bill were not properly explained to the Fijians, the military counteracted. The Fiji Law Society entered the debate, pointing out that the Qoliqoli Bill breached certain provisions of the constitution. 'By transferring to the landowners qoliqoli areas as defined in the Bill', the Society's *qoliqoli* subcommittee chair, Isireli Fa, stated:

> the state is in fact transferring to them the state's rights of sovereignty within these *qoliqoli* areas. The effect of this is that the *qoliqoli* could become autonomous areas whereby the owners of the *qoliqoli* could implement their own rules outside the regulation and control of the State.[20]

The upshot of the public debate on these two controversial Bills was to secure wide opposition support for Bainimarama, who was perceived as an honest man taking on a corrupt and self-serving government playing to the basest sentiments of people in a blatant effort to remain in power. The commodore's strictures became harsher, less compromising. Early in 2006, relations between the government and the military reached breaking

---

18 *Qoliqoli Bill 2006*, Bill No. 12 of 2006, preamble, available from: www.fijileaks.com/uploads/ 1/3/7/5/13759434/qoliqoli_bill_2006.pdf (accessed 4 May 2018).
19 *Radio New Zealand International*, 21 November 2006.
20 Isireli Fa, 'Fiji Law Society says Qoliqoli Bill is unconstitutional', *RNZ* Pacific, 2 November 2006.

point. The army staged a show of strength on the day parliament was dissolved in March, with 500 soldiers in full battle gear marching through the streets of Suva. The army's point was blunt; those who contemplated orchestrating violence to oppose a change of government would bear the full brunt of its force.

In fact, Bainimarama said publicly a few months before the election that a change of government would be good for Fiji. In the public eye, he was aligned with the opposition parties. As the campaign began in early 2006, the army sent teams of officers to Fijian villages to 'educate' the people about what it deemed to be the 'real' intentions behind the government's legislative agenda—to secure Fijian votes by plundering the public purse. A nebulous truce between the army and the government was negotiated by Vice-President Ratu Joni Madraiwiwi in mid-January 2006. Both men agreed to put 'the national interest' above everything else and to have regular consultation and dialogue, but the impression remained of simmering tension. A few months later, the deal collapsed. 'Qarase is trying to weaken the army by trying to remove me,' Bainimarama said.

> It has been his aim from day one. If he succeeds there will be no one to monitor them, and imagine how corrupt it is going to be. If civil servants speak out against the Government, they are sacked. If the provincial councils speak, their allocated funds are reduced, so we are the only hope of the silent majority.[21]

The army's claim that it, not the government, was the true champion of the public interest would be trumpeted loudly in the months ahead.

For its part, the government insisted that the army was simply an 'instrument of the state', not an institution outside or above it. 'The constitutional and statutory authority of the RFMF [Republic of the Fiji Islands Military Force] is strictly confined to maintaining and safeguarding national security within a democracy.'[22] The military's contention that the overarching security role it was given in the 1990 Constitution carried over into the 1997 Constitution was incorrect, Qarase argued, and he sought the intervention of the Supreme Court to clarify the issue. Section 94 of the 1990 Constitution gave the military the overall responsibility to ensure the security, defence and well-being of Fiji and its people at all times, and the army claimed that the section was incorporated into

---

21 See *Fiji Sun,* 1 November 2006.
22 Address by Laisenia Qarase to the GCC, 9 November 2006.

Section 112 (1) of the 1997 Constitution. The government argued that Section 94 had been repealed in its entirety. Section 112 (1) simply reads: 'The military force called the Republic of Fiji Military Forces established by the Constitution of 1990 continues in existence.'[23]

Qarase alleged further that Bainimarama had breached the understanding brokered by Vice-President Madraiwiwi on 16 January 2006. Under that agreement, Bainimarama 'would not make public statements without clearing them first with the Prime Minister'. He said, 'I met with the Commander under these arrangements. The problem that immediately arose was he expected me to virtually follow his orders'. Finally, Qarase claimed that the military was 'being used or influenced by unscrupulous people opposed to certain items of legislation introduced by the Government', and suggested that the commodore was 'being manipulated by those with a certain political agenda'.[24] There is no doubt that Qarase had in mind the tourism industry which was vehemently opposed to the Qoliqoli Bill.

The tension between the military and the government went underground from March to May (2006) as Fiji held its 10th general election since independence in 1970.[25] After several weeks of generally amiable campaigning, but with the usual allegation of vote rigging and electoral malpractices—which international observer teams deemed far-fetched[26]—Qarase's SDL Party was returned to power with 36 of the 71 seats in the House of Representatives. The Fiji Labour Party won 31 seats, the United People's Party and independents two each. Minor parties and disgruntled independents, who had briefly threatened to upset the conventional wisdom about the dominance of the two main parties, vanished without a trace. The SDL was clearly the party of choice among Fijians, winning over 80 per cent of the Fijian communal votes, compared to 51 per cent in 2001. Qarase's assiduous courting of the Fijian voters, through special assistance programs and grants for the indigenous community, and open

---

23   The Fiji Human Rights Commission, in a 32-page report released in early January 2007, generally endorses the military line. It is also highly (hyper)critical of the policies and practices of the Qarase Government.
24   Qarase, Address to the Nation, 1 November 2006.
25   Brij V. Lal, *Islands of Turmoil*, covers this subject. The 2006 election is discussed at pp. 251–64. See also Brij V. Lal, 'Chance Hai: On the hustings, 1999 and 2006', in *Intersections: History, Memory, Discipline*, ed. Brij V. Lal (Canberra: ANU Press, 2012), pp. 79–101, doi.org/10.22459/IHMD.11.2012.
26   Including the Commonwealth Secretariat and the South Pacific Forum in Suva. I should note that both the Human Rights Commission and the military allege that there were irregularities in the election process, although no evidence has so far been produced before the courts.

appeal to Fijian nationalism paid good dividends. The overwhelming majority of the Indo-Fijian voters—83 per cent—rallied behind Labour, leaving its main rival among Indo-Fijians, the National Federation Party, the main opposition party up to that point, gasping for political breath.

A narrow but clear victory for the SDL led the country to breathe a sigh of relief. Although it was impolitic to say so at the time of the campaign, the silent though widespread feeling in the country was that there would have been rumbling in the countryside, perhaps something more, if Labour had won the election. Qarase played the race card effectively to rally the Fijians behind him. One of the central planks in the SDL campaign was that Fiji was not yet ready for a non-Fijian prime minister. Chaudhry became the targeted focus of Fijian animus. Qarase also said that he found the idea of compulsory power sharing embedded in the multiparty Cabinet idea 'abhorrent': multiethnic Cabinet yes, multiparty Cabinet no.[27]

But as soon as the election results were known, Qarase did an astounding about-turn. Confident in the driver's seat, he welcomed, to most people's utter surprise, the concept of a multiparty Cabinet as the best way forward for Fiji. Indeed, he became its most vocal and enthusiastic proponent. Instead of offering Labour miniscule ministries of little electoral significance or fiscal viability, as he had done in 2001, he now offered substantial portfolios, including agriculture, trade and commerce, labour, industrial relations, urban development and health. Whether Qarase's about-turn was a Machiavellian plot to coopt and destroy Labour in a Cabinet dominated by the SDL, or whether it was a genuine gesture of power sharing, became a point of debate.

Qarase's offer put Labour in a quandary. At first Labour leader Chaudhry protested that the ministries his party was offered were those 'in a mess', only to be told by the electorate to join the government to help clean it up. Whatever calculations lay behind Qarase's offer, the mood in the country was enthusiastically in favour of the power-sharing arrangement which the usually combative Labour leader could only ignore at his political peril. Chaudhry offered a list of Labour names to Qarase but insisted that he be allowed to allot the portfolios among his nominees. That, Qarase rightly argued, was the prerogative of the prime minister. Chaudhry then manoeuvred to have himself appointed Leader of the Opposition, clearly an absurd proposition given that nine of his members were in the Cabinet.

---

27 The 1997 Constitution provides that any political party with more than 10 per cent of seats in the House is constitutionally entitled to be invited to serve in Cabinet.

Moreover, his demand was in direct breach of the Korolevu Declaration he himself had signed in 1999. 'Any party that participates in Cabinet is deemed not to be in Opposition.'[28] President Ratu Josefa Iloilo rejected Chaudhry's offer—as he had to.

Labour insiders said that Chaudhry was personally not keen on the idea of any multiparty Cabinet that he himself did not lead, and that he, in any case, thought would collapse under the weight of its own internal problems and contradictions.[29] Some of his Labour ministers, such as Krishna Datt and Poseci Bune, now in the twilight of their political careers, wanted the concept to succeed. They acknowledged the difficulties but promised to persist. Chaudhry demanded from his ministers a strict adherence to Labour policies as the basis for their participation in Cabinet. That caught the Labour ministers between the proverbial rock and a hard place. They could not ignore the directive of the Labour Parliamentary Caucus, but they also had to acknowledge the prime minister as their leader of government.

The Labour Party was split. When Datt questioned if Chaudhry's style was appropriate in the new environment that was attuned more to consensus and compromise rather than the confrontation characteristic of the Westminster system, and went on to praise Qarase's consultative style in contrast to his own leader's, the internal dissension became public. Chaudhry initiated disciplinary action against the dissidents. Subsequently, Datt and Bune were expelled for questioning the authority of their leader and for bringing the party 'into disrepute'. It must be said, parenthetically, that there cannot be too many parties in the post-Stalinist world that expel senior members for questioning their leader's political judgment or the way in which the party is run.

Several problems emerged only too clearly. One was the absence of any ground rules for the operation of the multiparty Cabinet, which created confusion about roles and responsibilities of the ministers from parties diametrically opposed to each other in their policies. Strangely, neither Qarase nor Chaudhry, both vying for political advantage over the other, saw the urgency of the matter. By the time the subject was resurrected for discussion, a coup was in train.

---

28 Korolevu Declaration, Section 3 (b), a copy of which was subsequently published as a Parliamentary Paper.
29 This is based on conversations with some of the members of the Labour Party in Cabinet. But see also Maika Bolatiki, 'FLP crisis poses threat', *Fiji Sun*, 19 September 2006.

Another problem was Chaudhry's reluctance to be in the Cabinet, which compounded the difficulties of his ministers. According to the Westminster convention, ministers were required to maintain Cabinet solidarity and confidentiality of its proceedings. Chaudhry was the leader of the Labour Party, but not privy to Cabinet discussions. This situation accentuated his angst and frustration, which he then vented upon his dissenting ministers. He publicly criticised government policies that his own ministers had had a hand in formulating, in effect playing the role of a de facto opposition leader—a role in which he thrived. In November, Qarase offered Chaudhry the portfolios of Deputy Prime Minister and Minister of Finance. Chaudhry dithered, fearing cooption and marginalisation. He now wanted multiparty Cabinet ground rules to be finalised before he would consider the offer.

There had, however, been no such insistence when he nominated nine of his party members for Cabinet. Many thought the working out of the multiparty Cabinet was not Chaudhry's priority; disciplining dissidents in his party and asserting his iron grip on the party machinery was. 'In a strange twist of destiny', as he put it, he accepted the same portfolios from the military but not from a democratically elected government. Had Chaudhry been less tepid about the multiparty Cabinet, and participated in it, Bainimarama might—just might—have considered the situation differently, deterred by a strong display of multiethnic unity on the political front between the leaders of the two main communities in Fiji.

Chaudhry's personal reluctance to be in a multiparty Cabinet was understandable, if only in narrow, self-serving political terms, but Qarase's behaviour made matters worse. Instead of adopting confidence-building measures with his Labour partner in government, he insisted on rushing through parliament the controversial Bills relating to amnesty and the foreshore. Their passage was important for him to consolidate his ethnic Fijian constituency, particularly the hard nationalist fringe that had given SDL its unequivocal support. It was good politics but bad policy. Second, Qarase appointed controversial people to key portfolios. Ratu Naiqama Lalabalavu, convicted for inciting mutiny in 2000, was appointed to the crucial Fijian Affairs ministry. His colleague, Ratu Josefa Dimuri, was appointed to the Senate. Josefa Vosanibola, the controversial Home Affairs minister, was back in his old portfolio despite the military's strong objection to his appointment. The statutory boards were filled with pliant political appointees. Chanting the mantra of popular mandate (in much the same counterproductive way as Chaudhry had done in 1999), the government gave the appearance of studied indifference to its critics.

Making matters worse for the government were revelations in the courts of massive vote-buying scams in the Agriculture Ministry. Bainimarama accused the government of fostering dissent in the army. Land Forces Commander Jone Baleidrokadroka's challenge to Bainimarama in January 2006 was cited as one example of this. Baleidrokadroka was dismissed from the military and faced the charge of indiscipline and insubordination, but then it was discovered that he was short-listed for the post of Commissioner of Prisons. People wondered if the 'revolving door' of the past was at play again. The sluggish growth of the economy and the allegation that the government was virtually bankrupt and living on borrowed money compounded its problem and encouraged open questioning of the government's competence to run the country.

By early October 2006, the army's cup of disillusionment was full. Bainimarama asked the government to resign, giving it a three-week ultimatum, as he left on an inspection tour of Fijian soldiers serving in peace-keeping missions in the Middle East. 'We don't need any special powers to legalize our move in demanding the government to resign,' the commander said.

> And we don't have to take over because the military will walk into the office of the Prime Minister and demand his resignation. If the people want us to do this, we will. At this stage, Fiji needs good governance and the military will demand their resignation. There is nothing illegal about this.[30]

His uncompromising stance was hardening by the day. The government predictably protested its innocence and refused to resign.

For its part, the military, under Acting Commander Esala Teleni, reiterated its criticism. Its strident statements, backed by a publicly expressed willingness to use force to remove the government, created high tension in the country and scared neighbours such as Australia and New Zealand into backing Qarase, with Australia sending a couple of naval ships to evacuate its citizens in the event of an emergency. The entry into Fiji of Australian SAS personnel carrying arms and communication equipment

---

30   *Fiji Times*, 17 October 2006.

without proper authorisation or customs clearance in Fiji, increased talk of a foreign invasion, with the government's tacit support. It was learnt later that Qarase had thrice unsuccessfully asked Australia and New Zealand for military assistance to confront the Fiji military. Fortunately for Fiji, the request was rejected. Taking on the highly trained and professional Fijian soldiers on Fijian soil would have resulted in bloodshed on an unprecedented scale.

The government made matters worse for itself by trying to remove Bainimarama while he was overseas and have him, again unsuccessfully, replaced by another senior officer, Colonel Ratu Meli Saubulinayau. This inept move strengthened the commander's standing, among his troops and in the country at large, as a man proudly defending Fiji's national sovereignty. The National Alliance Party, headed by former Military Commander Ratu Epeli Ganilau, a high chief in his own right, condemned the government, calling its action to remove 'the military commander in absentia and without even informing him' alarming.[31] His sentiments were echoed widely. Bainimarama also feared that the Qarase Government might implement the 2006 *Defence White Paper*, which repeated the recommendations of the *Security and Defence Review* of 2004 that the size of the military forces be halved.[32]

More alarming, on the local scene, was the deteriorating relationship between the military and the police force, with the Fiji Police Commissioner, Andrew Hughes, coming under strident attack for seemingly promoting the government's (and according to his critics Australia's regional) agenda. But there was another reason for the tension between the military and the Police Commissioner. Hughes was nearing the end of his investigation of the commander regarding his 'treasonous' statements about the government. Bainimarama had dubbed his campaign to get rid of the government as a 'clean-up' campaign, and Hughes said he wanted to 'find out what it means in the context of my broader responsibility for

---

31 *Fiji Times*, 3 November 2006.
32 The 2004 *Security and Defence Review* argued that the Republic of Fiji Military Forces were:

   too top heavy and cumbersome for the size of the force and will need drastic revision once the options outlined above are decided. The rank structure is also grossly distorted, for example there are 80 warrant officers class 1 and 159 warrant officers Class II in a force that would justify no more than 10 and 30 respectively at that rank. The same applies for officers. There are 8 colonels and 23 lieutenant colonels when half that number would be excessive in the current force.

I am grateful to Professor Stewart Firth for this information.

maintaining law and order in Fiji'.[33] Allegations against Bainimarama included disobedience of law and order, seditious comments, unlawful removal of a container of ammunition from the wharf, alleged plotting to overthrow the government, unlawfully obtaining from the president an order to abort a commission of enquiry against himself, and an investigation into the deaths of rebel soldiers in the November 2000 mutiny. Bainimarama dismissed Hughes's accusations as not being 'in the interest of crime prevention and investigation but to remove me from office as a result of political pressure on the Police Commissioner to silence the RFMF'.[34]

Hughes went further, appealing directly to the soldiers. 'I repeat a warning made a few weeks ago to the military, officers and troops in the military that they cannot commit unlawful acts and say I was only following orders.'[35] Five senior officers were already facing charges of committing unlawful acts. Most in the military were 'decent, honest and law-abiding honourable professionals, who should not have their reputations tainted. Think of your families and I don't want to see costly mistakes happen'. The military was being manipulated.

> In 2000 there were people behind George Speight, shadowy, operating in the shadows, manipulating and influencing rebels and we suspect the same applies here. There are individuals, groups and organizations behind this inciting and manipulating the commander and others to do what they are doing. Tell everyone hiding in the shadows who were involved in the conspiracy to destabilize the Government that they need to think again because the investigation is getting closer.[36]

Hughes had a commendable record as police commissioner, the best in recent years, but his increasingly public outbursts about 'shadowy characters' and about the need for justice to prevail and his appeal to soldiers above the head of the commander, created the impression that he was doing the government's bidding. The fraught relationship between the military and the police force broke down completely. Bainimarama demanded Hughes's immediate resignation.

---

33   *Fiji Times Online*, 25 November 2006.
34   *Fiji Sun*, 11 November 2006.
35   *Fiji Times Online*, 25 November 2006.
36   ibid.

While tension mounted, Qarase turned to the GCC to resolve the impasse, seeking its 'support and understanding of the approach I am taking to seek a resolution to this'. After describing the legislative processes of government, he outlined the importance to the Fijian people of the controversial Qoliqoli Bill and the Indigenous Claims Tribunal Bill.[37] These Bills, Qarase argued, were an integral part of the government's 'Blueprint for the Protection of Fijian and Rotuman Rights and Interests, and the Advancement of their Development'—the racially based affirmative action policies in favour of indigenous communities— which were endorsed both by Bainimarama and the interim Cabinet on 11 July 2000.[38] Qarase, in an address to the GCC, said, 'It was wrong to ignore the pleas and oft-expressed wishes of the Fijians over these historical grievances', adding that 'so long as the undercurrents of unhappiness and discontent associated with them continue, we can never be assured about long term stability in Fiji'.[39] Under the auspices of the blueprint, the government had already transferred Crown Schedule A and B from the government to the Native Land Trust Board.[40] A Fijian Trust Fund had been established to give the GCC an independent source of income. Qarase did not need to repeat other policies in education and in the transport industry (such as giving special grants to Fijian-run schools and denying them to Indo-Fijian schools where often the majority of the students were Fijians, and reserving 50 per cent of all new taxi licences to Fijians). Seen in the broad context, all these measures were designed to ensure the 'paramountcy of Fijian interests'.

Was Qarase wise in seeking the support and intervention of the chiefs in resolving the impasse? The GCC had often been called upon in the past (in 1987 and again in 2000) to adjudicate matters of national interest. At one level, Qarase argued, the crisis was between the government and an institution of the state. 'But when we look deeply into it,' he said, 'we see that this concerns the relationship between a Fijian-led government and a Fijian-led army. It is about us, *koi keda saka na I taukei kei Viti kei*

---

37 This Bill's purpose is to enable Fijians to present cases concerning long-standing grievances about the alienation of some of their ancestral land and to seek compensation or return. Around 500 claims have been lodged thus far.
38 'Blueprint for the Protection of Fijian and Rotuman Rights and Interests, and the Advancement of their Development', presented to the GCC by Qarase, 3 July 2000.
39 Qarase, Address to the GCC, 1 November 2006.
40 Land which as deemed vacant or without an owner as decided by the Native Land Commission set up after Cession in 1874.

Rotuma [indigenous people of Fiji and Rotuma].' It was for this reason that he had sought the Council's 'blessings to the Commander and to me, as we find our way to the path of peace and reconciliation for all'.[41]

Bainimarama differed. For him, the impasse was a political problem to be resolved by the government in consultation with the military. He accused Qarase of evading his responsibility as the duly-elected leader of the government. Further, the commander did not see the Council as a neutral or appropriate body to adjudicate the dispute. Many of its members had supported the coups of 1987 and 2000, and some of them occupied senior positions in government. Bainimarama said:

> I say Qarase lied from the beginning when he was elected to lead the country and did the opposite of what is expected of a Prime Minister in laughing at the rule of law by releasing coup perpetrators and coming up with racist policies that has [sic] divided this country more than ever.[42]

As for the GCC itself, Bainimarama was adamant that the military would not listen to them and that it was 'wrong for them to be involved in making any decisions'. Bainimarama's dismissive attitude towards the chiefs was unprecedented and could have had far-reaching consequences. The *Fiji Sun* editorialised:

> The chiefs have been treated with contempt. They have been reviled as never before by being told [by Bainimarama] to go and drink homebrew under a mango tree as they could be of no further use. Where it will all end is difficult to predict but it does seem inevitable that the GCC will emerge from whatever process takes place a diminished force at least in the public mind.[43]

The GCC's quiet endorsement of the coup compromised its position, especially as the coup was against a Fijian leader who was their staunch champion.

---

41   See also Maika Bolatiki, 'Fijian state versus Fijian army', *Fiji Sun,* 11 November 2006.
42   *fijilive,* 12 November 2006.
43   15 December 2006. See also the *Fiji Sun* editorial of 20 December where the paper asked:

> Are we seeing the beginning of the end of a chiefly system unable to integrate with this rapidly evolving world in which we live? Probably not. But we may be witnessing the first signs of a society unsure of its changing relationship with its history as the outside world inexorably alters the way in which we see ourselves and our place in it.

Further, 'There is a strong case for arguing that the chiefs have diminished in status as a result of the GCC's stand-off with the army commander and it is difficult to see how they can reverse that'.

How the GCC reacts as events unfold would be watched with considerable interest. The 1987 coups were staged in the name of the chiefs and conventional understandings of their place in the larger scheme of things; the 2006 coup was a complete reversal. In the longer perspective, the damage that the military had done to the role and function of traditional chiefs in modern society may eventually be seen as a far more significant effect of the military coup than the damage it had done to the institutions of parliamentary democracy. The latter could be repaired, as Fiji's recent experience suggests, but the damage to the indigenous cultural and social institutions may prove to be irreparable.

As the standoff between the military and the government escalated, the budget debate in parliament in November 2006 created further acrimony. Public attention and angst focused on the proposed increase in value added tax (VAT) from 12.5 per cent to 15 per cent except on basic consumer items such as powdered milk, tea, flour, sharps, tinned fish and kerosene. The government argued that the tax was considered worldwide as 'increasingly important as a source of revenues', and that it was 'one of the fairest and most efficient methods of taxation'.[44] One hundred and twenty countries had it, including many in the Pacific Islands. Labour rejected the tax outright and used the occasion to mount a spirited attack on the government's overall economic performance. Apart from causing internal dissension in the Labour Party when two of its ministers (Krishna Datt and Poseci Bune) decided to support the budget so as not to jeopardise the multiparty Cabinet, it raised a huge public outcry. The government's credibility as the manager of the nation's economy was at its lowest ebb. Amongst the nation's poor, sympathy was shifting towards the military.

In early November, Bainimarama repeated his 'non-negotiable' demands for the police to drop all investigations against him, for all Cabinet members who were involved in the 2000 coup and had served prison terms to be removed, for Police Commissioner Andrew Hughes to resign, for the police force's lightly armed Tactical Response Unit to be disbanded and for the two controversial Bills to be withdrawn. In late November, taking the opportunity of Bainimarama's private visit to New Zealand for a family celebration, New Zealand Prime Minister Helen Clark arranged a meeting between the commander and Qarase in an effort to break the

---

44   Budget Speech, 22 November 2006.

impasse.⁴⁵ To the military's demand that the government publicly declare that the coup of 2000 was illegal and that all those associated with it had to be removed from office, Qarase agreed to:

> develop, without delay, a renewed and fully resourced public education programme, to take to the public and the villages of Fiji, an information programme aimed at ensuring the wide public awareness and understanding that the events of 2000 were illegal.⁴⁶

Those found by due process to have associated themselves with illegal activities would be prosecuted.

On the controversial Bills, Qarase agreed that if the Bills were found to be 'legally or constitutionally unsound', they would be suspended (the military wanted them dropped). On the investigations against Bainimarama, Qarase agreed that if the appropriate Fiji Government authorities (Solicitor-General, Director of Public Prosecutions and the Commissioner of Police) recommended that the charges be dropped, the government would heed their advice (the military wanted the charges dropped forthwith). Andrew Hughes's contract was up for renewal, and the government agreed to accept the military's concerns when reviewing his position (the military wanted immediate termination of his contract). There would be no foreign military or police intervention in Fiji's affairs. Qarase agreed to 'undertake a review of the Police Tactical Response Unit'. The military's concerns about corruption and good governance would be addressed through new legislation dealing with leadership conduct, freedom of information and through the establishment of an Anti-Corruption Agency. And finally, regarding the military's concerns about force structure, allowances and terms of reference and conditions of employment would be addressed by an independent committee.

Qarase had conceded to virtually all of Bainimarama's demands, going as far as he could, although his critics argued that the prime minister was merely buying time by attempting to give the impression that action would follow when he had no such intentions. In any event, he had acknowledged his weakness and starkly demonstrated the relative power of elected office versus the military. But the commander repudiated the 'deal' as soon as he returned to Fiji. His mind had already been made up long before his New Zealand visit. The 'clean-up' campaign was fully

---

45   *Fiji Daily Post*, 3 December 2002.
46   ibid.

activated, although no one knew precisely what the military had in mind. Strategic facilities around the country were secured, police ammunitions seized, access to the president channelled through the military.

At 6 pm on 5 December 2006, Commodore Bainimarama announced the military takeover:

> We consider that Fiji has reached a crossroads and that the government and those empowered to make decisions in our constitutional democracy are unable to make these decisions to save our people from destruction.

He misguidedly invoked the 'doctrine of necessity'[47] in defence of his action and declared a state of emergency. But no 'exceptional circumstances' existed in the country. The duly elected government was in office. The prime minister had not advised the president to dissolve parliament, and the executive in the Westminster system is obliged to act on the advice of the prime minister. Claiming that the president was being put under undue pressure and prevented from exercising his constitutional powers, Bainimarama assumed his executive powers. The constitution, the commander claimed, was still alive. His coup, therefore, was constitutional. In truth, it was anything but.

A state of confusion ensued about the fate of the constitution, the commander's conduct under it, the meaning and implications of the doctrine of necessity, the impact of impending sanctions. However, none was more confusing than the behaviour of the president. In his mid-80s, frail and reportedly suffering from Parkinson's disease, he was conspicuous by his absence from the public eye. Conflicting statements issued under his name compounded the problem. It was claimed that the president had sanctioned Bainimarama's action—the two were reportedly close—but then came the claim that the president was still in charge. The removal from office of Vice-President Madraiwiwi, a former High Court judge, deprived the country of sane advice. Exactly a month after the coup, on 5 January 2007, Bainimarama re-installed the president whose powers he had temporarily appropriated. The president then appointed the interim administration, with the commodore at its head.

---

47 The doctrine authorises the executive to intervene if the government is unable to discharge its responsibilities in the event of an emergency such as massive civil disorder. But the doctrine is limited in its scope, and the executive is obliged to return power to the government once the emergency is over.

The confusion continued. The constitution had not been abrogated, at least formally, although the commander's edicts were in breach of its essential spirit. Many chief executive officers and political appointees of statutory bodies were sacked. Senior military officers were appointed to the police and prison services. Civil liberties remained precariously intact under the ever-vigilant eye of the military, although abuse of human rights began to surface. Travel bans on those involved in the coup were imposed by Australia, New Zealand and the European Union, and sanctions and cancellation of defence and sporting engagements were enforced. The Commonwealth suspended Fiji's membership from its foreign ministers meeting. The economy suffered from a decline in the tourist sector and the country's sugar industry, which was already under considerable strain from the projected cessation of preferential access to the European Union. The concurrent announcement by Emperor Gold Mines that it would cease its operations, with a loss of 1,500 local jobs, also had its effect. And the emigration of the best and the brightest, already high, continued apace, draining the country of talent and skill it could ill afford to lose. All this was predictable.

But some things were not. On the political front, the fraught relationship between the army and the GCC was something that would not have been predicted even six months previously. In the past, the GCC, as the umbrella body of the Fijians, exercised great moral and legal authority over the affairs of the indigenous community. It had endorsed the coups of 1987 and, less overtly, 2000. After the 2006 coup it was fractured and hobbled and ineffectively led. It was a frustrated bystander in a saga involving the Fijians. Fijians were divided, and the GCC was unable to provide its accustomed leadership. There was grumbling in the *vanua* (the land) about the military and its dismissive attitude to the chiefly body. Some provinces had asked their sons and daughters in the army to return home. It is unlikely that they did; for them, the military was their *vanua*, which had given them a place in society and was the source of their livelihood.

The potential for fragmentation and division in the indigenous community along provincial and regional lines had surfaced openly since the coup of 2000. It had been accentuated by the departure of the 'mana' and authority of the paramount chiefs who had been able to provide overarching leadership to their people. This was cause for grave concern. Compared to the other coups, there was a greater danger of the weakening of the moral authority of the basic ethnic Fijian institutions. There were many Fijians who thought that the military, the GCC and other elected leaders were not acting in their best interests. The question then arose: What institution could claim to represent all ethnic Fijians?

Unlike 1987 and 2000, neither race nor the protection of indigenous rights was an issue in 2006. This crisis was widely perceived as a tussle for power between a Fijian military and a Fijian government. As a result, the kind of intense international agitation that accompanied the earlier crises, largely at the behest of Indo-Fijian communities abroad, did not eventuate. Nor was there much sign of active or effective local protest. A part of the reason was that the issues were not starkly defined in racial or ethnic terms. Many supported Bainimarama's stated intentions for staging the coup, ridding the country of bad governance and corruption, but they disapproved of his methods. More puzzling was the quiescent reaction of the indigenous Fijians, the overwhelming majority of whom had supported Qarase's party just a few months previously. One reason might have been that their traditional institutions, the GCC and the Methodist Church, had changed sides and supported the coup, even if it was out of necessity rather than by choice. But culturally, military prowess and demonstration of physical strength, not abstract ideology, were highly esteemed virtues in Fijian society, which might have partly explained the Fijians' accommodating response. 'Fijians very quickly shift to where power lies,' a Fijian elder told me. 'We are a pragmatic people.'

From overseas—Australia, New Zealand, the Pacific Islands Forum and Commonwealth Secretariats, the United Nations Security Council— came unequivocal support for the Qarase Government. In their staunch commitment to the rights of the democratically elected government, they allowed no understanding or sympathy for Bainimarama and others. The sharpness of New Zealand's reaction was probably attributable, in part at least, to its failed attempt to broker a peace between Qarase and Bainimarma and the feeling that the latter acted in bad faith from the outset, having no intention of engaging in meaningful negotiation. Australia's displeasure probably arose from seeing its foreign policy initiatives in the region falter. Despite decades of benign engagement with the region through a series of bilateral and multilateral initiatives, Australia's reputation was at its lowest in decades. That said, there was no denying genuine dismay in both Wellington and Canberra at the overthrow of a democratically elected government in Fiji.

The reaction of the Melanesian Spearhead Group (MSG) (Papua New Guinea, Solomon Islands, Vanuatu) was at odds with the response of its bigger neighbours. At the meeting of its foreign ministers in Honiara on 12 January 2007, the MSG declared that 'the political situation in Fiji is an internal matter that can only be resolved by the people of Fiji using constitutional and democratic processes'. The ministers were content with the assurance that the 'rule of law and human rights will be observed, and that a democratic government through the holding of a general election would be held within a reasonable time frame'.[48]

The MSG's lack of sympathy for Qarase's government was surprising as on 30 October 2005, the Government of Papua New Guinea had awarded the then Fijian Prime Minister the 'Star of Melanesia', for bringing political stability to Fiji and for promoting business and commerce in the region.[49] The MSG's reaction put the Melanesian states at odds with the views of their larger neighbours—Australia and New Zealand—and with international organisations such as the European Union, the Commonwealth Secretariat and the United Nations. It was suggested that the Melanesian reaction may, in part, have been due to their then hostile attitude to Australia in particular. Be that as it may, the MSG's support for the military coup in Fiji was to come in time to be seen as short-sighted and ultimately counterproductive.

In the Indo-Fijian community, there had always been a marked lack of sympathy for the Qarase Government, which came upon the back of George Speight's coup in 2000. They were victims of the Qarase Government's many racially based pro-Fijian policies in education, the civil service and the public sector generally. The government had not given the impression of being interested in the welfare of the non-Fijian community. 'What was on offer', wrote an Indo-Fijian academic, 'was a dismal public management record, a race-based resource allocation regime, continuing tolerance of public racial abuse of a community by colleagues, and a range of exclusionary policies'.[50]

---

48 From the press release of the meeting, issued on 13 January 2007.
49 The other awardees were Sir Allan Kemakeza of the Solomon Islands and Ham Lini Vanuarora of Vanuatu.
50 Subhas Appana, 'Can't blame our Indians now', *Fiji Times Online*, 22 December 2006.

Many in the Qarase Government supported the 2000 coup and even benefited from it. Their sudden conversion to democracy was therefore politically expedient and unconvincing. For these reasons, many Indo-Fijians, now making up around a third of the population, silently supported Bainimarama's so-called 'clean-up' campaign. But it would be wrong to suggest that Indo-Fijians, as a community, had rallied behind the commander. They had not. Their condemnation of the coup had been expressed through muted murmurs rather than the vigorous campaigns that greeted past crises. Nonetheless, some nationalist Fijians were accusing Indo-Fijians of providing the military with moral and even financial support. They therefore bore the brunt of Fijian anger redirected against the military, and they unwittingly got caught in the crossfire between the military and Fijians opposed to it.

Unlike 1987 or 2000, calls for a sympathetic understanding of the military's position came from unlikely quarters. Fr Kevin Barr is one of Fiji's more enlightened church leaders. In a newspaper article, he wrote: 'If we look at the military takeover from the perspective of democracy, it stands condemned in principle. However, there is another perspective which needs to be considered.' He went on:

> Does the protection of 'democracy and the rule of law' have to be the only consideration when a military takeover has occurred? Is 'democracy' to be understood only in its narrow Western context and to be measured only by the criteria of free and fair elections? Are wider considerations such as those of social justice also relevant and important in assessing what has happened recently in Fiji? Could it be that the future in Fiji will be more truly democratic and people-centred, more just and more inclusive because of the Military takeover and clean-up?[51]

Questions such as these were being asked throughout the country, by members of all ethnic groups and social classes, suggesting the unpopularity of the Qarase Government's six years in office.

The 2006 coup was visible in Suva, whereas in the sugarcane belt of Western Viti Levu and in Vanua Levu its impact was barely noticeable, beyond a few stray military checkpoints on the periphery of urban centres. In 1987, and to a lesser extent in 2000, life in the Indo-Fijian

---

51 Paulo Baleinakorodawa, Kevin Barr and Semisi Qalowasa, 'Crisis brings uncertainty: What about opportunity?' *Fiji Sun,* 17 December 2006.

areas was severely disrupted. In 1987, boycotts against the coup in the sugar industry affected the cane belt severely; in 2000, Indo-Fijian areas on the Rewa Delta were terrorised for food (cattle, root crops), forcing many to flee to refugee camps in Lautoka. The 2006 coup left a different impression. Incidents of violent crime and burglary in urban areas were noticeably down. People felt personally safe on the streets and in their homes. The military's determination to prevent a breakdown in law and order had its impact, and was an important reason for the gathering public support. Nevertheless, recent concerted efforts to quell dissent did raise concern among human rights activists.

It has been asked whether removing Qarase and Commodore Bainimarama from their respective offices would have helped resolve the impasse. Personality did play a part and Qarase was more accommodating and moderate in public, as he had to be, though his critics argued that he was dangerously deceptive; a reassuring face of Fijian nationalism, the very soul of sweet reasonableness. Qarase is a self-avowed Fijian nationalist who is not necessarily antagonistic to the other communities. Bainimarama, heading an almost exclusively Fijian institution, the military, is an avowed multiracialist, although in television interviews he appears awkwardly assertive, even dogmatically authoritarian. His multiracialism may be a legacy of his education at the elite multiracial Marist Brothers High School in Suva. Qarase is a product of the exclusively Fijian (Queen Victoria School) and the European (until the early 1960s) Suva Boys Grammar.

But this crisis went beyond personalities. It was clear that the military sought a more enlarged, permanent public role for itself. It did not wish to remain simply an institution of the state, but sought to play an important role in the affairs of the state. 'Prevention is better than cure', a senior military officer told me. 'It is better to prevent the mess from taking place in the first place than to be called to clean it up afterwards.' He was referring to the role the military had to play in rescuing the country from the crisis of 2000. He cited Thailand, Indonesia, Pakistan and Turkey as models. Along with parliament and (until recently) the GCC, the military regarded itself as a major centre of power in Fiji and it was there to remain.

Could the crisis have been avoided? Bainimarama was adamant that he would have proceeded with his 'clean-up' campaign whatever the cost, but he had stated his intention to take on the government almost three years previously. His intention to execute the coup was probably the longest announced in recent history. His tactic differed from those employed by Sitiveni Rabuka in 1987. Then, Rabuka delivered a single, surgical strike on a single day, abrogated the constitution immediately and soon afterwards declared Fiji a republic. His actions stunned the nation. In 2006, Bainimarama deposed the government through 'death by haemorrhage' over a long period. His demands were clear and his intention unmistakable. He hoped that unrelenting pressure would crack the government and force it to accede to his demands. But the SDL Government, buoyed by overwhelming Fijian support in the May 2006 elections, and riding high on the wave of enthusiastic public support for the multiparty government concept, did not take the military's threat as seriously and as early as it could and should have. Indeed, for the most part, the government was determined to clip the commander's wings. Clumsy efforts to have him sacked when he was out of the country and to reduce the military's budget fuelled tensions. The government's attempt, to foster dissent among the officer corps against Bainimarama, failed. On the contrary, its actions only strengthened support for him. By the time the government realised the resoluteness of the military's position it was too late. The military had crossed its Rubicon.

Many questions remained to ponder, and only time would provide the answers. Would Commodore Bainimarama be the charismatic messiah who would lead Fiji away from the path of corruption, bad governance and the era of racially polarised politics towards a better future for all its citizens. Or would he, like one of his military predecessors, Sitiveni Rabuka, succumb to hubris and take his country back into the cul-de-sac of despair and disillusionment? Would the multiracial 1997 Constitution, once hailed as the saviour of the nation, remain intact, its lights undimmed, or would it be emasculated and eventually snuffed out if it conflicted with the agenda and interests of those in power? Would the military, henceforth, insist on having a far greater, far more visible public role in Fiji or would the fundamental tenets of parliamentary democracy be allowed to prevail? Would the institutions of law and order be allowed to exercise their proper function or would they do so only under the close supervision of the military? Would a parliamentary democracy of the Westminster type, with all its faults and flaws, return to Fiji or would it be allowed to exist only at the sufferance of the military?

Appendix

Andrew Hughes's Letter

The following letter from Fiji Police Commissioner Andrew Hughes (2003–2006) to the New Zealand Police Commissioner Howard Broad is about resolving the imminent political crisis in Fiji in 2006 following Commodore Frank Bainimarama's public threat to overthrow the democratically elected government of Qarase. Hughes recommends the desirability and importance of arresting and charging Bainimarama while he was on a visit to New Zealand to attend mediation talks between himself and Prime Minister Laisenia Qarase arranged by the Government of New Zealand. The New Zealand police had evidence of Bainimarama in a video conference with his loyal senior staff in Fiji urging them to kidnap Hughes to force the already beleaguered Fijian Government to capitulate to his ever-expanding demands. Technically, the matter was within the jurisdiction of the New Zealand police but the then New Zealand Foreign Minister Winston Peters opposed the idea in favour of a diplomatic solution (which Hughes predicted would never materialise). Had the New Zealand police acted on Hughes's advice, fully supported by the Fijian National Security Council, the course of Fijian history would have been very different.

Andrew Hughes's assessment was made during a rapidly unfolding series of events, but it was prescient in important respects. As he predicted, the coup took place soon after Bainimarama returned to Fiji in early December. His assessment of Bainimarama as 'cunning, self-obsessed, stubborn, manipulative, divisive, ruthless individual with a short temper accompanied by a propensity to violence' has been echoed by many other observers, including Michael Green, the New Zealand High Commissioner during the 2006 crisis in his book Persona Non Grata.[52] *The New Zealand mediation talks in early December 2006 bore out Hughes's prediction that compromise was not a word in Bainimarama's vocabulary and that he would renege on any undertaking that did not meet his demands in their entirety. Similarly, his fear about the impartiality and professionalism of state institutions under Bainimarama has been vindicated. Just to take one example, all the local commissioners of police have been senior military officers, Brigadier General Iowane Naivalarua, Commodore Esala Teleni and Brigadier General Sitiveni Qilihio. His acolytes*

---

52 Michael Green, *Persona Non Grata: Breaking the Bond: Fiji and New Zealand, 2004–2007* (Auckland: Dunmore Publishing, 2013).

staff the senior echelons of the Fijian military and civilian administrations. Hughes correctly surmised that at the time of the 2006 coup, many in the military and the civilian population were 'sitting on the fence' who might have opposed Bainimarama's plans if the commodore was not on the scene. Loyalty in Fiji is always contingent, not absolute or principled. Hughes writes about 'shadowy characters' behind Bainimarama but does not identify them. We now know that among them were leading Indo-Fijian businessmen who are amongst Bainimarama's staunchest supporters.

In a separate note, Andrew Hughes answered, in writing, 48 questions put to him about aspects of the 2006 crisis. He said early in his tenure he had cordial relations with Frank Bainimarama that deteriorated rapidly as the police began investigating his role in the mutiny and other related matters around November 2000. He formed an opinion early on that Bainimarama was suffering from post-traumatic stress disorder from an attempt on his life by rebel soldiers during the mutiny, and that he ordered their brutal deaths (mentioned in the letter). Hughes was asked about the role of Fiji High Court Judge Nazhat Shameem in the crisis. He replied that she was a 'key advisor to the Commodore', and was very 'close' to him. He mentioned the speculation about the nature of the relationship between the two, adding: 'There was some intelligence in this regard that was shared with me by Australia'. I should add, for the record, that Hughes had mentioned this to me in an informal interview in Canberra in 2007. The actual truth of the matter may never be known. All we have at present is Police Commissioner Andrew Hughes's statement. Hughes also says that Bainimarama sought advice from a wide range of sources, which, he says, included Muslims and Gujarati businessmen and, most surprisingly of all, the Fiji Human Rights Commissioner, Shaista Shameem, the elder sister of the judge. The true murky history of the 2006 coup, the mixture of motivations behind it, the identity of the key players behind the scenes, the amount of money that exchanged hands, the promises made, may never be known, but Andrew Hughes's letter will remain an indispensable document as a starting point for future researchers. For that reason it is being published in full.

Andrew Charles Hughes (6 June 1956–28 August 2018) was recommended for the position of Fiji Commissioner of Police by the Australian Federal Police. Before his Fiji posting, he was Chief Police Officer of the Australian Capital Territory. After being removed from his position by Bainimarama, he was appointed to head the UN's Police Division from 2007–2009.

IN-CONFIDENCE

28 November 2006
Mr Howard Broad
Commissioner
New Zealand Police
(Hand delivered)

Dear Howard,

The purpose of this letter is to formally seek your re-consideration of the decision not to arrest Commodore Frank Bainimarama under the provision of Section 117 (e) of the Crimes Act 1961 of New Zealand. At the outset let me state that I do recognize and appreciate that any decision in this regard is yours, however the gravity of the situation that confronts the nation of Fiji, its democratically elected government and its people, compels me to write to you to state my case in the strongest possible terms. I would not even contemplate influencing your statutory responsibilities in any other circumstances.

You have previously acknowledged that you are satisfied with the sufficiency of evidence, so I will not discuss this point.

You have told me that it is the public interest issue which is now being exercised.

Public interest

From my reading of Section 117 (e), its applicability to the current situation is that it includes, 'an overseas jurisdiction.' Would it not be reasonable to consider the public interest in a broader sense to include the public interest in the overseas jurisdiction that is being perverted, defeated etc.? Not necessarily exclusively in a legal sense, but more from a moral obligation as a 'good neighbour', especially in the case of Fiji with which New Zealand has strong and mutually beneficial interest across a wide range of common areas.

If that line of argument is followed, does it not then follow that the relevant authorities in that overseas jurisdiction are best placed to determine the best public interest that will inevitably be impacted by any decision made in New Zealand? Where the balance lies is ultimately a matter for New Zealand. In Fiji, the National Security Council chaired by the Prime Minister and comprised of the Attorney-General, Minister for Home

Affairs and Immigration, Minister for Foreign Affairs and Minister for Finance and National Planning, with the Commissioner of Police and the Chief Executive Officer of Home Affairs as co-opted members, considered that an arrest in New Zealand was <u>by far</u> the best, (and perhaps the only substantial option left), to avoid a destabilisation and likely replacement of the Government of Fiji.

I now turn to two scenarios. One where Commodore Bainimarama is allowed to return to Fiji and the other where he is arrested in New Zealand and charged with offence(s) under Section 117 (e).

Commander returns to Fiji

His intention when he threatened to 'force the government to resign' and then 'clean up the government' is now clear. He openly admits he is intending to severely destabilize or remove the democratically elected government. From reliable, intelligence sources we know that the first phase will occur soon after his return, likely to be on or shortly after 4 December 2006. According to leaked information regarding their Operation Plan (codenamed Arch Angel 2), the Commissioner of Police will be taken hostage and held to ransom at the Detention Centre at Queen Elizabeth Barracks to cause the government to 'throw in the towel' on the 8 demands (which I understand are known to you). This is unlikely to occur because many of the demands are either unreasonable, or impossible for the government to carry out. The concept for my incarceration was communicated to his close shorts by Bainimarama himself via a video conference to RFMF Headquarters from Wellington on Friday evening of last week. No action is to be taken in this regard by RFMF until he returns, but the order will be given shortly after he returns by the Commodore himself. Consistent with his statement that there will not be a coup, my 'arrest' will likely be on the basis that I am a threat to national security following the execution of a search warrant by Police on the office of the president recently.

(As an aside, and at the risk of introducing subjectivity into what must be a completely objective assessment, the Detention Centre was the sight of the brutal bashing murders of 4 Counter Revolutionary Warfare Soldiers that were taken by the Military from the Central Police Station cells under orders by Commodore Bainimarama. We have reason to believe he then ordered their beatings. The extent of the injuries that caused their deaths are the most horrific I have ever seen (from photographic evidence) in

30 years of policing. Eyeballs were hanging out of sockets, bodies pulped beyond recognition as being those of human beings. In one case, the bones of their right shoulder of the victim were protruding out the back of the victim on the opposite side of his body. The prospect of being captured and detained in the facility by these people is not one which I look forward to. It is also a reason why his demand for all investigations into the Military to be dropped cannot be contemplated).

Concurrent with this action will be the attack on the Police Tactical Response Unit where presumably, members of the PTR will be incarcerated and ill-treated. The Assistant Commissioner Operations Samuela Matakibau, aged 50 years, a long-serving loyal and capable officer is known to be the person held responsible by the RFMF for the development of the PTR. He could also be targeted. He has already drawn on his superannuation savings to send his family to the United States to stay with relatives.

If, or more likely when, the 9 demands cannot be met, the Minister for Home Affairs & Immigration, The Honorable Josefa Vosanibola, aged in his 60s, is next on their hostage list under Arch Angel 2. His 'arrest' could also be 'justified' on the grounds of national security because he is seen to be behind the 'unlawful removal' of the commander. Recent intelligence indicates that have also included the Prime Minister, Mr Laisenia Qarase, as a future hostage.

The Commodore has publicly attacked the Deputy Commissioner, Mosese Driver, aged 58 years and the Assistant Commissioner Crime, Keveuli Bulamainaivalu, aged 59 years (a 40 year police veteran), because of their publicly expressed loyalty to me as their Commissioner and for simply doing their job. I suspect Superintendent Waisea Tabakau, the lead investigator into the treason allegations, whose identity and recent visit to New Zealand to provide evidence against the Commodore to New Zealand authorities, will also be earmarked by him for special attention. In preparation for this course of action the RFMF has been training so called 'Kidnap Squads.'

The public threats from the Commodore that 'The Commissioner of Police should pack his bags and leave Fiji, or I'll pack them for him,' is another indication of his contempt for the office of the Commissioner and his role. Interestingly, the RFMF did not deny plans to kidnap me when they were stated as the reason I would not attend the launch today of the annual sporting challenge between the two services. If that was not cause enough for concern, the threats were broadened on Monday 27 November 2006 to include my family. They were repatriated to Australia today and my personal effects are now in storage. It is no longer possible, nor safe for me to live in my home of the past 3 and a half years.

The commander has no respect for any public authority. He has publicly scoffed at and ignored the GCC ('They should sit under a Mango tree and drink home brew') was his public response to the GCC's attempt to mediate in dialogue between him and the Prime Minister. As an aside, the psychiatrist in the mediation team regards him as being unstable, a view widely held by non-professionals as well [as], parliament, the Prime Minister (publicly labelling him a liar and a supporter of the 2000 Coup), government, the churches, the Supreme Court, the community, his overseas counterparts, the Auditor-General, the Police Commissioner and every other civil authority in Fiji. He has openly defied the due process of the law by surrounding himself with heavily armed bodyguards of between 20 and 25 in number. When arriving from overseas he is met airside by around 100 armed military personal, in disregard of airport security. This is simply to avoid arrest. On two occasions in the recent past one of his senior cohorts (Pita Driti) has publicly warned the Police not to attempt to arrest him, ominously stating that it would be 'unwise.' He clearly regards himself as above the law. The very thing he claims he is fighting for.

The Commodore's intention is to appoint himself President and commander in chief. This was documented by a source who was taking official Minutes (PROTECTED) when the Commodore told this to the President himself before leaving for New Zealand last week. His 'shadowy supporters' as I have referred to them publicly, will then be appointed to key positions. Ratu Epeli Ganilau as Minister for Home Affairs, Mahendra Chaudhry as Prime Minister, etc., etc.

His choice for my replacement is an ex Police Inspector Naipote Vere. He is regarded by my Chief Officers as arrogant, racist (hates Indians), vindictive and vicious fellow. Following the coup of 1987, he personally arrested the then Assistant Commissioner Administration, Chandra Dell [Deo] and dragged him through Nausori Police Station and Central Police Station as an act of intimidation. The arrest was under the order of Sitiveni Rabuka. What will become of my Indian Officers under his leadership?

How will he treat those targeted by Bainimarama for replacement? What will become of the others on the target list, including the Prime Minister and senior Cabinet Ministers?

The Fiji Police has undergone significant reforms over the past years, too numerous to list here. The impact of the reforms are more important. I enjoy a public approval rating that has reached 92% and never gone below 79%. 84% of the respondents believe the Force is now doing a better job than it was 12 months ago. Complaints against Police have dropped by 50%. Fiji Police won the Commitment to Business Excellence Award in 2005. In 2006 we won the coveted Achievement Award at the recent Service Excellence Awards, one of only 4 Ministries out of 46 to do so. In public opinion polls I have ranked as the 5th most popular person in Fiji. The Prime Minister is even higher. In stark contrast, the Commodore has only 18% from indigenous Fijians. His support from the Indo-Fijians is higher. This could be due to his attacks on the SDL Government and support for the Indo-Fijian dominated Labor Party. In any event, the Indo-Fijian community were extraordinarily tolerant and nonviolent in terms of showing their collective disapproval on issues.

What will become of the Force, the reforms and more importantly its service delivery to the people of Fiji? Will it retain its independence or will it become an instrument of oppression under Bainimarama's dictatorship?

Last week 15 members of the 19 strong Association of Christian Churches Forum (ACCF) came to visit me at Force Headquarters. The support of the other 4 members was communicated through their spokesperson at the meeting. They were effusive in their support for me and the stance against the Commodore I am taking. They represent 600,000 followers, including the most influential church in Fiji, the Methodist Church. They are praying for me to succeed in bringing Bainimarama under the rule of law. (At their instigation we all stood, held hands and prayed in my conference room. A very moving experience). They referred to Bainimarama as being 'possessed by the devil.' PROTECTED. This may seem unusual and perhaps an insignificant event by Bew [*sic*] Zealand and Australian common practice, however the power of The Church in Fijian society should not be underestimated. They are preaching to their congregations, including members of the RFMF, key messages in respect of supporting the Commissioner of Police.

The impact on the economy, Fiji's international reputation, including its membership of the Commonwealth, are [sic] self-evident. It will be a puppet government under an unstable military dictator. Will other undesirable foreign interest fill the void left by New Zealand and Australia? Will Fiji become a base for 'Transnational Organized Crime and Terrorism?'

Bainimarama is arrested and charged in New Zealand

Although there can be no guarantees, it is the firm view of the NSC and the Police leadership that widespread and lasting disorder is unlikely. Right minded Colonels similarly hold this view and moreover, that they can contain any disturbance to the barracks. Colonel Meli Sabulinau [Sabulinayau] (who was, and legally still is the presidentially appointed Commander RFMF following government's recommendation last month that Bainimarama be suspended while the Force investigations proceed, and was himself suspended by the president in this process), was met by Deputy Commissioner Driver today. The Colonel is confident that he can take control this time, if the Commodore in [sic] not in Fiji, and especially if he is arrested and charged overseas, rather than just the subject of local Police investigation. He believes timing will be crucial, as will a public announcement of his appointment by Government House.

We have pledged our full support in this process, as has government. The avenue to achieve this is Vice-President Ratu Joni Madraiwiwi, who is able to influence the president. Unlike last time, there are no documents to prepare, sign and have leaked to RFMF to derail the process. The presence of the two other most highly respected colonels in Fiji, unlike last time when they were both overseas, is a further significant factor in favour of Colonel's Meli's appointment and acceptance by the RFMF on this occasion. The Commodore has revealed his intention to remove the government. Previously his intention was veiled and open to interpretation. Removing the government is not a popular course for RFMF membership. At a recent briefing of senior RFMF Officers by Captain Teleni in which the RFMF concept of operation was unveiled, they all walked out when he was distracted momentarily away from the venue, is a clear illustration of the lack of support for the Commodore's intended course of action.

It is important at this point to recall that the Operation commences with a criminal act of kidnapping the Commissioner of Police. This in itself is not a coup in the Commodore's way of thinking. It is a process designed to force the government to agree to his demands, clearing the way for fresh demands. He does not require complete support of the RFMF to achieve this outcome. Just a core group of supports and his Kidnap Team.

This outcome is supported by our knowledge that Bainimarama rules the Military by fear. The more he gets away with things, the more powerful and feared he becomes. Despite this there are cracks in the RFMF. It is not a unified and united outfit. These cracks will widen if he is off the scene and this can be exploited to provide support for Colonel Meli, as he himself envisages. It is our assessment that most members of the RFMF are sitting on the fence, waiting to see what happens, prepared to take the path of least resistance, or to follow the direction that the strongest wind blows, and primarily concerned with their pay packets. The vast majority of them are decent Fijians who would not contemplate breaking the law in their own right.

As at 0800 hours today, only 791 Territorial Force members have marched in, out of about 3,000. Even the RFMF has expressed its surprise publicly at the very low turnout. Most of those who marched are the unemployed ones who are eager to receive (or possibly receive) the $18 per day allowance. When they marched in earlier this month, many were not fed for the first 24 hours. Some have only received $20 for the time they spent in camp. The RFMF Budget is overspent by $3.8m as at 22 October 2006. LPOs are not being honoured. Creditors are withdrawing goods and services. The Western Division RFMF (the second largest) is known to be against any unlawful action. This position was confirmed by the Divisional Police Commissioner to me today. He is in regular contact with his RFMF counterparts and they remain, in his assessment, loyal to the government and quietly supportive of my stance.

During the 2006 General Election, police who received the votes from the RFMF members deployed overseas on peacekeeping duties (over 800 in number) reported that 100% voted for the SDL Party. This is probably indicative of the support SDL enjoys among the wider RFMF. This is not surprising considering the vast majority of its members are indigenous Fijian. There is no political motivation to follow the Arch Angel 2 Plan as its principal architect is removed.

In the scenario that Fiji authorities believe is most likely, order will quickly be restored in the RFMF, damage to the economy from the continuing impasse minimized, and the Police/Military relationship can be rebuilt with me continuing as Commissioner of Police. In short, there will be a collective sigh of relief from the overwhelming majority of the population, and overwhelming majority of the RFMF.

The British High Commissioner to Fiji, Roger Sykes, also believes that the arrest of Bainimarama in New Zealand is the best option. He described it as 'cutting off the viper's head.' PROTECTED. The British presence in Fiji is small compared to New Zealand and Australia, but not insignificant.

In so far as the impact would be against New Zealand citizens, it is important to note that the RFMF usually issues warnings before strong action is taken. Coupled with this somewhat redeeming feature in an otherwise twisted leadership culture (although I suspect the grandstanding, projection of power and media attention feeds certain egos), is the fact that New Zealanders (and indeed Australians) are generally, almost universally, liked by Fijians. They admire our successes economically, educationally, technologically and most importantly to them, in Rugby. There is no latent resentment or hostility waiting to [*sic*] the opportunity to boil over. Look at my acceptance as an example of this general respect. Despite Bainimarama's vitriolic public attack on me, my base of popular support remains intact.

Criminal elements target expatriates for the same reason they target Indo-Fijian business people—their relative wealth, not because they are of a particular race. I should add at this juncture that there is no connection with the home invasion on the AFP Officer based at the Australian High Commission and the present political situation. He was targeted for his vehicles which were used later that morning in a failed attempt to rob a service station. This group has been identified and suspects are being chase. Regrettably, such incidents are relatively commonplace.

Turning to his closest cohorts, Captain Teleni and Colonel Pita Driti. Teleni is a classic example of what I have described above in respect of bending with the strongest breeze. He has no inherent leadership qualities and his naval background is not a natural point of endearment with the Army (The Commodore has overcome this through his charismatic leadership style and through his record of taking care of the welfare and pay of the troops).

Colonel Driti is not a respected leader. He is disliked by the troops and regarded as a theorist rather than a soldier's soldier. Quite opposite to Colonel Meli, Brigadier Iowane and former Colonel Seravakula who were extremely influential and command respect, All 3 have stood up to the Commodore in the recent past (and suffered the consequences in the case of two of them). Seravakula escaped to a UN job, but fortuitously he is back in Fiji for the Rabuka trial (His moderating influence should Bainimarama be arrested will be enormous). Meli and Seravakula are very high Chiefs. Bainimarama is either a low ranking Chief, or without any chiefly status. Opinions on this are divided between the two. Whatever the case, his chiefly status is not a factor in his favour. This means there will be no 'traditional insult' in his incarceration. Meli, Seravakula and Iowane are supporters of the Police and understand the importance of Law.

I believe once the Commander is arrested and charged, Teleni will go into survival mode and seek indemnity to 'tell all.' His character is weak and he will not be able to stand up to Colonel Meli if the Commodore is out of circulation. He is concerned about the Police investigation and upcoming charges into the unlawful removal of ammunition from Suva Wharf last month. Driti will most likely meld into the background similarly concerned over his future survival.

Will the New Zealand strategy or mediation/conciliation succeed?

As stated above, Commodore Bainimarama has a track record of walking away from previous attempts when the outcomes do not fit with his own agenda in its entirety. There is no room for compromise in his mind. I have worked with him for 3 and a half years. In my assessment he is a cunning, self-obsessed, stubborn, manipulative, divisive, ruthless individual with a short temper accompanied by a propensity to violence. I have caught him out lying to me on several occasions. He simply cannot be trusted.

My senior officers have grown up with him, they have played sport together, trained together, worked together as junior officers and up through the ranks. Diverse as my senior officers are in age, ethnic and religious backgrounds, personalities and personal values and beliefs, the opinion of him is unanimously and exactly the same as I have concluded above.

With the greatest respect to the efforts and intentions of the New Zealand Government, he will play along until his demands are not, or simply cannot, be met and then he will walk away from the talks, confident in his own mind that everyone is to blame because they did not meet his demands.

Conclusion

I believe the risk of violence resulting from RFMF members loyal to Bainimarama should he be arrested is low. The risk that any violence would be specifically targeted at New Zealand citizens is marginal and will be limited to Suva, not the tourist areas in The West where the Military are quite openly loyal to government and the police. I further believe that the risk of violence and long term instability should Bainimarama be allowed to return to Fiji is very high. With respect, I therefore conclude that you have overestimated the risk factor should he be arrested in New Zealand and underestimated the risk factors should he be allowed to return and continue with his plans unimpeded by civil authorities.

I further suggest, again with the greatest of respect and appreciation for the best intentions of the New Zealand Government, that a mediated diplomatic solution will not succeed unless all of the outcomes align perfectly with his demands, including fresh demands to his increasingly growing list. Moreover based on his recent track record I question whether this fellow deserves this opportunity.

His arrest in New Zealand would demonstrate in Fiji that no one is above the law, that the Rule of Law will always prevail. This is an important message to break the coup cycle once and for all. Failure to do this will reinforce that whoever controls the military can control the government.

If Bainimarama can be arrested and charged in New Zealand to allow sufficient time measured in days, not weeks, for Colonel Meli to exercise his current presidential appointment as Acting Commander RFMF, with the option left open for the Attorney-General to consider the public interest afresh in terms of prosecuting him, and with the benefit of gauging the success of Meli's appointment and the reaction (if any) from RFMF, then this will be a compromise that will give Fiji authorities the time it needs to resolve this problem and the opportunity for New Zealand authorities to redeem themselves in the eyes of Bainimarama and his supporters by not proceeding to prosecution and releasing him.

If the outcome is as the Fijian authorities confidently predict, the Fiji investigation and charges can proceed with a view to his extradition from New Zealand to Fiji for the substantive offences of Treason and Sedition and others. New Zealand intervention is therefore a short term one.

As stated above the National Security Council and the Fiji Police are firmly of the view that Bainimarama's arrest in New Zealand will produce the desired result in the short term to allow sufficient time for both the appointment of a new Commander and the justice process to take their respective courses and for the Government of Fiji to regain control of its long term future. This is in everyone's interests, not just the public interest of New Zealand.

No man should be allowed to hold a country, and a region, in his unbridled, absolute and unaccountable power.

Yours sincerely

Andrew Hughes
Commissioner of Police
Fiji Police

18
Entrenching illegality[1]

Democracy remains an article of faith—always. That is, it stands by the faith citizens have in themselves to arrive at proper decisions affecting their common future, and the faith they have in each other respecting that faith and its processes and outcomes. This renders democracy precarious because anyone at any time with sufficient resources can knock it over and down. All it takes is 'bad faith.' That is, anyone can destroy democracy by simply losing faith in what it is by its very nature.

— *Fiji Daily Post*[2]

However much I may sympathize with and admire worthy motives, I am an uncompromising opponent of violent methods even to serve the noblest of causes.

— Mahatma Gandhi[3]

To put on the garment of legitimacy is the first aim of every coup.

— Barbara W. Tuchman[4]

---

1 Originally appeared as 'This process of political reconciliation: Aftermath of the 2006 Fiji Coup', in *State, Society and Governance in Melanesia Project Discussion Paper* 2 (2007), 21 pages.
2 Editorial, *Fiji Daily Post,* 21 April 2007.
3 Mahatma Gandhi, *Young India,* 11 December 1924, p. 406.
4 Barbara W. Tuchman, *A Distant Mirror: The Calamitous 14th Century* (New York, NY: Ballantine Books, 1978), p. 399.

This chapter tells the story of how Frank Bainimarama sought to entrench his coup through a variety of coercive and noncoercive means, including using well-meaning civilians and the churches to provide him with a rationale for his intervention. He began increasingly to project himself as a selfless national leader.

Commodore Josaia Voreqe (Frank) Bainimarama told Fiji on the afternoon of 5 December 2006:

> We consider that Fiji has reached a crossroads and that the government and all those empowered to make decisions in our constitutional democracy are unable to make these decisions to save our people from destruction.

The military, which had 'observed the concern and anguish of the deteriorating state of our beloved Fiji', had, therefore, 'taken over the government as executive authority in the running of the country'. Those fateful words ended the long-running saga of escalating tension and mounting war of words between Laisenia Qarase's Soqosoqo Duavata ni Lewenivanua (SDL) Government and the Republic of Fiji Military Forces.[5] The following day, President Ratu Josefa Iloilo met Commodore Bainimarama and signed a military order dissolving parliament and inaugurating a military administration. Bainimarama assumed the Office of President. A month later he was sworn in as prime minister when he restored Ratu Josefa as president.

Resuming formal executive authority on 4 January 2007, Ratu Josefa thanked Bainimarama for 'having the courage to step in', and for 'handing back all my executive powers'. Noting that 'decisive decisions needed to be made', he added ominously (for a titular head of state), 'in any case given the circumstances, I would have done exactly what Commodore Josaia Voreqe Bainimarama did since it was necessary to do so at the time'.[6] This statement directly contradicted his press release of 5 December in which he 'neither condone[d] nor support[ed] the actions of the military today, which is clearly outside the constitution, contrary to the rule of law and our democratic ideals'.[7] Ratu Josefa's opposing pronouncements were mystifying. Perhaps he was not the free agent the world imagined—or wished—him to be. Soon after the takeover, he was shielded from the

---

5   For the causes of the 2006 coup, see Chapter 17.
6   From a typescript of Ratu Josefa Iloilo's speech circulated to the media.
7   Quoted in a Letter to the Editor, 'President's speech', *Fiji Times,* 6 January 2007.

public by the military, which issued statements in his name. The president was a frail, fading figurehead, a decent man but ineffectual, a curious onlooker in the drama taking place around him—and in his name. Wittingly or unwittingly, he became the military's fount of legality and legitimacy. And so sadly he has remained.

Mandate and the doctrine of necessity

Announcing the formation of an interim administration, Iloilo outlined what he would call the 'President's Mandate'. This included upholding the constitution; facilitating legal protection and immunity from both criminal and civil offences for the military; recognising the right of the military to suspend, dismiss or remove from office anyone it thought appropriate; steadying economic growth and 'correcting the economic mismanagement' of the previous government; restructuring the Native Land Trust Board to 'ensure more benefits flow to the ordinary indigenous Fijians'; creating an anticorruption unit in the Attorney-General's Office to eradicate systematic corruption; introducing a Code of Conduct to improve 'governmental and institutional transparency'; and preparing Fiji for democratic elections 'after advanced electoral office and systems are in place and the political and economic conditions are conducive to the holding of such elections'. The astonishing scope of the mandate showed the interim administration had no intention of relinquishing power anytime soon, raising the unhappy, and once unthinkable, spectre of Fiji becoming the Pacific's version of Southeast Asia's Burma.

More troubling was the patent illegality of the president's action. The president gave, or, more accurately, was reported to have given, a mandate that was never his to give in the first place.[8] In the Westminster system as adopted in Fiji, the president should act on the advice of the prime minister as the head of an elected government. The power that the president exercises in 'his own deliberate judgement' is carefully prescribed and limited, to be used in exceptional circumstances and then only for short periods of time. The proper course of action for

---

8   Section 96 (1) of the Fiji Constitution provides that:

   in the exercise of his or her powers and executive authority, the President acts only on the advice of the Cabinet or a Minister or of some other body or authority prescribed by this Constitution for a particular purpose as the body or authority on whose advice the President acts in that case.

the president to authorise would have been the prompt restoration of the deposed government. But illegal and improper though it was, the military and the interim administration recited the mandate as their overarching charter—their mantra of legitimacy.

Just as the 'President's Mandate' was misconceived, so, too, was the legal principle the military invoked to validate the overthrow of the Qarase Government. The coup, Bainimarama told the nation on 5 December, was justified by the 'doctrine of necessity'. The doctrine has a long pedigree, going back to the American Revolution.[9] In recent times, the doctrine has been confined within strict limits. In a landmark judgement of the Grenada Court of Appeal in 1986, these limits were carefully prescribed. For the 'doctrine of necessity' to be enforced, it said:

i. an imperative necessity must arise because of the existence of exceptional circumstances not provided for in the Constitution, for immediate action to be taken to protect or preserve some vital function of the State;

ii. there must be no other course of action reasonably available;

iii. any such action must be reasonably necessary in the interest of peace, order, and good government; but it must not do more than is necessary or legislate beyond that;

iv. it must not impair the just rights of citizens under the Constitution;

v. it must not be one the sole effect and intention of which is to consolidate or strengthen the revolution as such.[10]

Clearly, then, the 'doctrine of necessity' only applies in cases of extreme emergencies—civil strife, a calamitous natural disaster, massive breakdown of law and order—when the duly elected government of the day is unable to govern. It is to be the last resort in the absence of any other option. In 2006, the Fijian state was under no fatal threat. The newly elected government was grappling with the normal problems governments in developing countries face: a sluggish economy; failing public infrastructure; ailing health and education services; allegations of corruption. The Qarase Government was by no means perfect: complacent about its well-advertised shortcomings; pandering to the Fijian nationalist

---

9   Quoted in Venkat Iyer, 'Courts and constitutional usurpers: Some lessons from Fiji', in *Dalhousie Law Journal* 28(1) (2005): 47–68, at p. 37.

10   Judgment of Haynes P in *Mitchell v. Director of Public Prosecutions [1986] LRC (Const)* 35, 88 in the Court of Appeal, Granada. See also Venkat Iyer, 'Restoration constitutionalism in the South Pacific', *Pacific Rim Law & Policy Journal* 15(1) (2006): 39–72, at p. 60.

fringe with whose support it had won the elections; quietly tolerant of widely reported cases of misdemeanours in government and statutory organisations; rewarding political loyalists with lucrative appointments to boards and diplomatic missions. All that said, many in Fiji felt the country was turning a new corner, especially after the May 2006 elections with the advent of the multiparty cabinet comprising both SDL and Fiji Labour Party (FLP) members.[11]

Questions about the validity of the 'doctrine of necessity'[12] led the military to modify its position by invoking the 'doctrine of effectiveness'—that is, the military was the de facto government because it was effectively in control of the country. But effectiveness is more easily asserted than demonstrated. In the now famous Chandrika Prasad case,[13] the Fiji Court of Appeal demanded a 'high civil standard' of proof of acquiescence on the part of the populace, requiring the regime to show that any conformity and obedience to it stemmed from 'popular acceptance and support as distinct from tacit submission to coercion or fear of force'.[14] 'The burden of the proof of efficacy,' the court ruled, 'lies on the *de facto* government seeking to establish that it is firmly in control of the country with the agreement (tacit or express) of the population as a whole.' This test the military would almost certainly have failed. Reports of interrogation at the military barracks and abuse of human rights were simply too publicly well known to ignore.

The legality or illegality of the events of 5 December is moot, Bainimarama has said repeatedly. Everyone should accept the reality of what happened and 'move on'. But even as the events unfolded, the military gave the impression of not being overly constricted by legality. They had the guns, they had deposed the government, and that, as far as they were concerned, was that. The military knew that its claim to be working within the ambit

---

11   The 1997 Constitution provides that any political party with more than 10 per cent of seats in parliament (eight seats or more) is constitutionally entitled to be invited to serve in Cabinet. Labour had significant portfolios including Agriculture, Health, Housing, Labour and Industrial Relations, Environment and Commerce and Trade.
12   Raised, among others, by Brij V. Lal in the Fiji media.
13   *The Republic of Fiji and AG vs Chandrika Prasad 2000,* The Court of Appeal, Fiji Islands on Appeal From the High Court of Fiji Islands Civil Appeal No. ABU0078/2000S. High Court Civil Action No. 217/2000, available from: www.fijihosting.com/pcgov/docs_o/chandrikaprasad_ruling_appeal.htm (accessed 4 May 2018).
14   Quoted in Iyer, 'Courts and constitutional usurpers', pp. 55–56. See also George Williams, 'The case that stopped a coup? The rule of law and constitutionalism in Fiji', *Oxford University Commonwealth Law Journal* 1(1) (2001): 73–93, doi.org/10.1080/14729342.2001.11421385.

of the 1997 Constitution was similarly fraught, but this pretension served as a useful façade and foil. In truth, the military was working not so much within the spirit of the constitution as in breach of it.

Appointment of the interim administration

The publicly stated aim of the coup was to eradicate corruption in government. It was not a coup, Bainimarama said, but a 'clean-up' campaign. He pleaded for help to 'take the country forward'. Soon after taking over government, the military announced that all ministerial positions in the new interim administration would be filled by application only. The applicants would have to have at least 'ten years' experience in the workforce, be of sound character and must never have been declared bankrupt'.[15] Further, they would promise not to stand in future elections to prevent conflict of interest. Hundreds applied, including an elderly Indo-Fijian taxi driver who thought himself a suitable candidate for Minister of Transport because he knew about pot holes and corrupt transport officials, so he told me. But the most prominent members of the interim administration, such as FLP leader Mahendra Chaudhry and National Alliance Party (NAP) leader Ratu Epeli Ganilau, did not apply. Instead, they were 'invited' into the line-up. The much-touted show of transparency in the appointment of the interim administration turned out to be just that: a show. Bainimarama missed an important opportunity to make a fresh start with fresh faces—or to show nonpartisanship by including some SDL members.

The inclusion of Chaudhry in the ministerial line-up was one of the surprises in the interim administration, although his ceaseless hostility to the Qarase Government and lukewarm condemnation of the coup should have signalled his new political disposition.[16] 'A strange twist of destiny' was how he described his new situation,[17] although on 6 December, a day after the coup, he had promised 'never [to] be part of an illegal set up because he believe[d] in democracy and the rule of law'.[18] Such are the processes

---

15 These appeared in all the daily newspapers in Fiji.
16 His closest Labour ally and often his spokesman Lekhram Vayeshnoi, Interim Minister of Youth and Sports, described the coup as a 'Godsend'. See *fijilive*, 22 June 2007.
17 Mahendra Chaudhry, 'A strange twist of fate', *Fiji Times*, 10 January 2007.
18 'It's illegal, Chaudhry', *Daily Post*, 6 December 2006. See also *Fiji Sun*, 9 December 2006: 'I will not be part of anything that is not constitutional'. Chaudhry's supporters raise the Mara defence, 'My country needs me'.

of political transformation in Fiji. More important, Chaudhry accepted four senior ministries for himself: finance, sugar, national planning and public enterprise.[19] He had been offered the finance portfolio (along with the deputy prime ministership) by Qarase weeks before the coup but had declined. Chaudhry's membership of the interim administration gave it a multiracial face and a large, if often silent and puzzled, Indo-Fijian base.

But Chaudhry's participation in the interim administration came at a cost. Many Fijians opposed to the coup now saw it not so much as a military overthrow of a democratically elected government as much as an 'Indian'—Chaudhry's—coup against a Fijian government. The interim administration, in which Chaudhry was easily the most experienced politician, was seen as his 'handmaiden'.[20] Never their favourite, Chaudhry became a powerful lightning rod of the Fijian nationalists. 'Race' was once again in the picture.

Along with Chaudhry, Ratu Epeli Ganilau was another leader whose inclusion in the interim administration caused comment. A high chief, the eldest son of former President Ratu Sir Penaia Ganilau, former army commander and President of the Great Council of Chiefs (GCC), the founding leader of the NAP, a latter-day version of the original Alliance, Ganilau had a distinguished pedigree. But he was also a failed politician. His party had won only around 6 per cent of the votes in the May 2006 elections. But he, and fellow failed NAP member Manu Korovulavula, were among the ministerial line-up. Others included former Speaker of the House Ratu Epeli Nailatikau, Ganilau, a son-in-law of late President Ratu Sir Kamisese Mara, as well as the ever politically agile (not to say opportunistic) Poseci Bune, a publicly unacknowledged member of the Mara family. The Mara dynasty was widely seen as having been intimately associated with the military and the interim administration. Ratu Mara's youngest son, Tevita Uluilakeba, was Commander of the Army's Third Fiji Infantry Battalion.

In the eyes of many Fijians opposed to the coup, the military and the Mara clan morphed into one indistinguishable entity. Broadly speaking, the interim administration was made up principally of Labour and NAP figures, leading many to the cynical conclusion that those defeated at the

---

19   The last portfolio was taken away from him by his arch rival, former Labour Member of Parliament Poseci Bune , who expelled from the party for insubordination.
20   This is Madraiwiwi's description in a talk, 'Mythic constitutionalism: Whither Fiji's course in June 2007', delivered in Canberra at The Australian National University, 5 June 2007.

polls had entered the corridors of power under the cover of guns. Were they among the 'shadowy characters' that Police Commissioner Andrew Hughes had talked about on the eve of the coup, aiding and abetting the military's plans?[21] Bainimarama might have enjoyed more public support for his claim to transparent governance and for his own leadership had he appointed people of genuine national stature not discredited by past failures or charges of improper behaviour. However it is looked at, the interim administration lacked lustre and vigour.

Politicisation of public institutions

For reasons already mentioned, there was muted public condemnation of the military coup of 5 December. But the reaction from and within two quarters perplexed the public. One was the Human Rights Commission, especially its director Dr Shaista Shameem. She had long been at loggerheads with the Qarase Government, which, she felt, had ignored her complaints about the unconstitutionality of some of its policies (such as the race-based affirmative action policy)[22] and sought to politicise her office and thus undermine her effectiveness. By 2006, her cup of disillusionment with the government was full, and the coup provided an opportunity to retaliate.

In a wide-ranging report on the coup made on her own initiative, Shameem made a number of claims.[23] She argued that the Qarase Government was founded on an illegality. After the resolution of the 2000 coup, she asserted, the president had erred by appointing an interim administration headed by Qarase, not Chaudhry. Both the High Court of Fiji as well as the Fiji Court of Appeal had ruled, in the Chandrika Prasad case in 2001, that the purported abrogation of the 1997 Constitution was invalid, which should have restored the Labour Coalition to power. This was not done. Between the judgment of the High Court and that of the Court of Appeal, the 2001 election had taken place, bringing Qarase to power, making the issue moot. Nonetheless, Shameem argued, 'The cases are still relevant for the important constitutional principles that the courts

---

21 In an interview with ABC's *Lateline*, 23 November 2006.
22 As part of the Fijian 'blueprints' designed by the Qarase Government to offer assistance to indigenous Fijians lagging behind in various fields.
23 Doctor Shaista Shameem, Director, 'The assumption of executive authority on December 5th, 2006 by Commodore J.V. Bainimarama, Commander of the Republic of Fiji Military Forces: Legal, Constitutional and Human Rights Issues', Report, 4 January 2007.

established'. The army was not the culprit, Shameem asserted, but the GCC and others who prevented the army from carrying out its proper national security function. But the military was neither as innocent nor as hobbled as Shameem implies. It was the army after all that had advised the president that 'as a matter of national interest we cannot afford to have Mr Chaudhry and his group back'.[24] For the military, preserving law and order, which might be jeopardised if Chaudhry was returned to power, took precedence over constitutionalism.

Shameem also wrote scathingly of the Qarase Government, which, she argued, did everything in its power to undermine the constitution, especially the entrenched Bill of Rights:

> The Qarase Government was involved in massive violations of human rights in Fiji, constituting crimes against humanity, and made serious attempts to impose ethnic cleansing tactics in Fiji. The Commission attempted to thwart such inroads into constitutionality by a combination of persuasion and warnings, but ultimately, its funding was reduced, and even foreign government funding politicised by adverse reports on the Commission's investigations and analysis of government's abuse of human rights and fundamental freedoms.[25]

Some of the force of her case was vitiated by the sharp rhetorical excesses of her prose. 'Ethnic cleansing' and 'crimes against humanity' do not ring true to me or correlate to reality in Fiji. Ethnic discrimination, distasteful though it always is, cannot be equated to 'ethnic cleansing' and the wrenching violence invariably associated with it (as in former Yugoslavia or Rwanda). Shameem's frustration with the stalling tactics of the Qarase Government regarding her various reports on the abuse of human rights and of the breach of the constitution itself is evident and probably coloured her diagnosis of the situation.

On legal and constitutional matters, Shameem's judgments have been questioned. A response prepared by a group of senior Fiji lawyers and released anonymously to the public (for fear of retribution by the military) accused Shameem of being innocent of fundamental constitutional

---

24   Quoted in Brij V. Lal, *Islands of Turmoil: Elections and Politic in Fiji* (Canberra: Asia Pacific Press, 2006), p. 220, doi.org/10.26530/OAPEN_459301.
25   Shameem, 'The assumption of executive authority on December 5th, 2006 by Commodore J.V. Bainimarama'.

principles.²⁶ They disputed her understanding of the constitutional role of the military in the public life of Fiji. Instead of being the supreme arbiter of the national interest, the military operated under civilian control. The Qarase Government was not as unresponsive to criticism and public opinion as Shameem alleged. Were the elections unfair? The lawyers argued that the general elections 'were the most transparent and closely observed in the country's history'. They were as robust in their response as Shameem was in her report:

> What emerges from the Report is a pathological dislike of Prime Minister Qarase and his two Governments. The tragedy is that in confusing the latter with its apparent approval of the RFMF's perspective in relation to its own actions, the Report has compromised the Fiji Human Rights Commission and Shameem's own standing as well as set back the cause of human rights in Fiji.²⁷

That it sadly had done.

Another institution similarly embroiled in controversy after the coup was the judiciary. The causes of the division in it go back to the aftermath of George Speight's attempted coup in May 2000. Differences arose in the judicial ranks over Chief Justice Timoci Tuivaga's advice supporting the military's proposal to abrogate the 1997 Constitution to resolve the impasse.²⁸ In this stance, he was reportedly supported by two other fellow judges, Michael Scott and Tuivaga's successor as Chief Justice Daniel Fatiaki. Justices Nazhat Shameem and Anthony Gates opposed the advice. With time, coalitions formed; feelings on the bench hardened and rifts deepened. Bainimarama's coup provided Fatiaki's opponents, within the judiciary and outside, the opportunity to derail him. On 15 January 2007, Fatiaki was sent on enforced paid leave, pending an investigation into:

> the involvement of certain members of the judiciary in the events of 2000, the subsequent politicisation of the Judicial Bench, in particular the Magistracy and numerous instances of corruption, irregularities and gross inefficiency in the Judiciary.²⁹

---

26 J.V. Bainimarama, 'A Response to the Fiji Human Rights Commission Director's Report on the assumption of executive authority by Commodore J.V. Bainimarama, Commander of the Republic of Fiji Military Forces', n.d., but ca mid to late January 2007.
27 The lawyers are all known to me but I am under an obligation not to reveal their identities.
28 For more discussion, see Lal, *Islands of Turmoil*, pp. 200–01.
29 Republic of Fiji Military Forces, press release, 15 January 2007.

A tribunal of competent outside judges was promised to undertake the task, but after six months nothing had happened. A speedy resolution of the chief justice's saga was the principal recommendation of a LAWASIA mission to Fiji.[30]

The suspension of the chief justice was one issue of concern. There were others including, especially, the manner in which his successor was appointed. Sensing public disquiet and confusion, on 6 December 2006, the judges of the High Court issued a statement reassuring the public that they remained 'committed to their judicial oaths to uphold the constitution and do right to all manner of people in accordance with the law', uphold the rule of law and for all courts to remain open and accessible to the public as normal.[31] Meanwhile, with Fatiaki on leave, the Judicial Services Commission, which appoints judges and magistrates and is chaired by the chief justice, was convened by Justice Nazhat Shameem,[32] with the President of the Fiji Law Society Devenesh Sharma in attendance. They appointed Anthony Gates as acting chief justice. Criticising Gates's acceptance of the appointment as a 'breach of trust', Fatiaki said, 'They could have called me but they did not … It does not mean that if I am on forced leave, that I cannot come in and call a meeting of the Commission'.[33] That view, perfectly reasonable, was not the point: minds had already been made up that Fatiaki should go. The matter was before the courts, though in the opinion of at least one distinguished lawyer, the appointment of Anthony Gates as acting chief justice was in breach of the constitution.[34]

Concern was expressed about the civil service. After 5 December, a number of senior civil servants were either sacked or sent on leave because of their alleged closeness to the Qarase Government and because of doubt about their loyalty to the interim administration.[35] Some were sacked because of alleged mismanagement and corruption. The travel bans imposed by Australia and New Zealand were to discourage replacements from outside.

---

30 Report of visit to Fiji by LAWASIA Observer Mission, 25–28 March 2007.
31 This is from a media release issued on 6 December 2006.
32 Justice Shameem is Dr Shaista Shameem's younger sister.
33 See 'Gates broke trust: Fatiaki', *Fiji Times,* 18 January 2007. 'How Gates reached the top', *Fiji Sun,* 5 March 2007, reveals the contents of confidential minutes of the proceedings that led to Gates's appointment.
34 'Opinion Re Judicial Services Commission of Fiji – Recommendation for Appointment of Acting Chief Justice', by James Crawford SC, Whewell Professor International Law, University of Cambridge and Barrister, Matrix Chambers, Gray's Inn. The Opinion was issued on 20 February 2007. Other (similar) advice came from James Dingemans, QC of James Hawkins, Temple, London.
35 Among them were Jioji Kotabalavu, chief executive officer in the Prime Minister's Office, Solicitor General Nainendra Nand and the chief executive officer of the Public Service Commission, Anare Jale.

The drain of talent and experience was one problem plaguing the civil service. Another was its collapsing morale. A number of senior military personnel had recently been transferred into the service, blurring the line between the military and the civil service. Among them were Captain Esala Teleni as commissioner of police, Captain Viliame Naupoto, as head of the immigration department, Lt Col Iaone Naivalarua as commissioner of prisons and Lt Commander Eliki Salusalu as manager of the Government IT Centre. Land Forces Commander Pita Driti was Fiji's new High Commissioner to Malaysia and his chief of staff, Mason Smith, was earmarked for Fiji's Mission to the United Nations. The appointment of military personnel to civil and diplomatic service was not new in Fiji. After the 1987 coups, a number of senior military personnel were appointed to the public service, some even as district commissioners.[36] None of them was a spectacular success. Their appointments caused bitterness and frustration among senior civil servants bypassed or sidelined and a similar crisis of confidence in the civil service.[37] With the departure of talent from the civil service, and from Fiji generally, the problem acquired a graver complexion.

The church, the chiefs and the Indians

While the December coup was no surprise, it elicited different responses from the two major communities. Among Fijians, there was much confusion and puzzlement. How could this crisis have come to pass, they asked. One senior Fijian civil servant had talked to me optimistically about the '60:40 solution' to Fiji's political problem.[38] In the very near future, Fijians would constitute around 60 per cent of the total population and Indo-Fijians around 40 per cent. Fijian numerical preponderance would then translate into permanent political domination, ending the decades-long Fijian fear of 'Indian domination'. But, just when the prize was within reach, the coup jolted that dream. Fijians were puzzled and confused and divided in their response to the coup. Many, it would seem, opposed it, but there were also some (such as some members of the Kadavu Council,

---

36 For instance, Colonels Kacisolomone, Lomaloma and Kaukimoce. Isekia Savua was posted as Fiji's representative to the United Nations.
37 See 'Militarising our police or policing the military', *Daily Post*, 13 June 2007. The collapsing morale in the civil service was the subject of Jioji Kotabalavu in his address in Canberra at The Australian National University, 5 June 2007.
38 In fact, various projections put the Indo-Fijian population at around 37 per cent—and declining.

for instance) who supported it, along with elements of the Fijian middle class and those who had had independent careers, as well as Fijians living abroad. However, no clear-cut pattern of response emerged from the Fijian community, especially from those on Bainimarama's side.

One reason for this was the paralysis of the most important institutions of Fijian society, the Methodist Church and the GCC. In 1987, and to a lesser extent in 2000, the Methodist Church had rallied its supporters behind the coups, promising to make Fiji a Christian state complete with the enforced observance of the Sabbath. Since over 80 per cent of Fijians are Methodists, the power and reach of the church was considerable. The church's task was easier then because the 'other' was visibly different: non-Fijian and non-Christian. Soon after the December coup, the Methodists pledged support to the military, more in hope than conviction that the military intervention might bring better times.[39] Then the church leadership went quiet as the military imposed its hold on the country. Six months later, the church was beginning to assert its views. In June, the Methodist Church and the Association of Christian Churches said, 'The nation and our people have suffered enough. It's only proper that the nation be returned to democratic rule of law at an early opportunity.'[40] The Methodist Church was likely to have taken a harder line against the interim administration as it strove to regain its pride of place in Fijian cultural hierarchy.

Like the Methodist Church, the GCC too vacillated in the early days of the coup, giving the military the benefit of the doubt.[41] 'We need to work hand in hand and move forward as a country so we can rebuild this nation,' said council chair Ratu Ovini Bokini.[42] 'The council fully supports the interim ministerial appointments.' But, with time, dissension surfaced. Some resentment arose from the disrespectful manner in which Commodore Bainimarama had treated the council, telling the chiefs to refrain from meddling in politics, to relax and drink homebrew under a tree.[43] Such symbolic humiliation and disrespect for the highest umbrella organisation of Fijians was unprecedented. Some members of the council

---

39 'Methodists pledge support', *Fiji Sun,* 11 Jan 2007.
40 'Churches want early return to democracy', *fijilive,* 13 June 2007.
41 An overarching consideration of the GCC is in Robert Norton, 'The Great Council of Chiefs in Fiji's era of crisis and reform', manuscript in my possession.
42 'Chiefs approve', *Fiji Sun,* 11 January 2007. Several chiefs from Western Viti Levu trooped up to the Queen Elizabeth Barracks to show their 'appreciation' to the military.
43 Bainimarama himself is a chief though he does not use the honorific chiefly title 'Ratu'.

were also part of the deposed Qarase Government. The most vocal among them was Ro Teimumu Kepa, the Roko Tui Dreketi and former Minister of Education. A Fijian nationalist and a silent supporter of Speight's coup, she, along with many others, was now a transformed and principled democrat opposed to Bainimarama's coup.[44]

The impasse between the military and a palpably hobbled and humiliated Council of Chiefs came to a head over the appointment of the vice-president, following Ratu Joni Madraiwiwi's resignation soon after the coup when he refused to facilitate the military's plans. The issue was pressing in view of the president's indifferent health and his need for regular medical check-ups overseas. Normally, the vice-president and, in his absence, the Speaker of the House of Representatives, would act as head of state. But since the parliament was dissolved, there was no speaker. The chief justice, next in line, was not a citizen. The interim administration nominated former Speaker of the House and current Minister of Foreign Affairs Ratu Epeli Nailatikau for the position, regarding his appointment a foregone conclusion. Moreover, cultural protocol required respecting the president's choice: he was, after all, Tui Vuda, the paramount chief of Western Viti Levu. Confident about the outcome, the military did no prior canvassing with the chiefs. Bainimarama did not attend the meeting.

In the end, only Lau, led by Ratu Mara's son, Ratu Tevita Uluilakeba, endorsed Nailatikau. The opposition was led by Kepa who argued that the nomination, coming from an illegal interim administration, was illegal. Kepa preempted the issue, which was before the High Court. The interim administration's ineptness was part of the reason for the debacle. But Chairman Ovini Bokini's inability or failure to orchestrate a consensus solution compounded the problem. One member of the council told me that council should have kept meeting until a consensus was reached. Consensus, after all, is how the council has always conducted its business, though it has to be said that in the strained, postcoup atmosphere, consensus might not have been possible. Hubris on one side and incompetence on the other won the day.

---

44 She was not alone in her newfound respect for law and order and the rule of parliamentary democracy. Among the more astonishing examples was Mere Samisoni, a SDL Member of Parliament and a prominent Speight sympathiser.

The interim administration reacted swiftly to the council's snub, suspending the GCC on 12 April, saying that it 'will only be reconvened if, and when, the interim government sees it appropriate'.[45] Bainimarama denounced the council as a haven for anticoup politicians who were manipulating it to advance their own personal and political agendas. 'The council,' he continued, 'was a security threat in our efforts to move the country forward.'[46] The GCC's suspension caused consternation. But contrary to widespread fears, the GCC itself was not disestablished. It is a constitutionally recognised body and since the 1997 Constitution remained in force, so did the council. One purpose of the review of the council's membership was to orchestrate a more pliant membership of the council. But the power of the Minister of Fijian Affairs was limited as most of the 55 members of the GCC were elected independently by the provincial councils. Perhaps more than seeking to influence the council, the military was attempting to demonstrate its place in the new scheme of things, an altered political landscape where the council did not hold its traditional sway and was indeed 'subservient' to the government.[47]

Beyond the legality or illegality of the issue lay broader, more troubling questions. How much permanent damage had the military done to the status and reputation of the GCC? The council was in a bind, buffeted from within and without, and rudderless in unfamiliar waters. A *Fiji Sun* editorial put the matter succinctly:

> Commodore Bainimarama is no respecter of chiefly tradition and protocol. To commit such acts [snubbing the GCC] and get away with them will be widely seen as a massive insult. But it also represents a heavy blow to the status and standing of the chiefs and tends to undermine their relevance in a rapidly evolving society such as ours. Seldom can Fiji's highest traditional body have been so insulted in the past and, worse still, the culprit remain neither punished nor even chastised.[48]

---

45   'State suspends GCC meetings', *Fiji Times*, 13 April 2007. See also 'The vestige of Fijian identity', *Fiji Daily Post*, 15 April 2007.
46   'Address by the Interim Prime Minister Commodore Voreqe Bainimarama', 12 April 2007, on the Republic of Fiji Military Forces website, 31 May 2007.
47   This is the assertion of Interim Fijian Affairs Minister Ratu Epeli Ganilau. See 'Chiefs subservient to State: Minister', *Fiji Times*, 9 June 2007.
48   'A blow to tradition', *Fiji Sun*, 9 December 2006.

The Indo-Fijian community was widely, if erroneously, accused by many Fijians of instigating the coup and benefiting from it.[49] In Madraiwiwi's words, the 'Fijian heartland' saw the 2006 overthrow as 'an Indian coup'.[50] Some described it as a Muslim coup, given the alleged association of some prominent Muslims with the interim administration.[51] The Muslim connection, if there was one, was more a coincidence than an established connection. Some of the most prominent opponents of the coup were also Muslim, such as Shameema Ali and Imrana Jalal. The Indo-Fijian community was divided. There were undoubtedly those who were victims of the Qarase Government's race-based affirmative action policies who therefore saw no reason to mourn its demise. Qarase's pandering to the nationalist fringe disenchanted others. There were some whose support for the coup was motivated by revenge and grudge: 'Thank God', 'And about time'. The boot was on the other foot. But there were also many who were genuinely confused, perplexed and undecided. They may have approved of the removal of the Qarase Government, but not the method used to do it.

An example of an Indo-Fijian–led opposition to the coup was the hard-hitting submission the Fiji Islands Council of Trade Unions (FICTU), representing 18,000 members of the total 33,000 unionised workers in Fiji, made to the UN Visiting Mission.[52] It alerted the mission to the abuse of human rights in the country, and the 'misery and suffering of the ordinary citizens, the working class, farmers and the under-privileged'. It proposed the removal of Bainimarama as prime minister to enable the president to appoint a 'qualified civilian as interim prime minister' and the replacement of politicians and failed candidates in the 2006 elections in the interim administration by 'qualified civilians of repute'. Further, the council urged the preservation of the 1997 Constitution and a speedy return to parliamentary democracy. The FICTU was not alone in its critical response to the coup.

---

49 'Where to Now, Bainimarama?' *Daily Post*, 13 June 2007 for a representative expression of this view.
50 In his address in Canberra at The Australian National University, 5 June 2007.
51 The list includes the Attorney-General (Khaiyum), a controversial High Court Judge (Nazhat Shameem), Director of the Human Rights Commission (Shaista Shameem), Military's Chief Legal Advisor (Colonel Aziz), lawyer and recently appointed chairman of the Electoral Commission (Dr Sahu Khan).
52 Fiji Islands Council of Trade Unions, *Submission to the UN Mission*, 27 April 2007. The mission was sent to make an independent and confidential assessment of the situation in Fiji.

The National Federation Party, representing about 15–20 per cent of the Indo-Fijian population, was equally forthright in its denunciation. The party 'condemned the coup from day one and continues to do so', it told the UN Visiting Mission.[53] The party said the December coup was not a:

> clean-up campaign as the military and the interim administration claim it to be. Just like the previous coups, it is about power, even if it means achieving it through the barrel of the gun. The fact that the key players in the current administration are those who either badly lost in the last general elections or came out second best is testimony to this fact.

It urged the United Nations to work towards a speedy return to parliamentary democracy in Fiji. There were many in the Indo-Fijian community who shared that thought.

Response of civil society

Soon after the coup, some nongovernmental organisations (NGOs) attempted to form a broadbased anticoup coalition and even sent a delegation to the military. They suggested the appointment of a representative Presidential Commission of Truth, Justice and Reconciliation to, among other things, 'clarify the Truth regarding the events of 2000 coup and mutiny' and to consider ways of ending 'this abhorrent cycle of coups and attempted coups, and to put in place concrete measures to ensure the prevention of such conflicts in the future'.[54] The Citizens Constitutional Forum (CCF), formed in 1993 and active for years in the defence of human rights and good governance, also condemned the coup, though in decidedly (and uncharacteristically) measured tones, in marked contrast to its previous ringing denunciations of the past coups. On 4 December it called the coup illegal, but in the same breath added that 'the CCF does not hold the Qarase Government blameless in this crisis either—it has a track record of illegal activities over the past six years'.[55] It too had been

---

53 National Federation Party, *Submission to the United Nations Fact Finding Mission*, 24 April 2007.
54 From a draft of press release. The NGOs represented in the coalition included FemLINKPACIFIC, Fiji Women's Rights Movement, Fiji Women's Crisis Centre, Citizens Constitutional Forum and Pacific Centre for Public Integrity.
55 See Citizen's Constitutional Forum, Towards a Sustainable Constitutional Democracy, 4 December 2006, available from: www.ccf.org.fj (accessed 6 April 2018).

singed by the ongoing conflict with the Qarase Government, questioning its legality and constitutional foundation. Perhaps that bruising experience tempered its response. It preferred 'engagement' with the military and the interim administration to public confrontation.

But not all NGOs were critical of the coup.[56] Among the most notable was the Ecumenical Centre for Research, Education and Advocacy, founded in 1990 by the Reverend Paula Niukula 'to address the social, religious, economic and political issues that confront Fiji'.[57] Its current director Fr Kevin Barr asked whether a military overthrow of an elected government that was racist and discriminatory was necessarily an evil thing. If the coup in fact led to improvements in human rights and social justice, and to the alleviation of poverty and eradication of corruption and racial discrimination, should it be considered such a bad thing after all? Under the Qarase Government, Barr argued, democracy was being seriously undermined.

> Democracy was being manipulated in the interests of a group of extreme nationalists and rich elites. It was not working in the interests of all Fiji citizens. There was little concern for the poor, the ordinary workers, and for Indo-Fijians. There was serious mismanagement and some evidence of corruption. Hence although democratically elected by a small margin, the Qarase government was not a democracy that worked in the interests of all the people and sought to bring about justice for all.[58]

The last, Barr continued, is of paramount importance.

> The aim of democracy is surely to build a just society—the ordering of society to bring about social justice for all. If this does not happen, does that 'democracy' deserve to stay in power? Yet how can it be removed particularly when it has a history of manipulating the race card and possibly tampering with the electoral process?

---

56   Most human rights NGOs seem to oppose the coup while those concerned with social justice seem to support it.
57   See Ecumenical Centre for Research, Education and Advocacy's (ECREA's) website, available from: www.ecrea.org.fj (accessed 6 April 2018).
58   Kevin Barr, 'A flawed democracy', *Fiji Times,* 9 April 2007; see also his 'Does democracy benefit people', *Fiji Sun,* 3 April 2007.

Barr saw promise and opportunity in Bainimarama's coup and counselled patience and understanding. His views, expressed in newspaper columns, attracted criticism from opponents and planted the suspicion that many Catholics were like-minded and supported the coup.[59]

Barr's position raised many troubling questions. Which government, except in utopian democracy, works in the interests of 'justice for all'? Which government in Fiji has ever worked 'in the interests of all the people of Fiji'? And which government has not manipulated the race card? These questions did not excuse the Qarase Government's record, they simply put the issue in perspective. The race-based electoral system provided the incentive for ethnic manipulation, and Qarase, like other leaders in the past, including Chaudhry, played it to his advantage. Proposing solutions to deep-seated problems at gunpoint, without the support of the majority of the population, was both myopic as well as counterproductive. Military intervention exacerbated ethnic tension and hostility, and without interethnic accommodation and understanding, there could be no resolution of Fiji's deep-seated problems. People's participation in formulating and resolving problems were important, within the overarching framework of parliamentary democracy. What Barr ignored was that the military had set itself up as the ultimate guardian and arbiter of the national interest, over and above everyone else. What would happen if a democratically elected government failed to live up to the military's expectations in delivering social justice programs? Strengthening the basic tenets of parliamentary democracy, respecting the verdict of the ballot box in free and fair elections, would be a better way of resolving the country's problems than the short-cut of military intervention.

In April 2007, a group of NGOs and some interested former Fiji citizens, with an international public service background, formulated a charter to assist the government in drawing up a national plan for a better Fiji. Thoughtful and visionary, *Building a Better Fiji for All: A People's Charter for Change and Progress* outlined steps and programs necessary to 'rebuild Fiji into a nonracial, culturally vibrant and united, well governed, truly

---

59 See Archbishop Petero Mataca, 'Let's put common good first', *Fiji Times*, 29 September 2006 where he expressed criticism of the Qarase Government's resource policies. See also his 'Reflections on democracy', *Fiji Times*, 3 July 2007, where he urges his readers not to be 'obsessed with being politically correct' about 'the legality of this or the illegality of that', but to ponder about 'higher goals'. For an early optimistic assessment of the coup, see Andrew Murray, 'Observations on the current situation in Fiji', 26 January 2007, typescript sent to the author. Murray is a Senior Lecturer in Philosophy at the Catholic Institute of Sydney.

democratic nation that seeks progress and prosperity through merit-based equality of opportunity and peace'.[60] The National Council itself would comprise 40 members, 25 from Fiji's civil society, 13 from the interim administration and two co-chairs.

The vision the charter endorses is unexceptionable. There can be no argument with the view that:

> the vast majority of Fiji's people aspire for and deserve a country, including a system of governance, that is characterised by stability, transparency and accountability, as well as the prevalence of law, order and peace.

Nor could one argue that:

> Fiji needs to become a more progressive and a truly democratic nation; a country in which its leaders, at all levels, emphasise national unity, racial harmony and the social and economic advancement of all communities regardless of race or ethnic origin.

The spirit of the vision enunciated by the council was already part of the 'compact' of the 1997 Constitution, which specified broad principles for the governance of the country. The real problem for Fiji was not the vision but the willingness of its leaders, both military and civilian, to respect the rule of law.

The council proposed to act as a moral watchdog over the policies and performance of the government. But what would be the role of the parliament or political parties in that case? And what if the policies of the elected government of the day were at variance with those espoused by the national council? Idealistic and utopian, the charter effectively sought to remove the practice of politics in the processes of governance. Madraiwiwi's questions were asked by many. 'Is this a genuine effort at drawing the people of Fiji together? Or is it merely an attempt by the Interim Government and its cohorts to cloak them in some mantle of popular acclaim?'[61]

---

60   The document was initially for restricted circulation but later posted on different websites, including *fijilive*.
61   Address in Canberra at The Australian National University, 5 June 2007.

There was a further question. Did an interim administration have the constitutional authority to promulgate policies of far-reaching significance? In an important ruling in 2001 concerning the legitimacy of the Asesela Ravuvu Constitution Review Committee appointed by the Qarase-led interim administration, Justice Anthony Gates wrote:

> Unusual programmes of expenditure or reformist projects are the prerogative of an elected government. A lawful government needs to be buttressed by holding the confidence of the House of Representatives, and by acting within the Constitution with the two other bodies of Parliament, namely, the Senate and the President. Moving in advance of the will of Parliament in reformist fields, however well-intentioned, is not an act which the courts will validate under the necessity doctrine. The authorisation for the expenditure of public funds for such reform work is similarly outside the permitted scope of work of a caretaker Cabinet. Such authorisation is unlawful.[62]

Justice Gates's views are as relevant to the case of the People's Charter promoted by the interim administration as they were in stopping the work of the Asesela Constitution Review Committee in 2001.

External response

The military had not expected the kind of uproar it provoked among Fiji's neighbours and international trading partners when it executed the coup. After all, its rationale for the military intervention was good governance, and the promotion of a 'corrupt-free' society. The military had not conducted a coup; it had started a 'clean-up' campaign. It was doing precisely what the aid agencies and neighbouring countries had wanted from the island governments all along. The reaction, particularly from Australia, New Zealand but also from the United States and the European Union, was sharp and unequivocal. Whether Australia and New Zealand could have done more to prevent the crisis remains an open question, though susceptible to doubt, given Bainimarama's disposition. Nonetheless, one observer remarked that 'Canberra appeared more intent on stopping a military intervention than addressing the causes of the deepening volatility', with John Howard's 'repeated support for

---

62   Quoted in Iyer, 'Courts and constitutional usurpers', 65.

his Fijian counterpart [giving] no incentive for Qarase to modify his domestic agenda'.⁶³ New Zealand's reaction was probably coloured by Bainimarama's reneging on a truce it had brokered between him and Qarase in late November 2006.

Both Australia and New Zealand condemned the military takeover in ringing terms, imposing travel bans on members of the interim administration, their families and all who accepted appointments from it or were identified as its sympathisers and supporters. The military's place was in the barracks, Australian Foreign Affairs Minister Alexander Downer told Bainimarama firmly, not in the political arena.⁶⁴ New Zealand banned all ministerial level talks with Fiji, tightened travel restrictions on military personnel and civil servants appointed by the interim administration, froze the new Recognised Seasonal Employer Scheme that would have provided Fiji workers temporary visas to work in New Zealand, cancelled training for Fiji soldiers, stopped new development assistance schemes and suspended training programs for Fiji's public sector under the regional governance programs.⁶⁵ A new low in diplomatic relations between Fiji and New Zealand was reached in mid-June 2007 when Fiji expelled New Zealand High Commissioner Michael Green for 'being in our face' since the coup, according to Bainimarama. Green was, by wide consensus, an exemplary diplomat, unobtrusive and informed and accessible to the public. The interim administration, citing the Geneva Convention, refused to elaborate.⁶⁶ As the *Fiji Times* put it:

> The military and the interim Government must have known that their actions were not going to be greeted with joy by much of the rest of the world. They must have known and expected criticism. Maybe it has been a harder road than they anticipated.⁶⁷

It had.

---

63 Richard Herr, 'External influences and the 2006 Fiji Military Coup', unpublished paper. See also Steven Ratuva, 'Coups and international reaction', posted on *fijilive*.
64 'Downer shares views on Fiji', *Fiji Times*, 22 June 2007.
65 'Fiji loses foreign friends', *Fiji Sun*, 12 December 2006.
66 In April 2007, Bainimarama refused to see a visiting senior US State Department official and threatened to open up Loftus Street (where the American embassy is located) to the public, only to retract his threat when the enormity of the consequences of his action dawned upon him. So the threat of reprisal against foreign embassies was not new.
67 Editorial, *Fiji Times*, 15 June 2007; Bainimarama's reaction is reported in the *Fiji Times*, 19 June 2007.

The travel bans had an immediate and decisive effect. Many qualified people in Fiji had refused appointment from the interim administration for fear of being banned from travelling to the countries where many had close families. Many senior civil servants and police vied for lucrative jobs in international organisations and security contracts with international security services that they did not wish to risk. Labour mobility was a fact of life in Fiji and the diasporic dimension of the crisis was real. Travel bans had similarly discouraged foreign nationals from accepting positions in administrations that their own countries regard as illegal. This created a conundrum. Australia and New Zealand wanted to promote good governance and a speedy return to parliamentary democracy and yet their (perfectly understandable) policies and reactions hindered the outcome they desired. On the Fijian side, a military that had overthrown a democratically elected government professed puzzlement at the reaction of the international community to its extralegal action despite its planned promotion of good governance, even if it was under the cover of guns. Was there room for a middle course between indignation and engagement, between the legitimate defence of fundamental principles on the one hand and a pragmatic appreciation of the realities on the ground on the other? A 'slowly recuperating constitutional convalescent' needed all the help it could get.[68]

The countries of the Pacific Islands reacted cautiously to the coup in the beginning. A meeting of the Melanesian Spearhead Group's Ministers of Foreign Affairs in Honiara in mid-January 2007 saw the Fiji crisis as essentially an 'internal matter' to be resolved by the people of Fiji itself, warning against any foreign intervention.[69] Its response was probably coloured by the Melanesian countries' criticism of Australia's policy in the region, especially its mounting confrontation with the Solomon Island Sogovare Government and a diplomatic rift with Papua New Guinea. But their limited and vague support was short-lived when it dawned on them that Fiji's sickness was bad for regional cooperation generally. The hard line adopted by Australia and New Zealand might also have shifted their thinking. On 1 December 2006, the Forum Foreign Affairs Ministers met in Sydney to discuss the impending crisis and resolved to send an Eminent Persons Group (EPG) to Fiji to assess the underlying causes and the nature of the overthrow of the Qarase Government, and

---

68   These apposite words are Rod Alley's, Private communication, 20 June 2007.
69   MSG Ministers of Foreign Affairs Meeting: Outcome Statement, 13 January 2007; Also *Radio New Zealand International*, 15 January 2007.

'to recommend steps towards the restoration of democratic government, within the boundaries of the Constitution and the rule of law'.[70] The four-person EPG was chaired by Vanuatu's Foreign Affairs Minister and Deputy Prime Minister Sato Kilman and comprised Faumuina Liuga, Samoa's Minister for Natural Resources and Environment, Sir Arnold Amet, retired Chief Justice of Papua New Guinea, and General Peter Cosgrove, retired Chief of the Australian Defence Force.

The EPG report was blunt. The military takeover of the Qarase Government was 'unconstitutional and unacceptable', it said. The military should retreat to the barracks and civilian rule be restored as soon as possible, Bainimarama should vacate the position of interim prime minister and the state of emergency should be lifted. Further, the EPG report called on the military to continue to uphold the constitution, respect Fiji's domestic and international obligations, cease interference in the work of the judiciary and other accountable institutions and to end all abuse of human rights. The interim administration was asked to adopt a 'roadmap with measurable milestones, which included holding general elections between eighteen months to two years, if not sooner', and delink the military's 'clean-up campaign from a national time-table for elections except in those areas directly related to the electoral process'.[71]

The interim administration's response to the EPG report was measured,[72] with the Forum Foreign Affairs Ministers meeting in Vila on 6 March 2007 recommending that the forum maintain a 'staged process of engagement with the interim administration'.[73] To that end, the ministers set up a 'Pacific Islands Forum–Fiji Joint Working Group on the situation in Fiji' among whose task it was to assess whether an election could be held based on the current boundaries and registered within the time frame

---

70 This formed the core of the EPG's Terms of Reference. The report, marked for 'Forum Eyes Only: Confidential', was leaked to the media and published on the internet the moment it was printed and long before it was formally submitted to the Forum Ministers' meeting for their deliberation. Such is the reach and power of the internet.
71 I have a copy in my possession. It should also be available in the National Archives in Suva. I was brought over from Canberra to meet with the Eminent Persons Group in Suva.
72 Although the Fijian wing of the Fiji Labour Party described the EPG report as 'a piece of rubbish', its spokesperson, Maika Moroca, said: 'The so-called Forum Persons Group can go to hell with their report because it does not hold recommendations that are constructive enough to enable Fiji's economic recovery and return to democratic rule without corruption' (*Fiji Times,* 20 February 2007). It is highly unlikely that this statement could have been released without the tacit approval of the party hierarchy.
73 Forum Foreign Affairs Ministers' Meeting, 16 March 2007, Port Vila, 'Outcome Statement', PIFS (07) FFAMM.3.

specified by the EPG.[74] The group reported in May that 'from a technical point of view', parliamentary elections could be held in the first quarter of 2009, or even earlier (November 2008) if the Bureau of Statistics was able to conduct an earlier census. The second major recommendation was for 'minimal changes to the current electoral provisions and procedures before the next election'. Only those changes designed to reduce or eliminate abuse in the campaign and the voting process to 'reflect the voter's clear intention' were to be contemplated.

The group's recommendation conflicted with the interim administration's own Road Map for the Return to Parliamentary Democracy.[75] According to that document, Fiji would be ready for general elections and full restoration of parliamentary democracy only in 2010 (or possibly later), after the country's finances were stabilised, the economy resuscitated and electoral boundaries drawn up after a new census. The interim administration also envisaged a review of the constitution to rid it of 'provisions that facilitate and exacerbate the politics of race'. But these fundamental changes, desirable though they might be, could not legitimately be undertaken by the interim administration—that was the responsibility of an elected parliament. Whatever else may be the case, the next general elections in Fiji would have to be held under the 1997 Constitution.

After weeks of silence, Bainimarama issued a confusing series of statements in mid-June. First, he rejected any externally imposed timeframe for holding the next general election.[76] Fiji, and not the international community, would decide when the elections were to be held, he said. Two days later, he told a news conference that elections would be held after the 'President's Mandate' (see above) had been fulfilled and the objectives of December 2006 accomplished.[77] A day later, he agreed, 'in principle' that general elections could be held within the time frame specified by the EPG provided the international community lent Fiji a helping hand.

---

74 The Group was chaired by Papua New Guinea's High Commissioner to Fiji. The Expert Group was co-chaired by Dr Paul Harris (NZ) and Barrie Sweetman (Fiji). Its two other members were Dr Kesaia Seniloli (Fiji) and Bruce Hatch (Canada). Titled 'Report of the Independent Assessment of the Electoral Process in Fiji, 14–25 May 2007', it is available on *fijilive* and other websites, though this document, like many others cited in this essay, was sent to me by email.
75 Described in a speech by Commodore Bainimarama at the Queen Elizabeth Barracks on 20 February 2007.
76 'We will say when elections to be held, says interim PM', *Fiji Times,* 17 June 2007.
77 Interview on *FijiVillage.com,* 19 June 2007.

Whether this was a genuine commitment or a tactical ploy to deflect public criticism remains to be seen. Australia and New Zealand remained unconvinced. The *Fiji Times* wrote:

> It is very likely now that Australia, New Zealand and other democratic countries that deal with us will take a much closer look at the situation and withdraw even further, taking with them more of their aid money and their trade.
>
> ...
>
> Where they will differ from the views held by Commodore Bainimarama is that they will see a former democratic country now ruled by the gun, no matter what 'shopfront' the regime puts up. Military men are in most of the key positions of power in the civil service and the interim Cabinet cannot be seen as independent.[78]

The timing of the general election was crucial in the context of Fiji's ongoing aid negotiations with the EU, which matters to Fiji. Fiji sells sugar to it under a preferential agreement, and its aid to Fiji's ailing sugar industry is estimated at around FJ\$400 million.[79] In April 2007, when a Fiji delegation led by Foreign Affairs Minister Ratu Epeli Nailatikau (and comprising Finance Minister Mahendra Chaudhry and Attorney-General Aiyaz Saiyed-Khayium) went to Brussels, the EU reiterated Article 9 of the African, Caribbean, Pacific – European Community (ACP–EC) Cotonou Agreement that 'Respect for human rights, democratic principles and the rule of law constitute the essential elements of the Partnership Agreement'.[80] The EU undertook to 'continue and deepen the political dialogue with Fiji' provided certain conditions were met. These included respect for democratic principles, including holding parliamentary elections by March 2009, consulting widely within Fiji before adopting major legislative changes, respecting the rule of law and protecting human rights and the fundamental freedoms of its citizens, and protecting the independence and integrity of the judiciary, among other similar undertakings. Any derogation from the undertaking Fiji had given would jeopardise future aid to Fiji. This fear haunted the nation— the loss of aid for an industry whose collapse would cripple the country. The EU (and Australia and New Zealand for that matter) would not relax

---

78   Editorial, *Fiji Times,* 18 June 2007.
79   See *Fiji Sun,* 10 May 2007.
80   This comes from 'Opening of Consultations with the Republic of Fiji Islands under Article 96 of the Cotonou Agreement (Brussels), 18 April 2007'.

sanctions until Fiji went beyond the 'in-principle' undertaking it had given to returning Fiji to parliamentary democracy within the specified time frame. The EU's Commissioner for External Relations Benita Ferrero-Waldner had said that the 'most important thing is to see whether the commitment will materialise'.[81] Frustrated with outside pressure to meet the deadlines and honour its undertakings, Bainimarama threatened to postpone elections indefinitely.[82] That would compound Fiji's already considerable economic problems, and corrode its vital relationship with its powerful neighbours.

Warfare in cyberspace

The reaction to the 2006 coup was different from responses to previous coups in many ways, but one is novel: the intervention of cyberspace. In 1987, the latest invention was the facsimile machine, which allowed the military effectively to shut down Fiji's contact with the outside. In 2000, the national boundaries were more porous with the advent of email, transmitting massive amounts of information in real time. In 2006, the most notable innovation was the emergence of 'blogsites', enabling ordinary people with access to the internet worldwide opportunities to exchange news, ideas, information and comments about political developments in Fiji without the mediation of state licensing or the authorisation of the gatekeepers and agenda-setters of the mass media.[83] The speed of cyber communication was astounding—and confounding.

The sites differed in the depth and range of coverage and commentary, but all condemned the coup to varying degrees. Many carried opinions and information in the Fijian language, which suggests that they were run by indigenous Fijians or others intimately familiar with Fiji language, culture and protocol. As with cyberspace generally,[84] some of what passed for accurate information or analysis was petty prejudiced and partial,

---

81 'EU/Australia agree on sanctions', *fijilive*, 26 June 2007.
82 'Critics put elections in limbo: Bainimarama', *fijilive*, 3 July 2007.
83 These are too numerous to mention but among the more prominent ones are: *Why Fiji is Crying, Rere Vaka Na Kalou Ka doka Na Tui, Intelligentsya, Name and Shame, Discombobulated.*
84 An introduction to some of the complex issues raised by the use of cyberspace is in Steven Gan, James Gomez and Uwe Johannen (eds), *Asian Cyberactivism: Freedom of Expression and Media Censorship* (Bangkok: Friederic Naumann Foundation, 2004).

sometimes defamatory, frequently vituperative, always provocative, on occasions treasonous.[85] One website, on 20 June 2007, advised its readers thus:

> Destabilize the country. Make it ungovernable. Every act of resistance you engage in makes it difficult for the regime to govern and stay in control. The government is economically unstable, so your objective should be to complete destabilize that economic fulcrum.[86]

Attack businesses that make money for the regime, the site encouraged its readers. 'Attack their assets.' A few days later, the same website encouraged its readers to attack tourists to bring that industry to its knees. Other sites named and shamed people that they thought had supported the coup. Yet others sought to foster dissent in the ranks of the military. The enemy was identified, targeted, vilified, judged and hanged. It was verbal warfare at its most brutal and visceral.

When they first appeared, most sites condemned the coup as the work of a power-crazed 'military junta'. But with time, and especially after Madraiwiwi's address in early June 2007, a new interpretation began to emerge, insidiously portraying the military overthrow as an 'Indian' coup against the Fijian people. Chaudhry was identified as the villain of the piece and he became the object of vitriolic anger of the anticoup bloggers. In the minds of most anticoup bloggers, Chaudhry's connection to the coup had been irrevocably established. The blogsites seemed to reflect a wider, developing Fijian view of the coup as being fundamentally anti-Fijian as opposed to being anti the Qarase Government. Bainimarama's derisive treatment of the GCC touched a raw nerve and inflamed passions, which may have proved difficult to subdue in the short term. A potentially dangerous chasm, with grave implications for future interethnic accommodation, seemed to be opening.

---

85   And witty and humorous too. Thus: 'Machiavelli Chaudhry', 'Bainimahendra', 'Komanda Bai Karaik', 'Commodore Frankenstein' (Bainimarama), 'Rebel without a clue' (military spokesman Major Leweni Neumi), RFMF: 'Ratu Frank's Military Force', 'Pusi': Helen Clark, 'Big Moma Bernie': Bernadette Rounds-Ganilau, Laufitu 'Zsa Zsa Gabor' Malani, and others too impolite to repeat.
86   This site from which this quote was taken has since been disestablished, but similar views were common on most anticoup websites.

Where to now?

With the lifting of the Public Emergency Regulation on 1 June 2007, the first phase of the crisis came to an end. In that period, there were violations of human rights that brought condemnation from local activists as well as international organisations. There was evident tension in the vital organs of the state, as well as fear and uncertainty in the public sector as people were fired or sent on leave pending investigation. Prosecutions were still pending. The violent deaths of young Fijian men in either military or police custody—Nimilote Varebasaga, Sakiusa Rabaka and Tevita Malasabe—aroused profound public anger and anguish about the 'stunning sounds of silence from top-down',[87] and about the slow pace of investigation into the tragedies. The blame was laid at the door of the interim administration. The state of law and order was critical to its future.

There were other challenges as well. For a start, a number of cases contesting the legality of the military takeover were to come before the courts in the next few months. On the face of it, the verdict looked certain. How could it be otherwise? But whether the military would respect the ruling was another matter. Bainimarama had made it abundantly clear that 'Qarase will not come back', while the deposed prime minister was determined to remain in political harness, convinced, with justification, that he had the support of the silent Fijian majority. Whether the verdict of the courts would unravel the initiatives instigated by the interim administration (such as the Fiji Independent Commission Against Corruption) and order the status quo reinstated, or whether the military would simply abrogate the constitution to legalise the revolution it began, remained questions to be watched closely. Equally closely watched were to be the interim administration's various commitments to donor organisations, such as the EU, particularly about returning Fiji to early parliamentary democracy. The international community was not likely to let up on Fiji anytime soon. Neither was it lulled into complacency by insincere promises.

If returning the country to parliamentary democracy is one major challenge for the interim administration and for the people of Fiji as a whole, another is to revive the economy. The ailing state of Fiji's sugar industry, requiring regular and massive infusion of funds, is too well known to require mention. A lot would depend on Fiji abiding by the

---

87 Editorial, *Daily Post*, 13 June 2007.

undertaking it had given to the EU. The severe downturn in the tourism industry, expected after the coup, dented Fiji's economic prospects, though it would bounce back with political stability. The Governor of the Reserve Bank of Fiji, Savenaca Narube, identified three other major challenges to the Fijian economy.[88] The first was the low rate of growth at around 2.4 per cent over the previous five years, whereas double that rate would be needed to absorb the school-leaving population. The second challenge was to raise the investment in the economy to over 25 per cent of the gross domestic product, and to promote more local investment. And the third was to narrow the widening gap between import and export. None of these problems was insurmountable, but the atmosphere of uncertainty and anxiety about the country's future, the deepening unemployment and poverty levels in the country (around 34 per cent in 2002–03 from around 29 per cent in 1991)[89] would make their resolution difficult. With talks of retaliatory trade and aid bans in the air, wrote the *Fiji Times*:

> the nation watches as the economy continues to slump and more families feel the effects of redundancies, reduced working hours, pay cuts and the reduction of financial assistance meant for the poor and the underprivileged.[90]

Fiji subsequently experienced an emotional rollercoaster ride for 12 months. First there were the general elections conducted, by wide consensus, in a free and fair manner. Then there was the euphoria caused by the advent of the multiparty Cabinet. Genuine multiethnic reconciliation seemed within reach. But then came the coup and with it a drastically altered landscape. The interim administration made a strenuous, but ultimately failed, attempt to entrench itself in the public consciousness as an instrument for the good of the country. Some of its leading lights were too tainted by chequered pasts or private ambitions for power and glory to have any chance of winning public affection or esteem. Important institutions of the state were politicised, their impartiality impaired, their effectiveness undermined. A third of the nation lived in poverty. Squatter settlements mushroomed. An escalating war of words between

---

88 'Economic crisis looms', *Fiji Sun,* 12 May 2007.
89 Wadan Narsey, 'Truth behind our poverty', *Fiji Times,* 10 June 2007. For a more extensive treatment, see Satish Chand, 'Poverty and redistributive politics in post-independence Fiji: 50/50 by 2020', manuscript in my possession, courtesy of the author.
90 Editorial, 'Keeping a promise', *Fiji Times,* 21 June 2007. For a brief survey of postcoup economic trends, see Biman C. Prasad, 'Fiji's economy in the doldrums: Possibilities for a way forward?' presented to the Pacific Cooperation Foundation, Wellington, Seminar, Fiji at the Crossroads – Again? 8 June 2007.

the interim administration's supporters and opponents filled the air (and cyberspace) about whether the coup was the best or the worst thing that could have happened to Fiji: whether Bainimarama was the saviour of the nation or its destroyer; whether, from the ashes of the coup, the phoenix would eventually rise in the form of a truly representative democracy unencumbered by the politics of race and ethnicity; whether, in the end, the coup was worth all the pain and suffering it caused. Time would tell. In the meantime, half of the Fiji population, disaffected, disenchanted and disapproving of the unfolding events, watched in sullen silence.

19
The strange career of a 'clean-up' coup[1]

> There should be no romanticism that international public opinion or even international diplomatic or economic pressure can defeat a coup without determined strong defense by the attacked society itself.
>
> — Gene Sharp and Bruce Jenkins[2]

This reflective piece, more in the nature of a short history, takes a look at the meandering journey of Bainimarama's coup from its inception to its conclusion, the responses it provoked and the manner in which it attained its goal. It repeats some of the points made in the earlier chapters.

The date, 5 December 2006, may well go down in the annals of modern Fijian history as the date when the country dramatically changed course; a turning point when the country finally turned. It is surely beyond dispute that the twentieth century, with its assumptions and understandings about the nature and structure of Fiji's political culture, effectively ended not in 2000, but in 2006 when Commodore Bainimarama executed his military coup. The break with the past was decisive and irreversible. An improbable coup had largely succeeded in destroying the foundations of the old order,

---
1 Originally appeared as 'The strange career of Commodore Frank Bainimarama's Fiji 2006 coup', in *State, Society and Governance in Melanesia Project Discussion Paper* 9/2013 (Canberra: The Australian National University, 2013).
2 Gene Sharp and Bruce Jenkins, *The Anti-Coup* (Cambridge, MA: Albert Einstein Institution, 2003), p. 36.

and a new one was promised to 'take the country forward'. Everyone accepted that a race-based electoral system was counterproductive for a multiethnic democratic society, that gender inequality in any shape or form was indefensible, that all citizens should have equal rights, and that citizenship should be race neutral. Change in a society, as in any living organism, is inevitable, constant, though often it is more easily asserted than actually effected. But the larger question inescapably is change for what purpose? To what end, at what pace, on whose terms, under what conditions, through what means, at what price? That was the conundrum at the heart of the political debate in Fiji. I will not attempt to answer that question here. My purpose is not to speculate about what Fiji's future might look like under Bainimarama, but to understand the constellation of forces that have served to consolidate the commodore's coup. That, I hope, may provide us with some pointers for the future.

Origins of the crisis

The roots of Fiji's political turbulence in the late twentieth century reach back to the origins of its modern history in 1874 when Fiji became a British Crown Colony. The policies that the colonial government enunciated at the time had the overall effect of creating a racially segregated society in which each of the three principal ethnic groups, the Fijians, the Indo-Fijians and the Europeans, had their own distinctive understandings of their place in the larger scheme of things. Fijians assumed, or were encouraged to assume, that in the governance of the colony their interests would remain paramount. Indo-Fijians, invoking promises made by both the imperial and the colonial governments, sought parity with other groups. And the Europeans claimed privilege on account of their preponderant contribution to the colonial economy and ethnic and cultural affinity with the ruling elite. The position hardened as independence approached in the 1960s, with the threat of violence, made periodically, to maintain the racially segregated order.

The essential features of that order were entrenched in the Independence Constitution of 1970 by the political leaders of the three communities. The constitution was never put to referendum or even an election but adopted after a feel-good, self-congratulatory debate in the House of

Representatives.[3] Fiji had a mix of racial and cross-racial seats whose logic dictated an appeal for unity in one's own community and fragmentation in the opposition's. This appeal was sufficient to form government. Fijian victory would be assured if Fijians remained politically united with the support of an over-represented European group, which the fear of 'Indian dominance' ensured. For a while, the formula worked. The mood in the immediate postindependence period was celebratory. Fiji was a 'symbol of hope to the world', Pope John Paul II had intoned during a fleeting visit in 1986, which eventually morphed into the national slogan, 'Fiji: The Way the World Should Be'.

In truth, of course, things were not as rosy. None of the underlying problems about the nature of power sharing among the different communities, the kind of political culture Fiji needed to have for its multiethnic population, whether a racial electoral system should continue, or the terms and conditions of leasing agricultural land, were resolved. Instead they were brushed aside by a government entrenched in power and likely to remain so for a long time.[4] The logic of racial politics inevitably dictated the political agenda of governance. In time, unsurprisingly, every issue of public policy, whether affirmative action in the allocation of tertiary scholarships, appointments to or promotion in the civil service, in diplomatic postings, the deployment of development aid, came to be viewed through the prism of ethnic interests. Indigenous Fijians demanded a bigger share of government largesse on the supposed grounds of being the more disadvantaged community, while the Indo-Fijians asked for a fairer share of state resources based on need rather than ethnicity. By the late 1970s and early 1980s, the two ethnic groups were not as homogenous as they had been portrayed to be, divided by class and regional interests, and by ancient prejudices and modern greed. Disadvantage stalked Fijian and Indo-Fijian communities in roughly equal measure. Public perceptions and policies were markedly at variance with the reality on the ground.

Race was only one of the facts of life, not *the* fact of life as the leading politicians of the day proclaimed from the self-created safety of their ethnic compartments. But racial politics became the order of the day

---

3   See Brij V. Lal (ed.), *Fiji: British Documents on the End of the Empire* (London: The Stationery Office, 2006); see also Brij V. Lal, *Broken Waves: A History of the Fiji Islands in the Twentieth Century* (Honolulu: University of Hawaii Press, 1992), pp. 212–13.
4   Lal, *Broken Waves*.

with Fijians determined not to relinquish or even equitably share power with others. Tension simmered beneath the surface, frequently threatening to erupt at election times. The signs of imminent rupture were visible throughout the 1970s and 1980s.[5] They were there when Sakeasi Butadroka launched his 'Fiji for Fijians' Fijian Nationalist Party, with its platform to deport all Indo-Fijians to India. They were visible in the manufactured constitutional crisis of April 1977 when the ruling Alliance Party temporarily lost power to the National Federation Party because of a split in the indigenous Fijian communal vote. They were lurking beneath the surface in 1982 when the opposition came close to winning power, leading the Great Council of Chiefs (GCC) later that year to demand outright Fijian control of government. They came to the fore in May 1987 when a democratically elected multiracial Labour Coalition Government was ousted in a military coup with the quiet support of the luminaries of the Fijian establishment. They were present in the 1990 Constitution, which put political power back in the hands of the Fijians. They were present on the sullen faces of many nationalist-leaning Fijian parliamentarians who voted for the 1997 Constitution and then promptly orchestrated a campaign against it. And they were there in 2000 when George Speight attempted his improbable putsch, which deposed another Labour Coalition Government. Throughout the 1990s, as in the 1960s, the battle lines were drawn between those who wanted the political architecture of Fiji to reflect indigenous concerns and aspirations entrenched in the constitution itself and those who favoured a more democratic, inclusionary model of nonracial polity. Fiji was revisiting the unresolved debates of the earlier decades. Bainimarama promised finally to close the door on the obsessive and enormously counterproductive racial politics of the past.

The transformation scene

Fiji on the eve of the 2006 coup was a very different place to what it had been in 1987. The changes had a direct bearing on the fate of the Bainimarama coup. Among the factors that changed the fundamental character of the broader Fiji society was the demographic transformation in the country. In 1987, Indo-Fijians were around 49 per cent of the total population, but since then the percentage has declined substantially

---

5   ibid.

because of a continuing lower birth rate and increased emigration. Now, they are around 30–34 per cent of the population and declining (the latest 2017 Census has dispensed with racial categories for population data). Any Indo-Fijian who can leave will leave. That is the incontrovertible truth about contemporary Fiji. Indigenous Fijians (*iTaukei*), on the other hand, are closer to 60 per cent of the population, and confident of continued demographic dominance. The changed demographic equation has forever disappeared the expediently manufactured threat of 'Indian domination' that cast such a dark shadow over political debate in Fiji for much of the twentieth century. The 'wolves at the door' syndrome is dead. The second important consequence of the change is the opening up of space for democratic debate within Fijian society itself about issues once considered taboo: the relevance of the chiefly system; its privileges and priorities; its role in the modern political arena; and about the distribution of power, about the barriers and boundaries that kept people apart. It is a change with profound implications both for indigenous Fijians as well as for Fiji.

The years leading up to the 2006 coup were unhappy ones for Indo-Fijians. Governments elected with their support were unceremoniously deposed, not once but twice. They faced the wrath of militant Fijian nationalists (in the Taukei Movement, for example, led by Apisai Tora and Inoke Kubuabola), the religious extremism of the Methodist Church led by Manasa Lasaro, Viliame Gonelevu and Tomasi Raikivi, among others. They were deprived of fundamental human rights in the 1990 Constitution and in the racially discriminatory programs that flowed from it. Sitiveni Rabuka, many felt, was bad enough, even though he had publicly apologised for his actions in 1987, and helped bring about a fairer, more democratic constitution in 1997. But Laisenia Qarase, eventually deposed by Bainimarama, was not much better. Though a well-educated man and long-term head of the Fiji Development Bank, he extended the scope of the racially discriminatory policies of affirmative action in his so-called Fijian 'blueprint', let his ministers go unreprimanded for making racially provocative speeches in parliament (one of them, Asenaca Caucau, called Indo-Fijians 'noxious weeds') and gave the overall impression of caring little about non-Fijians. In his second term, with an eye on the verdict of history, he changed, became more inclusive and gave the Labour Party senior portfolios under the power-sharing provisions of the 1997 Constitution, but by then it was too late; the cup of Indo-Fijian disillusionment had been overflowing for some time. Among those most deeply embittered by Qarase's reign were Indo-Fijians who had left Fiji in personally unhappy circumstances. They never forgave him. Instead, they looked to Bainimarama to right the wrongs of the past and supported his military adventure from the comfort and safe distance of their overseas homes.

Those Indo-Fijians who remained in Fiji were trapped in despair and hopelessness, disillusioned by the bitter wrangling of heightened racial politics of which they were invariably on the receiving end. Many agricultural leases that began to expire under the *Agricultural Landlord and Tenant Act* were not renewed, the formerly productive farm land reverting to bush.[6] Some Fijian landowners wanted to enter commercial agriculture themselves, but other leases were not renewed for political reasons as a punishment for Indo-Fijians' refusal to accept Fijian political paramountcy. The idea that land was power, Fijian power, was well understood and opportunistically deployed. Whole areas in the sugar belt emptied. Most displaced tenants searched for a place in the mushrooming squatter settlements fringing urban centres, looking for jobs and opportunities that were rare even at the best of times. This is where around 15–20 per cent of Fiji's population now lives, most below the poverty line. Among the poorest people in Fiji are landless Indo-Fijian labourers. Given their predicament, it is understandable why they responded to Bainimarama's call to end corruption in Fiji and chart a new course. Many belatedly realised that little has changed in the new regime: the cast of characters was different, but the overall pattern of things was much the same. But Bainimarama remained their man, their buffer against a whole variety of forces arrayed against them, including the wrath of *iTaukei* nationalists. That unspoken fear was a powerful cementer of support behind the regime. But how long would Fijian military power shield Indo-Fijians and others from Fijian nationalists? Sooner rather than later, the realisation would dawn that democracy and the rule of law, rather than the rule of one man, is the best guarantor of citizens' rights.

Indigenous Fijian society was similarly undergoing profound social and economic changes in the 1980s and 1990s. Geographer Gerard Ward writes:

> The contradiction in native Fijian village economy and life are far more marked in the mid-1980s than in the mid-1960s. The choice in favour of change has probably been made already, even

---

6 Padma Narsey Lal, *Ganna: Profile of the Fiji Sugar Industry* (Lautoka: Fiji Sugar Commission, 2008).

if unconsciously in most cases. The test will be whether or not the social and political attitudes and policies can change quickly enough to keep up. If the coherence of native Fijian society and its hierarchical structure is a pillar of native Fijian political and economic systems, it is a pillar whose foundations and inherent strength are being weakened to an extent which is not always recognised by politicians or planners.[7]

On the contrary, Fijian political leaders and their advisors were still refurbishing the old system, trying to stem the tide of change against archaic structures whose time had long passed.

By the early 2000s, the urban drift was moving apace, with nearly 40 per cent of indigenous Fijians living in urban or peri-urban areas, exposed to all its challenges and opportunities. A more modern-minded Fijian middle class of self-made men and women was beginning to emerge, ironically benefiting from the affirmative action policies of previous Fijian governments. Fijian children were attending so-called 'Indian' schools, such as Suva Sangam, Suva Muslim High, Indian College, Mahatma Gandhi Memorial and others in larger numbers than ever before even though the Qarase Government was providing special assistance to only Fijian-designated schools. This was a far cry from the days when Fijian children attended only designated indigenous Fijian schools for fear of losing their culture and in response to various incentives provided by organs of the Fiji Administration. The break with the past was not abrupt, but there was sufficient movement to indicate a gradual shift to a new way of life in a new environment. Many in this group were now ready to listen to the self-empowering rhetoric Bainimarama employed when he took over.

Ward referred to the hierarchical structure of the native Fijian society. That structure, as O.H.K. Spate pointed out as early as 1959, was fast losing its relevance in the face of modern challenges.[8] It had had its uses in the past, providing guidance and leadership to a people living in the rural subsistence sector and effectively isolated from the broader social and economic environment, but had become a burden when borders and boundaries of Fijian society were becoming porous and all too

---

7   R. Gerard Ward, 'Native Fijian villages: A questionable future?' in *Fiji: Future Imperfect*, ed. Michael Taylor (Sydney: Allen & Unwin, 1987), pp. 33–45, at p. 45.
8   O.H.K. Spate, *The Fijian People: Economic Problems and Prospects* (Suva: Government of Fiji Legislative Council Paper 13, 1959), pp. 6–7.

often transgressed with impunity. The chiefs were losing their role as the gatekeepers of their people, and many lacked the skills to make them relevant to the requirements of the modern age influenced by forces of change fundamentally beyond their comprehension. When Bainimarama pushed them aside and abolished the GCC altogether, there were obligatory murmurs of protest, but its disbandment was not universally mourned among ordinary Fijians who could now begin to dream of their own place in the sun. The chiefly abuse of power and privilege over the decades had taken its toll on the loyalty and unquestioning support of their people.

Paramount chiefs ruled the Fijian roost throughout the twentieth century. Until his death in 1958, Ratu Sir Lala Sukuna was the unchallenged voice of his people in the councils of state, most notably as Secretary for Fijian Affairs in postwar Fiji.[9] In the second half of the century, the most prominent high chiefs were Ratu George Cakobau, the Vunivalu of Bau, Ratu Edward Cakobau, Ratu Penaia Ganilau and Ratu Kamisese Mara. They, and especially Mara, were groomed for national political leadership by the departing British.[10] Their large, looming presence on the national stage promoted the impression of Fijian political unity against the ever-present 'threat' of Indian domination. They were also like the banyan tree under which nothing much grew. But the coup of 1987, carried out ostensibly to preserve the unity and chiefly leadership of the Fijian people, and silently blessed by the leading chiefs of the day, unwittingly unravelled the carefully crafted structures of traditional Fijian leadership. The illusion of their invincibility and indispensability to the nation's future, carefully nurtured until then, was gone. Sitiveni Rabuka's ascendancy in the 1990s brought him in direct conflict with Ratu Mara, who had his own dynastic ambitions as well as his well-known view that the business of government was rightfully the prerogative of the chiefs. The clash between the two men reflected a larger subterranean tension in indigenous Fijian society; a larger clash of class interests. In any event, by 2006, all the paramounts were gone. Their progenies lacked lustre and national presence, there were no clear successors in sight, and many chiefs were variously embroiled in personal controversies over matrimonial and financial matters. There was thus a clear vacuum when Bainimarama arrived on the scene. As well as

---

9   Deryck Scarr, *Ratu Sukuna: Soldier, Statesman, Man of Two Worlds* (London: Macmillan Education, 1980).
10 Deryck Scarr, *Tuimacilai: A Life of Ratu Sir Kamisese Mara* (Adelaide: Crawford House Publishing, 2008).

having the backing of the military, he had few competitors. In time, many chiefs who had initially opposed the coup apologised to Bainimarama and sought forgiveness for their impudence, no doubt in the expectation of some reward from the regime. Why else would chiefs ask forgiveness from a man who had so brazenly undermined their status and power?

The world of Fiji in 2006 clearly was vastly different to the Fiji that existed in the 1970s or even the 1980s. Travel and technology had revolutionised people's perceptions of themselves and the world in which they lived. Work places and playing fields had become more multiracial. Television was a prominent presence in most homes and so, too, by the first decade of the twenty-first century was the internet (email, Facebook, blogsites). Old ways had lost their meaning and relevance. The citizens of Fiji were also citizens of the virtual world of Googlisthan and open to new ideas. The real irony was that high chiefs themselves, such as Ratu Epeli Nailatikau, the military-appointed President of Fiji, joined in the chorus of denunciation of chiefly privileges and prerogatives of which they themselves were long-time beneficiaries. Whether this was rank opportunism (they had few employable skills) or genuine conversion it is difficult to say.

Commodore Bainimarama

Enter Commodore Frank Bainimarama. Born on 27 April 1954, he had joined the Fijian navy in 1975, rising through the ranks to become the Chief of Staff of the Republic of Military Forces in November 1997, and its commander two years later when Brigadier General Ratu Epeli Ganilau, whose protégé he was, resigned to enter national politics—unsuccessfully as it turned out. Most observers have expressed surprise at the rapid rise and promotion of this unprepossessing naval officer from an unspectacular background. He was thought to be close to the Ganilau–Mara nexus of traditional Fijian politics. How mistaken that perception was became clear later; instead of being their guardian, he became their arch nemesis. As subsequent events would show, and keeping in tune with his characteristic mode of operation, he used the connection to ensconce himself in power, but then jettisoned it when it had outlived its usefulness. The old adage applies to him aptly: he has no permanent friends, just permanent interests. Now, subverting the old cultural order, the chiefs were doing his bidding, not the other way around. What Bainimarama lacked in formal education, he more than made up for in his finely honed skills of survival. There was no nuance or subtlety in his starkly etched view of the world. Dialogue and debate were alien to his nature.[11] He demonstrated again and again that it would be his way and no other way.

The first time Bainimarama came to prominence was in May 2000 during the Speight-led insurrection when Mahendra Chaudhry's Labour Government was held hostage in the Fijian parliamentary complex for 56 days. The military appeared at the time to be hobbled by internal divisions and provincial loyalties, completely at sea about how to contain the hostage crisis. To end the siege, Bainimarama signed an agreement (Muanikau Accord) with the Speight rebels to release all hostages, including Chaudhry, and surrender under immunity. He later repudiated the deal, though not for the last time, and Speight landed in jail. That was his modus operandi. During the same crisis, Bainimarama had led a delegation of senior military officers, including Brigadier General Ratu Epeli Ganilau and Brigadier General Sitiveni Rabuka, to ask President Mara to vacate his office in the interests of resolving the hostage crisis. That itself became a controversial initiative and the subject of further police investigation. Had Bainimarama committed a coup against the president? Mara's enforced and bitterly resented departure ended the century-old reign of the Tovata confederacy. It is not likely to return any time soon, if ever.

The other crucial event took place in November 2000, which scarred Bainimarama's life profoundly, according to those familiar with him. This was the mutiny in the Fiji military in which several loyalist soldiers were killed, with Bainimarama himself barely managing to escape assassination.[12] It was a scenario no one had previously imagined of Fijian soldiers spilling Fijian blood on Fijian soil. Bainimarama wanted the rebel soldiers caught and brought to justice—Fijian style. Several were brutally bashed to death, their bodies battered beyond recognition. The manner in which the mutiny was quashed caused public distress (and horror), but the commodore was determined to stamp his authority on the military by whatever means he could. To that end, he demanded a personal oath of loyalty to himself as the commander, not to the institution of the military.

---

11   Michael Green, *Persona Non Grata: Breaking the Bond: Fiji and New Zealand, 2004–2007* (Auckland: Dunmore Publishing Ltd, 2013).
12   Jone Baledrokadroka, 'Sacred king and warrior chief: The role of the military in Fiji politics', PhD thesis (Canberra: The Australian National University, 2013).

Those who could not oblige were sent packing, including several senior officers. There was no further dissent. The military became Bainimarama's unchallenged power base, ready and willing to do his bidding whatever that might be. And he rewarded that loyalty generously. 'I will always stand by my men,' he said repeatedly, to the delight of those under his charge but to the dismay of those who wanted perpetrators of violence to be brought to justice.

It was over the Qarase Government's handling of the military that permanently alienated the commodore from the government and strengthened his resolve to remove it from office. A new government elected in 2000 and headed by Qarase, initially with Bainimarama's endorsement, won office with the support of the Christian Alliance Matanitu ni Vanua (CAMV), a party supporting Speight and seeking his release from gaol and amnesty for other coup conspirators. To that end, the Qarase Government promised a Promotion of Reconciliation, Tolerance and Unity Bill to grant compensation to the victims of the 2000 coup and amnesty to its perpetrators. It was promoted as an effort to foster genuine healing and unity, but it was on all accounts an ill-advised move whose full significance and implications were not appreciated at the time. Bainimarama was incensed, and threatened to take action against the destabilisers. 'The military,' he said 'will dish out the same fate we dealt Speight and his group to anyone we think deserves this treatment.' He went further and threatened to sack the government. 'The RFMF must stop the Bill from passing or get rid of the Government if passed. We can recover without the Government; we cannot recover from the Bill.'[13]

There were other pieces of legislation, such as the Qoliqoli Bill to transfer the ownership of the foreshores from the Crown to its indigenous owners, which angered a large cross-section of the population, from small individual fishers to the barons of Fiji's powerful tourism industry. They orchestrated and financed opposition to it by supporting political groups, including the National Alliance Party of Fiji headed by Ratu Epeli Ganilau. Why was the Qarase Government in such a hurry to pass controversial legislation so early in its term and in the teeth of such fierce opposition, people asked? And why were political parties in government by virtue of the power-sharing provisions of the 1997 Constitution not consulted, especially the Fiji Labour Party? The main motivation, it

---

13 Republic of Military Forces, media release, n.d.

seems, was to placate the nationalist elements in the governing coalition, to prevent the tail wagging the dog. In the end, bowing to public pressure, the government agreed not to push ahead; but by then it was too late, the damage had been done. For many, Bainimarama's rhetoric became distinctly appealing. He emerged from the confrontation with his stature enhanced, as a figure on the side of the wider public standing against a corrupt government concerned only with its own survival.

For its part, the government tried to rein in an increasingly bellicose and belligerent Bainimarama. It sought in late 2006 to sack him, but the government's choice, Colonel Saubulinayau, a respected soldier, head of the Strategic Unit in Suva and former Acting Land Forces Commander, succumbed to the military's pressure to decline the Commission from the president; soon afterwards, he left the military for good. Bainimarama brushed aside a government-commissioned White Paper that recommended trimming the top-heavy end of the military. The government's decision not to renew Bainimarama's contract was similarly disregarded. Police Commissioner Andrew Hughes's investigation of Bainimarama's role in the crisis of 2000 was the last straw that broke the camel's back. By then, Bainimarama was far gone in his determination to sack the government. He wanted to strike before he was struck down. That he did on 5 December 2006.

The official narrative of the 2006 coup presents Bainimarama as a noble patriot motivated by nothing less than a passionate desire to clean the country of corruption and steady the course towards a united, prosperous, nonracial future, breaking decisively with the country's hobbled past and failed policies of nation building. He would return to the barracks once his mission was complete, he said; he had no interest in politics; a political career had never entered his mind, he declared—as all illegal usurpers of power do. No one in his interim administration would be standing for election so that decisions would not be tainted by allegations of political self-interest. Anyone wanting to serve alongside him would have to apply and would be selected on merit. His policies and programs would be open and transparent, above board. To a population subjected to a decade or more of corruption, abuse of office, the plundering of the public purse for petty political advantage, Bainimarama's words were music to the ear.

But soon the hopes vanished as old practices and patterns of behaviour returned. Government tenders were offered without a competitive process of assessment. Corruption was easy to allege but far more difficult to substantiate and successfully prosecute, as the regime-established Fiji Independent Commission Against Corruption (FICAC) found out. The same abuse of the judicial process occurred in getting favoured (or family-related) prisoners released early from jail. Allegations of massive interference with the judiciary refused to disappear despite the strenuous efforts of regime supporters. The auditor-general's report had not been released since 2007. The police force was placed under Bainimarama's deputy, Commodore Esala Teleni, who promptly sought to evangelise it with his fundamentalist Christian beliefs through the New Methodist Church headed by his brother Atu Vulaono.[14] He proclaimed town after town to be 'crime-free' in the face of massive evidence to the contrary and much public derision. Loyal senior military officers were placed in charge of strategic government departments to the bitter disappointment of career civil servants and contrary to Bainimarama's promise not to allow anyone to 'personally benefit' from his regime. In 2013, most of these senior military officers received astonishingly large salary increases—the largest in Fijian history. The politics of patronage was alive and well.

Beyond the rhetoric of 'clean-up' campaign, Bainimarama initially had no clear, overarching narrative for his military intervention. As it became clear later, the coup was more about saving Bainimarama's bacon than it was about saving the nation. As the regime was floundering around looking for justification, there entered a group of former Fiji technocrats with a plan to provide Bainimarama with an 'exit strategy'. The group was led by John Samy, a former Fiji economist and recently retired from the Asian Development Bank—as bona fide a technocrat as any—with a resolve to correct the mistakes of the past. His career in the Fiji civil service had unceremoniously ended in 1987, to his enduring bitterness. He now wanted to return to Fiji to give 'something' back, at a modest fee of FJ$12,000 tax-free per month. He helped establish a National Council for Building a Better Fiji in 2007 to make recommendations to create a just and fair society, promote unity and national identity, have transparent and accountable government, ameliorate the condition of the disadvantaged in all communities, mainstream indigenous Fijians in a progressive society, and share interfaith dialogue. These values were generally included in the 1997 Constitution but had to be reiterated anew to provide an appearance of newness to the military regime.

---

14 Lynda Newland, 'The new Methodism and old: Churches, police and state in Fiji, 2008–2009', in *The Round Table: The Commonwealth Journal of International Affairs* 101(6) (2012): 537–55, doi.org/10.1080/00358533.2012.749094.

In August 2008, the council published its People's Charter for Change, Peace and Prosperity. The charter was based on a number of 'pillar principles', which included, among others, the abolition of the racial voting characteristic of Fiji that had been used for much of the twentieth century, the adoption of a proportional representation voting system, and entrenching the principles of good, accountable, transparent governance, and effective delivery of public services—all unexceptionable aspirational goals. The charter proposed that its principles be incorporated into the 1997 Constitution, which, it said, would continue to remain the supreme law of the land. That work completed, the constitutional impasse would come to an end, the army would return to the barracks and the country would be prepared for the next general elections. The charter would become Bainimarama's exit strategy. Nothing of the sort happened.

The charter charade, with all its obvious flaws and faults, had bought Bainimarama valuable time to consolidate his position. It had given his military adventure an aura of purposefulness and the charter a tentative nod of approval from the international community. The Commonwealth Secretariat lauded his proposal to start a political dialogue with key stakeholders, including the various political parties. It sent its envoy, Sir Paul Reeves, the former chair of the Fiji Constitution Review Commission, to facilitate the process, but he was ignored by the regime, and the dialogue process unceremoniously dumped in characteristic Bainimarama fashion. He adopted the charter principles as the foundation of his 'Roadmap Back to Democracy' to 'mend the ever widening racial divide that currently besets our multiracial nation', but then proceeded in April 2009 to abrogate the 1997 Constitution. The principles of accountability and transparency were disregarded as Bainimarama proceeded to run the country by decrees, many of which were unchallengeable in a court of law. The decrees infringed basic human rights, such as the right to free speech, and the right of association and assembly, and trade union rights were emasculated. International fact-finding missions, from the International Bar Association and the International Labour Organization, were denied entry. Drunk on decrees, the regime pushed ahead with no accounting to the public for its policies or deeds or for the disbursement from the public purse. The arrogance of unearned power was again on full display.

Sources of support

How did all this come to pass? How did the commodore manage to consolidate his grip on the country with such apparent ease? Among other things, he used the strategic deployment of the tactics of fear and violence. Opponents and alleged opponents of the coup were targeted by the military, taken to the Queen Elizabeth Barracks and subjected to psychological torture, beatings and general harassment. There were threatening phone calls at night, stoning of vehicles and homes of regime critics, attempted arson. Fiji had experienced wanton acts of violence before, especially after the September 1987 coup, but nothing quite like this—systematic, relentless and brutal. There was no investigation and no charges were laid, which was not surprising as the police commissioner himself was a senior military officer. Violence, or the threat of violence, became an inescapable reality of post-2006 Fiji. Land Forces Commander Pita Driti, now languishing in jail for purportedly plotting against his former boss, told dissenters in 2010 that they 'will be in for something really hard in terms of how we will treat them this year'.[15] Bainimarama himself threatened, 'We'll need to shut people up', so as not to endanger reforms he had set in train.[16] Fear is a powerfully disabling emotion, but as Cicero says, it is not a lasting teacher of duty.

Another tactic was the complete clampdown of the local media, especially after the abrogation of the 1997 Constitution in April 2009. Military censors were placed in television and newspaper editorial rooms, vetting items for broadcast or publication. Editors, who stood up to the regime's intimidation, such as Russell Hunter of the *Fiji Sun*, were deported. The home of Netani Rika, the uncompromising editor of the *Fiji Times*, was targeted by a fire bomb. News-wise, Fiji was an area of complete darkness. Even when formal restrictions were lifted, reporters prudently exercised deliberate self-censorship for fear of retribution from the regime. The upshot was that people read or heard only what the regime allowed to be published or broadcast. On the internet, antiregime blogsites mushroomed, spreading information and deliberate disinformation, but only a small percentage of the Fiji population had access to them. The country ran on rumour and gossip with the regime's spies everywhere. Understandably, overt dissent disappeared, or went underground.

---

15 Pita Driti, Fiji Broadcasting Corporation, interview, n.d.
16 Republic of Fiji Military Forces, press release, n.d.

Compounding the problem was the public's diminished confidence in law enforcement and judicial institutions. The police force was under the command of a military officer (Commodore Esala Teleni succeeded by Brigadier General Ioane Naivalarua). Convicted police officers received early release from prison, and reports of police brutality that were captured on video and screened around the world went uninvestigated. Bainimarama's defiant declaration to 'stand by his men' dampened enthusiasm for diligent investigation. There was similarly diminished confidence in the impartiality and independence of the judiciary. The regime denied interference, but revelations by departing judges were sufficiently credible to be dismissed easily. As Justice Randal Powell said in August 2011, 'The Fiji military regime's idea of an independent judiciary is one that does the government's bidding', adding that the judges appointed 'would know that if they start pursuing an independent line, there can be consequences'.[17] Justice Marshall similarly complained of 'progressive inroads into the independence of the judiciary'. In the civil service, the presence of senior military officers as permanent heads of department, with direct access to Bainimarama and in effect accountable to him personally and no one else, had its own consequences.

We turn now to the response of the different communities to the coup and subsequent developments. Let me begin with the Indo-Fijians. Contrary to popular perception, the community was not united in its response to the coup. On one hand, there were many who were opposed to the military takeover. These included political parties (the National Federation Party, nongovernmental organisations, cultural organisations—Sangam, for example) as well as prominent individuals (Wadan Narsey, Shamima Ali, Imrana Jalal, to name just a few). On the other hand, significant sections of the community, if not actively supporting the coup, adopted a 'wait-and-see' approach, giving Bainimarama the benefit of the doubt. Among them were the dispossessed, the disinherited and the desperate; victims of previous coups and of the racially discriminatory affirmative action policies that followed in their wake. They knew firsthand what corruption was, and they believed the military's 'clean-up' campaign rhetoric.

Less understandable was the response of the 'intellectual class', which, with one or two notable exceptions, silently supported the coup. This group included vice-chancellors of the three universities who differed from

---

17   Jon Fraenkel, 'Fiji: Melanesia in review', in *The Contemporary Pacific* 25(3) (2012): 370–89, at p. 384, doi.org/10.1353/cp.2012.0046.

each other only in the enthusiasm with which they backed the regime and its purported aims. The vice-chancellor of the regional University of the South Pacific was, according to his own staff, a particularly 'ardent' supporter of the regime. The message their pliant behaviour sent was well understood by their subordinates. Inevitably a culture of silence ensued. The universities became training factories serving the interests of power rather than being engaged in the pursuit of truth as the conscience of society. Others talked vaguely about ethical and unethical coups, straining at the edges to justify the unjustifiable. They were joined by many Indo-Fijian expatriates, 'retired re-treads', according to some antigovernment bloggers, in the twilight of their careers who had left the country in personally unhappy circumstances but who now returned to lend a helping hand—for a handsome fee, of course. Some are belatedly beginning to rue their poor judgement but the damage has already been done.

Moral leaders of the Indo-Fijian community were among the early cheerleaders of the coup. Among them was Dewan Maharaj, the President of Fiji's largest Hindu organisation, the Sanatan Dharam Pratinidhi Sabha, and the owner of one of the country's largest printing companies working closely with the regime. The Arya Samaj, the much smaller but very well connected Hindu reformist organisation, was not far behind. The Fiji Muslim League was in the regime's corner but kept its presence quiet. Some have claimed that the 2006 coup was a Muslim coup, given the presence of so many of that faith in the regime or easily counted among its supporters. Aiyaz Sayed Khaiyum was the vain, voluble and highly visible attorney-general, the second most powerful person in government after Bainimarama himself. Others who were often mentioned as regime supporters and sympathisers included the former High Court Judge Nazhat Shameem, former Chair of the Fiji Human Rights Commission Shaista Shameem, and many others of lower rank and visibility. Understandably, they have all strenuously denied complicity. The claim about large Muslim support is far-fetched. There are many Muslims who did not support the coup. There was no Muslim conspiracy; it is just that some prominent individuals who opportunistically backed the regime happened to be of the Muslim faith. That said, it is true that the leadership of the Fiji Muslim League has always had a cosy relationship with the power elite of Fiji, including, for many decades, with the Alliance Party of Ratu Mara in the hope of getting separate Muslim representation in parliament. That dream is now evanescent.

The most enigmatic question in Fiji is Khaiyum's relationship with Bainimarama. It is no secret that Khaiyum is deeply distrusted by the military and disliked by a wide spectrum of *iTaukei* society for his brazen manners and ideological zeal. As Brigadier General Pita Driti's treason trial in late 2013 revealed, there was some talk among sections of the military of eliminating him altogether. Many Fijians saw him as the evil genius behind the throne manipulating Bainimarama, the prime mover of policies that have destroyed or seriously impaired *iTaukei* institutions under the current regime. What hold does this man then have over the prime minister? It is far too simplistic to see him as the wily manipulator of an otherwise innocent, well-meaning Bainimarama. Khaiyum's loyalty to the commodore was complete and unbreakable. He was politically ambitious but did not have an independent power base of his own. He was a nondescript lawyer before 2006. He burned his bridges with virtually everyone. Bainimarama was all he had. Khaiyum was nothing before Bainimarama, and he will become nothing after him. Doors to him in Australia and New Zealand are, and will remain, firmly shut. He is an anathema to international civil society organisations for the draconian decrees he authorised. That was why he showed all the passion of the twice converted in his slavish attachment to the military leader. For his part, Bainimarama had an acute understanding of his attorney-general's vulnerability and used it to his full advantage. He knew that Khaiyum would never be a threat to him and that he would diligently do his, Bainimarama's, bidding. He always delivered whatever the cost. And the commodore places absolute, unconditional loyalty high on the list of virtues he most prizes. Convergence of mutual interest rather than conspiracy underpins the relationship between the prime minister and his attorney-general. Once Khaiyum has outlived his usefulness, he too, like so many others before him, will be left to fend for himself.

The most important Indo-Fijian leader who backed the coup and joined the Bainimarama Cabinet in early 2007 as its Minister of Finance was the Fiji Labour Party leader Mahendra Chaudhry. Why would a leader of Chaudhry's background, a victim of two previous coups, join the military regime? Chaudhry defended his decision on the high moral ground that his intervention was motivated by nothing other than a desire to save his country from complete financial collapse after the coup. That might have been so, but he was also a man deeply embittered by the policies of the Qarase Government, unforgiving in his anger at being dislodged from power at the hands of Fijian nationalists in 2000. This was his chance to take his revenge on them. Revenge and retribution loomed large in his thinking. Chaudhry is an experienced trade unionist, and he probably thought that he could use his vast experience to manipulate the situation to his political advantage. As former New Zealand High Commissioner to Fiji Michael Green puts it, 'Chaudhry would not stand in the way of a coup, let alone use his considerable influence to prevent one'.[18]

Chaudhry lasted a year and a half in the regime when he was forced out of his finance portfolio. Soon afterwards, he became an implacable foe of the regime but from the sideline—a much diminished figure, his reputation for probity dimmed and his political base fragmented. His erstwhile colleagues have founded parties of their own (such as the People's Democratic Party), citing irreconcilable differences with their former leader. Chaudhry's joining the military regime had certain important consequences. In the first place, it bought Bainimarama valuable time to consolidate his position. Chaudhry's company portrayed him in a favourable light, not as a military dictator but as a leader determined to put Fiji on a different, more progressive path. Once Chaudhry had served his purpose, Bainimarama discarded him, as was his wont. Chaudhry's support for the regime also put a large section of the Indo-Fijian community behind it. And it stifled local and overseas opposition to the coup regime. In 1987, overseas trade unions led international opposition to the coup, especially in Australia and New Zealand. In 2006, they were confused to see the main trade union leader inside the coup Cabinet, urging restraint rather than sanctions.

More than a decade after the coup, the Indo-Fijian community is still divided. There are many gravy train riders who have done well out of the regime through lucrative contracts, tenders and the like. Many businessmen support the regime because, they say, an authoritarian regime is easier to deal with, though most have transferred their assets and moved their families offshore, especially to Australia and New Zealand. They have nothing to lose but their bank overdrafts should Fiji falter again. Others lent support in the hope of handouts. Many want respite from the constant turbulence that has characterised Fiji for the past two decades. On the whole, the early euphoric support for the regime has largely evaporated because of disillusionment with its practices, although many Fijians continued to see an Indo-Fijian's hand behind the regime.

---

18   Green, *Persona Non Grata,* p. 168.

On the Fijian side, initially there was confusion and anger: anger because a Fijian-dominated government had been deposed by a Fijian military, and confusion about what to do next. The deposed prime minister Laisenia Qarase was self-exiled in his Mavana village in the remote Lau province for several crucial months, depriving his supporters of a rallying point, a symbolic figure of resistance. His former fairweather ministerial colleagues were nowhere to be seen or they were maintaining discreet silence in the hope of picking up crumbs from the table. The GCC and Methodist Church (to which the majority of Fijians belong) were unceremoniously sidelined by Bainimarama. The GCC is now abolished, and the Methodist Church has been prevented from holding its annual convention. The Provincial Councils are in a limbo, their heads now appointed by the regime, not elected by the people themselves. They were once the cornerstone of rural Fijian administration, now they are a pliant tool of the regime. Fijian society is a leader-driven society, and the absence from the public stage of traditional leaders has been keenly felt. All the traditional channels of communication and guidance have been summarily disabled. Overall, Fijians have shown a pragmatic assessment of the situation in Fiji. They will shift to wherever the power lies. Their support for the regime is contingent, not absolute. Silence, in this instance, does not mean consent. To quote Robert Louis Stevenson, 'Cruelest lies are often told in silence'.[19]

By contrast, Bainimarama could count on the unswerving loyalty of his troops. The size of the military, and certainly its annual budget, increased substantially. Recruits came from all parts of the country. Many were often high school dropouts, with few skills and otherwise unemployed. Bainimarama gave them an identity and a purpose, a mission, and they repaid him with unswerving loyalty. Bainimarama's hold on the military was complete despite occasional murmurs of mutiny. Soldiers swore an oath of loyalty to him as the Commander of the Fiji Military Forces rather than to the institution of the military. Senior officers entered the civil service to carry out 'Bainimarama's mission'. In a very real sense, Bainimarama became in his own right the paramount chief of a new *vanua*: the Fijian military.

---

19 Robert Louis Stevenson, *Virginibus Puerisque and Other Papers,* 2nd edn (London: Chatto and Windbus, 1887 [1881]).

Beyond the military, Bainimarama presented himself as a new kind of Fijian: modern, multiracial and self-made, impatient with the protocol and hierarchy of traditional Fijian society. In his life and accomplishments many commoner Fijians saw possibilities for themselves for independence and self-realisation. For far too long, indeed for much of the twentieth century, indigenous Fijian and national politics had been dominated by high chiefs and their families while they themselves had been taken for granted and consigned to the shadows. Bainimarama gave them hope and a chance to shine. Many welcomed positions and promotions in the civil service with the departure of the incumbents. For some, Bainimarama's coup slowly morphed into a 'Fijian coup', fulfilling the long-held goals of the Fijian nationalists.

What of the reaction of Others—that is, non-Fijians and non–Indo-Fijians. A blanket generalisation is inappropriate because there are both supporters and dissidents amongst them, but it is beyond doubt that a significant section of them silently backed the coup and rallied to provide the nascent military regime support by accepting senior administrative and diplomatic postings (Winston Thompson, Peter Thomson, among many others). The ever adaptable Jim Ah Koy, a prominent local businessman, *iTaukei* one day, a General Voter another, and for a while Fiji's Ambassador to China, jumped on the bandwagon and joined the chorus condemning 'old politicians' of whom he was one himself. For much of the twentieth century, Europeans and part-Europeans had provided the prop for the Fijian establishment. They were useful for their electoral and financial support but not much besides. It was the fear of 'Indian domination' that had put them in the Fijian corner, but that fear was now gone and they were on their own. With the dismantling of that establishment, the Others saw freedom at last from the shadows and shackles of the past. Their support for the regime too is contingent, not absolute; they will move to wherever power lies. To the ranks of the local supporters came some old European expatriates now in their twilight years and others with hopes of cashing in on the Fijian crisis, with their own blogsites chanting the mantra of multiracialism and proclaiming Bainimarama the new messiah for Fiji. There is no doubt that there are many who believe in the prospect of a genuine democracy under Bainimarama's leadership, but naked self-interest is barely concealed in many calculations.

Civil society and nongovernmental organisations (NGOs) generally opposed the coup, but there were some, such as the Citizens Constitutional Forum, which initially adopted an 'indeterminate' position, hoping that bad means might lead eventually to good ends.[20] In the end, it fell afoul of the regime and, in August 2013, its head, the Reverend Akuila Yabaki, was charged for republishing an article locally that questioned the independence of the Fiji judiciary. The Methodist Church was hobbled, but the Catholic Church, or at least some of its leading figures, expressed an understanding of and sympathy for Bainimarama's policies. Archbishop Petero Mataca accepted appointment as co-chair of the National Council for Building a Better Fiji, and senior priest Fr Kevin Barr became a prominent, indeed often combative, supporter of the coup through his newspaper columns. He believed in Bainimarama's purported aims of the coup and placed 'social justice' ahead of 'human rights' in his agenda. The coup was not the ideal way to change government, Barr and others like him appeared to be saying, but if it served as an instrument for progressive social reform, it might not be such a bad thing after all. But even Barr, for all his vocal public support for it, was not spared the regime's wrath when he made some mildly mocking remarks about Fiji's increasing closeness to China. Bainimarama texted him, calling him a 'Fucked up priest', saying several times, 'Fuck U arsehole. Stay well away from me.' Barr relayed the abusive messages to his close friends, and they soon found their way in the cyberspace.[21] For good measure, Bainimarama threatened to revoke Barr's missionary visa. Bainimarama's intemperate outburst was not uncharacteristic or unexpected—it fitted into a pattern of behaviour that did not tolerate dissent or disagreement.

By 2010, Bainimarama was confidently ensconced in power. His enjoyment of it was palpable. He had worn down or otherwise harassed his opponents into sullen silence, at least for the time being. Force and fear were an important part of his modus operandi. He had the civil service under the control of handpicked military men and regime-friendly bureaucrats. The military was fully behind him. Businessmen came calling, with offers of support and further investment. He made frequent foreign visits on various missions, leaving his eager attorney-general in charge. With the assistance of experienced foreign policy hands, such as Peter Thomson, Fiji's Representative to the United Nations, the regime began to explore a newer place for Fiji in regional and international affairs.

---

20 Green, *Persona Non Grata*, p. 167.
21 *Fiji Today,* 16 January 2013.

The wider world

The 2006 coup was widely condemned. It could not be otherwise. The Pacific Islands Forum invoked the Biketawa Declaration (2000), which enjoined respect for the rule of law and 'upholding the democratic processes and institutions which reflect national and local circumstances, including the peaceful transfer of power'.[22] The European Union invoked the Cotonou Agreement and the Commonwealth the Harare Declaration, both of which recognise the individual's 'inalienable right to participate by means of free and democratic political process in framing the society in which he or she lives'. Australia and New Zealand imposed travel bans on the regime's closest supporters and cancelled defence cooperation with the Fijian military. The attorney-general, to his enduring annoyance, was stripped of his Australian permanent residency. All this was predictable, though the Fiji regime was probably shaken by the vehemence of the condemnation. Its narrative of a 'good coup' and 'clean-up' campaign was clearly not finding traction with its neighbours or the international community.

At first stumbling, Fiji soon began to strike back. It adopted a 'look north' policy. China responded enthusiastically. An emerging global giant, it was already looking for fresh fields for new resources (timber, minerals, marine produce). Fiji's overture came at an opportune time, and China provided soft loans and development assistance (building roads, bridges, dams). For its part, Fiji played the 'China card' to the maximum, hoping to force Australia and New Zealand into a more accommodating stance towards the regime. That hope remained unfulfilled but not before igniting a debate, in Australia at least, about whether engaging with the rogue regime might not be in its national interest despite serious imperfections in the regime's proposed constitution and the overarching role for the military in the political life of the country.[23] The Australian Labor Government remained unconvinced, demanding a more demonstrable commitment to restoring the country to full parliamentary democracy before relaxation could be contemplated, but the 2013 Coalition Government expressed a willingness to engage with Fiji. Sooner rather than later, it would discover the dangers of accommodating a mercurial regime determined to have

---

22 Pacific Islands Forum Secretariat.
23 Richard Herr and Anthony Bergin, 'Abbot must bring Fiji in from the cold', *Australian*, 13 September 2013.

its own way and no other way. The truth is that it was the Fijian military that created the mess in Fiji in the first place; that it was Fiji that ruptured diplomatic relations with Australia by expelling its high commissioner from Suva; and that it was Fiji that was the recalcitrant partner in the relationship between the two countries.

Within the region, Fiji worked assiduously to fragment opposition to the regime. These included taking a more prominent role in the Melanesian Spearhead Group (MSG) of which it had largely been a dormant and late-joining member in the past. Vanuatu outdid the others by conferring upon Bainimarama a high chiefly title—Chief Warwar—this upon a man who had undermined the chiefly system in Fiji. Fiji tried to orchestrate anti-Australia sentiment among MSG members and in the region more widely, painting it as a big white neo-colonial power insensitive to the needs of small Pacific Island states. There is, for a variety of reasons, a reservoir of resentment against Australia in the region and Fiji tried to tap into it. But in the end, Fiji's courting of the MSG was opportunistic and cynical. In private, some Melanesian leaders concede as much, but they are also acutely aware of Fiji's regional influence—as the home of vital regional institutions such as the University of the South Pacific and the hub of regional air and sea transport connections. Fiji attacked Australia and New Zealand for being bullies in the region, but was not shy about playing that role itself.

Fiji mercilessly pilloried the Pacific Islands Forum for its unwillingness to endorse the legitimacy of the coup by its Secretary-General, Samoan Judge Tuiloma Neroni Slade. The ridiculing and belittling comments about Bainimarama by the Samoan Prime Minister Tuilaepa Malielegaoi incensed the Fiji regime even further, although it was refreshing to see a Pacific leader show his courage of conviction. To bypass the Forum, Fiji began to explore the possibility of setting up a rival organisation. It convened separate meetings with selected island leaders (to which Australia and New Zealand were pointedly not invited) on the eve of the Pacific Islands Forum annual meetings. These separate meetings attempted to showcase Fiji's leadership of the region. In August 2013, Fiji spearheaded the move to establish a new Pacific Islands Development Forum as an alternative space to raise development issues in small Pacific Island states. This it did with the support of some local NGOs, such as the International Union for the Conservation of Nature (IUCN) who sought more influence and recognition in the region. Predictably, Samoa rejected the idea as a political ploy by Fiji to regain its former leadership role.

Whether it would amount to much more than a regional talkfest in the absence of financial backing from Australia and New Zealand, the region's traditional donor countries, remains to be seen. Fiji, for its part, hoped that its newfound friends in in the developing world would stand by it in its future confrontations with its traditional neighbours and partners.

Beyond the region, Fiji opened embassies in South Africa, Brazil and the United Arab Emirates and, as a new member of the Non-Aligned Movement, signed memoranda of understanding with Iran and North Korea. Russia became a newfound friend, and Fiji contributed a large peacekeeping force in the Golan Heights. It chaired the summit of G77. Fiji campaigned strongly, but in the end unsuccessfully, against Australia's drive for a seat on the UN Security Council, hoping for an eventual place there for itself as the representative of the Oceania region. How these manoeuvres will unfold in the future remains unclear, but the Fiji regime's determination to break away from the traditional pattern of diplomatic relations is beyond dispute. Fiji now considers itself far too important to be restrained by the protocols of regional politics in the South Pacific. As Bainimarama has said:

> We have gone beyond the region to chair the G77, the biggest voting bloc in the United Nations. We are leading the Pacific small islands developing states at the United Nations. We are leading players in the MSG. We have joined the Non-Aligned Movement. So it is no big deal for us to return to the Forum.[24]

Fiji's illusion of grandeur and glory on the global stage are starkly etched.

There has been much adverse comment in Fiji about Australia and New Zealand. From within Fiji and from sections of the Australian commentariat, including the Australia–Fiji Business Council, have come calls for Australia to reengage with Fiji. The most cogent response to this question has come from the late Michael Green, in his book *Persona Non Grata*. Green was New Zealand's High Commissioner to Fiji from 2004 to 2007, when he was expelled from Fiji. 'The pro-engagement proposition,' Green argues:

> is grounded in delusion about Bainimarama. He is not interested in advice or assistance unless it is to sustain him in power to implement his agenda in entirety. He is uncomfortable with the

---

24   Quoted in *fijilive*, 16 September 2013.

clash of ideas, negotiation and compromise, all critical elements to effectively functioning democracies. He is not interested in expert opinion if it does not conform to his understanding of the way things should be.[25]

Barr and other early supporters of the commodore's would attest to that.

Green goes on to point out the gap between Bainimarama's words and deeds. The commodore presents himself as a champion of good governance, but his actions belie that claim. As already mentioned, the military budget ballooned under his watch. He defied the elected government's White Paper recommendations to trim the top-heavy military to a more sustainable size. The Compulsory Supervision Order was used (as it had been by Qarase) to effect the early release of prisoners, including his brother-in-law who was jailed for manslaughter. He went to prison on full pay and was appointed a permanent secretary upon release. The abuse of human rights of escaped prisoners by police and the military went unpunished, including the barbaric beating of escaped prisoners captured on video that horrified the world. Bainimarama accused Qarase of practising cronyism but he himself was not above appointing loyalist soldiers to Cabinet, to senior positions in the civil service and to statutory organisations. 'The fact is that Bainimarama does not trust civilians, with a few exceptions, and prefers to appoint people to whom he can give orders with confidence that they will be carried out.'[26] Evidence from around the world suggests that 'military services routinely make bad governments, because they have a culture of command-and-obey and thereby cannot cope with dissent, disobedience, defiance or a "clash of ideas" in any way, shape or form'.[27]

One of the strong justifications Bainimarama had for his coup against the Qarase Government was that it was giving succour to the coup plotters of 2000 through the Promotion of Reconciliation, Tolerance and Unity Bill, a claim that many in Fiji believed. But he was himself not above giving favours to key coup strategists. Berenado Vunibobo, Speight's foreign policy advisor, was appointed Fiji's Representative to the United Nations. Colonel Pita Driti was nominated for the post of High Commissioner

---

25 Green, *Persona Non Grata*, p. 270.
26 ibid., p. 271.
27 ibid.; see also Brij V. Lal, 'The strange career of Commodore Frank Bainimarama's 2006 Fiji Coup', *State, Society and Governance in Melanesia Program Discussion Paper 2013/8* (Canberra: The Australian National University, 2013), p. 14.

to Malaysia, which was declined by Malaysia. The biggest travesty of all was the appointment of Inoke Kubuabola, first as High Commissioner to Papua New Guinea and later as Fiji's Foreign Minister. He was a founding member of the nationalist Taukei Movement in 1987, a key, self-confessed architect of the 1987 coups,[28] an advisor to Speight and a staunch defender of the racist, widely discredited 1990 Constitution. Another Taukei Movement member and 1987 coup supporter who found a place in Bainimarama's Cabinet was the octogenarian Filipe Bole. Understandably, Bainimarama's commitment to promoting open and transparent governance sounded unconvincing enough to foreign governments not to give their unqualified stamp of approval to the Bainimarama narrative.

After the abrogation of the 1997 Constitution in April 2009, a new constitution was always in prospect although with little sense of urgency as the country was being run by a plethora of decrees flowing almost daily from the attorney-general's chambers. In August 2012, the regime finally appointed a Constitution Commission headed by the distinguished Kenyan constitutional lawyer Professor Yash Ghai to draft a new constitution for Fiji. Ghai's choice was intriguing. Perhaps the regime, certainly the attorney-general, thought he might be more sympathetic to the regime's hopes and aspirations. Khaiyum was his law student in Hong Kong, and Ghai had surprisingly refrained from expressing an opinion on Bainimarama's coup. In the end, doubts about Ghai proved baseless. He proved himself to be the peerless constitutional engineer of integrity he always had been, even though he was let down by one of his fellow commissioners who was widely believed to have been the military regime's mole on the Commission.

After an extensive process of consultation (over 7,000 submissions were received), Ghai produced a Draft Constitution that was comprehensive, progressive, participatory and inclusive. A new nonracial electoral system with closed-list proportional representation (PR) at its heart was proposed, the voting age lowered to 18, a certain percentage of seats in parliament was to be reserved for women, the civil society was encouraged to participate in the political process (a part of a National Assembly that would help elect the president). The multiparty power-sharing concept of the 1997 Constitution was rejected. The Senate, as a house of review, was

---

28   Brij V. Lal, *Power and Prejudice: The Making of the Fiji Crisis* (Wellington: New Zealand Institute for International Affairs, 1988, reprinted 1990).

gone, as was the constituency system central to the Westminster system. The GCC was stripped of its former constitutional role in appointing the president and exercising an oversight role over Fijian affairs and it was accorded the status of a civil society organisation. Immunity would be granted to those who had participated in the coup, but only after they publicly acknowledged their role in it. Closure would only come after full disclosure. And while the military was placed firmly under civilian control, serving men and women would be free to disobey illegal orders. The military's preference for a guardian role for itself, with the responsibility to 'ensure at all times the security, defence and well-being of Fiji and its people' and to protect the legacy of 2006 was firmly rejected. It was the elected representatives of the people, not an unelected military, whose responsibility it would be to protect the will of the people.

The Ghai Draft proposed a measured movement in a new direction. It was presented to the president on 21 December 2012. The draft was to have gone to the president and then be presented to a hand-picked Constituent Assembly for final ratification. But the draft proved to be stillborn. The military was miffed and Bainimarama disgruntled with, among other things, the recommendations regarding immunity and the limited public role for the military. The president rejected it on 10 January 2013, dismissing it as a backward-looking document that, if adopted, would lead to 'financial and economic catastrophe and ruin'.[29] The draft's proposal to have a people's assembly elect the president would be an 'anathema to democratic representation'. It was not the president's prerogative to pass judgement on the Ghai Draft, but he was, after all, a creature of the military, its pliant tool with a record of doing its bidding and living the good life on the public purse. The much-touted Constituent Assembly was also summarily discarded. In a symbolic act of humiliation, a special contingent of police officers burned the printer's copies of the draft in Ghai's anguished presence on 12 December 2013. Once again, Bainimarama had the last laugh. He had managed to convince, or con, the international community into believing that the Ghai exercise was genuine, and he managed to secure overseas funds for it as well, but when the Commission refused to rubberstamp the military regime's agenda, it was unceremoniously disbanded. Sadly, one of its members continued to sing the praises of the military regime.

---

29 Office of the President, press release, 10 January 2013.

A new constitution, prepared by lawyers in the attorney-general's chambers with no public consultation, was promulgated on 6 September 2013 by the president. It differed only in minor details from the Draft Constitution the regime released on 21 March of the same year. There are many positive, forward-looking features in it. The new constitution has retained the regime's non-negotiable 'universal principles' of a common and equal citizenry, a common name 'Fijian' for all citizens, a secular state, an independent judiciary, good and transparent governance, entrenchment of economic and cultural rights, nonracial voting, the open list proportional representation system and a lower voting age. All this is commendable, but the constitution contains provisions that make mockery of the Westminster system of government. The powers of the prime minister and the attorney-general are considerably enhanced. The consultative provisions governing the role of the Leader of the Opposition are gone. The prime minister chairs the 'independent' Constitutional Offices Commission. The chief justice is appointed by the president on the advice of the prime minister and the attorney-general (rather than the Leader of the Opposition). The military is entrusted with maintaining the 'wellbeing' of the citizens of Fiji without overarching civilian oversight.

Parliament is reduced to playing a pliant role in the governance of the country. The provisions of the various draconian decrees curtailing the freedom of speech, assembly and association remain. The Bill of Rights is impressive in its comprehensiveness, but so are the derogations from it. And the constitution devised by 'we the people' cannot be changed without 75 per cent of votes in parliament and an equal percentage in a national referendum. In other words, it is virtually impossible to change, except through another coup. In the words of the former Vice-President Ratu Joni Madraiwiwi, other 'disturbing provisions' include 'disrupting the balance of power between different arms of state (s. 133), limiting political rights (s. 6), shielding decrees from legal challenge (s. 173), and expanding the role of the army (s. 130)'. He argues that not

> only do these run contrary to the government's own non-negotiable principles that set the bar for a quality document, but also they pose serious implications for the cultivation of a democratic culture and strengthening the rule of law.[30]

---

30   Joni Madraiwiwi, 'Treading in Moses' footsteps: Fiji's fourth constitution', *Constitutionnet*, 30 September, 2013.

The new constitution's fatal flaw, which may well be its undoing, is that it lacks legitimacy, is not founded in popular will, but was decreed into existence after a façade of hurried public consultation.

Bainimarama is convinced that he has completed the first phase of his 'glorious revolution' that began in 2000 when he stamped out the Speight insurrection. This is pure spin-doctoring: there was no popular uprising against the elected government of the day, and there was nothing glorious at all about the naked grab for power through a military coup. But in the absence of a free media, the regime has had its way with words unchallenged. The oxygen of free and unfettered speech in Fiji is in very short supply. In his address to the Certified Practising Accountants in Nadi in August 2013, Bainimarama outlined what he hoped to accomplish when he began his journey: a just, fair and nonracial society where 'everyone has a place in our national life … I am convinced that for all the challenges, history will eventually judge us favourably,' he said, 'because our revolution—that's what it is—has finally laid the foundations for a fairer, more equal society and the development of a modern, progressive state'.

There are many in Fiji who believed him, as they have believed him in the past, just as there are many who doubt his commitment to restoring the country back to true parliamentary democracy.[31] Michael Green doubts if a genuinely democratic system will emerge in Fiji. 'At best, it will be a guided democracy, like Indonesia's under Suharto or perhaps Singapore's under the Lee dynasty.'[32] Professor Yash Ghai is also among the sceptics. 'I doubt if he [Bainimarama] has read the constitution. He just repeats what his Attorney-General tells him.'[33] Commodore Bainimarama as an empty vessel for his attorney-general's agenda is a sobering thought, but it is a thought shared by many in Fiji.

In the end, Fiji's problems are as much constitutional as they are political. Even a deeply flawed constitution can be made to work if there is a will to do so. But will the military relinquish power voluntarily? Will it respect rather than preempt the verdict of the ballot box when the time comes? Does Bainimarama have the taste and temperament for the cut and thrust of robust democratic debate? Can he negotiate and compromise? His own

---

31 Stephanie Lawson, 'Indigenous nationalism, 'ethnic democracy', and the prospects for a liberal constitutional order in Fiji', in *Nationalism and Ethnic Politics* 18(3) (2012): 293–315, doi.org/10.1080/13537113.2012.707495.
32 Green, *Persona Non Grata*, p. 270.
33 *Australia News Network*, 23 October 2013.

record manifestly suggests otherwise, but he, like all of us, should be given the benefit of the doubt. The coup has succeeded, mainly through force and fear and other unsavoury means, to be sure: there has been violence, blood has been spilt, careers have been destroyed and innocent citizens have suffered. The social and moral, not to say the economic, costs have been incalculable, but that it has now entrenched itself into the body politic of Fiji is beyond doubt.

Bainimarama has summarily swept aside many institutions, structures and processes of Fijian political life. Posterity may forgive his transgressions as unfortunate but inevitable acts necessary to wrench the country away from its hobbled past towards a new future; forgiven, that is, if he shows a largeness of mind and vision to rise above personal ambition for power to create a truly democratic, progressive, just and fair society in Fiji. It has been done before in Fiji and it can be done again. To be sure, Frank Bainimarama is no Sitiveni Rabuka, lacking, as he does, the latter's intellectual agility, political deftness and a profound capacity for self-transformation and forgiveness. But he could use the power in his hands to rise above the fray and effect a genuine political transformation and be remembered by history not just as another ordinary coup maker but as the maker of a modern Fiji. That is his opportunity and challenge. For now, though, it is difficult to say whether the faint glow on the horizon is of a new dawn breaking or the glimmers of a funeral pyre dying.

20
Between a rock and a hard place[1]
Indo-Fijians, 2014

In the 2014 General Election, an overwhelming majority of Indo-Fijians voted for Bainimarama's Fiji First Party. At first glance this looks curious, a people who were the target of previous military coups supporting a coup leader. It was ironic, to be sure, but in the circumstances understandable: the reaction of a vulnerable people seeking stability and security, or even an illusion of it. This chapter examines the political predicaments of Indo-Fijians in the early years of the twenty-first century.

In the September 2014 General Elections, an estimated 80 per cent of Indo-Fijians voted for Commodore Frank Bainimarama's newly formed Fiji First Party.[2] The extent of the support was startling even though Indo-Fijians have a history of splitting their votes more frequently than indigenous Fijians. In the 1972 General Elections, for instance, 24 per cent of Indo-Fijian votes went to the Alliance Party, with that figure declining significantly over the decades as coups and ensuing convulsions soured

---

1   Originally appeared as 'Fiji Indians and the Fiji General Elections of 2014: Between a rock and a hard place and a few other spots in between', in *The People Have Spoken: The 2014 Elections in Fiji*, ed. Stephen Ratuva and Stephanie Lawson (Canberra: ANU Press, 2016), pp. 69–82, doi.org/10.22459/TPHS.03.2016.
2   Eric Larson, 'Fiji's 2014 Parliamentary Election', *Journal of Electoral Studies* 36 (2014): 235–39, doi.org/10.1016/j.electstud.2014.10.001; Brij V. Lal, 'In Frank Bainimarama's shadows: Fiji, elections and the future', *The Journal of Pacific History* 49(4) (2014): 457–68, doi.org/10.1080/00223344.2014.977518.

race relations and deepened the divide between the two communities.[3] However viewed, the Indo-Fijian shift away from traditionally Indo-Fijian parties to Fiji First is significant, even potentially historic. Several factors are responsible. On the one hand was the Bainimarama Government's ruthless use of incumbency to its enormous advantage and to the manifest disadvantage of the opposition parties, inventing and bending rules as it went along, and its generous and unaccounted use of the public purse for electioneering.[4] On the other was a deep sense of fear and foreboding among the Indo-Fijian voters: fear of revenge and retribution from Fijian nationalists should the regime lose, and foreboding about their future without the illusion of security provided by the Fijian military. Muzzling of the media through coercive decrees, suppressing dissent and disabling rival centres of power (of the trade unions and nongovernment organisations (NGOs), for instance, or the Methodist Church and the Great Council of Chiefs (GCC)) contributed their share. And then there were those who made hay while the sun shone or, as the local expression goes, an omelette from eggs broken in the melee. But just as one swallow does not a summer make, so one election, held under a new and controversial constitution promulgated by a political party intent on remaining in power at all cost, cannot tell us much about the future pattern of political culture in a country with a history of military coups. Contrary to the official narrative, Fiji's future stability is far from assured. Nevertheless, what is clear with the advantage of hindsight is that, wittingly or unwittingly, Indo-Fijian voters have for the time being rejected one model of democracy for another. They prefer the rule of a single strongman within an overarching architecture of democracy to the principles of representative democracy of the type enshrined in the conventional Westminster system, which Fiji had inherited at independence in 1970. There is change, no doubt, but whether that change is an aberration or permanent, superficial or significant, and whether it will necessarily serve the long-term interests of the Indo-Fijians, and of Fiji more generally, remains an open question.

---

3   Ahmed Ali, 'The Fiji General Election of 1972', *The Journal of Pacific History* 8 (1973): 171–80, doi.org/10.1080/00223347308572230; Brij V. Lal, *Islands of Turmoil: Elections and Politics in Fiji* (Canberra: Asia Pacific Press, 2006), doi.org/10.26530/OAPEN_459301.
4   Jon Fraenkel, 'The remorseless power of incumbency in Fiji's September 2014 Election', *The Round Table: The Commonwealth Journal of International Affairs* 104(2) (2015): 151–64, doi.org/10.1080/00358533.2015.1017255.

Any analysis of the 2014 Fijian General Elections and of Indo-Fijian political behaviour would have to begin with the political environment in which these took place. To begin with, 2014 was clearly not 1970, 1990 or even 2000.[5] All the fundamental and familiar markers of the Fijian political framework had changed. The assumptions and understandings that had governed Fijian political discourse for nearly half a century were gone—gone with the leaders who had engineered them, most notably Ratu Sir Kamisese Mara, the long-reigning prime minister and the preeminent Fijian leader of the second half of the twentieth century who died in 2004.[6] The 2013 Constitution, introduced in controversial circumstances without public consultation,[7] had several features that differentiated it from its predecessors. Communal voting was abolished, although not the practice of voting along ethnic lines. The voting age was reduced from 21 to 18, enfranchising a cohort that had come of age in an environment corrupted by coups and endless talk of more coups and that yearned for another, steadier, coup-free future. A new electoral system, open list proportional, replaced the former Alternative Vote system of the 1997 Constitution, which itself had replaced the first-past-the-post (FFP) system adopted at independence. These factors influenced the outcome of the elections and the response of Indo-Fijian voters.

The years since independence had seen Indo-Fijian society change dramatically. In 1970, Indo-Fijians constituted around 50 per cent of the national population. They had overtaken the indigenous Fijians during World War II, spawning deep fears of 'Indian domination' among Fijians and Europeans. That fear, whether real or manufactured for political purposes, determined the course of Fiji's political development as it entered the decade of decolonisation in the 1960s. Fijian leaders refused to countenance any change towards internal self-government or independence except on their terms. This included the demand for full retention of the communal system of voting and a tacit acknowledgement of the principle of Fijian political paramountcy in the governance of the country. In other words, Fijian leaders would accept change,

---

5 Stewart Firth, 'Reflections on Fiji since independence', *The Round Table: The Commonwealth Journal of International Affairs* 101(6) (2012): 575–83, doi.org/10.1080/00358533.2012.749098.
6 Deryck Scarr, *Tuimacilai: A Life of Ratu Sir Kamisese Mara* (Adelaide: Crawford House Publishing, 2008).
7 Romitesh Kant and Eroni Rakuita, 'Public participation and constitution-making in Fiji: A Critique of the 2012 constitution-making process', *State, Society and Governance in Melanesia Program Discussion Paper 6/2014* (Canberra: The Australian National University, 2014).

including independence, only if they were assured of political control.[8] A contrived political arrangement devised by the departing British, with communal representation and European over-representation at its heart, delivered that outcome—papering cracks over fundamental issues that divided the country.

Fiji enjoyed fragile political stability during its early postindependence years, but beneath a placid surface and feel-good atmosphere lurked fears and phobias that would wreck its prospects. Fiji was a symbol of hope to the modern world, Pope John Paul II had intoned during his fleeting visit to Fiji in 1985, but that was more a comforting rhetoric than a reflection of actual reality.[9] Fijian control of the government depended on unity among Fijians and enough disunity among Indo-Fijians to win power. But neither group was homogenous, divided as they were (and still are) along regional, religious and cultural lines. Sakeasi Butadroka's Fijian Nationalist Party exposed the fissures among Fijians by polling 25 per cent of the Fijian communal votes in the April 1977 elections, enough to cause the defeat of the ruling Alliance Party. The lesson was quickly relearnt that Fijian political solidarity was the sine qua non for Fijian control of government. To that end, the Alliance made strenuous efforts, reclaiming lost ground with a handsome majority in the September elections of that year, helped by a massive split among Indo-Fijians about why they were unable to form government after narrowly winning the elections in April.[10] The embers from that distant split glowed for decades afterwards, energising factions and divisions that debilitated Indo-Fijian politics, and still do.

But the Alliance's victory had come at a cost not fully appreciated at the time. It irrevocably fractured the multiracial foundations of the Alliance Party. Its pro-Fijian tilt, evident in the appointments and promotions in the civil service, the allocation of tertiary scholarships, the reservation of Crown land, among other things, saw many founding fathers of the Indian Alliance, including Sir Vijay R. Singh and James Shankar Singh, both former Cabinet ministers, joining the National Federation Party

---

8   Robert Norton, '"A pre-eminent right to political rule": Indigenous Fijian power and multi-ethnic nation building', *The Round Table: The Commonwealth Journal of International Affairs* 101(6) (2012): 521–35, doi.org/10.1080/00358533.2012.749093.
9   The Fiji Visitors Bureau turned the Pope's words into 'Fiji: The Way the World Should Be' for tourism promotion.
10   Brij V. Lal, *In the Eye of the Storm: Jai Ram Reddy and the Politics of Postcolonial Fiji* (Canberra: ANU E Press, 2010), pp. 142–76, doi.org/10.22459/ES.11.2010.

(NFP). In 1982, when the NFP (24 seats) came close to defeating the Alliance Party (28 seats), the GCC, meeting at the historic island of Bau, opened for the first time by a reigning British Monarch, passed resolutions to change the constitution to entrench permanent political control of government.[11] When the Alliance was defeated at the 1987 polls by a nominally multiracial coalition of the Fiji Labour Party (FLP) and the NFP, the month-old government was overthrown in a military coup carried out by Lt Col Sitiveni Rabuka, the third-ranking officer of the Fiji Military Forces, but tacitly supported by the leaders of the defeated Alliance Party and by Fijians more generally. 'Fijian rights in danger' was the catch cry, and it caught on. The depth of Indo-Fijian anger and hurt caused by the coups was not fully apprehended at the time. Two decades later, Bainimarama would tap into it to his great electoral advantage.

The goals of the coup were entrenched in the decreed 1990 Constitution, allocating a disproportionate number of seats in parliament to indigenous Fijians, abolishing all multiracial voting in favour of communal voting, decreeing a race-based, legally unchallengeable, affirmative action program, and reserving the offices of the prime minister, governor-general, the commissioner of police and the commander of the military and heads of important government bodies (such as the civil service) for them. The Methodist Church, one of the principal instigators of the coup, added fuel to the fire by demanding a strict observance of the Sabbath, known popularly as the Sunday Ban. For that agenda of religious zealotry, it would pay an incalculable price two decades later. And the Taukei Movement, which had morphed into existence soon after the 1987 elections from a diverse group of Fijian nationalists, demanded the complete fulfilment of the 'aims of the coup'. Violence was threatened and begun in some places, and leases to Indo-Fijian tenants were not renewed. Race relations in Fiji were strained to breaking point in the postcoup years.

The Indo-Fijian reaction to all this was to try to emigrate. Emigration had been taking place in small numbers since the 1970s, mostly to North America and the United Kingdom, but after the coup, a trickle turned into a torrent. In two decades, over 120,000 mostly well-educated professional Indo-Fijians emigrated, depriving the country of much-needed skill and talent.[12] Many departed deeply embittered and their

---

11   ibid., p. 243.
12   Kishor Chetty and Satendra Prasad, *Fiji's Emigration: An Examination of Contemporary Trends and Issues* (Suva: University of the South Pacific School of Social and Economic Development, 1993).

sense of unjust treatment and rejection continued unabated for decades. Most never forgave Rabuka for the coups despite his repeated pleas for forgiveness and his convincing claim that he had acted at the behest of others.[13] Revenge and retribution loomed large in their minds—however vocally denied. The shoe, as the saying goes, was finally on the other foot or, to use a colloquialism, Fijians were now tasting their own medicine. So when Bainimarama deposed the Qarase Government in 2006, many in the Fijian diaspora openly supported him, as they still do, deriving perverse satisfaction at the treatment of the Fijian nationalists by the Fijian military, an eventuality they had never contemplated before—no one had—a Fijian military publicly taking on the Fijian establishment and winning. The overwhelming majority voted for Bainimarama's party.[14] His well-publicised visits to Sydney and Auckland to thank his supporters and benefactors, mostly Indo-Fijians, was proof enough of that. Bainimarama's words, spoken at the United Nations General Assembly in September 2013, were music to their ears: the coup-inspired emigration of Fiji citizens was 'one of the most shameful episodes of our history', he said, 'and I determined that this must never, never happen again. We must never allow a fellow citizen to be second class citizen, to be less than on equal of his neighbour'. No Fijian leader had ever spoken such words of remorse and regret in this way before an international audience.

The massive demographic transformation in Fiji was accompanied by profound changes in the life of the Indo-Fijian community post-1987. None was more significant than the changes in the sugar industry, once the lifeblood of the economy but now in visible decline.[15] One cause of this was the nonrenewal of 30-year-old leases expiring under the *Agricultural Landlord and Tenant Act*. Leases were not renewed for many reasons. Among them was the genuine desire of some landowners to join the industry as cultivators themselves, attracted by the possibility of making a decent living that they saw, or thought they saw, Indo-Fijian tenants making. Closer acquaintance would reveal the appearance of prosperity to be deeply deceptive. Many Indo-Fijians were actually keen to give up farming altogether for a more regular cash income just when

---

13   John Sharpham, *Rabuka of Fiji: The Authorised Biography of Major-General Sitiveni Rabuka* (Rockhampton: Central Queensland University Press, 2000).
14   The 2013 Constitution allowed Fiji nationals living overseas to vote if they were properly registered, whereas before voters had to be resident in Fiji for two years before the elections. The residency requirement exempted those on officially authorised absence overseas.
15   Padma Narsey Lal, *Ganna: Profile of the Fiji Sugar Industry* (Lautoka: Fiji Sugar Commission, 2008).

Fijians wanted to come in. But political motivation was not far behind. Under Marika Qarikau, the fiercely, almost irrationally, nationalist head of the Native Land Trust Board, an implicit condition for the renewal of leases was Indo-Fijian acceptance of Fijian political supremacy. Land was power, Fijian power, and he wanted to extract the maximum concession from its users: simple quid pro quo.

Nonrenewal led to an exodus of displaced tenants from the sugarcane belts of Fiji on an unprecedented scale, especially northern Vanua Levu, for the mushrooming squatter settlements around south-eastern Viti Levu, clogging the Suva–Nausori corridor. Life in these settlements was plainly squalid—without running water, electricity, sewerage facilities or employment and educational opportunities—but the evictees had nowhere else to go and no one would have them. In the Cunningham squatter settlement in Suva, the Fijian landlord demanded money for the conduct of religious functions by his Indo-Fijian tenants. Refusal to pay, it was clearly understood, would mean immediate removal. To these people living at the edge of poverty and destitution on the sufferance of others, with little hope or optimism, talk of democracy and good governance and the disclosure of the auditor-general's report withheld since 2006, was just that—talk, academic talk. They had heard of such things before, to no avail. What they wanted was relief and respite from misery.

Here the Bainimarama regime had the upper hand, freely dispensing goods and services from the public purse. Most importantly, the regime promised the squatters on state land 99-year leases—a dream come true for hundreds who had never imagined a place of their own—and their gratitude to Bainimarama was unbounded. The government also addressed the perennial problem of violent burglary in urban and peri-urban areas through active military patrols. On this frontier of lawlessness and violence, the voters knew that only Bainimarama could deliver. Often, the protocols of natural justice were blatantly breached. But the savage beatings of escaped prisoners beamed around the world to great consternation about the abuse of human rights in Fiji meant little to the squatters who were often themselves targets of violent crime. They saw Bainimarama as the upholder of law and order, a leader who was finally on their side. The impression created was of a government at last caring for a group that had long lived literally and metaphorically on the unlovely fringes of society. They therefore rallied behind Fiji First. As indeed did those who had fallen prey to a declining rural sector and were making a meagre living in urban and peri-urban areas as casual labourers, domestic helpers, mechanics, drivers, carpenters. Rural decline is on the increase and has been for some time, and will continue to swell the numbers of the desperate urban poor.

Bainimarama's rhetoric justifying the coup also attracted many Indo-Fijians to his side. His was not a coup, he said repeatedly, if unconvincingly in the face of undeniable evidence, it was a 'clean-up' campaign. He wanted to cleanse the country of corruption. His call resonated with ordinary citizens, who knew in their bones that greasing the palm had become an endemic feature of life in the country, and that things were getting worse by the day, not better. Many Indo-Fijians therefore gave him the benefit of the doubt, and their early support bought the military regime valuable time to consolidate itself. By the time people saw that there was more to the coup than what the commodore had claimed; that corruption and mismanagement in various guises were alive and well; that what was alleged was never actually proven in a court of law (no big fish were ever caught), it was too late.

Over time, Bainimarama, with the help of adroit image makers, including an American public relations company (specialists in refurbishing the image of dictators and tyrants around the world), was portrayed as a selfless soldier embarking on a path to remake Fiji into a modern, vibrant, nonracial society, with Singapore as a model in mind. He was steadily transformed, in the public eye, from a tongue-tied, temperamentally volatile, short-fused military strongman, into a man of the people, an appealing leader, modest and engaging, photographed sitting cross-legged on a mat with cheering uniformed school children, sharing a cup of tea with rural Indo-Fijian housewives, inspecting government projects in shorts and floral bula shirt. No leader had done that before. His 'visit diplomacy' to previously neglected areas in remote regions was good theatre: on horseback, riding through stony rivers and rough terrain, with admirers in tow. Would a 'dictator' ever do that, people asked? He was antipolitics, he said, and blamed 'old' politicians for all the ills of Fiji's past, overlooking the inconvenient fact that several 'old' politicians were serving in his own Cabinet and had played key roles in previous coups (such as Foreign Minister Inoke Kubuabola). And not altogether subtly, Bainimarama made it clear that it was he, and he alone, who stood between chaos and stability. There would be no coup as long as he was in charge, he told voters. People believed him. They had no reason not to. He was, after all, a former military commander still in touch with his former troops; his eyes and ears firmly in place among them.

Of all the leaders standing for the elections, Bainimarama was the only one who had the unquestioned loyalty of the military whose leaders had said often enough that they would prefer him to continue. It was understood, though unsaid (it did not need to be), that the military would move in 'to protect the constitution' if Bainimarama was dislodged. Some political parties had questioned the immunity provisions of the 2013 Constitution, which spawned fear and anger among the rank and file of the military. Bainimarama was on their side. The military needed him as much as he needed them. Mutual self-interest was set in concrete. No one wanted another coup. The attraction of stability and security to a people long at the receiving end of previous coups counted for a lot. People reposed their faith in the coup leader. He was a strong man of action. As he often said, time for talk was over, time for action was now. He had stood up to the GCC and the Methodist Church and hobbled them unceremoniously. He had stood up for Fiji against international opposition to his regime. Finer points about democratic principles and long-term implications of the government's policies, the inherent dangers of relying on the whims of one man to govern, did not register with the voters. It was often said that nothing good had happened in Fiji until Bainimarama had come on the scene, and that Fiji would revert to its failed past without him at the helm. It was a familiar tactic of military dictators and authoritarian leaders around the world who portray themselves as the very embodiment of the national spirit, indispensable to the destiny of the nation. Rabuka had done that in 1987 and Bainimarama was doing it now.

This narrative was given unfettered play in the local media, operating under severe restrictions imposed by the Media Decree. The *Fiji Sun* newspaper became an unabashed cheerleader for the regime, with screaming front-page headlines praising the government for everything it did or purported to do, while belittling the motivations and modus operandi of its opponents. Fiji had not seen such grovelling journalism before or such blatantly biased reporting. Unsurprisingly, Bainimarama was the newspaper's choice for the 'Person of the Year'. Radio stations, both commercial and state-owned as well as the Fiji Broadcasting Corporation (FBC) television station, were similarly proregime, the national broadcaster run by the younger brother of the regime's controlling attorney-general. A prominent Indo-Fijian radio announcer, a household name among Indo-Fijians, pretended neutrality in her questioning of candidates who appeared on her show, but then on the eve of the elections suddenly resigned to stand for Bainimarama's party. The Chief Executive Officer of the Media Industry Development

Authority, similarly professed impartiality but (unsuccessfully) stood for Fiji First. It was disturbing to see such boundaries crossed with such impunity and in full public view. Decency demanded some distance, but none was forthcoming. Now anything was possible, any transgression forgiven, if you were with Fiji First.[16]

In the upshot, the people heard only what the military regime wanted them to hear while neutral or contrary voices were noticeably absent from the public domain. The Media Authority, for its part, mouthed sophomoric platitudes about fairness and responsibility and accuracy and balance in reporting, but it was in truth itself nothing more than a coercive and compliant instrument of and for the regime.[17] Critics took to social media, but ordinary folk in the countryside, without access to the internet, were innocent of the contrary views and voices floating in the cyber traffic.[18] In the end, the regime's manipulation of the media was as unprecedented as it was complete. It had learned well from the example of authoritarian regimes around the world that consolidation and unhindered and unaccountable exercise of power required a pliant media. And it had all the power in its hands to bend the media to its knees (by giving Fiji TV six-monthly licences, for example, or imposing huge fines for breaches of the Media Decree, and by restricting foreign ownership of the local media).

Several aspects of the 2013 Constitution helped to attract Indo-Fijian voters to Bainimarama's Fiji First Party. One was the abolition of communal voting that had been a defining feature of all Fiji constitutions from the early twentieth century.[19] 'One person, one vote, one value' was the new mantra. In truth, all votes were not equal under the open list proportional system, as the results showed, but what the regime said went. Common roll had been the catch cry of the Indo-Fijian community since 1929 when they first got the franchise, and it had been the signature

---

16 By contrast, students who campaigned for rival political parties were threatened with cancellation of their scholarships, even as the regime encouraged the participation in politics of young people.
17 Petitions for the investigation of biased reporting from proregime sources and their refusal to publish views critical of the regime were routinely ignored. For instance, see Wadan Narsey's blog site *Fiji: For Freedom and Fairness*.
18 The most trenchant critiques of the practices and policies of the Bainimarama Government appeared on *Coupfourpointfive* and on Wadan Narsey's *Fiji: For Freedom and Fairness*; *fijileaks* made important revelations. On the proregime side were *Grubbsheet* and to a lesser extent Cros Walsh's blog site *Fiji: The Way It Was, Is and Can Be*.
19 Ahmed Ali, *Fiji and the Franchise: A History of Political Representation, 1900–1937* (iUniverse, 2007).

platform of the National Federation Party in the decolonising decade of the 1960s.[20] Fiji First told Indo-Fijian voters it was doing nothing more than meeting a demand the leaders of the Indo-Fijians had been making for generations and therefore deserved its votes, not its condemnation. To see former staunch NFP members such as Praveen Bala (now the Minister of Housing and Local Government) in the Fiji First line-up muddied the waters. Atul Patel, the eldest son of the founding father of the NFP, A.D. Patel, endorsed this common roll platform of Fiji First, and Faiyaz Koya, the elder son of another NFP founder and Opposition Leader, Siddiq Koya, stood as a candidate for Fiji First and is now Minister of Trade and Tourism (after a few short days as attorney-general).[21] Their actual and virtual presence behind Bainimarama swayed many voters who were asking why NFP was opposing a man who was giving them what the party had been asking for all along: political equality, equal citizenship and a common roll.

On the surface, the question was compelling: why indeed? The truth though was that Bainimarama's brand of strongman, military-backed democracy was not what the NFP had been fighting for. Their quest all along had been for genuine representative democracy with a robust parliament of men and women elected in their own right rather than riding on the coat-tails of their leader right at the heart of it. Their platform was for a parliament that would be the ultimate guardian of the country's freely adopted rather than unilaterally imposed constitution, not an unelected, ethnically lopsided military as the protector of multiracialism and as the arbiter of the national interest. NFP had stood all along for a democracy where power flowed from the ballot box, not from the barrel of a gun. Fiji First invoking the name of the NFP in support of its campaign platform was as incomprehensible as it was ironic.

Another feature of the 2013 Constitution that had a bearing on the outcome of the 2014 election was the lowering of the voting age from 21 to 18. This had been recommended by the Reeves Commission in 1996,[22] but was rejected by a subcommittee of the Parliamentary Select Committee chaired by none other than Inoke Kubuabola on the grounds

---

20   See Brij V. Lal (ed.), *A Vision for Change: A.D. Patel and the Politics of Fiji* (Canberra: ANU E Press, 2011), doi.org/10.22459/VC.11.2011.
21   His younger brother, Faizal Koya, stood for the NFP, saying 'I was born in NFP and I will die in NFP'.
22   Report of the Fiji Constitution Review Commission (Sir Paul Reeves, Tomasi Rayalu Vakatora and Brij V. Lal), *The Fiji Islands: Towards a United Future,* Parliamentary Paper, 34 (1996).

that in Fijian culture 18-year-olds were considered children, not adults. They were to be seen rather than heard.[23] In 2014, a third of the voters were below the age of 30. They had come of age during an era of coups in Fiji. They had very little knowledge or understanding of the country's past and, more to the point, no interest in it. History was not taught in schools, and what little was taught was sanitised, brushed clean of the mud and muck of the past, ignoring the unarguable fact that Fiji had a fractured past with little in the way of a common, unifying narrative. The new generation was obsessively focused on the internet-dependent present. Not the book but the Facebook was their source of information and knowledge and enlightenment. They believed Bainimarama when he blamed Fiji's ill-fated past on corrupt politicians; they believed him rather than the obvious truth that it was the military, aided and abetted by some 'old' politicians, that was the real cause of Fiji's problems. They liked his empowering rhetoric of nonracialism and common citizenship, his standing up for Fiji against Australia and New Zealand (though they all secretly hope to migrate there one day and not to Fiji's newfound friends in Iran and North Korea). And reflecting an international trend, a rich vein of antipolitical sentiment ran among the youth of Fiji, to Bainimarama's clear benefit. This is not to say that all young people voted for Fiji First, but a substantial number did, out of a curious combination of apathy, indifference, naiveté and misguided enthusiasm.

The new open list proportional system worked enormously to Bainimarama's benefit. In the new system, the 50 seats in the House of Representatives had to be contested from a single national constituency, dispensing with the constituency boundaries of the past. Voters had to vote for a single candidate (with no indication of their name of party affiliation), with the vote for the individual candidate being automatically counted for his or her party. Seats in parliament would be allocated in proportion to the votes a party won. All parties and independent candidates would have to meet the 5 per cent threshold for victory.

Theoretically, the open list system gives the voters, not the party, the power to choose whom they vote for, but Fiji First encouraged voters to cast their vote for one person, party leader Frank Bainimarama. And that is precisely what happened. Bainimarama got 202,459 votes, nearly 70 per cent of the votes cast for Fiji First and 40.8 per cent of all the votes cast. The system delivered handsomely for Fiji First, but whether it

---

23 This, I base on a conversation with a member of the committee.

augurs well for representative parliamentary democracy is another matter. What happens when Bainimarama is no longer around? Is Fiji fated to be governed from now on by strong men (and perhaps women too) backed by the military within an overarching illusion of democratic governance? In 2009, I wrote: 'A militarized democracy seems in the offing in Fiji.'[24] Sadly, that prospect is looking more and more likely.

Support for Bainimarama and his party seems to have been fairly widespread across the Indo-Fijian community. Major Indo-Fijian businessmen were in his camp, with financial donations and public expressions of support. Among the most prominent of them were C.J. Patel, the Tappoos, the Damodars and Gokals, the Diwan Maharajs and owners of big transport and construction companies. Their commitment to Fiji is questionable as many have substantial assets outside the country and often their families too, with permanent residency papers in order. It is a truism that businessmen everywhere have a cosy relationship with those in power, but the Fiji business community seems to be a particularly myopic lot. There is no sense of loyalty or allegiance to any cause or ideology beyond turning a profit for themselves. They will readily embrace the next person in power, whatever their political ideology, as long as their coffers are full.

Less easy to explain is the support given by Fiji's educational and moral leaders. The Vice-Chancellor of the University of the South Pacific (USP), Rajesh Chandra, an academic bureaucrat par excellence, was a strong supporter of the coup and its leader from the beginning. His staff took his cue, fearful of reprisals. USP's most vocal antiregime academic, Wadan Narsey, was forced to resign from the university, with the Vice-Chancellor acceding to the military regime's demand. Chandra knew which side of the bread was buttered, as the expression goes in Fiji, but he was also embittered by the denial, unfair as he saw it, of the top job at the regional university some years back because of Fiji's refusal to support his nomination. This was his way of getting back. The Vice-Chancellor of the Fiji National University (FNU), Ganesh Chand, a former Labour politician, refrained from public commentary, perhaps more out of necessity than choice, prudence rather than principle. The FNU is a government-funded institution, and not all members of staff were always supportive of him for a variety of reasons, both personal as well as political. Despite his services to the regime, Chand was removed from his position in December 2014. For the historical record, not all Indo-Fijian

---

24 Lal, *In the Eye of the Storm*, p. 444.

academics in Fiji or in the Fijian expatriate community were with the regime. There were many, me included, who opposed the coup through their writings and interventions in the media, but media censorship in Fiji and other forms of overt and covert harassment ensured that contrary narratives did not reach the mainstream public. We mostly talked in cyberspace through emails and blog sites and Facebook accounts.

From abroad, retired academics in the twilight of their careers and other former Fiji professionals returned to lend support and write in praise of the regime and its leader, ostensibly convinced by the regime's rhetoric of creating a new Fiji. Most had left Fiji disillusioned after previous coups, and were returning now to settle old scores and to set things right, often for lucrative fees or appointments and the small, transient privileges of fading limelight. Some were no doubt diligent, hoping to use the opportunity of the coup to restructure Fiji's political culture towards more nonracialism and accountable and effective governance. The National Council for Building a Better Fiji became the vehicle for their efforts on the clear premise that all changes made would be within the overarching framework of the 1997 Constitution. Bainimarama gave that undertaking, but then proceeded to abrogate the constitution in April 2009 after the council had completed its work and given the coup leader his much-heralded roadmap back to parliamentary democracy. He also discarded the political dialogue process he had been urged to undertake by the Commonwealth, among others. He reneged on his promise to the Pacific Islands Forum to hold elections in 2009. Promises were made only to be broken at will. The commodore tactically outmanoeuvred everyone; in the end, he had the last laugh.

It was often said before and during the campaign that the 2006 coup was a Muslim coup. This was supposedly due to the support, vocal or tacit, for it by many prominent Muslims, such as Aiyaz Saiyed Khaiyum, Shaista Shameem, former head of the Fiji Human Rights Commission, and her younger sister and former High Court Judge Nazhat Shameem, now in Geneva as Fiji's Ambassador to the United Nations after a short stint as a private legal practitioner in Fiji and destined, many believe, to even higher offices in Fiji.[25] The visible presence of Muslims in statutory

---

25   Michael Green, *Persona Non Grata: Breaking the Bond: Fiji and New Zealand, 2004–2007* (Auckland: Dunmore Publishing Ltd, 2013), p. 186, writes about Nazhat Shameem's deep disappointment with the Qarase Government for not nominating her for an international judicial post, urging the New Zealand Government to sponsor her instead. Only Shameem will ever know if her sense of disappointment with the Qarase Government was sufficient for her to adopt a 'softer' approach to the coup and all that followed.

organisations and government bodies reinforced that perception. But Muslims did not instigate the coup;[26] they were as divided over the event as other communities, and there are opportunists among Muslims as there are in other groups. What is beyond doubt, though, is that over time, as the picture of the political landscape became clearer, and realisation dawned that Bainimarama would be around for a long time, Muslim support firmed up for Fiji First. They voted in very large numbers for the party. Without that, Khaiyum, widely distrusted among Indo-Fijians and among most Fijians for his controlling ways, confrontational approach and palpable love of power, and whose large hand was seen in the dismantling of many Fijian institutions, would not have got the votes he did (13,753 or 2.8 per cent of the votes cast), more than the total votes cast for the FLP.

But Muslims were not the only ones who supported the military regime. It was the same with other communities as well as the reality of Bainimarama's determination to remain at the helm sank in. The leaders of the Arya Samaj were among its early supporters, with one of them, former high school teacher Kamlesh Arya, appointed High Commissioner to Australia without any discernible qualifications for that important position. The leaders of the largest Fijian Hindu organisation, the Sanatan Dharam, were not far behind; then National President Diwan Maharaj, the owner of Quality Print, was among the early prominent backers of the regime. One of the schools in Nausori run by that organisation invited Bainimarama for a function and the welcoming ceremony included washing his feet while he sat on a chair smiling enigmatically, whether in bemused amazement or in genuine puzzlement at this gesture, it is difficult to say. The abasing symbolism was arresting as an indicator of desperation. The ceremony is normally performed at serious religious or ritually significant occasions (washing the feet of deities, for instance, or formally welcoming a bridegroom at a wedding by the bride's side), not for ordinary mortals, let alone politicians. Self-interest obviously played a part as organisations vied for government handouts. There were many Hindus who made a show of supporting Bainimarama to prevent him from falling completely into the 'Muslim camp'. But there were other factors as well. Bainimarama's firm rejection of the Methodist Church's demand (and that of the Social Democratic Liberal Party (SODELPA) as well) that Fiji become a Christian state was widely welcomed by Hindus

---

26 Among the strongest opponents of the coup were Shameema Ali of the Women's Crisis Centre and Imrana Jalal, a human rights lawyer, both Muslims.

and Muslims. Many had witnessed firsthand the ugly religious bigotry of the late 1980s—the Sunday Ban, the ransacking, looting and burning of Hindu and Muslim places of worship—and they did not want those episodes ever repeated. Bainimarama's confrontational attitude towards the Methodist Church, preventing it from holding its annual conferences, insisting that the church dissociate itself from party politics, was welcome among most Indo-Fijians.

Alternative political parties could not match what Fiji First had to offer the Indo-Fijian voters. Let us take SODELPA. This was the old Soqosoqo Duavata ni Lewenivanua (SDL) under a new name, fulfilling the requirement that all political parties have English names.[27] SDL held bad memories for most Indo-Fijians. Its pro-Fijian policies under the Qarase Government (the Fijian 'blueprints', scholarship programs for indigenous Fijians, subsidies to Fijian-only schools, among others) had deeply disenchanted many. Racist utterances by some of its parliamentarians (Asenaca Caucau, for instance, who likened Indo-Fijians to 'noxious weeds' and went unreprimanded) were not forgotten or forgiven. Insult and humiliation hardly ever are among Indo-Fijians; hurtful memories last a long time. The renamed party began with a progressive agenda, but soon started espousing what can broadly be described as a pro-Fijian platform. Many Fijians were understandably angry with the Bainimarama regime for its dismissive policies towards Fijian institutions and protocols, such as abolishing the GCC, using 'Fijian' as the name for all Fijian citizens irrespective of ethnicity, appointing the chairmen of provincial councils, altering the formula of land rent distribution, and dismantling many racially based affirmative action programs.

Hoping to tap into what appeared to be a swelling pool of indigenous Fijian resentment and anger about the regime's policies, SODELPA soon jettisoned any pretence of being a multiracial party, becoming, instead, the vehicle for indigenous Fijian views and concerns. The GCC would be brought back, the party said, Christianity could become the state religion, and the name Fijian would be reserved for indigenous Fijians only. In short, SODELPA once again became the champion for the cause of Fijian paramountcy, though of a more subdued variety than that demanded by the supporters of the 1987 coups. It had little to say to the

---

27   Under the Political Parties (Registration, Conduct, Funding and Disclosures) Decree 4/2013. The Decree also required all parties to register or reregister with 5,000 signatures from registered voters, with specified numbers from each of the country's four administrative divisions.

nonindigenous citizens of Fiji. It fielded only three Indo-Fijian candidates out of 50, among them a former SDL Minister George Shiu Raj and one of the founders of the People's Democratic Party (PDP), Nirmal Singh. They all polled miserably. SODELPA's Fijian reach was strong but its urban base was fractured. The party would have to adopt a broader, more nonethnic platform if it was become a serious contender for power in Fiji.

Indo-Fijian voters had three other parties to choose from: FLP, People's Democratic Party (PDP) and the NFP. None of them got the traction they hoped for. FLP's fate was particularly tragic, winning only 11,670 (2.4 per cent) of the votes cast and without a seat in parliament for the first time in its history. Formed in 1985, the party had won government in 1987 in coalition with the NFP, only to be overthrown in a military coup after a month in office. Its founding leader Dr Timoci Bavadra died in 1989, and was succeeded by the long-time trade unionist Mahendra Chaudhry, secretary of the Fiji Public Service Association, after a short stint at the helm by Bavadra's widow, Adi Kuini Bavadra. Adept and politically astute, Chaudhry was also in a hurry to wrest the leadership of the Indo-Fijian community from the NFP, determined, in his own words, to 'finish NFP off'. To that end, throughout the 1990s, he deployed his considerable political capital, emerging victorious in the 1999 General Elections and becoming the country's first Indo-Fijian prime minister. But his government, too, was overthrown in a quasi-coup after a year in office. The policies of his successor, Laisenia Qarase, kept him out of government despite the power-sharing provisions of the 1997 Constitution by offering Labour miniscule ministries of no significance.[28] By the time Qarase honoured these after the 2006 elections, Chaudhry's cup of disillusionment was full. He concentrated all his efforts in derailing the Qarase Government in which several of his own senior party members were ministers, though he himself had opted to stay out. In that endeavour, he found an unlikely ally in the commander of the Fiji military forces, Commodore Frank Bainimarama, who had his own private grievance against the government besides genuine anger at proposed bills, in particular the Promotion of Reconciliation, Tolerance and Unity Bill, which could have granted amnesty to rebel soldiers involved in the mutiny in the military in November 2007 in which several loyalist soldiers had died.

---

28   The 1997 Constitution provided that any political party with more than 5 per cent of seats in the House of Representatives was entitled to be invited into Cabinet in proportion to its numbers.

Chaudhry did not use his considerable political weight to oppose the impending coup. As the late Michael Green, New Zealand's High Commissioner to Fiji, put it, 'Chaudhry would not stand in the way of a coup, let alone use his considerable influence to prevent one'.[29] Instead, he joined the military Cabinet in early 2007. This was significant. Widely recognised as the leader of the Indo-Fijian community, his joining the regime Cabinet brought considerable Indo-Fijian support to Bainimarama, bought him valuable time and helped him consolidate his position. A year and a half later, in August 2008, Chaudhry was forced out of the Bainimarama Cabinet—left voluntarily, according to Chaudhry—and became a relentlessly vocal critic of the regime. But the regime had the last laugh. On the eve of the elections, Chaudhry was convicted of breaching the country's *Bills of Exchange Act* for failure to declare ownership of foreign currency without the express permission of the Reserve Bank. As a result of the conviction, he was barred from contesting the elections. Without him, the Labour Party was nothing. Its makeshift leader, former academic Rohit Kishor, was an unimpressive novice. The party, which had once won the hearts and minds of the Indo-Fijian community and formed the government of the country, was in severe doldrums, lacking people's affection and support, and with the reputation of its leader now tarnished beyond repair. Indo-Fijians understandably saw no reason to vote for it.

The PDP was formed by a group including leading trade unionists that had broken away from Chaudhry's Labour Party over disagreements about his leadership style. PDP was genuinely multiracial with fine talent but with little political experience beyond the trade union circles. It lacked rural reach and political credibility, too, in the eyes of many. The Fiji Trade Union Congress maintained a low profile in the early days of the coup, and General Secretary Felix Anthony accepted the military regime's appointment to statutory boards. For him now to turn around and condemn the regime would sound incongruous. Nonetheless, the party had socially progressive policies about law and justice and about protecting rights and freedoms, about protecting workers' rights and media freedom, among many others. They were in truth unexceptionable, but they failed to impress the Indo-Fijian electorate attuned to other offers and other voices. PDP's policies on indigenous issues were sensitive and sensible, but they directly contradicted the policies of Fiji First. PDP declared

---

29 Green, *Persona Non Grata*, p. 168.

in its manifesto that it 'respects the central place of the *iTaukei* within Fiji's wider multicultural society and will pursue policies and programs consistent with the UN Indigenous Tribal and Peoples Convention'. Fiji First's policy, which many Indo-Fijians found more appealing, placed everyone on an *equal* footing, not giving any group prior rights and privileges. On the GCC, PDP recognised 'the important role of the GCC as an institution and the role of chiefs in modern Fiji'. Therefore, it would 'reinstate the GCC and will assist it promote indigenous customs and traditions and to improve the economic well-being of indigenous people', while being guided by its advice 'on all matters relating to the protection of indigenous rights and interests'.[30]

More Indo-Fijians were listening to Fiji First on indigenous rights, which emphasised 'mainstreaming' indigenous practices. Khaiyum had written about the 'sunset clause' on separate traditional institutions in his master's thesis at the University of Hong Kong, under the supervision of Professor Yash Ghai (who would later chair the ill-fated Fiji Constitution Commission whose report was unceremoniously discarded by the Bainimarama regime). And most Indo-Fijians saw the GCC as a part of the problem, not part of the solution, remembering its support for previous coups and its being out of touch with the realities of a modern Fiji in a rapidly globalising world. The fact that the PDP was new on the scene with little track record did not help its cause. It won 15,864 (3.2 per cent) of the votes cast. Soon after the elections its leader Felix Anthony rejoined the Fiji Trades Union Congress (FTUC), which, under the present dispensation, would prevent him from participating in electoral politics. Without his active participation at the helm, the party's future was uncertain. It was more likely to wither on the vine of public apathy and indifference.

Finally, there was the NFP, which won 27,066 (5.5 per cent) of the votes and three seats in parliament, ending its absence for over a decade. NFP is Fiji's oldest political party, founded in 1964, based in the Indo-Fijian community but with a nonracial platform, and in the vanguard of the movement for independence on the basis of a common roll. But it was communal representation that won the day and entrenched the 1970 Constitution. Communal politics took root and racial divisions hardened to the point where a government elected with Indo-Fijian support was

---

30 From the election manifesto of the People's Democratic Party.

deposed in a military coup. The decreed 1990 Constitution entrenched racial apartheid. Nonetheless, the NFP leaders, principally Jai Ram Reddy, worked tirelessly with the Fijian leaders, principally the coup maker Sitiveni Rabuka, to produce a moderate, multiracial 1997 Constitution. It was a massive achievement in the most unlikely of circumstances, but its significance was not appreciated by Indo-Fijians.

Politics of moderation always lose in an atmosphere of polarised racial politics, and Fijian politics in the 1990s were deeply polarised. Both Rabuka and Reddy fell in the 1999 General Elections. NFP did not win a single seat then, or in the 2001 and 2006 elections. There was talk of closing shop but the party persisted. It gained moderate momentum on the eve of the 2014 elections. It mattered that the party was led by a team untainted by a political past. Its leader was the academic economist Biman Prasad from the USP, and its president was a young Fijian lawyer, Tupou Draunidalo. Her elevation to the presidency fulfilled the party's founding nonracial vision. In the party's line-up were several Fijian women and men with successful professional careers of their own. A decade or so earlier, this would have been unthinkable, and likened to treachery. But it was to the party's credit that it had broadened its multiracial base to this extent. Its policies were principled, moderate and progressive, appealing more to the electorate's intellect than to its heart. Its credentials as a party of principle were credible. Like all other parties, the NFP had been in the wilderness for the previous eight years, and the military regime had done all it could to hobble its prospects. The constraints were considerable. So, too, were its achievements: three parliamentary seats, won in the most difficult of circumstances. The NFP has a future if it maintains its multiethnic character and outlook and continues to infuse fresh blood into the party.

Indo-Fijian support for Fiji First was due not only to the weaknesses and constraints of other parties; it was also due to its own strengths and appeal as well. From 2007 onwards, despite the downturn in the economy, Bainimarama spared little effort to win popular support, including among Indo-Fijian voters. He managed to do so to a large degree, as the voting figures showed. He exploited the military regime's power of incumbency to the maximum, pointing to its record of achievements and making specific promises to the electorate, especially in the lower socioeconomic strata. Their attraction was considerable. Electricity subsidy to low income families, water free of charge to those earning less than $30,000 a year, price control and removal of value added tax on basic food items and pharmaceutical items, free milk to all first-year primary school children, streamlining the Tertiary Education Loan Scheme, providing free education to preschool, primary and secondary students, giving 99-year residential leases to squatters on state land. These were some of the many promises the regime made—promises backed by a record of achievements, it was emphasised.

No other party could give such concrete promises and would probably not have been believed even if they did. While other parties struggled to get their messages through to the electorate, Fiji First used the full paraphernalia of government machinery and the services of a compliant media to campaign. It helped the party's fortunes that all the district commissioners were former military men, along with many heads of government departments, some of whom declared their intention to contest the election within weeks of resigning their public service positions. This made mockery of Bainimarama's promise at the time of the coup that no one in his administration would benefit politically or stand for elections. But no one seemed to be overly concerned about broken promises. It was all a part of the 'game' of politics. And in any case, it was said with no sense of irony about it at all that Bainimarama was standing not because he wanted to but because the people of Fiji would not have it any other way; and the will of the people had to reign supreme, over and above personal preferences. That, after all, was the essence of democracy.

After the elections, it was commonplace to blame Indo-Fijians for their short-sighted and self-centred choice and their unwillingness to consider the long-term implications of their actions. But with the advantage of hindsight, it is understandable why Indo-Fijians, by choice as well as necessity, voted the way they did. Taking a long-term view about democracy and governance is not a strong suit of a people struggling to make ends meet and keen to leave for other lands at the first opportunity. The best and the brightest of the Indo-Fijian community have left, are leaving, or will leave—leaving behind those who cannot migrate because they lack the skills or resources to do so. To them (the ones who had to stay behind), the immediate fulfilment of their pressing daily needs was what mattered. By this criterion, Fiji First had a clear advantage over its rivals. Democracy based on the will and whims of one strongman is dangerous, and Fiji may yet pay a heavy price for this; but for many this one strongman also stood for stability against chaos. Indo-Fijians knew well that if Bainimarama failed, they would be done for. More than anything else, ordinary people wanted peace and security, and insurance against future coups. Bainimarama offered to be the buffer, and he was believed. But what happens when the well runs dry, or when some other saviour appears on the horizon, who has a different agenda, a different vision, perhaps even a nationalistic one? Does the military, for all practical purposes an indigenous institution itself, really have a multiracial vision? Do the commodore's own supporters, many of whom were in previous coup camps, also have a multiracial vision? In 2014, Indo-Fijians made the pragmatic assessment that, for the moment, Bainimarama, with the military solidly behind him, was their man. Tomorrow, as they say, is another day.

Democracy has had an ill-fated history in Fiji, having to contend with military coups as the vehicle for effecting political change in the country. It was alive all these years more in its symbolism than in its substance, dependent on the goodwill of powerful men rather than implanted in the hearts of ordinary citizens or embedded in the sinews of its public institutions. It had few true defenders but many fairweather friends who habitually deserted it in its moments of greatest need. Democratic values have been steadily eroding in Fiji since the 1987 coups along with a disillusionment with politics and politicians. All this made the Indo-Fijian reaction in 2014 understandable, but it is also true that Indo-Fijians have, in the process, planted the seeds of a new political order, a new kind of democracy, which is fundamentally at odds with the principles of representative democracy. Putting it colloquially, placing all your eggs in one basket in an uncertain environment is never prudent and neither is pinning all your hopes on one man to be your saviour, however good or great that saviour might turn out to be. The rule of law, freely arrived at, is infinitely superior to the rule of a group of men, however well-intentioned they might be. Fiji is going through a massive process of transition from one order to another. Inevitably, there will be uncertainty, confusion, error, disenchantment and disappointment. The larger question is whether, to borrow words from Tom Stoppard's *Rosencrantz and Guildenstern are Dead*, 'Look on every exit as being an entrance somewhere else'.[31] For the sake of Fiji, one hopes it will be entrance to a better place. That remains to be seen, but something very much to hope for.

---

31 Tom Stoppard, *Rosencrantz and Guildenstern Are Dead* (London: Faber and Faber, 1966), Act One.

PART 3
Retrospection

Figure 3. Cartoon of Brij and Padma Lal, showing confirmation of their life ban from travelling to Fiji imposed by the Fijian Government

Source. *Truth for Fiji* website, March/April 2015. Anonymous cartoonist. Online: truthforfiji.com/jan---mar-2015.html. Used with the permission of *Truth*.

21

Exile and a land of memory: Brij V. Lal, Indo-Fijian scholar activist[1]

C.K. Chen

> You can muffle the drum, and you can loosen
> the strings of the lyre.
> But who shall command the skylark not to sing.
>
> — Khalil Gibran[2]

Kevin Chen was a postgraduate student at The Australian National University when he wrote the present chapter as an assignment for another course. The substance of his original paper is intact except for some minor stylistic changes and prudent pruning to remove repetition. He is a Malaysian citizen now working on strategic issues there. A transcript of the interview is deposited at The Australian National University along with my papers.

I first met Professor Lal—or Brij as he insists on being called—some years ago when I was doing a Masters in Asia Pacific Studies at The Australian National University. One course organised by Dr Mary Kilcline Cody regularly invited guest lecturers to the class. Brij gave one such lecture

---

1 Originally appeared in *Fijian Studies* 14(2) (2016): 143–59.
2 Khalil Gibran, *The Prophet* (New York, NY: Knopf, 1923; Ware: Wordsworth Editions, 1996), p. 27.

and I remember it vividly. He walked into the lecture room in Coombs Extension 1.04, a shortish man with a greying head of hair and a neatly trimmed beard. He was wearing thick black-rimmed glasses and a tweed jacket with elbow patches to boot, the quintessential professorial attire for a Canberra winter. Head down and his hands clasped behind his back, he slowly paced the front of the room as he was introduced. You somehow sensed that he was a practised performer.

'Fiji is a four-letter word,' he began. We were all slightly taken aback by this abrupt, unaccustomed beginning. There were some smiles, some puzzled looks (especially from students from cultures not used to having teachers banter), some looking at him with intense anticipation. 'No, not *that* four-letter word,' he said in mock disappointment after a short silence, to giggles and titters, 'you people with wicked minds.' He had already won us over. 'Think of wind, rain, surf, sand, love, coup, hurt, pity.' Suddenly, the mood changed. The man was serious, dead serious. This wouldn't be a frivolous talk, forgettable, of the sort all too common in classrooms these days. For the next 45 minutes or so, with scarcely a note, he delivered from the podium an oration about the making and unmaking of his country's history, how the Fijians, Indo-Fijians and Europeans struggled to find their place in the Fijian sun and the different metaphors they invoked in support of their causes. He talked repeatedly about Fiji being a land of missed opportunity, of its desolate political landscape hobbled by an obsession with the politics of race. The similarities between Malaysia and Fiji were alarming, the only difference being that while they are still contesting the basis of legitimacy and representation in Fiji, in Malaysia we have come to an accommodation about those fundamental questions.

The lecture has remained with me. History, for Professor Lal, was not an abstract, remote discipline, but a lived reality. As he said, he lived not above or beyond his history, but within it as an active, engaged observer. I remember asking him: 'How can you be objective when you are so involved in the history you write?' And he replied: 'Objectivity is overrated. As you well know, the Devil doesn't think God is objective.' We all laughed, but he had a serious point.

> I am passionate about the values of democracy and the rule of law, about the sanctity of the ballot box, and if that is being subjective, then I cannot help it. I am a human being first and foremost, an academic second.

Any country anywhere in the world would be proud to claim Professor Lal as its own, I remember thinking. And it is this man that the Fijian Government had banned from entering the country for life! I wanted to find out more about him and his mission.

I was in the Fijian Parliament on 15 March 2015 when the Lal saga unfolded. It was the last day of my two-month research study visit to Fiji and I decided to visit Fiji's new parliament to catch a session of parliamentary sitting. The new parliament, I was told, had been moved from the Old Battery Hill site in Vieuto to its pre-1987 location in the old wing of the government building. It was another one of those decisions made by decree, as part of the Fiji First Government's new image policy, its determination to mark a break from the past. The new chamber was impressively refurbished with modern gadgetry. I took my seat to witness what promised to be a fairly ordinary session.

Then, during mid-morning, opposition member Prem Singh asked a question that got my attention: 'What is the duration of prohibition from entering the country imposed on foreign passport holders?' 'It goes from twelve months to an indefinite period,' replied Minister of Immigration Lesi Natuva.[3] Whereupon Singh followed up with a supplementary question. 'Why are former Fiji citizens and current Australian passport holders Professor Brij Lal and Dr Padma Lal banned from entering Fiji since November 2009 and January 2010?'

The minister stood up to reply. Fiji, he said, was a sovereign state and it was up to the state whether to allow or disallow a foreigner to enter the country. That was stating the obvious. Then he said, referring to Brij: 'This particular person, he had been very vocal and opposed moves towards democracy after the events of 2006.' He went on:

> His actions were viewed by the Government of the day as prejudicial to peace, defence, public safety, public order and security of the Government of day. The decision by the former Minister of Defence, he was given a prohibited immigrant status immediately. We had reviewed the decision when I came into office, and after studying the case, I concurred with the decision made by the former Minister of Defence.[4]

---

3   Timoci Lesikivatukoula Natuva (born 1957) was elected to parliament in 2014 with 2,691 votes after a 30-year career in the Fijian military. He holds an MA in Strategic Studies from Deakin University and has had several stints on international peacekeeping duties as a senior officer attached to the United Nations.
4   These and the quotes following are from the Fijian Parliament's *Hansard* of 18 March 2015.

The minister referred to was none other than Commodore Frank Bainimarama, Natuva's superior officer in the military.

There was a slight commotion in the chambers as someone from the government side chimed in about the inappropriateness of mentioning names of persons in parliamentary questions. Speaker Jiko Luveni was caught off guard, but agreed with the government.[5] 'We are referring to particular cases,' an opposition member retorted. 'It is strictly necessary to name these individuals.' Another pointed to the freedom of speech authorised in the constitution, but by now a clearly flustered speaker had had enough. This was a legal matter, she ruled pointedly, and she would allow no further discussion of it. Later the minister told the media that the Lals had been given indefinite bans on returning to Fiji.

I returned to Canberra determined to probe deeper into the matter. Something about the Fijian episode had disturbed me in an unidentifiable way. Banning someone from entering a country was bad enough, but there was hope at the end that the decision might be reversed after a passage of time. But an indefinite ban and that, too, on former citizens, in this case clearly two very distinguished former citizens of Fiji? Padma, Brij's wife, is an environmental and resources economist who has worked in Fiji and the Pacific Islands. She is a recognised authority on the country's ailing sugar industry, I discovered.[6] And Brij's various accomplishments are reflected in the awards and honours he has received over the years, including an Order of Australia in the Queen's Birthday Honours List 2015 for his contribution to teaching and research in Pacific history. I wonder what all this said about a society proclaiming itself to be a 'democracy' that was so intolerant of free speech and so harsh on dissidents.

I realised on the plane back why the Fijian incident disturbed me. I am a Malaysian citizen of Chinese descent. Our family has lived in Malaysia for several generations. Malaysia is our only home, but we all know in our hearts what our place is in the larger order of things in the country. We have democracy, we have elections, we vote, and we live in hope, but we also know the limit of things. We have what we might call a 'glass house'

---

5   Jiko Luveni was also President of the Fiji First Party and she was frequently criticised by the opposition for her allegedly partisan rulings.

6   Padma Narsey Lal is author of the standard reference work *Ganna: Portrait of the Fiji Sugar Industry* (Lautoka: Sugar Commission of Fiji, 2009). She was employed by the International Union for the Conservation of Nature, an international nongovernment organisation in Suva. Before that she had been a sustainable development advisor at the Pacific Islands Forum Secretariat.

democracy, as the treatment of former Deputy Prime Minister Anwar Ibrahim shows. But for all that, Malaysia is still home. The thought of being separated from it for life is simply unbearable. As we say, the spirits of our ancestors, our guardian angels, roam the land. And, as far as I know, no one has ever been banned for life in Malaysia. That is a record to reckon with.

I knocked on the door of Coombs 4240. As I entered, I found a room exactly as described in one of Brij's essays—clogged with books and papers on the shelves and on the floor, family pictures on the wall, enlarged photos of Fiji, and mementos of various achievements.[7] It is an historian's office alright, full of memories. Brij looked at me surveying all this in amazement. 'Books keep me alive,' he said, reading my mind, 'connect me to our present and past. Books are the only things that really matter.' This is not a very subtle dig at my generation hooked on Google. I smile and let his comment pass. He is an historian after all, a man of the written word, immersed in the past, a harmless Luddite remnant in his own lifetime (as he said in the course of our conversation).

I turn to his latest entanglement with the Fijian authorities. I began by asking him about Bainimarama. 'Have you ever met him? Why do you think he is so adamant about keeping you out of Fiji?' No, he has never met the 2006 coup leader. As for his reaction:

> I wish I knew but I would guess it is not very complicated. No dictator or military leader wants to be contradicted, his narrative challenged, its false foundations exposed. No emperor wants to hear that he has no clothes on. I took the military regime on in my writings, in my speeches and radio interviews, and I exposed their lies and half-truths. I was a thorn in their side, and they had to get rid of me as soon as they could.

This was no self-aggrandising exaggeration. Canadian journalism academic Marc Edge has written somewhere that Brij was the one academic the Fijian regime hated the most, and he was regularly the target of virulent attacks by proregime bloggers.[8]

---

7   Brij V. Lal, 'Coombs 4240', in his *Intersections: History, Memory, Discipline* (Canberra: ANU E Press, 2012), pp. 127–38, doi.org/10.22459/IHMD.11.2012.
8   See Brij V. Lal, 'Caught in the web', in his *Intersections: History, Memory, Discipline,* pp. 279–86.

'You say "false foundations" but Bainimarama has talked about leading a "glorious revolution". Surely he could not have succeeded without popular support.' 'George Orwell got it right all those years ago,' Brij responded, 'One does not establish a dictatorship in order to safeguard a revolution; one makes the revolution in order to establish the dictatorship.'[9] He fetches apt quotes with amazing ease, but I am looking for concrete details. Brij replies calmly:

> When Bainimarama carried out his coup on 5 December 2006, he really had no clue beyond protecting his personal interests. It truly was about saving Bainimarama's bacon, not about saving the nation. His contract with the military was up for review and not likely to be renewed, the police were investigating his role in the resignation of President Mara in 2000, questions were being asked about the brutal murder of rebel soldiers in the November 2000 mutiny, and a White Paper had called the Fiji military top heavy. He was angered that various bills proposed by the government might limit his power, grant immunity to those involved in the 2000 coup. And so he struck before he was struck down.[10]

'And he got away with it?' 'But all this was carefully camouflaged as Bainimarama took the high moral ground.' He went on:

> No one serving in his administration would stand for elections in future to avoid allegations of conflict of interest. That promise was quietly abandoned. No one in the military would benefit from the coup. The contrary proved to be the case as military officers entered the civil service to staff senior positions or got posted as diplomats. There would be no abuse of the judicial process as allegedly happened under previous governments. One by one, convicted criminals close to the military marched out of jail after a few months on a Compulsory Supervision Order and were restored to their former positions. Judges complained of interference from the Attorney-General. But nothing was investigated, nothing was done. In truth, nothing could be done. All the power was on the other side.

---

9   George Orwell, *Nineteen Eighty-four (1984)* (London: Seeker and Warburg, 1949), p. 332.
10   See Jon Fraenkel, Stewart Firth and Brij V. Lal (eds), *The 2006 Military Takeover in Fiji: A Coup to End all Coups?* (Canberra: ANU E Press, 2009), doi.org/10.22459/MTF.04.2009; and in particular in that volume Brij V. Lal, 'Anxiety, uncertainty and fear in our land: Fiji's road to 2006', pp. 21–42.

Only a few usual suspects spoke up, while others chose the path of quiet acquiescence. 'Nothing comforts oppressors more than the silence and neutrality of the populace,' Brij says.

'How did an illegal coup morph into a nation-building exercise?' As Brij tells it, the rationale and the rationalisation for the coup came much later.

> It was the initiative of some Fijian expatriates who seized the coup as an opportunity to restructure Fijian society, economy and politics, convinced that they, rather than the politicians, had the answer to Fiji's deep-seated problems. They were convinced that a perfect template would inexorably lead in the course of time to a perfect society. A 'People's Charter' came along with a 'Roadmap' to lead Fiji back to parliamentary democracy. Bainimarama, floundering, grabbed the opportunity and consolidated his hold on power. By the time it was realised that he might have other agendas, other fish to fry, it was too late.

Once ensconced, he quickly dispensed with his former hangers-on. Bainimarama had the last laugh.

'And his hangers-on, as you call them?' 'They are now back home in New Zealand and Australia after pocketing handsome sums advising and consulting in Fiji.' A trace of bitterness crept into his voice as he recalled some 'supine' academics—Brij's words—'who continued to sing hollow, self-ingratiating praises of the regime from the comforts of their overseas homes in return for small favours or vacuous flattery in their desolate twilight years.'

When I put this to a person who initially supported Bainimarama, he said that Brij, as an historian, should 'know better than most that human history is complex and there are some imperfect successes and many failures and even reverses'. He said that the coup provided 'an opportunity for a more desirable direction for Fiji'. At first, Bainimarama was prepared to work within the provisions of the 1997 Constitution, but then changed his mind. 'We were not naïve or misguided or a complete failure. Some elements [of our platform] have been adopted in the regime's still illegitimate constitution and policies.' Clearly, the debate will go on about duplicity and broken promises and motivations and machinations behind the scenes.

'How did Bainimarama consolidate his hold on power so quickly and completely?' Brij is pithy. 'Force, fraud and fear.' He continued:

> In the first few years, the military terrorised people it saw as its opponents: beatings at the barracks, stoning of opponents' properties (houses and cars), threatening midnight calls. And no one was ever prosecuted. All this is conveniently forgotten now, but victims of thuggery and violence paid a heavy price for standing up for their beliefs. After the setting aside of the 1997 Constitution came a deluge of draconian decrees limiting free speech and freedom of association, the stacking of the judiciary and other branches of government. None of this could be challenged in a court of law. And fear, insidious fear, of punishment and retribution if you were caught criticising the regime.

This, Brij says, is the actual lived reality in a repressive state and the realisation that few will stand by your side. 'Often, you have to walk alone.'

But if it is a lived reality, it was not immediately apparent on the streets of Suva and the surrounding areas I had visited. People were wary about foreigners, but those who did talk had good things to say. Burglaries were down, I was told, and people in congested urban centres could sleep peacefully at night 'with their windows and doors open'. Brij said:

> Indo-Fijians wanted peace after so many years of turbulence when they were at the receiving end of racist taunts and barbs. They wanted the coups to end, they wanted the country to move on, make a living. And they knew only Bainimarama could deliver.

That rang true to my own experience of travelling around Suva, passed squalid squatter settlements, makeshift roadside stalls selling vegetables, the congested low-cost housing estates. Hope was a scarce commodity in these parts. Bainimarama was their beacon. 'What happens when he goes?' 'The rule of law rather than the rule of one man: that is the only way forward.'

'Getting the indigenous Fijians on side would have been a mammoth task?' 'That it was,' Brij said.

> Bainimarama adopted a two-pronged approach. First, he disabled all rival centres of power. He dispensed with the Great Council of Chiefs, hobbled the Methodist Church, the two pillars of the Fijian establishment. He disabled the Fiji Sugar Cane Growers Council, the power base of Indo-Fijian politicians in the sugar

belt,[11] and he curtailed the power of trade unions, all done by decree. Bainimarama had no rivals. Laisenia Qarase [the deposed prime minister] was nowhere to be seen. His former comrades suddenly were all silent. The paramount chiefs were all gone.[12] In a very real sense, Bainimarama was now a paramount chief in his own right, chief of the military whose loyalty to him was unquestioned. The timing for him could not have been better.

'And the carrot?'

With the help of foreign image makers,[13] Bainimarama began chanting the mantra of multiracialism, the need to build a race-free Fiji of equal citizens, make Fiji the Singapore of the Pacific, to create a level field for all citizens irrespective of birth. Indo-Fijians were already in his corner, and now many commoner Fijians responded as well, looking at last for their own place in the sun.

I had heard vague talk about this in Suva. The old structures and institutions had ceased to have any relevance to their lives. Open disparagement of the high chiefs was not the kind of reaction I had anticipated.

The surprising thing for me was how quickly the once revered structures collapsed. Brij pointed to the long-term causes of the decline: rural decline, urban drift, a modern education, the spread of the cash economy.[14] 'The past is another country to the modern generation,' Brij said. It was the same everywhere in the world, victims of 'modernisation' and 'development'. In the past, the ills of Fijian society were blamed on the Indo-Fijians and their alleged grasping eye on all things Fijian, especially land. But now their numbers were declining; they were no longer a convincing scapegoat.

When the general elections finally took place in September 2014 under a new open proportional representation system, everyone expected Bainimarama to win, but not by such a large margin. But he had all the trump cards in his hands: the public purse to be plundered at will, an extensive propaganda machinery, a leader with an instantly recognisable

---

11   In particular Indo-Fijian politician Mahendra Chaudhry, leader of the Fiji Labour Party and General Secretary of the National Farmers Union of Fiji.
12   The reference here is to Ratu Sir Penaia Ganilau, former governor-general and president, and Ratu Sir Kamisese Mara, independent Fiji's first prime minister and later president who died in 2004.
13   People in Fiji talked about Qorvis, a Washington DC–based public relations firm that specialises in refurbishing the image of authoritarian regimes around the world.
14   See studies in Michael Taylor (ed.), *Fiji: Future Imperfect?* (Sydney: Allen and Unwin, 1987).

name, periodic statements from the Fiji military that it would prefer Bainimarama to continue in office (and all that it implied), and opposition parties hobbled by various draconian decrees. Old constituency boundaries were abandoned in favour of a single national constituency. And the open list system would allocate seats in parliament in proportion to the votes parties got.

The logic in the system was self-evident.[15] A party should amass as many votes as possible. Fiji First, Bainimarama's party, urged its supporters to cast their votes for one person, Frank Bainimarama. Everyone knew who he was. And that is precisely what happened. Of the 496,364 votes cast, Fiji First got 293,714 or 59 per cent of the votes, and of that Bainimarama got 202,458 votes or more than two-thirds of the votes cast for his party. The next highest vote getter for the party was Aiyaz Saiyed Khaiyum with 13,374 (mostly Muslim) votes, covertly orchestrated through promises and patronage. Clearly Bainimarama had very long coat-tails from which his party benefited enormously. Three Indo-Fijian members got fewer than 1,000 votes and they became ministers in the Bainimarama Government. Six other ministers had come from the Fiji military.

Brij says:

> The Bainimarama Government was government of 'small people,' most with no record of public service or standing whatsoever. That was a common view in Fiji. People in Fiji seemed to look back to the old days when they had leaders they looked up to, were proud of. None of the Fiji First's Indo-Fijians, for example, had much standing in the community, getting elected on a handful of votes in the curious electoral system that Fiji has.[16] They know that the sole reason for their presence in parliament is Frank Bainimarama, and they are completely beholden to him, outdoing each other to do his bidding, keeping the commodore pleased at any cost. Bainimarama thrives on public adulation.

---

15   See Jon Fraenkel, 'Fiji's electoral system changes', *Pacific Islands Report,* January 2013.
16   There are exceptions, I was told in Suva that Mahendra Reddy was chair of the Fiji Commerce Commission and Praveen Bala was the military regime's administrator for Lautoka city. He was Ba town's long-time mayor as member of the National Federation Party.

21. EXILE AND A LAND OF MEMORY

'This is not democracy,' Brij says. 'Military dictatorship has been replaced by parliamentary dictatorship. Or perhaps, this is democracy Bainimarama-style.'

'But at least Fiji has a parliament, which is a step in the right direction?' 'But it is a parliament without teeth,' Brij replies.

> Parliamentary procedures are regularly subverted to get the government's agenda through. Parliamentary questions are carefully vetted to spare the government close scrutiny or embarrassment, and debate is prematurely guillotined to derive the Opposition of parliamentary time and media coverage. The Opposition is belittled and routinely ridiculed. The number of parliamentary sitting days has been reduced to just four weeks. Just four weeks a year, two or more of which would be taken up during the budget session in November. All the government voted as one in support of the change and the all the opposition members unanimously opposed it.

It is all a brutal numbers game. 'The government wants to change the flag. The overwhelming majority rejects the proposal to change, but Bainimarama brazenly declares that he has noticed a strong desire for change in the people.' 'In that case, why not a referendum?' 'No, because that would give a lie to his claim of popular support.'

Following that pattern of unilateral decision-making, Bainimarama announced in July 2015 that he would be prepared to resettle the entire Kiribati population of nearly 100,000 in Fiji if their island was imperilled by climate change. An admirable sentiment, but the people of Fiji were not consulted, there was no debate in parliament, no consideration of complex social and economic issues involved.

> Did anyone ask the residents of the squatter settlements what they thought of the Kiribati proposal? This is Bainimarama's way; he expects complete compliance and capitulation, not questions or criticism. In this military man's books, disagreement is disloyalty.

'Everyone says Khaiyum, an Australian-educated lawyer, is the mastermind of these sweeping changes.'[17]

> His is certainly a name to contend with, the most powerful person in government. He is a highly visible, voluble presence in Fiji, in the newspapers, on television, on radio as the *de facto* leader of the government. Australian author and journalist Kathy Marks has described him as 'ruthless, authoritarian and vindictive'.[18]

He appears as a curious combination of arrogance and affected false modesty, a description with which both his friends and foes agree. Khaiyum inspires fear for his vindictive streak, not respect or regard. Brij has called him 'unctuous' and 'condescending'. There is no love lost between the two.

'What was the reason for the seemingly unbreakable bond between Bainimarama and Khaiyum?' Wild, unfounded speculation abounded in Fiji, but Brij has a simpler theory—mutual interest in survival.

> One without the other would be like a fish without gills. Whatever else you say about Khaiyum, he delivers. He is no threat to Bainimarama. He does not have an independent power base of his own. He was a nondescript company legal secretary before 2006, and he will return to a nondescript career after Bainimarama. And Khaiyum needs Bainimarama. Without him, he will be politically dead. He knows he is widely distrusted by indigenous Fijians for his controlling ways and confrontational tone. They see him as the evil genius behind the Bainimarama throne. They would not mourn his departure from the political scene; on the contrary, they would rejoice in it.

A harsh assessment, but it has a large grain of truth, judging by my admittedly limited conversation with people in Suva.[19] The truth that power is transitory has not dawned on anyone. Hubris will be the cause of their downfall.

---

17   Aiyaz Saiyed-Khaiyum has an undergraduate law degree from the University of New South Wales in Sydney and a MA in Law from the University of Hong Kong. Before the coup, he was the company secretary of the Colonial Group of Companies, with some legal experience with the Australian law firm Minter Ellison.
18   'Bula Bully', *Good Weekend*, 21 June 2014, p. 29.
19   Among the names mentioned to me in Suva were those of Dewan Maharaj, owner of Quality Print, who was President of the Sanatan Dharam, and Kamlesh Arya, General Secretary of the Arya Samaj. The leaders of the South Indian community refrained from taking sides.

'Was 2006 a Muslim coup?' Many non-Muslims in Fiji had told me in somewhat hushed tones that it was and point out the number of Muslims suddenly in prominent places. 'No, it wasn't,' Brij says firmly.

> It was a case of opportunistic individuals who happened to be Muslims who used the coup to advance their own personal agendas or settle old grievances once they knew that Bainimarama would be around for a long time.

And he hastened to add that the leading functionaries of the Hindu groups were also backers of the coup, such as the leaders of Sanatan Dharam and Arya Samaj. They blamed the Muslims to deflect attention from themselves. 'They are all in the same coup canoe, all equally culpable.'

I return to Brij and his time in Canberra since his enforced departure from Fiji in November 2009 and ask him, 'Why did you continue to speak out on Fiji on radio, on television and in the newspapers?' 'I had no choice,' he says. 'The opposition in Fiji had been silenced through draconian decrees and threats of terrible violence. Fiji was thrashing about, blaming everyone else for its problems, especially Australia. They had to be confronted.' I said, 'Australia did not instigate the coup in Fiji, the Fijian military did.' Brij replied:

> The blame should be laid squarely at their door. Why does Fiji need such a large standing military?[20] And why is the Fijian military still almost wholly indigenous Fijian? When I remind Bainimarama that one of his senior ministers, Inoke Kubuabola, was a key architect of the 1987 coup and an ardent champion of Fijian rights in the 1990s, he gets upset.

He goes on:

> Fiji blames the Pacific Islands Forum for its exclusion from it. Well, what would you expect? Fiji violated solemn undertakings it gave to resolve its problems through democratic means and then complains when reminded of the flagrant breach? It cynically uses the Melanesian Spearhead Group, to which it was latecomer, to get sympathy and support for itself in the region. Fiji accuses Australia of being a big brother in the Pacific when it covets that role for itself.[21]

---

20   According to some accounts, the largest per capita army in the world.
21   See Brij V. Lal, 'Fiji: Fishing in troubled waters', *Security Challenges* 8(2) (2012): 85–92.

'How do you see Bainimarama's intervention in the larger perspective of Fijian history?' I ask. 'The military coup of 2006 marked the end of an era in modern Fijian history,' he says.

> All the parameters and paradigms of the twentieth century went out the window with that coup: the obsession with the politics of race and indigenous rights and the fears and phobias they generated, the disappearance of the traditional gatekeepers left on the margins by the forces of modernity engulfing the life of most ordinary Fijians.

Spoken in a true professorial manner, precise and eloquent.

'So what would be Bainimarama's legacy, his place in Fijian history?' There is a pause, and then:

> Bainimarama has destroyed one world whose destruction is not universally mourned, in fact, quietly, cautiously welcomed. And he says he has laid the foundations of a new one full of fresh potential and opportunity, but this is easy, self-satisfying talk. Bainimarama constantly recites the mantra of multiracialism, and many believe him. But it is almost certain the military does not, nor many of his close supporters, such as Inoke Kubuabola, a self-admitted architect of the 1987 coup. Beneath the surface of feel-good talk lurks sinister currents of racialism. The two main communities are further apart now than a decade ago, both deeply suspicious about each other's motives and motivations.

This is a sentiment widely shared in Fiji but rarely expressed publicly. The public narrative will be questioned only at one's peril. Brij dismisses the talk of Fiji returning to true parliamentary democracy any time soon. It is not representative democracy but the illusion of democracy, repressive democracy, run on the whims of two men. One of them goes and the whole structure would collapse. Brij returns to the metaphor about fish without gills. 'Fiji is a fragile democracy.'

From politics to the person. 'There must have been a human, personal cost to his isolation and exile.' He agrees, but what really gets him angry is the punishment meted out to his wife, Padma. She was expelled from Fiji in January 2010. 'Padma has never uttered a political comment in the public domain whatever her private feelings and views might be,' he says.

She broke no law, she has no criminal record. Why punish her for simply being married to me? She is a consummate professional person, totally dedicated to her field of resource and environmental economics. They destroyed her professional career. For the way they treated her, I shall never forgive the Fijian regime. We both will wear the ban as a badge of honour. They are the ones diminished by it.

All of Brij's siblings now live in Australia, and many members of the extended family are scattered around the world. Only his widowed sisters-in-law and some of his nieces and nephews live in Fiji. Technology has lessened the pain of isolation. There is daily cyber traffic in the form of emails, Facebook communication, blog sites. Fijian radio and television news can be freely accessed. Without these, exile would have been unbearable. It would have killed him. What he misses most, Brij says, is not being able to say a final goodbye to dear friends and family. His cousins with whom he grew up in Tabia, his childhood friends, are passing on and he is distressed that he cannot be in Fiji to be with them in their last moments. And there are birthdays and weddings he can't attend, especially as the eldest living member of his extended family. There are so many new members of the family whom he has never seen, and they cannot afford to travel overseas. He hopes that they will understand the reason for his absence, but with so much propaganda around, he can't be sure. And he dearly misses the familiar smell, sights and sounds of rural Fiji, which words and pictures cannot quite capture.[22]

Sixty, Brij says, is the age when the past begins to return, when long-gone days begin to acquire a golden glow, and for him his Fijian past has been returning with ever greater poignancy and intensity in the past few years. He has had health issues, I learn indirectly but didn't think it appropriate to raise it with him.[23] Some years ago, he and his wife bought a house in Suva, in the much sought-after Beach Road in Laucala Bay where they hoped to retire to live among friends and family and do volunteer work in the squatter community. His screensaver is a 180-degree crimson-coloured dawn view of the of the Laucala Bay area from his veranda, with Nukulau Island glistening in the distance. The tiny island, I learned, has a huge historic significance, as the landing place of the Indian indentured

---
22 See Brij V. Lal, 'Fare well, Fiji', in *Mr Tulsi's Store: A Fijian Journey* (Canberra: Pandanus Books, 2001), pp. 207–08.
23 These include diabetes Type II and glaucoma in both eyes, a degenerative eye condition requiring constant monitoring.

labourers, including Brij's grandfather, and the place where the infamous George Speight was briefly incarcerated. Now it is a picnic spot for Suva's nouveau rich. The scene is the first thing he sees as he opens his computer every day, after all these years, a haunting reminder of fading memories.

All exiles feed on hope, and Brij thought that Fiji would open a new chapter after the elections of September 2014 and allow him back into the country. Encouraged by friends in Fiji and elsewhere, he wrote to the Minister of Immigration, Lesi Natuva, a navy man: 'The values of democracy, the rule of law and the processes and protocols of constitutionalism are sacrosanct to us.' He had opposed the military overthrow of a democratically elected government because, as a former constitutional commissioner, one of the architects of the reports that led to the formulation of the 1997 Constitution, he had no alternative but to take the stance that he did. But, 'Fiji has a new constitution and a newly elected government. My stand was against the 2006 coup, but the coup succeeded and the matter is over now.' After a month, Natuva emailed Brij to say that he was free to travel to Fiji but that he should check with his senior Immigration Department officials.

Brij did. On 15 December, the Assistant Director of Immigration Edward Brown wrote back:

> The latest development into your case is that both you and your wife's names are still appearing on our system and we have established that the instructions to put your names on our Controversial List had been given by the Prime Minister's Office. As such we will be delivering a letter to that office tomorrow the 16th of December seeking their comments and endorsement that your names should no longer be on the list and that the both of you can now travel to Fiji.

There was no response from the Prime Minister's Office. Brij was asked to write to the permanent secretary of the department 'advising him of the predicament that you are in and of your intention to return to the country soon'.

There then ensued a long silence. On 10 June 2015, Brij wrote to senior immigration officials asking for a response. 'The government proudly proclaims its commitment to open, transparent and accountable governance but, at least on this instance, its practice breaches its proclamation,' he wrote in some exasperation. 'My wife and I want to know why we are banned from travelling to the land of our birth.' The reply came on 29 June. It was from Edward Brown.

> Through this email, I would like to advise you that you and your wife's cases were processed and submitted to the Honourable Minister for Defence, National Security and Immigration for his decision and I regret to advise that after careful consideration, a decision was reached that the status quo should remain. As such you and your wife are still prohibited from returning to Fiji.

What that recommendation was no one will never know. The email came on the date of Brij's and Padma's 40th wedding anniversary. They are the first Fiji-born people ever permanently exiled from the land of their birth.

'It must be a bit lonely at the top,' I joke. 'Give me Fiji any day,' he says. Brij does not glorify exile.

> 'Exile is a dream of a glorious return,' Salman Rushdie has written somewhere in *The Satanic Verses*. I do not feel that way. I am with Simone Weil who says that to be 'rooted is perhaps the most important and least recognized need of the human soul'. To be a real, active member of a living, vibrant community is far more preferable to a life of isolation in another place whose secrets you will never fully know and whose future you will never fully grasp. An exile's life will forever be a life of existential in-betweenity.

Fiji is close to Brij's heart; he cannot let it go, and Fiji's hold on him is deep. Brij points to a huge pile of completed survey forms on the squatter settlement of Wailea, near Vatuwaqa. He had a book in mind on how and why people had uprooted themselves from their former rural homes and settled there. He wanted to explore their dreams and hopes. He talks movingly about a young boy, 10, no more, from the settlement he had met, a student at Vishnu Deo Primary School, who knew—everyone knew—that his mother was a sex worker in Suva. How he coped with the taunts of people as he walked down the foul-smelling lane to his tin shack home, only he knew. He had met a policeman who lived among the squatters to save money to send his three girls to school to secure them good marriages and careers and, if Lady Luck smiled, a foreign passport. There was an old Indo-Fijian man, thin and dark and perennially shirtless, making a quid on the side selling marijuana to high school kids from wealthy homes. There was a painter of sorts, living in a makeshift structure of rotting corrugated iron gathered from the roadside, who dreamed of having an exhibition of his works in Australia! And he had met a young Indo-Fijian girl, 12 or 13, who had dreams of becoming a nurse who would come back and live and work among the squatters: such a noble ambition in this most improbable of places; so many memorable stories that will now go unrecorded. 'I hope that someone will one day bear testimony to that dreadful human experience.'[24]

'What now for you?' I ask. He won't be eating 'the bitter bread of banishment,' he says. Canberra is, and has been, a warm, welcoming home. He has many friends who provide protective company and sustain him in his dark moments. He enjoys the respect of his colleagues. He was sent into exile to silence his voice, to send a message of fear to Fijian dissidents everywhere. But they got him completely wrong. He will not bow before the fury of dictators. He says he has the uncomfortable but necessary habit as an historian of remembering what those in power want forgotten. They can deny him his birthright to return to his native homeland, 'but they can't steal my memory'. 'I may not be able to return alive, but my ashes will, to the sacred places of my childhood.' W.H. Auden comes to his mind: 'The lights must never go out, / The music must always play'.[25] The memory of banishment will heal in time, he says, but it will not be extinguished, nor allowed to be. 'All that is needed for tyranny to triumph is for men and women of goodwill to do nothing, to look the other way,' he says defiantly. For him, redemption for human beings, as for communities and nations, lies in active remembrance, not in wilful forgetfulness. He says, quoting Auden again: 'All I have is a voice / To undo the folded lie'.[26] Over coffee at the God's after our talk in his office, Brij remembered some lines from one of his favourite poets, W.S. Merwin, that reveal the anguish in his heart:

> what I live for can I seldom believe in
> who I love I cannot go to
> what I hope is always divided
>
> — W.S. Merwin[27]

---

24 Some of the experience of living in squatter settlement is captured in Brij V. Lal's 'A change of seasons', in *Turnings: Fiji Factions* (Lautoka: Fiji Institute of Applied Studies, 2008), pp. 151–72.
25 W.H. Auden, *Another Time* (London: The British Library, 1940).
26 ibid.
27 W.S. Merwin, 'Teachers', in *The Carrier of Ladders* (New York: Atheneum, 1970), lines 6–8.

22

'Of exits and entrances'

In dialogue with Doug Munro

> All the world's a stage,
> And all the men and women merely players;
> They have their exits and their entrances.
>
> — William Shakespeare[1]

What follows is the result of a series of email exchanges between Doug Munro and myself between September and November 2017. It provides the opportunity to elaborate on my valedictory lecture at The Australian National University in February 2016 (which I light-heartedly called my 'Extinguished lecture'—Chapter 23 in this volume). In the lead-up, several colleagues made suggestions as to the subjects I might broach, some of which were included in my lecture. Those that I could not include, or at least not as fully as I would have liked, were put aside for later consideration, as were a number comments after the lecture. The present contribution, written in retirement, is my response to them. I thank colleagues and friends who made suggestions and apologise if my responses do not fully address their concerns. And, as always, my deep gratitude to Doug for a 40-year friendship and fruitful working relationship.

---

1 William Shakespeare, *As You Like It,* in *William Shakespeare: The Complete Works,* ed. Peter Alexander, (London and Glasgow: Collins, 1951, reprint 1980), pp. 254–83, 2.7.140, 141.

DM: You have said often enough that your journey from a remote, sugarcane-growing village of Tabia on the island of Vanua Levu to the top of your profession has been an improbable one. It reminds me of a statement in the computer-animated film *Ratatouille* (2007) that 'Not everyone can be a great artist, but a great artist can come from anywhere'.[2] What made your journey possible? Can you account for the success you have had in your career?

BL: It is impossible to be certain about these things as there are so many intangible, even unknown, factors to consider, and I am not sure I can do justice to the question. To start with, though, I suppose you will have to take a certain amount of native talent for granted, but that by itself is not sufficient because I know many talented people who have not done well and many not-so-talented people who have gone far. I would say that, in my case, determination, luck and timing were crucial. Regarding determination, I am reminded of the words of the football coaching legend Sir Alex Ferguson: 'Forget ability, to achieve in life you need something extra inside you, a dynamo that says I am going somewhere'.[3] From early on, I was determined that a canefarmer's life would not be mine. That desire and determination has been vital for my success.

I was the fourth child in a family of eight. Middle children are not usually burdened with expectations, obligations and responsibilities. That has certainly been my experience. I was often left alone to dream, to read whatever books and papers were around, which was not much. I recognised as a child that I was more interested in the conversations of adults—about politics, news, village matters—than I was in what children of my own age were interested in. Things I observed or heard about left a deep impression on me, sent me spinning into the inner recesses of my imaginary world. So, a certain seriousness of purpose was evident early. I was my *girmitiya* grandfather's favourite grandchild and I remember to this day the stories he used to tell about his youthful days in India, stories of people and places, gods and goblins, food and festivals, games children played, the fabulous animals that roamed the land (elephants, bears, lions). They were full of magic and romance and adventure, probably

---

2 *Ratatouille* (2007), a computer-animated comedy film, produced by Pixar, released by Walt Disney Pictures.
3 John Brewin, 'Adversaries Mourinho and Klopp might be well served borrowing from each other', 27 October 2017, available from: www.espn.in/football/english-premier-league/23/blog/post/3245758/adversaries-jose-mourinho-and-jurgen-klopp-might-be-well-served-borrowing-from-each-other (accessed 27 May 2019).

vastly exaggerated. For grandfather, everything about India had a golden glow reflecting, I suppose, the nostalgia and longing of a ruptured life in a land far away from home. Grandfather connected me to a past that has remained with me.

My parents told us stories they had heard from their parents and elders, morality tales from the *Panchatantra,* the Indian book of fables, in the unlit silence of our thatched house where we all slept. Radio was new in the village and there was no electricity in the house, so these stories kept our imaginative life active, kept us connected to the frayed fundamentals of our ancestral culture. I sometimes recite the stories of my early childhood to my grandchildren, to their bemusement ('But Nana. Bears can't talk and elephants can't dance!'). One image from my childhood remains vivid in my mind. I still remember aeroplanes disappearing over the horizon, and wondered who the travellers might be, where they might be going, whether I too might one day go to faraway places that I imagined to be full of novel and exciting things we so lacked at home. My curiosity about the world around me developed early, and it has remained with me. I regularly attended Ramayana recitals in the village and often accompanied adults in reciting the text. It was a wonderfully enriching experience full of entertainment and enlightenment I now realise. The Hindi I picked up then is still with me, minus some of the earlier fluency.

DM: What was the extent of parental influence on your education? This is something you have said much about in your autobiographical writings.

BL: My parents certainly encouraged us to study hard so that we had the opportunities denied to them, and we did. Both my parents were illiterate, though my mother somehow picked up enough Hindi to be able to write her name. Father always affixed his thumbprint on documents. I had tough examples to follow. Both my older brothers were star performers at primary school, coming top of their class and it was expected as a matter of course that I would do the same. My quest for excellence, to be the very best I could be, began around this time. I always came first in my class. We were a poor family making a living from our leased 10-acre (4-hectare) farm growing cane, rice, vegetables, chickens and we had a cow. It was clear to us from the very beginning that there was no future on the farm for all six boys. We would have to make our future somewhere else. That was incentive enough to do well at school.

We did not know it then, but that small leased farm was our salvation; a bigger farm and who knows where we might be today. All my brothers except one left the farm and the village for good. We were the first generation of Indo-Fijians to make a living away from the farm in a profession other than that of our parents. So, I am immensely grateful for dodging 'the nightmares of our parents' generation', to use the words of another historian, James Walvin, who grew up in straitened circumstances in the Greater Manchester area during the 1940s and '50s.[4]

Village elders were also keenly aware of the importance of education. They raised funds from voluntary subscription and built a thatched-hut school in 1945, the Tabia Sanatan Dharam School. Shortly afterwards, primary education was put on a firmer footing, and it was expected that all school-age children would attend school even if for a few years. The Tabia School was started by orthodox Hindus—the whole settlement was predominantly Hindu—but there was no requirement that the headmaster should be one of their own faith. On the contrary, some of the early head teachers were Christian and Muslim (Austin Sitaram, Simon Nagaiya, Ashik Hussein). In my time, the headmaster was a South Indian (Subramani Goundan). There was something inherently noble about that attitude; the education of children was their top priority. I suspect some of that secular attitude rubbed off on us as we studied and played with kids of other faiths. In this respect, unfortunately, attitudes have hardened, and interfaith relations are not what they were or should be. Religious exclusivism is on the rise.

DM: Could you elaborate on what sort of teaching and teachers you got at the schools you went to?

BL: We were lucky in the teachers we had. Our teacher in the final year at Tabia, Mr Goundan, took his role very seriously. He held weekend classes for us, and before the Entrance Exam he asked all the boys to camp in school so that we could have extra night classes. One day he said that he would not be surprised if one of us might top the exam in Vanua Levu. That would be a matter of immense pride to him and to the whole village, just as the little certificates we got for writing little syrupy pieces about the great contribution the CSR was making to the economic development of

---

4   See James Walvin, *Different Times: Growing Up in Post-War England* (York: Algie Books, 2014), p. 202.

Fiji. We did not break any records, though I came reasonably close. Once we had passed the exam, it was assumed that we would proceed to high school, which most of us did.

Labasa Secondary School, now Labasa College, started in 1954. It was the island's premier school, and among the very best in the country, measuring its success with such schools as Natabua, Marist and Suva Grammar. It was a fully government-funded school and it attracted the best students and, more importantly, some of the best teachers as well. I had three teachers who had a profound influence on me: Vijay Mishra and Subramani (English) and Krishna Datt (History). They were all freshly graduated from New Zealand universities and all of them were teaching in Fiji for the first time. They took their role as teachers seriously and pushed us hard. All of them came from similar backgrounds to us and they understood our predicaments. They had gone places and so, they thought, could we. They introduced us to the broad sweep of world history, to the great works of English literature, to the pleasures of the imagination and the nobility of scholarly pursuit. No wonder they went far themselves. Vijay and Subramani became professors of English literature and Krishna, now, Santa Claus–like, a public figure in Fiji. My debt of gratitude to my teachers is immense.

DM: And then you went to university.

BL: Yes, this was the turning point in the lives of most of us. Started in 1968 as a regional institution, the University of the South Pacific, with its principal campus at Laucala Bay, produced generations of young people from the Pacific Islands who went on to become leaders of their respective nations. It opened new horizons for us, broke barriers of isolation, acquainted us with developments taking place all around us as our countries took the first tentative steps into nationhood. The people we met and the things we talked about planted the idea in us that we could play a part in the future of our countries; a naïve hope in retrospect, shattered before it saw the light of day. The university introduced me to students from other Pacific Islands about whom we had heard but never actually met, and this contributed to an awareness of being part of a wider region. And this, too, has remained with me.

The new university was also keen to prove itself as a centre of excellence in learning, eager to prove this to the outside world. At least it was at that time. I had some fantastic teachers who inspired us by their concern and commitment: June Cook, an Englishwoman fresh from a stint at the United Nations; Ron Crocombe, the Professor of Pacific Studies; Walter Johnson (visiting from Hawaii, and formerly of Chicago). I still remember being told of the joy and pride my teachers at the university felt when they learnt that I had won a prize at the University of British Columbia for being the most outstanding graduate student. They felt vindicated, especially as I was the very first USP student to do graduate work at a university overseas. These teachers were an integral part of my luck. So, a measure of talent, great timing and a very large dose of luck. To these things, I would attribute my success.

DM: After a lifetime of studying Fijian history and politics, what are your thoughts on where Fiji went wrong?

BL: Fiji's great tragedy of the twentieth century was the yawning gap between the rhetoric its leaders espoused about what the country was and what it aspired to be with the observable reality on the ground. Our leaders mindlessly parroted metaphors of our supposed success. Fiji: a three-legged stool, denoting harmony and balance when there was none; Fiji the way the world should be,[5] when it was the last thing that the world should have aspired to be. We averted our eyes from the deep chasms in our history; we wanted the world to believe that we were one united nation when we went on creating institutions that entrenched racial divisions in the country. Race was a fact of life, our leaders said, ignoring the fact that there were many other facts of life that were daily impacting on us. We were divergent in our attitudes and aspirations. One group wanted a nonracial common roll, the other a communal one. One group agitated against the continuation of colonial rule, while the other wanted its retention. We had a Westminster system of government, but with an unwritten rule: that indigenous Fijians must always control government.[6] When that assumption was overturned in 1987, the military was unleashed to restore the status quo. The illusion we had celebrated for so long was finally shattered. For much of our history, we had no overarching narrative of inclusion and common citizenship; we were not a single united political community but a collection of ethnicities sharing a common geographical space. No wonder things fell apart in the end.

---

5   These words attributed to Pope John Paul II were not the words he spoke. He actually said, 'Fiji could be a beacon of hope to the modern world.'
6   The 2013 Constitution defines all Fiji citizens as Fijians, while *iTaukei* is used to refer to indigenous Fijians. But for the period I am talking about, Fijian meant indigenous Fijian. In this paper I use the old terminology because of the time frame involved.

DM: Could you say more about Fiji's political leadership at the time?

BL: Let me take indigenous Fijian leaders alone for the moment. Fijian people had some great leaders. Perhaps the greatest of them in twentieth-century Fiji was Ratu Sir Lala Sukuna.[7] He was a man of exceptional personal attributes and achievements who would have stood tall in any society. But his vision for his people was, in my judgement, fundamentally flawed, backward-looking and, in truth, retrogressive. In the aftermath of World War II, he promulgated policies and recommended structures designed to revert Fijian society to its nineteenth-century moorings, in villages living under the guidance of traditional leadership.[8] His primary loyalty was the perpetuation of aristocratic Fijian leadership for the colony.

This, at a time when Fiji was opening up to new challenges and opportunities after the war. What, pray, was the need to send the cream of Fijian male population to fight Chinese communist insurgents in the jungles of Malaya? We became cannon fodder for British imperial ambitions and adventures in Southeast Asia. There was an unwritten expectation that the United Kingdom would look after the interests of the Fijian people, guard them against ambitions of the Indo-Fijian population, and our involvement in the Malaya campaign was quid pro quo. But by the mid-1950s, the UK was beginning to shed its colonies. It would put Fiji firmly on the path of decolonisation in the 1960s.[9] Meanwhile, the Fijian people lost valuable time and opportunities to develop educational facilities, trade, commerce and commercial agriculture. The effects would last a long time. It was not as if there were no deeply felt pleas for reform and restructure of aspects of the Fijian administration—by O.H.K. Spate in 1959,[10] for example, or the Burns Commission in 1960,[11] but these

---

7   See Deryck Scarr, *Ratu Sukuna: Soldier, Statesman, Man of Two Worlds* (London: Macmillan Education, 1980).
8   See Brij V. Lal, *Historical Dictionary of Fiji* (New York: Rowman & Littlefield, 2016), pp. 92–93.
9   Brij V. Lal (ed.), *Fiji: British Documents on the End of the Empire* (London: The Stationery Office, 2006); and more generally W. David McIntyre, *Winding up the British Empire in the Pacific Islands* (Oxford: Oxford University Press, 2014).
10   O.H.K. Spate, *Fijian People: Economic Problems and Prospects* (Suva: Legislative Council Paper 13/1959); R.G. Ward and O.H.K. Spate, 'Thirty years ago: A view of the Fijian political scene: Confidential report to the British Colonial Office, September 1959', *The Journal of Pacific History* 25(1) (1990): 103–24, doi.org/10.1080/00223349008572628; Spate, *On the Margins of History: From the Punjab to Fiji* (Canberra, National Centre for Development Studies, Research School of Pacific Studies, The Australian National University, 1991), pp. 99–117.
11   Sir Alan Burns, *Report of the Commission of Enquiry into the Natural Resources and Population Trends of the Colony of Fiji* (Suva: Legislative Council Paper 1/1960).

went unheeded. Preservation of the chiefly-led social order and battening down the hatches against proposed constitutional reform during the 1960s became the primary concern of the new generation of Fijian leaders.

Indo-Fijian leaders, very briefly, subscribed to the values of modernity, democracy, equality and egalitarianism. They wanted a nonracial political culture, but these things found no traction in the broader body politic. The fundamental truth of their vision is belatedly being realised in the aftermath of the coups in Fiji. If Fijian and European leaders (and senior colonial officials) had adopted a different, more inclusive approach, things might have turned out to be different. Preoccupation with race blinded people to other issues of broader national good.

DM: And then what happened?

BL: Well, the Fijian social order and the assumptions that underpinned it had been under siege for some time, and it came crashing down with Bainimarama's 2006 coup. The Great Council of Chiefs (GCC), the umbrella organisation of the indigenous community since the late nineteenth century, was unceremoniously abolished with absolutely no consultation with the Fijian people. Many traditional privileges were gone. The chiefly system itself was facing irrelevance in the daily lives of the people, and so on. Perhaps, in the early years of the twenty-first century, its time had passed as forces of modernity and egalitarianism buffeted all aspects of Fijian life. It is astonishing how little indignant protest there has been among indigenous Fijians themselves about the treatment meted out to their traditional institutions and values. That says a great deal about the state of affairs in the indigenous community.

The developments that have followed since 2006 have been promoted as unleashing a 'new revolution' to take Fiji away from the practices and politics of the twentieth century. There can be no doubt that it has marked a decisive break from the policies and politics of the twentieth century, which, if successful, has the potential to take Fiji into a new era. A race-based electoral system is a thing of the past. Every citizen of Fiji can now call himself or herself a 'Fijian'. Affirmative action policies and prior treatment afforded to certain groups are now history. Equal citizenship is in the offing. Most progressive-minded people will welcome these new developments.

DM: So a new era is at hand?

BL: That is another matter. Nearly all these changes have been forced through without consultation with the people or through their elected representatives in parliament.[12] The government uses the brute force of its numbers to bulldoze change through. The parliament is now a pliant institution, not a venue for vigorous national debate. Loyal former military personnel occupy important civilian positions. As I have mentioned, indigenous institutions have been hobbled or unceremoniously dumped. The language of much of the population, Fijian, is banned from being used in parliament (and so far there has been no howl of protest for reasons that are mystifying). The military is ostensibly in the barracks, but it enjoys a guardian role in the constitution, with the power to intervene to protect public interest, without the authorisation of parliament. It is, in fact, the interpreter rather than the enforcer of the duly constituted public will. The government base is fragile, extremely narrow. In truth, the government is run by one or two ministers, especially the attorney-general, who controls all the major ministries of government. Many of Bainimarama's former close supporters have been side-lined or sacked (Commander Lesi Natuva, Colonel Pio Tikooduadua, Commodore Esala Teleni, Brigadier General Mosese Tikoitoga, among others).

Getting back to your earlier question, the lessons of the past, indeed of common sense, have not been learned. In public life, means are just as important as the ends. Consent of the public, not coercion and intimidation, is the best way to lay the enduring foundations of change. Dialogue is a word missing from the government's lexicon. An illusion of democracy is no substitute for the substance of democracy. On all these grounds, the Bainimarama experiment leaves much to be desired. One hopes that Bainimarama does not go the way of one of his predecessors, Ratu Sir Kamisese Mara, taking to his grave the political infrastructure he put in place during his time as the nation's leader.[13]

---

12   See Yash Pal Ghai, 'Ethnicity, politics and constitutions in Fiji', in *Bearing Witness: Essays in Honour of Brij V. Lal,* ed. Doug Munro and Jack Corbett (Canberra: ANU Press, 2017), pp. 177–206, doi.org/10.22459/BW.07.2017.
13   See Brij V. Lal, 'Making and unmaking of a Fijian colossus, A review essay of Tuimacilai: A Life of Ratu Sir Kamisese Mara', *Fijian Studies* 13(1) (2015): 31–41, available from: fijianstudes.net/wp-content/uploads/FS/13(1)/FS-13-1-Lal-Mara.pdf (accessed 24 January 2017).

DM: Can you share your thoughts on the quality and legitimacy of the current government in Fiji?

BL: The prime minister and his ministers read carefully crafted set pieces by international public relations companies such as Qorvis, which specialise in refurbishing the images of dictators and tyrants in the developing world. The effect is impressive, but without their scripts in front of them, many sound vapid and obtuse. The official narrative has a complete, unfettered run in the media. Propaganda is paraded as fact and in time assumes an air of unassailable authority. So, Bainimarama says that his 2006 coup was a nation-saving intervention. The truth is the 2006 coup was not about saving the nation, it was about saving Bainimarama's bacon; an act designed to subvert police investigation into his role in suppressing the mutiny of November 2000 and other related matters. No one dare say what everyone privately knows: that Frank Bainimarama is in thrall of his attorney-general, perhaps excessively, unhealthily so, to his detriment. This dependency relationship does his credibility and public image no good, but he is probably not aware of it or does not care. Constantly out on the campaign trail when not on the conference circuit, he seems to need public adulation for self-affirmation. His supporters attribute many fine qualities to him, but no one thinks of him as an astute and incisive intellect. They will also agree that he is a man of very short fuse, rough language and a volatile temperament.

The actual work of running the government is done by his attorney-general. To use an historical analogy, he is Fiji's Cardinal Richelieu, the power behind the French throne. An old Indo-Fijian canefarmer from Rakiraki visiting Australia invoked an analogy from the days of the Colonial Sugar Refining Company (CSR). 'Janab Saiyid-Khaiyum,' he said, 'is like the senior "Kulambar", the estate overseer. Whatever the Kulambar saheb wants to get done is done. His word was final.' All this may be an unfair characterisation of the actual situation, but I suspect many in the cane belt would understand that sentiment.

Attorney-General Khaiyum controls all the agenda-setting portfolios of government: he is Attorney-General and Minister of Justice, Minister of the Economy (including finance and national planning), Minister of Public Enterprise, Minister of Civil Aviation, Minister of Communication, Minister of Public Service, Acting Minister of Education and Minister of Elections (while holding the office of Secretary-General of the ruling party). What does this kind of unprecedented and unhealthy concentration of power in the hands of one man say about the way the government is conducted and decisions made? And, so it goes. All this is public knowledge, but the coercive media environment in Fiji suppresses discussion of critical issues. As I have said before, democracy dies without the oxygen of free speech.

DM: Professor Yash Ghai has written that, for an historian, you have taken a keen interest in constitution and constitution-making. Could you remind us how this came about?

BL: There is a long and proud tradition at The Australian National University of professors taking an active role in political and constitutional matters, beginning with Jim Davidson, the foundation professor of Pacific history at the ANU.[14] There were others. Oskar Spate, the distinguished geographer, wrote that brilliant report on the social and economic problems and prospects of the Fijian people and later served on the Currie Commission whose report led to the establishment of the University of Papua New Guinea and on the Fiji Education Commission, which laid the foundations of Fiji's postcolonial education policy.[15] Closer to home, there was Ahmed Ali, an ANU graduate, who served as a minister and diplomat in Fiji. David Stone and Alan Ward were other precedents.

This tradition of practical involvement possibly had a bearing, but I suppose I had always had a passive interest in politics and public affairs. I used to follow the legislative council debates in the papers in the late 1960s and 1970s, attended political rallies in the 1970s, and was active in student politics at the university, being for a while the editor of the student newspaper, *Unispac*. The Fiji Broadcasting Commission asked me to chair their 1982 election panel discussions, which brought me into contact with the leading political figures of the day. It also gave me an insight into and interest in the way politics were practised on the ground—how the sausage was actually made, so to speak. Out of that experience came my edited book *Politics in Fiji: Studies in Contemporary History*.[16] I was dragging the fire-cart closer to the fireplace, and that engagement has persisted, along with the many frustrations it has spawned.

---

14   Doug Munro, 'J.W. Davidson – The making of a participant historian', in *Pacific Lives, Pacific Places: Bursting Boundaries in Pacific History*, ed. Brij V. Lal and Peter Hempenstall (Canberra: Journal of Pacific History, 2001), pp. 97–116.
15   Sir George Currie, *Report of the Commission on Higher Education in Papua and New Guinea* (Canberra: The Commission, 1964).
16   Brij V. Lal (ed.), *Politics in Fiji: Studies in Contemporary History* (Laie: Brigham Young University and Sydney: Allen & Unwin, 1986).

DM: But what catapulted you directly into the political arena?

BL: The Fijian Military Coup of 1987. The coup was a deeply wrenching experience for me, not least because I had witnessed the race riots in Albert Park in central Suva. A fledgling democracy, by no means perfect, to be sure, had been overthrown; the verdict of the ballot box hijacked. All that generations of leaders had fought for, all that effort to create a peaceful, stable, democratic society, had come to naught. Worse, many in Fiji were cheering at what had happened. I joined the forces of protest, and wrote a book about it, *Power and Prejudice: The Making of the Fiji Crisis*.[17] I was determined to put on record a thesis different to the one celebrating the coup. The coup, I believed then as I believe now, was a pyrrhic victory for indigenous nationalism and hugely counterproductive in the long run for the indigenous people themselves. It is no satisfaction to say that I have been proven correct. The coup forced me to think more deeply about the forces that had shaped Fijian history of the twentieth century. I was looking for clues that might help me understand the roots of Fiji's contemporary social and political ailments. Out of that quest came my *Broken Waves: A History of the Fiji Islands in the Twentieth Century*.[18] In this book, I showed my hand in favour of the values of democracy and modernity. I showed where Fiji had missed the opportunity to forge a different, more inclusive future for all of its people. Instead of building bridges of understanding and common citizenship, we were busily erecting walls of ethnic compartmentalisation, deepening distrust and fear among the citizenry.

Unbeknownst to me at the time, that book and my other publications were being read in Fiji by political leaders, including Mr Jai Ram Reddy, the Leader of the National Federation Party and the Leader of the Opposition. I was invited to address the 1993 annual convention of the party in Nadi at which I spoke on what kind of constitution was appropriate for Fiji. The independence constitution of 1970 had been thrown out by the military and replaced in 1990 by a constitution that gave indigenous Fijians complete control of government. The latter was a draconian document, completely inimical to the values of democracy and principles of justice and fairness. In my talk, I emphasised the need

---

17 Brij V. Lal, *Power and Prejudice: The Making of the Fiji Crisis* (Wellington: New Zealand Institute for International Affairs, 1988, reprinted 1990).
18 Brij V. Lal, *Broken Waves: A History of Fiji in the Twentieth Century* (Honolulu: University of Hawaii Press, 1992).

to move away from the country's preoccupation with race and to embrace a common future for all. The speech was widely disseminated through the media.

DM: That speech played a part in having you appointed to the Constitution Review Commission in the mid-'90s.

BL: It certainly did. When an independent three-person commission was established, under the chairmanship of Sir Paul Reeves, the former Governor-General of New Zealand, to review the 1990 constitution, Mr Reddy chose me to represent the opposition and, in effect, the Indo-Fijian community.[19] The appointment forced me to put my money where my mouth was, so to speak, and I worked very hard with my fellow commissioners to produce a document that would pave the way for a united Fiji. That is how my foray into constitution making came about. I am not a constitutional lawyer or a constitutional theorist, like Yash Ghai, but I have a good understanding of the values and principles that should underpin democratic constitutions in the modern world, what kind constitutional architecture is necessary for multiethnic societies as well as the training to put things in an historical perspective. My commitment to democracy and to freedom, justice and equality, my unalterable opposition to military coups that overthrow democratically elected governments, has landed me in trouble. In 2009, the Fijian military regime deported me from Fiji and banned me (and my wife) for life from entering the country.

DM: Why, then, do you continue to speak out?

BL: Because not to do so would for me be unconscionable. One cannot be neutral on a moral battlefield, and for me what is happening in Fiji raises both political as well as moral questions: the fate of democracy, the rule of law, freedom of speech. It has been said that I have forfeited my moral authority to speak on Fiji because I live outside. That is a fatuous argument. The issue of my residence or my citizenship or my ethnicity was never raised when the Fijian Parliament appointed me to serve on a commission to review the 1990 Constitution and to make recommendations for a new one. What should matter in the end is what you say, what your ideas are, not your place of residence, or your ethnicity

---

19 Report of the Fiji Constitution Review Commission (Sir Paul Reeves, Tomasi Rayalu Vakatora and Brij V. Lal), *The Fiji Islands: Towards a United Future,* Parliamentary Paper, 34 (1996). Vakatora has written his own story, including his experience on the Commission in *From the Mangrove Swamps* (Suva: self-published, 1998).

or class. Or, to use a sporting analogy, play the game, not the player. People who use this argument would be the first ones to leave if they only could, whereas I, while living outside, have devoted my entire professional life of over 30 years to researching and writing on Fiji. Travel and technology freely transgress national boundaries. National boundaries have become ever so porous. Students in Fiji listen to my lectures, read my books and discuss my ideas, which make mockery of the ban. This is such an obsolete and archaic way of dealing with dissent. There is no use pretending to be King Canute in this age of inexorable change.

I will speak out whenever and wherever I see injustice and oppression. That is just me. The media in Fiji is muzzled, and views of government's critics get a short shrift. Draconian decrees reduce the space for free speech which makes it even more necessary to speak out. Free speech is a vital part of a democratic society. My views are broadcast on Australian and New Zealand radio stations, and they all reach Fiji—much to the chagrin, no doubt, of the Fijian authorities.

DM: And there has been a deafening silence from academics.

BL: At all the three Fiji universities, all kinds of subtle, and not-so-subtle, pressures are put on academics to toe the line, to appease the government. The government uses its purse strings to extract acquiescence, as happened in the case of a prominent academic at one of the universities who was fired from his longstanding job. Public lectures not authorised by the hierarchy are prohibited, scuttled. Academics are told to be 'responsible' and 'balanced', but these are code words for compliance and acquiescence. All this is especially sad because the university was once a place of vigorous debate about critical national and regional issues, but this is no longer the case. The local scene is dismal. Perhaps out of frustration—though this might be too charitable—some local academics run private businesses on the side. Scholarship takes second place in their priorities. The government has its supporters among some ageing academics, in Fiji and in Australia and New Zealand, who parrot the government line and sing its praises, seeking a moment in the sun in their twilight years. Some retired former Fiji people returned to lend a helping hand to the government only to realise that they were dispensable; some were discarded and became strong critics. All too late. In view of all this, in an area of darkness for free speech and free thought, it becomes even more important to speak up. It becomes important not only to point a finger but to show your hand.

DM: It is said by some of your critics that you are elitist, insensitive to the demands made on fellow academics living and working in Fiji.

BL: I would readily plead guilty to the charge of being elitist. It goes without saying that any university worth its name is a place of merit and talent, not a social welfare agency. Its purpose above all should be to extend the frontiers of knowledge. This foundational principle has been diluted in recent years by the need for relevance and accountability and the demands of consultancies. I understand the imperatives that drive this push, but in every decent university, there must always be a space for curiosity-driven research. In some places, there is increasing demand for equity and inclusion and gender/ethnic/class balance in appointments and promotions.

Some of this is needed and can be justified given the historical legacy of white male domination in the academia. Diversity is enriching, but I have also seen mediocre people get through because they fit one or the other category, to their own detriment and to that of the institution. Diversity and merit are not mutually exclusive. You can espouse the principle of diversity in the same breath as the principle of merit. In my own work, I have sought to meet the highest standards of contemporary scholarship in my own discipline, not always successfully, I would have to admit, but that impregnable fortress of excellence remains the ideal.

I have had the great privilege of teaching hundreds of undergraduate and dozens of graduate students in my career. Not everyone aspires to excellence, content to get by; not everyone is equally talented. People come to university for a variety of reasons, with a variety of expectations. That is fine, but I have pushed hard those who aspire to excellence. Some students found this hard going, but at the end they were immensely grateful that I had taken them seriously. It is a source of great satisfaction to me that work done under my supervision has been published in top-rated scholarly journals and by respected academic presses. Some of my former students have become close friends. They include students from the Pacific Islands. An academic career is a great privilege and it deserves to be treated as such.

DM: What is your advice to early career researchers?

BL: Aim high. Do not be content with inferior work. Read widely. Be bold. Dare to be different. Spend time reading the classic works in your field. Pay attention to style, to language and composition. I know that for many of us English will be a second language, and so mastering its nuances will not be easy, but that is why we must work harder. Develop a voice of your own. Publish in the highest-ranked journals that the quality of your work will bear. All this is easier said than done, but there are few alternatives. Most experienced writers and scholars will tell you about the importance of revising your manuscript several times over if necessary. There is one other thing worth mentioning: the importance of having your prepublished work read by someone whom you respect and whose judgement you trust. The thought can be daunting, having to submit yourself to someone else's scrutiny. We all have egos that sometimes get in the way. But it benefited me greatly. I have a group of colleagues who, between them, have read virtually everything I have ever published. They put aside their own work to read and critique mine. And I have done the same with theirs. I also sometimes gave my prepublished work to my graduate students for their assessment, much to my benefit. Occasionally, the comments can be deflating but they give pause for thought, and that is a good thing.

DM: Have you grown and changed as an historian in your career? If so, how and in what ways?

BL: We all change with time and in response to changed circumstances, and I am no exception. I have moved away from quantification with which I began my career to a more literary exposition of history. I am more involved now. I write as an involved insider. I've always said that I write, not as some casual, disinterested bystander on the sidelines passing lofty judgement. I declare my hand at the outset so that the reader is fully aware of my stance. This is a different position to that with which I began. I came of age, so to speak, at a time when we were taught to be objective, to keep our personal opinions out of the narrative. Facts, we were told, spoke for themselves. I now know that facts don't speak for themselves; they speak only when spoken to, and they answer the questions we ask of them. Authorial intervention in the narrative is now commonplace when the partiality of evidence, in both senses of the word, is taken as given and when the fundamental unknowability of truth is freely acknowledged. But this was not the case a generation ago. I do not fully embrace the dogmas of cultural studies, but am sympathetic to aspects of it.

22. 'OF EXITS AND ENTRANCES

DM: But from the late '90s you have also been writing in a more creative vein.

BL: That is true. The discipline of history once drove my scholarly approach. It still does but I am now much more aware of the role of memory in capturing the texture of the human experience. The question that fascinates me now is how to write about pasts where written documents do not exist and where public memory is not properly archived. The question came to me when I began to think seriously about the social and cultural evolution of Indo-Fijian culture in the postwar years; how a people growing up in the shadows of indenture created a sense of community and gave it meaning and purpose, how they nurtured things that celebrated life and mourned its passing, how the frictions and petty conflicts were resolved—things like that. There is no archival record about these important questions. Memory is all we have to go by. So, I write about some actual incident that I myself have observed or been told about, but do so creatively, imaginatively at the interface of history and memory. As a trained historian, I can't invent facts—that is a cardinal sin in our profession—but I can breathe life into them through imaginative reconstruction. I addressed these questions by turning to my own experience of growing up in a village, Tabia, in rural Vanua Levu. I used the lens of that personal experience to reflect the larger patterns of change and evolution of my generation, but I gave flesh and blood to the bare bones of the factual truth: a conversation might be imagined, a scene described, a connection made, all to capture the nuances of the actual case in question. I have described this sort of writing as 'faction: using the tools of fiction to depict nonfictional truth'. A more widely known name for this sort of exercise is 'creative nonfiction'.

DM: Do you ever think about your legacy as a scholar, writer, activist? Do you care?

BL: It would be very unhuman not to care, but I don't spend much time on this subject. Certainly, the question was furthest from my mind when I was doing my work. I have always been deeply influenced by the philosophy of the Bhagvada Gita where Lord Krishna advises Arjuna, as he hesitates to go into battle against his own cousins, not to worry about the fruits of action, but to do things according to your sacred duty, dharma. I should like to think that an independent approach unhindered by some rigid theory or theoretical dogma is evident in my work. I have always striven to create my own text rather than slavishly follow someone else's. I find this approach immensely rewarding, both intellectually as well as emotionally. I have sometimes been accused of being an 'empiricist'. I happily plead guilty. I thrill to the particularities of the human experience in its infinite variety and complexity. Abstract thought leaves me cold, unmoved. That is the way I am, and I wouldn't want to change. I would be quite content to be seen as a student and follower of good English and American narrative historians whose works I still read for pleasure and instruction, though I can never even remotely hope to match their example: J.H. Plumb, G.M. Trevelyan, Thomas Babington Macaulay, Arthur Schlesinger Jr, Richard Hofstadter, C. Vann Woodward, and closer to home, Bill Gammage, Geoffrey Blainey and Ken Inglis, to name just a few. These masters of English prose teach us how to bring the lived human experience to the written page, how to make historical narrative sparkle.[20]

DM: Do you have any regrets as you close one important chapter of your life?

BL: Oh, yes, there are many things I now regret, more things of omission rather than commission. The kind of career I was able to carve out for myself, beginning from where I did, that improbable background of village life in Tabia in the postwar years; that kind of career was possible only through single-minded pursuit of scholarship over many years. Many things I cherished—music, sports—had to be put aside, or put on hold. I am incredibly lucky in having the family I have, thanks immeasurably to Padma's selfless devotion to the welfare of the family. She provided the 'enabling environment' that gave me the space to pursue my own work and inclinations unhindered: the long hours at work, the absentmindedness at home, the extensive and extraneous reading and writing on the side in spare time that had to be done to fill in the gaps in my education and training. A professional person in her own right, she is an integral part of the luck I talked about earlier. I now wish I had been a more active, involved partner on the home front. My children were tolerant of my various obsessions as they were growing up, but here too there is regret that I was not more involved with their lives. Regret, yes, but I am also enormously grateful for what I do have.

---

20 If I were to mention just two introductions to the art of fine historical writing, they would be A.J.P. Taylor, Robert Rhodes James, J.H. Plumb, Basil Diddle Hart and Anthony Starr, *Churchill: Four Faces and the Man* (London: Penguin, 1968), and Robin Winks and Marcus Cunliff (eds), *Pastmasters: Some Essays on American Historians* (New York: Harper, 1969). I have these two books on my writing desk for inspiration.

There is some sadness and regret that the world I inherited, which formed and deformed my life, will go with me. This is a universal generational phenomenon, I realise, but the rupture in my case—our case, the case of our generation from Fiji living overseas—is greater, the loss irrecoverable. Fiji has been my passionate life-long obsession, but for my children it is their father's land, not theirs, a place to visit, perhaps, but nothing much beyond that. The world that formed me is alien, incomprehensible, to them: a prehistoric village with no paved roads, no running water, no electricity, hardly any reading material around. They cannot imagine me being born in a thatched hut at home, delivered by an illiterate midwife. The music that moves me and fills my house has no meaning to them. My mother tongue is not theirs. My quite extensive library of rare Fiji books and papers, lovingly collected over a lifetime, will have to perhaps find home in a library somewhere other than the homes of my children. As the poet says, 'The old order changeth, yielding place to the new / And God fulfils himself in many ways.'[21]

There is little point revisiting words left unsaid, things left undone. I did the best I could in the time I had. I will not leave this world wondering if I have made something of my time on earth. To use the words of Mary Oliver, from her poem 'When death comes', which I love repeating:

> When it is over, I don't want to wonder
> if I have made of my life something particular, and real.
> I don't want to find myself sighing and frightened,
> or full of argument.
>
> I don't want to end up simply having visited this world.[22]

I stood up for what I believed in, things I considered to be right and just and true. That will do me as my epitaph. *Terminat auctor opus.*

---

21 Alfred Lord Tennyson, *Morte d'Arthur* (1842), available from: www.poetryfoundation.org/poems/45370/mrte-darthur (accessed 25 May 2019).
22 Mary Oliver, 'When death comes', in her *New and Selected Poems: Volume One* (Boston: Beacon Press, 1992), pp. 10–11.

23

ANU made me, but which ANU is mine?[1]

My Australian National University extinguished lecture

> Now all my teachers are dead except silence
>
> — W.S. Merwin[2]

Valedictory lecture delivered at The Australian National University on 2 February 2016. The title is not entirely original. Eugene Kamenka, the ANU historian of ideas, called his farewell lecture two decades ago 'Australia made me, but which Australia is mine?' My immeasurable thanks, again, to Doug Munro for reading a draft of this lecture and offering many helpful comments. I am also grateful to Nic Halter, who chaired the lecture and whose conversations helped shape my thoughts. Ganesh Chand critiqued the paper with insight. My colleague Clive Moore shared with me his own experience of retirement and the changing culture of the academy.[3]

---

1 Originally appeared in *Pacific Journal of Education* 1(1) (2017): 89–110.
2 W.S. Merwin, 'A scale in May', in *The Second Four Books of Poems by W.S. Merwin* (Port Townsend, WA; Copper Canyon Press, 1993).
3 See also Clive Moore, 'A glass still full: Retirement and the historian', *Pacific Journal of Education* 1(1) (2017): 57–71.

Once upon a time, a generation or so ago, professors appointed to chairs were expected, as matter of course, to give an inaugural lecture before their peers and the wider community. Professors were supposed to profess and a key element was via an inaugural lecture. They were expected to outline their field of research, their scholarly interests and the direction in which they intended to take teaching and research in their departments and how they wished to reconfigure their disciplines.[4] Clearly, the lectures were serious, even solemn, occasions. Professors were scholars of prestige and influence within and beyond the academy. They had something to say, as Manning Clark might put it. Their decisions decided the destinies and destinations of those under their charge. The culture of patronage was alive and well and powerful. But those days are long gone, and the times have changed. 'God Professors' are now mythical figures of ancient history and objects sometimes of some puzzled bemusement among the younger generation.

These days, it is grant-dispensing bodies, such as the Australian Research Council, and not heads of departments who decide the fate of scholars. Routinely, the ability to attract large grants now matters in university appointments and promotions. It is an important part of the 'selection criteria'. 'Being clubbable', as ANU Foundation Professor of Law Geoffrey Sawyer thought should be considered in making appointments, is today a blessed memory.[5] And the current intellectual climate is fractured, its assumptions and understandings contested. Authority and consensus in matters of scholarship, once widely understood and shared, have been displaced by notions of tentativeness and partiality and the ultimate unknowability of the world around us. Relativism rules the day. Affirming standards in matters of historical judgement will appear elitist and antiquarian.

So, instead of an agenda-setting inaugural lecture, I will content myself with an 'extinguished' lecture as I prepare to retire from the academy after nearly 40 years, 25 of them spent at The Australian National University. My focus is not what I would do—too late for that now—but what I have done and how I got to where I eventually did. The academic world I entered in 1977 is not the world I left behind when I retired at the end of 2015. They

---

4   I am thinking here of James Wightman Davidson's famous agenda-setting inaugural lecture, *Problems of Pacific History: An Inaugural Lecture Delivered in Canberra, 23 November 1954* (Canberra: The Australian National University, 1955).
5   S.G. Foster and Margaret M. Varghese, *The Making of the Australian National University, 1946–1996* (Sydney: Allen & Unwin, 1996), p. 105.

are in fact chalk and cheese. The sunny confidence we had in our ability to make a difference, to make the world a better place, our unshakeable faith in the nobility of our profession and its place in the broader cultural life of the community, have been shaken by the incessant demands of modern academic life and its relentless culture of accountability and demand for 'relevance'. The intellectual and cultural climate has changed, but so, too, has the technology of acquiring knowledge. The transition from the prehistoric age of the 'selectric' typewriter and the liquid whitener to the mystifying and ever changing offerings of the computer has not been easy and is the cause, dare I say it, of much private grief and frustration. The world has indeed 'become stranger, the pattern more complicated',[6] to use the words of T.S. Eliot (of whom I suspect the present generation would have no idea, but who was a cultural icon in our time. I still vividly remember listening to Eliot reading his *Love Song of J. Alfred Prufrock* on a scratchy gramophone in the final year of high school, courtesy of our English teacher—now professor—Subramani).[7]

It is easy, on an occasion such as this, for ageing academics to grind old axes, gripe about how the world has changed for the worse, about how universities are not what they once were or how they should be. I will not disappoint you. I will do all this in a contained, moderate fashion, accepting the Naipaulian dictum that the world is what it is: 'men who are nothing, who allow themselves to become nothing, have no place in it'.[8] What I would like to do is to provide, if I can, glimpses of times and circumstances that formed and deformed me and my generation, and to see how and why things have changed, for better or for worse. I want to bear truthful witness to my time and place, but I also fear that some might find this piece a depressing dirge, mourning for a time that has passed and will never return. My hope, though, is that at least some colleagues of my generation will find in my footsteps echoes of their own, a testimony to their experience in the academy as well.

Let me begin with a brief account of my background to provide some context to what follows. I was born in a rural, sugarcane-growing village in Vanua Levu, Fiji's second largest island, in a family of six boys and two girls, son of unlettered parents eking a meagre existence on a 10-

---

6   T.S. Eliot, *East Coker,* 1969, is available freely in several places and in various poetry anthologies. This quote is from memory.
7   T.S. Eliot, *Love Song of J. Alfred Prufrock* (1915), available from: www.poetryfoundation.org/poetrymagazine/poems/44212/the-love-song-of-j-alfred-prufrock (accessed 26 May 2019).
8   V.S. Naipaul, *A Bend in the River* (London: Alfred A Knopf, 1979), p. 1.

acre leased farm. Large families and leased land were the two staples of the Indo-Fijian community in the postwar years. Large families for reliable labour supply and as a bulwark against the depredations of the outside world, a hedge against old age and infirmity. Land was leased land because we could never really own the land on which we depended for our livelihood. We were tenants, literally and metaphorically, and so we have remained. It was understood, though never expressly stated, that there would be no future on the farm for all of us and that we would have to do well at school to find employment elsewhere.

We did. Primary education was put on a firmer footing in the 1940s as a result of reforms recommended by the New Zealand educationist F.B. Stephens. School-age children were expected, as a matter of course, to complete at least some years of primary schooling. We took to schools like duck to water, partly, I suspect, to escape the boredom and routine of life at home. I still have with me books I read in primary school over half a century ago. After eight years at the Tabia Sanatan Dharam Primary School (founded in 1945), I attended Labasa Secondary, now Labasa College, the island's premier secondary school, established in 1954. We were the last cohort of Fiji students to receive a 'colonial' education, sitting the New Zealand Certificate and New Zealand University Entrance exams, which had a couple of years earlier succeeded the Empire-wide Cambridge Junior and Senior Certificate exams. There was nothing about Fiji or the Pacific in what we studied at school. Our primary reference points were England, Europe, Australia and New Zealand. So, in our history class, we studied the Russian revolution, causes of World War I, the rise of Nazism and fascism, the unification of Italy and Germany, the Victorian gold rushes and the history of the Liberal Party in New Zealand. In English, we studied the classic works of English literature (Dickens, the Brontë sisters, D.H. Lawrence, Joseph Conrad, William Golding and Shakespeare). In geography, there was a bit on the industrial revolution and much more on the agricultural developments in Australia and New Zealand. We memorised the names of big mountains and rivers and cities. We were mesmerised by pictures of huge grain harvesters on endless brown plains. I can still recall exam questions about the irrigation problems in Renmark (South Australia) and the population problems of the Cook Islands, then a New Zealand territory. Some mistook Renmark for Denmark, and we had no idea about the Cook Islands. I still vividly recall a friend in Brisbane telling me about his Senior Cambridge English paper in the mid-1960s. There was a question on the 'Phenomenon of the Beatles'. He proceeded to write a long essay on the 'Phenomenon of the Beetles' then plaguing the country's coconut industry. And he still passed!

I have no problem with such a curriculum, but it has come in for criticism by postcolonial scholars, such as Edward Said, who have suggested that the colonising of the mind was an integral and insidious part of the broader imperial project of conquest and subjugation.[9] It might have been, but that for us was not the point, I now realise. That broadening experience of learning about other pasts and other places enlivened our lives and lessened our sense of isolation. We came from a limited, unwritten world just a generation out of indenture; we had no vocabulary or narrative of our own to speak of; we had no books at home except some religious texts that were invariably more revered than actually read. Our colonial education gave us indispensable tools to understand our world, to read and write. It widened our horizon and the value of that, for us living in prehistoric villages on the outer fringes of poverty, was immeasurable. A curiosity about the world that came from that early exposure has remained with me, along with a deep sense of the essential interconnectedness of humanity across barriers of class and colour. Nothing human is alien to me. I still smart at the words 'who cares' in discussions of problems in remote parts of the world. And books and reading—the magic of the printed word, the craftmanship of good prose, an elegant turn of phrase—retain for me a magic that has lasted a lifetime.[10]

After high school came university. The critical factor here was the opening of the University of the South Pacific (USP) in Suva in 1968. It marked a turning point in modern Fijian and Pacific Islands history.[11] Until then, a select number of students, bright, wealthy or well connected, went to universities in Australia and New Zealand and returned with tertiary qualifications. For the overwhelming majority of students in Fiji, tertiary education was simply beyond reach financially. The opening of the university changed that for good for bright students from poor

---

9   See Edward Said, *Orientalism* (New York: Vintage, 1978); and *Culture and Imperialism* (New York: Chatto and Eindus, 1994).
10   Recounted in Brij V. Lal, *Mr Tulsi's Store: A Fijian Journey* (Canberra: Pandanus Books: 2001), pp. 59–80.
11   See Brij V. Lal, 'Laucala Bay', in *Pacific Places, Pacific Histories: Essays in Honor of Robert C Kiste*, ed. Brij V. Lal (Honolulu: University of Hawai'i Press, 2004), pp. 237–58.

homes. Fiji would not be the same again.[12] The timing was right as well. The Pacific Islands were decolonising, and there was an urgent need for massive numbers of trained people to staff the bureaucracy of the newly independent states. Most of us went to university on government scholarships; me to train for a career as a high school teacher of English and history. Midstream into my education, good grades and the kindly interest of some teachers ensured that there were other plans in store for me.

The education we received at the USP was deliberately instrumentalist in content and orientation as signalled in the names of the foundation schools that constituted the university: School of Education, School of Social and Economic Development and School of Natural Resources. We were expected to be cogs, well-trained cogs, to be sure, but cogs nonetheless, in the wheels of national development programs. Most were. What we learnt at university was sufficient for the purposes of local employment, but not nearly enough to equip us for academic careers. Knowledge of the intellectual traditions and protocols of our disciplines had to be acquired privately, haphazardly, and many gaps remained. The situation has not changed much. Indeed, all the anecdotal evidence suggests that the education might have regressed as coups and ensuing convulsions have severely corrupted the culture of learning. This is one of the sad, hidden costs of Fiji's recent turbulent history.[13] Bright students now prefer degrees in subjects such as accounting, information technology, medicine and nursing, which might improve their chances of emigration. That is the ultimate prize everyone is looking for. The humanities have little cache. The absence of role models does not help. The best and brightest of Fiji have gone or are actively preparing to leave.

At university, we met students from other parts of the country and from across the region for the first time. A 'USP Mafia', as we were sometimes dubbed, was born and dispatched across our island region, often to occupy positions of power and influence in other countries. Our horizons expanded, and the friendships forged in those early undergraduate years

---

12   For accounts of the early institutional history of the university, see Ron Crocombe and Malama Meleisea (eds), *Pacific Universities: Achievements, Problems and Prospects* (Suva: Institute of Pacific Studies, 1988), pp. 35–188.
13   The Vice-Chancellor of a university in Fiji recently informed me that his library would discard books, including hundreds we (Padma and I) had donated from our personal library, to enlarge the space for digital learning. Students, he said, don't read books these days, nor, it seems, do many academics either.

have remained. We all shared the sense that something new and exciting was afoot as our newly minted nation states embarked on the path of independence. We all felt we had a role to play in shaping the destiny of our people.[14] We debated the nature and purpose of development, the kind of leaders we needed, we denounced neo-colonialism and the excesses of capitalism, we advocated the need for an egalitarian, classless society. It seems so naïve in hindsight, but the desire to contribute was real, palpable at the time. History could be made, and our generation was the one to do it. We were at the right time, at the right place. We fancied ourselves as the architects of our nation's future. In hindsight, such forlorn hope.

It was with this partially formed and, in truth, naïve intellectual mindset, full of parochial details about this and that, and without an overarching framework (class analysis, for instance) to give it some coherence and structure, that I arrived at the ANU in August 1977 via a master's degree at the University of British Columbia.[15] I remember that day well. It was cold, bone-chillingly cold, as I made my way from Bruce Hall (where I would stay for six months) to the Coombs Building. That hexagonal building, a maze really, was as formidable a place as I have ever encountered anywhere in the world.[16] In the building I encountered fellow graduate students—we were called research scholars then—at various stages of research and writing, confidentially talking about the latest trend in historiography, discussing the ideas of E.P. Thompson, Haydn White and Michael Foucault. Poststructuralism, postcolonialism and post other such 'isms' were the exciting buzz words of those days. Not to be familiar with them was to risk being seen as a bit of a simpleton. I realised early on that I had a lot of private reading to do just to keep up. I survived, but there were many terrifying moments of doubt and despair and desperation along the way. Three years later, having completed my dissertation, I left Canberra, to return permanently in 1990.

---

14   See the essays in Sione Tupounua, Ron Crocombe and Claire Slatter (eds), *Pacific Way: Social Issues in National Development* (Suva: Institute of Pacific Studies, 1976).
15   With a thesis on the early history of East Indians in British Columbia.
16   See Brij V. Lal and Allison Ley (eds), *The Coombs: A House of Memories*, with a foreword by William C. Clarke (Canberra: Research School of Pacific and Asian Studies, The Australian National University, 2006).

Canberra, when I arrived in the late 1970s, was a small town, which retained the trappings of a bush town and was slowly emerging from the long dark shadow of the White Australia Policy. Monoculturalism was writ large everywhere, in faces and places, with signs of the occasional ethnic restaurants and Indian spice shops in the outer desultory suburbs. For more variety and volume, we were advised to go to Queanbeyan, about 10 kilometres across the border in New South Wales. That town, we were told, was more representative of real Australia than Canberra (pot-holed roads, unkempt streets, the aimless wandering of unemployed youth), but the comparison was not reassuring. We hardly ventured out. My main preoccupation was getting my dissertation done in time. Canberra, in 1990, was a different place, robustly multicultural and outward looking. People of colour no longer stood out in a crowd. Multicultural festivals were an exuberant part of the city's cultural life. People making polite conversation at parties no longer expressed curiosity about our relatively fluent command of English or about where we came from. In short, advances in travel and technology between the 1970s and 1990s had ensured that we were no longer the strangers we once seemed to be. The openness and tolerance of Canberra, its embracing of diversity, are for me one of the more remarkable, and happily irreversible, transformations in Australian society in recent decades. This is what made Canberra such a happy home for us.

The ANU was no stranger to us. It was the world's leading centre for Pacific scholarship to which we had been perfunctorily introduced in our Pacific courses at the USP. We had all read issues of *The Journal of Pacific History* and other publications from the ANU. We debated the 'three Fiji' thesis of E.K. Fisk's *The Political Economy of Independent Fiji.*[17] And some of us had glimpsed O.H.K. Spate's magisterial 1959 report on the economic problems and prospects of the Fijian people.[18] So, ANU was vaguely familiar as a formidable place of fine scholarship, but it had never occurred to us, certainly not to me, that some of us might actually go there for graduate work, still less teach there. The route by which I came to the ANU 30 years ago has bemused my students for whom the whole story seems improbable, almost bizarre. Nothing quite like my experience occurs, or could possibly be allowed to occur today.

---

17 E.K. Fisk, *The Political Economy of Independent Fiji* (Canberra: The Australian National University Press, 1970), and unmistakable with the photo of a Fijian tapa cloth on the cover.
18 Published by the Government of Fiji as Legislative Council Paper 13/1959.

During the course of my master's research I had come across Charles Price's book *Great White Walls are Built*,[19] on restrictions on Asian immigration in the white settler dominions, and I thought I could expand the book's scope by focusing on the experience of Indian migrants. Accordingly, I wrote to Price at the ANU. He never replied. I later discovered that he did not think I had enough background in demography for the subject, but, impressed with my proposal, he forwarded it to the then director of the Research School of Pacific Studies (as it then was), Wang Gungwu. He too liked what he saw but his field was Chinese history. He therefore forwarded my application to the Vice-Chancellor, the distinguished South Asianist Anthony Low, who had no expertise in Indian immigration. Nevertheless, he took me on, sight unseen, and that is how I landed an ANU research scholarship.[20] That was how things were done then, none of the extensive committee screening process, none of the extensive paperwork required, complete with fully footnoted thesis proposal. All that Anthony required was evidence of the ability to do independent research, and my master's thesis provided that. My experience was not unique. The late Ahmed Ali, Fiji historian and politician, once told me that a chance conversation with Jim Davidson in Suva about constitutional developments in Fiji (he was then the secretary of the Alliance Party) secured him an ANU scholarship. Jim had intermittently been advising groups on constitutional matters since 1959.

Another fundamental difference with the present was that you were admitted to the graduate program only through an internationally competitive scholarship program. The fee-paying system did not exist then. In fact, we were given a research scholar allowance as well as subsidised housing. ANU was elitist, fiercely, unapologetically elitist, and prided itself on attracting the world's best (at least in theory), students and staff, and although it was not formally stated, it was well known that only in the most exceptional of circumstances would scholarships be awarded to students over 30. An early doctorate, it was felt, would result in a long and productive research and teaching career. That hope was not misplaced. Australia in the 1960s and 1970s was a place of expanding tertiary education, and jobs were there for those who wanted them. Now, the possession of a doctorate is nothing more than a licence to hunt, and

---

19   C.A. Price, *The Great White Walls are Built: Restrictive Immigration to North America and Australasia, 1836–1888* (Canberra: Australian National University Press, 1974).
20   Brij V. Lal, 'A *girmitiya* "sepoy"', *South Asia: Journal of South Asian Studies* 39(1) (2016): 244–50, doi.org/10.1080/00856401.2016.1124229.

job prospects are grim. A secure, lifelong academic career is not taken for granted, nor is it an entirely attractive prospect financially or job-satisfaction wise.

We hear a lot these days about course work for graduate students. There are seminars and workshops run by educational consultants on how to supervise—who themselves most likely have never supervised a single graduate student. One occasionally hears of threats of legal action by dissatisfied students for inadequate or unsatisfactory supervision, and it does sometimes happen. Fee-paying students want big bang for their bucks. A lot of 'massaging' goes on. Things were different for us. There was, for instance, no course work component to our doctoral degree. That was the American way of doing things. In the Australasian system, the undergraduate degree was solid, and a good honours degree was enough to get admission to the graduate program. It was assumed that the fundamentals of the discipline had already been acquired and that students would be intelligent and resourceful enough to pick up on their own whatever else was needed along the way. The main game was the completion of the research thesis, which, it was expected, would meet the highest standards of contemporary scholarship, as the phrase went. And it was expected that, in due course, the thesis would find life as a substantial published book. Most did. But I can now see the value of compulsory graduate seminars in theory and methodology when students come ill-prepared for advanced, independent research, and not only from the Pacific Islands but many from Australian universities as well. Assistance is expected, and given in a variety of ways, including help with the English language and the art of composition for foreign students.

We had no sense of entitlement, and were forever grateful for the small mercies that came our way. We simply made do with what we had. We were told at the outset that a request for an extension beyond three years was frowned upon and given very grudgingly. We would spend the first year preparing a thesis proposal and do any required additional reading on our topic, one year in the field (including learning a foreign language if that was required) and the last year writing up the thesis. I still remember vividly asking Ken Gillion, one of my supervisors, what I should read, where I should begin. He gently told me to go to the library, read everything I could on my subject and, if at the end of six months, I was not on top of the literature, I should ask myself what I was doing here! That advice, well-meant, was panic-inducing in one learning the basic alphabets of advanced, independent research.

The ANU is not now the university it was 30 years ago. Australia's counterpart to Oxford and Cambridge, it was modelled on the Johns Hopkins Institute of Advanced Studies.[21] The undergraduate component was added in 1960, a decade after it was founded, with the merger of the Institute and the Canberra University College, previously a constituent college of the University of Melbourne. Still, for the most part, and despite the two original campuses being contiguous, the two were quite separate entities, with different rhythms and responsibilities, one primarily undergraduate and the other postgraduate. A glass curtain separated the two, the relations strained by misperceptions, mischief and stereotypes. The denizens of the Institute thought rather well of themselves as privileged, chosen, citizens of the International Republic of Letters. Those in the School of General Studies primarily taught undergraduates and took the profession of teaching seriously. They were often disdainful of the Institute dwellers as drones who led a pampered life, some not publishing much at all. During my first six years as an academic at the ANU I held a joint appointment with the faculties and the Institute and observed the tension between the two from close quarters. These were real. But now the boundaries have disappeared with the creation of the college system that has integrated the two parts of the university, though not altogether satisfactorily.

The ANU, or at least the Institute, had a distinct and perhaps even an enviable place in the Australian university system: *primus inter pares*. Until the late 1950s and '60s, many Australian universities, and especially the pre–World War II ones, were geared primarily for undergraduate teaching.[22] For postgraduate training, many smaller ones sent their students to the ANU—certainly Pacific history. It took on the role once occupied by premier English universities, principally Oxford and Cambridge. The United States was then not on the radar of students aiming for postgraduate education. Among the few who journeyed across the Pacific were Greg Dening and Jill Kerr Conway (Harvard), Paul Bourke (Wisconsin), Peter Denis (Duke) and Dorothy Shineberg (Smith College). By the same token, very few American graduate students or academics came Down Under. Australia was not an attractive destination

---

21 Foster and Varghese, *The Making of the Australian National University* (Sydney: Allen & Unwin, 1996), pp. 5–7. The Johns Hopkins University, founded in Baltimore in 1876, emphasised research and postgraduate training over undergraduate teaching.
22 Clive Moore reminds me that the more established universities, and even newer ones such as James Cook University, had healthy postgraduate programs in European, Australian and regional histories.

for academic employment, though that situation has changed in recent decades. And now all Australian universities have some graduate programs as an integral part of their offerings. Federal grants for higher education are more widely and evenly distributed. The federal Block Grant that sustained ANU's privileged place has shrunk, and ANU academics now compete for research funds with their counterparts from other universities. ANU still regularly ranks among the top Australian universities but that cosy sense of unquestioned preeminence has long gone, to the delight of its rivals.

Given the purposes for which it was founded, the ANU spared little effort or expense in attracting the very best scholars in the various disciplines—people of genuinely distinguished international eminence. In my own field, there was Jim Davidson, a New Zealander who was at Cambridge when appointed as the world's first professor of Pacific history on the recommendation of Raymond Firth, one of the new university's academic advisors.[23] Davidson played a crucial role defining the new field of Pacific history, giving it purpose and identity, detaching it from its parent field of European expansion to a more island-centred focus. His influence was profound. Harry Maude came to the university after a career in the British Colonial Service in the Pacific and at the South Pacific Commission. There he wrote his classic *Of Islands and Men,* comprised of meticulously researched and carefully crafted papers.[24] Oskar Spate came to the university as the Foundation Professor of Geography from the London School of Economics and, after retirement in 1972 as the Director of the Research School of Pacific Studies, joined the Pacific history department to write his magisterial trilogy on Pacific exploration.[25] His most important work though, as he himself said, was his 1959 Fiji report.[26] There were other luminaries in the Coombs building whose presence gave the university its gravitas and greatness: Jack Golson in prehistory, R.G. Ward in human geography, Derek Freeman in anthropology, Stephen

---

23 Raymond Firth, 'The founding of the Research School of Pacific Studies', *The Journal of Pacific History* 31(1) (1996): 3–7. For follow-up, see Donald Denoon, 'Pacific Island history at the Australian National University: Place and the people', *The Journal of Pacific History* 31(2) (1996): 202–14, doi.org/10.1080/00223349608572818.
24 H.E. Maude, *Of Islands and Men: Studies in Pacific History* (Melbourne: Oxford University Press, 1968).
25 O.H.K. Spate, *The Pacific since Magellan,* 3 vols (Canberra: The Australian National University, 1979, 1983, 1988).
26 Spate's autobiographical account of his academic journey is in *On the Margins of History: From the Punjab to Fiji* (Canberra: National Centre for Development Studies, Research School of Pacific Studies, The Australian National University, 1991).

Wurm in linguistics, to name just a few. Now, they are forgotten names.[27] A later cohort in history included Gavan Daws, Hank Nelson, Deryck Scarr, Donald Denoon, Dorothy Shineberg, Niel Gunson and the ever-enterprising Robert Langdon, who led the Pacific Manuscripts Research Bureau (which I chaired for 20 years between 1993 and 2013). These are all names to conjure with; giants on whose shoulders we proudly stood. Among many of my younger colleagues, there is no consciousness of the past of the place, and no desire to know it either. Institutional memory is shallow and tattered and this, for me, is the cause for great sadness.

After three years as a PhD scholar at the ANU, I left in 1980, first for Fiji for a couple of years and then for nearly a decade at the University of Hawai'i. After teaching the department's bread-and-butter 'World Civilizations' course for several years, I wrote to Gavan Daws, chair of the department of Pacific and Southeast Asian History at the ANU, to see if they had a fellowship to enable me to complete a book on the history of twentieth-century Fiji.[28] They indeed had, giving me a fully funded fellowship and paying the travel expenses of my family as well. I doubt there was any advertisement for the fellowship. The department knew my record and that, for them, was enough. The book I wrote, *Broken Waves: A History of the Fiji Islands in the Twentieth Century*, was published by the University of Hawai'i Press in 1992, and it is still in print. I had delivered what I had promised. And that opened the doors to other opportunities that, in the course of time, saw me relocate from Honolulu to Canberra.

The world of the 1990s is in many ways as different to the world I will be leaving as the 1970s were from the 1990s. I have already spoken about the sense of community. It was real. All research scholars were housed in university townhouses concentrated in certain locations in Canberra: academic ghettos we jovially called them. The shared experience of raising young families, of exploring a new country, of communal socialising, generated camaraderie and friendships that transcended barriers and boundaries and fostered friendships that lasted. All that is a vanishing memory. We were welcomed warmly when we returned in 1990; perhaps with the knowledge that we might become long-term residents.

---

27 The one exception might be Freeman, the subject of Peter Hempenstall's recent book, *Truth's Fool: Derek Freeman and the War with Anthropology* (Madison: University of Wisconsin Press, 2017). Freeman is largely remembered for his longstanding debate on Samoa with Margaret Mead, the iconic American anthropologist and writer.
28 I have briefly discussed my Hawai'i experience in *Mr. Tulsi's Store* (Canberra: Pandanus Books, 2001), pp. 111–25.

Hank Nelson spent countless hours introducing me to Australian literature, history and popular and sporting culture.[29] Cricket was our mutual passion. He read my papers and gently corrected my prose with pencilled comments in the margin, a reminder to me of his time as a high school teacher; the same concern, the same compassion for someone whose command of the language was less than perfect. I can still hear him saying: 'Shorter sentences, mate, shorter sentences'. And, 'avoid however: a lazy writer's word'. Bill Gammage introduced our family to the Australian bush and much else besides. Through them, we met other like-minded friends. And Ken Inglis taught me by example about the nobility of historical craftsmanship. There were other colleagues from afar who put aside their own work to read mine. Foremost among them would have to be Doug Munro.[30] It is difficult to express how grateful I have felt for this kind of generous comradeship.

In the Coombs building, the Tea Room was the one indispensable social centre for everyone, academics, research scholars and visitors alike. It was the one place on the campus where the mighty and the minions mingled freely. Every day at 10:30 am and 3:30 pm, people got together for morning and afternoon tea. The topic of conversation could range from the footy results of the previous weekend and recent cricket scores to international and national politics to a discussion of research projects. As students, we picked up an enormous amount of information and insights (as well as gossip) from our senior scholars. If your work sparked their interest, they might arrange for a longer conversation over a lunch at University House. Otherwise, just participating in the rites and rituals of the academy in action in all its trivia and seriousness was enough bonus in itself. But now, the Tea Room has been closed down. It lies empty and forlorn, haunted by memories of conversations of yesterday. I can still hear the animated discussions that went on years ago. A sadness comes upon me every time I pass the place on my way to and from my office.

If Coombs Tea Room was an integral feature of our lives, so was the department. Our life and work was organised by and around the department. It gave our lives a sense of purpose and cohesiveness. By the 1990s, the age of the God Professors was long over. Now, senior academics

---

29 I have recalled this in 'Hank of Coombs', in *The Boy from Boort: Remembering Hank Nelson*, ed. Bill Gammage, Brij V. Lal and Gavan Daws (Canberra: ANU Press, 2014), pp. 75–88, doi.org/10.22459/BFB.07.2014.

30 Doug Munro and Jack Corbett (eds), *Bearing Witness: Essays in Honour of Brij V. Lal* (Canberra: ANU Press, 2017), doi.org/10.22459/BW.07.2017.

(reluctantly) took turns running the department, helped along by fiscal autonomy and a long-serving and dedicated staff. Our 'boss' in the Division of Pacific and Asian History was Dorothy Macintosh, a 20-year veteran who knew all the skeletons hidden in the cupboards, every secret that there was to know, but who was the very epitome of rectitude. She would gracefully forgive our occasional lapses in attention to detail and set the course straight with a gentle reprimand. She was protective and caring. We all felt a sense of shared interest in and loyalty to a real living community. But all that, too, is in the past now. The department now is a virtual entity, bereft of soul and companionship, like so much else. Our newer faculty, burdened by the pressure to perform constantly, have neither the time nor the energy or inclination to foster a sense of community. Many are here for a brief period and sooner rather than later will look for opportunities elsewhere. Technology has also played its part in gradually corroding the old spirit. There was a time when people came to their offices to do their work. Much of the academic work was done on campus. This fostered greater contact and interaction. But now with the advent of computers, the internet and the email, the need to travel to the office—and pay a heavy parking fee—is reduced. People increasingly work at home and come to campus to print or to attend seminars.

Along with the erosion of the sense of a cohesive community has gone a more relaxed atmosphere in the workplace. Academics then, as now, were serious people, many world leaders in their fields, but they also found time to have fun. The security afforded by the tenure system was certainly a crucial factor. You did not have to live from one grant to another. ANU Vice-Chancellor Ian Young's exhortation that academics should not only do first-rate research but also earn money for their university would sound somewhat offensive to the academics of the earlier generation, but it is a reality of academic life now. It wasn't so once. Freed of the tyranny of the grant cycle, academics 'enjoyed' life. Time was taken off to watch an absorbing day of test cricket. During the cricket season, we would walk in and out of Donald Denoon's office at all times of the day listening to the cricket commentary on his radio. For years, Hank Nelson and I would watch the first session of the first test on the television I had persuaded Hank to buy when he was the convenor so that we could watch world-breaking news in real time while still at work. The only breaking news we ever watched was the test match. No one minded our self-indulgence because everyone knew that we would burn the midnight lamp to complete our work.

People had fun of a more literary type as well. In the mid-1990s, I discovered quite by accident that several of my colleagues were writing creatively on the side. Tessa Morris-Suzuki wrote children's stories and poems.[31] Donald Denoon amusingly boasted that he had two unpublished novels to his credit; he has gone on to publish a couple since his retirement.[32] Mark Elvin, our professor of Chinese history, published three volumes of fantasy under his middle names John Mark Dutton.[33] Hank Nelson published literary pieces in the *Meanjin*. And I dabbled in some creative writing myself, which I called 'faction'. Seeing all the creativity flowing around me, I created a folder in the departmental room for colleagues to place their creative pieces in. They did, and the word spread. With that material I, in due course, started a literary journal, *Conversation,* published by Pandanus Books. Poetry, short fiction, nonfiction, photographs, memoir all found their way into its pages. It lasted for five years, establishing itself as a welcome and attractive vehicle for creative writers in the Canberra region. It brought a kindred creative community together. All that is a distant memory now. I am sure other narratives, other memories, are being created as I speak but I have no idea what they are.

It is beyond doubt that there has been a shrinkage in the quotient of loyalty people now owe to their place of work. Universities are no exception. 'Institutions do not owe you loyalty', is a phrase commonly heard in our corridors; and that sentiment is reciprocated in ample measure. There was a time when I was proud and possessive about my university. I was proud of the great minds that had worked here: Manning Clark, Nugget Coombs, Oskar Spate, among many others. ANU is the place where I would work out my professional career; it would not, for me, act as a springboard for more lucrative employment elsewhere. But that feeling is part of a vanished past. I once felt a part of a living community; now I am merely an employee, on a contract, to be dispensed with when there is a financial crisis or when I am no longer needed; made redundant. Occasionally we have been called 'service providers' for the student clientele. In view of all this, it is perfectly understandable why the younger academics are mobile, on the lookout for better opportunities elsewhere. The university asks for loyalty and dedication, but is not prepared to reciprocate.

---

31 Tessa Morris-Suzuki's book of poems is *Peeling Apples* (Canberra: Pandanus Books, 2005).
32 Including *Afterlife: A Divine Comedy* (Canberra: Pandanus Books, 2004).
33 I have two of these, *St Giles's Fair* (Canberra: Samara Press, 2000), and *Tiger's Island* (Canberra: Samara Press, 2000).

One service the Department of Pacific and Asian History at ANU did provide, but which has now been abandoned, was to hold annual workshops on aspects of the discipline. These were shoestring affairs but colleagues appreciated the opportunity of regular gatherings to exchange ideas and notes about research projects. From these gatherings came many edited volumes on various aspects of Pacific history.[34] The Department of Pacific and Asian History also acted as a generous host to colleagues visiting the ANU for various periods of time, providing facilities, free of charge, for research and writing.[35] In this way, it acted as a social hub of the discipline, fostering networks of camaraderie and collegiality across the globe. All that has gone, perhaps inevitably, as funds have shrunk and other Pacific centres of learning have emerged in recent decades.

Let me now turn to the culture of learning and scholarship in the contemporary academy. There is now an entirely legitimate demand that scholars should do research and publish regularly in the highest-ranked journals and by prestige publishers. These things are of material significance in appointments and promotions. Quality is judged by where research is published, as distinct from the content. The rigid application of the assessment formula is an imposition from the more quantifiable social sciences. This mechanical evaluation of scholarship is something I find distasteful to the point of being loathsome. We in the humanities don't measure our productivity on a yearly basis. But it is here to stay. I have paid my dues and published in the required places, but from the outset I decided that I would also publish to get read, not only to get ahead.

My first book, *Girmitiyas: The Origins of the Fiji Indians,* was published as a 150-page monograph by the Journal of Pacific History in 1983. It was widely and favourably noticed in reviews across the world and is now regarded as a foundational text in Indian indenture historiography.[36] I went places as a result of it. Today, it won't take me far because it is

---

34 For instance, Brij V. Lal (ed.), *Pacific Islands History: Journeys and Transformations* (Canberra: Journal of Pacific History, 1992); Donald Denoon (ed.), *Emerging from Empire: Decolonization in the Pacific* (Canberra: Division of Pacific and Asian History, The Australian National University, 1997); Brij V. Lal and Hank Nelson (eds), *Lines Across the Sea: Colonial Inheritance and the Post-Colonial Pacific* (Brisbane: Pacific History Association, 1995); and Brij V. Lal and Vicki Luker (eds), *Telling Pacific Lives: Prisms of Process* (Canberra, ANU E Press, 2008), doi.org/10.22459/TPL.06.2008.
35 Including many who were postgraduates of other universities: Doug Munro (Macquarie), Clive Moore (James Cook), Peter Hempenstall and Stewart Firth (Oxford). The department, in a very real sense, was a broad church.
36 Clem Seecharan, *Finding Myself: Essays on Race, Politics and Culture* (Leeds: Peepal Tree Press, 2015), pp. 114–40.

not published by a prestige publisher. My *Mr Tulsi's Store,* published by Pandanus Books, now defunct, was voted one of the Ten Notable Books of Asia and the Pacific by the San Francisco–based Kiriyama Prize in 2002 and was also an ACT Notable Book of the Year, but it wasn't published by a well-known commercial publisher. Nor was my *Chalo Jahaji: On a Journey through Indenture in Fiji.* Don't get me wrong. I have paid my dues and doffed my hat to the right gods, but, over time, I have been more concerned to make my work accessible to the people about whom I write. I am no longer concerned with the validation and approval of the academe. For that reason, too, I publish my work through an open-access press to reach the widest audience possible at the least expense. The ethical responsibility to 'give something' back has grown on me over time. I escaped censure because of my track record and seniority.

Throughout my working life, I stood at a remove from the preoccupation within the discipline about arcane theoretical issues. My work has benefited from an awareness of postcolonial theory, but theory informs rather than overwhelms my work. As someone once said jocularly to me, theory is like your underwear. It supports the system but it is bad form to display it publicly. To put it another way, I create my own text, the product of my individual imagination, rather than aspire to become a footnote in someone else's, or an academic groupie. My advice to my graduate students has been to be bold and imaginative and adventurous, and dare to be original. It may appear to be a daunting thought, but the alternatives are not worth considering. Life is too short to play the second fiddle.

'A lot of history is concealed autobiography,' distinguished Australian historian Ken Inglis has suggested. That rings true to me. It has been my good fortune to have worked on topics close to my heart: the history and politics of Fiji and the history and culture of the Indian diaspora, particularly in Fiji. For me a subject comes to life when head and heart come together. Abstract, theoretical concerns do not appeal to my imagination. I thrill to the particularities of the human experience. I live within my history and not above or beyond it, and I write accordingly. Oskar Spate's sage advice is what I have followed:

> The impartiality which evades responsibility by saying nothing, the partiality which masks its bias by presenting slanted facts with an air of cold objectivity—these are a thousand times more dangerous than an open declaration of where one stands; then at least those who disagree can take one's measure with confidence: 'that is why he said this'. The important points are that inference

must be based on evidence, as carefully verifiable as possible; and the choice must be made on the evidence and not from preconceived ideas.[37]

That, I hope, is the approach that has informed my work. History, for me, is about the illumination of problems, contemporary and past, and not simply a detached study of a discreet period of time. I am well aware that the past has an integrity of its own and it must be evaluated on its own terms, but my interest lies centrally in understanding the historical roots of the contemporary world and the influences that shaped it. I recognise the teleological tendencies and reductive capacity of this approach, but these difficulties are surmountable.

The discipline of history has been the engine of much of my work. I began my career as a quantitative historian, using the computer to analyse a massive amount of emigration data from 45,000 emigration passes. For my doctoral dissertation I continued that work in a milder form in my investigation of the indenture experience in Fiji.[38] Quantification provided a useful base data and it answered the 'what' questions of history, answering in the case of my early research the annual volume of migration to Fiji, the precise demographic data on the emigrants (their age, sex, marital status, the districts of origin and registration, the rejection rate between the time of recruitment and the time of embarkation, the mortality in the depots and on the voyage out). In later work, I used statistics to examine such questions as suicide among Indian immigrants, the gender dimension of plantation work and resistance and accommodation. Quantification yielded valuable results, in enabling me to see the shape and dimensions of an historical problem. From the very beginning, though, I was aware that quantification could answer only some questions and not others; questions related to the inner promptings of human motivation: why people behaved the way they did. Statistics could reveal the extent of mortality, for instance, but not the experience of dying. For that, I turned early on to the qualitative data, such as folksongs and oral narratives in various genres. The combination of the two approaches I found immensely rewarding.

---

37 O.H.K. Spate, 'Thirty years ago: A view of the Fijian political scene: Confidential report to the British Colonial Office', *The Journal of Pacific History* 25(1) (1990): 103–24, doi.org/10.1080/00223349008572628.
38 Brij V. Lal, 'Leaves of the banyan tree: Origins and background of Fiji's North Indian Migrants', 2 vols, PhD thesis (Canberra: The Australian National University, 1981). See also my 'Indian indenture historiography: A note on problems, sources and methods', *Pacific Studies* 6(2) (1983): 33–50.

Like most academics, I have continued to research and publish my amply referenced and properly researched work using the usual paraphernalia of academic presentation. These have included, among other things, biographies of Fiji leaders, studies of elections and surveys of political developments in Fiji. But from the mid-1990s, my interest extended beyond academic writing. This was in response to changes, fundamental changes, I was witnessing all around me as we toured throughout Fiji during our constitution review exercise. Nonrenewal of 30-year leases under the *Agricultural Landlord and Tenant Act* was fragmenting Fiji's long-settled agricultural community of Indo-Fijian tenants. That was where I grew up, but that world was disappearing before my eyes. It was a world that our indentured grandparents and parents built from bits and pieces of a remembered past as they sought to give structure and coherence to their chaotic lives. They built schools and temples and mosques, established a routine of rites and rituals to celebrate life and mourn its passing. Vanua Levu, my home island, was emptying; young men and women were seeking better futures in the urban areas of Viti Levu. They hoped eventually to move from there to some place overseas. And displaced farmers were clogging the squalid squatter settlements fringing the major urban centres in south-eastern Viti Levu where now between 15–20 per cent of Fiji's total population lives—with very dim hopes of a bright future. In time, the squatter settlements may come to be seen as the first essential step in a much longer journey of disruption and rupture.

There is nothing written about this massive transformation taking place in contemporary Fiji beyond a few anecdotal pieces in the local dailies. University research on the subject is scanty at best. I wanted to retrieve whatever I could from the debris of our remembered past, but that is easier said than done. In my old world, memory was not properly archived, and documentary records did not exist. All I had were the failing recollections of a passing generation who could provide me with a link to our beginnings as a community. I had little to go on except conversation with older folk. During each visit to my village and other similarly situated settlements, I collected whatever information I could get: about how schools and mosques and temples were built, how village disputes were resolved, how marriage negotiations were conducted, and breaches of the marital code were dealt with, and how the old ways eventually paved ways to the new when roads and radio came. From these curious intermittent jottings over time came an archive of information and anecdotes, which provided the material for my three books of creative nonfiction or faction, as I have called it: *Mr Tulsi's Store, On the Other Side of Midnight* and *Turnings*.[39]

My aim in faction writing is not necessarily to capture the factual accuracy of a particular experience, which would be impossible anyway. It is, rather, to capture its emotional truth, the spirit of the experience. You use your personal experience as a lens to refract the larger collective experience. The proof of the pudding is in the eating. Of all my books, these works of faction have evoked the greatest responses from unknown people right across the world. In my footsteps, they hear the echoes of their own. This kind of writing is not easy for someone who had been trained to use verifiable evidence in the social sciences, but it is immensely rewarding to capture the voices and faces of people beyond the range of official statistics, unwritten and unremarked, but whose everyday deeds keep the engine of life going. It enables me to bear witness to my—our—time and place and that, for me, is enough.

Finally, I am extremely grateful to the quirk of fate that brought me to the ANU. It has allowed me to follow my bent. It is from here that I spoke up for the values of democracy, the rule of law and the protocols and practices of constitutionalism, secure in the knowledge that my university would stand by me and the values I espoused. It allowed me to follow my instincts and imagination to explore research questions that I, and not some funding agency, wanted to explore. 'Curiosity-driven research' it is sometimes called. It has honoured my contributions and encouraged me on. It has given me and my family the company of men and women who have enriched our lives beyond measure. I could not in good conscience ask for more. But the world now is a different place to the one I entered a generation ago. It has 'become stranger, the pattern more complicated', to use again the words of T.S. Eliot. And I have become remnant in my own time. I trust I have 'done state some service',[40] as Oskar Spate used to say, or left a deposit of lime, as (from memory) Marshall Sahlins has said, that might nourish someone else's efforts. We all live with the certainty that in time—and hopefully not too soon—we will all become part of faded conversations, a minor footnote in someone else's text.

---

39   *Mr. Tulsi's Store* (2001) was published by Pandanus Books, Canberra; *The Other Side of Midnight* (2005) by the National Book Trust, New Delhi; and *Turnings* (2008) by the Fiji Institute of Applied Studies, Lautoka.
40   Oskar Spate, 'The salad days', in *The Coombs: A House of Memories,* ed. Lal and Ley, pp. 23–34, at p. 33.

When I wrote an earlier version of this chapter for oral delivery, I called it my 'Extinguished lecture' rather than my 'Valedictory lecture'. It seemed to be then, and perhaps even was, a clever play on words. It also turned out to be prophetic, an epitaph to a place and a moment in time. What I was not to know at the time was that the School of Culture, History and Language, of which I had long been a member, and which I had headed for a while, would face serious restructuring to the point of becoming unrecognisable; the noble dream of Pacific history shattered before our eyes and that, too, in a place where the discipline was founded and nurtured for over half a century.[41] Good colleagues would face retrenchment, others deployed elsewhere in the university and some seeking greener pastures beyond Canberra. To see something built over many long years, with a proud and honourable legacy, dismantled with the stroke of a pen was a deeply saddening experience. I felt lucky to be getting out when I did. My colleagues viewed the timing of my departure with envy. Now, it is time to move on. Robert Graves's *Goodbye to All That* has taken on a grimmer meaning.

---

41   The Department of Pacific and Asian History at ANU now has a single Pacific historian. But the teaching of Pacific history has declined significantly in Australian universities, sometimes in favour of more 'relevant' applied social sciences for which scholarships are relatively easy to get.

Bibliography

Archival repositories

England
House of Commons, Parliamentary Papers
Foreign and Commonwealth Office
Colonial Office

Fiji
National Archives of Fiji

India
National Archives of India (NAI)
Emigration Proceedings
Home Legislative Department (Emigration)

Cases and legislation

Agricultural, Landlord and Tenant Act [Cap 270], ed. 1978, available from: www.paclii.org/fj/legis/consol_act_OK/alata308/ (accessed 5 June 2019).

Bills of Exchange Act [Cap 227], ed. 1978, available from: www.paclii.org/fj/legis/consol_act_OK/boea148/ (accessed 5 June 2019).

C169 – Indigenous and Tribal Peoples Convention, 1989 (No. 169), available from: www.ilo.org/dyn/normlex/en/f?p=NORMLEXPUB:12100:0::NO::P12100_ILO_CODE:C169 (accessed 5 June 2019).

Declaration on the Rights of Indigenous Peoples, A/RES/61/295, available from: www.un.org/esa/socdev/unpfii/documents/DRIPS_en.pdf (accessed 5 June 2019).

Indigenous Claims Tribunal Bill 2006, Bill No. 11 of 2006.

Mitchell v. Director of Public Prosecutions [1986] LRC (Const) 35, 88, Court of Appeal, Granada.

Native Land Trust Act, [Cap 134], available from: www.paclii.org/fj/legis/consol_act_OK/nlta206/ (accessed 5 June 2019).

Promotion of Reconciliation, Tolerance and Unity Bill 2005, available from: www.fijibure.com/recon.htm (accessed 4 May 2018).

Qoliqoli Bill 2006, Bill No. 12 of 2006.

Republic of Fiji and AG vs Chandrika Prasad 2000, High Court Action No. HBC0217.00L, Lautoka.

Republic of Fiji and AG vs Chandrika Prasad 2000, The Court of Appeal, Fiji Islands on Appeal From the High Court of Fiji Islands Civil Appeal No. ABU0078/2000S. High Court Civil Action No. 217/2000.

Books, chapters, newspaper and journal articles

Aiono, Fanaafi Le Tagaloa and Ron Crocombe (eds), *Culture and Democracy in the South Pacific* (Suva: Institute of Pacific Studies of the University of the South Pacific, 1992).

Ali, Ahmed, 'Remembering', in *Bittersweet: The Indo-Fijian Experience,* ed. Brij V. Lal (Canberra: Pandanus Books, 2004), 71–87.

——, 'Resisting girmit', in *Girmitiya: Souvenir Magazine of the National Farmers Union* (Suva, 2004), 64–69.

——, 'The Fiji General Election of 1972', *The Journal of Pacific History* 8 (1973): 171–80, doi.org/10.1080/00223347308572230.

——, *A Society in Transition: Aspects of Fiji Indian History, 1879–1937* (Suva: School of Social and Economic Development, University of the South Pacific, 1976).

——, *Fiji and the Franchise: A History of Political Representation, 1900–1937* (iUniverse, 2007).

——, *Fiji: From Colony to Independence, 1874–1970* (Suva: School of Social and Economic Development, University of the South Pacific, 1977).

——, *Girmit: The Indenture Experience in Fiji* (Suva: Fiji Museum, 1979).

Amnesty International, *Fiji's Draft Constitution Falls Short on Human Rights Standards,* 25 April 2013.

Andrews C.F. and W.W. Pearson, *Indian Indentured Labour in Fiji* (Perth: Privately published, 1918).

Anthony, James, 'The 1968 Fiji By-Elections', *The Journal of Pacific History* 4(1) (1969): 135–38, doi.org/10.1080/00223346908572151.

Bainimarama, J.V., 'A Response to the Fiji Human Rights Commission Director's Report on the assumption of executive authority by Commodore J.V. Bainimarama, Commander of the Republic of Fiji Military Forces', n.d. but c. mid to late January 2007.

Bainimarama, Voreqe, 'Address by the Interim Prime Minister Commodore Voreqe Bainimarama', 12 April 2007, on the Republic of Fiji Military Forces website, 31 May 2007.

Baledrokadroka, Jone, 'Sacred king and warrior chief: The role of the military in Fiji politics', PhD thesis (Canberra: The Australian National University, 2013).

Belshaw, C.S., *Under the Ivi Tree: Society and Economic Growth in Rural Fiji* (London: Routledge and Kegan Paul, 1964).

Bhana, Surendra (ed.), *Essays on Indentured Indians in Natal* (Leeds: Peepal Tree Press, 1990).

Bhana, Surendra and Joy Brain, *Setting Down Roots: Indian Migrants in South Africa, 1860–1911* (Johannesburg: Witwatersrand University Press, 1989).

Bhana, Surendra, *Indentured Indian Emigrants to Natal, 1860–1902: A Study Based on Ships' Lists* (New Delhi: Promilla & Co., 1991).

Birbalsingh, Frank (ed.), *Indo-Caribbean Resistance* (Toronto: Tsar, 1993).

Bisnauth, Dale, 'The East Indian immigrant society in British Guiana, 1890–1930', PhD thesis (Mona, Jamaica: University of the West Indies, 1977).

Bissoondoyal, Uttama and SBC Servansing (eds), *Indian Labour Immigration* (Moka, Mauritius: Mahatma Gandhi Institute, 1986).

'Blueprint for Affirmative Action for Fijian Education', presented to the GCC by Laisenia Qarase, 3 July 2000.

'Blueprint for the Protection of Fijian and Rotuman Rights and Interests, and the Advancement of their Development', presented to the Great Council of Chiefs by Laisenia Qarase, 3 July 2000.

Brereton, Bridget, *A History of Modern Trinidad, 1783–1962* (Portsmouth: Heinemann, 1989).

Brownrigg, F.W., *Sultanpur Settlement Report* (Allahabad: Government Printer, 1898).

Burns, Alan, *Report of the Commission of Enquiry into the Natural Resources and Population Trends of the Colony of Fiji* (Suva: Legislative Council Paper 1/1960).

Burns, Sir Alan et al., *Report of the Commission of Enquiry into the Natural Resources and Population Trends of the Colony of Fiji* (Suva: Government of Fiji Legislative Council Paper 8 of 1961).

Burton, J.W., *Fiji of Today* (London: Charles H Kelly, 1910).

——, *The Call of the Pacific* (London: Charles H Kelly, 1912).

Butler, David, 'Instant history', *The New Zealand Journal of History* 2(2) (1968): 107–14.

Butterfield, Herbert, *History and Human Relations* (London: Collins, 1951).

Carr, E.H., *What is History?* (London: Penguin Books, 1964 [1961]).

Carter, Marina, *Lakshmi's Legacy: The Testimonies of Indian Women in 19th Century Mauritius* (Stanley-Rose Hill: Edition l'Ocean Indien, 1994).

——, *Voices from Indenture: Experiences of Indian Migrants in the British Empire* (Leicester: Leicester University Press, 1996).

Census of India (1921), available from: archive.org/details/cu31924014522746 (accessed 11 May 2018).

Chakravarti, N.R., *The Indian Minority in Burma: The Rise and Decline of an Immigrant Community* (London: Oxford University Press, 1971).

Chand, Satish, 'Poverty and redistributive politics in post-independence Fiji: 50/50 by 2020', manuscript in my possession, courtesy of the author.

Chapman, J.K., *The Career of Sir Arthur Hamilton Gordon: First Lord Stanmore, 1829–1912* (Toronto: University of Toronto Press, 1964), doi.org/10.3138/ 9781442652699.

Chetty, Kishor and Satendra Prasad, *Fiji's Emigration: An Examination of Contemporary Trends and Issues* (Suva: School of Social and Economic Development, University of the South Pacific, 1993).

Chief Justice to President of Fiji Law Society, 14 June 2000. High Court file CJ/WF/9.

Citizen's Constitutional Forum, *Towards a Sustainable Constitutional Democracy*, 4 December 2006, available from: www.ccf.org.fj (accessed 6 April 2018).

Cole, Anthony, 'Accidental deaths', in Lal, *Chalo Jahaji: On a Journey of Indenture through Fiji* (Suva: Fiji Museum, 2000; Canberra: ANU E Press, 2012), 324–36, doi.org/10.22459/CJ.12.2012.

Comins, D.W.D., *Note on Emigration from the East Indies to British Guiana* (Calcutta: Government Printer, 1893).

——, *Note on Emigration from the East Indies to St Lucia* (Calcutta: Government Printer, 1893).

Commonwealth Secretariat, *An Analysis of the Draft 2013 Constitution of Fiji within the Framework of Fundamental Commonwealth Values* (London: Commonwealth Secretariat, April 2012).

Constitution Commission [of Fiji], *A Guide to Constitution Making for the People of Fiji* (Suva: Fiji Constitutional Commission, August 2012).

Constitution Commission, Panel Report, *Seeking Cooperation, Toleration and Understanding of our Diversity: A Model of the People's Constitution,* National Archives of Fiji.

Coulter, John Wesley, *Fiji: Little India of the Pacific* (Chicago: University of Chicago Press, 1943).

——, *The Drama of Fiji: A Contemporary History* (Rutland, VT: Charles Tuttle and Company, 1967).

Crawford, C.E., *Azamgarh Settlement Report* (Allahabad: Government Printer, 1898).

Crawford, James, S.C., 'Opinion: Re Judicial Services Commission of Fiji – Recommendation for Appointment of Acting Chief Justice', Matrix Chambers, 20 February 2007.

Crocombe, Ron and Ahmed Ali (eds), *Foreign Forces in Pacific Politics* (Suva: Institute of Pacific Studies, 1983).

Crocombe, Ron and Malama Meleisea (eds), *Pacific Universities: Achievements, Problems and Prospects* (Suva: Institute of Pacific Studies, 1988).

Cross, Malcolm, 'East Indian–Creole relations in Trinidad and Guiana in the late nineteenth century', in *Across the Dark Waters: Ethnicity and Indian Identity in the Caribbean,* ed. David Dabydeen and Brinsley Samaroo (London: Macmillan Caribbean, 1996), 14–38.

Currie, Sir George, *Report of the Commission on Higher Education in Papua and New Guinea* (Canberra: The Commission, 1964).

Dabydeen, David and Brinsley Samaroo (eds), *Across the Dark Waters: Ethnicity and Indian Identity in the Caribbean* (London: Macmillan Caribbean, 1996).

——, *India in the Caribbean* (London: Hansib/University of Warwick, Centre for Caribbean Studies Publication, 1987).

Das Gupta, Ranajit, 'Factory labour in Eastern India: Sources of supply, 1855–1946: Some preliminary findings', *Indian Economic and Social History Review* 18(3) (1973): 277–329, doi.org/10.1177/001946467601300301.

Davidson, J.W., 'Constitutional change in Fiji', *The Journal of Pacific History* 1 (1966): 165–68, doi.org/10.1080/00223346608572086.

——, 'Understanding Pacific history: The participant as historian', in *The Feel of Truth: Essays in New Zealand and Pacific History,* ed. Peter Munz (Wellington: AW & AH Reed, 1969), 27–42.

Davidson, James Wightman, *Problems of Pacific History: An Inaugural Lecture Delivered in Canberra, 23 November 1954* (Canberra. The Australian National University, 1955).

Davis, Kingsley, *The Population of India and Pakistan* (Princeton: NJ: Princeton University Press, 1951).

Dean, Eddie and Stan Ritova, *Rabuka: No Other Way* (Sydney: Doubleday, 1988).

Dening, Greg, 'Reflection: On the cultural history of Marshall Sahlins and Valerio Valeri', *Pacific History Bibliography and Comments* (Canberra: Journal of Pacific History, 1986), 43–48.

——, *The Bounty: An Ethnographic History* (Melbourne: University of Melbourne, 1989).

Denoon, Donald (ed.), *Emerging from Empire: Decolonization in the Pacific* (Canberra: Division of Pacific and Asian History, The Australian National University, 1997).

Denoon, Donald, 'Pacific Island history at The Australian National University: The place and the people', *The Journal of Pacific History* 31(2) (1996): 202–14, doi.org/10.1080/00223349608572818.

——, *Afterlife: A Divine Comedy* (Canberra: Pandanus Books, 2004).

Desai, Ashwin and Goolam Vahed, *Inside Indenture: A South African Story, 1860–1914* (Cape Town: Human Sciences Research Council, 2007).

Deutscher, Isaac, 'From the Introduction (1961)', in his *Stalin: A Political Biography*, 2nd edn (New York: Oxford University Press, 1966), x–xi.

Duncan, Nicole, 'Death on Fiji plantations', in Lal, *Chalo Jahaji: On a Journey of Indenture through Fiji* (Suva: Fiji Museum, 2000; Canberra: ANU E Press, 2012), 291–323, doi.org/10.22459/CJ.12.2012.

Durutalo, Alumita, 'Elections and the dilemmas of indigenous Fijian politics', in *Fiji before the Storm: Elections and the Politics of Development,* ed. Brij V. Lal (Canberra: Asia Pacific Press, 2000), 73–92.

Durutalo, Simione, 'Internal colonialism and unequal regional development: The case of Western Viti Levu, MA thesis (Suva: University of the South Pacific, 1985).

Dylan, Bob, 'The times they are a-changin', on *The Times they are A-Changin'* (Columbia Records, 1964), line 17, lyrics available from: www.bobdylan.com/songs/times-they-are-changin/ (accessed 10 April 2019).

Ecumenical Centre for Research, Education and Advocacy's (ECREA's) website, available from: www.ecrea.org.fj (accessed 6 April 2018).

Field, Michael, Tupeni Baba, Uniasi Nabobo-Baba, *Speight of Violence: Inside Fiji's 2000 Coup* (Canberra: Pandanus Books, 2005).

Fiji Islands Council of Trade Unions, *Submission to the UN Mission,* 27 April 2007.

Fiji Labour Party, 'Submission to the Fiji Constitution Commission', 12 October 2012.

Fiji Legislative Council Debate, April 1961.

Fiji Legislative Council Debates, 1946.

Firth, Raymond, 'The founding of the Research School of Pacific Studies', *The Journal of Pacific History* 31(1) (1996), 3–7, doi.org/10.1080/00223349608572802.

Firth, Stewart and Daryl Tarte (eds), *20th Century Fiji: People who Shaped the Nation* (Suva: USP Solutions, 2001).

Firth, Stewart, 'Reflections on Fiji since independence', *The Round Table: The Commonwealth Journal of International Affairs* 101(6) (2012): 575–83, doi.org/10.1080/00358533.2012.749098.

——, 'The contemporary history of Fiji: A review article', *The Journal of Pacific History* 24 (1989): 242–46, doi.org/10.1080/00223348908572619.

Fisk, E.K., *The Political Economy of Independent Fiji* (Canberra: Australian National University Press, 1970).

Forum Foreign Affairs Ministers' Meeting, 16 March 2007, Port Vila, 'Outcome Statement', PIFS (07) FFAMM.3.

Foster, S.G. and Margaret M. Varghese, *The Making of the Australian National University, 1946–1996* (Sydney: Allen & Unwin, 1996).

Fowler, Glenn, '"A want of care"' in Lal, *Chalo Jahaji: On a Journey of Indenture through Fiji* (Suva: Fiji Museum, 2000; Canberra: ANU E Press, 2012), 237–90, doi.org/10.22459/CJ.12.2012.

Fraenkel, Jon, 'Fiji: Melanesia in review', in *The Contemporary Pacific* 25(3) (2012): 377–89, doi.org/10.1353/cp.2012.0046.

——, 'Fiji's electoral system changes', *Pacific Islands Report,* January 2013.

——, 'Melanesia in review: Issues and events 2013: Fiji', *The Contemporary Pacific* 25(2) (2014): 476–95, doi.org/10.1353/cp.2014.0032.

——, 'The remorseless power of incumbency in Fiji's September 2014 Election', *The Round Table: The Commonwealth Journal of International Affairs* 104(2) (2015), 151–64, doi.org/10.1080/00358533.2015.1017255.

Fraenkel, Jon and Stewart Firth (eds), *From Election to Coup in Fiji: The 2006 Campaign and its Aftermath* (Canberra: ANU E Press, 2007), available from: press.anu.edu.au/publications/election-coup-fiji (accessed 6 April 2018).

Fraenkel, Jon, Stewart Firth and Brij V. Lal (eds.), *The 2006 Military Takeover in Fiji: A Coup to End all Coups?* (Canberra: ANU E Press, 2009), doi.org/10.22459/MTF.04.2009.

France, Peter, *Charter of the Land: Custom and Colonization in Fiji* (Melbourne: Oxford University Press, 1969).

Frank, Anne, *Het Achterhuis. Dagboekbrieven 14 Juni 1942 – 1 Augustus 1944* (Amsterdam: Contact Publishing, 1947).

——, *The Diary of a Young Girl*, trans. Barbara Mooyaart-Doubleday (New York: Doubleday & Company; London: Valentine Mitchell, 1952).

Gammage, Bill, Brij V. Lal and Gavan Daws (eds), *The Boy from Boort: Remembering Hank Nelson* (Canberra: ANU Press, 2014), doi.org/10.22459/BFB.07.2014.

Gan, Steven, James Gomez and Uwe Johannen (eds), *Asian Cyberactivism: Freedom of Expression and Media Censorship* (Bangkok: Friederic Naumann Foundation, 2004).

Geoghegan, G., *Coolie Emigration from India* (Calcutta: Government Printer, 1874).

Ghai, Yash Pal, 'Ethnicity, politics and constitutions in Fiji', in *Bearing Witness: Essays in Honour of Brij V. Lal,* ed. Doug Munro and Jack Corbett (Canberra: ANU Press, 2017), 177–206, doi.org/10.22459/BW.07.2017.

Ghai, Yash and Jill Cottrell, 'A tale of three constitutions: Ethnicity and politics in Fiji', in *Constitutional Design for Divided Societies: Integration or Accommodation?* ed. Sujit Choudhr, (Oxford: Oxford University Press, 2008), 287–315.

Gill, Walter, *Turn North-East at the Tombstone* (Adelaide: Rigby, 1970).

Gillion, K.L., 'CF Andrews and Indians overseas', *Visva-Bharti News* (February–March 1971): 206–17.

——, *Fiji's Indian Migrants: A History to the End of Indenture in 1920* (Melbourne: Oxford University Press, 1962).

——, *The Fiji Indians: Challenge to European Dominance, 1920–1946* (Canberra: Australian National University Press, 1977).

Glasgow, Roy Arthur, *Guyana: Race and Politics among Africans an East Indians* (The Hague: Martin Nijhoff, 1970), doi.org/10.1007/978-94-010-3213-1.

Gordon, Arthur Hamilton, *Paper on the System of Taxation in Force in Fiji. Read before the Colonial Institute* (London: Harrison, 1879).

Gounder, Farzana, *Indentured Identities: Resistance and Accommodation in Plantation-Era Fiji* (Amsterdam/Philadelphia: John Benjamins Publishing Co., 2011), doi.org/10.1075/sin.15.

Government of Fiji, Legislative Council Paper 13/1959.

Green, Michael, *Persona Non Grata: Breaking the Bond: Fiji and New Zealand, 2004–2007* (Auckland: Dunmore Publishing, 2013).

Griffin, Arlene (ed.), *With Heart and Nerve and Sinew: Post-Coup Writing from Fiji* (Suva: Christmas Club, 1997).

Grynberg, Roman, Doug Munro and Michael White, *Crisis: The Collapse of the National Bank of Fiji* (Suva: USP Book Centre, 2002).

Harvey, Jane, 'Naraini's story', in Lal, *Chalo Jahaji: On a Journey of Indenture through Fiji* (Suva: Fiji Museum, 2000; Canberra: ANU E Press, 2012), 337–47, doi.org/10.22459/CJ.12.2012.

Hau'ofa, Epeli, *Tales of the Tikongs* (Auckland: Longman Paul, 1983).

Hempenstall, Peter, 'Tasman epiphanies: The "participant history" of Alan Ward', *The Journal of New Zealand Studies* 4–5 (2005–06): 65–80, doi.org/10.26686/jnzs.v0i4/5.107.

——, *Truth's Fool: Derek Freeman and the War with Anthropology* (Madison: University of Wisconsin Press, 2017).

Hennings, C.G., *The Indentured Indian in Natal, 1860–1917* (New Delhi: Promilla & Co., 1993).

Herr, Richard, 'External influences and the 2006 Fiji Military Coup', unpublished paper.

Herr, Richard and Anthony Bergin, 'Abbot must bring Fiji in from the cold', *Australian*, 13 September 2013.

Hiatt, Lester Richard and Chandra Jayawardena (eds), *Anthropology in Oceania: Essays Presented to Ian Hogbin* (Sydney: Angus and Robertson, 1971).

Inglis, K.S. (Kenneth Stanley), assisted by Jan Brazier, *This is the ABC: The Australian Broadcasting Corporation, 1932–1983* (Melbourne: Melbourne University Press, 1983).

International Senior Lawyers Project (ISLP), *Analysis of the Draft Constitution of Fiji released by the Interim Government of Fiji on 21 March 2013*, n.d.

Iyer, Venkat, 'Courts and constitutional usurpers: Some lessons from Fiji', *Dalhousie Law Journal* 28(1) (2005): 47–68.

——, 'Restoration constitutionalism in the South Pacific', *Pacific Rim Law & Policy Journal* 15(1) (2006): 39–72.

Jalal, Ayesha, *The Pity of Partition: Manto's Life, Times, and Work across the India-Pakistan Divide* (Princeton, NJ: Princeton University Press, 2013), doi.org/10.1515/9781400846689.

Jayaraman, R., 'Indian emigration to Ceylon: Some aspects of the historical and social background of the emigrants', *Indian Economic and Social History Review* 4(4) (1967): 319–59, doi.org/10.1177/001946466700400402.

Jayawardena, Chandra, 'Religious belief and social change: Aspects of the development of Hinduism in British Guiana', *Comparative Studies in Society and History* 8(2) (1965): 211–40, doi.org/10.1017/S0010417500004011.

——, 'The disintegration of caste in Fiji Indian rural society', in *Anthropology in Oceania: Essays Presented to Ian Hogbin,* ed. L.R. Hiatt and Chandra Jayawardena (Sydney: Angus and Robertson, 1971), 89–119.

——, *Conflict and Solidarity in a Guianese Plantation* (London: Athlone Press, 1963).

Judt, Tony, *On Being Austere and Being Jewish* (New York Review of Books, 13 May 2010).

Kamikamica, Josefata', Fijian native land: Issues and challenges', in *Research Papers of the Fiji Constitution Review Commission,* Vol. 1: *Fiji in Transition,* ed. Brij V. Lal, Paul Reeves and Tomasi Vakatora, (Suva: School of Social and Economic Development, University of the South Pacific, 1997), 259–90.

Kant, Romitesh and Eroni Rakuita, 'Public participation and constitution-making in Fiji: A Critique of the 2012 constitution-making process', *State, Society and Governance in Melanesia Program Discussion Paper 6/2014* (Canberra: The Australian National University, 2014).

Kelly, John D., *A Politics of Virtue: Hinduism, Sexuality, and Countercolonial Discourse in Fiji* (Chicago: University of Chicago Press, 1991).

Klass, Morton, *East Indians in Trinidad: A Study in Cultural Persistence* (New York: Columbia University Press, 1961).

Kotabalavu, Jioji, 'The collapsing morale in the civil service', address, The Australian National University, 5 June 2007.

Kuper, Hilda, *Indian People in Natal* (Cape Town: University Press, 1960).

La Guerre, John (ed.), *Calcutta to Caroni,* rev. edn (St Augustine: University of West Indies, 1985).

Lal, Brij V. (ed.), *Pacific Islands History: Journeys and Transformations* (Canberra: Journal of Pacific History, 1992).

——, *A Vision for Change: Speeches and Writings of A.D. Patel, 1929–1969* (Canberra: ANU E Press, 2011), doi.org/10.22459/VCSW.11.2011.

——, *Bittersweet: The Indo–Fijian Experience* (Canberra: Pandanus Books, 2004).

——, *Fiji Before the Storm: Elections and the Politics of Development* (Canberra: Asia Pacific Press, 2000, Canberra: ANU E Press, 2012), doi.org/10.22459/FBS.12.2012.

——, *Fiji: British Documents on the End of the Empire* (London: The Stationery Office, 2006).

——, *Pacific Places, Pacific Histories: Essays in Honor of Robert C Kiste* (Honolulu: University of Hawai'i Press, 2004).

——, *Politics in Fiji: Studies in Contemporary History* (Laie: Brigham Young University and Sydney: Allen & Unwin, 1986).

Lal, Brij V. and Allison Ley (eds), *The Coombs: A House of Memories,* with a foreword by William C. Clarke (Canberra: Research School of Pacific and Asian Studies, The Australian National University, 2006).

Lal, Brij V. and Hank Nelson (eds), *Lines Across the Sea: Colonial Inheritance and the Post-Colonial Pacific* (Brisbane: Pacific History Association, 1995).

Lal, Brij V. and Michael Pretes (eds), *Coup: Reflections on the Political Crisis in Fiji* (Canberra: Pandanus Books, 2001; Canberra: ANU E Press, 2008), available from: press.anu.edu.au/publications/coup/download (accessed 11 May 2017).

Lal, Brij V. and Peter Hempenstall (eds), *Pacific Lives, Pacific Places: Bursting Boundaries in Pacific History* (Canberra: Journal of Pacific History, 2001).

Lal, Brij V. and Vicki Luker (eds), *Telling Pacific Lives: Prisms of Process* (Canberra: ANU E Press, 2008), doi.org/10.22459/TPL.06.2008.

Lal, Brij V. and Yogendra Yadav (eds), *Bhut Len Ki Katha: Totaram Sanadyha's Fiji* [in Hindi] (New Delhi Saraswati Press, 1994).

Lal, Brij V., Paul Reeves and Tomasi Vakatora (eds), *Research Papers of the Fiji Constitution Review Commission,* Vol. 1: *Fiji in Transition* (Suva: Suva: School of Social and Economic Development, University of the South Pacific, 1997).

Lal, Brij V., Peter Reeves and Rajesh Rai (eds), *The Encyclopedia of the Indian Diaspora* (Honolulu: University of Hawai'i Press, 2006).

Lal, Brij V. 'The 1982 Fiji National Election and its aftermath', *USP Sociological Society Newsletter* 5 (1983): 3–17.

——, 'A change of seasons', in *Turnings: Fiji Factions* (Lautoka: Fiji Institute of Applied Studies, 2008), 151–72.

——, 'A *girmitiya* "sepoy"', *South Asia: Journal of South Asian Studies* 39(1) (2016): 244–50, doi.org/10.1080/00856401.2016.1124229.

——, 'A time to move', in Lal, *Chalo Jahaji: On a Journey of Indenture through Fiji* (Suva: Fiji Museum, 2000; Canberra: ANU E Press, 2012), 121–36, doi.org/10.22459/CJ.12.2012.

——, 'A vision for change', *USP Sociological Society Newsletter* 5 (1983): 3–17.

——, 'Anxiety, uncertainty and fear in our land: Fiji's road to 2006', in *The 2006 Military Takeover in Fiji: A Coup to End all Coups?* ed. Jon Fraenkel, Stewart Firth and Brij V. Lal (Canberra: ANU E Press, 2009), 21–41, doi.org/10.22459/MTF.04.2009.

——, 'Anxiety, uncertainty, and fear in our land: Fiji's road to military coup, 2006', in *The Round Table: The Commonwealth Journal of International Affairs* 96(389) (Apr 2007): 135–53, doi.org/10.1080/00358530701292447.

——, 'Bahut Julum: Reflections on the use of Fiji Hindi', *Fijian Studies* 3(1) (2005): 153–58.

——, 'Caught in the web', in *Intersections: History, Memory, Discipline* (Canberra: ANU E Press, 2012), 279–86, doi.org/10.22459/IHMD.11.2012.

——, 'Chance Hai: On the hustings, 1999 and 2006', in *Intersections: History, Memory, Discipline* (Canberra: ANU E Press, 2012), 79–101, doi.org/10.22459/IHMD.11.2012.

——, 'Chiefs and Indians: Elections and politics in contemporary Fiji', *The Contemporary Pacific* 5(2) (1993): 275–301.

——, 'Chiefs and thieves and other people besides: The making of George Speight's Coup', *The Journal of Pacific History* 35(3) (2000): 281–93, doi.org/10.1080/00223340020010571.

——, 'Coombs 4240', in *Intersections: History, Memory, Discipline* (Canberra: ANU E Press, 2012), 127–38, doi.org/10.22459/IHMD.11.2012.

——, 'Fare well, Fiji', in *Mr Tulsi's Store: A Fijian Journey* (Canberra: Pandanus Books, 2001), 207–08, doi.org/10.22459/MTS.03.2013.

——, 'Fiji: Fishing in troubled waters', *Security Challenges* 8(2) (2012): 85–92.

——, 'Fiji's Constitutional conundrum', *The Round Table: The Commonwealth Journal of International Affairs* 372 (2003): 671–85, doi.org/10.1080/0035853032000150663.

——, 'Hank of Coombs', in *The Boy from Boort: Remembering Hank Nelson*, ed. Bill Gammage, Brij V. Lal and Gavan Daws (Canberra: ANU Press, 2014), 75–88, doi.org/10.22459/BFB.07.2014.

——, 'Hinduism under indenture, in Lal, *Chalo Jahaji: On a Journey of Indenture through Fiji* (Suva: Fiji Museum, 2000; Canberra: ANU E Press, 2012), 239–60, doi.org/10.22459/CJ.12.2012.

——, 'In Frank Bainimarama's shadows: Fiji, elections and the future', *The Journal of Pacific History* 49(4) (2014): 457–68, doi.org/10.1080/00223344.2014.977518.

——, 'Indian indenture historiography: A note on problems, sources and methods', *Pacific Studies* 6(2) (1983): 33–50.

——, 'Kunti's cry', in Lal, *Chalo Jahaji: On a Journey of Indenture through Fiji* (Suva: Fiji Museum, 2000; Canberra: ANU E Press, 2012), 195–214, doi.org/10.22459/CJ.12.2012.

——, 'Laucala Bay', in *Pacific Places, Pacific Histories: Essays in Honor of Robert C Kiste*, ed. Brij V. Lal, (Honolulu: University of Hawai'i Press, 2004), 237–58.

——, 'Leaves of the banyan tree: Origins and background of Fiji's North Indian migrants', 2 vols, PhD thesis (Canberra: The Australian National University, 1981).

——, 'Making and unmaking of a Fijian colossus, A review essay of Tuimacilai: A life of Ratu Sir Kamisese Mara', *Fijian Studies* 13(1) (2015): 31–41, available from: fijianstudies.net/wp-content/uploads/FS/13(1)/FS-13-1-Lal-Mara.pdf (accessed 24 January 2017).

——, 'Murmurs of dissent', in Lal, *Chalo Jahaji: On a Journey through Indenture in Fiji* (Suva: Fiji Museum, 2000; Canberra: ANU E Press, 2012), 167–94, doi.org/10.22459/CJ.12.2012.

——, 'Rabuka's Republic: The Fiji snap elections of 1994', *Pacific Studies* 18(1) (1995): 47–77.

——, 'Rhetoric and reality: The dilemmas of contemporary Fijian politics', in *Culture and Democracy in the South Pacific,* ed. Aiono, Fanaafi Le Tagaloa and Ron Crocombe (Suva: Institute of Pacific Studies of the University of the South Pacific, 1992), 97–116.

——, 'The decolonisation of Fiji: Debate on constitutional change, 1943–1963', in *Emerging from Empire? Decolonisation in the Pacific*, ed. Donald Denoon (Canberra: Division of Pacific and Asian History, The Australian National University, 1997), 29–39.

——, 'The Fiji General Elections of 1982: The tidal wave that never came', *The Journal of Pacific History* 18(2) (1983): 134–57, doi.org/10.1080/00223348308572463.

——, 'The odyssey of indenture', in Brij V. Lal, *Chalo Jahaji: On a Journey of Indenture through Fiji* (Suva: Fiji Museum, 2000; Canberra: ANU E Press, 2012), 41–66, doi.org/10.22459/CJ.12.2012.

——, 'The strange career of Commodore Frank Bainimarama's 2006 Fiji coup', *State, Society and Governance in Melanesia Program Discussion Paper 2013/8* (Canberra: The Australian National University, 2013).

——, 'Veil of dishonour', in Brij V. Lal, *Chalo Jahaji: On a Journey of Indenture through Fiji* (Suva: Fiji Museum, 2000; Canberra: ANU E Press, 2012), 215–38, doi.org/10.22459/CJ.12.2012.

——, 'While the gun is still smoking', in *Intersections: History, Memory, Discipline* (Suva: Fiji Institute of Applied Studies, 2011; Canberra: ANU E Press, 2012), 39–57, doi.org/10.22459/IHMD.11.2012.

——, *A Time to Change: The Fiji General Elections of 1999* (Canberra: Department of Political and Social Change, Research School of Pacific and Asian Studies, Regime Change and Regime Maintenance in Asia and the Pacific, Paper no. 23, The Australian National University, 1999).

——, *Another Way: The Politics of Constitutional Reform in Post-Coup Fiji* (Canberra: Asia Pacific Press, 1998).

——, Ashutosh Kumar and Yogendra Yadav (eds), *Bhut Len ki Katha: Girmit ke anubhav. By Totaram Sanadhya* (The story of the haunted line: The experience of Girmit by Totaram Sanadhya), (New Delhi: Rajkamal Prakashan, 2012).

——, *Broken Waves: A History of the Fiji Islands in the Twentieth Century* (Honolulu: University of Hawaii Press, 1992).

——, *Chalo Jahaji: On a Journey of Indenture through Fiji* (Suva: Fiji Museum, 2000; Canberra: ANU E Press, 2012), doi.org/10.22459/CJ.12.2012.

——, *Crossing the Kala Pani: A Documentary History of Indian Indenture in Fiji* (Canberra: Division of Pacific & Asian History, Research School of Pacific and Asian Studies, The Australian National University, and Suva: Fiji Museum, 1998).

——, *Girmitiyas: The Origins of the Fiji Indians* (Canberra: Journal of Pacific History, 1983).

——, *Historical Dictionary of Fiji* (New York: Rowman & Littlefield, 2016).

——, *In the Eye of the Storm: Jai Ram Reddy and the Politics of Postcolonial Fiji* (Canberra: ANU E Press, 2010), doi.org/10.22459/ES.11.2010.

——, *Intersections: History, Memory, Discipline* (Suva: Fiji Institute of Applied Studies, 2011; Canberra: ANU E Press, 2012), doi.org/10.22459/IHMD.11.2012.

——, *Islands of Turmoil: Elections and Politic in Fiji* (Canberra: Asia Pacific Press, 2006), doi.org/10.22459/IT.08.2006.

——, *Mr Tulsi's Store: A Fijian Journey* (Canberra: Pandanus Books, 2001).

——, *Power and Prejudice: The Making of the Fiji Crisis* (Wellington: New Zealand Institute for International Affairs, 1988, reprinted 1990).

——, *The Other Side of Midnight* (New Delhi: National Book Trust, 2005).

——, *Turnings: Fiji Factions* (Lautoka: Fiji Institute of Applied Studies, 2008).

Lal, Padma Narsey, *Ganna: Profile of the Fiji Sugar Industry* (Lautoka: Fiji Sugar Commission, 2008).

Lal, Padma, 'Land, lomé and the Fiji sugar industry', in *Fiji before the Storm: Elections and the Politics of Development,* ed. Brij V. Lal (Canberra: Asia Pacific Press, 2000; Canberra: ANU E Press, 2012), 111–34, doi.org/10.22459/FBS.12.2012.

Lal, Padma, Hazel Lim-Applegate and Mahendra Reddy, 'Land tenure dilemma in Fiji: Can Fijian landowners and Indo-Fijian tenants have their cake and eat it too?' *Pacific Economic Bulletin* 16(2) (2001): 106–19.

Laqueur, Walter and George L. Mosse (eds), *Historians in Politics* (London: Sage Publications, 1974).

Laqueur, Walter, 'Introduction: Historians in politics', in Walter Laqueur and George L. Mosse (eds), *Historians in Politics* (London: Sage Publications, 1974).

Larmour, Peter, 'The decolonization of the Pacific Islands', in *Foreign Forces in Pacific Politics,* ed. Ron Crocombe and Ahmed Ali (Suva: Institute of Pacific Studies, 1983), 1–23.

Larson, Eric, 'Fiji's 2014 Parliamentary Election', *Journal of Electoral Studies* 36 (2014): 235–39, doi.org/10.1016/j.electstud.2014.10.001.

Lasaqa, *The Fijian People: Before and After Independence, 1959–1977* (Canberra: Australian National University Press, 1984).

Laurence, K.O., *A Question of Labour: Indentured Immigration into Trinidad and British Guiana, 1875–1916* (Kingston: Ian Randle Publishers, 1994).

Lawson, Stephanie, 'Indigenous nationalism, 'ethnic democracy', and the prospects for a liberal constitutional order in Fiji', in *Nationalism and Ethnic Politics* 18(3) (2012): 293–315, doi.org/10.1080/13537113.2012.707495.

Legge, J.D., *Britain in Fiji, 1858–1880* (London: Macmillan, 1958).

Macdonald, Barrie, 'The literature of the Fiji coups', *The Contemporary Pacific* 2(1) (1990): 198–207.

Madraiwiwi, Joni, 'Treading in Moses' footsteps: Fiji's fourth Constitution', *Constitutionnet,* 30 September, 2013.

Madraiwiwi, Ratu Joni, address to The Australian National University, 5 June 2007.

Mangat, J.S., *A History of Asians in East Africa, c. 1886–1945* (Oxford: Oxford University Press, 1969).

Mangru, Basdeo, 'Indian Government Policy towards indentured labour Migration to the sugar colonies', in *Across the Dark Waters: Ethnicity and Indian Identity in the Caribbean,* ed. David Dabydeen and Brinsley Samaroo (London: Macmillan Caribbean, 1996), 162–74.

——, 'Tadjah in British Guiana', in *Indo-Caribbean Resistance,* ed. Frank Birbalsingh (Toronto: Tsar, 1993), 13–26.

Mara, Ratu Kamisese, *The Pacific Way: A Memoir* (Honolulu: University of Hawai'i Press, 1997).

Mara, Ratu Sir Kamisese, 'Message from the Prime Minister', in *Fiji Independence Souvenir Magazine* (1970).

——, 'Preface', in Lasaqa, *The Fijian People: Before and After Independence, 1959–1977* (Canberra: Australian National University Press, 1984), v.

Mataitini, Ro Alipate, 'Forked tongues', a paper presented to the Fiji Workshop held at The Australian National University, 19 November 2001.

Maude, H.E., *Of Islands and Men: Studies in Pacific History* (Melbourne: Oxford University Press, 1968).

Mayer, A.C., *Peasants in the Pacific: A Study of Fiji Indian Rural Society*, 2nd edn (Berkeley: University of Californian Press, 1973).

Mayer, Adrian C., 'The organisation of Indian settlement in Fiji', *Man* 54(284) (1953): 1–3.

——, *Indians in Fiji* (Oxford: Oxford University Press, 1963).

McDonald, Ian, Joel Benjamin, Lakshmi Kallicharan and Lloyd Seawar (eds), *They Came in Ships: An Anthology of Indo-Guyanese Prose and Poetry* (Leeds: Peepal Tree Press, 1998).

McIntyre, W. David, *Winding up the British Empire in the Pacific Islands* (Oxford: Oxford University Press, 2014), doi.org/10.1093/acprof:oso/9780198702436.001.0001.

McMillan, A.W., *Hindustani Handbook: Specially Prepared for Colonial Use: Lessons in Grammar, Key to Exercises, Vocabulary, and Useful Information on Indian Religions, Customs, and Languages (Devanāgari and Roman Scripts)* (Suva: Government Printer, 1931).

Mellor, Norman and James Anthony, *Fiji Goes to the Polls, The Crucial Legislative Council Elections of 1963* (Honolulu: East–West Center Press, 1968).

Milner, Ian, 'Conversation with Charles Brasch', *Landfall* 25(4) (1971), 349.

Miłosz, Czesław, *The Issa Valley* (New York: Farrar, Straus and Giroux, 1981).

Milton, John, *Comus* (1637), in *The John Milton Reading Room: A Mask Presented at Ludlow Castle 1634,* available from: www.dartmouth.edu/~milton/reading_room/comus/text.shtml (accessed 18 April 2019).

Mishra, Kamal Kishore and Satendra Nandan (eds), *India-Fiji: Experiences to Remember* (New Delhi: Indian Council for Cultural Relations, 2012).

Mishra, Sudesh, *Tandava* (Melbourne: Meanjin, 1992).

Mishra, Vijay, *Bollywood Cinema: Temples of Desire* (London: Routledge, 2002).

Monar, Rooplall, 'Babu', in *They Came in Ships: An Anthology of Indo-Guyanese Prose and Poetry,* ed. Ian McDonald, Joel Benjamin, Lakshmi Kallicharan and Lloyd Seawar, (Leeds: Peepal Tree Press, 1998), 203–205.

Moore, Clive, 'A glass still full: Retirement and the historian', *Pacific Journal of Education* 1(1) (2017): 57–71.

Morris, William, *The Earthly Paradise* (New York and London: Routledge, 2002).

Moynagh, Michael, *Brown or White? A History of the Fiji Sugar Industry, 1873–1973* (Canberra: Australian National University Press, 1981).

MSG Ministers of Foreign Affairs Meeting: Outcome Statement, 13 January 2007.

Munro, Doug and Jack Corbett (eds), *Bearing Witness: Essays in Honour of Brij V. Lal* (Canberra: ANU Press, 2017), doi.org/10.22459/BW.07.2017.

Munro, Doug, 'In the wake of the *Leonidas:* Reflections on Indo-Fijian indenture historiography', *The Journal of Pacific Studies* 28(1) (2005): 93–117, available from: www.usp.ac.fj/fileadmin/files/Institutes/jps/DougMunro.pdf (accessed 5 April 2018).

——, 'J.W. Davidson – The making of a participant historian', in *Pacific Lives, Pacific Places: Bursting Boundaries in Pacific History,* ed. Brij V. Lal and Peter Hempenstall (Canberra: Journal of Pacific History, 2001), 97–116.

——, 'Review of Brij V. Lal, *Another Way*', *Pacific Economic Bulletin* 14(1) (1999): 115–17.

Munz, Peter (ed.), *The Feel of Truth: Essays in New Zealand and Pacific History* (Wellington: A.H. & A.W. Reed, 1969).

Murray, Andrew, 'Observations on the current situation in Fiji', 26 January 2007, typescript sent to author.

Naidu, Vijay, *The Violence of Indenture in Fiji* (Suva: World University Service, 1980).

Narsey, Wadan, *Fiji: For Freedom and Fairness,* available from: narseyonfiji.wordpress.com/ (accessed 24 January 2019).

National Federation Party, *Submission to the United Nations Fact Finding Mission,* 24 April 2007.

Nayacakalou, Rusiate, *Leadership in Fiji* (Melbourne: Oxford University Press, 1975).

Neville, H.R., *Ghazipur District Gazetteer* (Nanital: Government Printer, 1908).

Newland, Lynda, 'The new Methodism and old: Churches, police and state in Fiji, 2008–2009', in *The Round Table: The Commonwealth Journal of International Affairs* 101(6) (2012): 537–55, doi.org/10.1080/00358533.2012.749094.

Niehoff, Arthur and Juanita Niehoff, *East Indians in the West Indies* (Milwaukee: Milwaukee Public Museum, 1960).

Norton, Robert, '"A pre-eminent right to political rule": Indigenous Fijian power and multi-ethnic nation building', *The Round Table: The Commonwealth Journal of International Affairs* 101(6) (2012): 521–35, doi.org/10.1080/003 58533.2012.749093.

——, 'Accommodating indigenous privilege: Britain's dilemma in decolonizing Fiji', *The Journal of Pacific History* 37(2) (2002): 133–56, doi.org/10.1080/0022334022000006574.

——, 'Reconciling ethnicity and nation: Contending discourses in Fiji's constitutional reform', *The Contemporary Pacific* 12(1) (2000): 83–122, doi.org/10.1353/cp.2000.0027.

——, 'The changing role of the Great Council of Chiefs', in *The 2006 Military Takeover in Fiji: A Coup to End all Coups,* ed. Jon Fraenkel, Stewart Firth and Brij V. Lal (Canberra: ANU E Press, 2009), 97–115, doi.org/10.22459/MTF.04.2009.

'Opening of Consultations with the Republic of Fiji Islands under Article 96 of the Cotonou Agreement (Brussels), 18 April 2007'.

Orwell, George, *Nineteen Eighty-four (1984)* (London: Seeker and Warburg, 1949).

Pacific Island Report, 13 August 2001.

Papua New Guinea's High Commissioner to Fiji, Paul Harris, Barrie Sweetman, Kesaia Seniloli and Bruce Hatch, 'Report of the Independent Assessment of the Electoral Process in Fiji, 14–25 May 2007'.

Persaud, Sasenarine, 'Let the past go pass, my love', in *They Came in Ships: An Anthology of Indo-Guyanese Prose and Poetry,* ed. Ian McDonald, Joel Benjamin, Lakshmi Kallicharan and Lloyd Seawar (Leeds: Peepal Tree Press, 1998), 223–28.

Pillay, Raymond, *The Celebration: Collection of Short Stories* (Suva: South Pacific Creative Arts Society, 1980).

Poster, Mark, *Critical Theory and Poststructuralism: In Search of a Context* (Ithaca: Cornell University Press, 1989).

Poynting, Jeremy, 'East Indian women in the Caribbean: Experience and voice', in South Asian Women Writers: The Immigrant Experience, *Journal of South Asian Literature* 21(1) (Winter/Spring 1986): 133–80.

Prasad, Biman Chand, 'Fiji economy: Muddling through', *The Round Table: The Commonwealth Journal of International Affairs* 101(6) (2012): 557–73, doi.org/10.1080/00358533.2012.749096.

——, 'Fiji's economy in the doldrums: Possibilities for a way forward?' presented to Pacific Cooperation Foundation, Wellington, seminar: Fiji at the Crossroads – Again? 8 June 2007.

Prasad, Surendra (ed.), *Coup and Crisis: Fiji a Year Later* (Melbourne: Arena Publications, 1988).

Price, C.A., *The Great White Walls are Built: Restrictive Immigration to North America and Australasia, 1836–1888* (Canberra: Australian National University Press, 1974).

Prime Minister of Fiji, 'Address to the nation', Suva, 1 November 2006.

Qalo, Ropate R., 'The stamp of the man: Initial impressions', *The Journal of Pacific Studies* 22 (1998): 207–12.

——, *Small Business: A Study of a Fijian Family* (Suva: Privately published, 1997).

Ram Kumud, Kashi (ed.), *Hindu Sanskrit Fiji Dwip Men* (Tavua: Privately published, 1965).

Ratu Joni Madraiwiwi, 'Mythic constitutionalism: Whither Fiji's course in June 2007', talk, The Australian National University, 5 June 2007.

Ravuvu, Asesela, *The Facade of Democracy: Fijian Struggles for Political Control, 1830–1987* (Suva: Reader Publishing House, 1991).

Reddi, S.J., 'Labour protest among Indian immigrants', in *Indian Labour Immigration,* ed. U. Bissoondoyal and S.B.C. Servansing (Moka: Mahatma Gandhi Institute, 1986), 116–35.

Reddy, Jai Ram, 'Message', in *Girmit's Greatest Gift: Magazine of the Fiji Girmit Council* (Suva, 2004).

Registration, Conduct, Funding and Disclosures, Decree 4/2013.

Report of the Fiji Constitution Review Commission (Sir Paul Reeves, Tomasi Rayalu Vakatora and Brij V. Lal), *The Fiji Islands: Towards a United Future*, Parliamentary Paper, 34 (1996).

Report of visit to Fiji by LAWASIA Observer Mission, 25–28 March 2007.

Robertson, Robbie, 'Cooking the goose: Fiji's coup culture contextualised', *The Round Table: The Commonwealth Journal of International Affairs* 101(6) (2012): 509–19, doi.org/10.1080/00358533.2012.749095.

Robertson, Robbie and Akosita Tamanisau, *Fiji – Shattered Coups* (Sydney: Pluto Press, 1988).

Roth, G.K., *Fijian Way of Life* (Melbourne: Oxford University Press, 1953).

Routledge, David, *Matanitu: Struggle for Power in Early Fiji* (Suva: Institute of Pacific Studies, 1985).

Saha, Panchanan, *Emigration of Indian Labour, 1834–1900* (Delhi: People's Publishing House, 1970).

Said, Edward, *Orientalism* (New York: Vintage, 1978).

——, *Representations of the Intellectual* (New York: Chatto and Windus, 1996).

Samisoni, Mere, 'Thoughts on Fiji's third coup d'etat', in *Coup: Reflections on the Political Crisis in Fiji*, ed. Brij V. Lal and Michael Pretes (Canberra: Pandanus Books, 2001), 39–46.

Sanadhya, Totaram, *My Twenty-One Years in Fiji, and, The Story of the Haunted Line*, ed. and trans. John Dunham Kelly and Uttra Kumari Singh (Suva: Fiji Museum, 1991).

Sanders, R.T., 'Interlude', in Sir Alan Burns, *Fiji* (London: Her Majesty's Stationery Office, 1963), 149–76.

Sandhu, K.S., *Indians in Malaya: Some Aspects of their Immigration and Settlement, 1786–1957* (Cambridge: Cambridge University Press, 1969).

Saunders, Kay (ed.), *Indentured Labour in the British Empire, 1834–1920* (London: Croon Helm, 1984).

Scarr, Deryck, *Ratu Sukuna: Soldier, Statesman, Man of Two Worlds* (London: Macmillan Education, 1980).

——, *The Politics of Illusion: Military Coup in Fiji* (Sydney: NSWU Press, 1988).

——, *Tuimacilai: A Life of Ratu Sir Kamisese Mara* (Adelaide: Crawford House Publishing, 2008).

Schlesinger, Arthur, Jr, 'The historian and history', *Foreign Affairs* 41(3) (1963): 491–97, doi.org/10.2307/20029635.

——, 'The historian as participant', *Daedalus* 100(2) (1971): 339–58.

Schwartz, Barton M. (ed.), *Caste in Overseas Indian Communities* (San Francisco: Chandler Publishing Company, 1967).

Seecharan, Clem, *Finding Myself: Essays on Race, Politics and Culture* (Leeds: Peepal Tree Press, 2015).

——, *Tiger in the Stars: The Anatomy of Indian Achievement in British Guiana, 1919–1929* (London: Macmillan Education, 1997).

Shameem, Shaista, 'The assumption of executive authority on December 5th, 2006 by Commodore J.V. Bainimarama, Commander of the Republic of Fiji Military Forces: Legal, constitutional and human rights issues', report, 4 January 2007.

Sharma, Guru Dayal, *Memories of Fiji, 1887–1987* (Suva: Fiji Times, 1987).

Sharma, Vivekananda (ed.), *Fiji's Poet Laureate: Poems of Kamla Prasad Mishra* (New Delhi: Gaurav Prakashan, 1999).

Sharpham, John, *Rabuka of Fiji: The Authorised Biography of Major-General Sitiveni Rabuka* (Rockhampton: Central Queensland University Press, 2000).

Shepherd, Verene, *Transients to Settlers: The Experience of Indians in Jamaica, 1845–1950* (Leeds: Peepal Tree Press, 1993).

Sherlock, Sir Philip et al., *Education for Modern Fiji: Report of the 1969 Fiji Education Commission* (Suva: Government Printer, 1969).

Shlomowitz, Ralph, 'Infant mortality and Fiji's Indian migrants, 1879-1919', *Indian Economic and Social History Review* 23(3) (1986): 289–302, doi.org/10.1177/001946468602300303.

Sidal, Morven, *Hannah Dudley: Hamari Maa* (Suva: Pacific Theological College, 1997).

Siegel, Jeff, *Language Contact in a Plantation Environment: A Sociolinguistic History of Fiji* (Cambridge: Cambridge University Press, 1987).

Smith, R.T. and Chandra Jayawardena, 'Caste and social status among the Indians in Guyana', in *Caste in Overseas Indian Communities,* ed. Barton M. Schwartz (Berkeley CA: Chandler Publishing Company, 1967), 43–92.

Soares Ramessar, Marianne, *Survivors of Another Crossing: A History of East Indians in Trinidad, 1880–1946* (St Augustine: School of Continuing Studies, University of the West Indies, 1994).

Spate, O.H.K., *On the Margins of History: From the Punjab to Fiji* (Canberra: National Centre for Development Studies, Research School of Pacific Studies, The Australian National University, 1991).

——, *The Fijian People: Economic Problems and Prospects* (Suva: Government of Fiji Legislative Council Paper 13, 1959).

——, *The Pacific since Magellan,* 3 vols (Canberra: The Australian National University, 1979, 1983, 1988).

Spate, Oskar, 'The salad days', in *The Coombs: A House of Memories,* ed. Brij V. Lal and Allison Ley (Canberra: Research School of Pacific and Asian Studies, The Australian National University, 2006), 23–34.

Stanner, W.E.H., *South Seas in Transition: A Study of Post-War Rehabilitation and Reconstruction in Three British Pacific Dependencies* (Sydney: Australasian Publishing Company, 1953).

Subramani, 'Ramcharitramanas country', in *India-Fiji: Experiences to Remember,* ed. Kamal Kishore Mishra and Satendra Nandan, (New Delhi: Indian Council for Cultural Relations, 2012), 70–83.

——, *Dauka Puran* (New Delhi: Star Publications, 2001).

Sukuna, J.L.V., *Fiji: The Three-Legged Stool: Writings of Ratu Sir Lala Sukuna,* ed. Deryck Scarr (London: Macmillan Education, 1983).

Swann, Maureen, 'Indian Indians: Resistance and accommodation, 1890–1913', in *Essays on Indentured Indians in Natal,* ed. Surendra Bhana (Leeds: Peepal Tress Press, 1990), 117–35.

Taylor, Michael (ed.), *Fiji: Future Imperfect?* (Sydney: Allen & Unwin, 1987).

Thomson, David, *The Aims of History: Values of the Historical Attitude* (London: Thames and Hudson, 1969).

Thornley, Andrew, 'The Methodist Mission and Fiji's Indians, 1879–1920', *New Zealand Journal of History* 8(2) (1974): 137–53.

Tikasingh, Gerad 'Social change in the emerging East Indian community in late 19th century Trinidad', *Journal of Caribbean Studies* 1(2–3) (1980): 120–39.

——, *Trinidad during the 19th Century: The Indian Experience* (Trinidad: RPL Limited, 2012).

Tinker, Hugh, *A New System of Slavery: The Export of Indian Labour Abroad, 1834–1920* (London: Oxford University Press, 1974).

——, *The Ordeal of Love: C.F. Andrews and India* (London: Oxford University Press, 1979).

Tupounua, Sione, Ron Crocombe and Claire Slatter (eds), *Pacific Way: Social Issues in National Development* (Suva: Institute of Pacific Studies, 1976).

Tupper, C.L., *Note on Colonial Emigration during the Year 1878–1879* (Calcutta: Bengal Secretariat Press, 1879).

University of the South Pacific, *Calendar 1983* (Suva: University of the South Pacific).

Vakatora, Tomasi Rayalu, *From the Mangrove Swamps* (Suva: Privately published, 1988).

Vassanji, M.G., *The Book of Secrets* (Toronto: McClelland & Stewart, 1994).

Vertovec, Steven, '"Official" and "popular" Hinduism in the Caribbean: Historical and contemporary trends in Surinam, Trinidad and Guyana', in *Across the Dark Waters: Ethnicity and Indian Identity in the Caribbean*, ed. David Dabydeen and Brinsley Samaroo (London: Macmillan Caribbean, 1996), 108–30.

Walsh, W.H., *Philosophy of History: An Introduction* (New York: Harper Torchbooks, 1958).

Walvin, James, *Different Times: Growing Up in Post-War England* (York: Algie Books, 2014).

Ward, Alan, 'Comfortable voyagers? Some reflections on the Pacific and its historians', *The Journal of Pacific History* 31(2) (1996): 236–42, doi.org/10.1080/00223349608572821.

Ward, R. Gerard, 'Native Fijian villages: A questionable future?' in *Fiji: Future Imperfect*, ed. Michael Taylor (Sydney: Allen & Unwin, 1987), 33–45.

Ward, R.G. and O.H.K. Spate, 'Thirty years ago: A view of the Fijian political scene *confidential report to the British Colonial Office,* September 1959', *The Journal of Pacific History* 25(1) (1990): 103–24, doi.org/10.1080/00223349008572628.

Watters, Raymond Frederick, *Koro: Economic Development and Social Change in Fiji* (London: Clarendon Press, 1969).

Weller, Judith, *The East Indian Indenture in Trinidad* (Rio Piedras, Puerto Rico: Institute of Caribbean Studies, University of Puerto Rico, 1968).

Wiesel, Elie, 'Nobel Peace Prize acceptance speech', Oslo, 10 Dec. 1986.

Williams, George, 'The case that stopped a coup? The rule of law and constitutionalism in Fiji', *Oxford University Commonwealth Law Journal* 1(1) (2001): 73–93, doi.org/10.1080/14729342.2001.11421385.

Winks, Robin and Marcus Cunliff (eds), *Pastmasters: Some Essays on American Historians* (New York: Harper, 1969).

Yardan, Shanan, 'Earth is brown', in *They Came in Ships: An Anthology of Indo-Guyanese Prose and Poetry,* ed. Ian McDonald, Joel Benjamin, Lakshmi Kallicharan and Lloyd Seawar (Leeds: Peepal Tree Press, 1998), 242–50.

About the author

Brij Vilash Lal, AM, is an Emeritus Professor of The Australian National University and an Honorary Professor of the University of Queensland. Educated in Fiji, Canada and Australia, he taught at The Australian National University for 25 years until 2016 and, before that, at the University of Hawai'i at Mānoa for nearly a decade, with brief stints at the University of the South Pacific and the University of Papua New Guinea. His many awards and honours for scholarship and public service include Member of the Order of Australia, Centenary of Federation Medal of the Government of Australia, Officer of the Order of Fiji, Fellow of the Australian Humanities Academy, Distinguished Pacific Scholar Medal, and International Fellow of the Jawaharlal Nehru Institute of Advanced Studies, New Delhi. He was honoured with a Festschrift, *Bearing Witness*, in 2017. In 1999, the Fiji Millennium Committee selected him as one of 75 men and women who helped shape the history of twentieth-century Fiji. In 2009, he and his wife, environmental and resource economist Padma, were banned for life from returning to Fiji for his unflinching opposition to the culture of military coups in his native country. Brij and Padma have two children, Yogi and Niraj, and (so far) four grandchildren, Jayan Kenneth, Maya June, Ash Arjun and Ella Saras. They now live in Brisbane.